The Routledge Handbook of Service Research Insights and Ideas

The Routledge Handbook of Service Research Insights and Ideas offers authoritative coverage of current scholarship in the expanding discipline of service research.

Original chapters from the world's leading specialists in the discipline explore foundations and innovations in services, highlighting important issues relating to service providers, customers, and service design. The volume goes beyond previous publications by drawing together material from different functional areas, including marketing, human resource management, and service process design and operations. These topics are important in helping readers become knowledgeable about how different functional areas interact to create a successful customer experience.

This book is ideal as a first port of call for postgraduate students desiring to get up to speed quickly in the services discipline. It is also a must-read for academics new to services who want to access cutting-edge research.

Eileen Bridges is a Professor of Marketing at Kent State University, USA. She received her PhD from Northwestern University, USA. Her research interests include customer expectations, technology-based products, and services. She previously served on the faculty at Rice University, USA, and as Editor-in-Chief of the *Service Industries Journal*.

Kendra Fowler is an Associate Professor of Marketing at Youngstown State University, USA. She received her PhD from Kent State University, USA. Her research interests include services, retailing, and advertising.

The Routledge Handbook of Service Research Insights and Ideas

Edited by
Eileen Bridges and Kendra Fowler

Routledge
Taylor & Francis Group

LONDON AND NEW YORK

First published 2020
by Routledge
2 Park Square, Milton Park, Abingdon, Oxon OX14 4RN

and by Routledge
605 Third Avenue, New York, NY 10017

First issued in paperback 2022

Routledge is an imprint of the Taylor & Francis Group, an informa business

British Library Cataloguing-in-Publication Data
A catalogue record for this book is available from the British Library

Library of Congress Cataloging-in-Publication Data
Names: Bridges, Eileen, editor. | Fowler, Kendra, editor.
Title: The Routledge handbook of service research insights and ideas / edited by Eileen Bridges, Kendra Fowler.
Description: New York : Routledge, 2020. | Includes bibliographical references and index.
Identifiers: LCCN 2019037491 (print) | LCCN 2019037492 (ebook) |
ISBN 9780815372530 (hardback) | ISBN 9781351245234 (ebook)
Subjects: LCSH: Service industries–Research. | Customer services–Research. |
Customer relations–Research.
Classification: LCC HD9980.5 .R688 2020 (print) | LCC HD9980.5 (ebook) |
DDC 658–dc23
LC record available at https://lccn.loc.gov/2019037491
LC ebook record available at https://lccn.loc.gov/2019037492

ISBN 13: 978-1-03-240023-5 (pbk)
ISBN 13: 978-0-815-37253-0 (hbk)
ISBN 13: 978-1-351-24523-4 (ebk)

DOI: 10.4324/9781351245234

Typeset in Bembo
by Swales & Willis, Exeter, Devon, UK

Contents

Contents

Editors' introduction to the volume

Eileen Bridges and Kendra Fowler

This volume serves as a reference offering an introduction to current scholarship in the expanding discipline of service research. It is aimed at postgraduate students and others new to academic research in services; its goals are to provide access to the relevant academic literature and to assist readers in becoming familiar with the work of some of the leading academics as well as research trends in the field. It offers a unique approach by drawing together material from different functional areas, including marketing, human resource management, and service process design and operations. These topics are important in helping readers become knowledgeable about how different functional areas work together to create a successful customer experience.

Five thematic parts provide structure to the volume. Part I offers five chapters in foundational areas, including service-dominant logic (S-DL), service profit logic, customer-dominant service logic, and servitization of manufacturing industries. The second part addresses innovation in service organizations: it includes chapters on relevant typologies and frameworks pertaining to innovation, descriptions of innovation by front line employees and in service environments, and concludes with a chapter detailing how complex network analysis can be used to create cutting-edge service innovations. This is followed by Part III, which offers five chapters on approaches to organizing the service business. Thus, it includes such topics as customer engagement with front line service providers, front line provider emotions, service process design and management, configuring the service supply chain, and obtaining cost-effective service excellence. The fourth part of the volume addresses service design, delivery, and customer engagement. It begins by looking at digitization of services and managing customer performance in services, and then considers co-creation of customer value, integration of resources to create a customer journey, and finally customer engagement via social media participation. Part V deals with ethics, responsibility, and culture in services. It includes critical background in such important topics as organizational ethics, transformative service research, green services, not-for-profit services, and multicultural service environments. In summary, each chapter provides a balanced overview of current knowledge, identifying issues and discussing relevant debates in an analytical and engaging manner. Authors have also offered reflections on where each research agenda is likely to advance in the future.

Chapter authors represent many parts of the world and various research traditions. Contributors are listed alphabetically below, and their current affiliations are provided. Here, the five parts of the book that comprise 24 chapters are described in some detail.

Part I includes five chapters that provide background on several foundational theories that drive research in service management.

Chapter 1, by Stephen L. Vargo, Kaisa Koskela-Huotari, and Josina Vink, traces the evolution of service-dominant logic (S-DL) and summarizes its core ideas. In particular, it redefines service as the process of using one's resources for the benefit of another actor (or for oneself). There is variation in the extent to which service exchange is direct – an actor applies resources for the benefit of another actor in person – or indirect – an actor applies resources for the benefit of another actor through, for example, a good. This approach to understanding is consistent with the idea of value co-creation. The resulting framework includes five axioms: (1) Service is the fundamental basis of exchange; (2) Value is co-created by multiple actors, always including the beneficiary; (3) All social and economic actors are resource integrators; (4) Value is always uniquely and phenomenologically determined by the beneficiary; (5) Value co-creation is coordinated through actor-generated institutions and institutional arrangements. The authors compare S-DL to three other perspectives (service logic, customer-dominant logic and service science) that differ in terms of the actors and the outcomes that are involved in the value-creation process, concluding that all are subsets of S-DL. Finally, the chapter suggests how S-DL can be used to broaden the scope of service research to a more contextual, multi-actor view of exchange termed a 'service ecosystem.'

Chapter 2, by Jonathan J. Baker, Julia A. Fehrer, and Roderick J. Brodie, presents a broadened view of how innovations are introduced to a marketplace. Drawing on S-DL, marketplaces are described as ecosystems comprised of multiple actors governed by institutional arrangements, which dictate the rules and norms that coordinate innovation and value co-creation activities. The chapter examines innovation processes at several levels, including technological, business model, and marketplace innovation. For an innovation to be successful, it must be normalized (i.e., incorporated into standards of practice), represented (i.e., distinguishable from other practices), and integrated (i.e., allowing multiple actors to participate in and benefit from the innovation).

Chapter 3, by Christian Grönroos, observes that conventional management models depend on goods-based profit logic in which nearly all business functions (excluding sales and marketing) influence revenues only indirectly through maintenance of the quality of the product, and therefore are considered cost centers. Such functions are invisible to customers and contribute very little to either customer loyalty or willingness to pay. However, in practice, goods-centric interactions are increasingly rare. Instead, the new reality is that most of a firm's functions and processes are open, and include interactions with customers. As such, the majority of an organization can potentially impact its revenue-generating potential. Therefore, quality management and assurance must be extended, no longer focusing exclusively on technical outcomes, but also on assessing the behavioral aspects of a service process. Service profit logic (SPL), the topic of the present chapter, takes into account this new dynamic; therefore, it categorizes business functions into three types of processes, including (1) interactive, (2) supporting, and (3) 'back office' cost centers that are invisible from the customer perspective.

Chapter 4, on customer-dominant logic (C-DL), is by Kristina Heinonen and Tore Strandvik. These authors propose looking at service systems from the customer point of view rather than from the service provider point of view, which is justified because customers make choices from their own perspectives. The perspective chosen by researchers and/or service managers determines what they pay attention to and what they consider to be key challenges. The authors suggest that C-DL affords researchers and service managers the most encompassing view, so that they can examine patterns of customers' overt and covert activities and experiences. The difference between C-DL and the more traditional provider logics (e.g. S-DL) is discussed, and the implications of adopting C-DL are examined.

Chapter 5 was authored by Bernhard Dachs, Christian Lerch, and Michael Weschta, who define servitization as 'the practice of manufacturing firms to enrich their offerings of material products with services.' This chapter considers differences in how much servitization occurs across industries and countries, with some interesting interpretation of results. For instance, in addition to comparing means, it also considers heterogeneity within various industries, production characteristics, and firm size as a factor that may impact the degree to which a particular firm implements servitization. Motives and obstacles associated with servitization are discussed. Finally, digitization and the Internet of Things (IoT) are addressed as providing new momentum for servitization.

Part II includes four chapters describing various approaches to innovation in services.

Chapter 6, by Christian Kowalkowski and Lars Witell, describes various typologies and frameworks that are used in service innovation. This chapter reviews research on service innovation and discusses the models that are most often used, given the characteristics of the innovation and the context in which they are developed. In particular, the authors look at different modes of service innovation: assimilation, demarcation, and synthesis. Following discussion, they focus on the synthesis perspective, and provide four archetypes for service innovation – output based, process based, experiential, and systemic. A unifying framework helps with comprehension, although the authors recognize that divergent understandings will most likely continue.

Chapter 7, by Marit Engen, observes that front line employees play a key role in service innovation, working closely with customers and bringing in relevant knowledge that contributes to innovation. The chapter details how front line employees are able to engage in innovation, by becoming agents in roles that go beyond their specific job requirements. To become such agents, they require three essential elements: the ability to innovate, the willingness to innovate, and the opportunity to innovate. The supporting role of middle managers is also discussed and suggestions are made for future research.

Chapter 8, by Kendra Fowler, provides a brief summary of the seminal work and details new developments in service environment design that allow for innovative customer experiences. It begins by providing a brief overview of the service environment literature, including discussion of ambient conditions (e.g. lighting and music), spatial configurations, and aesthetic choices (e.g. décor and signage). Next, it explores expanded frameworks that consider how social, cultural, and even natural elements contribute to this environment. It also addresses the use of digital technology, the impact of the service environment on employees, and the expanded emphasis on customer co-creation and service that is provided by the environment.

Chapter 9, by Zhen Zhu and Dmitry Zinoviev, describes a process for identifying where the next service innovation is likely to take place. This process utilizes complex network analysis methods to map the conceptual structure of service innovation by detecting and delineating related themes and their interconnections. It is based on subject terms in academic articles which form domains; critical concepts, typical research methods, and prominent industry contexts of each domain are then used to define structural frameworks and identify gaps that signify potential opportunities.

Part III includes five chapters on topics that relate to organizing the service business, including planning for front line positions, design and management of the service process, and integration of these two aspects. It concludes with a study of cost-effective service excellence.

Chapter 10, by Ainsworth Anthony Bailey and Carolyn M. Bonifield, investigates the role of front line service employees, both as the 'face' of the organization and in customer engagement, regardless of channel of service delivery. This includes an understanding of who should fill the front line role, and what their goals should be when they interact with customers. In addition, functions performed by the front line in both offline and online service environments and specifically how they engender customer engagement are topics that are addressed. Finally, the chapter proposes a model of front line service employee–customer engagement and customer intentions to provide feedback, which considers employee involvement and investment in customer relationships, and employee–customer relationship quality.

Chapter 11, by Gianfranco Walsh and Mario Schaarschmidt, examines how front line service providers use and are affected by their naturally felt emotions. Although the authors propose that the results may differ in employees' primary and secondary jobs, and they study dual jobbers to allow for this possibility, no evidence of difference between the two jobs is apparent. Thus, for both first and second jobs, the findings indicate that: (1) job satisfaction predicts the use of naturally felt emotions, (2) service providers who are committed to employing prescribed display rules are less likely to deploy spontaneous, genuine emotions, and (3) front line providers who perceive display requirements as unjust are less likely to deploy spontaneous, genuine emotions. These findings offer managerial implications in that, if display of genuine emotions is preferred, it is important to have satisfied employees who need not be committed to specific display rules, particularly if they are viewed as unjust.

Chapter 12, by Steven W. Rayburn, Sidney T. Anderson, and Kendra Fowler, examines service process design, a structured approach to developing and managing service offerings. The chapter offers a brief review of the current state of service process design, calling attention to efforts related to collaborative design and the increased role of technology. A five stage design process is recommended for service providers when planning the service provision. Specific tools and techniques that designers can use to better meet customer needs and facilitate the planning and/or evaluation of service processes are suggested for each stage. Several new approaches to service process design are identified as opportunities for continued research.

Chapter 13, by Christoph F. Breidbach, Hendrik Reefke, and Tobias Widmer, provides background on the topic of service supply chain configurations and how value networks are created. It begins with an overview on the basics of service supply chain development, starting with goods supply chains; this is followed by a description of how supply chains changed over time as service operations matured. The chapter makes mention of S-DL and how this foundational thought process influences supply chain design: apparently, as services grow, there is a greater need for efficiency that drives out agility. Service supply chains can follow different strategic orientations, which are influenced by their position in the market. This chapter illustrates four possible configurations, enhancing theoretical understanding of service supply chains and potentially guiding managerial decision-making, and refers to how the choice relates to the resulting levels of customer engagement.

Chapter 14, by Jochen Wirtz, discusses cost-effective service excellence (CESE). It is based on and extends the article by Wirtz and Zeithaml (*JAMS*, 2018). CESE is defined as achieving low unit costs (i.e., high productivity) while delivering an industry-leading level of service quality. This chapter describes how CESE can be achieved through three strategic pathways: (1) a dual culture strategy that provides a comprehensive set of high-quality services at low cost, largely driven by leadership ambidexterity and contextual ambidexterity; (2) an operations management approach that reduces process variability, allowing increased use of systems, technology, robotics, and artificial intelligence, and/or (3) a focused service factory strategy that utilizes a highly specialized service operation, delivering a single type of service to a highly focused customer segment. All three strategies are discussed and research questions are proposed to guide future inquiry into the topic.

Part IV includes five chapters that examine service design, delivery, customer co-creation of value, and customer engagement.

Chapter 15, by Eileen Bridges, Charles F. Hofacker, and Chi Kin (Bennett) Yim proposes a framework describing which technology-enabled service processes will migrate from employee handling to customer handling. Therefore, two situations are considered: (1) a process that is performed by employees in person is digitized to hand off to customers in an IT-enabled format, and (2) a process that has already been digitized for employees requires fewer changes in order to hand off to customers in the form of a self-service technology (SST). Although the firm's decision to digitize a service process is considered, the more important topic is whether the firm should expect the digitized service process to be utilized directly by a service employee or by customers, which depends on the abilities and desires of the target market. Therefore, this chapter suggests a theory regarding service process migration to SSTs.

Chapter 16, by Enrico Secchi, Uzay Damali, David McCutcheon, and Stephen S. Tax, develops a model of customer performance while participating in service processes, and provides an integrated overview of a set of practices that services can adopt to minimize the risk of failure due to inadequate customer participation. Seven broad categories of such practices that can improve customer performance include task design, customer learning, customer selection, multi-channel strategies, customer incentives, gamification, and employee flexibility. The authors assess the trade-off between reducing the requirements of a service delivery process and enhancing customer attributes that improve their performance, including motivation, knowledge, and skills. The idea is to optimize across both, to minimize the risk that customers will be unable or unwilling to perform their co-creation duties.

Chapter 17, by Andrew S. Gallan and Josephine Go Jefferies, explains the concept of value co-creation and distinguishes it from other related terms, to elucidate how value is co-created among actors in service ecosystems. A review of the value co-creation literature covers a range of important topics, and highlights antecedents (system-level and individual factors), the value co-creation process (resource integration, resolution of knowledge asymmetry, and practices), consequences, and developing measures. A number of current health-care-related examples are provided. Finally, future research directions are offered, including a discussion of implications for transformative service research and service design and management.

Chapter 18, by Cátia Jesus and Helena Alves, provides an overview of how resource integration and direct/indirect interactions between actors and events involved in a value co-creation process can be used to explain the journey a consumer takes when participating in a service experience. The chapter focuses on the service process and its interaction with the customer journey. Similar to the customer's purchase decision process in buyer behavior, the customer journey is formed by three phases (pre-purchase, purchase, and post-purchase) with several distinct stages. The chapter presents a 'customer journey map' (CJM) highlighting how consumers integrate operant and operand resources to co-create value in a complex service experience at an example cultural experience (a 'Christmas Town' event). This clarifies how and what types of resources consumers integrate in co-creating value; fundamental elements and touchpoints are identified. Using the CJM, organizations can harness innovations to improve customer satisfaction.

Chapter 19, by Rodoula Tsiotsou, examines how social media allow active (i.e., interactive) or passive (i.e., one-sided) customer engagement. The purposes of this chapter are to review literature on customer engagement in social media, identify key elements and forms of customer engagement, and propose a conceptual framework that explains how and when customers engage in social media interaction. More specifically, the proposed framework suggests that both intrinsic (i.e., related to personal and social motives) and extrinsic (i.e., related to the social environment) motives contribute to consumer engagement, which can be passive or active in nature. The co-creation of value and relationship building are identified as outcomes of consumer engagement in social media.

Part V includes five chapters that relate to organizational ethics and responsibility, and deal with issues of culture and societal advantage.

Chapter 20, by Eileen Bridges, is reprinted from the author's article that appeared in the *Journal of Service Theory and Practice* (volume 28, issue 5), entitled, "Executive Ethical Decisions Initiating Organizational Culture and Values." This chapter reports on a qualitative study that develops new theory regarding how service executives make ethical decisions and the factors they take into account in doing so. It uses an executive interview method, involving a dozen in-depth interviews with high-level executives in successful service organizations. The resulting research propositions are grounded in the executives' personal backgrounds, values, organizational culture, and values, and describe their impact on strategic decisions. The emergent findings offer insights that are both interesting and surprising. The propositions developed relate that executives in organizations having more family-oriented cultures tend to be more externally focused, to use outcome-oriented approaches to ethical decision-making, and to take more analytical measures of success into account. In organizations that place greater value on diversity, propositions suggest that executives tend to be more internally focused, process-oriented in their approaches to ethical decisions, and to use a blend of intuition and analytical measures in evaluating decision outcomes.

Chapter 21, by Mark S. Rosenbaum, Karen Edwards, Germán Contreras Ramírez, and John Grady, provides an overview of transformative service research, which investigates how service, service providers, and service systems may enhance well-being, especially for those with potential vulnerabilities. The authors identify a current lack of understanding in the field regarding service experiences among key segments of potentially vulnerable consumers (i.e., those with physical disabilities, mental impairments, and the elderly). The chapter introduces the concept of 'service inclusion' and highlights the need for future research aimed toward enhancing the service experience and welfare of persons with such potentially limiting biophysical or psychosocial characteristics. The chapter concludes with a list of service frameworks/theories that may need to be re-envisioned to fully embrace the experience of all consumers and offers a framework showing how various resources can promote consumer well-being and attachment.

Chapter 22, by Michael J. Dorsch, William E. Kilbourne, and Stephen J. Grove, defines the concept of 'green service' and describes important challenges of achieving environmental sustainability. The chapter's purpose is to examine how micro- and macro-level factors influence the extent to which services can become environmentally sustainable; in so doing, it draws together what is and can be done within firms and at the societal level as a whole. For instance, 'greenprinting' is suggested as a tool to help organizations achieve environmental sustainability, and the environmental impact model is used to illustrate how societies need to encourage reduced production and more responsible consumption of goods and services to achieve environmental sustainability. Macro-level factors influencing the extent and rate to which the service sector can contribute to environmental sustainability are discussed, and ideas for continued research into green service practices are suggested.

Chapter 23, by Joshua Coleman and Marla Royne Stafford, provides an excellent overview of the history of not-for-profit services and a discussion of the transformation toward social enterprise, combining not-for-profit values with for-profit strategies. It takes an historical perspective that dates back to the birth of the United States, describing how not-for-profit services developed, including the political and economic influences. It offers detailed descriptions of how social enterprises arose to fill a gap between strictly not-for-profit and for-profit organizations. Five trends in not-for-profit services are discussed, including digital fundraising, redefining donors into customers, operating like a for-profit business, fostering sustainability, and investing in strategic and innovative partnerships.

Chapter 24, by Elten Briggs and Detra Y. Montoya, discusses challenges faced by service providers operating in multicultural environments. It specifically addresses how firms can enhance external service communications, interactive service delivery, and internal service orientation to solidify their relationships with ethnic minority consumers. This is done by applying concepts from the services marketing triangle as an organizing framework to describe challenges faced by service providers operating in multicultural environments. Specifically addressed are: (1) the relationship between the organization and its front line employees, who need to have a multicultural orientation, (2) the interaction between front line employees and consumers at the point of service delivery, and (3) marketing messages between the organization and its multicultural customers. The rationales for approaches to enhance multicultural communications, deliver service to multicultural audiences, and develop firm service orientation are discussed, and examples are provided to guide service firms in their quests for multicultural inclusion.

Contributors

Helena Alves: Professor, Department of Management and Economics, Universidade Beira Interior, Research Center in Business Sciences (NECE), Portugal. Chapter entitled 'Resource integration and co-creation: a customer journey approach.' This work was financed by National Funds through the FCT Foundation for Science and Technology – Project UID/GES/04630/2013.

Sidney T. Anderson: Assistant Professor, Department of Marketing, Texas State University, USA. Chapter entitled 'Service process design and management.'

Ainsworth Anthony Bailey: Associate Professor, Department of Marketing & International Business, College of Business & Innovation, University of Toledo, USA. Chapter entitled 'Modeling consumer engagement with front line service providers.'

Jonathan J. Baker: Lecturer, Department of International Business, Strategy & Entrepreneurship, Faculty of Business, Economics & Law, Auckland University of Technology, New Zealand. Chapter entitled 'Service-dominant logic and market innovation.'

Carolyn M. Bonifield: Associate Professor, Grossman School of Business, University of Vermont, USA. Chapter entitled 'Modeling consumer engagement with front line service providers.'

Christoph F. Breidbach: Senior Lecturer and Co-Lead, Service Innovation Alliance, UQ Business School, University of Queensland, Australia. Chapter entitled 'Service supply chain configurations: from agile to efficient value networks.'

Eileen Bridges: Professor, Department of Marketing and Entrepreneurship, Kent State University, Ohio, USA. Chapters entitled 'Service digitization and the provider-to-customer handoff,' and 'Executive ethical decisions initiating organizational culture and values.' The latter was originally published in *Journal of Service Theory and Practice* (2018), 28(5), 576–608; reprinted with permission.

Elten Briggs: Associate Professor and Chair, Department of Marketing, University of Texas at Arlington, USA. Chapter entitled 'Providing service in multicultural environments.'

Roderick J. Brodie: Professor, Department of Marketing, University of Auckland Business School, New Zealand. Chapter entitled 'Service-dominant logic and market innovation.'

Joshua Coleman: Assistant Professor, Department of Marketing, Missouri State University, USA. Chapter entitled 'The convergence of not-for-profit services and the social enterprise.'

Bernhard Dachs: Austrian Institute of Technology, Center for Innovation Systems and Policy, Vienna, Austria. Chapter entitled 'The servitization of manufacturing industries.' The author thanks the Anniversary Fund of the Austrian National Bank for its financial support through project number 17675, 'Industrie 4.0, services, and the competitiveness of Austrian manufacturing.' He also thanks Doris Schartinger, Werner Jammernegg, and the editors of this book for their helpful comments.

Uzay Damali: Assistant Professor, Department of Management, University of Wisconsin-La Crosse, USA. Chapter entitled 'Managing customer performance in services.'

Michael J. Dorsch: Professor, Department of Marketing, College of Business, Clemson University, South Carolina, USA. Chapter entitled 'Green services and the quest for sustainable environment: chasing a holy grail.'

Karen Edwards: Senior Instructor, Department of Retailing, College of Hospitality, Retail, and Sport Management, University of South Carolina, USA. Chapter entitled 'Transformative service research: thoughts, perspectives, and research directions.'

Marit Engen: Associate Professor, Inland School of Business and Social Sciences, Inland Norway University of Applied Sciences, Norway. Chapter entitled 'Front line employees as innovators.'

Julia A. Fehrer: Lecturer, Graduate School of Management, University of Auckland, New Zealand; Research Fellow, Department of Services Management, University of Bayreuth, Germany. Chapter entitled 'Service-dominant logic and market innovation.'

Kendra Fowler: Associate Professor, Department of Marketing, Williamson College of Business Administration, Youngstown State University, Ohio, USA. Chapters entitled 'Innovative service environments' and 'Service process design and management.'

Andrew S. Gallan: Assistant Professor, Department of Marketing and Director, Center for Services Marketing & Management, Florida Atlantic University, USA. Chapter entitled 'Value co-creation and its meaning for customers.'

Josephine Go Jefferies: Lecturer in Marketing, Newcastle University, Newcastle upon Tyne, UK. Chapter entitled 'Value co-creation and its meaning for customers.'

John Grady: Professor, Department of Sport and Entertainment Management, College of Hospitality, Retail, and Sport Management, University of South Carolina, USA. Chapter entitled 'Transformative service research: thoughts, perspectives, and research directions.'

Christian Grönroos: Professor Emeritus, Hanken School of Economics, Finland. Chapter entitled 'Service profit logic: ensuring customer willingness to pay.'

Stephen J. Grove: Professor Emeritus, Department of Marketing, College of Business, Clemson University, South Carolina, USA. Chapter entitled 'Green services and the quest for sustainable environment: chasing a holy grail.'

Kristina Heinonen: Professor, Department of Marketing, Centre for Relationship Marketing and Service Management, Hanken School of Economics, Finland. Chapter entitled 'Customer-dominant service logic.'

Charles F. Hofacker: Carl DeSantis Professor of Business Administration and Professor, Department of Marketing, College of Business, Florida State University, USA. Chapter entitled 'Service digitization and the provider-to-customer handoff.'

Cátia Jesus: Guest Assistant Lecturer, Department of Management and Economics, Universidade Beira Interior, Portugal. Chapter entitled 'Resource integration and co-creation: a customer journey approach.' This work was financed by National Funds through the FCT Foundation for Science and Technology – Project UID/GES/04630/2013.

William E. Kilbourne: Professor Emeritus, Department of Marketing, College of Business, Clemson University, South Carolina, USA. Chapter entitled 'Green services and the quest for sustainable environment: chasing a holy grail.'

Kaisa Koskela-Huotari: Assistant Professor, CTF Service Research Center, Karlstad University, Sweden. Chapter entitled 'Service-dominant logic: foundations and applications.'

Christian Kowalkowski: Professor of Industrial Marketing, Department of Management and Engineering, Linköping University, Sweden. Chapter entitled 'Typologies and frameworks in service innovation.'

Christian Lerch: Fraunhofer Institute for Systems and Innovation Research, Business Unit Industrial Innovation Strategies, Karlsruhe, Germany. Chapter entitled 'The servitization of manufacturing industries.' The author thanks Doris Schartinger, Werner Jammernegg, and the editors of this book for their helpful comments.

David McCutcheon: Emeritus Faculty Member, Peter B. Gustavson School of Business, University of Victoria, Canada. Chapter entitled 'Managing customer performance in services.'

Detra Y. Montoya: Clinical Associate Professor of Marketing, W.P. Carey School of Business, Arizona State University, USA. Chapter entitled 'Providing service in multicultural environments.'

Germán Contreras Ramírez: Center of Marketing Director, Management Department, College of Business, Externado University, Colombia. Chapter entitled 'Transformative service research: thoughts, perspectives, and research directions.'

Steven W. Rayburn: Associate Professor, Department of Marketing, Texas State University, USA. Chapter entitled 'Service process design and management.'

Hendrik Reefke: Lecturer, Logistics, Procurement and Supply Chain Management, Cranfield School of Management, UK. Chapter entitled 'Service supply chain configurations: from agile to efficient value networks.'

Mark S. Rosenbaum: Professor and Chair, Department of Retailing, College of Hospitality, Retail, and Sport Management, University of South Carolina, USA. Chapter entitled 'Transformative service research: thoughts, perspectives, and research directions.'

Mario Schaarschmidt: Assistant Professor, University of Koblenz-Landau, Germany. Chapter entitled 'Front line service providers with two jobs: antecedents of naturally felt emotions.'

Enrico Secchi: Assistant Professor, Michael Smurfit Graduate Business School, University College Dublin, Ireland. Chapter entitled 'Managing customer performance in services.'

Marla Royne Stafford: William F. Harrah Distinguished Chair, Executive Associate Dean of Academic Affairs, Harrah College of Hospitality, University of Nevada, Las Vegas, USA. Chapter entitled 'The convergence of not-for-profit services and the social enterprise.'

Tore Strandvik: Professor Emeritus, Department of Marketing, Centre for Relationship Marketing and Service Management, Hanken School of Economics, Finland. Chapter entitled 'Customer-dominant service logic.'

Stephen S. Tax: Professor of Service Management and Francis G. Winspear Scholar, Peter B. Gustavson School of Business, University of Victoria, Canada. Chapter entitled 'Managing customer performance in services.'

Rodoula H. Tsiotsou: Professor of Services Marketing and Director of Marketing Laboratory MARLAB, Department of Business Administration, University of Macedonia, Greece. Chapter entitled 'Social media and customer engagement.'

Stephen L. Vargo: Shidler College Distinguished Professor, Department of Marketing, Shidler College of Business, University of Hawai'i at Mānoa, USA. Chapter entitled 'Service-dominant logic: foundations and applications.'

Josina Vink: Associate Professor, Institute of Design, Oslo School of Architecture and Design, Oslo, Norway. Chapter entitled 'Service-dominant logic: foundations and applications.'

Gianfranco Walsh: Professor of Marketing, Friedrich-Schiller-University of Jena, Germany. Chapter entitled 'Front line service providers with two jobs: antecedents of naturally felt emotions.'

Michael Weschta: Master Student, Institute for Production Management, Vienna University of Economics and Business, Vienna, Austria. Chapter entitled 'The servitization of manufacturing industries.' The author thanks Doris Schartinger, Werner Jammernegg, and the editors of this book for their helpful comments.

Tobias Widmer: Marie Curie Early Stage Researcher, Logistics, Procurement and Supply Chain Management, Cranfield School of Management, UK. Chapter entitled 'Service supply chain configurations: from agile to efficient value networks.'

Jochen Wirtz: Professor of Marketing and Vice Dean Graduate Studies, NUS Business School, National University of Singapore, Singapore. Chapter entitled 'Strategic pathways to cost-effective service excellence.' The author gratefully acknowledges Valarie Zeithaml's contributions, without which this chapter would not have been possible. The editors of this book, Eileen Bridges and Kendra Fowler, provided encouragement and excellent, constructive feedback on an earlier version of this chapter, which helped to sharpen it further.

Lars Witell: Professor, Department of Management and Engineering, Linköping University, Sweden. Chapter entitled 'Typologies and frameworks in service innovation.'

Chi Kin (Bennett) Yim: Professor in Marketing, Faculty of Business and Economics, The University of Hong Kong. Chapter entitled 'Service digitization and the provider-to-customer Handoff.'

Zhen Zhu: Professor of Marketing, Sawyer Business School, Suffolk University, Boston, Massachusetts, USA. Chapter entitled 'Finding the next edge in service innovation: a complex network analysis.'

Dmitry Zinoviev: Professor of Mathematics and Computer Science, College of Arts and Sciences, Suffolk University, Boston, Massachusetts, USA. Chapter entitled 'Finding the next edge in service innovation: a complex network analysis.'

Part I
Foundations

Service-dominant logic

Foundations and applications

Stephen L. Vargo, Kaisa Koskela-Huotari, and Josina Vink

Introduction

Over the last several decades, there has been an explosion of interest in *services*. This has resulted in both an exponential increase in services-oriented, academic literature and a growing number of firms reorienting themselves toward services rather than manufacturing. It is sometimes assumed that this shift to a 'services economy' is also the motivation for the research stream known as service-dominant (S-D) logic (Vargo & Lusch, 2004, 2008, 2016, 2018). However, as noted by Lusch and Vargo (2018), S-D logic is not about explaining the emergence of the services economy; in fact, it is not even about services in the traditional sense that would equate services with intangible goods. Instead, S-D logic offers a metatheoretical framework that identifies *service* (singular)—the process of using one's resources for the benefit of another actor (or oneself)—rather than goods, as the fundamental basis of economic and social exchange (Vargo & Lusch, 2004, 2017). In other words, S-D logic argues for a processual view, through which exchange in preindustrialized, industrialized, and post-industrialized economies, can best be understood in terms of *service-for-service exchange*. What varies is the extent to which service exchange is direct—i.e., an actor applies their resources for the benefit of another actor in person—or indirect—i.e., an actor applies their resources for the benefit of another actor through, for example, a good, which acts as a vehicle for service delivery.

In this way, S-D logic uses *service as a perspective* to understand the *nature* of exchange throughout all sectors and contexts, rather than limiting the relevance of service to those settings in which the exchange outputs are distinguished by the archetypical services characteristics of intangibility, inseparability, heterogeneity, and perishability (Zeithaml, Parasuraman & Berry, 1985). This view reveals that service has a far more pervasive role in society than is generally recognized. Service has been important since well before the industrial revolution and its presence extends beyond what is now considered the 'services economy.' By shifting the understanding regarding the nature of service, S-D logic helps to open up the field of service research toward wider applicability as will be discussed later in this chapter.

Furthermore, understanding exchange as a process also brings forth additional insights about the *purpose* of exchange. It becomes clear that the aim of exchange is not to move around products or other exchange objects, but to share applied knowledge and skills with other actors to support what they are trying to accomplish. In other words, the purpose of exchange is to enable reciprocal value creation. As this is possible only through collaboration and exchange with a large number of actors, S-D logic calls this process *value co-creation* (Lusch & Vargo, 2006; Vargo, Maglio & Akaka, 2008) and the collectives, among which value co-creation occurs, *service ecosystems* (Lusch & Vargo, 2014; Vargo & Lusch, 2011). Recent developments within S-D logic involve the inclusion of the sociological concept of *institutions* as the coordination mechanism enabling and constraining value co-creation within service ecosystems (Lusch & Vargo, 2018; Vargo & Lusch, 2016). Hence, from the initial focus of trying to overcome the goods-versus-services division of exchange outputs, S-D logic has developed into a metatheoretical framework that can be used to explain individual, dyadic, 'market,' or societal level value co-creation. This development builds a foundation for enhancing and extending the impact of some of the core insights from service research.

In this chapter, first an overview of S-D logic is provided. This is done by describing the key developmental periods of S-D logic and the resulting metatheoretical framework, which can be crystalized into five axioms that represent the core ideas of S-D logic. Second, the similarities and differences between S-D logic and related approaches, including 'service logic,' 'customer-dominant logic,' and 'service science,' are discussed to aid scholars in distinguishing these alternative approaches from one another. Then, the applicability and implications of S-D logic are discussed through a synthesis of how S-D logic has been employed within service research, marketing, and other disciplines. Interwoven within this discussion are promising opportunities for future research.

S-D logic as an evolving metatheoretical framework

Over the past 15 years, S-D logic has gone through several evolutionary periods, starting from the initial article that revealed the preoccupation of academic marketing with a dominant logic based on the exchange of manufactured outputs, that is "goods," (Vargo & Lusch, 2004) and expanding to the current narrative of institutionally coordinated value co-creating service ecosystems such as the building blocks of societies (Vargo & Lusch, 2016). This section gives an overview of the evolution of S-D logic by highlighting its central developments and expanding aim.

Challenging goods-dominant logic

S-D logic resulted from an analysis of over four decades of shifting industry practices and pioneering work by scholars who observed that traditional approaches to marketing largely mischaracterized services as a type of market offerings without goods-like qualities (Lusch & Vargo, 2018). This mischaracterization fostered the belief that services were somehow inferior to goods as they could not be easily stored, homogenized, or separated from customer processes. The initial S-D logic article (Vargo & Lusch, 2004) suggested that this underlying mind-set prevailing in traditional marketing theory should be called goods-dominant (G-D) logic, as it sees value as embedded in tangible manufactured outputs and views the distribution of these outputs as the purpose of exchange. The article highlighted several developments, primarily in sub-disciplines of marketing, which were challenging and reframing the assumptions of this dominant worldview. One of the important sub-disciplines on which the initial ideas of S-D logic were built was services marketing. Services marketing and other emerging perspectives within marketing at the time shared an implied logic that placed more emphasis on the exchange of intangible resources over tangible resources, collaboration over competition, and relationships over transactions.

The main argument in Vargo and Lusch (2004) and subsequent work is that these emerging perspectives, together with other transformations taking place outside of marketing, were converging on a potentially transcending perspective, now known as 'service-dominant (S-D) logic.' Hence, initially S-D logic was, at least in part, a response to several calls emphasizing the fragmented nature of academic marketing and the need for a paradigm shift (see e.g. Achrol & Kotler, 1999; Parvatiyar & Sheth, 2000). Vargo and Lusch proposed that marketing thought was not so much fragmented but evolving toward a new dominant logic that integrates goods with service(s) and provides a richer foundation for the development of marketing thought and practice.

During the first years of S-D logic's development, its focus was mainly on tracing the historical unfolding of events that led to the development of the narrow, goods-based model of economic thought (e.g. Vargo & Lusch, 2004; Vargo & Morgan, 2005). The authors noted that G-D logic, which prevailed in much of the academic marketing literature at the time, frames exchange in terms of tangible units of output (i.e., goods) and views the production and exchange of goods as the core of business and economics (Vargo & Lusch, 2004; Vargo et al., 2008). This logic is closely aligned with neoclassical economics, which views actors as rational, profit- and utility-maximizing economic entities among whom information and resources flow easily within equilibrium-seeking markets. Others have referred to G-D logic, for example, as "manufacturing logic" (Normann, 2001) and "company-centric, efficiency-driven view of value creation" (Prahalad & Ramaswamy, 2004). S-D logic's main purpose was to develop an alternative logic of exchange and value creation that broke free from the conventional G-D logic as thoroughly as possible.

There are several problems with G-D logic, but some of the most important ones relate to where it focuses attention. As the name implies, G-D logic fosters goods-centricity. This means that tangible outputs such as goods are viewed as superior to any other form of exchange. G-D logic also places the firm as the central and only active actor in value creation. In other words, it posits that value is something that is produced by the firm and embedded in physical goods during the firm-controlled manufacturing processes and then distributed through the market to the value-destroying 'consumers.' Given this linear and firm-centric view on value creation, G-D logic is also preoccupied with the importance of what something is worth, usually in monetary terms, when exchanged. G-D logic's over-emphasis on goods, firms, and monetary value has led to several deeply ingrained dichotomies that constrain the development of a broader, more general view on economic and social exchange.

In contrast, in S-D logic the purpose of exchange is *value co-creation, which is facilitated through the exchange of service,* that is, the application of specialized resources for the benefit of other actors (and themselves), rather than goods, which are only occasionally used in the transmission of this service. This shift in how exchange is understood also implies a radical change in the meaning of value. G-D logic views value as something determined and produced by the producer that can be embedded in goods and defined in terms of its 'exchange value.' Alternatively, Vargo and Lusch (2004) proposed that value is actually determined by the beneficiary on the basis of the "value in use" that results from the beneficial application of the resources (e.g. knowledge and skills) exchanged. This explicit, foundational idea of S-D logic is built on a shift that has been implicitly highlighted previously by a number of scholars. For example, Kotler (1977, p. 8) noted that the "importance of physical products lies not so much in owning them as in obtaining the services they render." Echoing these views, Normann and Ramírez (1993) argued that tangible goods can be viewed as embodied knowledge or activities, and Coombs and Miles (2000, p. 97) stated that "material products themselves are only physical embodiments of the services they deliver, or tools for the production of final services."

Building on these alternative perspectives, S-D logic articulates an integrated framework for thinking about value co-creation as a reciprocal process perspective on exchange (Vargo & Lusch, 2004). The framework also strengthens and expands the declaration made by Bastiat (1848/1995) 150 years prior stating that "services are exchanged for services." In other words, S-D logic was grounded in an alternative logic of value creation, which argues that exchange is best understood in terms of *service-for-service exchange*, rather than exchange in terms of goods-for-goods or goods-for-money. This means that, in dyadic exchange, what the 'customer' provides back to the 'producer' in return for the service received can also be understood in terms of service exchange, albeit often as an indirect form of service exchange. In other words, the money that the 'customer' uses to 'pay' the 'producer' for the service, comes from earlier service exchanges between the 'customer' (then as a service provider) and the 'customer's customer.' The producer can then use this money to acquire a service from another 'producer.' Hence, the foundational basis of exchange is always service, although in industrialized economies it is often masked by indirect forms of exchange (e.g. goods and money).

When highlighting S-D logic as an alternative to G-D logic, it is important to emphasize that the argument is not so much that G-D logic is wrong, but that it limits understanding by focusing on special cases of exchange and value creation (e.g. goods-for-money), rather than the general case (service-for-service). Hence, Lusch and Vargo (2014) argue that, rather than seeing G-D logic and S-D logic as binary alternatives, G-D logic (or at least 'goods logic') should be seen as a special case nested within S-D logic, rather than replaced by it. In other words, the more general theory of S-D logic can explain the existence of G-D logic as a special case.

Moving beyond firm or customer-centricity

The initial S-D logic article (Vargo & Lusch, 2004) concentrated on how value creation needed to be reframed for understanding of dyadic exchanges (i.e., between a firm and a customer). However, the discussion soon evolved toward emphasizing that value co-creation takes place within and among multiple actors (e.g. Lusch & Vargo, 2006; Vargo & Lusch, 2008). Aligned with S-D logic, Gummesson (2008) claimed that the "marketing concept" and "customer-centricity" are too limited as a foundation for marketing and urged marketing scholars and educators to accept the complexity of marketing by moving toward a network-based stakeholder approach and balanced centricity. Similarly, S-D logic recognizes that the venue of value creation is value configurations—economic and social actors interacting and exchanging across and through networks.

To remove the restrictive nature of pre-assigned labels and allow a higher-level abstraction of actors that are part of value co-creation, traditional designations such as 'buyers,' 'sellers,' 'consumers,' 'roducers,' 'suppliers,' 'middlemen,' and many other role specific terms are avoided in S-D logic, unless they are being referenced in conjunction with the traditional literature. Instead, all actors are referred to as just that, 'actors,' which are seen as being similarly characterized in terms of resource integration and service exchange (Vargo & Lusch, 2011). This means that all actors provide service—applying resources for another's benefit—to receive similar service from others. In this way, S-D logic problematizes the taken-for-granted 'producer–consumer' divide in which humans are separated into active, value-creating actors and passive, value-destroying actors.

Vargo and Lusch (2011) have argued that business-to-business (B2B), rather than the traditional business-to-consumer (B2C) orientation of mainstream marketing, offers a better exemplar of the general actor-to-actor (A2A) orientation. This is because in B2B there are no actors that are strictly producers or consumers but, rather, all actors are considered to be enterprises, working to benefit their own existence by benefiting the existence of other enterprises. In this way, all B2B is service-for-service exchange—either directly or indirectly. However, according to Vargo and Lusch (2016), the A2A orientation and its generic actor designation should not be confused with a position that all actors are identical. Indeed, it is intended to do just the opposite, by dissociating actors from predesignated roles (e.g. consumers) and setting the stage for characterizing them in terms of distinctly constituted identities.

Furthermore, S-D logic zooms out beyond the traditional dyadic focus of firm and customer to a wider, more comprehensive configuration of actors in its perspective of value co-creation (Vargo & Lusch, 2011, 2016). S-D logic argues that value creation occurs at the intersections of activities of providers, beneficiaries, and other actors. It is recognized that actors continually integrate resources from multiple sources (Lusch & Vargo, 2014; Vargo & Lusch, 2011), including: 'private' (e.g. family, friends), 'market-facing' (e.g. firms and other 'market' actors), and 'public' sources (e.g. communal and governmental actors). Hence, value is created through the integration of resources by multiple actors in a specific context, rather than manufactured and then delivered (Vargo et al., 2008).

S-D logic also implies that the beneficiary is always an active participant in its own value-creation process—that is, a co-creator of value (Lusch & Vargo, 2006). In other words, for value to be perceived by the beneficiary and, thus, value creation to occur, the beneficiary's (e.g. customer) operant resources must also be integrated. Consider, for example, having dinner in a restaurant. Although the food is prepared and served by others, the diner must integrate her knowledge of the use of the cutlery, chewing, and so on with the provided meal for value-in-use to be perceived. However, it is important to note here, that the generic actor (or A2A) orientation makes all actors simultaneously providers and beneficiaries through direct and indirect service-for-service exchange (Vargo & Lusch, 2011). The beneficiary role in value determination should not be seen as implying that S-D logic is solely 'customer-centric,' as it also sees service providers as beneficiaries who determine value outcomes for themselves.

As actors, over time, specialize in applying certain kinds of knowledge and skills for one another, they become less self-sufficient and more dependent on one another (Vargo & Lusch, 2004; cf., Normann, 2001; Ridley, 2010). S-D logic's A2A orientation revealed several other insights that led to the increasing realization of the complexity and dynamics of value co-creation. First, this orientation confirms that value co-creation takes place in networks, because it implies that the resources used in service provision typically, at least in part, come from other actors (Vargo & Lusch, 2011). Second, it suggests a dynamic component to these networks, because each integration or application of resources changes the nature of the network in some way (Chandler & Vargo, 2011). This knowledge, in turn, highlights that a network view alone is inadequate and that a more dynamic systems orientation is necessary (Vargo & Lusch, 2011; Wieland, Polese, Vargo & Lusch, 2012).

Embracing the systemic and institutional nature of value co-creation

In the numerous elaborations and extensions of S-D logic, one of the most important has been a general *zooming out* to allow a more holistic, dynamic, and realistic perspective of value creation, through exchange, among a wider configuration of actors (Vargo & Lusch, 2016). S-D logic is based on an understanding of the interwoven fabric of individuals and organizations, brought together into networks and societies, specializing in and exchanging service to create value in the context of their everyday lives (Chandler & Vargo, 2011; Lusch & Vargo, 2014). It highlights the dynamic and complex nature of value co-creation by arguing that actors continually integrate, apply, and exchange available resources from multiple sources, for value co-creation (Vargo & Lusch, 2011). This zooming out to understand value creation has resulted in a major turn toward a systems orientation in S-D logic (Chandler & Vargo, 2011; Vargo & Lusch, 2011). It also made apparent the need to articulate more clearly the mechanisms—institutions—that enable and constrain the often massive-scale coordination involved in systems of value co-creation (Vargo & Lusch, 2016).

Institutions should not be confused with the more everyday use of the word referring to firms, governmental agencies, or any such organizations. Instead, institutions in a sociological sense, as used here, consist of formalized rules and less formalized norms defining appropriate behavior, as well as cultural beliefs and cognitive models, frames, and schemas encapsulating the often taken-for-granted assumptions and beliefs fundamental to guiding social action in different situations (Scott, 2014). In other words, *institutional arrangements*—sets of interrelated institutions—represent the structure of social systems that lend them their systemic form (Giddens, 1984). In a slightly narrower sense, institutional arrangements can be thought of as the "rules of the game" in a society (North, 1990), which enable and constrain the way resources are integrated and how value is both co-created and determined (Vargo & Akaka, 2012; Vargo & Lusch, 2016; Wieland, Koskela-Huotari & Vargo, 2016).

The metatheoretical framework of S-D logic not only accommodates institutional arrangements; their coordinating role is essential for a deeper understanding of the value co-creating processes. Both the systemic and institutional orientation of S-D logic are encapsulated in the concept of *service ecosystems*, defined as "relatively self-contained, self-adjusting system of resource-integrating actors connected by shared institutional arrangements and mutual value creation through service exchange" (Vargo & Lusch, 2016, pp. 10–11). The term ecosystem in the service ecosystems perspective is used because it denotes actor–environmental interaction and energy flow (Vargo & Lusch, 2016). In *service* ecosystems this energy flow is understood in terms of reciprocal service provision. A society can be seen as a service ecosystem or, more finely grained, as comprising nested and overlapping service ecosystems (Lusch & Vargo, 2014; Vargo & Lusch, 2011, 2016), which in turn are composed of assemblages and sub-assemblages of resource-integrating, service-exchanging actors that constrain and coordinate themselves through institutional arrangements (Vargo & Lusch, 2016).

For analytical purposes, these structural assemblages can be viewed at various levels of aggregation (Vargo & Lusch, 2017), sometimes identified as "micro," "meso," and "macro" (Chandler & Vargo, 2011). Previous S-D logic research tends to place individual and dyadic structures and activities at the micro level; midrange structures and activities, such as an industry and a brand community, at the meso level; and broader structures and activities, such as states, at the macro level (Chandler & Vargo, 2011; Lusch & Vargo, 2014). However, it should be understood that 'levels' connote relative perspectives, rather than absolute associations. One advantage of having a multilevel (of aggregation) systemic understanding of value co-creation is that one can take advantage of "oscillating foci" (Chandler & Vargo, 2011), which facilitates understanding of the connectedness and contextualization of value co-creation, in a manner that is not otherwise possible.

The five axioms of S-D logic

As discussed, S-D logic offers a framework of value co-creation that is applicable at all levels of aggregation. In terms of its level of abstraction, this framework can be described as metatheoretical; that is, it resides at a rather high level of abstraction (see Vargo & Lusch, 2017 for a more detailed discussion of levels of abstraction). Although there is recent and

ongoing work in this research stream targeted at more specific midrange theoretical developments (e.g. Storbacka, Brodie, Böhmann, Maglio & Nenonen, 2016), the primary focus of
S-D logic to date has been to build its metatheoretical framework (Vargo & Lusch, 2016).
This framework is captured in five axioms, some of which are implied in the above discussion, that are elaborated in the following sections.

Axiom 1: service is the fundamental basis of exchange

To understand the meaning of Axiom 1 'Service is the fundamental basis of exchange,' it is
important to recognize that S-D logic represents a shift in the *underlying logic of exchange*, rather
than a shift in the emphasis of the type of output that is under investigation. This shift of logic
is achieved by introducing a processual conceptualization of *service* (singular)—the application
of resources for the benefit of another—as the basis of exchange (Vargo & Lusch, 2004, 2008).
In other words, the concept of service focuses on the *process of serving* rather than on a type of
output, such as "services" (plural) or intangible goods. Consequently, S-D logic is not about
making services more important than goods, but rather about transcending the two types of
outputs through a common denominator—service, a process.

With the help of this processual conceptualization of the basis of exchange, exchange can be
understood as actors applying their competencies to provide service for others and reciprocally
receiving a similar kind of service (others' applied competencies or money as 'rights' for future
competencies) in return. However, direct service exchange is often masked by indirect service
exchange, which refers to providing service not in person but through a good (i.e., vehicle for
service provision) or monetary currency (i.e., rights for future service). These indirect forms of
service exchange are also part of the processual understanding of exchange as service and, therefore, the concept of service exchange in S-D logic is not tied to the distinct moments of direct
physical interaction among people (Vargo, 2008) as is the case in the conventional literature on
services (Lovelock, 1983; Zeithaml, Parasuraman & Berry, 1985).

Axiom 2: value is co-created by multiple actors, always including the beneficiary

As discussed, S-D logic not only reframes the nature of exchange, but also its purpose.
Whereas G-D logic would consider the purpose of exchange to be firm profit, S-D logic
argues that the purpose is value co-creation. When S-D logic talks about *value*, it does not
refer to profit or the worth of something. Instead, value is broadly defined as "an emergent,
positively or negatively valenced change in the well-being or viability of a particular system/
actor" (Vargo & Lusch, 2018, p. 740).

S-D logic's conceptualization of the process of value creation also significantly differs
from the linear and sequential creation and destruction of value emphasized in G-D logic
(Wieland et al., 2016). Rather than placing the firm as the primary value creator and focusing on the value-contributing activities among two actors (usually a firm and a customer),
S-D logic argues for the existence of more complex and dynamic exchange systems within
which value co-creation occurs at the intersections of activities of providers, beneficiaries,
and other actors (Vargo & Lusch, 2011; Wieland et al., 2012). In this view, for value co-
creation to occur, there must be integration of the beneficiary actor's resources with those
applied by the service provider and others. All of this, in turn, implies that every time value
emerges as a result of resource integration, it is always co-created by multiple actors.

To conceptualize the configurations of actors involved in value co-creation, the concept of *service ecosystem* was introduced in S-D logic (Lusch & Vargo, 2014; Vargo & Lusch, 2011). The service ecosystems perspective is a systemic view on value co-creation in which the activities of resource-integrating actors, preceding a specific instance of value determination by an actor, are seen as part of the value co-creation process. In other words, the service ecosystem perspective emphasizes that value creation does not just take place through the activities of a single actor (e.g. customer) or between a firm and its customers, but that value unfolds over time among a whole host of actors.

Axiom 3: all social and economic actors are resource integrators

As explained, S-D logic argues that all actors provide service (apply resources for the benefit of others) to receive similar service from others (other actors applying their resources) in the process of co-creating value (Vargo & Lusch, 2011). This means that all actors are both providers and beneficiaries of service and that the activities and characteristics of actors are not fundamentally dichotomous, as implied by the conceptual division of economic actors into producers and consumers. Hence, Axiom 3 'All social and economic actors are resource integrators,' with Axiom 1, implies the unrestricted, A2A orientation as previously discussed.

In addition to reframing the actors taking part in resource integration, S-D logic also implies changes in the way resources are understood. Resources, in S-D logic, are viewed *"as anything, tangible or intangible, internal or external, operand or operant, an actor can draw on for increased viability"* (Lusch & Vargo, 2014, p. 121, emphasis in original). The literature regarding resources in S-D logic recognizes that two broad types of resources are being integrated (Vargo & Lusch, 2004). *Operand resources*, such as natural resources, require action taken upon them to be valuable. *Operant resources*, such as knowledge and skills, are capable of acting on other resources to contribute to value creation. Aligned with many of the resource-based views (Barney, 1991; Penrose, 2009), S-D logic emphasizes the primacy of operant resources over operand resources in value co-creation. In other words, although operand resources often contribute to the co-creation of value, without the application of operant resources, such as knowledge, skills, and competencies, value co-creation does not occur (Vargo & Lusch, 2004).

It is important to understand that, in S-D logic, potential resources are realized in the context and through the application of other resources. In other words, *resources are not, they become* (De Gregori, 1987; Vargo & Lusch, 2004). This means that resources such as knowledge and skills, and the availability of other resources, determine the *resourceness* of potential resources (Koskela-Huotari & Vargo, 2016; Lusch & Vargo, 2014). Consider, for example, fire: the resourceness of fire only became available for humans once the knowledge and skills to control and apply fire for specific purposes were developed. Hence, potential resources become resources, when appraised and acted on through integration with other potential resources.

Axiom 4: value is always uniquely and phenomenologically determined by the beneficiary

As stated in S-D logic, value is considered to be an emergent outcome of the resource integration that maintains or increases the well-being of a particular actor. This value is phenomenologically determined by each actor in their (social) context (Chandler & Vargo, 2011; Edvardsson, Tronvoll & Gruber, 2011; Vargo & Lusch, 2008). This means that value is perceived experientially and differently by diverse actors in varying contexts, and that each instance of value co-creation can have multiple possible assessments, including negatively valenced ones (Vargo, Akaka & Vaughan, 2017).

The contextual and phenomenological nature of value determination should not, however, be confused with randomness or naive subjectivism. Instead, S-D logic argues that value determination, like value co-creation, is guided by social structure and the complex constellations of institutional arrangements influencing actors (Siltaloppi, Koskela-Huotari & Vargo, 2016; Vargo & Lusch, 2016). In other words, "value-in-context suggests that value is not only always cocreated; it is contingent on the integration of other resources and actors" (Lusch & Vargo, 2014, p. 23). The systemic and institutional conceptualization of value enables the reconciliation of value-in-use and value-in-exchange because it provides the means for considering how various aspects of value are informed by institutional arrangements both in use and in exchange (cf., Vargo et al., 2017).

Axiom 5: value co-creation is coordinated through actor-generated institutions and institutional arrangements

The need to articulate more clearly the mechanisms that enable and constrain the often massive-scale cooperation involved in value co-creation was made apparent by S-D logic's movement toward a systems orientation and, more specifically, the introduction of the service ecosystems perspective discussed earlier in this chapter (Vargo & Lusch, 2011, 2016). Hence, Axiom 5, 'value co-creation is coordinated through actor-generated institutions and institutional arrangements,' was added to emphasize the importance of institutions. Institutions are the "regulative, normative and cultural-cognitive elements that, together with associated activities and resources, provide stability and meaning to social life" (Scott, 2014, p. 56). They play a central role in value co-creation as they enable actors to accomplish an ever-increasing level of collaboration under time and cognitive constraints (Vargo & Lusch, 2016). This is because institutions allow actors to perform important operations without thinking about them (Simon, 1996; Whitehead, 1911). When shared, institutions result in a network effect that enables growing returns as the potential coordination benefit to all actors increases.

Within the value co-creation narrative of S-D logic, institutions take on an expanded role and provide the building blocks for the increasingly complex and interrelated resource-integration activities in nested and overlapping ecosystems organized around shared purposes (Vargo & Lusch, 2016). Hence, value in S-D logic is informed by the institutional arrangements guiding actors' resource-integration processes. This view on value draws on the studies viewing value as an experience (Prahalad & Ramaswamy, 2004), but extends the understanding of the context of experience to consider the contributions and influence of multiple actors and other resources involved in deriving and determining value (Akaka, Vargo & Lusch, 2013). Institutional arrangements not only coordinate the process of value co-creation among multiple actors, but also provide criteria for value determination (cf., Friedland & Alford, 1991).

S-D logic and related perspectives: similarities and differences

As S-D logic has evolved, a few seemingly similar perspectives have also been proffered. Among them are *service logic, customer-dominant logic,* and *service science.* All of these perspectives share common goals of exposing the limitations of G-D logic and the desire to capture the underlying logic of exchange and value creation. At first glance, they might seem very similar, and some scholars have even used them interchangeably. They do, however, have significant differences in their foundational assumptions and focus. Therefore, it is important to understand how S-D logic is different from these related perspectives.

Most notably, the perspectives differ in terms of how they conceptualize value and which actors are taken as the focal actors under study. All of the four perspectives significantly differ from G-D logic, which conceptualizes the outcome of value creation primarily in terms of value-in-exchange (i.e., the price of something) and considers the firm as the single active actor in the value-creation process. However, the four perspectives differ from each other in terms of whether they conceptualize the outcome of the value-creation process as value-in-use or value-in-context[1] and whether they view one, two, or more actors as 'central' in the value-creation process. Figure 1.1 shows the varying scope of these perspectives, S-D logic being the most expansive and holistic in that it accommodates all of the conceptualizations of value and different focal actors in value co-creation, incorporating the other perspectives as special, restricted perspectives.

As discussed, S-D logic's metatheoretical framework has evolved into a narrative explaining how the co-creation value-in-context occurs in multi-actor configurations conceptualized as service ecosystems. According to this narrative, each actor participating in the focal

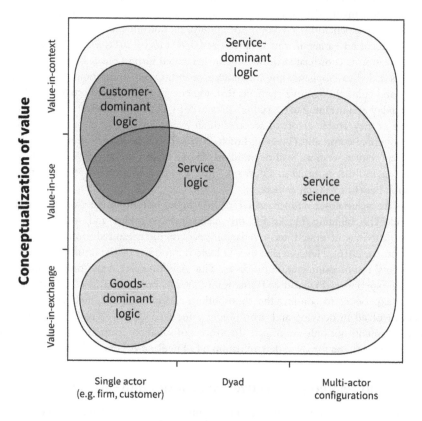

Figure 1.1 Comparing the conceptualization of value and focal actors of S-D logic and related perspectives.

exchange system creates and experiences value (positive or negative) guided by (partially) shared institutional arrangements that make up the context for joint value creation. Within this systemic understanding of value co-creation, perspectives such as service logic and customer-dominant logic, in which the views of the focal actors are more limited, can be seen as special, restricted cases of the more general S-D logic narrative. In other words, it is possible to *zoom in* to examine specific actors and their institutionalized roles and activities within value creation. However, S-D logic also advocates the importance of zooming out to understand the roles of other actors, as well as the institutional contexts of their actions. By elaborating the role of goods as an indirect form of service exchange, S-D logic can also accommodate something like a 'goods logic' to the extent that tangible outputs as service vehicles are included in exchange as a special case, but not seen as the foundational and therefore dominant basis of exchange.

Furthermore, the generalizable conceptualization of value-in-context in S-D logic makes it possible to *zoom in* to focus on specific institutionalized ways of determining value, such as value-in-exchange in which actors try to make sense of the (potential) value outcomes by giving monetary labels to them, or value-in-use in which the (potential) value outcomes are expressed in terms of the nature of the benefits that result as resources are integrated to accomplish a specific desired end. In other words, other perspectives using either a value-in-exchange and value-in-use conceptualization of value can be seen as special cases of S-D logic, which employs a more generalizable value-in-context conceptualization. Against this backdrop, the differences between S-D logic and service logic, customer-dominant logic and service science are discussed in more detail below.

Service logic

Service logic is discussed in a stream of literature that has stemmed from the criticism of Christian Grönroos (2008) toward S-D logic; he argues that S-D logic does not fully support an understanding of value creation and co-creation in a way that is meaningful for theoretical development and decision-making in business and marketing practice. Similar to the initial developments in S-D logic, service logic builds on the value-in-use conceptualization of value, which implies that value unfolds as customers use resources that they have purchased (Grönroos, 2008, 2011). Whereas S-D logic more explicitly advocates balanced centricity (Gummesson, 2008) and builds a contextual conception of value, service logic maintains the view of value as utility experienced by the customer. More specifically, service logic argues that "value is created by the user for the user" and that "the customer as the user and integrator of resources is a value creator" (Grönroos, 2011, p. 288). As the locus of value creation is viewed at the customer's end, the role of the service provider in service logic is not that of a value co-creator as S-D logic would argue, but rather that of a "value facilitator" (Grönroos, 2008, p. 307) with value solely created by the customer. Service logic views value as co-created only in select instances, specifically those in which there is direct, personal interaction between the provider and the beneficiary (Grönroos & Voima, 2013). Thus, although service logic theorizes about value creation between two actors (i.e., a dyad), the default position is more restricted, because the firm-centric view on value creation inherent in G-D logic is essentially replaced by one in which the customer is the sole, central actor. In doing so, service logic effectively replaces one central actor, the firm, with another, the customer.

Due to the strong focus on the dyad of the firm and the customer to conceptualize value creation, service logic has criticized S-D logic's systemic conceptualization of value co-creation on the grounds that it has overstated the extent of value co-creation (see e.g. Grönroos, 2011;

Grönroos & Voima, 2013). However, one could argue that, even in Grönroos and Voima's (2013) view of value creation, multiple actors are needed to enable each other's value-creation processes and, therefore, 'sole' value creation is not possible without narrowing the analysis of the process to only the activities performed by the customer. To break free from both of these restricted models, S-D logic argues that value creation does not simply take place through the activities of a single actor (e.g. customer) or between a firm and its customers but among a whole host of actors. Hence, in S-D logic, value is conceptualized as unfolding and influenced, over time, by a host of activities of various resource-integrating actors, both prior to and during a specific instance of value determination. In other words, interactions between actors separated by time and space are as much part of the systemic understanding of value co-creation as interactions occurring in person at one particular point in time and space. As stated, S-D logic therefore encourages zooming out to see the related, direct and indirect, activities of a full range of actors, as well as zooming in to see the activities of single actors in context. From this perspective, the conceptual difference between 'co-create' and 'facilitate' emphasized in service logic becomes questionable (Vargo & Lusch, 2016). The limited focus on one or two actors (customer and firm) can be seen as a very restricted view of the more general, systemic understanding of value co-creation.

Customer-dominant logic

Around the same time that the first service logic articles were published, another perspective was brought forward that was positioned as a customer-based approach to service (Heinonen et al., 2010; Heinonen, Strandvik & Voima, 2013). More specifically, this resulting perspective, called customer-dominant logic, "is a marketing and business perspective dominated by customer-related aspects instead of products, service, systems, costs or growth" (Heinonen & Strandvik, 2015, p. 472). Customer-dominant logic focuses on "value formation," by which customers interpret an offering (what a provider sells) in use in their everyday lives (Heinonen et al., 2013) coming rather close to the initial S-D logic understanding of value-in-context (Vargo et al., 2008), albeit with a single-actor interpretation. However, although customer-dominant logic recognizes two distinct processes of value formation, the customer's and the provider's, it emphasizes that the customer is in control in service situations and that managers should work to see through the lens of the customer (Heinonen & Strandvik, 2015).

In the initial customer-dominant logic article, Heinonen et al. (2010, p. 532) argued that even though S-D logic had widened the scope of marketing, it was still very production focused and "service provider-dominant" rather than "customer-dominant." This view has been maintained, more recently, by Heinonen and Strandvik (2015). The justification for this interpretation seems to be the S-D logic starting point, which includes the service provider in the value-creation equation. However, it ignores that S-D logic also recognizes, in any given value (co)creation occasion, that the beneficiary (e.g. customer) is the primary resource-integrating actor (Lusch, Vargo & O'Brien, 2007) and always the focal actor in value determination (Vargo & Lusch, 2008, 2016). Even more generally, it ignores the reciprocal nature of service provision in exchange (Vargo & Lusch, 2004) as well as the A2A orientation (Vargo & Lusch, 2011) of S-D logic, which sees all actors, simultaneously, as both service providers and beneficiaries. This means that, although the beneficiary's role in value determination is highlighted, it does not make S-D logic customer-centric (or provider-centric), as all actors are beneficiaries that determine value outcomes for themselves. Calling out one actor as "central" is not aligned with the systemic view of value co-creation within S-D logic. In short, S-D logic is inclusive of all actors involved in value co-creation, rather than limited by a more restricted view of the activities of a single party that determines value in a specific context. Arguably, it is also difficult to see what customer-dominant logic adds that is not already present in the market orientation and similar customer-focused orientations (e.g. Deshpande, Farley & Webster, 1993; Kohli & Jaworski, 1990).

Service science

A third related perspective to S-D logic is service science. Service science is "the study of service systems, which are dynamic value co-creation configurations of resources (people, technology, organizations and shared information)" (Maglio & Spohrer, 2008, p. 18). It differs from the other two perspectives discussed in that its philosophical underpinnings are directly drawn from S-D logic (Maglio & Spohrer, 2008; Maglio, Vargo, Caswell & Spohrer, 2009) and therefore it is much more closely aligned with S-D logic in terms of the two dimensions highlighted in Figure 1.1.

The connection between S-D logic and service science has been further extended as the concept of a service ecosystem was introduced to S-D logic (Vargo & Lusch, 2011). A service system in service science is defined as "a configuration of people, technologies and other resources that interact with other service systems to create mutual value" (Maglio et al., 2009). In other words, the unit of analysis in value creation according to service science is multi-actor configurations similar to those in S-D logic.

In its service ecosystems perspective, S-D logic advances the understanding of how socially constructed institutions, such as norms and meanings, mediate value co-creation (Vargo & Akaka, 2012; Vargo & Lusch, 2016). Spohrer and Maglio (2010, p. 159), on the other hand, emphasize the importance of socially constructed meaning in service systems and highlight the way in which "symbols guide both internal behavior and mediate interactions with other entities." As such, service science is closely aligned with S-D logic's institutional turn in understanding how value co-creation and the determination of value-in-context is coordinated. Recently, works drawing on the service ecosystems view have highlighted the importance of institutions as central drivers of the actions and interactions that enable innovation (Siltaloppi et al., 2016; Vargo, Wieland & Akaka, 2015). As innovation is one of the focal phenomena service science aims to further explain, an institutional turn opens up many opportunities for advancing service science and extending its conceptualization of value(-in-context) (Akaka, Koskela-Huotari & Vargo, 2019). Generally, however, the differences between S-D logic and service science should be seen in terms of emphasis rather than underlying philosophy. Thus, even the apparent differences are typically easily reconciled.

Applications and implications of S-D logic

As discussed throughout this chapter, S-D logic is evolving toward a general theory of value co-creation as the purpose of society (Vargo & Lusch, 2017), not simply for a particular subset of social activities studied by marketing or service scholars. Rather, S-D logic's metatheoretical framework offers a transcendent perspective that is broadly applicable across sectors, contexts, and disciplines. This section first gives an overview of vectors of 'diffusion' in service, marketing, and other research streams according to S-D logic, to highlight its applicability to a broad range of phenomena and disciplinary interests. Second, the chapter discusses how S-D logic and its service ecosystem view can contribute to advancing and expanding the scope of service research by outlining three characteristics of the metatheoretical framework and examples of their implications.

Applications of S-D logic

Along with the development of a more robust narrative, the axioms of S-D logic have been widely applied across a broad range of research streams and disciplines. For a more detailed description of vectors of diffusion in S-D logic, see Vargo and Lusch (2017). In the following section, examples of application areas of S-D logic in service, marketing, and other research streams are highlighted.

Service research

As a service-centered perspective on exchange, S-D logic has direct applicability across the areas of service research. Through the evolution of its overarching framework, S-D logic has helped to advance the conceptualization of a number of concepts and discussions in service research, such as *service innovation* (e.g. Lusch & Nambisan, 2015; Michel, Brown & Gallan, 2008), *service design* (e.g. Kimbell, 2011; Wetter-Edman, Vink & Blomkvist, 2018), *servicescape* (Akaka & Vargo, 2015; Nilsson & Ballantyne, 2014), and *customer engagement* (e.g. Brodie, Hollebeek, Juric & Ilic, 2011; Hollebeek, Srivastava & Chen, 2019). More generally, highlighting S-D logic's transcending view of service as a perspective, rather than focusing on services as a context of direct exchange, significantly extends the scope of service research from a narrow focus on business contexts where intangible outputs are sold, to exploring value co-creation processes in a variety of contexts in which exchange, regardless of the type of the exchange output, occurs. By elevating service research from something defined by an economic sector or specialized context, S-D logic also enhances the relevance of service research for marketing and many other disciplines.

Marketing

The metatheoretical framework of S-D logic has been used to inform a variety of research areas within marketing and is increasingly helping to guide the development of a general theory of the market. S-D logic has been taken up across many sub-disciplines of marketing, including *branding* (e.g. Halliday, 2016; Merz, He & Vargo, 2009), *supply chains* (Flint & Mentzer, 2006; Tokman & Beitelspacher, 2011), *consumer culture* (e.g. Arnould, 2007; Schau, Muñiz & Arnould, 2009), and *social marketing* (e.g. Luca, Hibbert & McDonald, 2015; Russell-Bennett, Wood & Previte, 2013). The most recent application areas also include *business models* (Wieland, Hartmann & Vargo, 2017) and *sales* (Hartmann, Wieland & Vargo, 2018). Traditionally, marketing has been understood as a small sub-domain of economics and business, focused narrowly on the techniques of the marketing department of a firm. S-D logic suggests, instead, that marketing should be understood as the study of value co-creation through markets, broadly applicable to economics, business, and society at large.

Other disciplines and research streams

S-D logic is evolving toward a general theory of value co-creation as the purpose of society, not simply for a particular subset of social activities (Vargo & Lusch, 2017). As it evolves, S-D logic is building a unified lexicon and systemic understanding of value co-creation that is broadly applicable across sectors and contexts. Already, S-D logic has informed and supported theorization in many disciplines and research streams outside of the traditional boundaries of service research and marketing, including: *engineering* (e.g. Isaksson, Larsson & Rönnbäck, 2009; Meier, Völker & Funke, 2011), *information systems* (e.g. Alter, 2010; Yan, Ye, Wang & Hua, 2010),

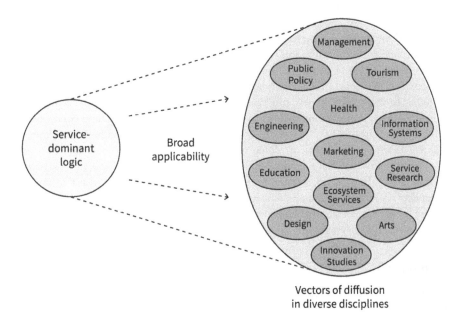

Figure 1.2 The broad applicability of S-D logic and existing vectors of diffusion in diverse disciplines.

tourism (e.g. FitzPatrick, Davey, Muller & Davey, 2013; Shaw, Bailey & Williams, 2011), *management* (e.g. Pels, 2012; Subramony & Pugh, 2015), *health* (e.g. Hardyman, Daunt & Kitchener, 2015; Rehman, Dean & Pires, 2012), *arts philosophy and creative industries* (e.g. Boorsma, 2006; Hearn, Roodhouse & Blakey, 2007), *design* (e.g. Chen & Vargo, 2010; Kimbell, 2011), *ecosystem services* (Matthies et al., 2016), *innovation studies* (e.g. Michel et al., 2008; Vargo et al., 2015), *public policy and administration* (e.g. Osborne, Radnor & Nasi, 2013), and *education* (e.g. Jarvis, Halvorson, Sadeque & Johnston, 2014). Figure 1.2 shows the broad applicability of S-D logic and existing vectors of diffusion within these different disciplines (for more details, see Vargo & Lusch, 2017). The application of S-D logic brings a unifying service perspective that enables the development of novel insights about the co-creation of value and supporting systems within these diverse research streams.

Implications of applying S-D logic

In addition to the axioms, S-D logic offers scholars and practitioners a mind-set that can help them to create parsimony amid complexity as well as to reconceptualize traditional concepts and develop new ones (Koskela-Huotari & Vargo, 2018). The next section describes some of the characteristics of the S-D logic mind-set and their implications for areas of service research, with support from illustrative examples.

Transcendence

The application of an S-D logic mind-set involves transcendence, that is, the reconciliation of some of the tensions and paradoxes within existing ways of thinking. Transcendence often involves creating higher-order abstractions that accommodate a broad range of specific phenomena. One central act of transcendence in S-D logic was the conceptualization of service (singular) that reconciled the dichotomy between goods and 'services' within G-D logic. Another example of this transcendent conceptualization can be found in the application of S-D logic to divergent discussions on the concept of innovation. Through the application of S-D logic, a conceptual inversion was made from a focus on innovation as output exchanged within a dyad (Michel et al., 2008), to innovation as new processes of value co-creation for multiple actors (Lusch & Nambisan, 2015). This inversion enabled the development of an overarching conceptualization of innovation as a process of changing the institutional arrangements guiding actors' integration of resources (Vargo et al., 2015). In doing so, the application of S-D logic offered a unifying perspective on innovation that includes both technical and nontechnical activities (Akaka, Vargo & Wieland, 2017). In addition, scholars have also begun applying S-D logic as a means to build a transcendent view that spans across human and natural systems (Matthies et al., 2016). In this space, S-D logic offers an alternative service-based view of ecosystems that may help to reconcile differences across living systems.

Accommodation

S-D logic is an accommodating mind-set that is capable of reconciling and synthesizing insights from various research streams. In fact, since its inception, S-D logic has built on the evolving literature across diverse research streams, as well as on shifting industry practices. As a metatheoretical framework, S-D logic is open to additional sources of input that align with its processual, systemic, and institutional orientation. Important sources of input include: institutional theory, practice theory, systems theory, complexity theory, and evolutionary theory (Vargo & Lusch, 2017). As S-D logic continues its development, it encourages input and ideas from other aligned research streams.

More generally, because of S-D logic's metatheoretical orientation and its arguably cohesive, explanatory narrative, S-D logic lends itself to simultaneous conceptual reconciliation across a wide array of other theoretical frameworks dealing with various aspects of network and system behaviors, governance, institutional processes, value creation, and similar phenomena. This, in turn, potentially affords the facilitation of cross-fertilization and interdisciplinary research, as well as practical application. For example, in discussions related to service design, a S-D logic mind-set has been used to integrate insights from design, pragmatism, and institutional theory to build a better understanding of how the embodied experiences of actors can trigger institutional work in service ecosystems (Wetter-Edman et al., 2018).

Likewise, because it is accommodating, S-D logic can also lend itself as a metatheoretical framework to interdisciplinary research areas, such as sustainability. Within S-D logic, value is understood in terms of well-being and the viability or survivability of the system (Vargo & Lusch, 2018). With that understanding, a general theory of value co-creation is of fundamental relevance to discourse about environmental and social sustainability. Through integration of other institutional and ecosystems theories, such as common resource governance (Ostrom, 1990), panarchy cycles (Gunderson & Holling, 2002), or autopoiesis (Maturana & Varela, 1980), S-D logic could aid in building a conceptual framework that supports the self-adjustment of service ecosystems in a way that acknowledges global resource limitations and the implications of climate change. Similarly, there have been preliminary links made between S-D logic and Corporate Social Responsibility (e.g. Enquist, Edvardsson & Petros Sebhatu, 2008), and there are promising opportunities for advancing this discussion through a service ecosystem view.

Transformation

Application of the S-D logic mind-set supports transformation in the sense that it allows new insights that were not previously possible. S-D logic not only provides a means of problematizing underlying assumptions within G-D logic, but also offers an alternative perspective that can help generate new and interesting conceptual and practical developments. For example, inspired by S-D logic, there is an evolving research agenda for a "public-service dominant" approach in the field of public administration (Osborne et al., 2013). Furthermore, when S-D logic's service ecosystems perspective is applied to the domain of public policy and administration, it shifts the focus from delivering services (direct exchange) to coordinating actors' value co-creation activities across levels of aggregation to address public concerns (Trischler & Charles, 2019).

As such, S-D logic provides a more holistic and systemic view of the role of government in shaping institutional arrangements, well beyond the traditional role of establishing legislation and providing services. Building on Scott's (2014) three pillars of institutions—regulative, normative and cultural-cognitive – the role of governments is expanded outside the limits of existing notions of policy to include all of the informal, taken-for-granted social structures guiding actors' integration of resources. In the case of public healthcare, for example, the application of S-D logic highlights the importance of governments shifting away from a dominant focus on contexts of direct exchanges, such as hospital services, toward shaping the institutional arrangements that influence how actors co-create well-being in their everyday lives (see e.g. Joiner & Lusch, 2016).

Conclusion

S-D logic argues that service—the process of using one's resources for the benefit of another actor—rather than goods is the basis of exchange. This core insight has enabled the development of a metatheoretical framework that reframes both the nature of exchange and its purpose and has significant consequences to the way value creation is understood across various levels of aggregation. More specifically, S-D logic and its service ecosystems perspective offer a more holistic, dynamic, and systemic understanding of the co-creation of contextual value among a wide configuration of actors. Applying the S-D logic mind-set can help to enable transcendence, accommodation, and transformation in both practice and theory. With widespread diffusion in service research, marketing, and a growing number of other disciplines, S-D logic offers a fruitful platform for interdisciplinary research collaborations that illuminate taken-for-granted assumptions inherited from neoclassical economics and together work toward strengthening an alternative understanding of a society.

Note

1 'Value-in-context' was originally introduced by Vargo et al. (2008) as a semantic improvement in relation to the more G-D logic-appropriate 'value-in-use.' However, over time, it has morphed into a more differentiated concept, emphasizing the contextual and systemic-specific nature of value.

References

Achrol, R. S., & Kotler, P. (1999). Marketing in the network economy. *Journal of Marketing*, 63(Special Issue), 146–163.

Akaka, M. A., Koskela-Huotari, K., & Vargo, S. L. (2019). Further advancing service science with service-dominant logic: Service ecosystems, institutions, and their implications for innovation. In

Maglio, P. P., Kieliszewski, C. A., Spohrer, J. C., Lyons, K., Patricio, L. & Sawatani, Y. (Eds.), *Handbook of service science* (Vol. 2, pp. 641–659). New York: Springer.

Akaka, M. A., & Vargo, S. L. (2015). Extending the context of service: From encounters to ecosystems. *Journal of Services Marketing*, 29(6/7), 453–462.

Akaka, M. A., Vargo, S. L., & Lusch, R. F. (2013). The complexity of context: A service ecosystems approach for international marketing. *Journal of International Marketing*, 21(4), 1–20.

Akaka, M. A., Vargo, S. L., & Wieland, H. (2017). Extending the context of innovation: The co-creation and institutionalization of technology and markets. In Russo-Spena, T., Mele, C., & Nuutinen, M. (Eds.), *Innovating in practice: Perspectives and experiences* (pp. 43–57). Cham and Switzerland: Springer International Publishing.

Alter, S. (2010). Viewing systems as services: A fresh approach in the IS field. *Communications of the Association for Information Systems*, 26(1), 196–224.

Arnould, E. J. (2007). Service-dominant logic and consumer culture theory: Natural allies in an emerging paradigm. In R. W. Belk & F. J. Sherry, Jr. (Eds.), *Research in consumer behavior: Consumer culture theory* (Vol. 11, pp. 57–78). Oxford, UK: JAI Press and Elsevier.

Barney, J. (1991). Firm resources and sustained competitive advantage. *Journal of Management*, 17(1), 99–120.

Bastiat, F. (1848/1995). *Selected essays on political economy* (S. Cain, Trans. G. B. Huszar Ed.). New York and Irvington-on-Hudson: The Foundation for Economic Education, Inc.

Boorsma, M. (2006). A strategic logic for arts marketing: Integrating customer value and artistic objectives. *International Journal of Cultural Policy*, 12(1), 73–92.

Brodie, R. J., Hollebeek, L. D., Juric, B., & Ilic, A. (2011). Customer engagement: Conceptual domain, fundamental propositions, and implications for research. *Journal of Service Research*, 14(3), 252–271.

Chandler, J. D., & Vargo, S. L. (2011). Contextualization and value-in-context: How context frames exchange. *Marketing Theory*, 11(1), 35–49.

Chen, H.-M., & Vargo, S. L. (2010). Service-oriented challenges for design science: Charting the "E"-volution. *Pacific Asia Journal of the Association for Information Systems*, 2(1), 1–15.

Coombs, R., & Miles, I. (2000). Innovation, measurement and services: The new problematique. In J. S. Metcalfe & I. Miles (Eds.), *Innovation systems in the service economy: measurement and case study analysis* (pp. 85–103). Norwell, MA: Kluwer Academic Publishers.

De Gregori, T. R. (1987). Resources are not; they become: An institutional theory. *Journal of Economic Issues*, 21(3), 1241–1263.

Deshpande, R., Farley, J. U., & Webster, F. E., Jr. (1993). Corporate culture, customer orientation, and innovativeness. *Journal of Marketing*, 57(1), 23–37.

Edvardsson, B., Tronvoll, B., & Gruber, T. (2011). Expanding understanding of service exchange and value co-creation: A social construction approach. *Journal of the Academy of Marketing Science*, 39(2), 327–339.

Enquist, B., Edvardsson, B., & Petros Sebhatu, S. (2008). Corporate social responsibility for charity or for service business? *Asian Journal on Quality*, 9(1), 55–67.

FitzPatrick, M., Davey, J., Muller, L., & Davey, H. (2013). Value-creating assets in tourism management: Applying marketing's service-dominant logic in the hotel industry. *Tourism Management*, 36 (June), 86–98.

Flint, D. J., & Mentzer, J. T. (2006). Striving for integrated value chain management given a service-dominant logic for marketing. In R. F. Lusch & S. L. Vargo (Eds.), *The service-dominant logic of marketing: Dialog, debate, and directions* (pp. 139–149). Armonk, NY: ME Sharpe.

Friedland, R., & Alford, R. R. (1991). Bringing society back in: Symbols, practices and institutional contradictions. In W. W. Powell & P. J. Dimaggio (Eds.), *The new institutionalism in organizational analysis* (pp. 232–263). Chicago, IL: The University of Chicago Press.

Giddens, A. (1984). *The constitution of society: Outline of the theory of structuration*. Berkeley, CA: University of California Press.

Grönroos, C. (2008). Service logic revisited: Who creates value? And who co-creates? *European Business Review*, 20(4), 298–314.

Grönroos, C. (2011). Value co-creation in service logic: A critical analysis. *Marketing Theory*, 11(3), 279–301.

Grönroos, C., & Voima, P. (2013). Critical service logic: Making sense of value creation and co-creation. *Journal of the Academy of Marketing Science*, 41(2), 133–150.

Gummesson, E. (2008) Extending the service-dominant logic: From customer centricity to balanced centricity. *Journal of the Academy of Marketing Science*, 36(1), 15–17.

Gunderson, L. H., & Holling, C. (2002). *Panarchy: Understanding transformations in human and natural systems*. Washington, DC: Island Press.

Halliday, S. V. (2016). User-generated content about brands: Understanding its creators and consumers. *Journal of Business Research*, 69(1), 137–144.

Hardyman, W., Daunt, K. L., & Kitchener, M. (2015). Value co-creation through patient engagement in health care: A micro-level approach and research agenda. *Public Management Review*, 17(1), 90–107.

Hartmann, N. N., Wieland, H., & Vargo, S. L. (2018). Converging on a new theoretical foundation for selling. *Journal of Marketing*, 82(2), 1–18.

Hearn, G., Roodhouse, S., & Blakey, J. (2007). From value chain to value creating ecology: Implications for creative industries development policy. *International Journal of Cultural Policy*, 13(4), 419–436.

Heinonen, K., & Strandvik, T. (2015). Customer-dominant logic: Foundations and implications. *Journal of Services Marketing*, 29(6/7), 472–484.

Heinonen, K., Strandvik, T., Mickelsson, K. J., Edvardsson, B., Sundström, E., & Andersson, P. (2010). A customer-dominant logic of service. *Journal of Service Management*, 21(4), 531–548.

Heinonen, K., Strandvik, T., & Voima, P. (2013). Customer dominant value formation in service. *European Business Review*, 25(2), 104–123.

Hollebeek, L. D., Srivastava, R. K., & Chen, T. (2019). SD logic–informed customer engagement: Integrative framework, revised fundamental propositions, and application to CRM. *Journal of the Academy of Marketing Science*, 47(1), 161–185.

Isaksson, O., Larsson, T. C., & Rönnbäck, A. Ö. (2009). Development of product-service systems: Challenges and opportunities for the manufacturing firm. *Journal of Engineering Design*, 20(4), 329–348.

Jarvis, W., Halvorson, W., Sadeque, S., & Johnston, S. (2014). A large class engagement (LCE) model based on service-dominant logic (SDL) and flipped classrooms. *Education Research and Perspectives (Online)*, 41, 1.

Joiner, K. A., & Lusch, R. F. (2016). Evolving to a new service-dominant logic for health care. *Innovation and Entrepreneurship in Health*, 3, 25–33.

Kimbell, L. (2011). Designing for service as one way of designing services. *International Journal of Design*, 5, 2.

Kohli, A. K., & Jaworski, B. J. (1990). Market orientation: The construct, research propositions, and managerial implications. *Journal of Marketing*, 54(2), 1–18.

Koskela-Huotari, K., & Vargo, S. L. (2016). Institutions as resource context. *Journal of Service Theory and Practice*, 26(2), 163–178.

Koskela-Huotari, K., & Vargo, S. L. (2018). Why service-dominant logic? In R. F. Lusch & S. L. Vargo (Eds.), *The SAGE handbook of service-dominant logic* (pp. 40–57). London, UK: SAGE Publications Inc.

Kotler, P. (1977). *Marketing management: Analysis, planning, implementation and control.* (3rd ed.). Upper Saddle River, NJ: Prentice Hall.

Lovelock, C. H. (1983). Classifying services to gain strategic marketing insights. *Journal of Marketing*, 47(3), 9–20.

Luca, N. R., Hibbert, S., & McDonald, R. (2015). Towards a service-dominant approach to social marketing. *Marketing Theory*, 16(2), 194–218.

Lusch, R. F., & Nambisan, S. (2015). Service innovation: A service-dominant logic perspective. *MIS Quarterly*, 39(1), 155–175.

Lusch, R. F., & Vargo, S. L. (2006). Service-dominant logic: Reactions, reflections and refinements. *Marketing Theory*, 6(3), 281–288.

Lusch, R. F., & Vargo, S. L. (2014). *Service-dominant logic: Premises, perspectives, possibilities.* New York: Cambridge University Press.

Lusch, R. F., & Vargo, S. L. (2018). An overview of service-dominant logic. In S. L. Vargo & R. F. Lusch (Eds.), *The SAGE handbook of service-dominant logic* (pp. 3–21). London, UK: SAGE Publications Inc.

Lusch, R. F., Vargo, S. L., & O'Brien, M. (2007). Competing through service: Insights from service-dominant logic. *Journal of Retailing*, 83(1), 5–18.

Maglio, P. P., & Spohrer, J. (2008). Fundamentals of service science. *Journal of the Academy of Marketing Science*, 36(1), 18–20.

Maglio, P. P., Vargo, S. L., Caswell, N., & Spohrer, J. (2009). The service system is the basic abstraction of service science. *Information Systems and e-Business Management*, 7(4), 395–406.

Matthies, B. D., D'Amato, D., Berghäll, S., Ekholm, T., Hoen, H. F., Holopainen, J., ... Toppinen, A. (2016). An ecosystem service-dominant logic? Integrating the ecosystem service approach and the service-dominant logic. *Journal of Cleaner Production*, 124, 51–64.

Maturana, H. R., & Varela, F. J. (1980). *Autopoiesis and cognition: The realization of the living*. Boston, MA: Reidel Publishing Company.

Meier, H., Völker, O., & Funke, B. (2011). Industrial product-service systems (IPS2). *The International Journal of Advanced Manufacturing Technology*, 52(9–12), 1175–1191.

Merz, M. A., He, Y., & Vargo, S. L. (2009). The evolving brand logic: A service-dominant logic perspective. *Journal of the Academy of Marketing Science*, 37(3), 328–344.

Michel, S., Brown, S. W., & Gallan, A. S. (2008). An expanded and strategic view of discontinuous innovations: Deploying a service-dominant logic. *Journal of the Academy of Marketing Science*, 36(1), 54–66.

Nilsson, E., & Ballantyne, D. (2014). Reexamining the place of servicescape in marketing: A service-dominant logic perspective. *Journal of Services Marketing*, 28(5), 374–379.

Normann, R. (2001). *Reframing business: When the map changes the landscape*. New York: John Wiley & Sons.

Normann, R., & Ramírez, R. (1993). From value chain to value constellation: Designing interactive strategy. *Harvard Business Review*, 71(4), 65–77.

North, D. C. (1990). *Institutions, institutional change and economic performance*. New York: Cambridge University Press.

Osborne, S. P., Radnor, Z., & Nasi, G. (2013). A new theory for public service management? Toward a (public) service-dominant approach. *The American Review of Public Administration*, 43(2), 135–158.

Ostrom, E. (1990). *Governing the commons: The evolution of institutions for collective action*. Cambridge, UK: Cambridge University Press.

Parvatiyar, A., & Sheth, J. N. (2000). The domain and conceptual foundations of relationship marketing. In J. N. Sheth & A. Parvatiyar (Eds.), *Handbook of relationship marketing* (pp. 3–38). Thousand Oaks, CA: SAGE Publications Inc.

Pels, J. (2012). The service dominant logic: A conceptual foundation to address the underserved. *International Journal of Rural Management*, 8(1–2), 63–85.

Penrose, E. (2009). *The theory of the growth of the firm*. (4th Ed.). Oxford, UK: Oxford University Press.

Prahalad, C. K., & Ramaswamy, V. (2004). Co-creation experiences: The next practice in value creation. *Journal of Interactive Marketing*, 18(3), 5–14.

Rehman, M., Dean, A. M., & Pires, G. D. (2012). A research framework for examining customer participation in value co-creation: Applying the service dominant logic to the provision of living support services to oncology day-care patients. *International Journal of Behavioural and Healthcare Research*, 3(3–4), 226–243.

Ridley, M. (2010). *The rational optimist: How prosperity evolves*. New York: HarperCollins Publishers.

Russell-Bennett, R., Wood, M., & Previte, J. (2013). Fresh ideas: Services thinking for social marketing. *Journal of Social Marketing*, 3(3), 223–238.

Schau, H. J., Muñiz, A. M., Jr., & Arnould, E. J. (2009). How brand community practices create value. *Journal of Marketing*, 73(5), 30–51.

Scott, W. R. (2014). *Institutions and organizations: Ideas, interests, and identities*. Thousand Oaks, CA: SAGE Publications Inc.

Shaw, G., Bailey, A., & Williams, A. (2011). Aspects of service-dominant logic and its implications for tourism management: Examples from the hotel industry. *Tourism Management*, 32(2), 207–214.

Siltaloppi, J., Koskela-Huotari, K., & Vargo, S. L. (2016). Institutional complexity as a driver for innovation in service ecosystems. *Service Science*, 8(3), 333–343.

Simon, H. A. (1996). *The sciences of the artificial* (Vol. 3). Cambridge, MA: MIT Press.

Spohrer, J., & Maglio, P. P. (2010). Toward a science of service systems. In P. P. Maglio, C. A. Kieliszewski, & J. C. Spohrer (Eds.), *Handbook of service science* (pp. 157–194). New York: Springer.

Storbacka, K., Brodie, R. J., Böhmann, T., Maglio, P. P., & Nenonen, S. (2016). Actor engagement as a microfoundation for value co-creation. *Journal of Business Research*, 69(8), 3008–3017.

Subramony, M., & Pugh, S. D. (2015). Services management research review, integration, and future directions. *Journal of Management*, 41(1), 349–373.

Tokman, M., & Beitelspacher, L. S. (2011). Supply chain networks and service-dominant logic: Suggestions for future research. *International Journal of Physical Distribution & Logistics Management*, 41(7), 717–726.

Trischler, J., & Charles, M. (2019). The application of a service ecosystems lens to public policy analysis and design: Exploring the frontiers. *Journal of Public Policy & Marketing*, 38(1), 19–35.

Vargo, S. L. (2008). Customer integration and value creation: Paradigmatic traps and perspectives. *Journal of Service Research*, 11(2), 211–215.

Vargo, S. L., & Akaka, M. A. (2012). Value cocreation and service systems (Re)formation: A service ecosystems view. *Service Science*, 4(3), 207–217.

Vargo, S. L., Akaka, M. A., & Vaughan, C. M. (2017). Conceptualizing value: A service-ecosystem view. *Journal of Creating Value*, 3(2), 1–8.

Vargo, S. L., & Lusch, R. F. (2004). Evolving to a new dominant logic for marketing. *Journal of Marketing*, 68(1), 1–17.

Vargo, S. L., & Lusch, R. F. (2008). Service-dominant logic: Continuing the evolution. *Journal of the Academy of Marketing Science*, 36(1), 1–10.

Vargo, S. L., & Lusch, R. F. (2011). It's all B2B … and beyond: Toward a systems perspective of the market. *Industrial Marketing Management*, 40(2), 181–187.

Vargo, S. L., & Lusch, R. F. (2016). Institutions and axioms: An extension and update of service-dominant logic. *Journal of the Academy of Marketing Science*, 44(4), 5–23.

Vargo, S. L., & Lusch, R. F. (2017). Service-dominant logic 2025. *International Journal of Research in Marketing*, 34(1), 46–67.

Vargo, S. L., & Lusch, R. F. (Eds.). (2018). *The SAGE handbook of service-dominant logic*. London, UK: SAGE Publications Inc.

Vargo, S. L., Maglio, P. P., & Akaka, M. A. (2008). On value and value co-creation: A service systems and service logic perspective. *European Management Journal*, 26(3), 145–152.

Vargo, S. L., & Morgan, F. W. (2005). Services in society and academic thought: An historical analysis. *Journal of Macromarketing*, 25(1), 42–53.

Vargo, S. L., Wieland, H., & Akaka, M. A. (2015). Innovation through institutionalization: A service ecosystems perspective. *Industrial Marketing Management*, 44, 63–72.

Wetter-Edman, K., Vink, J., & Blomkvist, J. (2018). Staging aesthetic disruption through design methods for service innovation. *Design Studies*, 55, 5–26.

Whitehead, A. N. (1911). *An introduction to mathematics*. Cambridge: Cambridge University Press.

Wieland, H., Hartmann, N. N., & Vargo, S. L. (2017). Business models as service strategy. *Journal of the Academy of Marketing Science*, 45(6), 925–943.

Wieland, H., Koskela-Huotari, K., & Vargo, S. L. (2016). Extending actor participation in value creation: An institutional view. *Journal of Strategic Marketing*, 24(3–4), 210–226.

Wieland, H., Polese, F., Vargo, S. L., & Lusch, R. F. (2012). Toward a service (eco)systems perspective on value creation. *International Journal of Service Science Management, Engineering, and Technology*, 3(3), 12–25.

Yan, J., Ye, K., Wang, H., & Hua, Z. (2010). Ontology of collaborative manufacturing: Alignment of service-oriented framework with service-dominant logic. *Expert Systems with Applications*, 37(3), 2222–2231.

Zeithaml, V. A., Parasuraman, A., & Berry, L. L. (1985). Problems and strategies in services marketing. *Journal of Marketing*, 49(2), 33–46.

2

Service-dominant logic and market innovation

Jonathan J. Baker, Julia A. Fehrer, and Roderick J. Brodie

Introduction

The dynamic, interdependent relationship between innovation and the (re)structuring of markets has been of interest to scholars for some time. However, although innovation and markets have been studied by scholars from numerous disciplinary backgrounds, a cohesive conceptualization of markets and innovation processes is lacking (Hauser, Tellis, & Griffin, 2006). This is especially pronounced with the differentiation between product-related innovation (e.g., new types or examples of consumer goods), and market-related innovation (e.g., new geographic markets or new market structures); see Vargo, Wieland, and Akaka (2015). In response, there have been repeated calls for broader conceptualizations that enable examination and theoretical development of complex, contemporary innovation processes (Ordanini & Parasuraman, 2011); processes that manifest as new types of goods, services, systems, business models, or, ultimately, markets. Such a perspective needs to reflect the features and challenges of contemporary times – the socially embedded nature of economic activities (Granovetter, 1985) and the importance of multiple actor groups in contributing to innovation processes. The ability of firms, collaborators, or social groupings to deliberately innovate markets is a research area that holds much promise for strategists, innovation practitioners, and many others (Kindström, Ottosson, & Carlborg, 2018; Nenonen, Möller, & Storbacka, 2017; Nenonen & Storbacka, 2018; Storbacka & Nenonen, 2015). However, this remains a nascent area of research.

The way innovation is conceived of and managed by firms has radically altered in recent times. Traditionally, innovation processes were seen as an internal firm responsibility, secretive and closed (Mele, Pels, & Storbacka, 2015). Now, 'open innovation' involves knowledge flows both within and across the boundaries of the firm (Alexy & Dahlander, 2014; Chesborough, 2006). Additionally, 'innovations' were generally thought of as tangible 'products' or 'inventions,' but many of the most visible, fast-growing, and valuable global firms today are primarily service providers and not goods manufacturers (e.g., the so-called 'FAANGs' – Facebook, Apple, Amazon, Netflix, and Google's parent company Alphabet).

In parallel, markets have traditionally been imagined to primarily comprise dyads of producers (as value creators) and consumers (as value destroyers), with both parties involved in exchanging goods for money (Vargo et al., 2015). However, global giants like Airbnb and Uber have no employees or capital invested in what are ostensibly their core service offerings (i.e., accommodation and transportation services, respectively); but are notable for their ability to bring together and coordinate a vast array of heterogeneous market actors on a global scale. Numerous other firms are innovating, disrupting, shaping, and creating markets through technology-driven service-delivery platforms in multiple industries. Examples include education providers Coursera and Udacity, personal and professional services platform Upwork, crowdfunding platforms Indiegogo and Kickstarter, peer-to-peer lenders LendingClub and Zopa, and social enterprises such as the Food Assembly (cf. Owyang, 2014). The success of these businesses cannot be suitably understood while adopting a 20th century perspective that sees firms as the primary creators of value that is realized only when tangible goods are sold to a particular target market segment.

Another issue with understanding innovation is that contemporary research examining collaborative innovation processes has a splintered approach. In trying to identify and explain innovation drivers or antecedents, research has typically adopted either a macro- (economic or institutional system), meso- (dyads or networks), or micro- (single firm) level perspective (Corsaro, Cantu, & Tunisini, 2012). Although these are valuable research contributions in themselves, their perspectives offer neither clear distinctions between the levels, nor a comprehensive multilevel understanding of innovation. For instance, a macro-level research lens might ascribe primacy to geographical or industrial network positions as drivers of innovation (Asheim & Coenen, 2005; Su & Chen, 2015), whereas a micro-level lens might identify internal firm competencies or product types as key (Garcia & Calantone, 2002). However, a comprehensive perspective that encompasses the multiple levels of innovation activity (micro-, meso-, and macro-) is not possible with such diversity of approach and concept. This is further complicated by the fact that every discipline adopts different conceptualizations and lexica to examine technology, people, organizations, and societies (Maglio & Spohrer, 2008); there are marked differences between the language and perspectives of sociology, economics, management, strategy, marketing, etc.

In sum, there is a pressing need for a comprehensive integrative perspective of innovation processes with some key characteristics. First, an integrative perspective must incorporate consideration of different settings and levels of aggregation. Hence, any such perspective must be capable of exploring the constraining and enabling social and institutional contexts in which these processes occur and the practices of the multiple actors that contribute to innovation processes (Vargo & Lusch, 2016; Vargo et al., 2015). Second, an integrative perspective must enable comprehensive consideration of innovations of diverse types including new goods, services, networks, business or social systems, processes, business models, or even markets (Wieland, Vargo, Akaka, & Barbeau, 2018). Last, and perhaps most importantly, such a conceptualization must provide a shared lexicon that enables people to coalesce around a collective perspective and understanding (Maglio & Spohrer, 2008). This allows scholars, managers, and others with different sets of practices and knowledge (from different domains), to benefit from a combination of unique perspectives.

As argued in this chapter, a transcendent conceptualization of innovation is found in Service-dominant (S-D) logic (Lusch & Vargo, 2014; Maglio & Spohrer, 2008; Vargo & Lusch, 2016). A conceptualization of innovation processes based in S-D logic is discussed in detail throughout this chapter, the remainder of which is organized as follows: in the next section, S-D logic is used to describe a unifying conceptualization for innovation. The third section outlines neo-institutional theory and the role of (de)institutionalization processes in the acceptance, normalizing, or embedding of innovations. The fourth section systematically reveals how the systemic and institutional perspective of S-D logic informs conceptualizations of technological, business model, and market innovation. The chapter concludes by presenting implications for theorists and practitioners alike.

Service-dominant logic

An S-D logic perspective asserts that all value is co-created by generic actors (sometimes many) involved in resource integration through service exchange (Vargo & Lusch, 2008). These actors are embedded within adaptive service 'ecosystems,' that are coordinated by overlapping, interrelated societal institutions (or 'institutional arrangements') (Lusch & Vargo, 2014; Vargo & Lusch, 2016). Furthermore, service ecosystems are layered or nested within one another (Koskela-Huotari, Edvardsson, Jonas, Sörhammar, & Witell, 2016). Examples of such ecosystems include a household or firm (on a microlevel), a community or collective (on a mesolevel), and a society or national economy (on a macrolevel). Maglio and Spohrer (2008) state that the smallest ecosystem is two individuals, whereas the largest is the global economy.

Viewing all actors as embedded in ecosystems, involved in processes of value creation for themselves and others, enables an understanding of modern, open, consultative, and inclusive firm-coordinated innovation processes (Vargo et al., 2015). These open innovation processes frequently comprise a broad type and number of actors (Huarng, Cervera, & Mas-Verdu, 2018). Additionally, an ecosystem conceptualization enables comprehensive understanding of innovation processes (and outcomes) at multiple levels. For example, this includes (1) innovation activities undertaken by (micro-level) individuals or organizations, or (meso-level) business networks (Möller, Rajala, & Svahn, 2005) and (2) innovations that manifest as new technologies, new business models (Fehrer, Woratschek, & Brodie, 2018), or new structures or shapes of markets (Storbacka & Nenonen, 2015).

Incorporating an institutional perspective into innovation processes is crucial, as institutions shape the social contexts in which innovation occurs. Paradoxically, institutions constrain the ability of actors to innovate (i.e., to move away from taken-for-granted practices, processes, assumptions, etc.), while also providing the institutionalized rules and norms that enable such entrepreneurial activity (Battilana & D'Aunno, 2009). By extension, when incumbent practices and technologies are disrupted, processes of deinstitutionalization effectively take place. Conversely, when innovative practices and technologies are diffused and established as accepted, new norms, expectations, and processes of institutionalization occur.

In sum, viewed from the S-D logic (i.e., service ecosystems) perspective, innovations – at any level of aggregation or in any context – reflect new, better ways for value co-creation processes to occur. Thus, value co-creation activities occur within institutionally embedded ecosystems. To elaborate on this argument, the next section introduces institutions and the mechanisms for undertaking institutional change.

Institutions

Institutions provide predictable structures and frames for people to go about their daily lives (Scott, 2001). Although often conceptualized simply as large organizations (e.g., universities or hospitals), institutions are the norms, practices, (formal and informal) rules, and shared understandings that provide psychological security and predictability for people within households, communities, countries, and even transnationally (Scott, 2001). Institutions can be formal (e.g., parliament, the justice system, legal marriage) or informal (e.g., how people greet each other or the act of applauding). They are generally stable and reproducible, but are capable of disruption and change. Most importantly, institutions provide humans with cognitive "short-cuts" as they go about their daily lives (Scott, 2001). Rather than having to assess and reassess every experience, action, and decision, institutionalized norms, beliefs, and expectations allow psychological security and certainty through heuristic pathways and social schemata (DiMaggio & Powell, 1991; Scott, 2001; Thornton, Ocasio, & Lounsbury, 2012).

All ecosystem actors exist within broader institutional contexts, where actors operating within a context may include individuals, groups, formal or informal organizations, collections of competitors, regulators, etc. (Edvardsson, Kleinaltenkamp, Tronvoll, McHugh, & Windahl, 2014). Sets of interrelated institutions – institutional arrangements (Koskela-Huotari et al., 2016) – guide the manner in which firms (and other actors) operate within an industry, market, or economy. For example, a formal institution (e.g., an industry regulator) shapes the way value co-creation activities can be enacted by a firm. Additionally, institutionalization is a key topic when examining innovation. For an innovation to be successful, it must become institutionalized (Vargo et al., 2015), which means that it must become an accepted, taken-for-granted norm, expectation, practice, or routine in people's lives. Accordingly, as an innovative technology becomes institutionalized, incumbent or pre-existing technology might become disrupted and obsolete through deinstitutionalization.

As all actors are themselves embedded within certain institutionalized social and cultural contexts, all interpretation of value by any market actor (e.g., customers, product users, brand communities, etc.) takes place within this broader, institutionalized socio-cultural frame (Edvardsson et al., 2014). The assessment of value is unique to all individuals and takes place within a particular social and cultural context that comprises, amongst other things, institutionalized norms, understandings, expectations, and rules. These institutional factors (e.g., that may manifest as trends, fashions, customs, etc.) constantly influence the interpretation of value by an actor (Edvardsson, Tronvoll, & Gruber, 2011). Hence, not only are institutions integral to the existence of service ecosystems and to how value co-creation activities can be coordinated, but also to the way value is uniquely interpreted by human actors embedded in market systems.

However, institutions do not simply have a top-down constraining influence on people, organizations, and communities. Instead, they provide rule structures within which people may modify or even break incumbent elements (Battilana & D'Aunno, 2009). Hence, there is an inherent tension between the agency an actor enjoys and the governing or coordinating institutional structure. This is known as the "paradox of embedded agency" (Seo & Creed, 2002, p. 226) and is best understood by remembering that institutions are structured and reproduced by the very practices enacted by people as they go about their daily lives (Giddens, 1984).

For example, the formal institution of a wedding, in any number of cultures and religions around the world, typically includes numerous formal and informal institutionalized behaviours (e.g., generally accepted dress codes, ceremonial activities, passages of text or scripture, etc.). People may adopt these behaviours and activities when they wed because time-honoured institutionalized norms and customs influence and shape their decision-making. As such, the institution of a wedding is constantly performed and enacted by those people who choose to engage with it. However, if all people in a particular culture collectively decided that formal weddings should take place in breweries with the bride and groom dressed as garden gnomes, that is what the institution of formal marriage would rapidly become in that culture. Furthermore, changes to formalized institutional rules around weddings in many parts of the world (such as same-sex weddings) have come about through changing social ideologies and political action such as advocacy for human rights.

Institutions operate as a duality (Giddens, 1984): although institutional structures provide a governing or influencing framework within which activities take place, ultimately an institutional structure is a (re)production of the very practices of the institutionally embedded actors (Battilana & D'Aunno, 2009). There is a reciprocal and interdependent relationship between the practices adopted and performed by actors and the resulting institutionalized behaviours, norms, belief systems, and expectations. When considering markets from an S-D logic perspective, as institutionalized practices evolve and change through innovation activities, then so do value co-creation processes, and vice versa (Akaka, Vargo & Wieland, 2017; Baker, Storbacka, & Brodie, 2018). This is a key concept when understanding market stability or change, which result from processes of (de)institutionalization of incumbent technologies, processes, and practices.

To understand how institutionally embedded actors might deliberately undertake institutional change, initially the theory of institutional entrepreneurship emerged (e.g., DiMaggio, 1988). Institutional entrepreneurship explores how actors embedded within a certain institutional context can break with accepted norms, rules, beliefs, and behaviours and leverage available resources to create change or disruption. This perspective marked a key development in institutional theory: institutional entrepreneurship argues that, although institutions themselves are deterministic in the way that they structure and coordinate lives, institutional actors are capable of creating change. However, institutional entrepreneurship has been criticized for positioning institutional entrepreneurs as endowed with extraordinary, superhuman abilities (Lawrence, Suddaby, & Leca, 2009) and for not suitably considering contextual influences on entrepreneurial action (Smothers, Murphy, Novicevic, & Humphreys, 2014). Accordingly, institutional entrepreneurship has been further expanded through the "institutional work" framework (Lawrence & Suddaby, 2006; Lawrence et al., 2009).

Institutional work unifies various strands of sociology and institutional theory beyond institutional entrepreneurship (DiMaggio, 1988) including social practice theory (Bourdieu, 1984, 1990; Schatzki, Knorr-Cetina, & von Savigny, 2001), structuration theory (Giddens, 1984), and deinstitutionalization (Oliver, 1991). Institutional work is defined as "the purposive actions of individuals and organizations aimed at creating, maintaining and disrupting institutions" (Lawrence & Suddaby, 2006, p. 215). Like S-D logic, this framework conceptualizes institutions as residing within "nested systems" at micro-, meso-, or macro- levels. However, these levels are arbitrary because they are interdependent and overlapping (Giddens, 1984).

Importantly, institutional work does not explore just the intentional activities of actors to undertake institutional change (i.e., by creating new or disrupting old institutions), but also institutional maintenance – maintaining stability or longevity in existing institutional arrangements. However, the dimensions of institutional disruption and creation are most pertinent to the present discussion of innovation processes. There is no one definitive list of the types of institutional work (Nenonen, Storbacka, & Frethey-Bentham, 2019). Nevertheless, a synthesis of various versions appears in Table 2.1. The crowdfunding platforms Kickstarter and Indiegogo are used as examples to illustrate institutional work.

Institutional creation can occur for a number of reasons. Political work is a particularly powerful instrument for the creation of new institutions, and so is change in belief systems, meanings, and boundaries (Lawrence & Suddaby, 2006; Zietsma & Lawrence, 2010; Zietsma & McKnight, 2009). The crowdfunding platforms Kickstarter and Indiegogo have significantly influenced the change in meanings and boundaries of the traditional funding process.

Table 2.1 Institutional work framework

Institutional outcome	Classification of work	Forms of institutional work
Creation	Political work	Vesting property rights through new rules
		New rules that redefine hierarchies and boundaries
		Advocatory activity through political or regulatory mechanisms
	Change in actor belief systems	Constructing peer-group relationships and functions within field boundaries
		Building and sustaining support of constituents
		Negotiating and envisioning common strategic objectives
		Normalizing practices through newly established peer group
		Selecting from available alternative practices
		Examining the ethical foundations of previously accepted practices
	Change in meanings and boundaries	Preserving elements of pre-existing rules, technologies, and practices makes change less abrupt
		Creating acceptance by sharing information
		Educating actors in required new skills and knowledge
Maintenance	Ensuring adherence to rules systems	Enabling continuation of institution through creating rules and agencies
		Policing institutional actors through compliance monitoring and enforcement
		Deterring institutional change through coercive barriers
	Reproducing existing norms and belief systems	Publicly valorizing positive and demonizing negative institutional actors
		Mythologizing an institution's history
		Embedding and routinizing accepted practices through education and ceremony
Disruption	Attacking or undermining institutional mechanisms	Disconnecting rewards and sanctions through state apparatus
		Undermining the ethical foundations of old practices
		Disassociating moral foundations for practices, rules, or technologies
		Undermining core assumptions and beliefs reduces perceived risk of innovation

Note: Compiled from Lawrence and Suddaby (2006), Battilana and D'Aunno (2009), Kraatz (2009), Zietsma and McKnight (2009).

Crowdfunding refers to efforts by artists and entrepreneurs to fund their ventures by drawing on relatively small contributions from sometimes very large numbers of individuals ('the crowd') using the internet, without requiring financial intermediaries (Mollick, 2014). The idea of patronage – a way of funding artists through patrons – has existed for centuries in the arts scene. For example, Archduke Rudolph of Austria was Ludwig van Beethoven's greatest patron, giving the famous composer funds to continue creating music. In turn, Beethoven composed music for him. However, the technological developments of the internet make the idea of patronage much more dynamic and accessible to both a broader group of actors and to new actors (Chua, 2017).

Institutional creation also involves changes to both concrete and abstract belief systems that actors rely on for understanding and interpreting. As new peer relationships emerge, and new peer groups are structured, innovative practices become accepted, normalized, and routinized (Lawrence & Suddaby, 2006). Barriers created by resistance to driving abstract understandings and beliefs can be overcome if institutionalized elements of old ways of doing things are replicated or mimicked (Hargrave & Van de Ven, 2009). In the case of crowdfunding, the funders establish new normalizing practices, such as pledging money for entrepreneurial projects, which is not new *per se*; however, it is executed by peers of ordinary people. Further, funders activate their social networks to support crowdfunding campaigns, a replication of existing practices in contemporary business and social environments (Fehrer & Nenonen, 2019). Kickstarter and Indiegogo, however, drove substantial change in fundamental beliefs of what funding processes could look like and how they are executed. This includes mechanisms for evaluating the viability of start-up projects – a highly public setting in which experimenting and fast failing are executed – and how potential markets for new goods and services are validated or shaped to be ready for an innovation (Fehrer & Nenonen, 2019). However, Kickstarter and Indiegogo also *maintain* several institutionalized elements of traditional funding processes. For example, entrepreneurs and artists still have to pitch their projects in the most convincing ways to receive funding, and crowdfunding platforms receive a management fee for connecting founders with funders and potential customers – similar to business angels and venture capitalists.

Finally, *disruption of institutions* occurs as a result of actors attacking or undermining the mechanisms that maintain incumbent institutional arrangements (Lawrence & Suddaby, 2006). This may be achieved in various ways. The ethical underpinnings of incumbent practices may be questioned as social ideologies evolve and change (Zietsma & Lawrence, 2010), or actors might use institutional systems such as lawyers, judges, and courts to question incumbents (Lawrence & Suddaby, 2006). For example, as crowdfunding grew in popularity and reached significant turnover – rising from $US 2.7 billion in 2012 to $US 34.4 billion in 2015 (Masssolution, 2016) – and with its global impact expected to grow even further (World Economic Forum, 2016), its legal status was questioned. As with many other successful platform business models, the legal status of crowdfunding was not precisely defined and was open to interpretation. Ambiguous legal status provides an opportunity for platform businesses to exploit, thereby disrupting incumbent institutions, although it involves fighting legal battles. With crowdfunding, various legal issues arise including equity funding regulations, intellectual property and patent regulations, copyrights, and trademarks (Murray, 2018). However, due to support from 'the crowd,' in the USA the government was put under pressure to adjust the law. In 2012, the Jumpstart Our Business Startups (JOBS) Act became law, and one of the key provisions was to instruct the Securities and Exchange Commission (SEC) to find ways to exempt crowdfunding from some of the more onerous provisions that restrict access to funds from non-registered securities offerings by non-accredited investors.

Most institutional work research has adopted the 'field' (mesolevel) or organization (microlevel) as the focal entity, but actors may undertake 'work' that impacts any one of the institutional levels (Lawrence & Suddaby, 2006). For example, institutional work might manifest in the micro-level practices of individual people or organizations, at the mesolevel in industry bodies, associations, or business networks, or at the macrolevel in national or even transnational institutional arrangements (Battilana & D'Aunno, 2009; Scott, 2014). Hence, an important contribution made by institutional work has been the integration of a practice-based approach to understanding changes that manifest at any one of the institutional levels (Hargrave & Van de Ven, 2009). Hence, institutional work offers a fresh perspective when exploring both the outcomes and the drivers of innovation at different levels of aggregation within a service ecosystem.

In summary, institutional considerations are crucial to understanding how actors can coordinate value co-creation activities in socially embedded ecosystems and how value is perceived and interpreted by ecosystem actors (Edvardsson et al., 2014). Additionally, the institutional work framework provides a means of understanding processes of (de)institutionalization of innovation in all contexts. The next section demonstrates how this institutional dimension is embedded in S-D logic, and how this institutional and systemic perspective enables S-D logic to provide a comprehensive consideration of the holistic and dynamic nature of innovation processes relating to technology, business models, and markets (Vargo et al., 2015).

An institutional and systemic perspective for market innovation

S-D logic views innovations that emerge from technological advancements as resulting from processes of (de)institutionalization. Likewise, Wieland, Hartmann, and Vargo (2017) argue that a systemic and institutional approach similarly shifts business model innovation to the study of how institutions are (re)formed. That is, they suggest through "an iterative and dynamic process involving a broad range of actors (i.e., firms, customers, other stakeholders, etc.) that institutionalization – the maintenance, disruption, and change of rules, norms, meanings, symbols – enables and constrains resource integration and value cocreation practices" (p. 68). Finally, S-D logic views markets as systems that emerge and continuously shape, and are shaped by, institutions and institutional arrangements (Vargo & Lusch, 2016; Vargo et al., 2017). This provides a lens through which to explore how versatile actors can consciously construct and reconstruct and thereby innovate markets (Araujo, 2007; Kjellberg & Helgesson, 2006; Mele et al., 2015; Storbacka & Nenonen, 2011). The following subsections elaborate on how the systemic and institutional perspective of S-D logic informs the conceptualizations of technological innovation, business model innovation, and market innovation, in order to provide a holistic framework.

S-D logic informed view of technological innovation

Traditional conceptualizations of technology and innovation have generally resided within different scholarly and practitioner disciplines and have largely been conceptualized within a goods-dominant (G-D) logic perspective (Koskela-Huotari, et al., 2016). Hence, the complex dynamics of modern markets and accelerating change have not been comprehensively understood. Such traditional perspectives have provided only "incomplete knowledge about the true nature and impact of service innovations" (Ordanini & Parasuraman, 2011, p. 4). Determining how to measure innovation success has also been heavily influenced by thinking grounded in neoclassical economics and G-D logic. For example, the success of innovation initiatives has often been measured in terms of patents or sales (Michel, Brown, & Gallan, 2008). However, patents are generally sought for new tangible goods, and sales are associated with increased value-in-exchange. Further, "most textbooks continue to conceptualise individual companies (and their R&D departments) as the main innovators" (Mele & Russo-Spena, 2015, p. 42). This is because traditional innovation practices have been typically closed – primarily comprising secretive R&D facilities in large corporations where company scientists imagine, design, build, and launch new ideas (Chesborough, 2006). However, such perspectives do not reflect the underlying reality that all value is co-created through the integration of resources by many actors, where the firm is an important actor, but only one actor in the service ecosystem.

Innovation is very often implicitly linked to technology; however, mainstream innovation literature often adopts a narrow conceptualization of technology. For instance, it may be related to digital and mechanical devices or artefacts. S-D logic, however, accentuates the interdependence of technology and innovation. S-D logic scholars have been drawn to Arthur's (2009, p. 28) more transcendent conceptualization of "technology as a means to fulfil human purpose … [which includes] technology as an assemblage of practices and components." Arthur argues that both "hardware" and "software" qualify as technology, so technology includes not just machines, devices, goods or artefacts, but also processes, organizations, institutions, etc. In sum, a technology is anything that achieves a human purpose. Hence, technology from an S-D logic perspective is seen in much the same way as products – both intangible and tangible.

Novel technologies are a product of evolutionary processes in that they are related in some way to the technologies that precede them, or as Arthur (2009, p.18) puts it, "evolution requires a mechanism of 'heredity.'" Accordingly, all new technologies (innovations) result through the combination of pre-existing technologies as "existing technologies beget further technologies" (Arthur, 2009, p. 21). From this perspective, it becomes obvious that technology is exclusively reliant on the development and deployment of human knowledge and skills (operant resources) to find solutions. Therefore, technology is both physical and social (Akaka et al., 2017) and any 'hardware' is an expression or manifestation of operant resources. Hence, much like any tangible good, 'hardware' is an indirect service provider.

In the era of mass customization, and growing technological and market complexity, many of the operant resources needed to remain competitive are located outside the firm (Cesaroni & Duque, 2013). These may include customers, research institutes, universities, suppliers, partners, brand fan groups, product users, etc. (Möller & Rajala, 2007). Although many of these actors play a critical role in enabling the process of value co-creation, when acting as sources of knowledge or inspiration for innovation, they also are operant resources for the firm (Ordanini & Parasuraman, 2011). For example, a group of customers might contribute ideas for service innovation through a focus group, whereas customer-facing staff might do so owing to on-the-job experiences with clients (Ordanini & Parasuraman, 2011). Meanwhile, actors with whom the firm has no financial relationship (e.g., brand fan groups) might serve as sources of inspiration for service innovation through ideas posted on blogs or social media (Harrison & Kjellberg, 2016). For example, a participant in quirky.com might contribute an idea for a new product, and others in the Quirky community may comment or make suggestions to improve the idea. If an idea is chosen to be manufactured, both inventor and contributors earn money (Quirky, 2018). Another example is a "wiki" (e.g., Wikipedia), which is co-created by numerous heterogeneous, willing actors. In all cases, actors with a monetary or non-monetary relationship – internal or external to the firm – can act as operant resources for innovation processes.

Contemporary perspectives perceive innovation processes as network activities, involving cooperation and collaboration by multiple actors both within and without the firm (Alexy & Dahlander, 2014). No longer is innovation perceived as primarily a closed, internal organizational act. Instead, an "open" innovation perspective "assumes that firms can and should use external ideas as well as internal ideas, and internal and external paths to market" (Chesborough, 2006, p. xxiv). Furthermore, past reliance on tangible goods as the vehicle for innovation has now been replaced with a focus on information-intensive offerings (Lusch & Nambisan, 2015) as experiential value assumes primacy over tangible product attributes, reflected in the success of firms like Facebook and Google. Indeed, the most innovative service firms are those that are the most collaborative, both with internal actors (especially customer-facing staff) and with external actors (especially business partners and customers), as described by Ordanini and Parasuraman (2011). In sum, actors participating in innovation processes individually and collectively act as operant resources. They bring their own unique goals, knowledge, capabilities and competencies, perceptions, power, position, and culture to the table (Corsaro, Cantu, & Tunisini, 2012, p. 786).

Adopting an S-D logic lens, innovation can occur through any one of four fundamental paths. These include (1) integrating existing resources and practices in different ways, (2) adopting new practices while using existing resources, (3) integrating new resources with existing practices, and (4) combining both new practices and new resources (Skålén, Gummerus, Koskull, & Magnusson, 2015). Any one of these combinations implicitly requires changes to service delivery or processes, which, in turn, may require modifications to the competencies of both firm and customers (Ordanini & Parasuraman, 2011). Consequently, this perspective requires a fundamental shift in mindset by firms. Rather than focusing on the maximization of value-in-exchange, instead firms need to focus primarily on maximizing the customer's realization and interpretation of value-in-use, in context (Sebastiani & Paiola, 2010). Hence, it is the collaborative integration of operant resources by multiple contributing actors that best enables innovation and new value propositions to emerge (Vargo et al., 2015).

S-D logic informed view of business models

The business model and business model innovation literatures feature considerable heterogeneity and a lack of cohesion in language and conceptualization (Zott, Amit, & Massa, 2011). A convincing singular definition of a business model has not yet been fully articulated (Wieland et al., 2017), and many of those that have are underpinned by a G-D logic. Teece's (2010, p. 172) definition of a firm's business model is the "design or architecture of the value creation, delivery, and capture mechanisms," which explicitly indicates the firm both creates and delivers value. Zott et al. (2011, p. 1020) posit a generic definition of a business model as "how firms do business" (which is tautological as well as something of a firm-centric perspective), although they do assert a systems approach is needed. Foss and Saebi (2017, p. 216) suggest that business models "can be conceptualized as 'complex systems,'" intimating a need to adopt a systems perspective.

Studies of business model innovation tend to adopt one of several approaches (Foss & Saebi, 2017). Some perceive business model innovation as a process, others as an outcome; some focus on changes to individual organizational characteristics as evidence (like pricing models or organizational boundaries), others on high-level attributes such as "targeted segments" or changes to the "value-chain" (Foss & Saebi, 2017). These studies all represent thinking grounded in the belief that firms create and deliver value to customers who are the consumers ('destroyers') of value. For example, a firm-centric perspective is present when defining business model innovation as "designed, novel, nontrivial changes to the key elements of a firm's business model and/or the architecture linking these elements" (Foss & Saebi, 2017, p. 201).

There is an emergent recognition of the importance of networks to business models. For example, Storbacka and Nenonen (2011, p. 248) assert that networks "define the resources that an individual market actor possesses and the ways that the market actor can interact with other market actors – and their resources." Mason and Spring (2011) recognize the interconnectedness between network actors (e.g., those in a supply chain or innovation network), and that business models evolve through interactions with other institutional actors. Moreover, Coombes and Nicholson (2013) contrast "open" models (that incorporate external stakeholders), with "closed" models. Open models reflect firms' reliance on customers for value realization (Prahalad & Ramaswamy, 2004a, 2004b), and the role of stakeholders (including customers) in open innovation processes (Chesborough, 2006). This contrasts with business models that exist as only internal to a single firm, where the firm is the sole actor responsible for innovation and value creation. Accordingly, this research recognizes the dynamic, systemic nature of value-creation networks (Vargo & Lusch, 2016).

Fehrer et al. (2018) draw on this systemic perspective of business model design when they analyse the value-creation and value-capture processes of platform business models. As many of the world's fastest growing companies are now peer-to-peer platforms that are representative of open models (e.g., Uber, Kickstarter, etc.), an actor-to-actor (A2A), rather than the firm-centric business-to-customer (B2C), perspective is needed. Platform businesses are enabled through sophisticated technology, and the institutionalized rules and norms that govern them are produced by the actors using the platforms. Hence, they operate as non-hierarchical entities (Fehrer et al., 2018). For example, both Uber drivers and riders get to rate each other after service experiences. Both sets of actors play a role as collective 'micro-regulators,' and governance of the ecosystem is democratized. In contrast, with taxi firms this role is traditionally performed by industry regulators and associations and through rules devised by taxi firms themselves. As such, governance of the traditional ecosystem is hierarchical.

With open business models, there is evidence of how value is co-created and systemically captured by various actors in the service ecosystem (Coombes & Nicholson, 2013), and each socio-culturally embedded service beneficiary has a unique interpretation of this value (Edvardsson et al., 2014). Hence, when adopting an S-D logic perspective of (1) service as the application of one's competencies for the benefit of another (Vargo & Lusch, 2004), and (2) all value being co-created through service-for-service exchange, "service strategy […] involves actors developing an understanding of how they can best serve themselves through service to others. The representation and performance of this understanding is captured in the *business model*" (Wieland et al., 2017, p. 926)

In summary, a firm's ability to coordinate activities between multiple actors requires considerably more recognition of systemic elements, including the institutional factors that both constrain and enable the practices of embedded actors, and the ability to connect and collaborate with various actors within the service ecosystem. So rather than being a firm-centric proposition, a business model is centred on the ability to maximize interaction between systemic actors (Wieland et al., 2017). This model is the bridge or conduit that enables firms to engage versatile actors in value co-creation processes.

S-D logic informed view of market innovation

There is an implicit relationship between innovation and market creation and change. However, ironically the 'market' has been under-researched in the marketing discipline for some years (Kjellberg et al., 2012; Vargo, 2007; Venkatesh, Peñaloza, & Firat, 2006). For example, Venkatesh et al. (2006, p. 252) assert, "Paradoxically, the term *market* is everywhere and nowhere in our literature." Early research examining the innovation of markets focused on new product markets, new geographical markets, or the entrepreneurs that drive or adapt to change (e.g., Schumpeter, 1947). Later, the effect of changing (tangible) technologies on markets became a focus for researchers (Kjellberg, Azimont, & Reid, 2015), although still largely conceptualizing markets as primarily comprising producer–consumer dyads (Vargo et al., 2015). Scholars have recently begun to explore how markets themselves are innovated (e.g., Kjellberg et al., 2012; Mele et al., 2015; Nenonen et al., 2014; Storbacka & Nenonen, 2015). This shifting focus reflects the need for research to adopt a considerably broader perspective than simply viewing markets as places where buyers and sellers come together to engage in economic transactions. Giesler (2008, p. 752) argues, "conceptualizing markets as systems of monetary transactions is a useful but distancing fiction. It should not give us licence to forget our cultural embeddedness in, and social responsibility for, the action in the market theatre."

Indeed, market change is a product of relational processes. For example, Rosa, Porac, Runser-Spanjol, and Saxon (1999) highlight how market definitions (e.g., product categories) are developed over time as producers, consumers, and others negotiate shared meanings. Humphreys (2010) tracks the influence of those in marketing and media on changing public discourse and influencing perceptions of what is considered legitimate or normal. While Kjellberg and Olson (2017) demonstrate that no market is isolated, but instead adjacent markets in similar fields influence new markets as they search for regulatory legitimacy.

Traditional perspectives of markets, underpinned by neoclassical economics, have seen markets as pre-existing, generally stable, and out of the firm's control. Instead, today markets are viewed from a systems perspective and conceptualized as complex adaptive service (eco)systems (Nenonen et al., 2019). These market systems involve multiple actors engaged in resource integration through service exchange. Markets are dynamic, malleable (Nenonen et al., 2014), and capable of great and rapid change (Vargo et al., 2015). Further, as ecosystems, contemporary markets feature multiple heterogeneous actors engaged in value co-creation activities, far beyond those conceived of in traditional industry-focused strategy literature (e.g., Porter, 1996). Indeed, the term 'actors' includes horizontal, vertical, economic, and social actors. For example, the successes of platforms (e.g., Google Play or the App Store) have hinged on recognition of this ecosystem character and on the open development responsibilities given to numerous contributors (Nenonen & Storbacka, 2018).

Adopting a neo-institutional theory perspective, markets are produced and structured (Giddens, 1984) through enacted micro-level practices, performed by market actors (Kjellberg & Helgesson, 2007). This approach to the study of markets runs parallel to the work of scholars in multiple disciplines within the broader social sciences who, in recent decades, have adopted a practice-level approach to understanding social phenomena (Scott, 2014) such as institutional change (Lawrence, Suddaby, & Leca, 2009). In the study of markets, a practice approach reflects the impossibility of clearly defining "the list of properties that is typical of [all] markets" (Kjellberg & Helgesson, 2007, p. 141), but instead recognizes that markets are generated through the practices enacted within them (Araujo & Kjellberg, 2011). Market practices are defined as "routine, micro-level interactions between multiple actors seeking to create value for themselves and others" (Kjellberg et al., 2012, p. 220). These practices encompass all concrete activities in the market (Spencer & Cova, 2012) including both market-*shaping* activities and market*ing* activities. This practice perspective reflects the duality of structure (cf. Giddens, 1984), in that practices collectively generate the market while the structure and function of the market necessarily shape the practices.

Accordingly, Kjellberg and Helgesson (2006) and Kjellberg et al. (2012) contribute a framework that specifies three classifications of practices in which market actors engage. First, *normalizing* practices are defined as those activities that shape, control, or create stability in markets and that establish normative objectives for market actors. Normalization might be undertaken by government, by a regulatory authority, or by a professional association or body; normalizing practices also includes all those practices perceived as standard and legitimate within a given field. Second, *representational* practices are the language, symbols, and signs used to represent (and re-present) concrete depictions and demonstrations of the market and its function. Last, *exchange* practices are those practices that enable the realization of economic exchanges and the exchange of market offerings (Kjellberg & Helgesson, 2007).

S-D logic scholars have adapted the markets-as-practice framework to more accurately reflect the notion of value 'co-creation' (e.g., Lusch & Vargo, 2014; Wieland, Koskela-Huotari, & Vargo, 2016). As co-creation is realized through A2A engagement, collaboration, and service-for-service exchange, resource-integrating actors are not limited to simply dyadic economic exchange as depicted by *exchange* practices (Wieland et al., 2016). Indeed, an S-D logic perspective includes both operant and operand resources as integral to value co-creation, and additionally actors in non-economic or indirect roles. For example, non-paying service users and members of brand communities engage in value co-creation activities (Vargo & Akaka, 2012; Wieland et al., 2016). Thus, in S-D logic's adaptation of the markets-as-practice framework, *exchange* practices are extended and reclassified as *integrative practices* (Lusch & Vargo, 2014; Wieland et al., 2016). In sum, the practices that market actors enact either *normalize* markets, *represent* markets (Kjellberg & Helgesson, 2007), or involve resource *integration* (Lusch & Vargo, 2014).

Ideas also play a part in the generation of markets in that they have a performative effect. Performativity implies that ideas, concepts, and theories do not just describe the market, but also create or format the market (Callon, 2007, 2009; Cochoy, 1998). The concepts, theories, and tools that managers (and other actors) bring to their work are not just used to interpret what is "the market," but also perform the market and shape what the market becomes. For example, the adoption and application of measuring devices (like market segmentation tools) (Kjellberg & Helgesson, 2007) and models and frameworks (like consumer behaviour models or brand strategy frameworks) (Mason, Kjellberg, & Hagberg, 2015) collectively define for managers what other actors populate the market, who is their competition, what is the 'industry' within which the firm exists, etc. Hence, as managerial models and devices, used to interpret or understand 'the market,' in turn shape and define the market, then markets are open to (re)definition and (re)creation by managers (Callon, 2010).

In sum, markets are in constant development as socio-materially constructed ecosystems (Araujo, Finch, & Kjellberg, 2010; Kjellberg & Helgesson, 2007; Kjellberg et al., 2012) and are "plastic" in that they can both retain and change shape (Nenonen et al., 2014). And like all other ecosystems of varying sizes, markets are continually performed via A2A engagement and collaboration (Wieland et al., 2016, p. 213). Market innovation can be driven by, and result in, considerably more elements than only changes to product and price (Nenonen et al., 2019). For example, representational elements such as symbols, terminology, and industry or product categorizations can change (Rosa & Spanjol, 2005), while market structure can be disrupted as supply chains or the number of competing firms are altered (Jaworski, Kohli, & Sahay, 2000). The types of customers, or the ways customers use or access products can evolve (Kumar, Scheer, & Kotler, 2000), and industry norms or regulations can change (Nenonen et al., 2019; Vargo & Lusch, 2016). Additionally, it is important to note that not all technological innovations lead to new market creation (Akaka et al., 2017). As discussed earlier, innovations must become institutionalized for a viable new market to form – which is to say new value co-creation processes must become normalized, accepted, and routinized, i.e., taken for granted.

Synthesizing the markets-as-practice framework (Kjellberg & Helgesson, 2007) and the institutional work framework (Lawrence & Suddaby, 2006) offers a powerful proposition for understanding (de)institutionalization processes involving technologies, business models, or market systems. This synthesis is depicted in Figure 2.1. Markets-as-practice categorizes the types of practices undertaken by market actors while the institutional work framework categorizes the types of actions actors take to create, disrupt, or maintain institutional arrangements. Different forms of institutional work can impact multiple market practices simultaneously. Furthermore, institutional arrangements do not have simply a top-down, deterministic effect by coordinating markets, but also provide the institutional rules and expectations that allow innovators to act (Battilana, Leca, & Boxenbaum, 2009). Hence, institutions are both constraining and enabling (Battilana & D'Aunno, 2009). This theoretical synthesis of market practices (Kjellberg & Helgesson, 2007) and institutional work (Lawrence, Suddaby, & Leca, 2009) is best explained with the use of an example.

Market innovation may occur as new business models emerge. Internet-streaming service providers like Netflix, Hulu, and Amazon Prime are responsible for substantial market shaping and have changed the way people watch television (Adalian, 2018). This is reflected in various

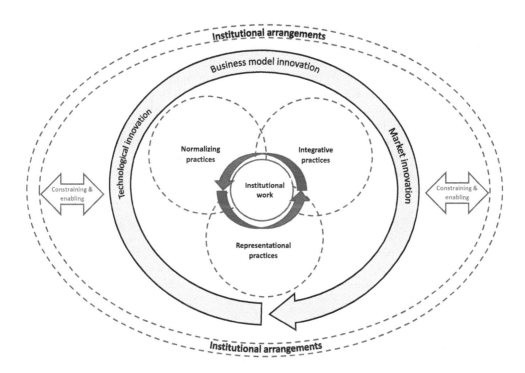

Figure 2.1 Market innovation occurs through an interdependent relationship between changing market practices and institutional arrangements.

examples of institutional disruption and creation work that has modified pre-existing institutionalized market practices related to traditional television network broadcasters or cable television providers. Internet-streaming companies are platforms that allow multiple actors, globally, to come together and engage in extensive value co-creation. The geographical limitations of network television and broadcaster middlemen of yesteryear are removed from consideration. However, internet streaming still maintains some institutionalized elements from traditional television watching (such as families gathering together around a television set; or collections of 43-minute episodes as 'seasons'; a plethora of viewing choices; etc.). However, internet streaming also introduces new elements that have become institutionalized (such as watching on demand, watching on various devices, binge-watching, personalization of content, and a user account that allows continued consumption of content while travelling the world).

When considering the creation of the market for internet streaming, the institutional work undertaken to change actors' belief systems, associated abstract meanings, and field boundaries is especially important (Ellis, Jack, Hopkinson, & O'Reilly, 2010; Lawrence & Suddaby, 2006). This has manifested in new peer-group relationships such as production companies creating cinema-quality movies for the small (-ish) screen (e.g., big-screen televisions), and sometimes very small screen (e.g., smartphones). Accordingly, new integrative practices have emerged, such as commissioning and contracting of content from major production houses for small-screen consumption (Adalian, 2018), together with licences to stream pre-existing content (Spangler, 2018), accessing video on-the-go, etc.

Normalizing practices have also changed; these include expectations of which companies produce content for the small screen; the quality of actors who might be involved – with numerous 'A-listers' involved in big-budget, live-streaming content (Sturges, 2018) – and the kinds of devices required to access content. Integrative practices have further been impacted – Netflix viewers have acquired abstract understandings, skills, and knowledge about behaviours such as 'binge-watching,' and technologies like 'smart televisions' have developed. Boundaries that existed between awards ceremonies (Usborne, 2018) (e.g., the Emmy Awards for television content and the Academy Awards for cinema) have been broken and blurred by Netflix content that can qualify for consideration in either (Sperling, 2017). Representational practices now include apps, internet browsers, and advertising-free delivery. Meanwhile, as cable television and broadcasting regulators may not have the same control over Netflix content as they once did over television networks, normalizing practices are further transformed as internet-streaming services are more impacted by internet regulators.

In summary, and reflecting Arthur's (2009) conceptualization of new technologies as novel combinations of pre-existing technologies, S-D logic sees new markets as ecosystems that result from dynamic reconfigurations of pre-existing markets (Vargo et al., 2015). Markets as ecosystems are the product of A2A resource integration through value co-creation processes (Wieland et al., 2016). The practices depicted in Figure 2.1 are carried out by actors when performing markets are integrative, normalizing, and representational in character (Lusch & Vargo, 2014). However, the institutionalized nature of these practices can be deliberately maintained, created, or disrupted through the purposive actions (institutional work) undertaken by market actors. As practices change, so do the nature and shape of the market system, and vice versa.

Although the institutional arrangements that govern value co-creation practices are constraining, they also provide rules, structures, belief systems, and norms that enable institutional actors to take action and generate change (Loasby, 2000) by engaging in institutional work (Lawrence & Suddaby, 2006). Hence, innovation of markets occurs through the (de)institutionalization of technologies and practices through changes to acceptance, normalization, and use by multiple actors over time, which manifest as new value co-creation processes.

Concluding remarks

This chapter set out to explore how best to understand innovation processes at multiple levels of aggregation – innovation that manifests as new products, processes, business models, and, ultimately, markets. Vargo and Lusch (2008, p. 9) characterize S-D logic as "a mindset, a lens through which to look at social and economic exchange phenomena so they can potentially be seen more clearly." An S-D logic lens represents an encompassing, meta-theoretic perspective and integrative lexicon (Brodie & Löbler, 2018) that can embrace various, diverse mid-range theoretical frameworks such as those from the technology, innovation, and strategic marketing literatures (Wieland et al., 2017). Thus, S-D logic provides a paradigmatic lens through which to understand the networked, sociological phenomena reflected in multiple disciplines.

A key feature of S-D logic is the service ecosystem, defined by Lusch and Vargo (2014, p. 161) as "relatively self-contained, self-adjusting systems of resource-integrating actors connected by shared institutional arrangements and mutual value creation through service exchange." A service ecosystem exists on multiple levels: individuals engaging in service exchange are an ecosystem, an organization is an ecosystem, a market is an ecosystem (Koskela-Huotari et al., 2016; Wieland et al., 2016), a field is an ecosystem, and the global economy is an ecosystem (Maglio & Spohrer, 2008). The ecosystem concept is considerably more inclusive than related constructs such as value chains, supply chains, or industries. Instead, an ecosystem is non-linear and includes all of the heterogeneous actors involved in value co-creation activity involving material and cultural elements, whether "producer," "consumer," "user," or any other actor (Mele et al., 2015; Storbacka & Nenonen, 2011). Hence, 'actors' include all horizontal, vertical, economic, and social participants.

All ecosystems are coordinated by interdependent and overlapping institutions (Vargo & Lusch, 2016), which not only provide the rules, norms, behaviours, and expectations for people's lives, but are also in turn reproduced by the practices enacted by embedded actors (Kjellberg & Helgesson, 2007). These institutional arrangements influence not only the ability of firms to coordinate value co-creation activities (both formally and informally), but also the unique interpretations of value by each ecosystem actor (Edvardsson et al., 2014).

Paradoxically, institutional arrangements provide the rules and resources that enable actors to engage in institutional work (Battilana & D'Aunno, 2009) and change what are normalized and routinized practices or beliefs (Lawrence, Suddaby, & Leca, 2009), replacing them with newly institutionalized alternatives – otherwise known as 'innovations.' It is only when a new technology is institutionalized that it can be considered a successful innovation, and it is a process of institutionalization that occurs when technology (both hardware and software, Arthur, 2009), or business models (Fehrer, Woratschek, & Brodie, 2018), or markets (Baker et al., 2018; Humphreys, 2010) are innovated.

There are important implications for managers when adopting an S-D logic lens. First, when examining incumbent innovation processes, managers need to be aware of the dominant logic that frames their approach to, and evaluation of, the purpose of the firm and the means of maximizing value (Mele, Colurcio, & Russo-Spena, 2014). When operationalizing innovation processes, there is a need to consider the development of all value propositions from the perspective of the service beneficiary, principally the customer (Skålén et al., 2015). After all, value is co-created *with* a service beneficiary, through time, in a particular social context. Value is neither embedded within tangible goods, nor is it realized at the time of sale. Hence, firms must become increasingly focused on maintaining and building relationships not only with customers, but also with other partners and collaborators within the broader value-creation network (Wieland et al., 2017).

By extension, a managerial focus on co-creation with multiple other actors requires a move from a largely competitive to a largely collaborative mindset. Deep understanding is required of how value propositions are perceived and used in practice, and of how value co-creation can be maximized for all actors. For example, when considering market innovation, a market that is growing in size or value will deliver growth to all actors even if each individual actor's market share remains static (Nenonen & Storbacka, 2018).

Skålén et al. (2015) note that innovations affecting value propositions might involve either changes to the resources to be integrated or to the practices to be employed when engaging in resource integration. Hence, firms must adopt flexibility not only in terms of what resources are to be employed, but also the practices with which to integrate them. As practices or resources change, so do value co-creation processes. However, to be successfully embedded as an innovation, any new value co-creation process needs to be institutionalized. The institutional dimension of ecosystems and value co-creation processes is the overarching commonality between innovation processes associated with products, business models, or markets. The institutional work framework (Lawrence, Suddaby, & Leca, 2009) provides a conceptualization of how actors create, disrupt, or destroy institutions (i.e., by engaging in processes of (de)institutionalization).

Being cognizant of broader societal institutional factors (e.g., beliefs, norms, and expectations) and systemic elements is critical for firms. As social ideologies change (sometimes radically, e.g., growing populism; concern for inequality), instability and complexity in markets can occur (Baker et al., 2018). In complex, fast-moving markets that feature frequent changes in technology and innovation, rapid processes of deinstitutionalization and institutionalization occur. In volatile contexts, these processes are recurrent, simultaneous, and overlapping (Zietsma & McKnight, 2009). It is critical that managers remember the importance of social construction of markets, through firm–customer dialogue (Rosa & Spanjol, 2005), inclusion of networked customers (Scaraboto & Fischer, 2013), or through the role of media and regulators (Humphreys, 2010; Kjellberg & Olson, 2017). In sum, market innovation is co-created by multiple heterogeneous actors and does not result from the actions of a sole actor working alone, whether an entrepreneur or a firm.

Last, adopting an S-D logic perspective has implications for strategists. The distinction between manufactured tangible goods and intangible services disintegrates as, in S-D logic, all value is seen to be derived from service-for-service exchange. Therefore, rather than attempting to formulate and operationalize simultaneous goods and 'services' strategies, a 'service' strategy is all that is required (Mele et al., 2014; Wieland et al., 2017). The focus of this service strategy must be on maximizing customers' interpretation and realization of value-in-use, in context, no matter the 'tangibility' of the value proposition. Additionally, by viewing markets as ecosystems, firms become embedded in contexts that are considerably more complex than often represented in the traditional strategy literature (e.g., Porter, 1996). Hence, strategic considerations must encompass considerably more elements than inherited wisdom dictates. Furthermore, a business model should not be perceived as a firm-centric proposition. Instead, it is the conduit to engagement and interaction with systemic actors (Wieland, et al., 2017), one that enables firms to engage all actors in value co-creation processes, including those related to all types of innovation.

References

Adalian, J. (2018). *Inside netflix's TV-swallowing, market-dominating binge factory*. Retrieved from www.vul ture.com/2018/06/how-netflix-swallowed-tv-industry.html.

Akaka, M. A., Vargo, S. L., & Wieland, H. (2017). Extending the context of innovation: The co-creation and institutionalization of technology and markets. In T. Russo-Spena, C. Mele & M. Nuutinen (Eds.), *Innovating in practice: Perspectives and experiences* (pp. 43–57). Cham, Switzerland: Springer International Publishing.

Alexy, O., & Dahlander, L. (2014). Managing open innovation. In M. Dodgson, D. M. Gann & N. Phillips (Eds.), *The Oxford handbook of innovation management* (pp. 442–481). Oxford, UK: Oxford University Press.

Araujo, L. (2007). Markets, market-making and marketing. *Marketing Theory*, 7(3), 211–226.

Araujo, L., Finch, J., & Kjellberg, H. (Eds.). (2010). *Reconnecting marketing to markets*. Oxford, UK: Oxford University Press.

Araujo, L., & Kjellberg, H. (2011). Shaping exchanges, performing markets: The study of market-ing practices. In P. Maclaran, M. Saren, B. Stern & M. Tadajewski (Eds.), *The SAGE handbook of marketing theory* (pp. 195–218). London, UK: SAGE Publications.

Arthur, W. B. (2009). *The nature of technology: What it is and how it evolves*. (1st ed.). New York: Free Press.

Asheim, B. T., & Coenen, L. (2005). Knowledge bases and regional innovation systems: Comparing nordic clusters. *Research Policy*, 34(8), 1173–1190. doi: 10.1016/j.respol.2005.03.013.

Baker, J. J., Storbacka, K., & Brodie, R.J. (2018). Markets changing, changing markets: Institutional work as market shaping. *Marketing Theory*, 19, Online, 1–28. doi: 10.1177/1470593118809799.

Battilana, J., & D'Aunno, T. (2009). Institutional work and the paradox of embedded agency. In T. B. Lawrence, R. Suddaby & B. Leca (Eds.), *Institutional work: Actors and agency in institutional studies of organizations* (pp. 31–58). Cambridge, UK: Cambridge University Press.

Battilana, J., Leca, B., & Boxenbaum, E. (2009). Agency and institutions: A review on institutional entrepreneurship. *Academy of Management Annals*, 3(1), 65–107. Retrieved from https://hal.archives-ouvertes.fr/hal-00802301.

Bourdieu, P. (1984). *Distinction: A social critique of the judgement of taste* (R. Nice, Trans.). Cambridge, MA: Harvard University Press.

Bourdieu, P. (1990). *The logic of practice*. Cambridge, UK: Polity Press.

Brodie, R. J., & Löbler, H. (2018). Advancing knowledge about service-dominant logic: The role of midrange theory. In S. L. Vargo & R. F. Lusch (Eds.), *SAGE handbook of service-dominant logic* (pp. 564–579). London, UK: SAGE Publications.

Callon, M. (2007). What does it mean to say that economics is performative? In D. MacKenzie, F. Muniesa & L. Siu (Eds.), *Do economists make markets? On the performativity of markets* (pp. 311–357). Princeton, NJ: Princeton University Press.

Callon, M. (2009). Elaborating the notion of performativity. *Le Libellio D'Aegis*, 5(1), 18–29. Retrieved from https://hal-mines-paristech.archives-ouvertes.fr/file/index/docid/460877/filename/Callon-_Libellio2009.pdf.

Callon, M. (2010). Marketing as an art and science of market framing: Commentary. In L. Araujo, J. Finch & H. Kjellberg (Eds.), *Reconnecting marketing to markets* (pp. 224–233). Oxford, UK: Oxford University Press.

Cesaroni, F., & Duque, L. C. (2013). Open innovation and service dominant logic: Application of foundational premises to innovative firms. *Harvard Deusto Business Research*, 2(1), 17–34.

Chesborough, H. W. (2006). *Open innovation: The new imperative for creating and profiting from technology*. Cambridge, MA: Harvard Business School Publishing Corporation.

Chua, Z. B. (2017). *Kickstarter: How a simple idea started a funding platform*. Retrieved from http://bworl donline.com/content.php?section=Technology&title=kickstarter-how-a-simple-idea-started-a-fund ing-platform&id=143201.

Cochoy, F. (1998). Another discipline for the market economy: Marketing as a performative knowledge and know-how for capitalism. In M. Callon (Ed.), *The laws of the markets* (pp. 194–221). Oxford, UK: Blackwell Publishers.

Coombes, P. H., & Nicholson, J. D. (2013). Business models and their relationship with marketing: A systematic literature review. *Industrial Marketing Management*, 42(5), 656–664. doi: 10.1016/j. indmarman.2013.05.005.

Corsaro, D., Cantu, C., & Tunisini, A. (2012). Actors' heterogeneity in innovation networks. *Industrial Marketing Management*, 41(5), 780–789.

DiMaggio, P. J. (1988). Interest and agency in institutional theory. In L. G. Zucker (Ed.), *Institutional patterns and organizations: Culture and environment* (pp. 3–22). Cambridge, MA: Ballinger.

DiMaggio, P. J., & Powell, W. W. (1991). Introduction. In W. W. Powell & P. J. DiMaggio (Eds.), *The new institutionalism in organizational analysis* (pp. 1–38). Chicago, IL: The University of Chicago Press.

Edvardsson, B., Kleinaltenkamp, M., Tronvoll, B., McHugh, P., & Windahl, C. (2014). Institutional logics matter when coordinating resource integration. *Marketing Theory*, 14(3), 291–309.

Edvardsson, B., Tronvoll, B., & Gruber, T. (2011). Expanding understanding of service exchange and value co-creation: A social construction approach. *Journal of the Academy of Marketing Science*, 39(2), 327–339. doi: 10.1007/s11747-010-0200-y.

Ellis, N., Jack, G., Hopkinson, G., & O'Reilly, D. (2010). Boundary work and identity construction in market exchanges. *Marketing Theory*, 10(3), 227–236. doi: 10.1177/1470593110373430.

Fehrer, J. A., & Nenonen, S. (2019). Crowdfunding networks: Structure, dynamics and critical capabilities. *Industrial Marketing Management*, in press. doi: 10.1016/j.indmarman.2019.02.012.

Fehrer, J. A., Woratschek, H., & Brodie, R. J. (2018). A systemic logic for platform business models. *Journal of Service Management*, 29(4), 546–568.

Foss, N. J., & Saebi, T. (2017). Fifteen years of research on business model innovation. *Journal of Management*, 43(1), 200–227. doi: 10.1177/0149206316675927.

Garcia, R., & Calantone, R. (2002). A critical look at technological innovation typology and innovativeness terminology: A literature review. *Journal of Product Innovation Management*, 19(2), 110–132. doi: 10.1111/1540-5885.1920110.

Giddens, A. (1984). *The constitution of society: Outline of the theory of structuration*. Berkeley and Los Angeles, CA: University of California Press.

Giesler, M. (2008). Conflict and compromise: Drama in marketplace evolution. *Journal of Consumer Research*, 34(6), 739–753. doi: 10.1086/522098.

Granovetter, M. (1985). Economic action and social structure: The problem of embeddedness. *American Journal of Sociology*, 91(3), 481–510.

Hargrave, T. J., & Van de Ven, A. H. (2009). Institutional work as the creative embrace of contradiction. In T. B. Lawrence, R. Suddaby & B. Leca (Eds.), *Institutional work: Actors and agency in institutional studies of organizations* (pp. 120–140). Cambridge, UK: Cambridge University Press.

Harrison, D., & Kjellberg, H. (2016). How users shape markets. *Marketing Theory*, 16(4), 445–468. doi: 10.1177/1470593116652004.

Hauser, J., Tellis, G. J., & Griffin, A. (2006). Research on innovation: A review and agenda for marketing science. *Marketing Science*, 25(6), 687–717. doi: 10.1287/mksc.1050.0144.

Huarng, K. H., Cervera, A., & Mas-Verdu, F. (2018). Innovation and service-dominant logic. *Service Business*, 12(3), 453–456.

Humphreys, A. (2010). Megamarketing: The creation of markets as a social process. *Journal of Marketing*, 74(2), 1–19. doi: 10.1509/jmkg.74.2.1.

Jaworski, B. J., Kohli, A., & Sahay, A. (2000). Market-driven versus driving markets. *Journal of the Academy of Marketing Science*, 28(1), 45–54. doi: 10.1177/0092070300281005.

Kindström, D., Ottosson, M., & Carlborg, P. (2018). Unraveling firm-level activities for shaping markets. *Industrial Marketing Management*, 68(2018), 36–45. doi: 10.1016/j.indmarman.2017.09.003.

Kjellberg, H., Azimont, F., & Reid, E. (2015). Market innovation processes: Balancing stability and change. *Industrial Marketing Management*, 44(2015), 4–12. doi: 10.1016/j.indmarman.2014.10.002.

Kjellberg, H., & Helgesson, C. F. (2006). Multiple versions of markets: Multiplicity and performativity in market practice. *Industrial Marketing Management*, 35(7), 839–855. doi: 10.1016/j.indmarman.2006.05.011.

Kjellberg, H., & Helgesson, C. F. (2007). On the nature of markets and their practices. *Marketing Theory*, 7(2), 137–162. doi: 10.1177/1470593107076862.

Kjellberg, H., & Olson, D. (2017). Joint markets: How adjacent markets influence the formation of regulated markets. *Marketing Theory*, 17(1), 95–123.

Kjellberg, H., Storbacka, K., Akaka, M., Chandler, J., Finch, J., Lindeman, S., … Nenonen, S. (2012). Market futures/future markets: Research directions in the study of markets. *Marketing Theory*, 12(2), 219–223. doi: 10.1177/1470593112444382.

Koskela-Huotari, K., Edvardsson, B., Jonas, J. M., Sörhammar, D., & Witell, L. (2016). Innovation in service ecosystems: Breaking, making, and maintaining institutionalized rules of resource integration. *Journal of Business Research*, 69(8), 2964–2971. doi: 10.1016/j.jbusres.2016.02.029.

Kraatz, M. S. (2009). Leadership as institutional work: A bridge to the other side. In T. B. Lawrence, R. Suddaby & B. Leca (Eds.), *Institutional work: Actors and agency in institutional studies of organizations* (pp. 59–91). Cambridge, UK: Cambridge University Press.

Kumar, N., Scheer, L., & Kotler, P. (2000). From market driven to market driving. *European Management Journal*, 18(2), 129–142.

Lawrence, T. B., & Suddaby, R. (2006). Institutions and institutional work. In S. R. Clegg, C. Hardy, T. B. Lawrence & W. R. Nord (Eds.), *The SAGE handbook of organization studies* (2nd ed., pp. 215–254). London, UK: SAGE Publications.

Lawrence, T. B., Suddaby, R., & Leca, B. (Eds.). (2009). *Institutional work: Actors and agency in institutional studies of organizations*. Cambridge, UK: Cambridge University Press.

Loasby, B. J. (2000). Market institutions and economic evolution. *Journal of Evolutionary Economics*, 10(3), 297–309. doi: 10.1007/s001910050016.

Lusch, R. F., & Nambisan, S. (2015). Service innovation: A service-dominant logic perspective. *MIS Quarterly*, 39(1), 155–175. doi: 10.25300/MISQ/2015/39.1.07.

Lusch, R. F., & Vargo, S. L. (2014). *Service-dominant logic: Premises, perspective, possibilities*. Cambridge, UK: Cambridge University Press.

Maglio, P., & Spohrer, J. (2008). Fundamentals of service science. *Journal of the Academy of Marketing Science*, 36(1), 18–20. doi: 10.1007/s11747-007-0058-9.

Mason, K., Kjellberg, H., & Hagberg, J. (2015). Exploring the performativity of marketing: Theories, practices and devices. *Journal of Marketing Management*, 31(1–2), 1–15. doi: 10.1080/0267257X.2014.982932.

Mason, K., & Spring, M. (2011). The sites and practices of business models. *Industrial Marketing Management*, 40(6), 1032–1041. doi: 10.1016/j.indmarman.2011.06.032.

Masssolution. (2016). *2015CF-RE crowdfunding for real estate*. Retrieved from http://reports.crowdsourcing.org/index.php?route=product/product&product_id=54.

Mele, C., Colurcio, M., & Russo-Spena, T. (2014). Research traditions of innovation: Goods-dominant logic, the resource-based approach, and service-dominant logic. *Managing Service Quality*, 24(6), 612–642.

Mele, C., Pels, J., & Storbacka, K. (2015). A holistic market conceptualization. *Journal of the Academy of Marketing Science*, 43(1), 100–114. doi: 10.1007/s11747-014-0383-8.

Mele, C., & Russo-Spena, T. (2015). Innomediary agency and practices in shaping market innovation. *Industrial Marketing Management*, 44(2015), 42–53. doi: 10.1016/j.indmarman.2014.10.006.

Michel, S., Brown, S., & Gallan, A. (2008). An expanded and strategic view of discontinuous innovations: Deploying a service-dominant logic. *Journal of the Academy of Marketing Science*, 36(1), 54–66. doi: 10.1007/s11747-007-0066-9.

Möller, K., & Rajala, A. (2007). Rise of strategic nets: New modes of value creation. *Industrial Marketing Management*, 36(7), 895–908.

Möller, K., Rajala, A., & Svahn, S. (2005). Strategic business nets: Their type and management. *Journal of Business Research*, 58(9), 1274–1284.

Mollick, E. (2014). The dynamics of crowdfunding: An exploratory study. *Journal of Business Venturing*, 29(1), 1–16.

Murray, J. (2018). *Crowdfunding legal issues for small businesses*. Retrieved from www.thebalancesmb.com/crowdfunding-legal-issues-for-small-businesses-398020.

Nenonen, S., Kjellberg, H., Pels, J., Cheung, L., Lindeman, S., Mele, C., ... Storbacka, K. (2014). A new perspective on market dynamics: Market plasticity and the stability–fluidity dialectics. *Marketing Theory*, 14(3), 269–289. doi: 10.1177/1470593114534342.

Nenonen, S., Möller, K., & Storbacka, K. (2017). Market innovation: Renewal of traditional industrial networks. In T. Russo-Spena, C. Mele & M. Nuutinen (Eds.), *Innovating in practice: Perspectives and experiences* (pp. 59–81). Cham and Switzerland: Springer International Publishing.

Nenonen, S., & Storbacka, K. (2018). *SMASH: Using market shaping to design new strategies for innovation, value creation, and growth*. Bingley, UK: Emerald Publishing Limited.

Nenonen, S., Storbacka, K., & Frethey-Bentham, C. (2019). Is your industrial marketing work working? Developing a composite index of market change. *Industrial Marketing Management*, 80, 251–265.

Oliver, C. (1991). Strategic responses to institutional processes. *Academy of Management Review*, 16(1), 145–179. doi: 10.5465/AMR.1991.4279002.

Ordanini, A., & Parasuraman, A. (2011). Service innovation viewed through a service-dominant logic lens: A conceptual framework and empirical analysis. *Journal of Service Research*, 14(1), 3–23.

Owyang, J. (2014, December 7). *Collaborative economy honeycomb 2: Watch it grow*. Retrieved from www.web-strategist.com/blog/2014/12/07/collaborative-economy-honeycomb-2-watch-it-grow/.

Porter, M. E. (1996). What is strategy? *Harvard Business Review*, 74(6), 61–78.

Prahalad, C. K., & Ramaswamy, V. (2004a). Co-creating unique value with customers. *Strategy & Leadership*, 32(3), 4–9.

Prahalad, C. K., & Ramaswamy, V. (2004b). *The future of competition: Co-creating unique value with customers*. Boston, MA: Harvard University Press.

Quirky. (2018). *How quirky works*. Retrieved from https://quirky.com/.

Rosa, J. A., Porac, J. F., Runser-Spanjol, J., & Saxon, M. S. (1999). Sociocognitive dynamics in a product market. *Journal of Marketing*, 63(1999), 64–77.

Rosa, J. A., & Spanjol, J. (2005). Micro-level product-market dynamics: Shared knowledge and its relationship to market development. *Journal of the Academy of Marketing Science*, 33(2), 197–216.

Scaraboto, D., & Fischer, E. (2013). Frustrated fatshionistas: An institutional theory perspective on consumer quests for greater choice in mainstream markets. *Journal of Consumer Research*, 39(6), 1234–1257.

Schatzki, T. R., Knorr-Cetina, K., & von Savigny, E. (2001). *The practice turn in contemporary theory*. London, UK: Routledge.

Schumpeter, J. A. (1947). The creative response in economic history. *The Journal of Economic History*, 7(2), 149–159.

Scott, W. R. (2001). *Institutions and organizations* (2nd ed.). Thousand Oaks, CA: SAGE Publications.

Scott, W. R. (2014). *Institutions and organizations: Ideas, interests, and identities* (4th ed.). Thousand Oaks, CA: SAGE Publications.

Sebastiani, R., & Paiola, M. (2010). Rethinking service innovation: Four pathways to evolution. *International Journal of Quality and Service Sciences*, 2(1), 79–94. doi: 10.1108/17566691011026612.

Seo, M., & Creed, W. E. D. (2002). Institutional contradictions, praxis, and institutional change: A dialectical perspective. *Academy of Management Review*, 27(2), 222–247. doi: 10.2307/4134353.

Skålén, P., Gummerus, J., Koskull, C., & Magnusson, P. (2015). Exploring value propositions and service innovation: A service-dominant logic study. *Journal of the Academy of Marketing Science*, 43(2), 137–158. doi: 10.1007/s11747-013-0365-2.

Smothers, J., Murphy, P. J., Novicevic, M. M., & Humphreys, J. H. (2014). Institutional entrepreneurship as emancipating institutional work. *Journal of Management History*, 20(1), 114–134. doi: 10.1108/JMH-06-2012-0047.

Spangler, T. (2018). *Netflix licensed content generates 80% of U.S. viewing, study finds*. Retrieved from https://variety.com/2018/digital/news/netflix-licensed-content-majority-streaming-views-2017-study-1202751405/.

Spencer, R., & Cova, B. (2012). Market solutions: Breaking free from dyad-centric logic and broadening the scope of S-D L. *Journal of Marketing Management*, 28(13–14), 1571–1587. doi: 10.1080/0267257X.2012.742453.

Sperling, N. (2017). *Netflix, the oscars, and the battle for the future of film*. Retrieved from www.vanityfair.com/hollywood/2017/11/netflix-the-oscars-the-battle-for-the-future-of-film.

Storbacka, K., & Nenonen, S. (2011). Markets as configurations. *European Journal of Marketing*, 45(1), 241–258. doi: 10.1108/03090561111095685.

Storbacka, K., & Nenonen, S. (2015). Learning with the market: Facilitating market innovation. *Industrial Marketing Management*, 44(2015), 73–82. doi: 10.1016/j.indmarman.2014.10.009.

Sturges, F. (2018, -10–27). Pretty risky: Has Julia Roberts's move from hollywood to TV drama homecoming worked? *The Guardian*. Retrieved from www.theguardian.com/tv-and-radio/2018/oct/27/julia-roberts-homecoming.

Su, Y., & Chen, J. (2015). Introduction to regional innovation systems in East Asia. *Technological Forecasting & Social Change*, 100(2015), 80–82. doi: 10.1016/j.techfore.2015.11.004.

Teece, D. J. (2010). Business models, business strategy and innovation. *Long Range Planning*, 43(2), 172–194. doi: 10.1016/j.lrp.2009.07.003.

Thornton, P. H., Ocasio, W., & Lounsbury, M. (2012). *The institutional logics perspective: A new approach to culture, structure, and process*. Oxford, UK: Oxford University Press.

Usborne, S. (2018, -04–17). Netflix's 'new world order': A streaming giant on the brink of global domination. *The Guardian*. Retrieved from www.theguardian.com/media/2018/apr/17/netflixs-new-world-order-a-streaming-giant-on-the-brink-of-global-domination.

Vargo, S. L. (2007). On a theory of markets and marketing: From positively normative to normatively positive. *Australasian Marketing Journal*, 15(1), 53–60. doi: 10.1016/S1441-3582(07)70029-0.

Vargo, S. L., & Akaka, M. A. (2012). Value cocreation and service systems (re) formation: A service ecosystems view. *Service Science*, 4(3), 207–217.

Vargo, S. L., Koskela-Huotari, K., Baron, S., Edvardsson, B., Reynoso, J., & Colurcio, M. (2017). A systems perspective on markets–Toward a research agenda. *Journal of Business Research*, 79, 260–268.

Vargo, S. L., & Lusch, R. F. (2004). Evolving to a new dominant logic for marketing. *Journal of Marketing*, 68(1), 1–17.

Vargo, S. L., & Lusch, R. F. (2008). Service-dominant logic: Continuing the evolution. *Journal of the Academy of Marketing Science*, 36(1), 1–10. doi: 10.1007/s11747-007-0069-6.

Vargo, S. L., & Lusch, R. F. (2016). Institutions and axioms: An extension and update of service-dominant logic. *Journal of the Academy of Marketing Science*, 44(1), 5–23. doi: 10.1007/s11747-015-0456-3.

Vargo, S. L., Wieland, H., & Akaka, M. A. (2015). Innovation through institutionalization: A service ecosystems perspective. *Industrial Marketing Management*, 44(2015), 63–72. doi: 10.1016/j.indmarman.2014.10.008.

Venkatesh, A., Peñaloza, L., & Firat, A. F. (2006). The market as a sign system and the logic of the market. In R. F. Lusch & S. L. Vargo (Eds.), *The service-dominant logic of marketing: Dialog, debate, and directions* (pp. 251–265). Armonk, NY: ME Sharpe.

Wieland, H., Hartmann, N. N., & Vargo, S. L. (2017). Business models as service strategy. *Journal of the Academy of Marketing Science*, 45(2017), 68. doi: 10.1007/s11747-017-0531-z.

Wieland, H., Koskela-Huotari, K., & Vargo, S. L. (2016). Extending actor participation in value creation: An institutional view. *Journal of Strategic Marketing*, 24(3–4), 210–226. doi: 10.1080/0965254X.2015.1095225.

Wieland, H., Vargo, S. L., Akaka, M. A., & Barbeau, B. (2018). A unifying perspective for the technological, business model, and market aspects of innovation. In S. L. Vargo & R. F. Lusch (Eds.), *SAGE handbook of service-dominant logic* (pp. 508–521). London, UK: SAGE Publications.

World Economic Forum. (2016). *Alternative investments 2020 the future of capital for entrepreneurs and SMEs*. Retrieved from www3.weforum.org/docs/WEF_AI_FUTURE.pdf.

Zietsma, C., & Lawrence, T. B. (2010). Institutional work in the transformation of an organizational field: The interplay of boundary work and practice work. *Administrative Science Quarterly*, 55(2), 189–221. doi: 10.2189/asqu.2010.55.2.189.

Zietsma, C., & McKnight, B. (2009). Building the iron cage: Institutional creation work in the context of competing proto-institutions. In T. B. Lawrence, R. Suddaby & B. Leca (Eds.), *Institutional work: Actors and agency in institutional studies of organizations* (pp. 143–177). Cambridge, UK: Cambridge University Press.

Zott, C., Amit, R., & Massa, L. (2011). The business model: Recent developments and future research. *Journal of Management*, 37(4), 1019–1042. doi: 10.1177/014920631140626.

3

Service profit logic
Ensuring customer willingness to pay

Christian Grönroos

The service reality

Unlike goods, service cannot exist without customers. Even if there are no buyers, goods can be manufactured and perhaps sold at a later date. From the beginning of modern service marketing research, it was observed that the customer is part of the service production process; therefore, if the customer is not present and willing to buy and consume, no service production can take place and the service provider is left with idle resources (Eiglier & Langeard, 1975). For example, if a restaurant is empty one evening, it still has to carry its costs, but without corresponding revenues. Moreover, by taking part in the service production process, customers actively influence the service they get (Eiglier & Langeard, 1975; Grönroos, 1978; Gummesson, 1979). Hence, service and the customers of a service firm are interconnected in critical ways, such that service requires a strong customer focus.

Neglecting customers has several negative effects. First, they may lose interest in the firm's service. In this case, revenues are lost, but the cost level remains unchanged (for some time at least). Second, customers may not be adequately informed about how to fulfil their roles in the service production process, which leads to deteriorating service quality. Either face-to-face service processes or digitized processes (where the customers are mostly faceless) might have been designed without taking into account the customers' own processes, levels of knowledge and skill, and personal wishes in an adequate way. The outcome is frustrated, dissatisfied customers, and in the end lost revenues.

Conventional approaches to revenue and cost management

According to conventional management wisdom and many management models, the business processes that cause costs and those that generate revenues are largely disconnected. One example of such models is conventional manufacturing productivity management. The quality of goods can remain unchanged when the input resources into the manufacturing process or the process itself are changed. Therefore, improved cost efficiency can be achieved without changes to the quality of the goods or loss of revenues. Another example is conventional marketing management. In this case, the sales and marketing function (which is more or less separated from the firm's other business processes) receives goods to sell that meet customer requirements, and they are expected to be able to generate revenues for the firm (Grönroos, 2015).

Both management models mentioned above are based on the assumption that revenues and costs stem from different sources. Managing revenues and managing costs are treated as separate processes, wherein only an indirect connection exists. Because of this indirect connection, sales and marketing can sell goods that other business functions produce. The cost of developing and producing a particular level of quality in goods, and the resulting interest in the goods created among customers and potential customers, has an impact on customer willingness to buy at a given price and therefore also on the firm's revenue-generating capability. However, the indirect connection between revenues and costs is only vaguely included in management models and in managerial decision-making. This may occur because a firm's production and administration are considered to be cost-generating functions and are treated as such by management, whereas revenue generation is considered the responsibility of sales and marketing.

The conventional models and the service reality

The management approach described in the previous section (i.e., separation of revenue- and cost-generating centres) is grounded in a goods manufacturing reality wherein customer perceptions of what a firm can offer are only slightly related to the manufactured good, and more closely related to how sales and marketing present and offer it. Viewed this way, production processes have only a distant, indirect effect on customer willingness to pay. Furthermore, the functions of business processes other than sales and marketing have no impact on a firm's revenue generation.

This reality belongs to the past for service firms, and especially for business-to-business (B2B) services. Increasingly, the offerings that customers buy and use include more service elements than tangible manufactured elements. As a result, many more of a firm's processes and activities influence customer perceptions and willingness to pay. Some examples include customer service, deliveries, maintenance, information, complaints handling, service recoveries, front line employee behaviour, service systems, and digital technologies and processes, which may have a profound impact on customer experiences and perceptions of the service. This influences not only the current quality perceptions of the offerings they have bought, but also their willingness to support the firm's revenue generation in the future. The service reality is much more complex than what the conventional models assume. Neglecting this leads to bad service and dissatisfied customers.

Firms' cost-creating and revenue-influencing processes, as well as the cost-related and revenue-related management decisions, are not as neatly disconnected and separated as many conventional models imply. Without considering the impact of capital, a firm's economic profit is basically a function of revenues and costs, where costs are subtracted from revenues to calculate the economic profit. In a service context, revenue- and cost-influencing processes and decisions are not completely separable, so an interesting and important question for management emerges: how does management decision-making influence a firm's profit in the much more complex reality of service firms? In other words, what does the *service profit logic* look like? In this chapter, this logic is analysed and discussed. Understanding service profit logic as a basis for management decision-making is not important exclusively for service firms, but for all kinds of firms that have complex customer relationships, in which a number of processes, activities, and interactions performed by business functions other than sales and marketing are experienced by customers and influence their perception of the firm's ability and willingness to help them. This is certainly the case in many B2B contexts. Therefore, the B2B reality is in many ways comparable to the service reality, and today the profit logic of B2B interactions resembles the profit logic of service firms. Hence, in this chapter the term 'service firm' includes B2B manufacturers that have customer interfaces going beyond mere goods.

A short note on *goods profit logic*

As was observed in the introductory section, from a conventional manufacturing viewpoint, how effectively sales and marketing functions manage to convince customers to buy goods determines the revenues generated for the firm, whereas the other firm business processes, such as production (but not including sales and marketing) drive costs.

In Figure 3.1 goods profit logic is schematically illustrated. The setting is straightforward, and managerial decision-making is in principle equally straightforward. From the customer point of view, manufacturing processes occur in a closed backstage area and do not influence perceptions of quality. (The same is true of other business functions.) Therefore, if sales and marketing make promises that appeal to customers, and a good that fulfills these promises is delivered, the customers can be expected to be satisfied and willing to pay for repeat orders of the same good. In this case, revenue management is a matter of successful sales and marketing and the existence of a wanted good, as indicated by the thick arrow in the figure. Manufacturing and the performance of other business functions are matters of cost management, as indicated by the broken arrow in the figure.

Viewing this goods-based profit logic, the implication is that revenues and costs are driven by separate processes. Consequently, the firm sees the management of revenues and that of costs as constituting different processes. Implications for revenues do not have to be taken into account when cost-related decisions are made, provided that such decisions do not influence the manufactured good's quality level. From the customer point of view, sales and marketing and the product itself are the only visible parts of the firm; all other business functions form a 'back office,' which is invisible to them and does not influence either their perceptions or willingness to pay. In situations where customers do not experience the processes and actions of functions other than conventional sales and marketing, and are only influenced by the quality of a standardized good, thinking along the lines of goods profit

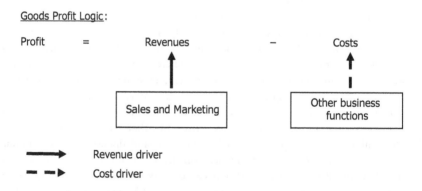

Figure 3.1 The goods profit logic of traditional manufacturing.

logic serves management well. However, as mentioned before, for many firms the customer interface is much broader and more complex. In a service context, where the interface between the firm and its customers includes other resources and processes than a single good alone (or may include no goods at all), adopting such a view of the profit logic causes management to neglect the customers. The risk that customers will experience bad service grows and, therefore, the risks increase that that the firm will lose customers and eventually face declining profitability.

The service firm's customer interface

The customer interface of service firms is different than that of conventional goods manufacturing firms, which means that the reality of service firms must also be different from the one the goods profit logic is based on. The customer experiences more than a pre-produced good and, consequently, the efforts of conventional marketing and sales are not the only reasons for a customer to decide to buy, and especially to buy repeatedly. The most important characteristic of services is that they are processes; when consuming them, customers are particularly exposed to these service processes. For instance, when eating at a restaurant, a guest experiences the architecture of the restaurant, the functionality of its systems, the attitudes and behaviours of its personnel, the influence of fellow guests and, of course, the composition of the menu and the attractiveness of the meal. A B2B example involves hiring the services of a management consultant. In this case, the client experiences the consultant's skills and knowledge, ability to implement the assignment and develop a solution, and general attitudes and behaviours.

In view of the broadened interface between service firms and their customers, what makes customers willing to buy repeatedly? Marketing and sales can create brand awareness as well as an initial interest in the firm and its offerings, which may result in a first purchase. However, what makes customers willing to continue buying? In principle, the answer is the same as in a goods-based business: it is necessary to help customers cope with their individual or business processes, while maintaining their interest in continuing as customers. However, it is important to note that, in service firms, the manufactured good is missing. Tangible items, such as meals in a restaurant or policy documents in a consultancy assignment, are not goods. They are goods-like resources which, together with a host of other resources, interact with each other and with the customers in the service process. Customer perceptions of how the service process functions, as well as the resulting outcomes, replace a pre-produced good. Therefore, this process and its outcomes influence customer perceptions of quality and determine their willingness to pay. The outcome of a service process is often considered a hygiene factor, whereas the process itself dominates the quality perception (Grönroos, 1984). Hence, the service process drives the service firm's revenue generation. The implications for service firms' profit logic and for service management are substantial.

The first implication relates to the dominating management mindset. Goods are outputs of manufacturing processes; customers buy and consume these outputs. Therefore, managers are used to thinking in terms of what manufacturing outputs do for customers. However, in service contexts, the customers do not exclusively experience outputs. The outcomes generated by the service processes may not even be the trigger that makes them interested in continuing as customers. For instance, the positive feeling after a good meal at a restaurant may make a customer satisfied with the outcome of the visit to this restaurant, but may not be a reason for him or her to return. If, on top of this, the experiences with the service process of the restaurant are considered excellent, the likelihood that he or she will return may increase. In service, process becomes a focus of management, because it is equally as important as the outcome (and in many cases is even more important). If the prevailing mindset causes managers to excessively concentrate on the outcome, thereby neglecting the importance of the process, service will suffer.

Another implication, which relates to the previous one, is both psychological and physical. In goods firms with broad customer interfaces, the manufactured goods are very much present in the minds of everyone, including strategic decision-makers, marketers and sales reps, and in the minds of the employees who interact with the customers in many capacities. In service firms, the service processes are often systematized, such that they are thought of as similar to goods manufacturing processes, and they are discussed using a goods terminology. However, the service processes remain processes, but their importance is disguised by the goods terminology used. As a consequence, these 'artificial goods' (i.e., services thought of as goods), are equally present in the minds of both service managers and providers. In such cases, managers and other employees both become preoccupied with goods and have a goods mindset. Strategies, sales talks, marketing campaigns, and other customer interactions start to revolve around these artificial goods, and the firm's focus on customers is lost. The omnipresent goods disguise the customers. This leads to dissatisfaction and eventually lost customers and lost revenues. Losing focus on the customers leads to mismanagement of the customer interfaces, which the customers experience as bad service. The point is to put the goods aside and focus on the customers instead, and on how to serve them well.

There are a number of other implications of the extended and complex customer interface. As customers experience the service processes and not their outcomes alone, the nature and scope of marketing and of customer perceptions of quality differ from what conventional models assume. Furthermore, productivity management, which traditionally is treated as an issue internal to the firm, must also include the external effects of productivity-related decisions. The competence level of employees (other than sales and marketing professionals) interacting with customers must be enhanced to include appropriate behavioural and communication skills, and the attitudes of such employees must be favourable toward interacting with customers. These challenges for management in service firms are addressed at some length in subsequent sections of this chapter.

Service profit logic

Because of service firms' broad customer interface, the whole firm cannot be treated as a back office, as it often is in manufacturing firms. The manufacturing firm's pre-produced good is replaced by the service process. The customer participates in parts, but not all, of this process. Therefore, the number of business processes that are open or closed to the customers must be carefully analysed. If customer interactions with a process open to them (such as interactions with the staff in a retailing store or with technicians doing repair work on installed equipment) are neglected by the firm, a negative impact on customer satisfaction may occur and the customers may be lost. If such processes are not planned and staffed with a customer focus in mind, the likelihood that the customers will not be served well increases and the risk of losing revenues grows. Today, in many open processes customers experience smart technologies and digitized encounters, such as when making hotel reservations and buying theatre tickets. Here, too, technologies that are not customer-friendly and processes that are malfunctioning will have negative effects on customers. In Figure 3.2, the service profit logic is schematically illustrated (Grönroos, 2015).

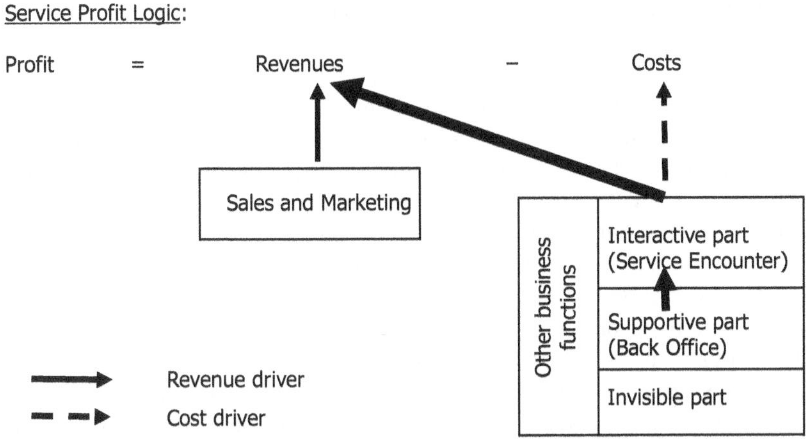

Service Profit Logic:

Profit   =   Revenues   –   Costs

Sales and Marketing

Other business functions

Interactive part
(Service Encounter)

Supportive part
(Back Office)

Invisible part

→ Revenue driver

⇢ Cost driver

Figure 3.2   Service profit logic: how profit emerges in a service context.

Source: Grönroos, Christian: *Service Management and Marketing: Managing the Service Profit Logic.* 4th edition. Chichester: John Wiley & Co, 2015, p. 72; slightly developed.

As mentioned above, and as the figure shows, conventional marketing and sales contribute to revenues, whereas other business functions create costs, as in goods profit logic. However, the major difference between service logic and goods logic is the thick arrow from the 'other business functions' box to revenues (see Figure 3.2). This arrow indicates that a service firm's processes (other than conventional sales and marketing) function and influence customer experiences, having a pivotal impact on customer satisfaction, willingness to pay, and therefore also on the firm's revenue-generating capacity. From a service profit logic point of view, depending on the impact on customers, such business functions and processes must be divided into three distinct categories, namely (1) interactive processes, (2) supporting processes, and (3) processes that are invisible from the customer perspective.

Interactive processes form the service encounter, wherein customers interact directly with the service firm's processes and resources. In these interactions, customers are exposed to and experience the attitudes, behaviours, and skills of front line service employees as well as the accessibility, functionality, and attractiveness of other resources, such as systems and smart technologies. In addition, the service environment and fellow customers, who may be in the service process at the same time, also influence customer experiences and quality perceptions. As service marketing research demonstrated very early, the service for a given customer and the level of satisfaction it generates emerge in such interactions (Eiglier & Langeard, 1975); also, the customer takes an active role in this service production process and influences it (Grönroos, 1978). The service encounter can be located at the service firm's premises, such as a bank office or a gym, or at the customer's premises, such as when repair and maintenance is performed on installed equipment. As indicated by the thick arrow in Figure 3.2, customer interactions with the service firm's interactive processes (i.e., the service encounter) have a direct impact on customer willingness to pay and therefore on the firm's revenue generation.

The firm's processes closed to the customers can be divided into two categories, namely processes that support the ability of interactive processes to serve and in that way influence willingness to pay and the firm's revenue-generating capability indirectly, and closed processes which have no impact on the customers. These will be discussed next.

Supporting processes form a back office that is mostly closed to the customers, such as the restaurant kitchen, a financial advisor's analytics support, or housekeeping in a hotel. Although such processes are not visible to customers, they are not without importance to customer perceptions of quality. If the supporting processes do not function properly or fail to have a customer focus, they will create problems for service employees and customer-serving systems during the service encounter, and the interactive processes will not be able to provide good service and favourable quality perceptions to customers. Hence, performance of the supporting processes has an indirect impact on customer willingness to pay and, therefore, an indirect impact on the service firm's ability to generate revenues. In Figure 3.2, this is indicated by the black arrow from the supporting processes to the interactive processes.

Finally, there may be functions and processes that neither directly nor indirectly influence the ability of the service encounter to provide good service. These are *invisible processes* (so-called because they are invisible to the customers). It is difficult to predetermine which processes belong in this category. However, parts of the firm's administrative routines and some manufacturing processes are probably such invisible processes. On the other hand, although they might be considered invisible processes, such activities as procurement, competence development, and many management processes should often be considered supporting processes. Real, invisible parts of the service firm can be managed and developed exclusively with their cost implications in mind.

Managerial implications of service profit logic

According to the conventional goods profit logic, business functions and processes (excluding marketing and sales) have either no impact or only an indirect impact on customer willingness to pay. Production processes are not visible to customers, and any interactions that do occur are expected to be very minor. Therefore, cost concerns dominate the management of these business functions. Provided that other business processes provide sales and marketing with goods, for which there is a market, sales and marketing are solely responsible for a manufacturing firm's revenues. In a service firm, on the other hand, the existence of large interactive parts of many processes makes the situation dramatically different. Cost and revenue management functions can no longer be kept apart. As far as the interactive processes (service encounter) and supporting processes (back office) are concerned, decisions regarding cost and revenue effects of actions to be taken have to be integrated. When actions that are expected to change cost levels are planned, the revenue effects of such actions must be considered simultaneously. This is not taken into account very well in conventional management models.

In summary, the need for integrating decisions that influence the firm's cost level, on the one hand, and decisions that steer the firm's revenue-generating capability, on the other hand, necessitated by service profit logic, has implications for a number of management decisions. In subsequent sections, the most obvious and important ramifications for decision-making are discussed. These relate to marketing management, organizing marketing in a customer-focused organization, quality management, productivity management, and competence development.

Marketing management

On a general level, "the ultimate objective of marketing is to make a firm meaningful to its customers" (Grönroos, 2015, p. 277). How this is achieved is explained by *promise theory*, according to which marketing is a matter of making promises effectively, and impeccably fulfilling expectations created by promises made (Calonius, 2006). If expectations are created through over-promising that cannot be fulfilled in regard to what a good or service can do for a customer, the firm making such promises becomes meaningless to the customer and marketing fails. For marketing to succeed there must be a balance between promise-making and promise-keeping. This is called the "promise management" view of marketing (Grönroos, 2009). The broader and more complex the customer interface is (e.g., in service), the more challenging it is to achieve such a balance. According to conventional marketing models, which include tactics such as the marketing mix and its 4 Ps (price, product, promotion, and place), only the actions of marketing professionals and sales representatives are expected to influence customer preferences and buying decisions. If the price, place, and promotion tactics manage to make customers interested in a good and persuade them to buy, the product should create customer satisfaction and repeat buying behaviour and, as a consequence, the firm becomes meaningful to customers.

Especially in the case of consumer goods, there is a fairly standardized good that is responsible for fulfilling expectations and keeping promises made. In this case, it is comparatively straightforward to create a balance between promise-making and promise-keeping. However, when moving toward customer relationships with broader customer interfaces beyond a standardized good, the management of promises becomes more challenging, and marketing more complicated. As service marketing research has demonstrated, if a firm is to avoid losing customers and thereby weakening its revenue-generation capability, the marketing concept has to be expanded considerably beyond the limited and restrictive models of conventional marketing (e.g., Grönroos, 1978; Gummesson, 1991).

Service profit logic explains why the marketing concept must be expanded. In the interactive processes of a service firm, a range of front line employees (whose main task is to produce and deliver the service) influence the perceptions of customers and their willingness to pay. Bank tellers, restaurant waiters, airline cabin personnel, management consultants, repair and maintenance technicians are examples of such front line employees. When interacting and communicating with the customers, front line service employees act as *part-time marketers* (Gummesson, 1991). Such employees demonstrate to customers that the offerings they select help them to cope with their processes in a satisfactory way. Perhaps even more than sales reps and full-time marketers do, part-time marketers create resales and make the customers willing to pay on a continuous basis. Moreover, they often have many more customer contacts than do full-time marketers and sales reps, and they meet customers at critical moments, which occur when customers experience what has been offered and form their quality perceptions (Gummesson, 1991). The efforts of part-time marketers are an integral part of the marketing process and are frequently more critical than those of external marketing and sales personnel.

In service marketing, the part of the marketing process which is the responsibility of part-time marketers is called *interactive marketing* (Grönroos, 2015). In conclusion, the total marketing process consists, on the one hand, of conventional external marketing, which aims to make promises and create sales, and, on the other hand, of an interactive marketing process. The objective of this part of the total marketing process is to demonstrate that the firm manages to keep promises made to customers and thereby create resales and up-sales, and also create favourable references, word-of-mouth, and social media exposures. The full-time marketing professionals and sales reps are responsible for making promises and getting customers, whereas the part-time marketers are responsible for fulfilling promises, keeping customers, and developing customer relationships.

Quality management

Traditionally, quality management has been considered a more or less technical issue, in which the technical outcome of the production process is managed. Thus, quality assurance relates to the technical specifications of the production output and quality management is largely an internal issue, in which the customer is not involved. However, as service profit logic demonstrates, service customers are exposed to more than the technical outcome of a service process and the effects of its quality. The service process, and how its interactive processes function, both provide an important impact on customer perceptions of quality. Consequently, the focus of quality management must not be restricted to ensuring that the outcome of the service process is good. In service, customer focus is an integral part of quality management. All aspects of the service process, such as the attitudes and behaviours of the employees and the functionality and attractiveness of the systems and digitized processes, must be managed from a quality perspective as well. Traditionally, such issues have no role in quality management. However, how the processes function may have a critical impact on how a customer perceives the quality of the service. For customers, the service outcome may be a hygiene factor, whereas the impact of the service process on perceptions of quality may determine whether customers become satisfied or not.

The first service quality model was published by Grönroos (1984). A more advanced version of this model is illustrated in Figure 3.3. In the model, five important quality-related aspects are introduced; these include (1) quality as a subjective individual perception; (2) quality as disconfirmation of expectations; (3) quality as a function of both the service process and the outcome of the service process; (4) image as a filter mediating experiences; and (5)

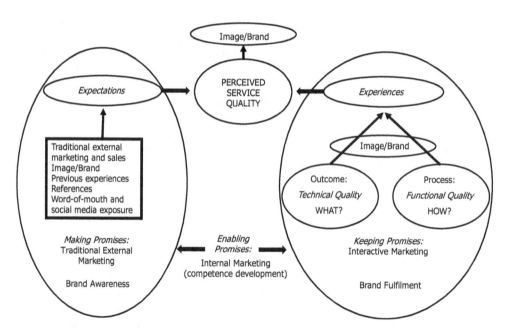

Figure 3.3 The relationship between quality, marketing, brand, and competence of (internal marketing) management.

Note: Adapted from Grönroos, Christian (1984) 'A Service Quality Model and its Marketing Implications,' *European Journal of Marketing*, 18(4), p. 40.

expectations management as an integral part of quality management. These aspects are discussed in detail next.

Quality as a subjective individual perception. Although some of the customer experiences with service may be objective, a considerable portion of the experiences are subjective (Grönroos, 1984). The outcome of the service process, which is what the customer is left with after the service is complete, may be fairly objectively experienced, but the service process is typically experienced subjectively. For example, the outcome of repair on a household appliance is fairly straightforward and objectively experienced; it functions again. However, the experiences related to the repair process are different. The accessibility of the repair firm, how time schedules are kept, and the attitudes and behaviours of the service employee(s) (such as attentiveness, willingness to listen, and communication with the customer) are experienced in a much more subjective way. Furthermore, customer knowledge bases and skill levels are not homogeneous; also, emotions influence how customers experience service processes, and these are not homogeneous either. Consequently, the perception of quality is not only subjective but differs between individuals as well. Therefore, service quality is a subjective perception, not an objective assessment.

Quality as disconfirmation of expectations. Customers seldom go into a service process with a blank mind. They have typically formed expectations about the service beforehand, and they relate their experiences with the service to such expectations. If expectations are met, the quality will probably be perceived to be positive. If they are not met, the quality of the service will be perceived to be low. This is called the "disconfirmation paradigm" (Oliver & Burke, 1999). Furthermore, in service research, it has been shown that by exceeding customer expectations, the service provider may create better overall perceptions of quality than occur by just meeting expectations. This is called creating "customer delight" (Oliver, Rust, & Varki, 1997). However, exceeding customer expectations by too great a margin may backfire. This may cause customers to believe that they have paid too much for the service.

Quality as a function of both process and outcome. The outcome of a service process influences customer perceptions of quality, of course, but as mentioned above, their experiences with the service process do that as well. This is explained by service profit logic. The service firm's interactive processes are open to the customers and the interactions that take place form the service for them, which has an important impact on the resulting perception of service quality. As indicated by the figure, the outcome of the service process, or *what* the customers get in the end, is labelled *technical quality*. The service process, or *how* this outcome is achieved, is said to generate *functional quality*. Hence, service is experienced in two dimensions, specifically outcome and process dimensions.

As was illustrated by the case of repair of a household appliance, the two service quality dimensions are normally experienced in different ways. The service outcome is experienced rather objectively, whereas the service process is experienced more subjectively. For example, making a hotel reservation on a booking site is not necessarily experienced in a similar way by two persons, although both might have managed to complete their reservations successfully and get the rooms they wanted. The fact that the technical quality outcomes of the reservation process (i.e., the room reservations) have been successfully accomplished is probably perceived by both individuals in a similar, rather objective manner. However, the processes of making the reservations are likely to be experienced differently. Some reasons for this may include the customers' skill levels and emotional states, as well as the preparedness and functionality of the website. In addition, external factors, such as time pressure, disturbing factors in the environment, and specific interactions between the customer and the website form the service's functional quality, and these are experienced in different ways. In situations where the technical outcome is critical to the customer, the importance of the functional quality impact is low or sometimes even insignificant. However, in most cases, although the technical quality has to be adequate, the functional quality dominates the customer experience and determines perceived quality. In such cases, the service firm must make sure that the technical quality is on an acceptable level, but the firm competes on the basis of the functional quality experience it manages to deliver.

Image as filter moderating experiences. The image of a firm can relate to its perceptions of quality. If a customer believes that a firm has a positive image, he or she might make excuses for negative experiences with the service (at least if these experiences are not viewed as extremely negative). Such negative experiences will have little or no impact on customer perceptions of quality. A firm with a neutral, unknown, or even negative image will not have the benefit of such a filter, and no such mediating effect will occur. Negative experiences may even be reinforced. Of course, continued bad experiences will diminish even the mediating filter effect offered by customer predisposition toward a positive image. In such cases, as indicated by the top of Figure 3.3, negative quality perceptions will cause the image to deteriorate. On the other hand, positive quality perceptions following a recent service experience will strengthen the image.

Expectations management as an integral part of quality management. Customer expectations influence perceptions of quality. This means that firms must manage customer expectations carefully. Leading customers to have expectations that are too high may destroy the perceived quality of a service (even if the service actually has a good level of quality). For instance, if a person goes to a pizza restaurant expecting a steak dinner, it is likely that he or she will be dissatisfied. If he or she, on the other hand, enters this restaurant expecting to get a good pizza, the quality perception has a chance to be good, or even delightful. As indicated by the figure, conventional external marketing activities, such as marketing communication and pricing, are responsible for the level of customer expectations created. In addition, any predispositions regarding the firm's image that are held by customers may influence their expectations. Hence, firm image appears in three places in the service quality model, including on the left-hand side (contributing to expectations), on the right-hand side (as a quality experience filter), and on the top (as image either reinforced or hurt by the quality perception). Furthermore, references and customer exposures to social media also have an impact on expectations. Finally, customer needs and values also contribute to their expectations.

Perceived service quality attributes. In the 1980s, research into service quality generated lists of service quality attributes. As part of the development of the SERVQUAL (service quality measurement) instrument, a set of five service quality determinants emerged (Parasuraman, Zeithaml, & Berry, 1985; Zeithaml, Parasuraman, & Berry, 1988). These five are *tangibles* (such as facilities and equipment), *reliability* (such as accurate service and no mistakes), *responsiveness* (such as willingness to serve), *assurance* (such as feelings of confidence in the service systems), and *empathy* (such as demonstrated understanding of customer needs and problems). These determinants relate primarily to experiences of the service process.

Another list of service criteria that impact perceptions of quality includes seven attributes (Grönroos, 1988, 2015). These are:

- *professionalism and skills*: the knowledge and skills of employees and the functionality of service systems and processes;
- *attitudes and behaviours*: how the employees treat their customers;

- *accessibility and flexibility*: how easily accessible the service firm's resources are and how they adapt to the customers' processes;
- *reliability and trustworthiness*: how well promises made to customers are kept;
- *service recovery*: how well mistakes and service failures are handled;
- *servicescape*: how the service environment supports the service experience, and;
- *reputation and credibility*: how well customers believe that the firm will provide value for money and represent values shared by them.

In the quality model of Figure 3.3, the first criterion represents the technical quality dimension, the last criterion represents the image factor, and the other five criteria represent the various functional quality dimensions.

Service brand management. A brand may be described as an image held by a person. Thus, image can be replaced with brand in the perceived service quality model, linking the model to brand management. Managing brands requires the creation of *brand awareness* in the minds of customers and potential customers, but for a brand image to emerge, *brand fulfilment* is also required (Berry, 1999; Grönroos, 2015). Brand fulfilment means that the customer experiences service which confirms his or her brand awareness. Only when actions creating brand awareness and delivering brand fulfilment support each other, can a brand that corresponds to a brand image wanted by the firm be created. As indicated in Figure 3.3, expectations management on the left side of the figure relates to creation of brand awareness, whereas the delivery of technical quality (outcome) and functional quality (process) on the right-hand side is responsible for brand fulfilment.

The link between service marketing and perceived service quality. Figure 3.3 and the discussion about the perceived service quality model also shows how the management of service quality is connected to service marketing and promise management. Expectations management, which includes sales and other conventional external marketing activities (such as marketing communication and pricing), aims to *make promises* that create expectations, triggering intentions to buy among customers and potential customers, and eventually lead to sales. As indicated by Figure 3.3, previous experiences of customers, the image or brand they hold, and their word-of-mouth and social media exposures also influence their expectations. The delivery of the technical quality (outcome) and the functional quality (process) should meet the expectations that promise-making has created (or perhaps even exceed them). From a marketing point of view, this is an interactive marketing process. Hence, full-time marketing activities that make external promises are on the left-hand side of the perceived service quality model in Figure 3.3, and interactive promise-keeping marketing implemented by the firm's 'part-time' marketers is on the right-hand side of the model.

Figure 3.3 also includes a third element of promise management, without which neither effective promise-making nor successful promise-keeping are possible, namely the development of a needed competence level among front line service employees, which ensures that they know how and are motivated to do a good job as part-time marketers. In service marketing research, this is called *internal marketing*. As shown in Figure 3.3, internal marketing efforts tie together external marketing and interactive marketing. Internal marketing is discussed in a subsequent section.

Organizing marketing in a customer-focused service firm

In service marketing research, as well as in practice, it was observed that a customer-focused organization cannot be very hierarchical (e.g., Carlzon, 1989). An unnecessarily hierarchical organization widens the gap between strategic management and the customer interface, causing management to lose contact with the challenges of providing good service and also with the work of service employees. It was also observed that marketing in service firms, including traditional external marketing as well as interactive marketing, is spread throughout the organization and cannot be organized in any conventional way (Grönroos, 1983; Gummesson, 1979). Service profit logic explains why this is the case. Many business functions and processes have customer contacts, and customer perceptions of quality (and their willingness to pay for this quality) are influenced by these contacts.

In service, marketing and customer-focused behaviours cause an organizational dilemma (Gummesson, 1979). Traditionally, marketing is considered the responsibility of a marketing department. This is such a deeply rooted thought that often 'marketing function' and 'marketing department' are used as synonyms in the marketing literature. However, making the marketing department fully responsible for all marketing activities leads to an organizational trap (Grönroos, 1983). Departments responsible for the many service processes in a firm, where interactions with customers occur and interactive marketing takes place, cannot be expected to report to a marketing department. For this department, marketing is the sole responsibility, but the other departments are primarily responsible for managing their processes successfully in a technical manner. Although marketing-like behaviour by the customer contact personnel is equally as important as well-performed jobs in a technical sense, for these individuals it is an additional requirement. Hence, if marketing is organized such that a marketing department is expected to take care of the firm's customers and manage all marketing activities, the total marketing processes will be managed only partially. Interactive marketing will be neglected.

The marketing department as an organizational trap also has a psychological side. The existence of such a department can create the illusion among employees and managers in other functions and departments that the responsibility for making customers satisfied (and willing to continue buying from the firm) rests exclusively with the marketing department. In departments other than marketing and sales, it is not uncommon that customers are considered more of a necessary evil than anything else. If no actions are taken to convince these employees and their managers that the responsibility to make customers satisfied (and interested in returning) rests on their shoulders, promises may be made by the marketing department, but promise-keeping will not function satisfactorily. Thus, the customers will not be satisfied and they may not return. Eventually, revenues are lost. Marketing has failed. A large and visible marketing department may even be counter-productive to successful marketing (Grönroos, 2015).

The conclusion of the organizational trap problem is that *in service firms marketing cannot be organized*, at least not into a single unit. The traditional external parts of marketing (such as marketing communication and pricing) can be organized into a separate department of full-time marketing specialists, as long as others in the organization realize that this department does not carry the sole responsibility for the firm's customers or for marketing activities. People in the rest of the organization must understand what the marketing department can do (i.e., make promises and create brand awareness), and what it cannot do (i.e., keep promises and deliver brand fulfilment). The service employees and their supervisors and managers must understand and accept that they carry the responsibility for satisfying the customers; that is, that they have a critical role in the firm's complete marketing process.

In summary, when the full-time marketers are organized into a separate department, marketing can only be instilled in the part-time marketers as a customer-focused attitude of mind, such that they understand and accept that they have dual responsibilities, namely to perform their tasks successfully in a technical sense *and* at the same time create a good marketing impact (Grönroos, 2015). As mentioned before, this is called *internal marketing* in the service marketing literature.

Productivity management

Conventional productivity management literature largely assumes that the quality of production outputs can be held constant when more cost-efficient production resources and processes are introduced. In this mindset, costs are considered variable, whereas the revenues generated by products are thought to be fixed. Productivity is, therefore, considered an internal cost efficiency issue. In very traditional production, this constant quality assumption and focus on cost efficiency hold. For service firms this is certainly not the case. For such firms, both costs and revenues are variable. As demonstrated by service profit logic, both revenues and costs are influenced by how the interactive processes (the service encounter) and support processes function. Depending on the type of resources used and the service production routines and processes at work, the cost level may be higher or lower.

Customer perceptions of service quality also depend on the type of resources used and the service production routines and processes at work. Thus, this affects their willingness to pay as well as the firm's revenue-generating capacity. This means that cost levels indirectly influence levels of revenue. Unless the firm can find lower-cost resources and processes, which at the same time are experienced as having better quality (e.g., internet banking), cost cuts will lead to revenue losses. Thus, higher cost efficiencies may or may not lead to lost revenues. In service firms, the risk is apparent that a conventional manufacturing productivity mindset will create a productivity management approach in which the search for cost efficiencies dominates and the corresponding effects on the firm's revenue-generation capability are neglected.

The ultimate goal of productivity management is to develop business processes that have a favourable impact on the firm's economic result. In traditional manufacturing (where costs are viewed as variable but revenues as fixed), because the quality of the production output can be kept stable, productivity management becomes a matter of cost efficiency management. This viewpoint can work in goods manufacturing industries. However, in service firms, such a mindset can be harmful. Because in service (unlike traditional manufacturing) both costs and revenues are viewed as variable, productivity/cost efficiency management can have a negative impact on the firm's economic result. Cost savings may, in fact, lead to decreased revenues.

As research into service productivity demonstrates, a new productivity mindset and model are required. Quality effects must always be taken into account (Grönroos & Ojasalo, 2004; Parasuraman, 2002). When decisions are made about how to change the resources and processes that are experienced by customers, both cost and revenue effects have to be taken into account simultaneously. Conventional productivity models are based on two assumptions: (1) production and consumption are separate, and (2) customers do not participate in the production process. Because of the first assumption, productivity management is an exclusively internal process and productivity improvements can be achieved in a closed system to which customers have no access. The second assumption implies that changes in the production system have no effects on customer perceptions and interests in buying the production output. As has been shown, both assumptions are incorrect in service. The interactive process of service production is open to the customers, and the customers participate in the service production process.

The Ojasalo service productivity model. Service productivity management requires models that integrate internal cost effects and external revenue effects (Grönroos & Ojasalo, 2004). Most publications on service productivity (e.g., Aspara, Klein, Luo, & Tikkanen, 2018; Calabrese & Spadoni, 2013; Parasuraman, 2002; Rust & Huang, 2012) consider the external effects due to customer perceived quality an endogenous factor that has to be taken into account, but do not include them as an integral part of productivity management. However, the Ojasalo model (Grönroos & Ojasalo, 2004; Ojasalo, 1999;) claims that this is not enough. Instead, both internal efficiency effects (costs) and external effectiveness effects (perceived quality and revenues) have to be integrated into a service productivity management model. The Ojasalo model is based on the fact that inputs into service production processes (resources and actions) are provided by both the firm and the customers; this change in production inputs influences customer perceptions of quality. Therefore, from a productivity point of view, the service production process consists of three separate subprocesses:

- service provider and customer producing the service in interactions (interactive processes; service encounter);
- service provider producing the service in isolation from the customer (back office);
- customer producing the service in isolation from the service provider.

In the first two situations, the service firm has to use resources that, while being as cost efficient as possible, do not harm perceptions of service quality to such an extent that more revenue losses than cost savings are created. In the third situation, the firm must ensure that customers are properly informed, such that they can engage with service production and consume the service in a way which enhances both their technical and functional quality perceptions and, thus, their willingness to pay.

According to the Ojasalo model, service productivity management requires a balance between actions that generate internal cost efficiencies and actions that generate external revenues. If seeking this balance is not an integral part of productivity-related decision-making, the risk that the ultimate goal of productivity management, that is, an improved or at least maintained economic result, will not be achieved. In addition to the internal efficiency (costs) and external effectiveness (perceived quality, revenues) variables, the Ojasalo model also includes a third variable, namely *capacity utilization.* A higher capacity level (e.g., more employees or more seating space in a restaurant) may have a positive effect on perceived service quality and revenues, but this may come at the expense of an increased cost level. A lower capacity level may reduce costs, but this may be achieved at the expense of reducing perceived service quality and also revenues.

In conclusion, service productivity management should aim to find a balance between actions that determine the cost level of service production and actions that impact customer perceptions of quality and willingness to pay, while finding a capacity utilization level which enables an optimal revenue/cost ratio and an optimal economic result. Hence, service productivity is a function of internal cost efficiency, external revenue effectiveness, and capacity utilization.

Service productivity as mutual learning. As services are ongoing processes, where relationships with customers develop and can exist for long periods of time, both the service provider and the customer learn from each other. This has effects on service productivity and productivity management. The service provider may find ways to adjust to the customer's level of knowledge, skills, and desires to be served. The customer, on the other hand, may learn how to engage with the service provider's processes, including what information is needed and what can be expected to take place. If the relationship continues, both parties may learn to recognize each other and develop a level of familiarity; in addition, the service firm may learn to provide service in a more cost-efficient and quality-enhancing way. This learning process is mutual and generates four potentially virtuous processes (Grönroos & Ojasalo, 2015), including:

A. Customer-driven process enhancing internal efficiency.
B. Provider-driven process enhancing internal efficiency.
C. Customer-driven process enhancing external effectiveness.
D. Provider-driven process enhancing external effectiveness.

The mutual learning process is illustrated in Figure 3.4 Processes A and B help to improve internal efficiency and thereby reduce the costs of producing service. Following the A process, the customer learns how the service process functions and this narrows the competence gap between the customer and service provider, resulting in more engaged and efficient customer participation in the process. Following the B process, the service provider learns about the customer's skills and desires and recognizes the customer's competence level. This enables the provider to allow the customer to be more engaged in the service process. As is the case with the A process, this has a positive effect on internal efficiency and the cost of producing service.

The C and D processes help to improve perceived quality and external effectiveness, and thereby have a positive effect on revenues. Following the C process, the customer learns

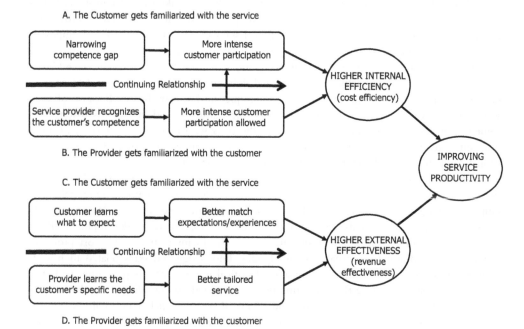

Figure 3.4 Service productivity as mutual learning.

Note: Adapted from Grönroos, Christian, and Ojasalo, Katri (2004) 'Service Productivity: Toward a Conceptualization of the Transformation of Inputs into Economic Results in Services,' *Journal of Business Research*, 57(4), p. 419.

what to expect from the service provider, which leads to a better match between his or her expectations and experiences with the service. From this, improved quality perceptions and higher external effectiveness result. Following the D process, the provider learns about the customer's specific knowledge level, needs, and desires, and thereby manages to tailor the service to better match customer needs. Both processes have a positive effect on external effectiveness as well as the service provider's revenue-generating capability.

From the two service productivity models, namely the service productivity model and the mutual learning model, the complicated nature of productivity management in service is evident. First, decisions about cost efficiency and about revenue generation cannot be made separately. Second, productivity in service is a dynamic issue. It changes, and when a customer relationship continues it has the potential to improve. However, if the service provider changes resources used in the process (e.g., by replacing an employee with someone who has no knowledge of the customers or by an automated system), what has been learned over time may be lost and service productivity harmed. Furthermore, productivity varies between customers: different customers need different amounts of time and resources, which must be taken into account in productivity management.

Competence development and internal marketing

The nature of the service profit logic (in which employees in many different interactive and support processes contribute to a firm's revenue generation capability) influences the types of skills and competencies required in an organization. Traditionally, full-time marketers and sales reps are the only persons who need to be able to handle customers and customer contacts. Typically, their training ensures that they know how to take care of customers at least on some level, and further customer-related competence development may improve this. For employees in other functional areas, technical skills to perform their tasks are important and continued training offered to them often relates to such technical skills. Such training to develop competencies is, of course, still necessary in service firms. However, in addition, employees engaged in interactive processes need skills and competencies to listen to customers, communicate with them, and react to their questions and problems. Because of some service employees' roles as part-time marketers, their attitudes and behaviours toward customers is of critical importance. They may be the ones who make or break the customers' willingness to pay and continue to support the firm's revenue generation. Therefore, traditional competence development takes new forms in service firms.

In human resource management, competence development is traditionally inward-oriented. As pointed out above, arranging competence development programmes related to employees' technical levels of knowledge and skills dominates. However, as demonstrated by service profit logic, such skills and, correspondingly, such competence development efforts, are not enough for employees working in a service firm's interactive or support processes. For them, in addition to internally oriented skills, knowledge and skills related to how to manage the firm's external interface are also of critical importance. As part-time marketers, they are the ones who bring the marketing process, initiated by the full-time marketing professionals and sales reps, to a successful end. Thus, they have dual responsibilities: first, to perform their technical tasks successfully and, second, when doing this, to do a successful part-time marketing job. The latter means that they ensure that promises made by the firm's conventional external marketing and sales are successfully kept, and thereby make the customers with whom they interact satisfied with what they get and willing to continue buying. In the best case, they will buy more and engage in favourable customer-to-customer communication. Traditionally, this second responsibility has not been a high-priority requirement for human resource management.

In summary, in addition to the required technical skills, service employees need to be trained to perform in a marketer-like manner. The internal processes and activities to accomplish this are called *internal marketing* (Ballantyne, 2003; Grönroos, 1990; Lings & Greenley, 2005; Piercy & Morgan, 1991). The term internal marketing is used to indicate that service cannot be successfully marketed to ultimate, external customers unless it is first marketed to the internal market of service employees. However, performing in a marketer-like manner does not mean making use of active selling and persuasion. Rather, it means that employees act in such a way that they satisfy customers and influence customer preferences and future buying decisions favourably, thereby supporting the firm's revenue generation. The same is true of employees in supporting processes as well. In this case, service employees in interactive processes are internal customers, who must be served as well as the firm's ultimate external customers. If internal marketing fails, it is likely that the firm's marketing process will also fail, leading to loss of revenues.

The overall purpose of internal marketing is to close the gap between the skills, knowledge, and competencies that employees need to successfully provide customers with good service, and the current levels, as well as to maintain desired behaviours (Grönroos, 2015). The goal of internal marketing processes and actions is, therefore, to instill and maintain customer-focused and service-minded attitudes and skills (such as communication and behavioural skills) among service employees, such that they contribute favourably to the firm's revenue generation.

Even in times of increasing digitization, customers and employees alike form a firm's most important assets. If the employees are not devoted to helping customers, then strategic decisions, planning of offerings and operational processes, development of administrative routines, and execution of such processes will be inward-based and resource-oriented, lacking customer focus. This results in unsatisfied customers, negative word-of-mouth, and loss of revenues. Because of the central role of employees on all levels, internal marketing is a strategic issue that relates to strategic decision-making as well as to tactical programmes and activities. In spite of this, internal marketing is frequently considered an unimportant set of activities (predominantly training and internal communication about the firm's products, marketing activities, etc.). However, such tactical activities are not sufficient. If the strategic backup is lacking, training and communication will be ineffective, and may even backfire. If employees, who have become motivated to serve customers and are equipped with adequate skills, realize that the firm does not wish to be a strategically customer-focused service firm, frustration and negative attitudes toward the employer are created.

Tactical internal marketing. Almost any internal activity can serve as a tactical internal marketing effort. Such activities should aim to make employees aware of new goods and services offered to the market (as well as new external marketing campaigns and promises made), and of new operational systems and routines and new technologies used in service production. Moreover, internal marketing efforts should ensure that employees also understand and accept how any new goods or services, marketing promises, systems, and technologies influence their performance in customer interfaces. Although there can be a large variety of tactical activities, the most common ones include:

- training;
- internal communication;
- systems and technology support;
- supervisory support.

In an internal marketing context, *training* aims to teach service employees to handle customer contacts in a marketing-like manner. Employees should also understand their roles in the firm's complete process of providing service to customers, and thereby also their roles in the marketing process. Ultimately, favourable attitudes toward adopting a customer focus and providing good service should be developed. However, to be successful, training must always be supported by other tactical actions as well as strategic policies.

Internal communication, using any distribution channels available, fulfils the need to inform employees about new service-oriented strategies, new goods and service products, and new ways of performing in either internal or external service encounters.

Systems and technology support are means by which a firm provides its employees with structures and supportive technologies to make it possible for them to provide good service. Without this support, it would be difficult for employees to perform in a customer-focused manner and provide good service. The firm's support processes (or back office) are one such supporting system ensuring customer-focused and service-oriented behaviour by employees in customer interfaces.

Supervisory support is the means by which employees receive support from their supervisors (such as advice, encouragement, guidance, etc.). If no such supervisory support exists, investments in training and in internal communications will be less effective, or even without effect.

Strategic internal marketing. If strategic backup is lacking, tactical internal marketing processes and activities will fail. The firm must want to be a service firm, and this must be reflected in at least four areas, which must be managed in a way that is motivating for employees; these include leadership and management methods, human resource policy, training policy, and planning systems (Grönroos, 2015).

Motivating leadership and management methods. In order to achieve continuity in training processes and other tactical internal marketing activities, the role of management is paramount. The leadership provided by management on all levels must demonstrate active support to the idea of customer focus and service orientation. This must be evident in strategic decisions, in decisions about resources, and in everyday contacts with employees. Empowering employees by giving them decision-making authority and thereby showing trust in them, providing feedback, and maintaining two-way communication channels internally are other examples of motivating leadership and management methods.

Motivating human resource policy. The human resource management approach must motivate employees to be customer focused and service-oriented. In many firms, customer contact jobs are the responsibility of the newest and least-trained employees. Often, they are hired on a part-time basis and their salaries are low. Such a human resource policy does not support customer focus and service-mindedness. Instead, human resource policy that is motivating includes hiring policies which encourage service-minded persons to apply, job descriptions and career plans which encourage customer focus and service orientation, and reward systems that appreciate customer-focused and service-oriented behaviours.

Motivating training policy. Traditionally, employees are trained primarily to perform their technical tasks. However, in a service firm the training policy must be different, to offer motivation for customer-focused and service-oriented behaviours. In addition to technical training, a substantial amount of training related to how to behave with customers and how to react to them and communicate with them is also needed. Training must be a continuous process. The training policy must aim to develop a holistic understanding of the firm's service strategy and marketing process, and of each employee's role. The training policy should be designed such that it creates favourable attitudes toward providing good service among employees and motivates them to deliver good service in all customer contacts.

Motivating planning systems. Frequently, employees feel frustrated because they have no way of influencing their work routines or processes. Service employees know from experience and first-hand customer feedback what works, what does not work, what could be improved, and how it could be improved. The frustration owing to being unable to contribute has negative impacts on motivation. Motivating planning systems means that the firm should make use of employees' knowledge of customer processes, needs, and wishes. To at least a minimal degree, employees should be involved in planning processes where their own work is planned. This has at least two important favourable implications: (1) the employees are more motivated and skilled to perform their tasks, and (2) tacit knowledge previously unknown to management is revealed. Tacit knowledge that is documented in this way can be used to improve operational processes and routines, use of technology, and even create new service strategies, thereby making operational processes more customer focused and strategies more service-oriented (Ballantyne, 2003).

Finally, it is important to understand that it is not enough to include service employees in customer contacts and support employees in internal marketing processes. Managers on all levels must also be involved.

Analysing customer focus readiness

Being a service firm is a strategic decision. The firm must decide to be or become a firm which aims to provide service to its customers rather than to deliver resources only. Because service cannot exist without customers, taking a service approach also introduces a customer focus. For a service firm, readiness for maintaining customer-focused relationships is, therefore, a necessity. In Figure 3.5, an illustration is provided of a customer relationship grid to be used for analysis of such readiness (Grönroos, 2017). This grid introduces two variables that are required to perform an analysis of firm readiness for customer focus and service provision.

For such an analysis the firm has to ask itself two questions:

> *Does the firm understand its customers' processes as well as its own processes? Does the firm understand its customers' quality-related experience as well as it understands the (technical) quality of its solutions?*

These two questions relate to the two variables in the relationship grid: (1) Is the organization mentally focused – including when executing its operations – on its customer or on its own processes?, and (2) Is the organization mentally focused – including when executing its operations – on its customers' definition of quality or on its own definition of (technical) quality?

The focus of the organization is understood collectively by both strategic managers and those planning and implementing strategies and policies. 'Mentally,' refers to the mindset in the organization that steers how the organization operates in its many customer interfaces, including delivery of goods, customer service processes, repair and maintenance, service recovery and complaints handling, invoicing, etc.

As indicated in the Figure 3.5, customer expectations can be expected to be positioned in the upper right-hand corner of the grid. Customers are naturally concerned with their own processes, which they expect to be helped. It can also be assumed that they expect the quality of the help, that is, the quality of service, to be sufficiently high according to their view of what constitutes good quality. As the perceived service quality model illustrates, this perception is not restricted to a good technical outcome quality, but includes functional process quality elements as well. Moreover, frequently the latter dimension dominates perceptions of quality.

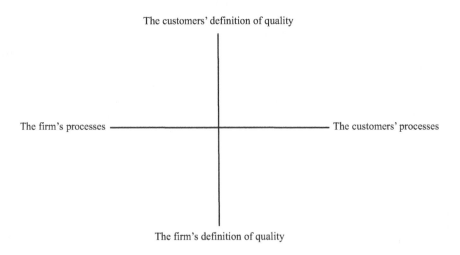

The customers' definition of quality

The firm's processes ———————————————————— The customers' processes

The firm's definition of quality

Figure 3.5 Relationship marketing grid: analyzing customer focus and service orientation.

Note: Based on Grönroos, Christian (2017) 'Relationship Marketing Readiness: Theoretical Background and Measurement Directions,' *Journal of Services Marketing*, 31(3), 218–225.

Typically, organizations are in the corridor from the upper right-hand side toward the lower left-hand side, as indicated in the figure. In order to be successful service providers, firms should be positioned as close to their customers as possible. However, it is not uncommon that firms find themselves in positions somewhere in the lower left quadrant of the grid. The mindset of strategic management is dominated by concerns about the firm's production processes and cost-efficient use of resources. In quality development and management, internal quality standards are predominant, guided by technical outcome quality aspects. However, operating based on such mental models lacks a thorough customer focus. Firms in the service sector (such as banks, insurance companies, transportation firms, etc.) that function like this often attempt to productize their services, trying to make them resemble goods. As a consequence, the customer remains distant, and insight is vague into their processes and how they define knowledge about quality.

To do an analysis of the firm's customer relationship readiness, that is, readiness to perform as a customer-focused service firm, proper analyses of customer processes and quality definitions are needed. The management approaches and models consistent with service profit logic and presented in this chapter provide guidelines and directions for such analyses. Conventional market research is insufficient to obtain the required insights. Instead, ethnographic methods are needed, in which customer processes, goals, values, wishes, life paths, etc., are revealed. Based on such insights, it is possible to define what constitutes customer perceptions of good quality, and to draw conclusions about what type(s) of help would fulfil their real needs. In mass markets, all customers cannot be studied in this way, of course, but typical customer archetypes can be found.

Conclusion

Conventional management models are based on goods profit logic, in which, from a management perspective, business functions and processes other than sales and marketing primarily create costs. (They influence revenues only indirectly through the goods produced.) This profit logic functions in cases where the interface with customers is limited to a fairly standardized good and the actions of conventional marketing and sales personnel. For customers, the rest of the firm is a 'back office,' which is not visible to them. However, such narrow customer interfaces are increasingly rare. Instead, customer relationships include a growing number of contacts between customers, employees, and systems representing a variety of business functions (other than sales and marketing). These functions may include personal service in a whole host of service establishments, customer contact centres, deliveries, installation, repair, maintenance, problem-solving and service recoveries, information seeking on websites, and the provision of service digitally. In traditional service firms, customers interact with parts of service processes (such as in bank offices, when operating an ATM, or when using internet banking).

The common thread in all of the situations mentioned above is that goods profit logic fails to describe how business functions and processes contribute to a firm's economic profit through influence on both revenues and costs. Functions and processes which are assumed to be back-stage and closed to customers become partially open interactive processes. Thus, customers are informed about how the firm functions, how trustworthy the firm, its employees, and its systems are, and how well the firm can be expected to perform. In other words, customer willingness to pay and contribute to a firm's revenues are influenced by processes that, in the traditional model, are considered back-office processes, closed and invisible to them. This leads to less than optimal management decisions regarding a number of crucial management areas, including marketing, quality management and assurance, productivity management, and competence development. Decisions about how to organize the marketing function may also be counter-productive to the development of a customer-focused organization.

Service profit logic takes the new reality for a growing number of customer relationships into account. This profit logic realizes that a part of a firm's functions and processes (other than sales and marketing) are open processes, where interactions with customers take place. The functioning of these interactive processes has a direct impact on customer willingness to pay and on a firm's revenue-generating capability. Some functions and processes are back-office processes and not open to the customers, but they are open to the interactive processes. If they do not perform well and support the interactive processes successfully, then customers will not be well served. Thus, backstage processes influence a firm's revenue generation as much as the interactive processes, but indirectly.

In this chapter, the term 'service firm' has been used. However, today this term means much more than what traditionally has been included. As the examples used in this chapter demonstrate, many elements in extended customer relationships (such as deliveries, installation, repair, maintenance, and problem recoveries) are typical for goods manufacturing firms that want to take better care of their customers. When manufacturing firms add such activities to their customer relationships, they move toward a service firm mode, regardless of whether this is formulated in the firm's strategy or not. (This may be called 'servitization.') After doing so, the economic result in such firms is determined by the nature of service profit logic.

References

Aspara, J., Klein, J., Luo, X. & Tikkanen, H. (2018). The dilemma of service productivity and service innovation. An empirical exploration in financial services. *Journal of Service Research*, 21(2), 249–262.

Ballantyne, D. (2003). A relationship-mediated theory of internal marketing. *European Journal of Marketing*, 37(9), 1242–1260.

Berry, L. L. (1999). *Discovering the soul of service*. New York: The Free Press.

Calabrese, A. & Spadoni, A. (2013). Quality versus productivity in service production systems: An organizational analysis. *International Journal of Production Research*, 51(22), 6594–6606.

Calonius, H. (2006). Contemporary research in marketing: A market behaviour framework. *Marketing Theory*, 6(4), 419–428.

Carlzon, J. (1989). *Moments of truth*. New York: Harper & Row.

Eiglier, P. & Langeard, E. (1975). Une approche nouvelle du marketing des service. *Revue Francaise de Gestion*, November, 97–113.

Grönroos, C. (1978). A service-orientated approach to the marketing of services. *European Journal of Marketing*, 12(8), 588–601.

Grönroos, C. (1983). *Strategic management and marketing in the service sector*. Cambridge, MA: Marketing Science Institute (also published in the UK by be).

Grönroos, C. (1984). A service quality model and its marketing implications. *European Journal of Marketing*, 18(4), 36–44.

Grönroos, C. (1988). Service quality: The six criteria of good perceived service quality. *Review of Business*, (St. John's University), 9(3), 10–13.

Grönroos, C. (1990). Relationship approach to marketing in service contexts: The marketing and organizational behavior interface. *Journal of Business Research*, 209(1), 3–12.

Grönroos, C. (2009). Promise management: Regaining customer management for marketing. *Journal of Business & Industrial Marketing*, 24(5/6), 351–359.

Grönroos, C. (2015). *Service management and marketing: Managing the service profit logic*. 4th edition. Chichester: John Wiley & Co.

Grönroos, C. (2017). Relationship marketing readiness: Theoretical background and measurement directions. *Journal of Services Marketing*, 31(3), 218–225.

Grönroos, C. & Ojasalo, K. (2004). Service productivity: Toward a conceptualization of the transformation of inputs into economic results in services. *Journal of Business Research*, 57(4), 414–423.

Grönroos, C. & Ojasalo, K. (2015). Service productivity as mutual learning. *International Journal of Quality and Service Sciences*, 7(2–3), 296–311.

Gummesson, E. (1979). The marketing of professional services: An organizational dilemma. *European Journal of Marketing*, 13(5), 308–318.

Gummesson, E. (1991). Marketing revisited: The crucial role of the part-time marketers. *European Journal of Marketing*, 25(2), 60–67.

Lings, I. N. & Greenley, G. E. (2005). Measuring internal marketing orientation. *Journal of Service Research*, 7(3), 290–305.

Ojasalo, K. (1999). *Conceptualizing productivity in services*. diss. Helsinki: Hanken School of Economics.

Oliver, R. L. & Burke, R. R. (1999). Expectation processes in satisfaction formation: A field study. *Journal of Service Research*, 1(3), 196–214.

Oliver, R. L., Rust, R. T. & Varki, S. (1997). Customer delight: Foundations, findings, and managerial insight. *Journal of Retailing*, 73(3), 311–336.

Parasuraman, A. (2002). Service quality and productivity: A synergistic perspective. *Managing Service Quality*, 12(1), 6–9.

Parasuraman, A., Zeithaml, V. A. & Berry, L. L. (1985). A conceptual model of service quality and its implications for future research. *Journal of Marketing*, 61(4), 41–50.

Piercy, N. F. & Morgan, R.A. (1991). Internal marketing: The missing half of the marketing program. *Long Range Planning*, 24(2), 82–93.

Rust, R. T. & Huang, M-H. (2012). Optimizing service productivity. *Journal of Marketing*, 76(2), 47–66.

Zeithaml, V. A., Parasuraman, A. & Berry, L. L. (1988). Communication and control processes in the delivery of service quality. *Journal of Marketing*, 64(April), 35–48.

4

Customer-dominant service logic

Kristina Heinonen and Tore Strandvik

Introduction

Customer-dominant logic (C-DL) was developed as an organizational perspective a decade ago, in response to an increasing need for organizations to focus on the customer (cf. Heinonen & Strandvik, 2015, 2018; Heinonen et al., 2010; Heinonen, Strandvik, & Voima, 2013; Strandvik & Heinonen, 2015). This perspective is an alternative to other perspectives on service, such as the *service-dominant logic* (S-DL) and *service logic* that are also presented in this book. The C-DL perspective applies to customers in different sectors, industries, and contexts irrespective of the label used (e.g., *consumer, citizen, client, buyer, shopper, patient, guest,* or *beneficiary*). The term *customer* includes individuals, groups of individuals, companies, and organizations who buy, use, and consume different market offerings from private, public, and not-for-profit organizations. Similarly, *service provider* is used herein to refer not only to commercial settings, but also to all types of noncommercial settings like public service, NGOs, municipalities, political parties, cultures, and institutions.

C-DL has been applied in studies related to service management, marketing, and consumer research, and its conceptual underpinnings have been scrutinized in connection with constructs such as customer value (Heinonen, Strandvik, & Voima, 2013), service experience (Lipkin, 2016; Tynan, McKechnie, & Hartley, 2014), customer-to-customer interactions (Rihova, Buhalis, Moital, & Beth Gouthro, 2013), service recovery (Cheung & To, 2016), brand communication (Strandvik & Heinonen, 2013), consumer engagement (Heinonen, 2018), and customer activity (Mickelsson, 2013). The C-DL concept has been used to describe various empirical contexts (e.g., tourism, Rihova et al., 2013; retail banking, Medberg & Heinonen, 2014; online communities/social media, Heinonen, 2011; Heinonen, Campbell, & Lord Ferguson, 2019; healthcare, Seppänen, Huiskonen, Koivuniemi, & Karppinen, 2017; business-to-business services, Strandvik, Heinonen, & Vollmer, 2018; and airline travel, Xu, Yap, & Hyde, 2016).

The notion of customer primacy was expressed by Drucker (1974, p. 61), who argued that all businesses start with customers: "It is the customer who determines what a business is." All markets and industries are faced with challenges emerging from technological developments, increasing international competition, environmental sustainability concerns, and aspirations for global good. To be competitive in the face of these challenges, there is a need to focus on understanding who the customer is and why they do what they do (Drucker,

1974). This is the starting point of C-DL: C-DL is a management perspective grounded in understanding customer logics. The purpose of this chapter is to discuss theoretical and practical implications of adopting a customer-dominant perspective of service business, by stressing the primary role of customers in markets and the difference between providers' and customers' logics. The contribution of the C-DL approach to current academic, societal, and business challenges is also discussed.

This chapter is structured into three sections. The first section outlines the setting for C-DL, including foundational characteristics. The second section presents C-DL as a service management approach, employing key concepts and arguments. The third section digs into implications of applying C-DL to current service research and practice, and identifies possibilities for further development. Differences from other service perspectives are also discussed in the third section. Finally, three cornerstones of C-DL are presented: dominant logics, the primacy of customers, and customer logic.

Dominant logics determine attention, focus, and action

To provide a background on C-DL, some aspects of the evolution of marketing thought are briefly presented, because marketing perspectives in academic research have evolved in response to changing business environments. These perspectives, that can be seen as mental sensemaking constructions, determine what factors are focused on and acted upon. However, all aspects of a perspective are not always expressed; there are also implicit understandings that comprise a perspective. Several marketing perspectives exist simultaneously among researchers and practitioners, which can provide both complementary and opposite explanations. Different perspectives may use the same concepts with different interpretations, or they might have different concepts for similar phenomena, adding to the conceptual diversity in marketing theorizing.

Academic marketing perspectives

Numerous perspectives, often called *schools of thought*, have emerged in the history of marketing, such as the *marketing management perspective, service marketing, relationship marketing, consumer culture theory*, and the *Industrial Marketing and Purchasing* (IMP) approach, to name a few (Fisk, Brown, & Bitner, 1993; Grönroos, 1982; Gummesson & Grönroos, 2012; Möller, 2013; Sheth & Parvatiyar, 1995). Marketing perspectives are characterized by their dominant aspects and their differences from other perspectives. The increased importance of services, inspired theorizing about service offerings in contrast to physical goods (Fisk et al., 1993). One major development in this vein was that all companies can be seen as service companies and can apply a service perspective to their businesses (Grönroos, 1982). This argument suggests that attention should shift from the outcome to the process of providing service. S-DL (Vargo & Lusch, 2004) was initially contrasted with *goods-dominant logic*, a term used to characterize the classic marketing mix approach. Relationship marketing, in turn, emphasizes customer relationships in contrast to a focus on transactions and onetime service encounters. The emergence of the IMP perspective in business-to-business marketing was based on the perceived need to refocus from an emphasis on transactions to an emphasis on interactions, relationships, and networks (Ford, 2011; Möller, 2013). A similar view emphasizing systems has been proposed in S-DL (Ford, 2011), changing the focus from dyads to systems of interactions (Vargo & Lusch, 2008). Such shifts in focus and scope, as well as in foundational assumptions, can lead to new concepts, models, and insights.

Heinonen and Strandvik (2015) summarized different marketing perspectives based on the focus and scope of each service perspective. They argued that a shift has occurred over time from a provider focus, through the current interaction focus, toward a customer focus. The scope of this perspective refers to shifts from considering transactions/encounters through relationships toward systems representing increasing contextual complexity. The resulting framework demonstrates key characteristics and differences between marketing perspectives. The traditional marketing perspective is a logical reference point in mapping the evolution of marketing thought, as it represents a combination of provider focus and transaction scope (Heinonen & Strandvik, 2015, 2018). Each shift from this reference point has represented some form of paradigm shift that has required the development of new concepts and a change of underlying ontological assumptions.

The initial shift from considering service encounters not only from the provider's point of view but also from the point of view of customer interactions led to the concept of perceived service quality (Grönroos, 1982). Likewise, the shift from managing separate service encounters to managing customer relationships resulted in a new stream of research and new business practice (Sheth & Parvatiyar, 1995). Currently, there is a strong interest in systems/network perspectives, which represent a shift from focusing on separate relationships to analyzing networks or systems of relationships based on interactions (Vargo & Lusch, 2017). In service research, this has resulted in employing concepts including: value-in-use, co-creation, engagement, and service systems (Chandler & Lusch, 2015; Maglio & Spohrer, 2008; Vargo & Lusch, 2016; Vargo, Maglio, & Akaka, 2008). The next step, shifting from a provider or interaction focus to a customer focus, as suggested here by C-DL, results in new interpretations of extant concepts and models, and creates a need for new conceptualizations.

It should be noted that all marketing perspectives have a view on customers, but employing a customer focus, as described here, means giving customers the primary role, which goes beyond what has been called 'customer orientation' in the provider-dominant perspectives. Customer orientation commonly refers to collecting and disseminating information about customer needs and wants (e.g., Kohli & Jaworski, 1990; Narver & Slater, 1990; Shapiro, 1988; Slater & Narver, 1998) in order to engage customers, hence considering the customer as an object. By changing the perspective to give the customer the primary role, the issue becomes how customers prefer to engage providers into their businesses and lives. Customers are hence seen as the drivers of potential business for a provider, but not as objects for providers' 'marketing' activities. The traditional focus on needs and wants is replaced by understanding customers' logics and contexts.

In service research, there are currently several service perspectives with somewhat different dominant features. The differences between have been discussed in a number of articles (c.f. Grönroos & Gummerus, 2014); further analysis is beyond the scope of this chapter. C-DL evolved in response to service logic (Grönroos, 2006) and S-DL (Vargo & Lusch, 2004), and shares some aspects of other perspectives, but has a different focus and scope. C-DL is not focused on the service (system) or interaction, but on the customer, demonstrating a contrast between providers and customers as the actors in markets. Service can be considered from the provider's and/or the customer's point of view; C-DL proposes that the customer point of view should dominate, and it is focused holistically on customers' lives. This is in contrast to S-DL, that is focused on systems of generic actors (Vargo & Lusch, 2008) and the service logic that is focused on the interaction between the provider and the customer (Grönroos, 2006). Such differences in stance between perspectives become visible in the interpretation and use of concepts (e.g., service, value, experience, and customers) as well as in suggestions and implications for research and practice. Questions that arise based on a customer-dominant perspective include: how do customers choose, engage, and combine service providers? What is the function and meaning of customer relationships from the customer point of view? What role do corporate brand images play for the customer? How do customer experiences of a good or service relate to their other activities, resources, and aspirations? These questions would not be in the foreground if not for a customer focus.

Marketing perspectives in business practice

Managers act according to their understanding of the business landscape and this mental model becomes their perceived reality (Normann, 2001). Marketing perspectives also play a significant role in practice and are represented by individual managers' mental models and sensemaking as demonstrated, for example, in a retail bank setting (Strandvik, Holmlund, & Lähteenmäki, 2018). Research on managerial cognition demonstrates the role of framing as it relates to individual managers, top management teams, and organizations. Although managers do not adopt pure theoretical marketing perspectives as such, they consciously or subconsciously include such influences in their mental models or theories-in-use of their business and markets. An emphasis on the mental models of individuals resonates with dominant logics research on an organizational level, and institutions research on an industry and societal level (Vargo & Lusch, 2016). The impact of theories-in-use was highlighted by Rydén, Ringberg, and Wilke (2015), who empirically identified four different archetypical mental models of how managers consider social media in marketing as manifestations of different underlying paradigm-level mind-sets . The dominant feature of each model was designated by different provider-consumer roles: "business-to-consumers," "business-from-consumers," "business-with-consumers," and "business-for-consumers." These were accompanied by corresponding marketing strategies, respectively: "sell and promote," "listen and learn," "connect and collaborate," and "empower and engage." In the first two, customers are passive and the provider is active. The third model stresses the significance of interaction with customers. In the fourth model, the provider is a part of an organic whole, together with customers. Interestingly, this empirically derived categorization of theoretical marketing thought corresponds largely to the map of marketing perspectives suggested by Heinonen and Strandvik (2015). As these examples indicate, the key issue is that managers' mental models influence what they see and do in their business practice on a strategic level. Dominant logics matter in theory and practice.

Without customers there is no business

The primacy of the customer is evident when considering that no company or organization can exist without customers, users, or supporters. As said in the introduction, the term *customer*, as employed in the label *customer-dominant logic*, is used in an inclusive manner covering all kinds of customers irrespective of the label used.

The reason for considering the customer role as the driving force in markets is anchored in the view that customers have a choice. Even in cases where customers do not have an explicit choice or do not recognize themselves as potential customers, such as when customers are vulnerable or are the recipients of public services (Bone, Christensen, & Williams, 2014; Fisk et al., 2018), customers should be a primary concern (even if this is in practice not always the case). The customer's choice, which from the provider's perspective represents competition, is a significant issue for service business, but has not been explored sufficiently in service research. The C-DL perspective considers competition not from the provider's point of view, but from the viewpoint of customers and what they perceive as alternatives based on their idiosyncratic logics. These logics represent holistic and evolutionary representations of each individual customer's sensemaking and mental models.

Markets are, from this perspective, constituted and driven by customer logics. This view can be seen as an alternative to extant understandings that markets should be constructed and shaped by providers or systems of providers (cf. Storbacka & Nenonen, 2011). The existence of the provider and its offered service is motivated by a need to provide cost-effective service with a transformative purpose. For example, many public services are not sufficiently based on supporting customers in their everyday activities, and by designing a service based on customer logics it may be easier to facilitate customers in their aspirations to be better off. Also, the activities and aspirations of noncustomers (i.e. individuals who are not currently purchasing or using a specific offering), represent another area in which providers should focus. Understanding customer, potential customer, and noncustomer logics is needed to truly enable service outreach to all potential customers – empowered as well as vulnerable – in commercial, public, and base-of-the-pyramid contexts. The following section elaborates on the customer logic notion from the viewpoint of a customer-dominant approach.

Customer logic as a holistic driving force

The concept of the *customer* represents, in itself, a key issue warranting further elaboration in terms of different customer roles and contexts, configurations of customer actors, and different aggregation levels. Such a focus on customer ecosystems provides insight into the portfolio of service providers used by the customer on one hand and the constellation of nonbusiness actors in the customer's context on the other hand. These issues are discussed next.

Idiosyncratic sensemaking

Customer logic captures holistically the mental model and sensemaking behind customers' choices and activities. It is a "coordinating concept in which the patterns of customers' overt and covert activities, experiences and goals are integrated" (Heinonen & Strandvik, 2015, p. 475). It represents "the identity of the customer" and how a customer's "different activities, experiences and resources are linked to each other, thereby forming a system of their own" (Heinonen & Strandvik, 2018, p. 5). Each customer has an individual logic based on a variety of factors, such as values, tasks, knowledge, capabilities, and traditions as well as future-oriented elements such as ambitions, aspirations, goals, dreams, and visions. Customer logic that is both cognitive and emotional drives customer perceptions and experiences. The logic is revealed in customer activities and decisions, what customers pay attention to, and what interpretations they make. It essential to understand what customers decide to buy (or support or use) and what they decide not to buy, as well as their reasons for these decisions. These issues are not sufficiently on the agenda in other service perspectives.

Although the phenomenological approach included in some service perspectives recognizes the influence of subjective experiences (Husserl, 1970), service perspectives do not explicitly account for internal consistency and holistic patterns in thoughts and behaviors of individual customers. As a consequence, logics and the diversity of logics are not generally recognized in these perspectives. Customer logics cannot be identified based solely on socio-economic segmentation criteria or external characteristics, but rather require an approach that identifies patterns or uses in-depth methods to understand customer reasoning and interpretations. Service providers have a major challenge in understanding customer logics, because they have their own perspectives and framing, both of which color their views of what would be 'logical.'

Customers and providers have different (albeit sometimes overlapping) perspectives, aspirations, and logics. Thus, there is a need to explore the differences, rather than assume there is a common interest that could override them. Because of diversity and heterogeneity in markets (Chalmers Thomas, Price, Schau, 2012), it is evident that different logics exist and the provider's main task is therefore to understand customer logics and align offerings and activities accordingly. It is important to recognize that there are several different customer logics; of course, a provider cannot bend its own activities to support all of them. On a higher systemic level, in value chains of provider–customer relationships, the contrast between provider logic and customer logic could be applied, giving a new view of value systems. In contrast to assumptions in the extant marketing literature, C-DL asserts that providers might influence, but cannot control, customer logics through tactics such as promotional activities or offering designs. It can be argued that customers are largely influenced in three ways: through their own experiences (including changes in their resources), through outside influence by other customers and providers, and through the impact of the larger social and institutional context in which they live.

Customer logics: individuals and aggregates

Customers perform different roles that may be divided among individuals or groups representing the customer. Shugan (2004, p. 25) comments that S-DL provides insight into the issue of different roles and units:

> For example, who is the customer of a hospital? Is it the patient who receives the service, the insurer who pays for the service, the admitting physician who refers the patient, the government regulator who specifies the service, or the employer who chooses the healthcare provider?

Although this may not be an inclusive list of customer roles and may not be relevant in all contexts, it points to the need to elaborate the *customer* concept in theory and in practice. For instance, the question as to who is the customer could be posed in a business-to-business context: is it the company, a representative of the customer company, a unit within the customer company, a team of individuals in different roles involved with the provider, or all of these? The same question applies in regard to a consumer visiting a supermarket: is the customer this one consumer, all of the individuals constituting the household, or only some of them? In service research, the customer is often considered to be the visible actor that has direct contact with the provider. It may be more sensible to posit that the visible actor is a special case and usually there are other individuals involved. The emphasis on customers and idiosyncratic sensemaking does not mean that this focus is on individuals only. Rather, the focus is on idiosyncratic customer logic in any customer unit, ranging from individuals, groups of individuals, and organizations to groups of organizations.

The concept of a 'customer' may refer to any unit acting as a customer, whether it is a consumer (single person buying for own usage), a collective of consumers (a family or a group of people buying for own usage), a company or any type of organization or a group of them (buying for business usage), or a region or a country (buying for governmental usage). Additionally, the one acquiring/purchasing something may be someone other than the one using it, further indicating the complexity of the notion of 'customer.' The main issue is the emphasis on the unit making choices regarding what to acquire/purchase (and for whose usage) to achieve its own goals.

The focus is as much on a single consumer, company, or organization as it is on the idiosyncratic logic of a group of consumers, companies, or organizations. The logic of a group of consumers resembles the research on shared meanings in marketplace cultures (Arnould & Thompson, 2005; Cova, 1997; Muniz & O'guinn, 2001). However, unlike these studies, in the C-DL stream of research, the individual and collective identities and logics of customers are equally prevalent and important (Heinonen et al., 2019). All experiences, activities, and value conceptions have an individual and collective characteristic, and the customer balances the influence of these factors (Heinonen et al., 2018). Although each customer applies his or her own logic, this does not mean that there are, in practice, an unlimited number of logics. Rather, it can be expected that contextual, social, cultural, and psychological factors influence and shape these idiosyncratic logics, resulting in a finite and reasonable number of clusters of logics from a service management point of view.

In addition to focusing on customer logics and applying systemic and relationship perspectives, service providers also need to consider the *customer's ecosystem*. In contrast to the service ecosystem notion focused on service-for-service exchange where customers are a part of a provider-driven service (cf. Chandler & Lusch, 2015; Vargo & Lusch, 2017; Vargo et al., 2008), the customer ecosystem implies that selected service providers are a part of a customer's (life) system. The service system notion and customer ecosystem notion are hence completely separate entities. Customer ecosystems are systems of actors, resources, and elements that are relevant to customers and linked to each other through different kinds of relationships. They consequently affect customers' choices, usage, and evaluations of service (Heinonen & Strandvik, 2015). This concept involves a shift from provider-driven coordination and co-creation in service ecosystems to customer orchestration of value formation in customer ecosystems. Therefore, it entails several implications for researchers and practitioners regarding how customers, configurations of value units, the scope of value formation, and relevant actor systems are conceptualized.

Characteristics of C-DL

The three propositions covered so far are: (1) 'Dominant logics determine attention, focus, and action,' (2) 'Without customers there is no business,' and (3) 'Customer logic is a holistic driving force'; these are cornerstones that characterize and differentiate C-DL. Dominant logics play a triple role, in the sense that they represent different paradigms or schools of thought in service research, managerial mental models in service business, and customers' mental models used to make sense of service alternatives in markets. The proposition that customers are necessary for business might sound like a truism, but in fact is surprisingly frequently overlooked both in practice (witness, for example, unsuccessful start-ups and innovations) and in theory (e.g., by focusing on the service provider and service itself rather than on customers). Introducing customer logic as a concept highlights the need to see the bigger picture beyond conceptualizations like needs, wants, expectations, and practices. Customer logic is grounded in customers' own contexts and experiences, which are not wholly influenced by service providers.

In C-DL, it is assumed that customer choices of services and providers are driven by idiosyncratic logic based on the customer's past, present, and future contexts. It can therefore be expected that there are a number of different customer logics, and that the value formation of service is embedded in the customer's context. It is certainly different from how value is formed for the service provider. For the service provider, value is formed through the provision of service, considering the restrictions that arise (e.g., insufficient capabilities, resources, and/or customer insights, and productivity/profitability requirements). Whereas a service provider focuses on the service provided, a customer considers how the service fits into his or her business or life. In *resource integration*, the logics meet (and sometimes clash). Providers can improve business value creation by understanding customer logics and creating business models and service offerings that are aligned with selected customer logics. Providers are becoming embedded in customers' lives, as opposed to customers being involved in companies' offerings. Sometimes the logics are too different from each other and it is not possible to create a business model that would enable a win-win situation.

The focus of C-DL is on seeing customers as the dominant actors and the nexus of service and value creation, whereas other perspectives continue to emphasize actions and processes dominated by a (system of) service provider(s). There is a dual meaning conveyed by the term *dominant*. The first meaning is the conventional one of seeing a perspective as a dominant logic, or, according to Prahalad and Bettis (1986, p. 491):

> a mind set or world view or conceptualization of the business and the administrative tools to accomplish goals and make decisions in that business. It is stored as a shared cognitive map (or a set of schemas) among the dominant coalition.

Second, the term is meant to communicate the primary position of the customer in the marketplace in a more specific sense. That is, the basic premise of C-DL is "positioning customer insight in the foreground in place of the type of offering … or the system of providers" (Heinonen & Strandvik, 2015, p. 473). Thus, the primacy of the customer is the key issue; the disruptive changes transforming the business environment and markets of any industry represent a critical argument for emphasizing the customer. Heinonen and Strandvik (2018, p. 1) further state that

> the most dramatic consequence is not the possibilities created for companies but rather the challenges that emerge as a result of customer behavior undergoing fundamental changes. Technology transformation has paved the way for empowered customers who are increasingly influencing businesses and markets, and the challenge for practitioners and researchers alike is to make sense of the role of these customers in such business environments.

In summary, customer behavior is changing: in many service categories, customers have more available alternatives as to which providers to engage. As a result, providers are facing challenges to being seen, chosen, and sustained as customer partners.

To understand how customers and societies are changing, it is important to understand the broader contextual setting of service. Layder's (2018) view on domains of social reality can be utilized to depict the ontological setting of service perspectives. Layder distinguishes between four interrelated social processes representing different social domains: *psychobiography*, *situated activity*, *social settings*, and *contextual resources*. He points out that each of these has its own properties and dimensions of power, time, and space. Social domains are intertwined, and social behavior is the result of influences from all domains. These domains represent different layers of social reality. Psychobiography refers to factors such as personal characteristics, motives, experiences, emotions, and relationships that evolve throughout a person's life. Situated activity refers to encounters and interactions in which people influence each other. These situated activities may be brief or regularly repeated over time, planned or emergent, significant or trivial, and are shaped by influences from the other domains. Social settings are formally or informally organized settings like families, business networks, organizations, religious groups, and other arenas in which everyday activities take place. The domain of contextual resources is a macrolevel construct and contains society-wide contexts, including for example, institutions, cultural values, and politics.

Layder's four social domains are used here to identify and structure key issues that drive service business decisions. Figure 4.1 depicts the four domains with changes resulting in challenges for service business. Both historical and future factors influence the present, but Layder (2018) suggests that the pace of change varies across different social domains. Taking a critical realist position, he argues that the classic *agency versus structure* debate in the social sciences can be resolved by considering different domains as separate but intertwined. Following this stance, C-DL's emphasis on customer idiosyncratic logic does not contradict the potential influence of other social domains, but it also does not assume that customers are dominated by their context. Different streams of research may differentially emphasize different domains: C-DL places more emphasis on the self-domain (psychobiography) in relation to situated activity, whereas, for example, S-DL approaches situated activity from a social setting domain perspective. This difference has consequences for what are considered interesting and relevant research issues from the perspective of each theoretical framework.

As indicated in Figure 4.1, the foundation of this model is based on distinct differences between provider and customer logic, as manifested by goals, resources, and activities. The situated activity incorporates separate encounters as well as connected interactions in relationships and systems. These are manifested through offerings as proposed by providers, as well as *needings*, which are representations of customer goals and aspirations. A needing is different

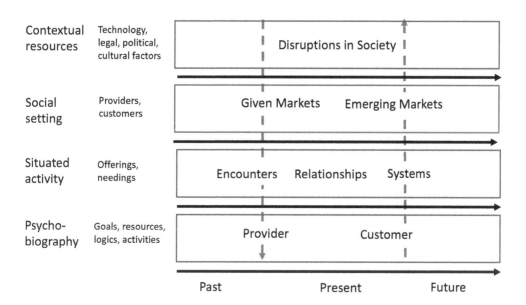

Figure 4.1 Changes and challenges for service businesses.

from the concept of *needs* or *wants*, and represents a customer's understanding of how a provider should contribute to his or her goals; it may also consider goodness-of-fit with other providers available (Strandvik, Holmlund, & Edvardsson, 2012). The social setting, from a C-DL perspective, involves an interplay between given and emerging markets as conceived by providers and customers. Finally, the contextual resources, in the C-DL view, refer to disruptions in society represented by legal, political, and cultural factors.

Although C-DL emphasizes the domain of self, all social domains are interrelated and represent important issues for researchers and managers to consider. The two main actors in a market, the service provider and the customer, can both be considered on the psychobiography/self level to have an agency-based trajectory, but they are also embedded in a structure of the situated activities, social setting, and context domains influencing them while also continuously changing. For example, the banking industry has significantly been affected by digitization as well as changes in regulations, which has changed the social setting (competition) and has affected situated activities (communication and interaction between the bank and its customers), and has forced banks to reconsider their business models and offerings. Customers have, as a result of these changes in different domains, adopted new logics, strategies, and practices for handling their financial affairs sometimes to the surprise of traditional banks following their traditional beliefs about customer behavior.

C-DL in business practice

Theoretical marketing perspectives have real and practical implications for societies and markets. The key issue is to focus on relevant and significant organizational and societal challenges "as opposed to trying to predict the next big theory" (Corley & Gioia, 2011, p. 24). Because the C-DL perspective is grounded in the everyday realities of individuals in different markets, it provides solid insights into the dynamics of societies and markets. There are indications that customers' power and roles will become larger in the future due to the development of information technology and increasingly dynamic markets (Lemon & Verhoef, 2016). Customers will, in practice, have more opportunities and tools to acquire information and compare offerings. At the same time, providers' influence on customers may weaken, because customers are active subjects and not passive objects for marketing activities any longer. This is also the case in settings where agency may not reside with the focal customer, but a representative of the customer (cf. Čaić, Odekerken-Schröder, & Mahr, 2018). Thus, markets are constituted and driven by customer logics manifested in customer activities and provider choices.

Many service marketing perspectives emphasize how providers – or systems, networks, or society as a whole – influence and control the customer, i.e. that customers are to be embedded in providers' contexts. C-DL departs from this view and suggests that rather than being interested in service as such, customers strive to achieve their goals by engaging service providers and being involved in societal agendas. The difference in the starting point is significant. Rather than focusing on how customers can be involved in service ecosystems, the emphasis is now on aspects of customer internal and surrounding environments, which are important to achieving customer goals and aspirations. This seemingly trivial shift in focus results in a number of central questions to reflect on: how can providers be involved in customers' lives? To what extent are customers controlled or influenced by service providers and contextual factors like technology, society, environment, and social setting? To what extent are they free to act in an autonomous manner? What are the implications of seeing customers as subjects in their own contexts, rather than as recipients and beneficiaries of different stakeholders' service-related activities? What is the practical consequence of going beyond investigating value co-creation between stakeholders in a service system and, instead, exploring customers' value formation within their own customer ecosystem? This dichotomy of orchestration and autonomy is especially evident in technology-based environments as exemplified by the three scenarios of the collaborative economy (Fehrer et al., 2018).

C-DL as a perspective on marketing emphasizes the mental models or mind-sets of individual managers and organizations. At an aggregate level, mind-sets have been conceptualized as "institutions" (Vargo & Lusch, 2016). C-DL assumes that provider logic is different than customer logics, simply because customers and providers have different goals, aspirations, and resources. Managers and organizations follow idiosyncratic provider logic; as a consequence, it is essential for them to understand the business logic employed by themselves, their managers, and other companies (cf. Rydén et al., 2015; Strandvik et al., 2018). Such logic directs a provider's attention and the framing of threats, opportunities, and actions. Similar to the extant research in strategic management and managerial sensemaking, it is evident that the logic a provider uses is challenging to capture and change (Jaworski, 2018). A provider's logic can be seen as based on its understanding of how to best achieve its goals, considering its resources and capabilities, and this logic becomes evident in its business model, strategies, offerings, and operations. In C-DL, it is assumed that the better the provider understands customer logics, the more potential it has to perform well. Importantly, provider and customer logics are not necessarily aligned. The difference in logics complicates the achievement of reciprocal cooperation and coordination.

The foundation of the customer-dominant perspective is based on a holistic view of customers embedded in their own context (and not that of the service system) and the notion of customer logic representing their subjective reasoning about employing service providers. Customers' configuration of service providers in use is usually less known to service providers, and represents a baseline for their experienced value formation. The key issue to consider when applying C-DL is the transition from an atomistic service-for-service focused provider-dominant view on customers to a holistic customer-dominant view on how customers orchestrate their lives in which providers merely play a part. Figure 4.2 presents the contrast between the customer and provider logics. It should be noted that the figure is a schematic representation, and in practice there are a number of different provider logics as well as customer logics.

Figure 4.2 illustrates the contrast between provider and customer logics. It provides essentially a holistic view on how logics can be seen to influence customers' and providers' actions and reactions in markets: the influence on intentions and plans (needing/value requirement and offering/value proposition) and activities and outcomes (value experience and provider performance). Several mismatches may emerge, depicted as Mismatch 1 to Mismatch 7. It is proposed that providers can benefit from understanding customer logics; reducing Mismatch 7 might reduce the other specified mismatches. Another suggested implication of the model is that conflict and avoidance are as likely as coordination, co-creation, and attraction. Provider and customer logics are largely hidden to the other party, and interpretations are often based on what is visible. For the provider, it may take effort to understand different customer logics. It is also proposed that both provider and customer logics materialize in structures and established activity patterns, which make them resistant to change.

Based on customer logic, which shapes past experiences and future aspirations, a needing or value requirement arises (Strandvik et al., 2012). The needing concept on the customer side mirrors the service offering on the provider side, and it is activated for the customer when needed. The needing is emergent and dynamically updated based on service offerings and provider performance in the marketplace.

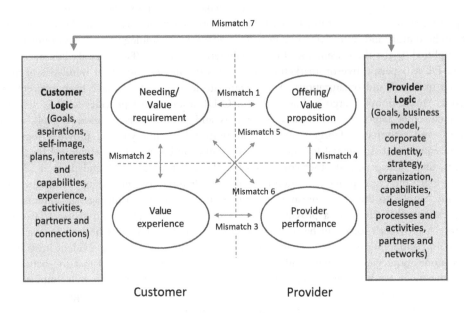

Figure 4.2 Differences between provider and customer logics.

Service offerings need to be designed and optimized for profitability and productivity reasons, and this leads to compromises in terms of features. The *value proposition* of an offering is an idealized representation of what will be performed in practice. Mismatch 1 in Figure 4.2 represents the mismatch between customer requirements and this proposed value of service. In this case the service promise does not fit the customer, but might be designed for other customers. Mismatch 3 indicates the difference between the provider view of the service performance and the customer interpretation thereof. There might be different standards of evaluation between the customer and provider or different foci. Mismatch 2 occurs when the customer's experienced value-in-use is not fulfilled. This may be caused by a combination of the other mismatches as indicated by the arrows. Mismatch 4 depicts the difference between the designed service offering and actual service performance; Mismatch 2 is only visible to the customer and Mismatch 4 is only visible to the service provider. Mismatch 5 depicts the disappointment experienced by a customer when the service offering communicated is not fulfilled as promised. Finally, Mismatch 6 may occur, for example, when customers evaluate service providers in relation to their requirements, based on providers' actual performance rather than on what is promised in marketing communication. The figure provides a diagnostic tool, similar to the Gap model of service quality (Parasuraman, Zeithaml, & Berry, 1985), for an increased understanding of the complexity of achieving fit between customers and providers in value creation, and explicates the anatomy of interactions, co-creation and resource integration.

To date, there is limited explicit research on customer logics and related concepts, such as customer ecosystems and customer activities, and thus there are many opportunities to contribute to a better understanding of how customers avoid, choose, retain, or switch providers. As customers are not necessarily individuals, but often represent collectives (families, companies, or organizations), the customer logic concept becomes even more multifaceted. However, more is known about provider logics than about customer logics; for example, the schools of thought in the marketing and service domains tend to take an idealistic, often normative, perspective on service business.

Implications of C-DL for current and future service research

This last section describes implications of applying a customer-dominant approach to service research and application. C-DL is discussed in relation to some current societal and market challenges debated in service research. This chapter suggests that the perspective used determines what elements researchers and managers pay attention to, and what they consider to be key challenges. The implications discussed herein are based on shifting the focus of different phenomena from a provider-dominant view to a customer-dominant view.

Value co-creation

Value co-creation – that is, the collaboration between different stakeholders in order to create value – has emerged as a key phenomenon in service research and value creation (Prahalad & Ramaswamy, 2000, 2004). Although it was originally depicted as a perspective on the collaboration between a customer and a company, it has shifted toward incorporating multiple stakeholders in a system (Bryson, Sancino, Benington, & Sørensen, 2017; Čaić et al., 2018; Payne, Storbacka, & Frow, 2008; Vargo & Lusch, 2016; Vargo et al., 2008). In addition to this shift, the common denominator in many co-creation studies is the assumption that value is based on shared logics and created in coordinated interactions between the customer and the service provider(s). Customers have been suggested as participants in co-creation to varying degrees. For example, McColl-Kennedy, Vargo, Dagger, Sweeney, and van Kasteren (2012) identified five co-creation practice styles of customers and showed how customers engage in different value co-creation activities, depending on their co-creation style. This model, although focused on interactions and the assumption that co-creation is the key issue of value creation, indicates that customers do, in fact, have differing preferences toward levels of co-creation.

C-DL provides another perspective on value creation, which is value formation. It is conceptualized with elements (designated by the questions who, what, how, when, and where) embedded in the customer's context and lifeworld (Heinonen et al., 2013). An implicit understanding of *formation* as a synonym of *emergence* is that the value experience is constantly changing. Value formation captures the idea of value experiences in customer lives. The "splintered society" introduced by Fletcher (2006) stresses a fragmented customer reality where the market is atomized and uncontrollable, paralleling the focus in C-DL on idiosyncratic customer logics.

A customer-dominant approach to value has several implications. Whereas the predominant focus on interactions and co-creation implies a provider agency and that the provider can orchestrate value creation, the C-DL assumes that it is not "always deliberately and mutually created" (Heinonen et al., 2013, p. 105). Moreover, instead of value being orchestrated by a service provider, including interactions and touchpoints, the customer-dominant approach recognizes value formation accumulates in the customer's own lifeworld (Heinonen et al., 2010). Therefore, the temporal and contextual perspective on value formation is further-reaching than traditionally assumed, and it involves multiple points of reference, not just the touchpoints designed by the service provider. Value formation also emerges as a social and experiential phenomenon through mental – and, for the provider, invisible – processes. It is, therefore, not an isolated event, but rather linked with other customers' realities (Heinonen et al., 2013). Value formation is thus always partially collective and shared (Arantola-Hattab, 2013).

The term *co-creation* is predominantly used in a broad and nonspecific way, assuming that all interactions offer different opportunities for mutual and harmonious value co-creation. Yet the nuances and challenges of value creation, such as the differences in deliberate collaboration, potential collaboration, and nonconscious influence, are not explicitly emphasized. The C-DL perspective provides analytical reasons to distinguish between mutually intentional co-creation, provider-driven value creation, customer-driven value creation, and spontaneous value creation (Grönroos, Strandvik, & Heinonen, 2015). Co-creation is consequently a special case of value creation. Furthermore, C-DL assumes that the value experience is fundamentally idiosyncratic and relative. This means that what is a benefit and what is a sacrifice is customer-specific and cannot be determined beforehand by the provider.

Customer engagement

Customer engagement – customer connection to and investment in an object – has recently received increasing interest within both academic research and business practice. It has been explored from different perspectives and contexts, such as online communities, social media, work, big data, brands, and co-creation (Brodie, Ilic, Juric, & Hollebeek, 2013; Dessart, Veloutsou, & Morgan-Thomas, 2015; Jaakkola & Alexander, 2014; Kahn, 1990; Kunz et al., 2017). Customer engagement is frequently seen from the perspective of cognitive, emotional, or behavioral dimensions (Brodie, Hollebeek, Juric, & Ilic, 2011). A customer-dominant approach to engagement shifts and broadens the focus of engagement in several ways, particularly in relation to the object of engagement.

Although customer engagement addresses customer experiences and perceptions, it can be argued that engagement research is not sufficiently customer-centric, as it revolves around customer reactions to provider-defined aspects, with the object of engagement being frequently a provider's offerings or brands (Heinonen, 2018; Kunz et al., 2017). For instance, in a conceptual study by Brodie et al. (2011), the focal engagement object was described as a course/module, brand, product, and organization. A systemic approach to engagement, such as engagement in actor networks, revolves around customer service experiences (Li, Juric, & Brodie, 2018) or uses a service ecosystem as the primary unit of analysis (Alexander, Jaakkola, & Hollebeek, 2018). A customer-dominant approach, in contrast, suggests a change in the unit of analysis, from the service point of view to aspects of customer lives that create strong cognitive, emotional, or behavioral reactions. Therefore, instead of a provider-defined object, the object of a customer-dominant approach to engagement is a customer-defined target, such as customer areas of interest, activities, or lifestyles. Such an emphasis would be focused on broader aspects of customers' lives, such as their aspirations and goals in life, as opposed to merely focusing on their relationship to an offering or brand. Additionally, C-DL would rephrase the engagement issue; rather than being a question of how providers can engage customers in provider activities, it becomes a question of how customers choose to engage with the providers in their activities.

Transformative service, social inclusion, and societal welfare

Transformative service research (TSR) has emerged as an important area investigating how service can advance societal well-being; this research is focused on uplifting changes that improve individual and societal well-being (Anderson & Ostrom, 2015; Anderson et al., 2013). TSR indicates three key research areas: (1) destruction of value and negative service, (2) the role of collectives and social phenomena in well-being, and (3) the influence of customer activities (co-production and co-creation) on their well-being (Anderson & Ostrom, 2015). Additionally, TSR research focuses on global challenges (e.g., poverty, vulnerable customers, minorities, food waste, and social inclusion) (Baron, Patterson, Maull, & Warnaby, 2018; Bone et al., 2014; Fisk et al., 2016, 2018; Loomba, 2017; Reynoso, Valdés, & Cabrera, 2015).

A customer-dominant approach can contribute to the nascent research on the transformative nature of service and its influence on societal welfare. By adopting the C-DL, researchers and practitioners can contribute to the alleviation of issues related to social inclusion, customer well-being, and societal welfare (Fisk et al., 2018; Rosenbaum et al., 2011). Specifically, C-DL can provide a foundation for understanding different types of customers through the concept of *customer logic* and the idiosyncratic sensemaking. Moreover, C-DL acknowledges the primary role of customer tasks, activities, and experiences and how these enable customers to achieve life goals. The key issue is focusing on how service can support this achievement; therefore, C-DL can contribute to the understanding of how well-being is achieved through service and the customer ecosystem. In other words, C-DL provides a broader context regarding how customers engage in and perform daily activities to achieve life goals and aspirations.

Digital transformation, big data, and automation

Connectivity, transparency, and unpredictability are transforming the business landscape (Kunz et al., 2017; Porter & Heppelmann, 2014). Digital transformation and disruptive technologies (e.g., artificial intelligence, machine learning, robotics, automation, and big data) are driving this transformation (e.g., Wirtz et al., 2018; Wuenderlich et al., 2015). The sheer volume, variety, velocity, and veracity of data provide the opportunity to create substantial value for both customers and companies (Wedel & Kannan, 2016). Disruptive technologies provide opportunities for companies to connect with customers, engage in continuous dialogue, create more efficient activities and synergies between processes, and learn about market realities (e.g., Bohnsack & Pinkse, 2017; Broekhuizen, Bakker, & Postma, 2018; Caro & Sadr, 2018). Disruptive technologies and the associated business transformation have implications for customers in terms of more alternatives and opportunities, informed decisions, support in the execution of different activities, and better connections and networks to relevant entities (Di Pietro et al., 2018; Govindarajan & Ramamurti, 2018; Wuenderlich et al., 2015).

Researchers are interested in exploring how service interactions and processes change with technology, such as envisioning "service robots in the frontline" (Wirtz et al., 2018), human–robot interactions in elderly care (Čaić et al., 2018), and automation of service operations (Breidbach et al., 2018). In practice, a major challenge seems to be initiating change in mental models to utilize the possibilities provided by digitization (Holmlund, Strandvik, & Lähteenmäki, 2017; Rydén et al., 2015). Industries (e.g., finance) with strong institutional logic are experiencing radical changes in their markets that may require business model innovations. For example, a study on online interest communities identified four different value formation profiles based on the underlying customer logics and thereby indicated the shift to the customer domain and the continuous interplay of individual and collective experiences (Heinonen et al., 2019). C-DL can contribute to the need to understand how technologies are embedded in customer lives, how they can potentially provide support in performing everyday tasks and activities, and their role in achieving life goals.

Market dynamics

The dynamism of markets and marketing phenomena such as customer experiences and value is increasingly important and has received some research attention. Most markets and providers are going through major transformations due to the emergence of disruptive technologies and changes in political, social, and institutional structures (Holmlund et al., 2017; Nenonen et al., 2014; Strandvik et al., 2018). Although market dynamism, transformation, and disruption are increasingly evident, the research on these issues from a customer perspective is still emerging; for instance, despite the abundant research on customer value, existing research has predomintly taken a static view of this issue, focusing on elements, antecedents, and consequences of value (creation). Indeed, most approaches in marketing are based on models and concepts that describe structures and stable states (Blocker, 2012) rather than change. This is logical when considering that providers are restricted by their mental models, resources, and structures. Providers cannot, therefore, easily change their strategies, business models, or service offerings, as these were carefully created to fulfill the goals of the company based on its specific capabilities and there is an investment in these past choices. More research is needed to understand how and why value emerges and changes (Beverland & Lockshin, 2003; Corsaro & Snehota, 2010; Eggert, Kleinaltenkamp, & Kashyap, 2019). We argue that adaptation to changes or disruptions in the marketplace is facilitated by applying a customer-dominant perspective.

C-DL asserts that marketing phenomena should be considered from perspectives that emphasize change, emergence, flow, and development. Accordingly, models and concepts need to include directions, goals, aspirations, frustrations, and disappointments, which describe sensations in a constant state of flux. Such changes have implications for markets and relationships between providers and customers. Although the primary focus of market dynamics is typically on managers, regulators, and organisations (Mele et al., 2018), it is increasingly important to recognize customers in such a dynamic environment. C-DL can provide a customer perspective on market dynamics, directing the interest of managers and researchers toward changes in customer perceptions, experiences, or evaluations. Managers might consider, for example, how value emerges, how it grows, and how it declines or even dissolves completely. Thus, the focus is on change itself and on the forces creating change. As society and business environments are changing, it is both theoretically and practically relevant to study how customer behavior is changing.

The dynamism discussed above also relates to customer logic. In situations of change, caused by customer-internal, market-related, or society-related factors, the most significant challenge for service providers is to understand customers' reasoning, i.e. logics. Although idiosyncratic customer logic is semi-stable, idiosyncratic logic can change in different ways, as customers are influenced by different sources. For instance, customers come from different backgrounds and have different aspirations, leading to a continuous emergence of new logics and new logic clusters. Moreover, disruptive changes in the marketplace may be caused by the introduction of new societal-level ideas about environment protection, causing customer logics to change for some customers, leading to abandonment of meat consumption. In other, less dramatic situations, customers may become more critical toward and informed about service providers based on information in social communities. This extends the market-scripting literature addressing markets as manager's social constructions (Storbacka & Nenonen, 2011). Markets are, in this literature, seen as configurations of mental models and as a consequence business models and practices. This literature tends to apply a systems and co-creation perspective drawing also on S-DL (Storbacka & Nenonen, 2015). C-DL adds to the literature by suggesting that the success of market scripting, that is conscious activities by the focal market actor (typically a provider) to change mental models, may be conditioned by customers' mental models, e.g., their logics. We argue that customer logics are evolving, but cannot be shaped by a single provider or service category alone; customer logics are related to the holistic context taken into consideration by the customer, including the past, present, and future. Markets would hence be defined, emerge, and dissolve based on what customers are ready to buy (and pay for in commercial settings).

Concluding remarks

Almost all markets and service categories are faced with increased dynamism and a need for transformation. The transformative capacity of service relates to the ability to align business practices with rapidly changing market demands. Although multiple sources contribute to such transformation, in this chapter it is argued that the most substantial changes emanate from improved customer ability to influence markets and market-related activities. As a result, businesses need to prioritize customers as the primary stakeholders in markets.

This chapter focuses on customers in the broad sense, and it is argued that all organizations have customers, regardless of their label. C-DL thus has relevance to, and is applicable to, any commercial or noncommercial setting in which a provider or system of providers serves customers for some purpose. By explicitly emphasizing customers, C-DL can provide a fresh lens to alleviate issues related to transformative service.

Highlighting the primacy of customers involves focusing on understanding customers holistically. This refers to an interest in customers' idiosyncratic sensemaking, as well as in the drivers and restrictors of individual behaviors, cognitions, and emotions. This chapter recognizes that customer individual and subjective logics are distinct from provider logics, and also asserts that, at both the individual and aggregate levels, customers choose which providers to involve in the process of achieving life goals and tasks. The distinction between customer and provider logics constitutes the key element of C-DL and reveals theoretical and practical challenges that would otherwise remain overlooked. For researchers, the key challenge is to move away from emphasizing interactions and touchpoints to exploring customers' tasks, activities and goals. For practitioners, the focus on customer logic highlights the importance of understanding the issues that are important for customers which may be small details for the provider. It also indicates the need for providers to involve themselves in customers' lifeworlds.

References

Alexander, M., Jaakkola, E., & Hollebeek, L. (2018). Zooming out: Actor engagement beyond the dyadic. *Journal of Service Management*, *29*(3), 333–351.

Anderson, L., & Ostrom, A.L. (2015). Transformative service research: Advancing our knowledge about service and well-being. *Journal of Service Research*, *18*(3), 243–249.

Anderson, L., Ostrom, A. L., Corus, C., Fisk, R. P., Gallan, A. S., Giraldo, M., … & Shirahada, K. (2013). Transformative service research: An agenda for the future. *Journal of Business Research*, *66*(8), 1203–1210.

Arantola-Hattab, J. (2013), *Family as a customer experiencing co-created service value* (doctoral thesis). Helsinki, Finland: Hanken School of Economics.

Arnould, E. J., & Thompson, C. J. (2005). Consumer culture theory (CCT): Twenty years of research. *Journal of Consumer Research*, *31*(4), 868–883.

Baron, S., Patterson, A., Maull, R., & Warnaby, G. (2018). Feed people first: A service ecosystem perspective on innovative food waste reduction. *Journal of Service Research*, *21*(1), 135–150.

Beverland, M., & Lockshin, L. (2003). A longitudinal study of customers' desired value change in business-to-business markets. *Industrial Marketing Management, 32*(8), 653–666.

Blocker, C. (2012). The dynamics of satisfaction and loyalty after relational transgressions. *Journal of Services Marketing, 26*(2), 94–101.

Bohnsack, R., & Pinkse, J. (2017). Value propositions for disruptive technologies: Reconfiguration tactics in the case of electric vehicles. *California Management Review, 59*(4), 79–96.

Bone, S. A., Christensen, G. L., & Williams, J. D. (2014). Rejected, shackled, and alone: The impact of systemic restricted choice on minority consumers' construction of self. *Journal of Consumer Research, 41*(2), 451–474.

Breidbach, C., Choi, S., Ellway, B., Keating, B. W., Kormusheva, K., Kowalkowski, C., & Maglio, P. (2018). Operating without operations: How is technology changing the role of the firm? *Journal of Service Management, 29*(5), 809–833.

Brodie, R., Hollebeek, L, Juric, B., & Ilic, A. (2011). Customer engagement: Conceptual domain, fundamental propositions, and implications for research. *Journal of Service Research, 14*(3), 252–271.

Brodie, R. J., Ilic, A., Juric, B., & Hollebeek, L. (2013). Customer engagement in a virtual brand community: An exploratory analysis. *Journal of Business Research, 66*(1), 105–114.

Broekhuizen, T. L., Bakker, T., & Postma, T. J. (2018). Implementing new business models: What challenges lie ahead? *Business Horizons.* https://doi.org/10.1016/j.bushor.2018.03.003.

Bryson, J., Sancino, A., Benington, J., & Sørensen, E. (2017). Towards a multi-actor theory of public value co-creation. *Public Management Review, 19*(5), 640–654.

Čaić, M., Odekerken-Schröder, G., & Mahr, D. (2018). Service robots: Value co-creation and co-destruction in elderly care networks. *Journal of Service Management, 29*(2), 178–205.

Caro, F., & Sadr, R. (2018) Internet of Things (IoT) in retail: Bridging supply and demand. *Business Horizons.* https://doi.org/10.1016/j.bushor.2018.08.002.

Chalmers Thomas, T., Price, L. L., & Schau, H. J. (2012). When differences unite: Resource dependence in heterogeneous consumption communities. *Journal of Consumer Research, 39*(5), 1010–1033.

Chandler, J. D., & Lusch, R. F. (2015). Service systems: A broadened framework and research agenda on value propositions, engagement, and service experience. *Journal of Service Research, 18*(1), 6–22.

Cheung, F. Y. M., & To, W. M. (2016). A customer-dominant logic on service recovery and customer satisfaction. *Management Decision, 54*(10), 2524–2543.

Corley, K. G., & Gioia, D. A. (2011). Building theory about theory building: What constitutes a theoretical contribution? *Academy of Management Review, 36*(1), 12–32.

Corsaro, D., & Snehota, I. (2010). Searching for relationship value in business markets: Are we missing something? *Industrial Marketing Management, 39*(6), 986s–995.

Cova, B. (1997). Community and consumption: Towards a definition of the "linking value" of product or services. *European Journal of Marketing, 31*(3/4), 297–316.

Dessart, L., Veloutsou, C., & Morgan-Thomas, A. (2015). Consumer engagement in online brand communities: A social media perspective. *Journal of Product & Brand Management, 24*(1), 28–42.

Di Pietro, L., Edvardsson, B., Reynoso, J., Renzi, M. F., Toni, M., & Guglielmetti Mugion, R. (2018). A scaling up framework for innovative service ecosystems: Lessons from Eataly and KidZania. *Journal of Service Management, 29*(1), 146–175.

Drucker, P. F. (1974). *Management: Tasks, responsibilities, practices.* London: Heinemann.

Eggert, A., Kleinaltenkamp, M., & Kashyap, V. (2019). *Mapping value in business markets: An integrative framework.* Industrial Marketing Management, *79,* 13–20.

Fehrer, J. A., Benoit, S., Aksoy, L., Baker, T. L., Bell, S. J., Brodie, R. J., & Marimuthu, M. (2018). Future scenarios of the collaborative economy: Centrally orchestrated, social bubbles or decentralized autonomous? *Journal of Service Management, 29*(5), 859–882.

Fisk, R. P., Anderson, L., Bowen, D. E., Gruber, T., Ostrom, A. L., Patrício, L., & Sebastiani, R. (2016). Billions of impoverished people deserve to be better served: A call to action for the service research community. *Journal of Service Management, 27*(1), 43–55.

Fisk, R. P., Brown, S. W., & Bitner, M. J. (1993). Tracking the evolution of the services marketing literature. *Journal of Retailing, 69*(1), 61–103.

Fisk, R. P., Dean, A. M., Alkire, L., Joubert, A., Previte, J., Robertson, N., & Rosenbaum, M. S. (2018). Design for service inclusion: Creating inclusive service systems by 2050. *Journal of Service Management, 29*(5), 834–858.

Fletcher, W. (2006). The splintered society. *International Journal of Market Research, 48*(4), 387–388. https://doi.org/10.1177/147078530604800402.

Ford, D. (2011). IMP and service-dominant logic: Divergence, convergence and development. *Industrial Marketing Management*, 40(2), 231–239.

Govindarajan, V., & Ramamurti, R. (2018). Transforming health care from the ground up. *Harvard Business Review*, 96(4), 96–104.

Grönroos, C. (1982). An applied service marketing theory. *European Journal of Marketing*, 16(7), 30–41.

Grönroos, C. (2006). Adopting a service logic for marketing. *Marketing Theory*, 6(3), 317–333.

Grönroos, C., & Gummerus, J. (2014). The service revolution and its marketing implications: Service logic vs service-dominant logic. *Managing Service Quality*, 24(3), 206–229.

Grönroos, C., Strandvik, T., & Heinonen, K. (2015). Value co-creation: Critical reflections. In J. Gummerus & C. von Koskull (Eds.), *The Nordic School: Service marketing and management for the future* (pp. 69–81). Helsinki and Finland: CERS, Hanken School of Economics.

Gummesson, E., & Grönroos, C. (2012). The emergence of the new service marketing: Nordic School perspectives. *Journal of Service Management*, 23(4), 479–497.

Heinonen, K. (2011). Consumer activity in social media: Managerial approaches to consumers' social media behavior. *Journal of Consumer Behaviour*, 10(6), 356–364.

Heinonen, K. (2018). Positive and negative valence influencing consumer engagement. *Journal of Service Theory and Practice*, 28(2), 147–169.

Heinonen, K., Campbell, C., & Lord Ferguson, S. (2019). Strategies for creating value through individual and collective customer experiences. *Business Horizons*, 62(1), 95–104.

Heinonen, K., Jaakkola, E., & Neganova, I. (2018). Drivers, types and value outcomes of customer-to-customer interaction: An integrative review and research agenda. *Journal of Service Theory and Practice*, 28(6), 710–732.

Heinonen, K., & Strandvik, T. (2015). Customer-dominant logic: Foundations and implications. *Journal of Services Marketing*, 29(6/7), 472–484.

Heinonen, K., & Strandvik, T. (2018). Reflections on customers' primary role in markets. *European Management Journal*, 36(1), 1–11.

Heinonen, K., Strandvik, T., Mickelsson, K.-J., Edvardsson, B., Sundström, E., & Andersson, P. (2010). A customer-dominant logic of service. *Journal of Service Management*, 21(4), 531–548.

Heinonen, K., Strandvik, T., & Voima, P. (2013). Customer dominant value formation in service. *European Business Review*, 25(2), 104–123.

Holmlund, M., Strandvik, T., & Lähteenmäki, I. (2017). Digitalization challenging institutional logics: Top executive sensemaking of service business change. *Journal of Service Theory and Practice*, 27(1), 219–236.

Husserl, E. (1970). *The crisis of European sciences and transcendental phenomenology: An introduction to phenomenological philosophy*. Chicago, IL: Northwestern University Press.

Jaakkola, E., & Alexander, M. (2014). The role of customer engagement behavior in value co-creation: A service system perspective. *Journal of Service Research*, 17(3), 247–261.

Jaworski, B. J. (2018). Reflections on the journey to be customer-oriented and solutions-led. *AMS Review*, 8(1–2), 75–79.

Kahn, W. A. (1990). Psychological conditions of personal engagement and disengagement at work. *Academy of Management Journal*, 33(4), 692–724.

Kohli, A. K., & Jaworski, B. J. (1990). Market orientation: The construct, research propositions, and managerial implications. *Journal of Marketing*, 54(2), 1–18.

Kunz, W., Aksoy, L., Bart, Y., Heinonen, K., Kabadayi, S., Villaroel Ordenes, F., & Theodoulidis, B. (2017). Customer engagement in a big data world. *Journal of Services Marketing*, 31(2), 161–171.

Layder, D. (2018). *Investigative research*. London: SAGE.

Lemon, K. N., & Verhoef, P. C. (2016). Understanding customer experience throughout the customer journey. *Journal of Marketing*, 80(6), 69–96.

Li, L. P., Juric, B., & Brodie, R. (2018). Actor engagement valence: Conceptual foundations, propositions and research directions. *Journal of Service Management*, 29(3), 491–516. https://doi.org/10.1108/JOSM-08-2016-0235.

Lipkin, M. (2016). Customer experience formation in today's service landscape. *Journal of Service Management*, 27(5), 678–703.

Loomba, A. P. (2017). Reconstructing lives: Transformative services for human trafficking survivors. *Journal of Services Marketing*, 31(4/5), 373–384.

Maglio, P. P., & Spohrer, J. (2008). Fundamentals of service science. *Journal of the Academy of Marketing Science*, 36(1), 18–20.

McColl-Kennedy, J. R., Vargo, S. L., Dagger, T. S., Sweeney, J. C., & van Kasteren, Y. (2012). Health care customer value cocreation practice styles. *Journal of Service Research*, *15*(4), 370–389.

Medberg, G., & Heinonen, K. (2014). Invisible value formation: A netnography in retail banking. *International Journal of Bank Marketing*, *32*(6), 590–607.

Mele, C., Russo-Spena, T., & Tregua, M. (2018). The performativity of value propositions in shaping a service ecosystem: The case of B-corporations. In *Social dynamics in a systems perspective* (pp. 175–194). Cham: Springer.

Mickelsson, K.-J. (2013). Customer activity in service. *Journal of Service Management*, *24*(5), 534–552.

Möller, K. (2013). Theory map of business marketing: Relationships and networks perspectives. *Industrial Marketing Management*, *42*(3), 324–335.

Muniz, A. M., & O'guinn, T. C. (2001). Brand community. *Journal of Consumer Research*, *27*(4), 412–432.

Narver, J. C., & Slater, S. F. (1990). The effect of a market orientation on business profitability. *Journal of Marketing*, *54*(4), 20–35.

Nenonen, S., Kjellberg, H., Pels, J., Cheung, L., Lindeman, S., Mele, C., & Storbacka, K. (2014). A new perspective on market dynamics: Market plasticity and the stability–fluidity dialectics. *Marketing Theory*, *14*(3), 269–289.

Normann, R. (2001). *Reframing business: When the map changes the landscape*. Chichester: John Wiley & Sons.

Parasuraman, A., Zeithaml, V. A., & Berry, L. L. (1985). A conceptual model of service quality and its implications for future research. *Journal of Marketing*, *49*(4), 41–50.

Payne, A. F., Storbacka, K., & Frow, P. (2008). Managing the co-creation of value. *Journal of the Academy of Marketing Science*, *36*(1), 83–96.

Porter, M. E., & Heppelmann, J. E. (2014). How smart, connected products are transforming competition. *Harvard Business Review*, *92*(11), 64–88.

Prahalad, C. K., & Bettis, R. A. (1986). The dominant logic: A new linkage between diversity and performance. *Strategic Management Journal*, *7*(6), 485–501.

Prahalad, C. K., & Ramaswamy, V. (2000). Co-opting customer competence. *Harvard Business Review*, *78*(1), 79–90.

Prahalad, C. K., & Ramaswamy, V. (2004). Co-creation experiences: The next practice in value creation. *Journal of Interactive Marketing*, *18*(3), 5–14.

Reynoso, J., Valdés, A., & Cabrera, K. (2015). Breaking new ground: Base-of-pyramid service research. *The Service Industries Journal*, *35*(13), 695–709.

Rihova, I., Buhalis, D., Moital, M., & Beth Gouthro, M. (2013). Social layers of customer-to-customer value co-creation. *Journal of Service Management*, *24*(5), 553–566.

Rosenbaum, M. S., Corus, C., Ostrom, A. L., Anderson, L., Fisk, R. P., Gallan, A. S., Giraldo, M., Mende, M., Mulder, M., Rayburn, S. W., Shirahada, K., & Williams, J. D. (2011). Conceptualization and aspirations of transformative service research. *Journal of Research for Consumers*, *19*, 1–6.

Rydén, P., Ringberg, T., & Wilke, R. (2015). How managers' shared mental models of business–customer interactions create different sensemaking of social media. *Journal of Interactive Marketing*, *31*, 1–16.

Seppänen, K., Huiskonen, J., Koivuniemi, J., & Karppinen, H. (2017). Revealing customer dominant logic in healthcare services. *International Journal of Services and Operations Management*, *26*(1), 1–17.

Shapiro, B. P. (1988). *What the hell is market oriented?* (pp. 1–3). HBR Reprints.

Sheth, J. N., & Parvatiyar, A. (1995). The evolution of relationship marketing. *International Business Review*, *4*(4), 397–418.

Shugan, S. M. (2004). Finance, Operations, and Marketing Conflicts in Service Firms, in Day, G. S., Deighton, J., Narayandas, D., Gummesson, E., Hunt, S. D., Prahalad, C. K., Rust, R. & Shugan, S. M. Invited commentaries on "Evolving to a new dominant logic for marketing." *Journal of Marketing*, *68*(1), 24–26.

Slater, S. F., & Narver, J. C. (1998). Customer-led and market-oriented: Let's not confuse the two. *Strategic Management Journal*, *19*(10), 1001–1006.

Storbacka, K., & Nenonen, S. (2011). Scripting markets: From value propositions to market propositions. *Industrial Marketing Management*, *40*(2), 255–266.

Storbacka, K., & Nenonen, S. (2015). Learning with the market: Facilitating market innovation. *Industrial Marketing Management*, *44*, 73–82.

Strandvik, T., & Heinonen, K. (2013). Diagnosing service brand strength: Customer-dominant brand relationship mapping. *Journal of Service Management*, *24*(5), 502–519.

Strandvik, T., & Heinonen, K. (2015). Essentials of customer dominant logic. In J. Gummerus & C. von Koskull (Eds.), *The Nordic School: Service marketing and management for the future* (pp. 111–127). Helsinki and Finland: CERS, Hanken School of Economics.

Strandvik, T., Heinonen, K., & Vollmer, S. (2018). Revealing business customers' hidden value formation in service. *Journal of Business & Industrial Marketing.* https://doi.org/10.1108/JBIM-11-2017-0259 (EarlyCite).

Strandvik, T., Holmlund, M., & Edvardsson, B. (2012). Customer needing: A challenge for the seller offering. *Journal of Business & Industrial Marketing, 27*(2), 132–141.

Strandvik, T., Holmlund, M., & Lähteenmäki, I. (2018). "One of these days, things are going to change!" How do you make sense of market disruption? *Business Horizons, 61*(3), 477–486.

Tynan, C., McKechnie, S., & Hartley, S. (2014). Interpreting value in the customer service experience using customer-dominant logic. *Journal of Marketing Management, 30*(9–10), 1058–1081.

Vargo, S. L., & Lusch, R. F. (2004). Evolving to a new dominant logic for marketing. *Journal of Marketing, 68*(1), 1–17.

Vargo, S. L., & Lusch, R. F. (2008). From goods to service(s): Divergences and convergences of logics. *Industrial Marketing Management, 37*(3), 254–259.

Vargo, S. L., & Lusch, R. F. (2016). Institutions and axioms: An extension and update of service-dominant logic. *Journal of the Academy of Marketing Science, 44*(1), 5–23.

Vargo, S. L., & Lusch, R. F. (2017). Service-dominant logic 2025. *International Journal of Research in Marketing, 34*(1), 46–67.

Vargo, S. L., Maglio, P. P., & Akaka, M. A. (2008). On value and value co-creation: A service systems and service logic perspective. *European Management Journal, 26*(3), 145–152.

Wedel, M., & Kannan, P. K. (2016). Marketing analytics for data-rich environments. *Journal of Marketing, 80*(6), 97–121.

Wirtz, J., Patterson, P. G., Kunz, W. H., Gruber, T., Lu, V. N., Paluch, S., & Martins, A. (2018). Brave new world: Service robots in the frontline. *Journal of Service Management, 29*(5), 907–931.

Wuenderlich, N. V., Heinonen, K., Ostrom, A. L., Patrício, L., Sousa, R., Voss, C., & Lemmink, J. G. (2015). "Futurizing" smart service: Implications for service researchers and managers. *Journal of Services Marketing, 29*(6/7), 442–447.

Xu, Y., Yap, S. F. C., & Hyde, K. F. (2016). Who is talking, who is listening? Service recovery through online customer-to-customer interactions. *Marketing Intelligence & Planning, 34*(3), 421–443.

5

The servitization of manufacturing industries

Bernhard Dachs, Christian Lerch, and Michael Weschta

Introduction

All modern economies are service economies. Services overtook manufacturing industries in terms of output and employment and became the dominant sectors in all European countries and the US. This structural change toward the tertiary sector is known as 'tertiarization.'

However, there is another type of tertiarization: in recent years, there is a tendency in manufacturing firms to complement or replace their output of physical goods with service offerings. This trend takes place at the level of goods, not sectors. This trend may be referred to as 'servitization' (Baines & Lightfoot, 2013; Vandermerwe & Rada, 1988), to distinguish it from tertiarization as defined above. Other terms that describe service offerings by manufacturing firms include *product-related services* (Frambach, Wels-Lips, & Gündlach, 1997), *product-service systems* (Mont, 2002; Tukker & Tischner, 2006), *service infusion* (Brax, 2005), or *integrated solutions* (Brax & Jonsson, 2009; Davies, Brady, & Hobday, 2007). Examples of services offered by manufacturing firms include:

- an electronics firm also develops software and provides software updates;
- a railway manufacturer offers training to client staff;
- a car manufacturer provides financing to clients;
- a brewery sells third party products in addition to its own products;
- a producer of machinery provides installation, maintenance, and recycling of old equipment;
- a gas turbine manufacturer operates the equipment for the client;
- a chemical company produces for clients and documents the production process, its emissions, etc., to assist clients in meeting legal requirements.

A rich literature on the servitization of manufacturing has evolved in the past 30 years (Gebauer, Fleisch, & Friedli, 2005; Mathieu, 2001a, 2001b; Oliva & Kallenberg, 2003; Vandermerwe & Rada, 1988). There are also some recent review papers (Baines, Lightfoot, Benedettini, & Kay, 2009; Carlborg et al., 2014; Kowalkowski, Gebauer, & Oliva, 2017; Luoto, Brax, & Kohtamäki, 2017; Rabetino, Harmsen, Kohtamäki, & Sihvonen, 2018; Tukker, 2015) and a textbook (Baines & Lightfoot, 2013). Servitization is a cross-disciplinary topic; Baines et al. (2009) identify five research communities that have contributed to this literature.

A basic definition for servitization, which works for most contexts, is brought forward by Vandermerwe and Rada (1988, p. 314), in one of the most frequently cited papers on the topic: they regard servitization as the practice of companies to enrich their offerings of material products with immaterial services. This can include different types of services, such as services related to the physical good, but also more product-independent services focusing on the processes of the client (Mathieu, 2001a).

Various authors provided taxonomies of different service offerings by manufacturing firms based on the value proposition (Kindström & Kowalkowski, 2014). Such taxonomies differentiate between services that support products versus customer processes (Oliva & Kallenberg, 2003), or distinguish between firms that sell the utility derived from a good as a service, rather than selling the good itself. Terms such as 'Pay-Per-Use,' 'Operator Models,' 'Availability Contracts,' and 'Integrated Solutions' describe these kinds of services. Thus, servitization is changing the core businesses of companies – including what companies offer to their customers, and the ways companies generate revenue. Moreover, servitization is seen as a path toward greater sustainability (Bellos & Ferguson, 2017; Tukker, 2015).

Servitization is closely related to digitization, the diffusion of information and communication technologies (ICTs) in the economy. Blinder (2006) argues that ICTs made services more standardized and tradable over the last 30 years, bridging the divide between physical goods and services. Thus, servitization is one of the drivers of a convergence between manufacturing and services (De Backer, Desnoyers-James, & Moussiegt, 2015). Moreover, digitization also allows new services by manufacturing firms based on the Internet of Things (IoT) and Industrie 4.0 (Paschou, Adrodegari, Perona, & Saccani, 2017; Rymaszewska, Helo, & Gunasekaran, 2017). These technologies offer new insights into how customers use a firm's products, which in turn provides new approaches to service provision and value generation.

In recent years, some excellent literature surveys on servitization have been published which discuss the phenomenon in detail (Baines et al., 2009; Carlborg et al., 2014; Kowalkowski et al., 2017; Luoto et al., 2017; Rabetino et al., 2018; Tukker, 2015). Therefore, the next section in this chapter focuses on the 'Empirical evidence for servitization.' Following that, 'Motives for servitization' briefly discusses the motives of manufacturing firms to offer services, and 'Obstacles to servitization' deals with issues that cause servitization to be more difficult. Finally, 'Digitization and servitization' provides insights into the recent literature on firm decisions to digitize and servitize; the chapter closes with 'Conclusions.'

Empirical evidence for servitization

This chapter provides empirical evidence for servitization of manufacturing firms from two sources: first, it employs data from the supply tables of input-output statistics. These supply tables were compiled by the WIOD (World Input-Output Database) project (Dietzenbacher, Los, Stehrer, Timmer, & de Vries, 2013). The second data source is the European Manufacturing Survey (2015), a firm-level survey that collects data on innovation in manufacturing.

Macroeconomic evidence for servitization

Input-output statistics relate the inputs of goods, capital, and labour to outputs of goods and services in an economy. In particular, supply tables – as a part of input-output statistics – keep track of which industry produces what good or service in an economy. The focus is on the primary output of the industry, but non-characteristic outputs, such as electricity produced by the pulp and paper industry, or transport services provided by the steel industry, are also recorded. This makes input-output data one of the rare sources allowing comparison of the servitization of manufacturing across countries.

Figure 5.1 depicts the share of services in manufacturing output for various countries, and breaks down total service output into three different types of services. Small- and medium-sized economies such as Finland, Sweden, the Netherlands, Australia, or Belgium reveal the highest shares of servitization. In contrast, larger countries (including the US and Japan) show only moderate or low levels of servitization. The UK and Germany, large countries which are characterized by medium levels of servitization, are exceptions. One possible explanation for this pattern is market size and specialization: large domestic markets offer suppliers of goods-related services more opportunities for specialization outside the boundaries of manufacturing firms and allow more division of labour between manufacturing and service providers.

Some countries (including France, Taiwan, Russia, and Mexico) report no service output for manufacturing firms, and the value for China is close to zero. This does not mean that there is no servitization in these countries; it is unlikely that French manufacturing firms offer no services, because neighbouring countries in the European Union reveal considerable service output in manufacturing. More likely, this is instead the effect of different statistical practices, rather than a lack of service offerings from manufacturing firms in these countries.

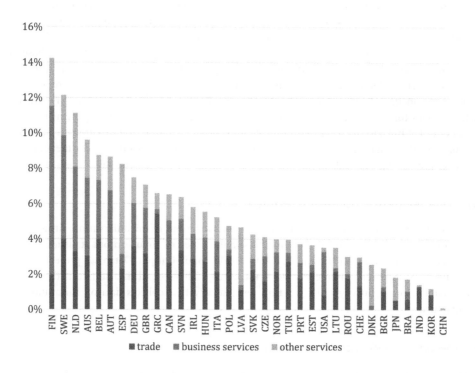

Figure 5.1   Share of services in total output of manufacturing firms, 2014.

Note: Sources include WIOD (2016) and see Dietzenbacher et al. (2013); own calculations.

Thus, results based on input-output statistics describing servitization should be interpreted cautiously.

Comparing the results from input-output statistics with previous findings at the country level (Neely, 2008; Neely, Benedetinni, & Visnjic, 2011), it becomes apparent that the biggest outlier is the United States. Neely et al. (2011) reported that the US was the country with the highest level of servitization in their sample. These authors focused on groups of companies and not on individual enterprises, so it is possible that the service business of some US-based company groups is organized into independent firms, which are not regarded as manufacturing but as service firms. Thus, the service business would not have been counted as manufacturing output by input-output statistics. For China, Neely et al. (2011) observed a surge in service output of manufacturing firms between 2007 and 2011, which is also visible in the present data (see Figure 5.2). However, the level of servitization was still very low in China in 2014.

In addition to providing the total service share, Figure 5.1 also breaks down total service output into three different types of services, two of which constitute the majority of the service output of manufacturing firms. First, manufacturing firms are engaged in considerable trading activities, in particular wholesale trade. Trade services account for 10% of total output of manufacturing in Luxembourg, and for 3%–5% of total manufacturing output in Greece, Belgium, Sweden, Malta, and Germany. The vast majority of trade services, however, are generated by retail and wholesale trade in all countries.

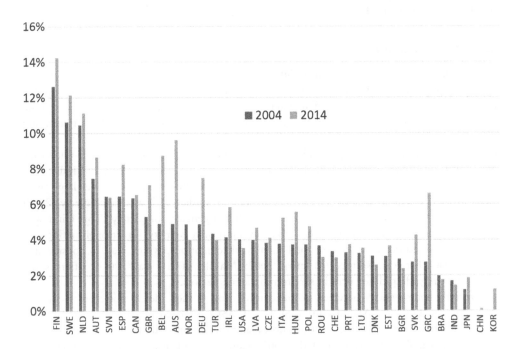

Figure 5.2 Share of services in the output of manufacturing firms, 2004 and 2014.

Note: Sources include WIOD (2016) and see Dietzenbacher et al. (2013); own calculations.

Business services are a second relevant category of total service output. This includes a heterogeneous group of activities, such as computer and software services, accounting and consulting, technical and R&D services, and advertising. Some of these services have very close ties to manufactured products, such as technical services or consulting. The third category – 'other services' – consists of a broad spectrum of different activities, which are all considerably smaller than the first two categories.

The median annual growth rate of service output in manufacturing across countries was 5%, which is higher than the median growth rate of the corresponding output of physical products in the period 2004–2014. As a result of the faster growth of services, the share of services in total manufacturing output increased from 2004 to 2014 in the majority of countries (see Figure 5.2).

The largest increases in the share of services in manufacturing output are found in Australia, Greece, Belgium, Germany, and Luxembourg. Luxembourg had a value of 19.6% for 2004, so it is excluded from Figure 5.2 because it is so large as to be off the scale. In absolute terms, service output increased most in Korea, China, Slovakia, and Poland. However, as can be seen in Figure 5.2, servitization in Korea and China started from very low initial levels.

Despite considerable differences between the countries, input-output data show that servitization is a global phenomenon, which is also taking place in emerging economies. Differences between countries may result from different statistical practices; however, they may also be related to factors of national specialization which are not yet well understood. One of these factors is the sectoral composition of the manufacturing sector in each country, given that different industries reveal different degrees of servitization. Other factors that may impact the overall degree of servitization measured in a country include the size distribution in manufacturing, export intensity, the presence of lead users for services in the country, and the diffusion of IoT and Big Data.

Servitization and firm characteristics

It is difficult to make sense of country differences without systematic evidence of the underlying firm population and, more generally, the incentives and obstacles firms face due to different sizes, different sectors, or different stages of the value chain. Unfortunately, very little attention has been given to differences in the characteristics of firms that offer services, and how these differences relate to the servitization process. Baines et al. (2009, p. 555) observe that '… the majority of these [exemplars] are large multinationals supporting high-value capital equipment.' One example is offered in the highly cited article by Oliva and Kallenberg (2003) describing the equipment industry. Moreover, case studies typically cover large firms (e.g., Fischer, Gebauer, & Fleisch, 2012). Quantitative studies such as that of Neely (2008) consider firm size, but typically neglect sectoral heterogeneity completely. This blind spot seems surprising, because servitization – like any innovative activity – is strongly influenced by firm characteristics as well as sectoral framework conditions, which lead to considerable heterogeneity between sectors (Malerba, 2002; Marsili, 2001). Lay (2014) offers some impressions regarding differences in servitization across sectors.

To study heterogeneity between manufacturing firms in more detail, this chapter employs data from the European Manufacturing Survey (EMS) completed in 2015. At the company level, EMS surveys the utilization of techno-organizational innovations in the manufacturing sector. The data for this chapter include 3,067 manufacturing firms with at least ten employees from nine European countries (Austria, Croatia, Denmark, Germany, the Netherlands, Slovenia, Serbia, Spain, and Switzerland). Results are calculated based on 2,269 firms that gave information on service turnover. There are 1,505 firms reporting a positive service turnover, so approximately half of all firms in the sample are servitized.

Figure 5.3 presents sectoral differences in servitization as measured by the average service turnover. It includes turnover from services that are directly invoiced to the client, as well as indirect service turnover as generated by product-service systems or integrated solutions.

The data show that machinery and manufacturers of transport equipment are the most servitized sector, generating 15% and 13% of their turnover from services, respectively, whereas the average share across all sectors is about 10%. The manufacturing of computers, electronics and optical products, the metal sectors, and electrical equipment sit in the middle of the distribution, whereas the producers of plastic products, the pulp and paper industry, and the chemical industry are less servitized. The least servitized sector in the figure is the food industry. Firms in this sector deliver a total service turnover of only 3%.

Considering the share of indirect service turnover as an indicator of clients' willingness to pay, it seems that this willingness is highest in machinery and transport equipment, and lowest in the food industry. The food industry is also the sector where the share of indirect service revenues as a share of total turnover is highest, which points to a low willingness of clients to pay for additional services.

These results put the body of case studies on servitization into perspective – some of the best-known cases (including Rolls-Royce, Alstrom, ABB, and Caterpillar) come from the

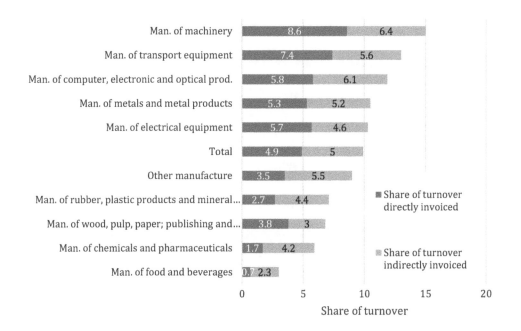

Figure 5.3 Share of direct and indirect turnover from services in manufacturing firms by sector, 2014.

Note: Sources include European Manufacturing Survey (2015); own calculations.

most servitized sector, and it is no coincidence that very little evidence exists in regard to the food industry.

Servitization is closely related to the physical products of a firm and how they are produced. Thus, one of the most important determinants of servitization at the firm level is production characteristics, such as product complexity and lot size. Figure 5.4 shows the relationship between these two production characteristics and the share of service turnover of firms. There is a positive relationship between product complexity and the share of direct and indirect service turnover: complex products need more training, support, maintenance, etc., in the form of services, and this increases the potential for servitization and turnover of services.

Manufacturing firms producing in single lot sizes exhibit distinctly higher service turnover than firms producing in small/medium lot sizes, or even in large lot sizes. Consequently, there is a negative relationship between lot size and the share of service turnover. This is a clear indication that servitization and customization go hand in hand; it may be that firms that produce individual products follow a goods dominant logic (Vargo & Lusch, 2004) to a much lower degree than do mass producers, because individual products require more interaction with the client. However, it may also be that big lot manufacturing produces goods that require less assistance in the form of services by producers.

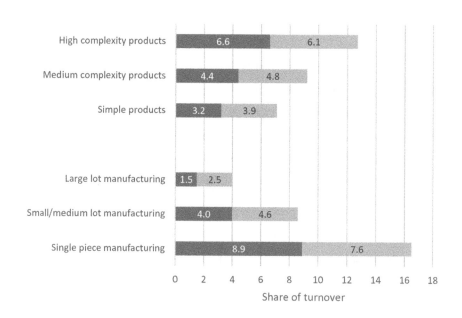

Figure 5.4 Share of direct and indirect turnover from services in manufacturing firms by production characteristics, 2014.

Note: Sources include European Manufacturing Survey (2015); own calculations.

The servitization literature pays little attention to the question of whether small or large firms are better suited for servitization. Neely (2008) showed that the share of servitized firms increases with firm size in a sample that is limited to firms with more than 100 employees, but did not investigate this further. Kowalkowski, Witell, & Gustafsson (2013) reported that SMEs often lack the knowledge or the resources needed for successful servitization.

Contrary to these findings, the present data show that small companies (49 or fewer employees) generate a total share of 11 % of turnover in services; medium-sized companies (50 to 249 employees) generate a share of 10%, and large companies (250 and more employees) a service share of 9%. This indicates that small firms have advantages in servitization, which may be due to faster decision processes, more agility, and greater willingness to specialize to the needs of the customer. There is, however, evidence from a previous paper using EMS data (Dachs et al., 2014) that the relationship between firm size and servitization is U-shaped, with higher servitization levels for small firms on the one hand and also for very large firms (1,000 or more employees) on the other hand.

Motives for servitization

Servitization is increasing in the majority of countries, which leads to the question, what are the drivers and motives of this process? To find the reasons that manufacturers offer services, it is necessary to look at the potential benefits. Mathieu (2001b) suggested three types of benefits that firms can derive from servitization, which subsequently found wide recognition in the literature. She distinguished between financial benefits, strategic benefits, and marketing benefits, and discussed all three in detail. These categories are utilized below.

The *financial benefits* of servitization are well documented in the literature: services foster revenue growth in manufacturing firms (Eggert, Hogreve, Ulaga, & Muenkhoff, 2014). Moreover, Reinartz and Ulaga (2008) report that services often provide higher margins than physical products. In contrast, the evidence presented by Neely (2008) indicates that profitability of servitized firms is lower than it is in pure manufacturing firms. A possible explanation brought forward by Visnjic Kastalli and Van Looy (2013) is a U-shaped relationship between profitability and service offerings, wherein profitability first decreases as servitization increases, and then increases after a threshold is reached (see also Kohtamäki, Partanen, Parida, & Wincent, 2013). Another financial benefit from servitization is the generation of revenues over the entire life cycle of a product (Cohen & Whang, 1997; Lockett, Johnson, Evans, & Bastl, 2011). Furthermore, services can help firms to diversify their sources of earnings and reduce their vulnerability to demand shocks related to manufactured goods. Oliva and Kallenberg (2003, p. 163) point out the importance of the installed base (the number of products of a firm in use) to servitization. A large installed base can be an asset for firms that aim to increase their service revenue, because it means many potential clients for services. However, a large installed base also indicates that the market for the product is mature/saturated, and servitization is a reaction to sluggish revenue growth.

A second motive for servitization is to gain *strategic benefits*. These benefits are primarily related to gaining competitive advantage and avoiding commoditization. Product differentiation via services can help to reduce price competition in mature product markets (Baines & Lightfoot, 2013; Gebauer, Gustafsson, & Witell, 2011). Service characteristics such as employee qualifications, friendliness, and responsiveness may be harder for competitors to copy than are design and other features of physical artefacts. Additional strategic advantage arises when a service provider can 'lock in' customers to their services (Neely, 2008, p. 104). In addition, product differentiation may hamper potential market entrants.

Finally, the servitization literature assumes that services provide *marketing benefits* to manufacturing firms. Services and the interactions involved in service provision can help to build deeper relationships and greater loyalty between clients and suppliers than can simply selling physical products (Penttinen & Palmer, 2007; Vandermerwe & Rada, 1988). Vandermerwe and Rada (1988, p. 321) make the point that if a company sends a service team to work together with a customer, they can find out if their current product is right for the customer's needs, which can serve as market research. Mey Goh and McMahon (2009) and Dachs et al. (2014) point out that information gathered in the process of service provision can benefit the innovation processes of firms and can help manufacturers to design better and more reliable products. Visnjic, Wiengarten, Neely (2016) stress the complementarities between service business model innovation and product innovation that benefit the longterm performance of firms.

Obstacles to servitization

If services can provide additional revenues, barriers to entry, improved customer relationships, and better market information to manufacturing firms, why is there so little servitization? The answer to this question lies in some pervasive obstacles that have been identified in the literature. The 'service paradox' in manufacturing firms observed by Gebauer et al. (2005) brings these obstacles to the point: successful servitization requires considerable investment as well as substantial changes in organizational structure and mindset. However, manufacturing firms are frequently risk-averse and locked into their current business models for tangible products.

Servitization requires that firms develop a service-dominant logic on innovation, in contrast to the goods-dominant logic prevalent in many manufacturing firms (Lusch & Nambisan, 2015; Vargo & Lusch, 2004). In order to become a successful service provider, a firm needs to change:

> from thinking about the purpose of firm activity as *making something* (goods or services) to a process of *assisting customers in their own value-creation processes*; from thinking about *value* as something *produced* and sold to thinking about value as something *co-created* with the customer and other value-creation partners; ... from thinking of *customers as targets* to thinking of *customers as resources*.
>
> *(Vargo & Lusch, 2008, p. 258)*

A goods-dominant logic focuses on a high division of labour in a factory, and on the separation of production and consumption to increase control and productivity. These characteristics are not appropriate for many services, for two reasons. First, modularity is too low for an extensive division of labour in many services and, second, the exchange and interaction with customers is essential for services provision ('co-creation'). Thus, managerial ignorance of service-dominant logic and over-emphasis of risks can become a self-fulfilling prophecy, contributing to the service paradox.

Neely (2008, p. 113) contributes quantitative evidence that servitization can lead to lower profits, especially for large firms. In addition, this author found a disproportionately high share of bankruptcies among servitized firms in his sample (Neely, 2008, p. 108). Eggert et al. (2014) provide evidence that only firms having both decentralized decision-making processes and loyal customers can expect favourable financial results from servitization. Eggert et al. (2014) and Witell and Löfgren (2013) both found evidence that points toward a low willingness of customers to pay for services as an obstacle to servitization in manufacturing firms (see also Neely, 2008, p. 115). Firms that have provided services in the past as an add-on, free of charge, are especially vulnerable. A low willingness to pay is one reason, among others, that many firms provide services and physical goods in bundles and invoice them indirectly (see the section entitled 'Servitization and firm characteristics'). Another solution may be to make services more visible and measurable, with the help of ICT.

Digitization and servitization

The strongest push toward servitization today can be expected from new digital technologies in manufacturing, such as the IoT (or Industrie 4.0), 3D printing, advanced robotics, artificial intelligence (AI), blockchains, and cybersecurity. The OECD (2017, p. 26) speaks of these developments as 'the next production revolution.'

Much discussion focuses on the IoT, which allows firms to gather detailed information on the status of goods and components, their usage by clients, potential failures, and other performance indicators. Such data are collected using networked sensors inside the production equipment, in aircraft engines, trucks, trains, and others. Data collected by these sensors may be the basis for new or considerably improved IoT-enabled services (*digital servitization*). A central role for the development of these services will have methods to analyze Big Data.

There is a broad consensus in the policy literature that the IoT can help firms in the process of servitization. Documents often mention complementarities between IoT, new business models, and new service offers by manufacturing firms. For example, the OECD (2017, p. 35) finds that 'another notable effect of the IoT is to make industry more services-like. This is because manufacturers can provide customers with new pay-as-you-go services based on real-time monitoring of product use.' The widely recognized recommendations of the German National Academy of Science and Engineering (acatech) on Industrie 4.0 discuss new business models and partnership opportunities that are enabled by Industrie 4.0 (Kagermann, Wahlster, & Helbig, 2013, p. 22).

The idea of a technology push in servitization has also been addressed in the academic literature (Ostrom, Parasuraman, Bowen, Patrício, & Voss, 2015; Paschou et al., 2017; Rust & Huang, 2014). This is an important research direction, because most contributions do not relate servitization to technological innovation. However, Paschou et al. (2017) observed that the literature on servitization and the literature on digitization developed somewhat in isolation from each other.

A part of the literature on digital servitization discusses the technological foundations of the trend. Fleisch, Weinberger, and Wortmann (2015) explained the connection between Industrie 4.0 and services, using an approach that puts an emphasis on bridging the digital and physical worlds. Gorldt, Wiesner, Westphal, and Thoben (2017) introduced the concept of a Cyber-Physical Product-Service System (CPSS). This is an intelligent product that provides monitoring, controlling, and data processing, and acts as a bridge between the physical and the digital worlds; it also acts as the technological basis for services. Rymaszewska et al. (2017) proposed a conceptual framework of how the IoT enables servitization. Baines and Lightfoot (2013) discussed how manufacturers can deploy ICT for the delivery of services, and Naik, Schroeder, Ziaee Bigdeli, and Baines (2017) analysed (with the help of the affordance theory) how digital capabilities enable servitization.

The literature on digital servitization provides a large number of examples for digital service offers by manufacturing firms. Table 5.1 provides a categorization of IoT-based services offered, based on various articles and book chapters that are primarily from Germany. Digital services are classified into five groups, from services that support the customer in the selection of the right product, to services that help the customer to operate the product in the most efficient way. In all five groups, the interaction of the service provider with the client is essential and the data gathered from the client and processed by the service provider are in the centre of the interaction.

Asset management and information services (Table 5.1, rows 1 and 2) provide a closer interaction with customers. Rymaszewska et al. (2017) argue that IoT helps firms to better

Table 5.1 Types of digital services by manufacturing firms

Asset/stock management services Using data from the customer's operations to ensure that the customer has the optimal assets/materials	• Selection of suitable products for the customer (Gebauer et al., 2017) • Using operational data to discover and fulfil customer demand for new products and functionalities (Jüttner et al., 2017; VDI/VDE, 2016) • Web-based monitoring and replenishment of inventories/vendor-managed inventory (Breitfuß et al., 2017; Gebauer et al., 2017)
Information services Providing processed external data or information that support the customer's activities	• Providing environmental data that are relevant for optimizing the product use (Gebauer et al., 2017) • Providing benchmarks using data from different customers (Kaufmann, 2015) • Introducing new forms of interaction with the customer (Coreynen, Matthyssens, & Van Bockhaven, 2017)
Maintenance services Using product data and/or remote access to improve/innovate maintenance	• Predictive maintenance/condition-based maintenance (Gebauer et al., 2017; Jüttner et al., 2017; OECD, 2017; Rymaszewska et al., 2017) • Remote services (Jüttner et al., 2017)
Monitoring services Capturing data from the product (and processing them), then returning them to the customer	• Providing an analysis of operational and feedback data to the customer (Cenamor et al., 2017; Gebauer et al., 2017) • Providing (real-time) condition data to customer (Cenamor et al., 2017; Gebauer et al., 2017) • Providing real-time location data to customer (Gebauer et al., 2017) • Providing analysed data about the product environment to the customer (Lassnig, Stabauer, Güntner, & Breitfuß, 2017) • Providing monitoring services that include products of competitors (Jüttner et al., 2017) • Providing scanning services for customized production (Coreynen et al., 2017).
Optimization services Using product data to improve the customer's use of the product	• Optimizing fleet operations (Gebauer et al., 2017; OECD, 2017) • Providing consulting on how to make product use more efficient, based on recent operational data (Jüttner et al., 2017; VDI/VDE, 2016) • Recalibrating/updating smart products according to recent operational data (e.g., per remote access/automatically) (Gebauer et al., 2017; Herterich, Eck, & Uebernickel, 2016; Jüttner et al., 2017; VDI/VDE, 2016)

Source: own compilation.

serve their customers because it provides firms with real product usage data. Before IoT, servitized manufacturers had to rely on their expertise to offer services. In a survey among machine building companies, Lichtblau et al. (2015, p. 51) found that product development was the most frequent purpose of analysing product usage data. Rust and Huang (2014) stressed that information technology can deepen and personalize service relationships. Cenamor, Rönnberg Sjödin, and Parida (2017) concluded that information modules (*in a platform approach to servitization*) should replace both good and service modules as the core modules for successful servitization. Moreover, the data generated from services are not necessarily attractive only for manufacturers. Some authors (e.g., Fleisch et al., 2015; VDI/VDE, 2016) suggest that revenue can be generated – within the terms of the service contract with the client – by selling data to third parties.

Another type of IoT-based service is new maintenance and monitoring services (Table 5.1, row 3 and 4). Real-time data collected by sensors from equipment can be used for detailed performance monitoring and the prediction of failures. This not only leads to reduced warranty costs for the producer (Gebauer, Joncourt, & Saul, 2017), but it also saves maintenance costs for the client (Jüttner, Windler, Schäfer, & Zimmermann, 2017). Similarly, as connected products make it possible to react to changing customer requirements by applying small upgrades, manufacturers can shorten response times and speed up innovation cycles, without introducing a new product every time (Lerch & Gotsch, 2015, p. 50; Rymaszewska et al., 2017, p. 102).

Finally, equipment manufacturers can use customer data to optimize the use of their equipment, even if the equipment is operated by the client (Table 5.1, last row). This, however, needs detailed regulation to control what the equipment manufacturer is allowed to do. This may be a first step toward operator-based models.

Table 5.2 provides a classification of different revenue models that were identified in the literature in the context of digital servitization. The sample is small, but from the examples it is apparent that IoT offers firms new opportunities to generate income.

Indirect service sales (Table 5.2, row 1) are a well-known strategy of manufacturing firms to increase the attractiveness of their physical products with service. Transaction-based models were also used by manufacturing firms in the past, but these are considerably facilitated by the data generated by IoT. This is even more true for outcome-based and usage-based revenue models, where services are billed according to the outcome per unit of use. Here, the IoT can create the technological basis for a much larger diffusion of such revenue models and act as a driver for servitization.

Recent research identified some *necessary conditions* and *potential obstacles* to digital servitization. Challenges which arise from goods-dominant logic are also relevant in digital servitization. In order to deal with large amounts of data, companies need a range of new ICT capabilities (Ardolino et al., 2018; Cenamor et al., 2017). This includes identification and tracking of products and users, geo-localization, condition monitoring, timing and intensity assessment, data analysis, prediction, visualization, and others. AI is key for a number of these capabilities. Moreover, it is not always understood that new/innovative entrants could threaten existing business models, even in niches (VDI/VDE, 2016). Due to reduced product and technology life cycles, companies must speed up their innovation processes, requiring more resources to which not all companies have access. Furthermore, the adoption of fast and agile innovation methods, which are advantageous for developing software, can clash with an existing culture that is useful in developing physical products (Fleisch et al., 2015, p. 14).

To offer IoT-based services, a provider must ensure that customers are ready to use these services. This includes having the right technical equipment, such as smart products, among

Table 5.2 Revenue models used in digital servitization

Indirect service sales Services are provided free of additional charge as part of a product or package	• Smart services that are not billed, but are monetarized through facilitated product sales (Jüttner et al., 2017) • Service component as additional option to be purchased with the product (Rymaszewska et al., 2017)	**PRODUCT SALES**
Transaction-based Products are sold, and services are paid per transaction	• Purchase of spare parts and repair service (Obermaier, 2016) • Purchase of a product (Ziegler & Rossmann, 2017)	
Service contract Separate from product purchase; guarantees the customer a performance level, maintenance is the responsibility of the supplier	• Fixed service fee for maintenance and an availability guarantee (Obermaier, 2016; Rymaszewska et al., 2017)	
Outcome-based revenue model A service or product is priced according to its outcome or success, which is measured by capturing data. Product ownership may not be transferred	• Pay for savings (Obermaier, 2016) • Pay for process improvements (Jüttner et al., 2017) • Pay for performance/availability (Baines & Lightfoot, 2013; Kaufmann, 2015) • Pay for deterioration of the product (Kaufmann, 2015)	
Usage-based revenue model A product or service is paid for per unit of use, while ownership is not transferred. Usage may be measured by IoT	• Pay-per-hour/month (Baines & Lightfoot, 2013; Lassnig et al., 2017; OECD, 2017) • Pay-per-mile (Gebauer et al., 2017; VDI/VDE, 2016) • Pay-per-unit (Kaufmann, 2015; VDI/VDE, 2016)	**SERVICE SALES**

Source: own compilation.

other requirements. Contrary to conventional servitization thinking, a large installed base can be an obstacle for digital servitization if the installed equipment is not capable of being integrated into the new business model (VDI, 2016, p. 16). Finally, the provider may need to ensure that a customer's employees have the skills and technical abilities to use the services (Bruhn & Hadwich, 2017).

An important factor in digital servitization is also the mindset of the customers: some customers might have an aversion to new technology and/or might be concerned about data security (Bruhn & Hadwich, 2017). Systems security is especially important in usage- or outcome-based revenue models (VDI/VDE, 2016). Customers might also be worried about a drain of their know-how (Kagermann et al., 2013 p. 22). Kaufmann (2015, p. 24) observed that customers are often reluctant to share data or authorize its use, until they have been convinced about the value of its potential benefits.

Conclusion

Servitization is the practice of manufacturing firms to enrich their offerings of material products with services. Evidence from input-output tables indicates that servitization is increasing, both in absolute and in relative terms, in the majority of countries. Small- and medium-sized economies in Europe reveal the highest levels of servitization to date. Manufacturers of machinery and transport equipment are the most servitized industries, generating 15% and 13% of their turnover from services, respectively.

The literature provides various reasons for firms to servitize; strong motives include financial advantages, such as higher and more stable revenues. Services can also help firms to differentiate their products from those of competitors, and can provide a more appealing value proposition to their clients. However, servitization strategies require considerable financial investment as well as organizational change, and firms may be unwilling to commit to such a service-dominant logic. These factors also explain why firms might be disappointed by the economic results of the new service business. (The servitization literature provides many examples of manufacturing firms that failed to generate satisfying benefits from services.)

New production technologies such as the IoT or Industrie 4.0 provide a new momentum for servitization. The IoT generates large amounts of data regarding how clients use the equipment, which may lead the way to a better understanding of the needs of customers. In addition, such data provides an opportunity for new services, or for new outcome- or usage-based revenue models. However, it is a huge step from unstructured usage data to services that create value for the consumer. A part of the value proposition to the customer lies in the analysis and interpretation of the data. Thus, digital servitization requires investments in new capabilities by firms, a recurrent topic in the servitization literature.

The results of this chapter provide some conclusions for managers. Managers can expect a continuation of the servitization trend because, on the one hand, the saturation in many mature markets will tempt firms to look for new sources of revenue in services. On the other hand, technological change that comes with the IoT will open opportunities for new services. To grasp this opportunity, firms need a clear servitization strategy, must be prepared for change, and must be ready to invest considerably in new competencies.

For academic research, scholars should consider heterogeneity between firms in servitization, and how this heterogeneity relates to servitization intensity and strategies. Important dimensions that are related to differences are the home country, business sector, firm size, production technologies, export orientation, and position in the value chain. These factors are often underappreciated sources of variation in observed servitization strategies and performance.

Finally, trends such as Big Data or the IoT point to the growing importance of new technologies for servitization. In the past, the academic literature on servitization and on digitization developed somewhat in isolation from each other. A stronger integration of these two research streams, such as by investigating the interrelations between technological innovation and servitization strategies, is a fruitful direction for future research.

References

Ardolino, M., Rapaccini, M., Saccani, N., Gaiardelli, P., Crespi, G., & Ruggeri, C. (2018). The role of digital technologies for the service transformation of industrial companies. *International Journal of Production Research, 56*(6), 2116–2132.

Baines, T. S., & Lightfoot, H. W. (2013). *Made to serve: How manufacturers can compete through servitization and product-service systems*. Chichester: Wiley.

Baines, T. S., Lightfoot, H. W., Benedettini, O., & Kay, J. M. (2009). The servitization of manufacturing: A review of literature and reflection on future challenges. *Journal of Manufacturing Technology Management*, *20*(5), 547–567.

Bellos, I., & Ferguson, M. (2017). Moving from a product-based economy to a service-based economy for a more sustainable future. In Y. Bouchery, C. J. Corbett, J. C. Fransoo, & T. Tan (Eds.), *Sustainable supply chains: A research-based textbook on operations and strategy* (pp. 355–373). Cham: Springer International Publishing.

Blinder, A. S. (2006). Offshoring: The next industrial revolution? *Foreign Affairs*, *85*(2), 113–128.

Brax, S. A. (2005). A manufacturer becoming service provider: Challenges and a paradox. *Managing Service Quality: An International Journal*, *15*(2), 142–155.

Brax, S. A., & Jonsson, K. (2009). Developing integrated solution offerings for remote diagnostics: A comparative case study of two manufacturers. *International Journal of Operations & Production Management*, *29*(5), 539–560.

Breitfuß, G., Mauthner, K., Lassnig, M., Stabauer, P., Güntner, G., Stummer, M., ... Meilinger, A. (2017). Analyse von Geschäftsmodell-Innovationen durch die digitale Transformation mit Industrie 4.0. Salzburg: Salzburg Research.

Bruhn, M., & Hadwich, K. (2017). Dienstleistungen 4.0: Erscheinungsformen, Transformationsprozesse und Managementimplikationen. In M. Bruhn & K. Hadwich (Eds.), *Dienstleistungen 4.0: Geschäftsmodelle – Wertschöpfung – Transformation. Band 2. Forum Dienstleistungsmanagement* (pp. 1–39). Wiesbaden: Springer Fachmedien Wiesbaden.

Carlborg, P., Kindström, D., & Kowalkowski, C. (2014). The evolution of service innovation research: A critical review and synthesis. *The Service Industries Journal*, *34*(5), 373–398.

Cenamor, J., Rönnberg Sjödin, D., & Parida, V. (2017). Adopting a platform approach in servitization: Leveraging the value of digitalization. *International Journal of Production Economics*, *192*, 54–65.

Cohen, M. A., & Whang, S. (1997). Competing in product and service: A product life-cycle model. *Management Science*, *43*(4), 535–545. doi:10.1287/mnsc.43.4.535.

Coreynen, W., Matthyssens, P., & Van Bockhaven, W. (2017). Boosting servitization through digitization: Pathways and dynamic resource configurations for manufacturers. *Industrial Marketing Management*, *60*, 42–53.

Dachs, B., Biege, S., Borowiecki, M., Lay, G., Jäger, A., & Schartinger, D. (2014). Servitisation of European manufacturing: Evidence from a large scale database. *The Service Industries Journal*, *34*(1), 5–23.

Davies, A., Brady, T., & Hobday, M. (2007). Organizing for solutions: Systems seller vs. systems integrator. *Industrial Marketing Management*, *36*(2), 183–193.

De Backer, K., Desnoyers-James, I., & Moussiegt, L. (2015). *Manufacturing or services: That is (not) the question. The role of manufacturing and services in OECD economies*. Paris. OECD Science, Technology and Industry Policy Papers No. 19.

Dietzenbacher, E., Los, B., Stehrer, R., Timmer, M. P., & de Vries, G. J. (2013). The construction of world input-output tables in the WIOD project. *Economic Systems Research*, *25*(1), 71–98.

Eggert, A., Hogreve, J., Ulaga, W., & Muenkhoff, E. (2014). Revenue and profit implications of industrial service strategies. *Journal of Service Research*, *17*(1), 23–39.

European Manufacturing Survey. (2015). *Fraunhofer Institute for Systems and Innovation Research*. Available at: www.isi.fraunhofer.de/en/themen/industrielle-wettbewerbsfaehigkeit/fems.html#tabpanel-367861728.

Fischer, T., Gebauer, H., & Fleisch, E. (2012). *Service business development: Strategies for value creation in manufacturing firms*. Cambridge: Cambridge University Press.

Fleisch, E., Weinberger, M., & Wortmann, F. (2015). Business models and the internet of things. In I. P. Žarko, K. Pripužić, & M. Serrano (Eds.), *Interoperability and open-source solutions for the internet of things* (pp. 6–10). Cham: Springer.

Frambach, R. T., Wels-Lips, I., & Gündlach, A. (1997). Proactive product service strategies: An application in the European health market. *Industrial Marketing Management*, *26*(4), 341–352.

Gebauer, H., Fleisch, E., & Friedli, T. (2005). Overcoming the service paradox in manufacturing companies. *European Management Journal*, *23*(1), 14–26.

Gebauer, H., Gustafsson, A., & Witell, L. (2011). Competitive advantage through service differentiation by manufacturing companies. *Journal of Business Research*, *64*(12), 1270–1280.

Gebauer, H., Joncourt, S., & Saul, C. (2017). Transformation von Unternehmen: Technologien und Geschäftsmodelle. In M. Bruhn & K. Hadwich (Eds.), *Dienstleistungen 4.0: Geschäftsmodelle –*

Wertschöpfung – Transformation. Band 2. Forum Dienstleistungsmanagement (pp. 299–313). Wiesbaden: Springer Fachmedien Wiesbaden.

Gorldt, C., Wiesner, S., Westphal, I., & Thoben, K.-D. (2017). Product-Service Systems im Zeitalter von Industrie 4.0 in Produktion und Logistik: Auf dem Weg zu Cyber-Physischen Product-Service Systemen. In M. Bruhn & K. Hadwich (Eds.), *Dienstleistungen 4.0: Geschäftsmodelle – Wertschöpfung – Transformation. Band 2. Forum Dienstleistungsmanagement* (pp. 363–378). Wiesbaden: Springer Fachmedien Wiesbaden.

Herterich, M. M., Eck, A., & Uebernickel, F. (2016). *Exploring how digitized products enable industrial service innovation:an affordance perspective.* In Proceedings of the 24rd European Conference on Information Systems (ECIS), Istanbul.

Jüttner, U., Windler, K., Schäfer, A., & Zimmermann, A. (2017). Design von Smart Services: Eine explorative Studie im Business-to-Business-Sektor. In M. Bruhn & K. Hadwich (Eds.), *Dienstleistungen 4.0: Geschäftsmodelle – Wertschöpfung – Transformation. Band 2. Forum Dienstleistungsmanagement* (pp. 335–361). Wiesbaden: Springer Fachmedien Wiesbaden.

Kagermann, H., Wahlster, W., & Helbig, J. (Eds.). (2013). *Umsetzungsempfehlungen für das Zukunftsprojekt Industrie 4.0. Abschlussbericht des Arbeitskreises Industrie 4.0.* Berlin: acatech: Deutsche Akademie der Technikwissenschaften e.V.

Kaufmann, T. (2015). Datenzentrierte Geschäftsmodelle. In *Geschäftsmodelle in Industrie 4.0 und dem Internet der Dinge: Der Weg vom Anspruch in die Wirklichkeit* (pp. 11–30). Wiesbaden: Springer Fachmedien Wiesbaden.

Kindström, D., & Kowalkowski, C. (2014). Service innovation in product-centric firms: A multidimensional business model perspective. *Journal of Business & Industrial Marketing, 29*(2), 96–111.

Kohtamäki, M., Partanen, J., Parida, V., & Wincent, J. (2013). Non-linear relationship between industrial service offering and sales growth: The moderating role of network capabilities. *Industrial Marketing Management, 42*(8), 1374–1385.

Kowalkowski, C., Gebauer, H., & Oliva, R. (2017). Service growth in product firms: Past, present, and future. *Industrial Marketing Management, 60*, 82–88.

Kowalkowski, C., Witell, L., & Gustafsson, A. (2013). Any way goes: Identifying value constellations for service infusion in SMEs. *Industrial Marketing Management, 42*(1), 18–30.

Lassnig, M., Stabauer, P., Güntner, G., & Breitfuß, G. (2017). Studienkatalog zur digitalen Transformation durch Industrie 4.0. Salzburg: Salzburg Research.

Lay, G. (Ed.). (2014). *Servitization in industry.* Heidelberg: Springer.

Lerch, C., & Gotsch, M. (2015). Digitalized product-service systems in manufacturing firms: A case study analysis. *Research-Technology Management, 58*(5), 45–52.

Lichtblau, K., Stich, V., Bertenrath, R., Blum, M., Bleider, M., Millack, A., … Schröter, M. (2015). Industrie 4.0-Readiness. Aachen: IMPULS-Stiftung des VDMA.

Lockett, H., Johnson, M., Evans, S., & Bastl, M. (2011). Product service systems and supply network relationships: An exploratory case study. *Journal of Manufacturing Technology Management, 22*(3), 293–313.

Luoto, S., Brax, S. A., & Kohtamäki, M. (2017). Critical meta-analysis of servitization research: Constructing a model-narrative to reveal paradigmatic assumptions. *Industrial Marketing Management, 60*, 89–100.

Lusch, R. F., & Nambisan, S. (2015). Service innovation: A service-dominant logic perspective. *MIS Quarterly, 39*(1), 155–175.

Malerba, F. (2002). Sectoral systems of innovation and production. *Research Policy, 31*(2), 247–264.

Marsili, O. (2001). *The anatomy and evolution of industries: Technological change and industrial dynamics.* Cheltenham, UK and Northampton, MA: Edward Elgar.

Mathieu, V. (2001a). Product services: From a service supporting the product to a service supporting the client. *Journal of Business & Industrial Marketing, 16*(1), 39–61.

Mathieu, V. (2001b). Service strategies within the manufacturing sector: Benefits, costs and partnership. *International Journal of Service Industry Management, 12*(5), 451–475.

Mey Goh, Y., & McMahon, C. (2009). Improving reuse of in-service information capture and feedback. *Journal of Manufacturing Technology Management, 20*(5), 626–639.

Mont, O. K. (2002). Clarifying the concept of product–service system. *Journal of Cleaner Production, 10*(3), 237–245.

Naik, P., Schroeder, A., Ziaee Bigdeli, A., & Baines, T. S. (2017). Enabling servitization by affordance. Edinburgh: Paper presented at the 24th EurOMA Conference.

Neely, A. (2008). Exploring the financial consequences of the servitization of manufacturing. *Operations Management Research, 1*(2), 103–118.

Neely, A., Benedetinni, O., & Visnjic, I. (2011). *The servitization of manufacturing: Further evidence.* Cambridge: Paper presented at the 18th European Operation Management Association Conference.

Obermaier, R. (2016). Industrie 4.0 als unternehmerische Gestaltungsaufgabe: Strategische und operative Handlungsfelder für Industriebetriebe. In R. Obermaier (Ed.), *Industrie 4.0 als unternehmerische Gestaltungsaufgabe: Betriebswirtschaftliche, technische und rechtliche Herausforderungen* (pp. 3–34). Wiesbaden: Springer Fachmedien Wiesbaden.

OECD. (2017). *Enabling the next production revolution: The future of manufacturing and services.* Paris. Organisation for Economic Co-operation and Development.

Oliva, R., & Kallenberg, R. (2003). Managing the transition from products to services. *International Journal of Service Industry Management, 14*(2), 160–172.

Ostrom, A. L., Parasuraman, A., Bowen, D. E., Patrício, L., & Voss, C. A. (2015). Service research priorities in a rapidly changing context. *Journal of Service Research, 18*(2), 127–159.

Paschou, T., Adrodegari, F., Perona, M., & Saccani, N. (2017). *The digital servitization of manufacturing: A literature review and research agenda.* Paper presented at the RESER conference 2017. Bilbao, Spain.

Penttinen, E., & Palmer, J. (2007). Improving firm positioning through enhanced offerings and buyer–seller relationships. *Industrial Marketing Management, 36*(5), 552–564.

Rabetino, R., Harmsen, W., Kohtamäki, M., & Sihvonen, J. (2018). Structuring servitization-related research. *International Journal of Operations & Production Management, 38*(2), 350–371.

Reinartz, W., & Ulaga, W. (2008). How to sell services more profitably. *Harvard Business Review, 86*(5), 90–96, 129.

Rust, R. T., & Huang, M.-H. (2014). The service revolution and the transformation of marketing science. *Marketing Science, 33*(2), 206–221.

Rymaszewska, A., Helo, P., & Gunasekaran, A. (2017). IoT powered servitization of manufacturing: An exploratory case study. *International Journal of Production Economics, 192*, 92–105.

Tukker, A. (2015). Product services for a resource-efficient and circular economy: A review. *Journal of Cleaner Production, 97*, 76–91.

Tukker, A., & Tischner, U. (2006). Product-services as a research field: Past, present and future. Reflections from a decade of research. *Journal of Cleaner Production, 14*(17), 1552–1556.

Vandermerwe, S., & Rada, J. (1988). Servitization of business: Adding value by adding services. *European Management Journal, 6*(4), 314–324.

Vargo, S. L., & Lusch, R. F. (2004). Evolving to a new dominant logic for marketing. *Journal of Marketing, 68*(1), 1–17.

Vargo, S. L., & Lusch, R. F. (2008). From goods to service(s): Divergences and convergences of logics. *Industrial Marketing Management, 37*(3), 254–259.

VDI/VDE. (2016). Digitale Chancen und Bedrohungen: Geschäftsmodelle für Industrie 4.0. Düsseldorf: Verein Deutscher Ingenieure e.V.

Visnjic, I., Wiengarten, F., & Neely, A. (2016). Only the brave: Product innovation, service business model innovation, and their impact on performance. *Journal of Product Innovation Management, 33*(1), 36–52.

Visnjic Kastalli, I., & Van Looy, B. (2013). Servitization: Disentangling the impact of service business model innovation on manufacturing firm performance. *Journal of Operations Management, 31*(4), 169–180.

Witell, L., & Löfgren, M. (2013). From service for free to service for fee: Business model innovation in manufacturing firms. *Journal of Service Management, 24*(5), 520–533.

World Input-Output Database. (2016, November). Retrieved from www.wiod.org/release16.

Ziegler, M., & Rossmann, S. (2017). *Digital machinery decoded: A practical guide for machinery companies to navigate digital transformation and outperform competition.* Stuttgart: Porsche Consulting.

Part II

Innovation in service operations

6

Typologies and frameworks in service innovation

Christian Kowalkowski and Lars Witell

Introduction

Services are fundamental for competitiveness across firms and markets (Ostrom, Parasuraman, Bowen, Patricio, & Voss, 2015; Vandermerwe & Rada, 1988). Technological advances have had significant effects on the development of service innovations; as Rust (2004, p. 24) puts it, "the service revolution and the information revolution are two sides of the same coin." Service innovation is increasingly regarded as a key source of differentiation and growth, not only in service firms but also in manufacturing firms (Kowalkowski, Gebauer, & Oliva, 2017). As Theodore Levitt (Levitt, 1972, p. 42) pointed out almost 50 years ago:

> Everybody is in service. Often the less there seems, the more there is. The more techno-logically sophisticated the generic product (e.g., cars and computers), the more dependent are its sales on the quality and availability of its accompanying customer services (e.g., display rooms, delivery, repairs and maintenance, application aids, operator training, installation advice, warranty fulfillment). In this sense, General Motors is probably more service-intensive than manufacturing-intensive. Without its services its sales would shrivel.

As the importance of services for businesses and economies has increased, the body of schol-arly work on service innovation has grown. This topic is regarded as a strategic priority for ser-vice research (Ostrom et al., 2015) and the number of publications on the topic has grown considerably, especially in the past two decades (Carlborg, Kindström, & Kowalkowski, 2014; Witell, Snyder, Gustafsson, Fombelle, & Kristensson, 2016). Service innovation research has its roots in the analysis of technological innovation for manufacturing firms (Gallouj & Weinstein, 1997) and it has focused primarily on outputs and processes, as evidenced by the fact that it builds on the traditional distinction between product and process innovation (Abernathy & Townsend, 1975; Utterback & Abernathy, 1975). This view still dominates innovation research and policy making (e.g., Adner & Levinthal, 2001; Freel, 2003; Roper, Du, & Love, 2008), as seen in the OECD *Oslo Manual* (OECD, 2018, p. 21), which refers to the duality of innovation as a process and as an outcome. First published in 1992, the *Oslo Manual* has become an inter-national reference guide for policymakers and researchers for collecting and using data on innov-ation. Although mainstream innovation literature has long regarded service industries as having low innovation frequency (e.g., Barras, 1986; Baumol, 1967; Pavitt, 1984), this view has recently been challenged, and the expanding field of service innovation research has become more diversified in its approaches and theoretical foundations (Carlborg et al., 2014; Helkkula, Kowalkowski, & Tronvoll, 2018; Toivonen & Tuominen, 2009).

This chapter synthesizes the extant research on service innovation; it discusses different perspectives and views of service innovation focusing on characteristics, categories, models, and innovation modes. It brings together literatures that are typically treated separately, and identifies the shared and specific understandings of what service innovation is and what implications it has for theory and practice. It begins by providing synopses of four recent service innovation literature reviews. Second, it synthesizes prior research according to characteristics, core models, and innovation modes. Following this, the fivefold innovation framework by Miles (2016) is discussed; this framework builds on the influential works of Gallouj and Weinstein (1997) and Coombs and Miles (2000). Next, a typology of four theoretical service innovation archetypes is discussed and compared to prior empirical work. Finally, the chapter discusses why different perspectives, despite criticism, continue to exist in parallel and are likely to continue to do so also in the future—in academic research as well as in practice.

State-of-the-art research on service innovation

A synopsis of four recent literature review articles covering the past 30 years in service innovation indicates this research takes place in a developing field, consisting of different perspectives, definitions, conceptualizations, and frameworks (Carlborg et al., 2014; Gallouj & Savona, 2009; Snyder, Witell, Gustafsson, Fombelle, & Kristensson, 2016; Witell et al., 2016). Most of these reviews use three critical perspectives from service innovation research (assimilation, demarcation, and synthesis) to describe and analyze the field (Coombs & Miles, 2000). Briefly, *assimilation* suggests that service innovation is based on technological innovations in manufacturing firms, *demarcation* differentiates innovation in the service sector from that in the manufacturing sector, and *synthesis* creates an integrative view broad enough to encompass innovation in both service and manufacturing (see also Ordanini & Parasuraman, 2011).

Gallouj and Savona (2009) reviewed the literature concerning innovation in services a decade ago, and framed the debate about what it was at that time as well as how it was conceptualized over the previous 20 years. They put forward the evolving concept of value and emphasized how service output is ill-defined and incorrectly measured. They attempted to reclassify literature based on whether it primarily assimilated to or differentiated from traditional conceptualizations of innovation in manufacturing sectors. Building on the assimilation, demarcation, and synthesis views of service innovation, they concluded that assimilation remained the dominant perspective in service innovation research. Furthermore, they observed that knowledge about the diffusion of service innovations was, at the time, primarily built on research in information technology (IT) and the reverse product cycle (Barras, 1986), which does not apply to most services.

Carlborg et al (2014) focused on the evolution of service innovation research and provided an analysis of 128 articles published between 1986 and 2010. Their focus was on the progression of service innovation research, including both topicality and perspective. Their analysis revealed that this research could be grouped not only by topic, but also into three phases of evolution that characterized dominant views on service innovation: formation, maturity, and multidimensional.

In the formation phase (1986–2000), scholars developed rationales for service innovation that relied on theories and models different from those applied to traditional goods innovation, and many publications adopted a clear demarcation between the two. The service offering itself was the primary focus of these studies. The research stream then moved on to involve customers (e.g., Alam, 2002) and describe ways to organize new service development (NSD) projects in the maturity phase (2001–2005). It also saw more attempts to contribute to the elaboration of an integrative, synthetist approach. In the multidimensional phase (2006–), service innovation research became more diversified and fragmented, emphasizing linkages between innovation and business strategy. Scholars like Karniouchina, Victorino, and Verma (2006) called for more multidisciplinary research, reflecting the evolving view of service innovation as a multidimensional concept along the lines of Coombs and Miles' (2000) synthesizing approach as well as the emphasis of service-dominant logic (S-D logic) on service as the common denominator of the exchange process. Rather than using the plural 'services,' which implies units of output, S-D logic uses the singular term 'service' to refer to the "application of specialized competences (… knowledge and skills), through deeds, processes, and performances for the benefit of another entity or the entity itself" (Vargo & Lusch, 2008, p. 26).

As the field continues to diversify, Carlborg et al. (2014, p. 385) argued that "the service innovation concept becomes all-encompassing, [and] identifying the exact loci of service innovation research becomes more difficult." These authors suggested that the dominant research perspective has shifted among the three phases from assimilation toward demarcation and, more recently, to a synthesis view of service innovation.

Witell et al. (2016) reviewed 1,301 service innovation articles in academic journals between 1979 and 2014, covering a wide range of research disciplines, including marketing, management, and operations research. They identified key characteristics of 84 definitions of service innovation, according to different perspectives (assimilation, demarcation, synthesis) and concluded that although "the concept is widely used, few research papers have explicitly defined service innovation" (Witell et al., 2016, p. 2863). The use of perspectives beyond assimilation has introduced new aspects, such as change, customers, and value, into definitions of service innovation. For example, the business model concept found its way into definitions of service innovation (Enz, 2012), but the definitions still do not focus on value capture for multiple actors. In addition, the authors suggested that claims of the prevalence of the synthesis perspective are not definitive; research using all perspectives is still published.

Breaking from the focus on alternative research perspectives, the same set of authors provided an extensive review of 1,046 articles and used it as a platform for analyzing how categories can help clarify the concept of service innovation (Snyder et al., 2016). Service innovation outcomes are captured with a range of categories and comprise four main types: (1) degree of change, (2) type of change, (3) newness, and (4) means of provision. First, a service innovation can be based on completely new core characteristics or improvements to existing core characteristics (Gallouj & Weinstein, 1997). Second, referring to the duality of innovation as a process and as an outcome, a service innovation can be based on changes in the core characteristics related to the output or service provision. Third, newness is emphasized through the use of newness as a basis for the categorization of service innovations. Traditionally, newness to the market has been a key to defining service innovation, but the business press and policymakers have changed the focus to being new to the firm (Toivonen & Tuominen, 2009). Finally, a service innovation can be provided in a new way through technology or new organizational arrangements (van der Aa & Elfring, 2002).

In summary, literature reviews show that service innovation is often treated as an empirical phenomenon with little theoretical conceptualization to capture its essence. Witell et al. (2016, p. 2863) concurred, arguing that the wide "variety in definitions limits and hinders knowledge development of service innovation." Carlborg, Kindström, and Kowalkowski (2014, p. 386) further emphasized that most of the existing literature focused on development processes, so "additional studies ... should broaden the focus from a narrow focus on the innovation process only to gain a better understanding of interactions with the customer as well as other stakeholders in the organization's service ecosystem."

Understanding service innovation

This section synthesizes the extant research on service innovation. It outlines different perspectives and their views of service innovation, focusing on characteristics, models, and modes of service innovation, and discusses how these can be used in describing different perspectives on service innovation.

Characteristics

Prior studies explain and define the concept 'service innovation' in different ways. Some studies use a general definition, whereas others use dimensions or categories to define the concept (Gallouj & Weinstein, 1997). A general definition explains service innovation by describing the innovation's core characteristics (e.g., Ostrom et al., 2010). For example, the Organisation for Economic Co-operation and Development (OECD) (2018) defines innovation as a new or improved product (good or service) and/or process that differs significantly from what has previously been made available to potential users (i.e., product) or brought into use (i.e., process). Menor and Roth (2007) suggest that service innovation—either an addition to current services or a change in the delivery process—is an offering not previously available to customers that requires changes in the competencies applied by service providers and customers.

A service innovation may involve changes in several dimensions of an existing service (Carlborg et al., 2014). This follows a view in which a product is defined as a set of characteristics. Hence, a service is based on the provider's characteristics, client competencies, technical characteristics, and final users' service characteristics (Gallouj & Weinstein, 1997; Saviotti & Metcalfe, 1984). This multidimensional view is more prominent in more recent research (e.g., Amara, Landry, & Doloreux, 2009; Helkkula et al., 2018; Rubalcaba, Michel, Sundbo, Brown, & Reynoso, 2012). When dimensions are changed to define service innovation, there may be multiple changes to an existing offering. The plethora of dimensions available suggests that service innovation is becoming a broader concept and that firms have increasing potential for innovation.

Core models

The theoretical underpinnings of existing core models for service innovation are quite varied. Three theoretical foundations used in core models of service innovation are "Lancasterian representation" (the product defined as a set of service characteristics) (Lancaster, 1966), "dynamic capabilities" (a firm's ability to integrate, build, and reconfigure resources) (Teece, Pisano, & Shuen, 1997), and "S-D logic" (the application of knowledge and skills for the benefit of actors) (Lusch & Vargo, 2006). The framework suggested by Gallouj and Weinstein (1997), which is based on a Lancasterian view, describes service innovation according to characteristics, such as offerings, technology, and competencies of customers and other actors (e.g., policymakers). A service innovation results from changes in any of these characteristics (Gallouj & Savona, 2009). Using this approach, six modes of service innovation emerge, including: radical, incremental, improvement, formalization, ad hoc, and recombinative innovations. Gallouj and Weinstein (1997) argue that recombinative service innovation is a "fundamental mode of creating innovations," which lies at the heart of innovation in services; that is, it depends on an ability to explore and mobilize an extended set of resources and competencies (knowledge and skills). Different degrees of novelty are captured through three of the different modes (radical, incremental, and improvement service innovations). Ad hoc forms of innovation are constructions of solutions to customer-specific problems and hence not immediately reproducible; therefore, they rely on institutional formalization innovation to achieve the required degree of standardization of the various characteristics. The framework focuses on what is offered and type of innovations, but lacks a systemic perspective (because it focuses on the supplier-customer dyad).

Den Hertog, van der Aa, and de Jong (2010) based their conceptualization of service innovation on a dynamic capabilities approach and suggested a conceptual framework with six dynamic service innovation capabilities: (1) signaling user needs and technological options; (2) conceptualizing; (3) (un)bundling; (4) co-producing and orchestrating; (5) scaling and stretching; and (6) learning and adapting. Successful innovators outperform their competitors in at least some of these innovation capabilities. The authors argue that novelty can range from "new to the firm" to "new to the world," but do not elaborate on what the differences mean for the conceptualization or practice of service innovation. They do, however, make three remarks related to implementation: (1) because dynamic capabilities come at a cost, an organization has to be selective in nurturing existing and developing new capabilities; (2) because a dynamic capability cannot be created overnight, service innovations are built on and related to historically grown capabilities; and (3) although most elements can be transferred between organizations, adaptation of dynamic capabilities is needed to become a successful service innovator.

Koskela-Huotari, Edvardsson, Jonas, Sörhammar, and Witell (2016) drew on S-D logic to conceptualize service innovation as a process that unfolds through changes in the institutional arrangements governing actors' resource integration practices in service ecosystems. Four case studies were used to illustrate the interdependent patterns of breaking, making, and maintaining the institutionalized rules of resource integration. Results indicated that institutional work allows actors to co-create value in novel and useful ways by: a) including new actors, b) redefining the roles of involved actors, and c) reframing resources within service ecosystems. Although effort is required to break and make the institutional rules in order for innovation to occur, at the same time institutional maintenance is needed for these changes to become an integral part of institutional structures.

Perspectives on service innovation

Two influential publications use different terminologies to suggest that there are three broad perspectives on service innovation (Coombs & Miles, 2000; Gallouj & Weinstein, 1997). Gallouj and Weinstein (1997) distinguished between a *technologist* perspective, which considers the diffusion of technological innovations derived from the manufacturing sector (e.g., Barras, 1986), and a *service-oriented* perspective, which focuses on non-technological forms of innovation such as consultancy services. Coombs and Miles (2000) distinguished between an *assimilationist* perspective and a *demarcationist* perspective. Assimilation assumes that frameworks and models used when discussing manufactured product innovation are equally applicable to the service context—whether technological or non-technological—and this perspective is often forwarded by economists and statisticians (Miles, 2016).

The prevalence of assimilation in many organizations may be explained by the view of services as 'innovation laggards.' This approach can be traced back to Pavitt's (1984) sectoral taxonomy for innovation, in which the service sector is largely a passive adopter of technology and recipient of innovations from elsewhere. Essentially, it means that service innovation is equated or reduced to the adoption and use of technology. As Gallouj and Savona (2009) point out, such perspective strives to assimilate services within established frameworks used for manufacturing sectors and physical goods. Demarcation, on the other hand, stresses the unique characteristics of services (Rathmell, 1966; Shostack, 1977). Consequently, this approach proposes specific models and frameworks that comprehend the specificities of service offerings and processes (e.g., Edvardsson & Olsson, 1996), and this perspective is common in marketing and management research (Carlborg et al., 2014; Miles, 2016).

As a response to the multidimensional nature of service innovation, Gallouj and Weinstein (1997) and Coombs and Miles (2000) proposed a third distinct perspective that transcends the other two, which they refer to as *integrative* or *synthetist*. Specifically,

> it encompasses both goods and services. Secondly, it applies both to technological innovation itself and to the non-technological forms of innovation. It can be seen as a way of clarifying and making more operational functional approaches that have proved to be too general.
>
> (Gallouj & Weinstein, 1997, p. 539)

Although service innovation literature traditionally falls into either the assimilation or demarcation perspective (Carlborg et al., 2014), contemporary research increasingly emphasizes adopting synthesis to understand and study service innovation (e.g., Drejer, 2004; Helkkula et al., 2018; Rubalcaba et al., 2012).

A fivefold framework for service innovation

Miles (2016) recently argued that the two traditional perspectives referred to by Gallouj and Weinstein (1997) and by Coombs and Miles (2000) can be better described in terms of two distinct dimensions. First, service innovation can focus on technological or non-technological elements (techno- versus servo- approaches). Second, emphasis can be placed on either similarities or differences between services and goods or on sectors (assimilation versus demarcation). In combination, the two dimensions provide an innovation framework with four categories (see Figure 6.1).

A *techno-assimilation* approach would stress industrialization of services, similar to the industrialization of manufacturing processes, based on prototypical manufacturing characteristics (Bowen, Siehl, & Schneider, 1989). This echoes Levitt's (1972) production-line approach to service. *Techno-demarcation* emphasizes technological innovation, such as Barras' (1986) attempt to characterize service innovation. Next, the *servo-demarcation* approach is common in studies of NSD that often highlight salient characteristics of services, as opposed to NSD that distinguishes it from product development models applied to goods (e.g., de Brentani, 2001; Kindström & Kowalkowski, 2009). Finally, *servo-assimilation* has relevance to research and practice that investigate the service features of all economic activities (Miles, 2016), such as new social practices and processes through market innovation (Vargo, Wieland, & Akaka, 2015).

Ultimately, a synthesis approach transcends assimilationist and demarcationist perspectives (Coombs & Miles, 2000; Gallouj & Weinstein, 1997) by integrating insights from service and manufacturing industries, with studies employing techno- and servo-approaches (Miles, 2016). The case for synthesis finds its rationale in the worldwide growth of the service sector and the

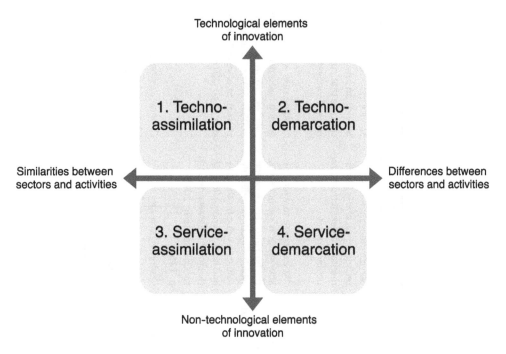

Figure 6.1 Service innovation dimensions.

Note: Based on Miles (2016, p. 15).

servitization of manufacturing firms (Vandermerwe & Rada, 1988). Accelerating technological development has blurred the lines between service and manufacturing sectors (Carlborg et al., 2014). Hence, the increasing role of technology in services (Breidbach et al., 2018), the "dematerialization of resources" (Normann, 2001), and the growth of "anything-as-a-service" business models (Kowalkowski & Ulaga, 2017) are likely to lead to further intertwinement between the manufacturing and service sectors. Today, service activities such as engineering, R&D, design services, and consulting are part of various integrated goods-service offerings (i.e., solutions) that enable firms to integrate more closely with customers and other stakeholders in ecosystems (Valtakoski, 2017). Consequently, services are part of innovation processes across the whole economy; therefore, "a simple distinction between manufacturing and services is unsustainable—a more integrated perspective is required" (Miles, 2016, p. 28).

Synthesis is the final approach to service innovation in the fivefold framework of Miles (2016). Theoretically and conceptually, it resonates with the S-D logic of marketing, which provides an overarching view of how value is co-created (Lusch & Vargo, 2006). A synthetist approach could facilitate the study of innovation in general and enable a better understanding of the relationship between the development of new technologies and new markets (Vargo et al., 2015).

Table 6.1 summarizes the five perspectives on service innovation, including typical definitions, key characteristics, and key models. Next, the five perspectives are discussed in greater detail, before moving on to examine theoretical archetypes of service innovation.

Table 6.1 Perspectives on service innovation: definitions and characteristics

Perspective	Techno-assimilation	Techno-demarcation	Servo-assimilation	Servo-demarcation	Synthesis
Description	Knowledge on product innovation holds for services, and innovation is based on technological change	Service innovation is based on technology and is fundamentally different from product innovation	Knowledge on product innovation holds for services, and innovation is based on non-technological change	Service innovation is non-technological and is fundamentally different from product innovation	Service innovation should provide an integrative perspective that concerns all types of innovations
Typical definition	"Technology-based inventions, driven by the emergence of new markets or new service opportunities" (Ko & Lu, 2010 p. 164)	"Fundamental change in services that represent revolutionary changes in technology or service benefits" (Cheng & Krumwiede, 2010 p. 162)	"A new way of business thinking to reform relatively conservative and inflexible operational procedures and processes, which can transform organizations to better meet the needs of their markets" (Kuo, Kuo, & Ho, 2014 p. 697)	"As the extent to which new knowledge is integrated by the firm into service offerings, which directly or indirectly results in value for the firm and its customers/clients" (Salunke, Weerawardena, & McColl-Kennedy, 2011 p. 1253)	"Finding new ways of co-solving customer problems" (Michel, Brown, and Gallan, 2008 p. 50) or "improved cocreation of value" (Helkkula, et al., 2018, p. 293)
Key characteristics	Significant, product process, risk, capability	Process, firm	Organization, management, market	Customer, change	Change, customer, more value
Exemplar models	Sectoral technological taxonomy (Miozzo & Soete, 2001)	The reverse product cycle (Barras, 1986)	Oslo Manual (OECD, 2018)	An integrated service development model (Edvardsson, 1997)	System of characteristics and competencies (Gallouj & Weinstein, 1997)

Techno-assimilation

The extension of manufacturing concepts to service organizations and industries has received considerable attention, especially in the 1970s and 1980s before service research became an established part of business and management research (e.g., Bowen et al., 1989; Chase, 1978). Manufacturing approaches to service provision, such as substitution of people for technology, detailed division of labor, service standardization, and decoupling the client from the service organization, can be applied to increase the efficiency of service provision. Today, these theories are more nuanced, as service operations have followed a trend similar to that encountered in manufacturing/production principles—from mass production logic to lean service production (Kowalkowski & Ulaga, 2017).

The concept of innovation associated with the assimilation perspective is reflected in the innovation indicators suggested by the OECD *Oslo Manual* (OECD, 2018). Almost all examples in the manual imply application of novel hardware and software; the only exceptions are innovations centered on the location of services (e.g., home delivery, pickup of rented vehicles, and provision of management contact points for outsourced services on-site rather than remotely), or application of procedures and methods which in practice are likely to involve new technical support (e.g., the implementation of a new reservation and projects management system). Although in principle the manual does not exclude non-technological product innovation (e.g., a new insurance contract, a new financial product, or a new field of expertise in consultancy) or non-technological process innovation (methodologies, protocols, etc.), Djellal, Gallouj, and Miles (2013) find that these formulations tend to work against inclusion of such cases.

Techno-demarcation

The introduction of the reverse product cycle model is often viewed as the beginning of research on service innovation (Carlborg et al., 2014; Miles, 2016). Barras (1986) described the reverse product cycle, in which service firms use new technologies as a first step to improve efficiency, improve quality of existing services, and then introduce new services. The reverse product cycle highlights central features, such as the importance of knowledge and competencies in service industries, although it has been criticized for neglecting non-technological characteristics of service innovation (Gallouj & Savona, 2010; Gallouj & Weinstein, 1997). It focuses on IT-based innovation, but as Djellal, Gallouj, and Miles (2013) point out, services also use other types of technologies such as physical, chemical, and biotechnological systems (e.g., cooking, refrigeration, transportation, materials handling, and health services).

The reverse cycle model describes the developments at a particular historical period when IT was being adopted across service industries. Such a view is reductionist and, rather than providing the basis for a theory of service innovation, it provides a theoretical lens on the diffusion of technological innovation from manufacturing to the service sector (Gallouj & Weinstein, 1997). The limitations of this view are further underlined by recent developments in industry. Rather than diffusing technological innovation from manufacturing, new technology-based service companies are increasingly driving innovation. Examples include platform companies (such as ride-hailing service firm Uber, online marketplace Airbnb, or retailer and internet conglomerate Alibaba Group), streaming media service providers (such as Netflix or Spotify), and startup firms in the financial technology sector.

Servo-assimilation

A servo-assimilation perspective acknowledges that service innovation, in contrast to product innovation, is frequently based on non-technological change such as organizational innovation (e.g., Kuo et al., 2014). At the same time, the underlying assimilation view is that knowledge on product innovation also holds for services. Using a model applicable to innovation in general, Nijssen et al. (2006) find that willingness to cannibalize current organizational skills and routines plays an important role for service innovation.

The importance of non-technological innovation more broadly was recognized by Abernathy and Clark (1985), who separated innovation into two domains of innovative activities: technology/production and market/customer. In their view, the non-technological 'market/customer' side of innovation focuses on service channels, relationships with the customer base, customer applications, customer knowledge, and modes of customer communication. Non-technological innovations may be particularly prominent, not only as a result of radical technological innovation, but also due to large-scale market changes, as in the case of liberalization and privatization of formerly publicly controlled sectors such as railroads and aviation (cf., Davies, 2004). Although many empirical studies and policy documents (e.g., OECD, 2018) increasingly include more service industries and non-technological forms of innovation, thereby striving to expand the scope of innovation to encompass the service features of all economic activities, Djellal et al. (2013) argue that there is still progress to be made. This is especially true for non-technological product (output) innovations, non-technological process innovations, ad hoc innovations (e.g., tailor-made services), innovations in integrated goods-service offerings (i.e., solutions), social innovation, and user-driven innovations that are initiated by consumers for their own use without direct intervention of a firm.

Servo-demarcation

For decades, scholars have described service activities and industries as being distinct from manufacturing. Miles (2016) finds that many of those who have highlighted key characteristics of services and NSD come from the management and marketing disciplines (e.g., Edvardsson, 1997). Supported by arguments that services require novel theories, models, and indicators, proponents of a service-demarcation approach often call attention to a number of unique characteristics of, and preconditions for, service innovation in general and NSD in particular. For example, many new services do not require as large an initial investment as goods development projects do (e.g., patent applications, manufacturing facilities, physical prototypes), but tend to be more resource-intensive at the back end of development projects (Kindström & Kowalkowski, 2009).

Co-production requires, among other things, increased customer centricity which means that in NSD projects, more interaction with and feedback from customers is usually required (Drejer, 2004; Edvardsson, Gustafsson, Kristensson, Magnusson, & Matthing, 2006). Furthermore, as compared to manufacturing, the overall R&D intensity in service firms is relatively low, because service firms typically do not pursue conventional R&D (Hipp & Grupp, 2005; Hollenstein, 2003; Miles, 2016). Literature on the servitization of manufacturing industries implies that offering services has become increasingly important for traditional manufacturers. However, this shift is seldom reflected in actual innovation work:

Investing resources in product development is obvious for any leading manufacturer. The very same companies typically invest only a negligible share of their development resources in new services, and even fewer pursue service research in a scientific sense ... service innovation often becomes a concern only once the new product is ready to launch.

(Kowalkowski & Ulaga, 2017 p. 149).

To conclude, in addition to general frameworks and models, servo-demarcation provides conceptual and empirical contributions that aim to identify sector-specific innovation behaviors. For instance, these might include theories developed in the field of retailing (Djellal et al., 2013) or service-specific traits within manufacturing (Kindström & Kowalkowski, 2009).

Synthesis

Schumpeter (1934) viewed innovation as a novel combination of new and existing knowledge. Although his thinking influenced the synthesis perspective, Witell et al. (2016) point out that in certain ways his conceptualization of service innovation moves away from the original ideas. Schumpeter (1934) argued that the process of developing a new offering should be differentiated from the process of its commercialization and from evaluation of the outcome, but a synthesis perspective views service innovation as including both the development process and its outcome. Furthermore, such a 'neo-Schumpeterian' view of service innovation (e.g., Drejer, 2004; Flikkema, Jansen, & Van Der Sluis, 2007; Sundbo, 1997; Toivonen & Tuominen, 2009) emphasizes that economic development is driven by the emergence of new combinations (i.e., innovations) that are economically more viable than previous solutions (Witell et al., 2016).

As Hill (1977) points out, even for identical output, the same activity may be classified as a good or a service, depending on the responsibilities of the firm in the production process. From an innovation perspective, such classifications can be irrelevant—and even misleading—to the effort to understand value creation and the success and failure of service innovations (Kindström & Kowalkowski, 2014). For example, the decrease of manufacturing's share of GDP worldwide largely reflects price reductions for goods relative to services (*The Economist*, 2005). "Regardless of sector size or importance though, the division between service and manufacturing may be artificial. The service sector seemingly has become a catch-all for everything that does not qualify as manufacturing" (Kindström & Kowalkowski, 2014 p. 96).

Referring to Gallouj and Weinstein (1997) and other studies (e.g., Carlborg et al., 2014; Gago & Rubalcaba, 2007; Rubalcaba, Gago, and Gallego, 2010) suggests that the synthesis perspective is now widely represented in studies of service innovation. Furthermore, Vargo, Wieland, and Akaka (2015) argue that the separation between technological and non-technological innovation has made it difficult to develop an integrative approach for studying innovation in general. However, Miles (2016, pp. 27–28) suggests that it may be "more accurate to say that there is much research that aims to contribute to the elaboration of an integrative [synthesis] approach but that a consolidated view is yet to be established (or at least to be widely agreed upon)." A recent conceptualization that contributes to the synthesis approach is the service innovation typology by Helkkula et al. (2018). Identifying four distinct theoretical archetypes, they embed elements of traditional perspectives while acknowledging the multidimensional nature of service innovation. Such conceptual work may complement the five empirically driven perspectives proposed by Miles (2016) and presented in Table 6.1, addressing calls for theoretical integration and advancing a consolidated view.

In the next section, the Helkkula, Kowalkowski, and Tronvoll (2018) typology is discussed in relation to different theoretical lenses and illustrated by a mini case example, which illustrates how the conceptualization might be empirically applied.

Four theoretical archetypes of service innovation: a typology

Based on the synthesis approach to service innovation, which transcends two broad empirically driven perspectives (assimilation/technologist and demarcation/service-oriented), Helkkula et al. (2018) strove for theoretical integration by proposing a typology of theoretical archetypes. Responding to calls for an overarching framework (e.g., Gallouj & Savona, 2009; Rubalcaba et al., 2012) or typology (Carlborg et al., 2014), they draw on synthesis and S-D logic to present four archetypes—output-based, process-based, experiential, and systemic—each informed by distinct theories and different underlying assumptions. Prior to this, innovation research in general (and service innovation research in particular) has focused primarily on output and process, which are the first two archetypes. However, recent research has moved beyond these traditional conceptualizations to provide a more experiential and systemic understanding of service innovation (Edvardsson & Tronvoll, 2013; Helkkula, Kelleher, & Pihlström, 2012). The two archetypes cited here include the social aspects of service innovation and broaden its scope beyond firm-centered production activities, processes, and offerings. In Table 6.2, the four archetypes of service innovation are differentiated in terms of characteristics and roles of actors.

A key contribution of the *output-based* archetype of service innovation is the characterization of innovation in terms of measurable activities and items. Theoretically, this archetype is rooted in an assimilation perspective that equates service innovation with output; that is, the scope of the innovation is measured as the number of new services launched. Service innovation is an economic concept that should provide benefits to its developer, typically the supplier firm (Toivonen & Tuominen, 2009). Although research acknowledges the role of customers in relation to innovation output, traditional assessments build on a neoclassical economic view that separates production from consumption, and resonates with the early, unidirectional Schumpeterian innovation model of entrepreneurship that brings innovations to markets (Laursen & Salter, 2006). It also resonates with Nobel Memorial Prize recipient Simon S. Kuznets' influential system of national accounts (e.g., Kuznets, 1966), including its use to measure productivity and to set production targets across different sectors of the economy (Fogel, 2000).

The *process-based* archetype of service innovation contributes by focusing on activity and time span; it applies to any change in the service creation process that influences value creation, including shifts in roles, competencies, skills, practices, norms, and behaviors of a firm's employees or customers (Helkkula et al., 2018). Service innovation is regarded as an activity rather than an output and, as opposed to a closed production system, the customer is seen as a potentially active participant in the production process. Interdependence patterns and divisions of work can vary largely between different service processes (Larsson & Bowen, 1989), and process innovations can alter customer involvement and disposition to participate in various ways (Chase & Apte, 2007). Although it is common in the literature to conceptually distinguish between process- and output-based service innovation (e.g., Menor & Roth, 2007), it may be difficult to discern the beginning and end of a process and how it relates to the output.

The key contribution of the *experiential* archetype is its ability to focus on the individual service innovation experience and how the customer makes sense of it. Because such experiences involve individual sensemaking, they are not objective (Helkkula et al., 2018). Customers, supplier employees, and all other engaged actors perceive this value individually and subjectively in their own social context, co-creating value through experience

Table 6.2 Archetypes of service innovation: characteristics and roles of actors

	Output-based archetype	Process-based archetype	Experiential archetype	Systemic archetype
Foundation of the research approach	Product innovation management	New service development, operations management	Phenomenological (experientially determined) value	Social systems, living systems, industrial networks
Innovation focus	Attributes of the service innovation (e.g., new technology)	Service innovation process; architectural elements (phases) of the customer's service consumption	Beneficiaries' experiences while using the service and in the wider phenomenological context, extending beyond a specific service offering	Resource integration by actors engaged in the services ecosystem
Description of service innovation	An offering not previously available to the firm's customers requiring modifications in the sets of competencies applied by the service providers and/or customers	A change in the service creation process requiring modifications in the sets of competencies applied by service providers and/or customers	An individual experience of something new or revised	A reconfiguration of resources, actors, and institutional arrangements to enable service innovation
Focus on value creation	Creating outputs (to various extents) with valuable attributes	The process of applying new ideas or current thinking in fundamentally different ways	Co-creating valuable service experiences through service innovations	Integrating available resources within the service ecosystem in a specific context
Role of main actors	Companies that innovate offerings; customers as either passive adopters or active co-developers	Companies that manage the process; actors who attend the process, such as customers	Customers or any other beneficiary in the service innovation phenomenon	Different elements of the system that make resources available for value creation
Role of focal firm	To produce new service offerings	To enable new service processes	To facilitate valuable experiences	To integrate market and other resources in a novel and viable way
Role of employees	To take the new service to the market; launching, selling, and marketing activities	To divide work between front line employees who interact with customers, and backstage employees who produce in isolation	To facilitate customers' experiences of value	To integrate market, private, and other resources in a novel and viable way
Role of customer	To generate ideas and provide inputs and feedback on new	To more or less actively provide	To experience the service innovation	To integrate private resources with other available resources

(Continued)

Table 6.2 (Cont.)

	Output-based archetype	Process-based archetype	Experiential archetype	Systemic archetype
	service concepts before they are launched, or following launch ('after-innovation')	inputs to the service production process	phenomenon in his/her social context	in a novel and viable way
Other relevant actors	Suppliers and service partners	Service partners and other customers (in individual collective phases)	Other individuals in the social setting	All other actors involved in the service ecosystem

Based on Helkkula et al. (2018, p. 290)

(Rubalcaba et al., 2012). This conceptualization of service innovation in terms of the experience of engaged actors is seldom the starting point in innovation literature. However, Helkkula et al. (2018) argue that this archetype has attracted growing attention precisely because of its focus on the experience of the user/beneficiary, and it resonates with the rapidly growing stream of literature on customer experience (e.g., Lemon & Verhoef, 2016).

Finally, the *systemic* archetype contributes by focusing on resource integration by actors in the ecosystem. It resonates with the view of Rubalcaba et al. (2012) that the unit of analysis for service innovation research should be the service ecosystem rather than the service offering. Furthermore, it builds on the notion that individual firms cannot successfully launch a new offering or orchestrate the required networks without connecting to multiple actors in the ecosystem. These actors are guided by social values and institutional arrangements that influence how resources are accessed and integrated. The novel value creation enabled by a service innovation must therefore be understood as part of a collective, embedded in a social system (Helkkula, Kowalkowski, & Tronvoll, 2018). Traditionally, only market-facing resources controlled by a firm are considered when attempting to understand service innovation. However, from a systemic view, both private-facing resources controlled by a customer and public-facing resources controlled by society become key elements in service innovation. In addition, changes in institutions and institutional arrangements (Lawrence & Suddaby, 2006) are seen as an integral part of service innovation.

A combined value-centric view of service innovation

Classification schemes and taxonomies including the service innovation dimensions of Miles (2016) or the modes of innovation described by Gallouj and Weinstein (1997) are used to categorize phenomena based on empirically observable, measurable characteristics (Bailey, 1994). Such classifications generally refer to either-or notions (McKelvey, 1975), which means that a service innovation is either in a specific category or it is not. For example, Gallouj and Weinstein (1997) conceptualize six distinct categories. By contrast, typologies describe conceptually derived, interrelated sets of 'ideal' types. In practice, such ideal theoretical archetypes might not exist in isolation (Brodie, 2014; Doty & Glick, 1994); hence, the four archetypes are not mutually exclusive.

Adopting a synthesis perspective, Helkkula et al. (2018) present a combined, value-centric view of service innovation. The authors' idea is to exploit the strengths of each archetype while overcoming their limitations, by integrating them within an overarching view that conceptualizes service innovation in terms of value co-creation. Although prior research examines different types or modes of innovation in isolation rather than in parallel, in practice, service innovation opportunities and challenges can be better addressed by drawing on all four archetypes. Regarding service innovation as improved value creation for the benefit of customer, a supplier and/or other actors require a combined view. As Helkkula et al. (2018, p. 285) point out,

> no single theoretical archetype alone can capture the complexity of value cocreation in service innovation because of its phenomenological appearances. The combined typology of archetypes in service innovation distinguishes theoretical lenses, facilitating their practical application and so bridging theory and practice in pursuit of novel value cocreation.

Thus, a shared view of service innovation enables theory building and allows for better operationalization of service innovation in further (empirical) research (Witell et al., 2016).

Case illustration: from radio broadcasting to webcasting

In practice, service innovation seldom involves only one archetype. To improve understanding of how the four theoretical archetypes relate to empirical phenomena, consider an example of an innovative shift in audio service transmissions. This innovation changed how organizations provide access to and how customers consume such services, from radio broadcasting to webcasting. From an output- and process-based view, this shift represents technological (product) innovations.

In 1920, wireless broadcasts by radio waves began in the UK, and many other countries followed soon thereafter. Over the coming decades, broadcasting took several forms (primarily AM and FM stations, and later digital and satellite radio). In many households, the (analog) radio became the favored source for media consumption, especially before the breakthrough of television. With radios becoming available in cars, and devices becoming increasingly cheaper and more portable, radio output and consumption increased. However, audio frequency limitations and costs of broadcasting (including expensive licenses, regulations, and capital investments required for digital radio) limited the potential for growth of audio services. The shift to webcasting (the first internet radio service was launched in 1993) enabled greater freedom to broadcast, and has enabled organizations and individuals to set up internet radio studios at low cost. Recently, online access by any suitable device has increased output even further, increasing customer flexibility and choice. Changes in the processes of delivering and accessing radio represent innovations from a process-based view.

Although the shift to webcasting required customers to invest in new technology (as did the shift in some countries from analog to digital radio), it has provided them with greater freedom, as internet technologies enable customers to access audio services anywhere and anytime. From an experiential view, innovation has changed the individual experience and the social context. Initially, most households had one radio device, which shaped the (collective) experience of radio listening. Innovation has changed phenomenologically determined value for the individual and potentially shifted the service experience from social/collective to domestic/individual. Finally, from a systemic view, the shift has changed the service ecosystem, introducing new actors and resources (broadband and mobile infrastructure, devices, apps, etc.) and establishing new rules and norms. Although traditional radio

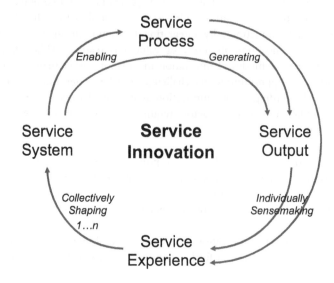

Figure 6.2 The narrative of value-centric service innovation.

Note: Based on Helkkula et al. (2018, p. 293).

broadcasters also provide webcasting, its availability has enabled worldwide distribution of audio services from a wide range of new niche actors.

Figure 6.2 illustrates how the four service innovation archetypes improved understanding of the shifts in radio listening behavior. Technological innovations changed the service processes, generating new ways of accessing audio services, from broadcasts to webcasting. Next, service process and output influenced the service experience through individual sensemaking. Collectively, the service experience shaped the ecosystem. Such reconfiguration then enabled new and improved service processes and additional outputs. A combined value-centric view allows for the application of the archetypes in combination. In practice, firms need to balance innovation efforts: Witell et al. (2016) and Helkkula, Kowalkowski, and Tronvoll (2018) argue that NSD projects can be more effectively managed by combining the archetypes—as shown by the value-centric view in Figure 6.2—to exploit their benefits and holistically explore new opportunities for value creation.

Discussion

This section offers reflections on the use of terminology, modes of service innovation, and the use of different perspectives. One key question to be addressed is whether research on service innovation is mature enough to move toward using one term, one mode, and one perspective, or if parallel existing paradigms continue to be required.

Terminology for service innovation

Different perspectives on service innovation apparently agree on only one issue—a service innovation is a new service (Witell et al., 2016). As this chapter shows, such a view of service innovation is not sufficient to capture the essence of the service innovation concept—because all new services should then be viewed as innovations. Schumpeter (1934) argued that innovation not only creates value for the entrepreneur, but also changes the market in such a way that other firms imitate and follow. This suggests that the concept of newness cannot relate solely to a single individual or firm perspective; it has to consider either the entire market or the world in order to remain relevant.

Witell et al. (2016) emphasized that differences in perspectives should be mirrored in different labels for what an innovation is (such as "innovation" for assimilation, "services innovation" for demarcation, and "service innovation" for synthesis). If the labels are used in this way, they are consistent with the origin and key characteristics used in each perspective (see Miles, 2016; Vargo & Lusch, 2008). Using the labels consistently would be beneficial for academics and practitioners when they read research and develop managerial implications, because it would clarify what implications can be attributed to each specific view of service innovation.

Put together, combine, and recombine

Arthur (2009) suggested that as more new technologies become available, larger solution space and more new services can be created. This logic is based on the idea that service innovation concerns recombining resources in novel ways. Lusch and Nambisan (2015) described service innovation as the rebundling of resources, to create novel resources that are beneficial to some actors. This is consistent with the Schumpeterian view of innovation, making "carrying out of new combinations" the core of how service innovation takes place (Schumpeter, 1934 p. 66). The recombinative view of innovation is also apparent in the literature on product innovation, which is the foundation for the assimilation perspective on service innovation. Henderson and Clark (1990) call this "architectural innovation" and view it as reconfiguration of an established system to link together existing components in new ways.

Service innovation takes advantage of new combinations of resources derived from existing knowledge and technology. Gremyr, Löfberg, and Witell (2010) and Gremyr, Witell, Löfberg, Edvardsson, & Fundin (2014) suggested that service innovations are often recombinative, and that new services often go through a series of changes before succeeding on the market. Service research typically emphasizes the recombinative aspect of service innovation, but it also involves changing the resources that are recombined, or even breaking apart existing service (Gallouj & Savona, 2009). Gremyr et al. (2014) provide an example of how Volvo combined changes in technology with a new business model and new service content, enabling the company to introduce a new service on the market and integrate it with the core product offering to create an innovative solution. Although recombinatory innovation typically focuses on the service offering (Gallouj & Weinstein, 1997), it also has bearing on the reconfiguration of the service ecosystem, as put forward by the systemic archetype in the Helkkula et al. (2018) typology. Such reconfiguration of resources can enable new offerings, processes, and experiences.

Synthesis as a potential replacement for assimilation and demarcation

Currently, there are many perspectives on service innovation, and it makes sense to seek a unifying approach, perhaps a synthesis perspective or a value-centric view. However, there are good reasons that the different perspectives continue to exist in parallel, and they are all likely to be used in the future, both in theory and practice. This is true, in part, because different perspectives emphasize different traits and characteristics of service innovations. If one wants to emphasize the technological view of service innovations, an assimilation perspective fits best, whereas if the customer view is the main characteristic of the service innovation, either a demarcation or a synthesis perspective should be selected. Alternatively, an experiential and/or process-based archetype could pinpoint this view. Furthermore, as shown by research on service development in manufacturing (e.g., Gremyr et al., 2014; Kindström & Kowalkowski, 2009), a demarcation perspective may be particularly helpful when pursuing service innovation in goods-dominant companies.

To be able to provide a synthesis perspective, many models become rather abstract and may be more difficult to apply in practice and operationalize in research studies. An example is suggested by the many broad survey studies on service innovation activities. These typically measure output and process-based innovations, which can be defined and measured using company data, whereas experiential and systemic innovation are more challenging to capture and compare in such studies. In summary, this is the price to be paid when one attempts to comprehend the different views through one perspective and model.

Conclusion

The present chapter reviews an exhaustive list of research on service innovation, and has attempted to create structure and provide summaries and guidelines on how researchers and managers can view this topic. Although the chapter focuses on certain specific models for service innovation, there is not one best way to view it. Taking a contingency perspective, the choice depends on the characteristics of the service innovation which core models best describe the context (firm, market, offering, beneficiary, ecosystem, etc.) where the service innovation is being developed.

This chapter distinguishes and describes the characteristics and core models present in several different perspectives on service innovation. The five perspectives focus on technological or non-technological elements (techno- versus servo- approaches) and similarities or differences between services and goods (assimilation versus demarcation) as well as a unifying synthesis perspective. In addition, the chapter describes four archetypes for service innovation—output-based, process-based, experiential, and systemic. Taken together, the perspectives and archetypes of service innovation provide a nuanced view that can guide researchers to better study and understanding of service innovation.

Advice to future researchers would include being consistent in terminology that describes service innovation and how it can be understood. Previous research has often been vague in describing what perspective it has adopted and what aspects best characterize a service innovation. It is important to observe that not all new services are innovations and that not all firms are innovative—and making a contradictory suggestion would diminish the value of the 'service innovation' concept.

References

Abernathy, W. J., & Clark, K. B. (1985). Innovation: Mapping the winds of creative destruction. *Research Policy*, 14(1), 3–22.

Abernathy, W. J., & Townsend, P. L. (1975). Technology, productivity and process change. *Technological Forecasting and Social Change*, 7(4), 379–396.

Adner, R., & Levinthal, D. (2001). Demand heterogeneity and technology evolution: Implications for product and process innovation. *Management Science*, 47(5), 611–628.

Alam, I. (2002). An exploratory investigation of user involvement in new service development. *Journal of the Academy of Marketing Science*, 30(3), 250–261.

Amara, N., Landry, R., & Doloreux, D. (2009). Patterns of innovation in knowledge-intensive business services. *Service Industries Journal*, 29(4), 407–430.

Arthur, W. B. (2009). *The nature of technology: What it is and how it evolves*. New York, NY: Simon and Schuster.

Bailey, K. D. (1994). *Typologies and taxonomies: An introduction to classification techniques*. Thousand Oaks, CA: SAGE Publications.

Barras, R. (1986). Towards a theory of innovation in services. *Research Policy*, 15(4), 161–173.

Baumol, W. J. (1967). Macroeconomics of unbalanced growth: The anatomy of an urban crisis. *American Economic Review*, 57(3), 415–426.

Bowen, D. E., Siehl, C., & Schneider, B. (1989). A framework for analyzing customer service orientations in manufacturing. *Academy of Management Review*, 14(1), 75.

Breidbach, C., Choi, S., Ellway, B., Keating, B. W., Kormusheva, K., Kowalkowski, C., ... & Maglio, P. P. (2018). Operating without operations: How is technology changing the role of the firm? *Journal of Service Management*, 29(5), 809–833.

Brodie, R. J. (2014). Future of theorizing: Increasing contribution by bridging theory and practice. In L. Moutinho, E. Bigné, & A. K. Manrai (Eds.), *The Routledge companion to the future of marketing* (pp. 88–104). New York, NY: Routledge.

Carlborg, P., Kindström, D., & Kowalkowski, C. (2014). The evolution of service innovation research: A critical review and synthesis. *Service Industries Journal*, 34(5), 373–398.

Chase, R. B. (1978). Where does the customer fit in a service operation? *Harvard Business Review*, 56(6), 137–142.

Chase, R. B., & Apte, U. M. (2007). A history of research in service operations: What's the big idea? *Journal of Operations Management*, 25(2), 375–386.

Cheng, C. C., & Krumwiede, D. (2010). The effects of market orientation and service innovation on service industry performance: An empirical study. *Operations Management Research*, 3(3–4), 161–171.

Coombs, R., & Miles, I. (2000). Innovation, measurement and services: The new problematique. In J. S. Metcalfe & I. Miles (Eds.), *Innovation systems in the service economy, measurement and case study analysis* (pp. 85–103). Boston, MA: Kluwer Academic.

Davies, A. (2004). Moving base into high-value integrated solutions: A value stream approach. *Industrial and Corporate Change*, 13(5), 727–756.

de Brentani, U. (2001). Innovative versus incremental new business services: Different keys for achieving success. *Journal of Product Innovation Management*, 18, 169–187.

Den Hertog, P., van der Aa, W., & de Jong, M. W. (2010). Capabilities for managing service innovation: Towards a conceptual framework. *Journal of Service Management*, 21(4), 490–514.

Djellal, F., Gallouj, F., & Miles, I. (2013). Two decades of research on innovation in services: Which place for public services? *Structural Change and Economic Dynamics*, 27(C), 98–117.

Doty, D. H., & Glick, W. H. (1994). Typologies as a unique form of theory building: Toward improved understanding and modeling. *Academy of Management Review*, 19(2), 230–251.

Drejer, I. (2004). Identifying innovation in surveys of services: A schumpeterian perspective. *Research Policy*, 33(3), 551–562.

The Economist. (2005). Industrial metamorphosis. *The Economist*, 377(8446), 69–70.

Edvardsson, B. (1997). Quality in new service development: Key concepts and a frame of reference. *International Journal of Production Economics*, 52(1/2), 31–46.

Edvardsson, B., Gustafsson, A., Kristensson, P., Magnusson, P., & Matthing, J. (2006). *Involving customers in new service development*. London: Imperial College Press.

Edvardsson, B., & Olsson, J. (1996). Key concepts for new service development. *Service Industries Journal*, 16(2), 140–164.

Edvardsson, B., & Tronvoll, B. (2013). A new conceptualization of service innovation grounded in SD logic and service systems. *International Journal of Quality and Service Sciences*, 5(1), 19–31.

Enz, C. A. (2012). Strategies for the implementation of service innovations. *Cornell Hospitality Quarterly*, 53(3), 187–195.

Flikkema, M., Jansen, P., & Van Der Sluis, L. (2007). Identifying neo-schumpeterian innovation in service firms: A conceptual essay with a novel classification. *Economics of Innovation and New Technology*, 16(7), 541–558.

Fogel, R. W. (2000). *The fourth great awakening and the future of egalitarianism.* Chicago, IL: University of Chicago Press.

Freel, M. S. (2003). Sectoral patterns of small firm innovation, networking and proximity. *Research Policy,* 32(5), 751–770.

Gago, D., & Rubalcaba, L. (2007). Innovation and ICT in service firms: Towards a multidimensional approach for impact assessment. *Journal of Evolutionary Economics,* 17(1), 25–44.

Gallouj, F., & Savona, M. (2009). Innovation in services: A review of the debate and a research agenda. *Journal of Evolutionary Economics,* 19(2), 149–172.

Gallouj, F., & Savona, M. (2010). Towards a theory of innovation in services: A state of the art. In F. Gallouj & F. Djellal (Eds.), *The handbook of innovation and services: A multi-disciplinary perspective* (pp. 27–48). Cheltenham, UK and Northampton, MA, USA: Edward Elgar Publishing.

Gallouj, F., & Weinstein, O. (1997). Innovation in services. *Research Policy,* 26(4/5), 537–556.

Gremyr, I., Löfberg, N., & Witell, L. (2010). Service innovations in manufacturing firms. *Managing Service Quality: An International Journal,* 20(2), 161–175.

Gremyr, I., Witell, L., Löfberg, N., Edvardsson, B., & Fundin, A. (2014). Understanding new service development and service innovation through innovation modes. *Journal of Business & Industrial Marketing,* 29(2), 123–131.

Helkkula, A., Kelleher, C., & Pihlström, M. (2012). Characterizing value as an experience: Implications for researchers and managers. *Journal of Service Research,* 15(1), 59–75.

Helkkula, A., Kowalkowski, C., & Tronvoll, B. (2018). Archetypes of service innovation: Implications for value cocreation. *Journal of Service Research,* 23(3), 284–301.

Henderson, R. M., & Clark, K. B. (1990). Architectural innovation: The reconfiguration of existing product technologies and the failure of established firms. *Administrative Science Quarterly,* 35(1), 9–30.

Hill, T. P. (1977). On goods and services. *Review of Income and Wealth,* 23(4), 315–338.

Hipp, C., & Grupp, H. (2005). Innovation in the service sector: The demand for service-specific innovation measurement concepts and typologies. *Research Policy,* 34(4), 517–535.

Hollenstein, H. (2003). Innovation modes in the Swiss service sector: A cluster analysis based on firm-level data. *Research Policy,* 32(5), 845–863.

Karniouchina, E. V., Victorino, L., & Verma, R. (2006). Product and service innovation: Ideas for future cross-disciplinary research. *Journal of Product Innovation Management,* 23(3), 274–280.

Kindström, D., & Kowalkowski, C. (2009). Development of industrial service offerings: A process framework. *Journal of Service Management,* 20(2), 156–172.

Kindström, D., & Kowalkowski, C. (2014). Service innovation in product-centric firms: A multidimensional business model perspective. *Journal of Business & Industrial Marketing,* 29(2), 96–111.

Ko, H. T., & Lu, H. P. (2010). Measuring innovation competencies for integrated services in the communications industry. *Journal of Service Management,* 21(2), 162–190.

Koskela-Huotari, K., Edvardsson, B., Jonas, J. M., Sörhammar, D., & Witell, L. (2016). Innovation in service ecosystem: Breaking, making, and maintaining institutionalized rules of resource integration. *Journal of Business Research,* 69(8), 2964–2971.

Kowalkowski, C., Gebauer, H., & Oliva, R. (2017). Service growth in product firms: Past, present, and future. *Industrial Marketing Management,* 60, 82–88.

Kowalkowski, C., & Ulaga, W. (2017). *Service strategy in action: A practical guide for growing your B2B service and solution business.* Scottsdale, AZ: Service Strategy Press.

Kuo, Y. K., Kuo, T. H., & Ho, L. A. (2014). Enabling innovative ability: Knowledge sharing as a mediator. *Industrial Management & Data Systems,* 114(5), 696–710.

Kuznets, S. (1966). *Modern economic growth: Rate, structure, and spread.* New Haven, CT and London: Yale University Press.

Lancaster, K. L. (1966). A new approach to consumer theory. *Journal of Political Economy,* 74(2), 132–157.

Larsson, R., & Bowen, D. E. (1989). Organization and customer: Managing design and coordination of services. *Academy of Management Review,* 14(2), 213–233.

Laursen, K., & Salter, A. (2006). Open for innovation: The role of openness in explaining innovation performance among UK manufacturing companies. *Strategic Management Journal,* 27(2), 131–150.

Lawrence, T. B., & Suddaby, R. (2006). Institutions and institutional work. In S. R. Clegg, C. Hardy, T. B. Lawrence, & W. R. Nord (Eds.), *Handbook of organization studies* (2nd Edition, pp. 215–254). London: SAGE Publications.

Lemon, K. N., & Verhoef, P. C. (2016). Understanding customer experience throughout the customer journey. *Journal of Marketing*, 80(November), 69–96.

Levitt, T. (1972). Production-line approach to service. *Harvard Business Review*, 50(5), 41–52.

Lusch, R. F., & Nambisan, S. (2015). Service innovation: A service-dominant logic perspective. *MIS Quarterly*, *39*(1), 155–175.

Lusch, R. F., & Vargo, S. L. (2006). *The service-dominant logic of marketing: Dialog, debate, and directions.* Armonk, NY: M. E. Sharpe.

McKelvey, B. (1975). Guidelines for the empirical classification of organizations. *Administrative Science Quarterly*, 20(4), 509–525.

Menor, L. J., & Roth, A. V. (2007). New service development competence in retail banking: Construct development and measurement validation. *Journal of Operations Management*, 25(4), 825–846.

Michel, S., Brown, S. W., & Gallan, A. S. (2008). Service-logic innovations: How to innovate customers, not products. *California Management Review, 50*(3), 49–65.

Miles, I. (2016). Twenty years of service innovation research. In M. Toivonen (Ed.), *Service innovation: Novel ways of creating value in actor systems* (pp. 3–34). New York, NY: Springer (Translational Systems Sciences, vol. 6).

Miozzo, M., & Soete, L. (2001). Internationalization of services: A technological perspective. *Technological Forecasting and Social Change*, *67*(2–3), 159–185.

Nijssen, E. J., Hillebrand, B., Vermeulen, P. A., & Kemp, R. G. (2006). Exploring product and service innovation similarities and differences. *International Journal of Research in Marketing*, *23*(3), 241–251.

Normann, R. (2001). *Reframing business: When the map changes the landscape.* Chichester, UK: John Wiley & Sons, Ltd.

Ordanini, A., & Parasuraman, A. (2011). Service innovation viewed through a service-dominant logic lens: A conceptual framework and empirical analysis. *Journal of Service Research*, 14(1), 3–23.

Organisation for Economic Co-operation and Development (OECD). (2018). *Oslo manual: Guidelines for collecting, reporting and using data on innovation.* Paris, France: OECD Publishing.

Ostrom, A. L., Bitner, M. J., Brown, S. W., Burkhard, K. A., Goul, M., Smith-Daniels, V., Demirkan, H., & Rabinovich, E. (2010). Moving forward and making a difference: Research priorities for the science of service. *Journal of Service Research*, 13(1), 4–36.

Ostrom, A. L., Parasuraman, A., Bowen, D. E., Patricio, L., & Voss, C. A. (2015). Service research priorities in a rapidly changing context. *Journal of Service Research*, 18(2), 127–159.

Pavitt, K. (1984). Sectoral patterns of technical change: Towards a theory and a taxonomy. *Research Policy*, 13(6), 343–373.

Rathmell, J. M. (1966). What is meant by services? *Journal of Marketing*, 30(October), 32–36.

Roper, S., Du, J., & Love, J. H. (2008). Modelling the innovation value chain. *Research Policy*, 37(6-7), 961–977.

Rubalcaba, L., Gago, D., & Gallego, J. (2010). On the differences between goods and services innovation. *Journal of Innovation Economics*, 5(1), 17–40.

Rubalcaba, L., Michel, S., Sundbo, J. Brown, S. W., & Reynoso, J. (2012). Shaping, organizing, and rethinking service innovation: A multidimensional framework. *Journal of Service Management*, 23(5), 696–715.

Rust, R. T. (2004). If everything is service, why is this happening now, and what difference does it make? Invited commentaries on "evolving to a new dominant logic for marketing." *Journal of Marketing*, 68(January), 23–24.

Salunke, S., Weerawardena, J., & McColl-Kennedy, J. R. (2011). Towards a model of dynamic capabilities in innovation-based competitive strategy: Insights from project-oriented service firms. *Industrial Marketing Management*, 40(8), 1251–1263.

Saviotti P. P., & Metcalfe, J. S. (1984). A theoretical approach to the construction of technological output indicators. *Research Policy*, 13, 141–151.

Schumpeter, J. A. (1934). *Change and the entrepreneur.* Cambridge, MA: Harvard University Press.

Shostack, G. L. (1977). Breaking free from product marketing. *Journal of Marketing*, 41(April), 73–80.

Snyder, H., Witell, L., Gustafsson, A., Fombelle, P., & Kristensson, P. (2016). Identifying categories of service innovation: A review and synthesis of the literature. *Journal of Business Research*, 69(7), 2401–2408.

Sundbo, J. (1997). Management of innovation in services. *Service Industries Journal*, 17(3), 432–455.

Teece, D. J., Pisano, G., & Shuen, A. (1997). Dynamic capabilities and strategic management. *Strategic Management Journal*, 18(7), 509–533.

Toivonen, M., & Tuominen, T. (2009). Emergence of innovations in services. *Service Industries Journal*, 29(7), 887–902.

Utterback, J. M., & Abernathy, W. J. (1975). A dynamic model of process and product innovation. *Omega*, 3(6), 639–656.

Valtakoski, A. (2017). Explaining servitization failure and deservitization: A knowledge-based perspective. *Industrial Marketing Management*, 60, 138–150.

van der Aa, W., & Elfring, T. (2002). Realizing innovation in services. *Scandinavian Journal of Management*, 18(2), 155–171.

Vandermerwe, S., & Rada, J. (1988). Servitization of business: Adding value by adding services. *European Management Journal*, 6(4), 314.

Vargo, S. L., & Lusch, R. F. (2008). Why "service"? *Journal of the Academy of Marketing Science*, 36(1), 25–38.

Vargo, S. L., Wieland, H., & Akaka, M. A. (2015). Innovation through institutionalization: A service ecosystems perspective. *Industrial Marketing Management*, 44(1), 63–72.

Witell, L., Snyder, H., Gustafsson, A., Fombelle, P., & Kristensson, P. (2016). Defining service innovation: A review and synthesis. *Journal of Business Research*, 69(8), 2863–2872.

7

Front line employees as innovators

Marit Engen

Introduction

Front line employees (FLEs) – those having regular customer contact – traditionally have an important role in the service literature. In the decade from 1980 to 1990, when studies of service quality dominated the research field, FLEs were argued to have key positons in service delivery processes, to ensure quality and provide customer satisfaction (e.g. Grönroos, 1984, 1990; Normann, 1984; Parasuraman, Zeithaml, & Berry, 1985). Beginning with the new millennium, growing attention on service innovation as a critical research field slowly brought the focus around to FLEs as essential actors and contributors to new service development and service innovation (e.g. de Brentani, 2001; Edvardsson, Gustafsson, Johnson, & Sanden, 2000; Ordanini & Parasuraman, 2011; Sundbo, 1997).

The FLEs' boundary-spanning roles, working in-between the organization and the customers, have positioned these employees as potential carriers of valuable knowledge relevant for the innovating organization (Engen & Magnusson, 2015; Karlsson & Skålén, 2015; Melancon, Griffith, Noble, & Chen, 2010). Even so, in the article by Ostrom, Parasuraman, Bowen, Patrício, and Voss (2015) on 'Service research priorities,' the relevance of FLEs *appears* to be less compelling as the context of how service is delivered and experienced has evolved (p. 134, italics in original). Despite this, these authors identify nine important employee-related topics to address in future research, one of which states; "incorporating the 'voice of the employee' in service innovation" (Ostrom et al., 2015, p. 135). As knowledgeable actors, FLEs may contribute and play an important role in service innovation processes. However, having knowledge and being suited to take on a role does not necessarily imply that an employee is *able* to take on the role.

Although acknowledged as valuable, FLEs are rarely portrayed as the leading actors in studies of service innovation (Engen & Magnusson, 2018; Sundbo, Sundbo, & Henten, 2015). The literature tends to present FLEs as playing an important part, and argues for the involvement of FLEs (e.g. Åkesson, Skålén, Edvardsson, & Stålhammar, 2016; Karlsson & Skålén, 2015; Ordanini & Parasuraman, 2011). However, service innovation processes are typically orchestrated by someone else (e.g. managers). Thus, in service innovation studies, FLEs are primarily perceived as contributors to innovation processes (e.g. idea makers) and are not themselves viewed as innovators or initiators of innovation processes (Kesting & Ulhøi, 2010).

This chapter takes a somewhat different approach and makes a distinction between agency and involvement in innovation processes. In other words, there is a difference between being an agent and being involved. Involvement is often applied without identifying what this means for the implicated actors. Generally, involvement in organizational activities can, according to Ang (2002), hold both active and passive aspects; however, as someone else (e.g. managers) is responsible for involving an employee, it suggests a somewhat passive point of departure. Viewed a different way, becoming agents implies that FLEs can construct their own actions within their workplaces (Giddens, 1984). In this view, FLEs are described as knowledgeable actors, where a central premise lies in the actors' opportunity to act on their knowledge. However, to be able to 'act differently,' they need not only to have the knowledge, but also to have the option and power to make a different choice (Giddens, 1984). Accordingly, the meaning of 'becoming agents' in service innovation processes suggests that employees are not merely subjugated to organizational processes, but they practise agency, understood as situations where employees make choices and exert influence on their work practices (Eteläpelto, Vähäsantanen, Hökkä, & Paloniemi, 2013). FLEs' potential to practise agency has its boundaries. An employee's actions are influenced by constraining and enabling arrangements, based on both conditions of the workplace as well as the employee's personal characteristics (Billett, 2012; Eteläpelto et al., 2013). *The aim of this chapter is therefore to develop new understanding of how FLEs may innovate by practising agency, and how they can construct their roles as agents in service innovation processes.*

The next section outlines the central theoretical perspectives to service innovation, focusing in particular on how FLEs are positioned and portrayed in service innovation processes. Based on further theory development and backed with empirical examples, a framework for understanding FLEs as agents is subsequently introduced. The chapter ends with a discussion of implications for service innovation research.

Service innovation

Service innovation, as a research field, has evolved from being marginal and neglected (Miles, 2000) to representing a rich, complex, and dynamic field, in which new approaches and contributions are continually introduced. In fact, a rapidly growing number of studies have left the concept of service innovation as broadly and loosely defined (Rubalcaba, Michel, Sundbo, Brown, & Reynoso, 2012; Witell, Snyder, Gustafsson, Fombelle, & Kristensson, 2016). Owing to the goal of this chapter, it is necessary to bring attention to some aspects of how service innovation is commonly understood and framed.

A general understanding of innovation is provided by Schumpeter (1934), who views innovation as carrying out 'new combinations,' combining existing ideas and resources in novel ways. This definition is applicable for most perspectives and disciplines, as almost all innovations reflect existing knowledge, combined in new ways (Lundvall, 2010). Although Schumpeter focused on the solitary role of the firm to carry out such combinations, service innovation is viewed as a more open and interactive process. It is a process relying on various sources of knowledge, thus involving different actors across different practices, organizations, industries, and sectors (Chesbrough, 2003, 2011; Lusch & Nambisan, 2015; Vargo, Wieland, & Akaka, 2015, 2016; von Hippel, 1988). Furthermore, service innovation is not a concept or an activity reserved for service firms or service industries. The broadened perspective of the service-based view of innovation blurs the border between goods and services, and refers to a specific approach to business innovation (Rubalcaba et al., 2012). A broad approach to service innovation is further highlighted through the service-dominant logic (S-D logic) perspective, in which services are seen as value co-created practices, and service innovation is not simply a new offering, but improved customer value co-creation (Michel, Brown, & Gallan, 2008; Patrício, Gustafsson, & Fisk, 2018; Vargo & Lusch, 2008).

The S-D logic and service ecosystem perspectives represent process views of service innovation, where multiple actors engage in co-creating processes and integrating resources in new and novel ways (Helkkula, Kowalkowski, & Tronvoll, 2018; Koskela-Huotari, Edvardsson, Jonas, Sörhammar, & Witell, 2016; Skålén, Gummerus, von Koskull, & Magnusson, 2015). A process view is central for discussing FLEs as innovators. It allows us to consider phenomena dynamically, in terms of movement, activity, events, change, and temporal evolution instead of what is produced, or output (Langley, 2007, p. 271). This chapter turns attention toward FLEs: how they act, understanding the premises for their actions, and what may follow from these acts. At the same time, it is important to view FLEs within the frame of where they act. Hence, the chapter follows the process perspective of organizing for service innovation provided by Rubalcaba et al. (2012), in which FLE frameworks for action are set within a balanced approach to service innovation, and they are viewed as actors stationed in-between the processes for management and customers.

Following this background, the chapter's framework, which offers a balanced approach to service innovation, is presented. To deepen understanding of how FLEs can become agents within the balanced approach, a practice-based approach to innovation is subsequently introduced to extend the model (e.g. Brown & Duguid, 1991; Ellström, 2010; Høyrup, 2012).

A balanced approach to service innovation

The balanced approach advocated in this chapter views service innovation processes through a dual lens, in which innovation is seen as being driven by the whole organization (Fuglsang & Sundbo, 2005). The framework combines the necessity of strategic directions for innovation with the recognition of including ideas that emerge throughout the organization. Thus, the duality aspect is reflected through the concept of strategic reflexivity (Fuglsang & Sundbo, 2005; Sundbo, 2003), seen as a form of instrument for managing the chaos that innovation processes constitute (Sundbo & Fuglsang, 2002). Although strategy marks the need for organizations to change, reflexivity refers more to processes of how and when to change (Sundbo, 2003). Reflexivity and interpretation are not actions that are preserved in one distinct group. Strategic reflexivity needs to lean on an organization that is described as dual, in which the duality reflects two structures within the organization (Fuglsang & Sundbo, 2005; Rubalcaba et al., 2012). The two structures include a hierarchical one, defined as managerial, and a loosely coupled interactive one, in which both employees and managers are expected to participate. The strategy (hierarchy) functions as a guideline for the ideas that employees and managers are expected to contribute (loosely coupled); thus, the structures are dependent on each other and need to be combined in order to ensure an innovation process that is continuous and inclusive.

Employees, middle managers, and top managers, although representative of different structures within the organization, are viewed as important contributors to both interpreting the current situation and contributing ideas to processes that are ongoing and emergent. The ideas that typically emerge from employees through bottom-up processes need to be coordinated, developed, and fitted within the strategic course of the organization and ongoing top-down processes (Saari, Lehtonen, & Toivonen, 2015). Hence, the organization adopts a dual and balanced approach to innovation activities (Rubalcaba et al., 2012; Sundbo, 2003).

FLEs are seen in this perspective as particularly important idea generators (Rubalcaba et al., 2012). FLEs are often the first and only point of contact between the organization and the customer. Customers can therefore be seen as part of the FLE work arena, and the interaction point is the key for highlighting FLEs as knowledgeable actors who can stimulate innovation (e.g. Lages & Piercy, 2012; Ordanini & Parasuraman, 2011; Sørensen, Sundbo, & Mattsson, 2013; Sundbo et al., 2015). Employee work practices are more than an arena for bringing in customer-based knowledge. Karlsson and Skålén (2015) find that FLEs contribute practice knowledge ('know how') and product knowledge ('know what') in addition to customer knowledge, depending on the phase of the service innovation process. Engen and Magnusson (2015) argue similarly, that FLEs contribute both use knowledge and technology knowledge in service innovation processes. 'Use knowledge' refers to knowledge gained as a user (customer value), whereas 'technology knowledge' refers to knowledge of the organization, specifically work routines (Lüthje, 2004). Both types of knowledge are necessary to succeed at innovation (von Hippel, 1994). In Åkesson et al. (2016), FLEs are found to incorporate valuable customer-based knowledge throughout the innovation process. Furthermore, employee work practices are seen as an important arena for testing what really works, as well as modifying and adjusting new ideas.

As previously stated, the positioning of FLEs as contributors to service innovation is well demonstrated in several studies. FLE knowledge of customers, combined with their knowledge of practice, make FLEs apt as innovators. However, FLE knowledge is more than what they know; their knowledge is also embedded in situated activity (Dougherty, 2004). This implies that, when FLEs are invited to contribute to innovation outside their practice, only part of their knowledge is transferred and integrated into service innovation processes. A core piece of knowledge in a practice-based approach to innovation is how employees continuously enact their jobs, while at the same time they reshape their jobs (Price, Boud, & Scheeres, 2012), creating new solutions from and based in employee work practices. These are ongoing processes (Hernes, 2014), which do not necessarily feature clear starting points or endings, as with a more well-defined project. Through such working and learning processes, FLE practices change and (may) become part of the organization's innovations. The duality displayed here is central in the balanced approach to service innovation, as it argues for balancing ideas and innovation activities both top-down and bottom-up (Rubalcaba et al., 2012; Saari et al., 2015). However, the premises for employees to act and contribute, and how they go about it within the duality, are more vaguely described.

A distinction can be made between FLEs in the management-led and strategy-based innovation processes versus the bottom-up processes. In the management structure, innovating initiatives are determined by managers; hence, FLEs participate by either being invited or requested to participate (e.g. Åkesson et al., 2016). This does not imply that employee involvement is less valid; it is simply based on different premises (Engen & Magnusson, 2018). In bottom-up processes, a core notion is how ideas originate from interaction of employees; it is based on the input of active employees that initiate, support, and even drive the processes themselves (Høyrup, 2012; Kesting & Ulhøi, 2010). To be able to understand FLEs as agents in service innovation processes, it is important to view their actions from their positions. Consequently, this chapter introduces a practice-based approach as a viewpoint to understand FLEs in the act of innovating (Russo-Spena & Mele, 2012).

The practice of FLEs

The use of the term 'practice' in organizational studies differs in both label and definition from common usage of the term (see Corradi, Gherardi, & Verzelloni, 2010 for a review). However, a central premise for all practice-based approaches is the recognition that knowledge is situated in collective action (Dougherty, 2004; Lave & Wenger, 1991) and is seen as a participative social process (Corradi et al., 2010). Following Wenger (2000), learning is viewed as a dynamic, two-way relationship between people and the social learning systems in which they participate. Hence, learning is not exclusively for an individual, but involves the entire community (Gherardi, Nicolini, & Odella, 1998). A community can be any group of people who engage in a process of collective learning and sharing cultural practices, such as a tribe around a campfire or a group of housekeepers at a hotel (Wenger, 2000). When the term 'community' is applied in a workplace, the socialization process utilizes on-the-job learning as an ongoing social activity to discover what is to be done and when and how to do it, according to set routines.

It is also important to understand why things are done as they are, as well as the expectations regarding what it means to be a member of the community (Gherardi et al., 1998). The emphasis is directed toward what is done and how it is done, and not necessarily the grouping that is included in the community. Following Gherardi et al. (1998, p. 279):

> Communities of practice are just one of the forms of organizing: it is not a way to postulate the existence of a new informal grouping or social system within the organization, as a way to emphasize that every practice is dependable on social processes through which it is sustained and perpetuated, and that learning takes place to the engagement in that practice.

Thus, the practice refers to the work being done, and how people go about doing the work (Brown & Duguid, 2001). The community is useful in understanding the relationship between the members, the ongoing activities and processes, and how knowledge, both tacit and explicit, is transferred and new knowledge created (Carlile, 2002; Gherardi et al., 1998).

Turning to the practice of FLEs, a central aspect is that they are not really employed to innovate. FLEs might be thought of as 'ordinary employees,' in the sense that they are not specifically assigned to the innovation tasks of the organization, which may be more appropriate to an R&D department (Kesting & Ulhøi, 2010). The asset provided by FLEs who become agents is therefore deeply connected to their everyday work (Høyrup, 2012; Kesting & Ulhøi, 2010), and their work practice location is a site for learning and innovation. A central notion in the practice-based perspective is how the innovation process is embedded within the employee work practices, their experiences, and reflections, which link learning, innovation, and organization of work. Following Brown and Duguid (1991), learning represents the bridge between working and innovating. Sharing work practice amongst or by a group creates a site for an effective loop of insight, problem identification, and learning, and thereby knowledge production. The same community is then a significant repository for developing, maintaining, and reproducing knowledge (Brown & Duguid, 2001), where the innovative potential lies in the community's way of seeing the world anew (Brown & Duguid, 1991) and redefining the work practice (Dougherty, 2004).

FLE innovative potential

The balanced approach to service innovation views innovation as emergent; strategy frames the innovation processes as a "stream of incremental innovations" (Rubalcaba et al., 2012). FLEs – their ideas, problem-solving abilities, and knowledge – represent the key for realizing the stream. The workplace and/or work processes of FLEs constitute the arena for change (Orlikowski, 1996); this is also an arena for learning and innovation (Ellström, 2010; Nilsen

& Ellström, 2012). The perspective acknowledges how new ideas often emerge from the employee–client interface and, when implemented, represent a new form of innovation for organizations. Such new forms include ad hoc innovation (e.g. Gallouj & Weinstein, 1997) and bricolage innovation, where FLEs do things differently, changing their practice and making use of resources at hand (Fuglsang & Sørensen, 2011). Both ad hoc and bricolage innovations have in common that they are not necessarily based on an intended or pre-planned process, but represent innovation that comes both from and within FLE work practices (Fuglsang & Sørensen, 2011; Gallouj, 2002; Sundbo, 1998).

Bricolage innovations typically represent practice-based innovation processes where managers are not necessarily aware of the activities (Fuglsang, 2010). FLEs enact their jobs, interact with each other, and reconstruct their work practices. However, FLEs may also be couriers of ideas that go beyond the borders of their work practices, where the options to act on these ideas rest outside their control (Engen & Magnusson, 2015; Fuglsang & Sørensen, 2011). The few studies that follow bottom-up processes initiated by FLEs point to the importance of a front-office climate that values creativity, as well as general organizational support (Sørensen et al., 2013). Middle managers are identified as having an important role in coordinating innovation activites, because they are in between employees and top management (Fuglsang & Sørensen, 2011; Saari et al., 2015). Engen and Magnusson (2015) show that middle managers have three roles (facilitator, translator, and gatekeeper) that endorse FLE roles and activities in service innovation processes in different ways. As a facilitator, the middle manager supports and organizes FLEs to participate in innovation activities (e.g. by organizing arenas for idea generation and development). As a translator, a key task is to provide FLEs with information that may guide their ideas alongside the organization's chosen strategic direction. Finally, as a gatekeeper, the middle manager fulfills an important task, which is making sure that the employees get feedback on their ideas.

In summary, the innovative potential of FLEs may be actuated based on either individual or job-conditioned arrangements. To have knowledge and the ability to innovate does not necessarily imply that an employee will do so. Therefore, it is important to identify what makes FLEs tick and triggers them to act on their knowledge, even though they are not invited or expected to innovate. The next section of the chapter draws on FLEs' own stories, to explore how their voices can be incorporated into the organizational processes.

Methodological background of the stories

The stories in the following section are extracted from 53 interviews with FLEs from a wide spectrum of workplaces. The respondents include nurses, engineers, massage therapists, fitness workers, food safety inspectors, and bank employees. In addition, 30 interviews with middle managers and higher level managers are included. These interviews derive from three separate studies, all with the primary aim of better understanding the role of FLEs in service innovation processes. The three studies include:[1] (1) a multiple case study set in (a) a spa-resort, (b) a multinational telecom equipment and service provider, (c) a public sector hospital, and (d) a public sector rehabilitation centre; (2) a single case study of a regional savings bank; (3) a single case study of a public sector agency with food safety as the sphere of activity.

The data analyses are based on cross-case synthesis, a technique that is applicable when the individual cases, or parts of them, have been conducted as independent research studies (Yin, 2009). The analyses of the interviews were narrowed down and framed by the aim of this chapter to understand FLEs as agents in service innovation processes, with the idea that they practise agency. Hence, the analyses followed the questions: how do employees contribute, with what, and why do they engage in innovation activities? The analyses followed phenomenological principles, which implied extraction of condensed meaning from the different interviews that were subsequently sorted in 'themes' (Boyatzis, 1998; Brinkmann & Kvale, 2015). The themes representing the FLE stories were constructed irrespective of context, to provide a generic picture of how FLEs describe themselves as actors engaged in innovation activities, and how they are enabled to act in service innovation processes.

In the next section, the stories of various FLEs are discussed. Portrayals of FLEs as agents are emphasized, elucidating how they are able to construct their participation in innovation activities.

Stories by FLEs

Three key themes emerged from the analyses of the interviews. These themes depict aspects of how FLEs become agents in service innovation processes: (1) the employees' workplace-related knowledge and skills indicate that they have the *ability* to innovate, (2) they are interested and motivated to continuously alter and improve their workplaces, so they show *willingness* to innovate, and (3) because they are given access to resources, the employees have the *opportunity* to innovate. Figure 7.1[2] illustrates how all of these aspects intertwine, and further shows that all three aspects need to be present in order for FLEs to act as agents.

Although the model presented in Figure 7.1 identifies how FLEs can become agents, it also recognizes how employees are hindered from practising agency by three intersections. Reasons for the latter include: (1) Willingness-Opportunity, in which employees lack knowledge relevant for innovation, and therefore are less apt to engage in innovation activities, (2) Ability-Opportunity, in which FLEs may lack motivation to engage in innovation activities, and (3) Ability-Willingness, in which employees may be prevented from acting on their knowledge due to limited access to resources.

As indicted by the model, FLEs have different stories to tell depending on where they 'stand' in the model. Excerpts of their stories are presented next, focusing on the three aspects facilitating employees as agents.

Figure 7.1 Front line employees (FLEs) as agents of service innovation processes (SIP).

FLE ability to innovate

FLE abilities are highly connected to their work practices. The following quotation encapsulates this well:

> We are specialists in different fields, so we come up with ideas based on our expertise (FLE, spa-resort).

The stories from employees all carry similar messages: that their ideas are based on what they do, as stated by two employees working at a savings bank:

> I suggest ideas on things I believe could work better

> The ideas deal a lot with improving our work processes. It does not mean that everything has to be new and spectacular; it can be that old ways are done a bit smarter."

Quotations point to how FLEs get ideas while working. Furthermore, they explicate that these ideas typically fit within the frame of incremental innovations, alongside ongoing employee practices. A food inspector explains innovation activities as part of a continuous process:

> It [innovation] is something that emerges in the group, because we want to do a good job. I do not believe that it happens systematically; I do not feel that someone says 'now today we are placing improvement on the agenda.' It is part of what we do, and a continuous process where we consider if what we do can be improved.

As customers are part of the work processes, the ideas typically use customer value creation as a point of departure. For instance, one of the employees at the savings bank developed a spreadsheet so that customers could more easily understand their benefits if they decided on rental activity. The spreadsheet was developed based on employee experiences regarding customer struggles to understand the profits of rental activities.

In addition to being an arena for learning, the work practices also carry an important function, facilitating employee innovation activities, as expressed by two of them:

> My colleagues are excellent resources. We use a lot of time to discuss amongst each other (FLE, saving bank).

> We talk together, all of us that work together in the region […] we ask questions of how to do something [...] If a colleague has experienced a smart way to do something, naturally this is shared and discussed (FLE, food safety).

The work practice is also described as an arena for collaboration and idea development. An employee at the savings bank explains it in the following way:

> My co-workers are excellent resources. We spend a lot of time discussing. […]. We have what we call a 'blackboard meeting' every Tuesday. One of the topics on the weekly agenda is 'ideas for improvements'. We post ideas, and then throughout the whole week we can add and build on the ideas by using post-its. After a week, we have a discussion and decide whether to go further or not. If we do decide to go further, we organize a small group that meet regularly before deciding on what to do and implement the changes (FLE, savings bank).

This quotation indicates the central core of FLEs becoming agents. They work, they get ideas, and they collaborate, actions that are initiated and driven by the employees themselves:

> I believe the informal arenas are important, where you can meet and discuss inspections you have made, or discuss some input you have received over a cup of coffee. In my opinion, that is where ideas emerge, and where you are able to talk about them. [...] It is easier to take part in idea development at the informal meetings. You get to use the time differently and it feels less formal and strict (FLE, food safety).

FLEs' ability to innovate is deeply rooted within their work practices, which include their potential as well as their limitations. Because employees are preoccupied with their work, that is what they get ideas about, as stated by one employee at the spa-resort: "I do not see myself as influencing the whole resort, but [it is] foremost to be able to influence the part where I belong." A common theme throughout the stories is how the work practices represent a corner-stone for employee innovation activities. Work is also demonstrated as essential for the next aspect, which is the FLE willingness to contribute to service innovation.

FLE willingness to innovate

FLE willingness to innovate is related to individual characteristics, in addition to being influenced by the working environment, including colleagues and managers. This is illustrated by two quotations:

> I still have a lot of energy and enthusiasm to get my ideas through, to be able to make changes. I think it is about two things: who I am as a person and the fact that I have yet to receive that many no's to my initiatives (FLE, spa-resort).

> I consider us to be a really enthusiastic and committed group, who wants to do things better. But it can be hard to get everyone on board. I think it is like this: the further away from the origin that the key holder for further development or implementation sits, the more difficult it seems to be. So it can be a bit frustrating that you have ideas and then it just stops (FLE, food security).

The above quotations point to how employees can be part of two different 'innovation loops,' one being more positive than the other. The commitment to engage in innovation activities seems to come from within the employees themselves. Most of their stories are about how they take an interest in their job and profession, and their enthusiasm to engage in doing things better for their colleagues as well as for their clients and customers. Colleagues are important for support as well as for collaboration; however, innovation initiatives also require support from management, as indicated above.

Although employee engagement in innovation activities is seen by many as positive, it is also described as hard work; most employees feel the need to be heard in order to be motivated to innovate:

> I think it is like this: I have received a response and have been shown trust by my managers and my colleagues. You get feedback, like 'yes, this works well', and that makes you dare to take the next step (FLE, spa-resort).

"Our manager listens to us, and is willing to try what we suggest. It seems like he often agrees with us, and allows us to try it out" (FLE, savings bank).

Positive feedback triggers the employees and provides them with a kind of security regarding who they are as innovators. Yet, when they have to struggle to be heard, it can result in the opposite effect:

> I get the feeling that they [management] make the decisions. If we try to explain that this is not the best way to do it, we get the response that 'well, it has been decided'. Instead of listening to us who knows [...] so I think a lot of people have given up, as it is difficult to be heard (FLE, food security).

The above quotations are parts of stories in which FLEs have what can be described as an inner drive, wanting to contribute. Some employees lose interest in contributing when, for instance, they feel they are not being heard. However, some stories are told by employees who, to a lesser extent, want to contribute. They are, as the following quotation points to, satisfied when they can stick to the daily routines.

> I have come to the understanding that as long as everything works well, there is no point in making changes. I am a bit conservative like that. So I rarely propose any suggestions; no I don't do that (FLE, food security).

Although present, the attitude expressed above is quite rare amongst the employees. Some state that they do not see themselves as being very innovative, and that they quite seldom get new ideas. However, they do address the topic as though they like to contribute together with colleagues, for instance in informal groups discussing ideas and improvements.

FLEs' willingness to innovate is rooted in their work practices, in addition to being influenced by their individual characteristics. Some employees are genuinely more creative than others. However, the main story lies in the support by co-workers and managers that leads to engagement in innovation activities in the long run. As previously stated, having knowledge and being willing to innovate are necessary but not sufficient; employees may still not be able to act. In the next section, stories of how employees gain the opportunities to innovate are presented.

FLE opportunity to innovate

FLE opportunity to innovate can be characterized by two different stories. Both are dependent on having access to resources. The first is about how FLEs engage in bricolage innovation, where they initiate, develop, and enact new solutions based on resources that they can access and control themselves. The second describes how innovations may be co-developed and implemented together with managers or, on the other hand, they may be stopped. This distinction is commented on by one employee as follows:

> We do not have a special system [for ideas]. We address it as it comes along, and we discuss in the hallway or on a coffee break. [...] When it comes to the daily small ideas for improvement, we address them right away. When there are other ideas, like those that, for instance, are rule-governed, that is a different process (FLE, food security).

The two types of innovation processes that are described above are based on quite different ideas and innovation activities. The first is informal and doesn't necessarily go beyond the work practice of the employees involved. It is therefore a 'limited process' in regard to scope and scale; the ideas the employees come up with are small, the time from when the ideas emerge until they are implemented in practice is short, and only a few people need to be involved. These bricolage innovations are part of the work practice and part of the employee continuous improvements. Thus, FLEs are able to act on their knowledge, assuming that they want to, because no one needs to know or needs to be asked. The second type of process has a different story. In this case, FLEs come up with ideas that go beyond their own work practice and/or they need resources outside their control for development and implementation. They come forward as important idea makers for the organization as a whole:

> These employees are my main source for ideas […] it is imperative that they are part of the development processes (middle manager, food security)

> I am totally dependent on using my employees to create the best processes […]. They are the ones closest to the customers and know what the customers need (middle manager, savings bank).

An opportunity to engage in innovation activities is not something that is solely based on the employee and his/her colleagues. It is also based on the relationship between the closest manager (here defined as the middle manager) and the employees.

> A lot of the new things that are done, and the way they are done, are based on ideas from front line employees. It changes the ownership. They approach me with an idea or solution, and then we try it out. It changes how we address problems and how we choose to solve them, and their motivation increases (middle manager, savings bank).

The middle manager apparently views encouragement as an important task, and mentions different ways and arenas to cultivate FLE participation in innovation processes. These include blackboards, sticky notes, regular idea development meetings, and having innovation activities as a fixed agenda item in unit meetings. The managers also point to the importance of 'being there' by taking part in informal meeting opportunities, such as coffee breaks.

The middle managers describe themselves as somewhat 'stuck in the middle.' Similar to the FLEs, they are not employed to innovate. These activities come in addition to daily operations, and being an innovation manager is not described as an effort-free role:

> It takes a lot of work to move forward the ideas. It is a balance how much effort and time I can spend on it; I cannot push further all ideas I receive (middle manager, food security).

Middle managers also state that some ideas require resources they themselves do not control. Therefore, they might find themselves in a similar position to the FLEs, being dependent on others to be able to act and engage in innovation activities.

The managers tell a variety of stories. Some see innovation as an important extra role in which they want to engage. Others do not recognize innovation as part of their work assignments. Therefore, the opportunities for FLEs differ, depending on the possibilities within their units, especially the support and facilitation from their managers.

FLEs are provided with opportunities to innovate based on their access to, and control of, resources and/or the possibility of collaborating with their managers. Both types of processes are also conditioned on employee willingness to participate in innovation processes. As described above, not all employees see themselves as active idea makers; having the opportunity to innovate does not ensure that a particular employee will take it.

In summary, the stories as described above show how FLEs can become agents and assets for their organizations based on their knowledge and skills, willingness to contribute, and, when given an opportunity, their contributions. At the same time, the model presented in Figure 7.1 indicates that personal characteristics, working conditions, and attributes of the work environment influence employee roles as agents. In addition, middle managers come forward as important enablers for FLE intentions to practise agency.

FLEs as agents of service innovation processes

As the stories elucidate, by being able, willing, and afforded the opportunity, FLEs can become agents of service innovation processes. This discussion encompasses how employees construct their innovation activities based on their knowledge, skills, and willingness, and whether or not they are constrained by access to resources. It shows how employee potential to practise agency is constrained and enabled, both by the employees themselves and by conditions in the workplace. The stories demonstrate the importance of employee work practices. This constitutes an arena for working, learning, and support, between employees and customers, amongst colleagues, and between employees and middle managers.

The balanced approach to service innovation was previously described as dependent on two different structures working together (Rubalcaba et al., 2012). One is hierarchical, managerial, and sets strategy, and the other is loosely coupled, interactive, and allows employees and managers to act and contribute ideas. The stories indicate how the "stream of incremental innovations" described by Rubalcaba et al. (2012) can be rooted in the work practices of FLEs. The stories suggest that it is through the activities of everyday work life that employees create alterations or reproduce their work processes. It is from the work practices that problems and/or opportunities arise (e.g. interacting with customers or colleagues) and solutions can be developed and implemented. Accordingly, the ideas or innovation processes emerge from and within FLE work practices.

Employees may, to a certain point, act upon the ideas by themselves. One example is given by bricolage innovations, where employees initiate and enact new solutions without necessarily having the awareness (or approval) of managers. They become agents of service innovation processes by their own initiative and control. However, employees can also come up with ideas that need support and resources outside their control. Under these conditions, middle managers play an important role in creating the workplace as an environment for FLEs to practise agency. As enablers, these managers provide employees with support, as well as creating arenas for collaboration so that the employees can develop their ideas further. This is similar to management functions found in previous studies (e.g. Engen & Magnusson, 2015; Saari et al., 2015). When employees need resources they do not control themselves, they can turn to their managers for the opportunity to act as agents. Therefore, middle managers are identified in enabling roles, influencing the willingness of FLEs to innovate, and providing them with opportunities to do so.

Middle managers are positioned between the structure of FLEs and top management, so they need to coordinate and integrate the ideas that emerge from the work practice within the organization (e.g. Fuglsang & Sørensen, 2011; Saari et al., 2015). Several middle managers brought forward how they had to "work hard" to get commitment and approval from top management in order to secure further development and implementation of employee ideas. However, they did not always succeed. Therefore, although the stories indicate that there is a difference between being an agent and being involved, the ability of employees to construct their participation in service innovation is still, to a great extent, dependent on managers.

The stories of FLEs represented here are in line with findings from previous research that argue that FLEs are potential contributors of relevant knowledge for organizational innovation activities (e.g. Åkesson et al., 2016; Engen & Magnusson, 2015; Karlsson & Skålén, 2015; Sundbo et al., 2015). Introducing agency provides a more nuanced image of how FLEs may contribute to service innovations as agents. Certainly, viewing FLEs as agents does not rule out the relevance of involving FLEs in management-led and -controlled processes. It is more a matter of introducing a perspective in which FLEs are given different prerequisites to act within the work processes. The mandate for employee innovation activities in management-led processes is often predefined, whereas practice-based processes are (as previously argued) closer to the employee domain (both in terms of knowledge and domain of interest). When practising agency, FLEs may add to a given strategic course, and nuance and strengthen it through ongoing processes alongside practice in organizations.

Managerial implications

This chapter illustrates how FLEs, together with colleagues and middle managers, can construct their participation in service innovation and thereby contribute to organizational innovation activities. It is important for managers to recognize that FLEs not only contribute knowledge that is important to innovating, but also contribute knowledge that is often novel and hidden from managers. When an organization fails to incorporate such knowledge, opportunities that arise from the front line are easily missed. However, when FLEs are enabled to practise agency, they contribute practice-based knowledge through ongoing innovation processes.

Organizations need to recognize middle managers and their roles in creating opportunities for FLEs to become agents. Opportunities are created in different ways through facilitation and support. It is imperative that managers understand that to practise agency it is necessary for employees to have access to resources, such as time, as well as arenas for discussions and idea development.

Middle managers are important, but so is top management. A balanced approach to innovation rests on the premise of a dual organization: the two structures are dependent on each other. Top management plays a significant role in enabling middle managers to handle their roles. In order for middle managers to facilitate the employees, they also need resources, encouragement, and support from their managers. It is top management's responsibility to (indirectly) facilitate FLEs in becoming agents in service innovation processes; furthermore, they should design a structure that enables a balanced approach to innovation.

In this chapter, agency helps to enable and understand FLEs as innovators. Understanding the relation between agency, practice, and innovation opens up a fruitful angle to innovation studies in general and practice-based innovation in particular. The stories provided by FLEs are used to create an understanding of them as agents. Agency is influenced by conditions within the workplace as well as by the person who practises agency. This chapter illuminates only some of these factors. Research that further explores how the socio-cultural conditions of a workplace affect employee agency in innovation activities would add to understanding of how practices are renewed and ideas are developed and enacted. Eteläpelto et al. (2013) point out the importance of power relations and work cultures. These factors can influence both relationships between employees and relationships between managers and employees, and therefore they represent an interesting angle for future empirical studies.

The stories provided in this chapter offer a generic image of FLEs as agents. However, based on particular employees' type of work and context, the premises for practising agency would likely differ, and could be another avenue for further research. Furthermore, the stories indicate that there are individual differences between employees as regard to their willingness to innovate. Employee commitment and motivation to work, as well as work-related goals, are all factors intertwined with agency (Eteläpelto et al., 2013). How these factors influence employee willingness to innovate represents a promising opportunity for further studies.

Notes

1 The first study was part of a research project at Karlstad University, Service Research Centre. The second was a case study designed as a collaborative between two Master students and the chapter author as supervisor. The students conducted the interviews as part of a data collection for their Master thesis: 'Jamesson & Knudsen, 2017: A case study of middle managers influence on employee-driven innovation. Lillehammer.' The third study was a research project at Inland Norway University of Applied Sciences.
2 A version of the figure was first published in Engen (2016). In this chapter, new empirical data is included and the discussion elaborated.

References

Åkesson, M., Skålén, P., Edvardsson, B., & Stålhammar, A. (2016). Value proposition test-driving for service innovation: How frontline employees innovate value propositions. *Journal of Service Theory and Practice, 26*(3), 338–362.

Ang, A. (2002). An eclectic review of the multidimensional perspectives of employee involvement. *The TQM Magazine, 14*(3), 192–200. doi:10.1108/09544780210425856.

Billett, S. (2012). Explaining innovation at work: A socio-personal account. In S. Høyrup, M. Bonnafous-Boucher, C. Hasse, M. Lotz, & K. Møller (Eds.), *Employee-driven innovation: A new approach* (pp. 92–107). Basingstoke: Palgrave Macmillan.

Boyatzis, R. E. (1998). *Transforming qualitative information: Thematic analysis and code development.* Thousand Oaks, CA: SAGE.

Brinkmann, S., & Kvale, S. (2015). *InterViews: Learning the craft of qualitative research interviewing.* (3rd ed.). Thousand Oaks, CA: SAGE.

Brown, J. S., & Duguid, P. (1991). Organizational learning and communities-of-practice: Toward a unified view of working, learning and innovation. *Organization Science, 2*(1), 40–56.

Brown, J. S., & Duguid, P. (2001). Knowledge and organization: A social-practice perspective. *Organization Science, 12*(2), 198–213.

Carlile, P. R. (2002). A pragmatic view of knowledge and boundaries: Boundary objects in new product development. *Organization Science, 13*(4), 442–455.

Chesbrough, H. W. (2003). *Open innovation: The new imperative for creating and profiting from technology.* Boston, MA: Harvard Business School Press.

Chesbrough, H. W. (2011). *Open services innovation: Rethinking your business to grow and compete in a new era.* San Francisco, CA: Jossey-Bass.

Corradi, G., Gherardi, S., & Verzelloni, L. (2010). Through the practice lens: Where is the bandwagon of practice-based studies heading? *Management Learning, 41*(3), 265–283.

de Brentani, U. (2001). Innovative versus incremental new business services: Different keys for achieving success. *Journal of Product Innovation Management, 18*, 169–187. doi:10.1111/1540-5885.1830169.

Dougherty, D. (2004). Organizing practices in services: Capturing practice-based knowledge for innovation. *Strategic Organization, 2*(1), 35–64. doi:10.1177/1476127004040914.

Edvardsson, B., Gustafsson, A., Johnson, M. D., & Sanden, B. (2000). *New service development and innovation in the new economy*. Lund: Studenlitteratur.

Ellström, P.-E. (2010). Practice-based innovation: A learning perspective. *Journal of Workplace Learning, 22*(1/2), 27–40.

Engen, M. (2016). Frontline employees as participants in service innovation processes; Innovation by weaving. (PhD), Lillehammer University College, Lillehammer.

Engen, M., & Magnusson, P. (2015). Exploring the role of front-line employees as innovators. *The Service Industries Journal, 35*(6), 303–324. doi:10.1080/02642069.2015.1003370.

Engen, M., & Magnusson, P. (2018). Casting for service innovation: The roles of frontline employees. *Creativity and Innovation Management, 27*(3), 255–269. doi:10.1111/caim.12263.

Eteläpelto, A., Vähäsantanen, K., Hökkä, P., & Paloniemi, S. (2013). What is agency? Conceptualizing professional agency at work. *Educational Research Review, 10*, 45–65. doi:10.1016/j.edurev.2013.05.001.

Fuglsang, L. (2010). Bricolage and invisible innovation in public service innovation. *Journal of Innovation Economics*, (1), 67–87. doi:10.3917/jie.005.0067.

Fuglsang, L., & Sørensen, F. (2011). The balance between bricolage and innovation: Management dilemmas in sustainable public innovation. *The Service Industries Journal, 31*(4), 581–595. doi:10.1080/02642069.2010.504302.

Fuglsang, L., & Sundbo, J. (2005). The organizational innovation system: Three modes. *Journal of Change Management, 5*(3), 329–344. doi:10.1080/14697010500258056.

Gallouj, F. (2002). Innovation in services and the attendant old and new myths. *Journal of Socio-Economics, 31*(2), 137–151.

Gallouj, F., & Weinstein, O. (1997). Innovation in services. *Research Policy, 26*, 537–556. doi:10.1016/S0048-7333(97)00030-9.

Gherardi, S., Nicolini, D., & Odella, F. (1998). Toward a social understanding of how people learn in organizations: The notion of situated curriculum. *Management Learning, 29*(3), 273–297.

Giddens, A. (1984). *The constitution of society. Outline of a theory of structuration*. Cambridge: Polity Press.

Grönroos, C. (1984). A service quality model and its marketing implications. *European Journal of Marketing, 18*(4), 36–44. doi:10.1108/EUM0000000004784.

Grönroos, C. (1990). *Service management and marketing. Managing the moments of truth in service competition*. Toronto: Lexington Books.

Helkkula, A., Kowalkowski, C., & Tronvoll, B. (2018). Archetypes of service innovation: Implications for value cocreation. *Journal of Service Research*, doi:10.1177/1094670517746776.

Hernes, T. (2014). *A process theory of organization*. Oxford: Oxford University Press.

Høyrup, S. (2012). Employee-driven innovation: A new phenomenon, concept and mode of innovation. In S. Høyrup, M. Bonnafous-Boucher, C. Hasse, M. Lotz, & K. Møller (Eds.), *Employee-driven innovation: A new approach* (pp. 3–33). Basingstoke: Palgrave Macmillan.

Karlsson, J., & Skålén, P. (2015). Exploring front-line employee contributions to service innovation. *European Journal of Marketing, 49*(9/10), 1346–1365.

Kesting, P., & Ulhøi, J. P. (2010). Employee-driven innovation: Extending the license to foster innovation. *Management Decision, 48*(1), 65–84. doi:10.1108/00251741011014463.

Koskela-Huotari, K., Edvardsson, B., Jonas, J. M., Sörhammar, D., & Witell, L. (2016). Innovation in service ecosystems: Breaking, making, and maintaining institutionalized rules of resource integration. *Journal of Business Research, 69*(8), 2964–2971.

Lages, C. R., & Piercy, N. F. (2012). Key drivers of frontline employee generation of ideas for customer service improvement. *Journal of Service Research, 15*(2), 215–230. doi:10.1177/1094670511436005.

Langley, A. (2007). Process thinking in strategic organization. *Strategic Organization, 5*(3), 271–282. doi:10.1177/1476127007079965.

Lave, J., & Wenger, E. (1991). *Situated learning: Legitimate peripheral participation*. Cambridge: Cambridge University Press.

Lundvall, B.-Å. (2010). Introduction. In B.-Å. Lundvall (Ed.), *National systems of innovation: Toward a theory of innovation and interactive learning* (pp. 1–20). London: Anthem.

Lusch, R. F., & Nambisan, S. (2015). Service innovation: A service-dominant logic perspective. *MIS Quarterly, 39*(1), 155–176.

Lüthje, C. (2004). Characteristics of innovating users in a consumer goods field: An empirical study of sport-related product consumers. *Technovation, 24*(9), 683–695. doi:10.1016/S0166-4972(02) 00150-5.

Melancon, J. P., Griffith, D. A., Noble, S. M., & Chen, Q. (2010). Synergistic effects of operant knowledge resources. *Journal of Services Marketing, 24*(5), 400–411. doi:10.1108/08876041011060693.

Michel, S., Brown, S. W., & Gallan, A. S. (2008). An expanded and strategic view of discontinuous innovations: Deploying a service-dominant logic. *Journal of the Academy of Marketing Science, 36*(1), 54–66. doi:10.1007/s11747-007-0066-9.

Miles, I. (2000). Services innovation: Coming of age in the knowledge-based economy. *International Journal of Innovation Management, 4*(4), 371–389. doi:10.1142/s1363919600000202.

Nilsen, P., & Ellström, P.-E. (2012). Fostering practice-based innovation through reflection at work. In H. Melkas & V. Harmaakorpi (Eds.), *Practice-based innovation: Insights, applications and policy implications* (pp. 155–172). Lahti: Springer.

Normann, R. (1984). *Service management: Strategy and leadership in service businesses.* New York: John Wiley & Sons.

Orlikowski, W. J. (1996). Improvising organizational transformation over time: A situated change perspective. *Information Systems Research, 7*(1), 63–92.

Ordanini, A., & Parasuraman, A. (2011). Service innovation viewed through a service-dominant logic lens: A conceptual framework and empirical analysis. *Journal of Service Research, 14*(1), 3–23. doi:10.1177/1094670510385332.

Ostrom, A. L., Parasuraman, A., Bowen, D. E., Patrício, L., & Voss, C. A. (2015). Service research priorities in a rapidly changing context. *Journal of Service Research, 18*(2), 127–159. doi:10.1177/ 1094670515576315.

Parasuraman, A., Zeithaml, V. A., & Berry, L. L. (1985). A conceptual model of service quality and its implications for future research. *Journal of Marketing, 49*(4), 41–50.

Patrício, L., Gustafsson, A., & Fisk, R. (2018). Upframing service design and innovation for research impact. *Journal of Service Research, 21*(1), 3–16. doi:10.1177/1094670517746780.

Price, M. O., Boud, D., & Scheeres, H. (2012). Creating work: Employee-driven innovation through work practice reconstruction. In S. Høyrup, M. Bonnafous-Boucher, C. Hasse, M. Lotz, & K. Møller (Eds.), *Employee-driven innovation. A new approach* (pp. 77–91). Basingstoke: Palgrave Macmillan.

Rubalcaba, L., Michel, S., Sundbo, J., Brown, S. W., & Reynoso, J. (2012). Shaping, organizing, and rethinking service innovation: A multidimensional framework. *Journal of Service Management, 23*(5), 696–715.

Russo-Spena, T., & Mele, C. (2012). 'Five co-s' in innovating: A practice-based view. *Journal of Service Management, 23*(4), 527–553. doi:10.1108/09564231211260404.

Saari, E., Lehtonen, M., & Toivonen, M. (2015). Making bottom-up and top-down processes meet in public innovation. *The Service Industries Journal, 35*(6), 325–344. doi:10.1080/02642069.2015.1003369.

Schumpeter, J. A. (1934). *The theory of economic development: An inquiry into profits, capital, credit, interest, and the business cycle.* Cambridge, MA: Harvard University Press.

Skålén, P., Gummerus, J., von Koskull, C., & Magnusson, P. R. (2015). Exploring value propositions and service innovation: A service-dominant logic study. *Academy of Marketing Science, 43*(2), 137–158. doi:10.1007/s11747-013-0365-2.

Sørensen, F., Sundbo, J., & Mattsson, J. (2013). Organisational conditions for service encounter-based innovation. *Research Policy, 42*(8), 1446–1456. doi:10.1016/j.respol.2013.04.003.

Sundbo, J. (1997). Management of innovation in services. *The Service Industries Journal, 17*(3), 432–455. doi:10.1080/02642069700000028.

Sundbo, J. (1998). *The organisation of innovation in services.* Fredriksberg: Roskilde University Press.

Sundbo, J. (2003). Innovation and strategic reflexivity: An evolutionary approach applied to services. In L. V. Shavinina (Ed.), *The international handbook on innovation* (pp. 97–114). Amsterdam: Elsevier Science.

Sundbo, J., & Fuglsang, L. (2002). Innovation as strategic reflexivity. In J. Sundbo & L. Fuglsang (Eds.), *Innovation as strategix reflexivity* (pp. 1–16). London: Routledge.

Sundbo, J., Sundbo, D., & Henten, A. (2015). Service encounters as bases for innovation. *The Service Industries Journal, 35*(5), 255–274. doi:10.1080/02642069.2015.1002478.

Vargo, S. L., & Lusch, R. F. (2008). Service-dominant logic: Continuing the evolution. *Journal of the Academy of Marketing Science, 36,* 1–10. doi:10.1007/s11747-007-0069-6.

Vargo, S. L., Wieland, H., & Akaka, M. A. (2015). Innovation through institutionalization: A service eco-systems perspective. *Industrial Marketing Management*, *44*, 63–72. doi:10.1016/j.indmarman.2014.10.008.

Vargo, S. L., Wieland, H., & Akaka, M. A. (2016). Innovation in service ecosystems. *Invited Paper Journal of Serviceology*, *1*(1), 1–5.

von Hippel, E. (1988). *The sources of innovation*. New York: Oxford University Press.

von Hippel, E. (1994). 'Sticky information' and the locus of problem solving: Implications for innovation. *Management Science*, *40*(4), 429–439. doi:10.1287/mnsc.40.4.429.

Wenger, E. (2000). Communities of practice and social learning systems. *Organization*, *7*(2), 225–246. doi:10.1177/135050840072002.

Witell, L., Snyder, H., Gustafsson, A., Fombelle, P., & Kristensson, P. (2016). Defining service innovation: A review and synthesis. *Journal of Business Research*, *69*(8), 2863–2872.

Yin, R. K. (2009). *Case study research : Design and methods*. (4th ed.). Thousand Oaks, CA: SAGE.

8

Innovative service environments

Kendra Fowler

Introduction

The roots of service environment research can be traced back more than four decades to Kotler's (1973) work on atmospherics, which is described as the design of buying environments "to produce specific emotional effects in the buyer that enhance his purchase probability" (Kotler, 1973, p. 50). Specifically mentioned in this seminal work were ambient conditions related to four of the five senses (sight, sound, scent, and touch) and their use in creating attention, conveying information, and influencing affect. The following decades saw advances in the topic, as academics began to build frameworks to explain in more detail how components of the buying environment come together to influence the buyer's response. Bitner (1992) coined, and other researchers subsequently adopted, the term "servicescape" to describe marketer-designed buying environments. In the years since, the servicescape literature has expanded considerably to include additional elements of the designed environment, to more fully explain the buyer's response, and to reflect the complexity of an increasingly digital world.

In this chapter, the extant research on service environment research is synthesized. The first section of the chapter illustrates servicescape literature's place within the wider spectrum of research exploring customer–provider interaction. Next, Bitner's (1992) explanation of the servicescape is discussed. Frameworks that build upon her original model (e.g., Rosenbaum & Massiah, 2011) as well as new conceptualizations that greatly expand the scope of the servicescape (e.g., Akaka & Vargo, 2015) are then highlighted. The distinguishing features of the various frameworks are described, implications for theory and practice are highlighted, and the chapter concludes with a discussion of the dynamic nature of servicescape research and the ways in which technological innovations might shape future service environments.

Background (service encounters to service ecosystems)

Before delving into servicescape research, it is important to place the literature in the wider service marketing context. Service marketing research encompasses a varied spectrum of study. At one extreme is the service encounter (Surprenant & Solomon, 1987), the dyadic interaction between a customer and service provider. At the other is the service ecosystem (Vargo & Lusch, 2010), a more expansive perspective that considers multiple consumers and service providers as well as the socio-historic context and institutions that influence the focal interaction. As servicescape research provides the backdrop for the interaction between actors engaged in a service experience, a brief description of the interaction continuum is necessary.

Early research in service marketing centered on "dyadic interactions (short-or long-term) between firms and customers that are influenced by peripheral phases and actors (e.g. other customers), which, in turn, influence satisfaction with a particular core service offering" (Akaka & Vargo, 2015, p. 455). This interaction between the customer and the service provider became known as the "service encounter" (Surprenant & Solomon, 1987), with investigations typically considering the roles and expected behaviors within the dyad and how interactions impact perceptions of quality and service outcomes. Dyads between various sets of actors have been examined. For example, Arnould and Price (1993) explore the relationship between river guides and river rafting participants, discovering that underlying cultural scripts influence the behavior of the consumer as well as expectations for both the customer's and the service provider's behavior. Mukherjee, Pinto, and Malhotra (2009) study the influence of power perceptions in the educator–student dyad and suggest that managing students' complaining behavior can lead to increased student satisfaction and retention. Still other research considers business dyads. For example, to examine the perceived relationship quality between two businesses, Holmlund (2001) proposes a model that distinguishes between process and outcome aspects of dyadic relationship interactions and further considers how quality can be developed within each domain. This approach assumes the whole relationship becomes the service offering, "which, in turn, reflects the inter-linking of two firms' value creation process" (Holmlund, 2001, p. 33).

Other researchers argue that dyadic service relationships do not cast a wide enough net to capture the entire service marketing process; the models are "limited in the sense that they are only focusing on two-part relations, disregarding the influence by one or several other actors" (Andersson-Cederholm & Gyimóthy, 2010, p. 266). In their qualitative study of the business travel market, Andersson-Cederholm and Gyimóthy (2010) find that a triad conceptualization (traveler, service provider, corporate client) best describes the shifting roles, positions, and relations among the parties and showcases the "complexity of service interrelations, illuminating tensions and ambivalence among the three actors" (p. 277). In a similar vein, Childerhouse, Luo, Basnet, Ahn, Lee, and Vossen (2013) study triads consisting of a supplier, a business customer, and an associated logistics services provider, and identify integration of information between partners as a key relationship stabilizer, with the actor that serves as an information conduit having the most influence on the triad.

Other researchers go a step further, to consider networks larger than just three actors. Maglio and Spohrer (2008, p. 18) describe such networks as service systems – "value-co-creation configurations of people, technology, value propositions connecting internal and external service systems, and shared information" with the smallest service system comprised of a single individual and the largest the global economy. Maglio and Spohrer (2008, p. 19) suggest value is created from "resources with rights (people and organizations), resources as property (technology and shared information), physical entities (people and technology), and socially constructed entities (organizations and shared information)."

Like Maglio and Spohrer (2008), Tumbat and Belk (2013) suggest that a wider view must be taken to understand issues involving "participant performances in the co-construction of marketplace experiences" (p. 49) and introduce the notion of a "performancescape" – a marketplace "substantively and communicatively staged and managed not only by service providers but also, to some extent, by consumers" (p. 56). Thus, a performancescape expands upon the elements typically included in the servicescape (those designed and managed by the service provider) to also consider consumers' active participation in molding the service environment. In their study of commercial mountaineering expeditions on Mount Everest, Tumbat and Belk (2013) find that in the performancescape, the skills and the knowledge of customers and service providers have a great potential to shape the service experience for everyone involved. These authors further suggest that similar situations exist in more commonplace service industries such as healthcare, education, and law "because in these contexts, service providers and their clients interact over long periods of time and invest substantial amounts of time, money, and effort in managing and utilizing their performances" in order to create value (Tumbat & Belk, 2013, p. 57). Nilsson and Ballantyne (2014) suggest that the environment in which these interactions take place can enhance or detract from the value propositions offered, support or constrain resource integration between actors, and/or influence the value-creation outcomes.

Vargo and Lusch (2010) advocate for the widest possible interpretation of the interaction between actors, the service ecosystem. According to these authors (p. 176), a service ecosystem is "a spontaneously sensing and responding spatial and temporal structure of largely loosely coupled, value-proposing social and economic actors interacting through institutions, technology, and language to (1) co-produce service offerings, (2) engage in mutual service provision, and (3) co-create value." This expanded view "broadens the time/place dimensions that conventionally restrain research in service encounters and servicescapes beyond physical, social, symbolic and relational dimensions to consider the multiplicity of institutions across a wider socio-historic space" (Akaka & Vargo, 2015, p. 459) and allows researchers to consider a broader range of market offerings. Examples of offerings that have been examined using the more expansive service ecosystem framework include sport marketing (Tsiotsou, 2016), health promotion (Luca, Hibbert, & McDonald, 2016), retailing and entertainment (Di Pietro et al., 2018), and tourism (Winkler & Nicholas, 2016). Research related to service ecosystems will be covered in more detail in the section of this chapter entitled *Broadening servicescape to the service ecosystem*.

In summary, service marketing research considers the interaction between actors in a service experience, with a wide array of possible actor configurations from dyads to dynamic ecosystems. At the point of interaction, the actors and various resources come together to form value co-creation configurations (Maglio & Spohrer, 2008). Servicescape research sits at the crossroads of these resources, as it explores the environment where various actors and accompanying resources come together to participate in exchange. The next section of the chapter presents the foundations of servicescape research and highlights more recent research that continues to follow the same perspective.

Servicescape foundations

As mentioned previously, Kotler's (1973) work on atmospherics was one of the first to specifically identify the environment as a key component of consumers' perceptions regarding a service. More than a decade later, Baker (1986)'s classification schema categorizes environmental elements into ambient, design, or social factors. In addition to her schema, Baker (1986) puts forth a number of propositions, based on Mehrabian and Russell (1974), suggesting how each environmental factor could impact consumer approach and avoidance behaviors.

Building upon these earlier works, Bitner (1992) proposes an expanded typology and coins the term "servicescape" to describe the service environment. According to Bitner (1992), a servicescape is comprised of the dimensions of the physical surroundings including "all of the objective physical factors that can be controlled by the firm to enhance (or constrain) employee and customer actions" (p. 65). These dimensions include (1) ambient conditions (background conditions of the environment such as temperature, lighting, noise, music, and scent), (2) spatial layout and functionality (the layout of the objects within an environment and their ability to facilitate goal accomplishment), and (3) signs, symbols, and artifacts (items that serve as implicit or explicit signals of the service provider's offerings and image). Although described separately, the dimensions are thought to work synergistically, and are perceived by employees and customers as a holistic pattern of interdependent stimuli (Bitner, 1992). Each of these dimensions is described in turn below along with some contemporary examples of the research being done in each area.

Ambient conditions

Ambient conditions impact the five human senses (sight, sound, scent, touch, and taste). Although all have been studied in the servicescape context, ambient conditions related to sight, sound, and scent tend to have the largest bodies of research. Spence, Puccinelli, Grewal, and Roggeveen (2014) argue that visual aspects of the service environment often attract the most attention and resources from service providers and therefore also garner the most research attention. Research into visual ambient conditions typically concerns color or lighting choices. For example, Rafaeli and Vilnai-Yavetz (2004) evaluate the impact of a color change of the public buses in Israel; Bogicevic, Bujisic, Cobanoglu, and Feinstein (2018) consider how color choices influence satisfaction with hotel rooms; Bellizzi, Crowley, and Hasty (1983) investigate the ability of color to attract customers to a retail display; and Dijkstra, Pieterse, and Pruyn (2008) show that the color of hospital rooms can impact patient stress levels as well as cognitive appraisals of the room. Lighting research suggests that consumers touch more items with the addition of retail display lights (Summers & Hebert, 2001), and utilizing bright cool lighting (as opposed to soft warm lighting) increases the time consumers are willing to spend in a store and intentions to purchase (Briand Decré & Pras, 2013).

Sound is also a well-researched ambient condition within the servicescape literature. A meta-analysis of 32 studies by Garlin and Owen (2006) suggests that appropriate background music (defined in terms of tempo, familiarity, and liking) can produce positive effects on affective, attitudinal/perceptual, temporal, and behavioral variables. More specifically, results from the meta-analysis suggest that slower tempo, lower volume, and familiar music produce the best results. A study by Ferreira and Oliveira-Castro (2011) similarly finds that consumer perceptions of a shopping mall can be changed with the manipulation of the background music and that selecting music with high preference and quality ratings can increase the daily revenue of stores within the mall.

Scent studies in the servicescape literature generally find that appropriately scented retail environments (defined as congruent with the store or merchandise) can entice consumers to stay longer and spend more (Spangenberg, Sprott, Grohmann, & Tracy, 2006), enhance perceptions of the retail space and the quality of the goods sold (Chebat & Michon, 2003), and help consumers to form a holistic impression of the store (Ward, Davies, & Kooijman, 2003). These finding are interesting given that many consumers may not even be aware of the scent within the environment. Research suggests, however, that ambient condition manipulations may be effective even when they go undetected (Russell & Snodgrass, 1987) and that in addition to producing results among consumers, scent may also be effective at enhancing the attitudes of service employees (Fowler & Bridges, 2012). Some researchers caution, however, that different experimental designs can substantially affect outcomes, and as such should be interpreted with care (Teller & Dennis, 2012).

Space and function

Space and function represent the second dimension of Bitner's (1992) framework. Space includes

> the ways in which machinery, equipment, and furnishings are arranged, the size and shape of those items, and the spatial relationships among them. Functionality refers to the ability of the same items to facilitate performance and the accomplishment of goals.
>
> *(Bitner, 1992, p. 66)*

Space and function are often studied in retailing contexts and include studies related to shelving (e.g., Eisend, 2014), checkout queues and configurations (e.g., Wang & Zhou, 2018), and store layout decisions (e.g., Yapicioglu & Smith, 2012).

Shelf space allocation and management have probably been discussed and debated as long as there have been stores. Retailers faced with finite selling spaces must make decisions regarding the size and location of the space devoted to the various goods that are sold within the store. Such allocation decisions impact the attention the good receives and can help to legitimatize new goods offerings (Curhan, 1973). Recent research on shelf allocation supports the assertion that increasing shelf space can improve sales and, perhaps even more importantly, finds that once sales have improved, the shelf space can be reduced without a dramatic decrease in sales, provided the space reduction is carried out systematically (Eisend, 2014).

A second area of interest in relation to space and function is the checkout queue and management. Wang and Zhou (2018) compare supermarket queues with individually designated servers to queues that are shared by two servers and find that pooling (queues shared by two servers) has an indirect negative effect on service time. Although not incorporated into their study, the authors suggest that future research should consider the impact that the queuing system and wait time have on customer perceptions of the store. Other researchers have studied the consequences of using mobile self-checkout. As retailers begin to incorporate mobile self-checkout, many simultaneously introduce exit inspections in an effort to reduce shrink (i.e. disappearance of merchandise). Hoehle, Aloysius, Chan, and Venkatesh (2018) investigate the impact of these exit inspections and identify five specific dimensions – tolerance for unfair process, tolerance for changes in validation process, tolerance for inconvenience, tolerance for mistrust, and tolerance for privacy intrusion – that may negatively impact customer perceptions of the service encounter.

Finally, another popular topic in regard to space and function is the "decompression zone," the entrance area of a retail store. Described by industry expert Paco Underhill (2008) as a place where shoppers mentally decompress and switch their mind-set from the outside world to the act of shopping, the decompression zone is often considered ineffective space, in that consumers are not yet in a state of mind to interact with a store's marketing messages or begin the purchasing process. Pham (2013) notes that the majority of the research on the decompression zone is descriptive in nature and conducted by industry experts, resulting in very low status among academics. Pham (2013)'s call for more empirical research into the effects of the decompression zone was answered by Otterbring (2018) who found through a series of field studies that placing goods at the store entrance tends to increase sales for these goods, but does not influence overall spending in the store.

Signs, symbols, and artifacts

The final dimension of the servicescape articulated in Bitner's (1992) framework includes signs, symbols, and artifacts. These elements encompass a wide variety of objects and materials (e.g., signage, artwork, flooring, display fixtures, etc.) that help to convey to the customer the "meaning of the place and norms and expectations for behavior" (p. 66). As this is the most heterogeneous of Bitner's (1992) three servicescape dimensions, the related research is also quite diverse. Some research addresses the shapes of objects in the servicescape. For example, Liu, Bogicevic, and Mattila (2018) conduct experiments manipulating the shapes of furniture, fixtures, and decorations at restaurants and healthcare facilities and find that shape cues in the interior design influence interpretation of experiential services; circular shapes convey warmth and angular shapes suggest competence.

Other research considers more specifically how signage impacts the consumer experience. Signage may be informative and directional; it may be used for identifying certain service offerings or servicescape elements, and/or it may be used for to communicate rules of behavior (Bonfanti, 2013). A study by Newman (2007) focuses on the informative nature of signage and observes that clear signage helps consumers find their way in a servicescape, inducing positive consumer moods leading to more positive impressions of the service provider. Similarly, other research finds that signage can help direct individuals to less crowded service areas (Wakefield & Blodgett, 1996) and improve consumer perceptions of service quality (Fodness & Murray, 2007).

Adaptations and expansions of Bitner's framework

As seen in the previous section, much of the research that builds upon Bitner's (1992) conceptualization of the servicescape considers the effect that the built service environment (ambient conditions, function/layout, signs/symbols/artifacts) has on consumer perceptions of and behaviors toward the service provider. More recent servicescape research, however, includes additional elements and even highlights some outside the direct control of the service provider. Rosenbaum and Massiah (2011, p. 481) suggest an expanded servicescape framework would include "built (i.e. manufactured, physical), social (i.e. human), socially symbolic, and natural (environments) dimensions." According to these authors, although the built environmental elements selected by the service provider impact consumer perceptions and behaviors, other factors are equally as important. The social dimension is made up of the interactions among individuals (customer–customer, customer–employee, or employee–employee) and the emotions expressed during these interactions. The socially symbolic dimension includes all elements that possess specific evocative meanings and help signal group membership. Finally, the natural environment uses natural stimuli (plants, landscape paintings, etc.) to overcome the mental fatigue associated with prolonged exposure to draining cognitive tasks.

Pizam and Tasci (2019) take a similar approach in conceptualizing what they call the experiencescape. This framework takes what the authors call a "stake-holder centric" view of the servicescape (including the perspective of consumers, employees, and relevant others) and embeds the framework within the hospitality culture. Like the Rosenbaum and Massiah (2011) model, the experiencescape includes dimensions of Bitner's (1992) original framework including a functional component (which corresponds to Bitner's dimensions of layout/function and signs/symbols/artifacts and Rosenbaum and Massiah's physical dimension), and a sensory component (which corresponds to Bitner's ambient conditions). Like Rosenbaum and Massiah (2011), Pizam and Tasci (2019) also include components related to social interaction, the influence of culture (Rosenbaum and Massiah's socially symbolic dimension), and natural elements. Servicescape research emphasizing each of the additional dimensions (social, socially symbolic/cultural, and natural) is described below.

Servicescape research with social emphasis

Tombs and McColl-Kennedy (2003) suggest expanding the servicescape model to more specifically focus on the social dimensions. Their new framework, dubbed the social servicescape, suggests that the purchase occasion influences consumer reaction to and acceptance of social density and expressed emotions of others within a servicescape, which in turn influences consumer affective and cognitive responses and behaviors. Empirical tests of the social servicescape have been carried out in several service contexts. For example, in the restaurant industry Hanks, Line, and Kim (2017) find the impact of social density is dependent on the type of restaurant, with the greatest negative impact occurring in family dining establishments where consumer perceptions might be that staff are not equipped to handle large crowds. These authors find that social density in fine dining and sports bars, on the other hand, has negligible impact on consumer perceptions, as these venues are often crowded and consumers might expect the staff to be well trained and accommodating. Also within the restaurant industry, Harris and Ezeh (2008) investigate social elements related to the service provider's behavior and image and find that "the inclusion of these variables leads to nearly 59 percent of variations in [customer] loyalty" (p. 409).

When tested in the hotel industry, the presence of both employees and other customers significantly impacts customer satisfaction and behavior, even when the customer is not directly interacting with the employees or other customers (Line & Hanks, 2019). Similar findings are evident in the retail industry as well. According to research by Lucia-Palacios, Pérez-López, and Polo-Redondo (2018), social support from either sales associates or shopping companions with similar shopping preferences can alleviate shopper stress in crowded retail environments. The impact of other consumers on the social experience within a retail setting therefore plays an important role shaping the intentions of customers and perceptions of service quality (Brocato, Voorhees, & Baker, 2012).

Servicescape research with socially symbolic emphasis

Within the socially symbolic dimension, Rosenbaum (2006) suggests that consumers assign meanings to consumption environments based on the social environment proffered. As those meanings become linked to social support, the consumption environment takes on increased significance. The work in this area largely centers on the service provider as a third place, a public place hosting "regular, voluntary, informal, and happily anticipated gatherings of individuals beyond the realms of home and work" (Oldenburg, 1999, p. 16). The interactions of individuals within the service setting result in commercial friendships, which provide consumers with companionship and emotional support, positively impacting their loyalty to the service provider (Rosenbaum, 2006). Even temporary happenings such as concerts and cultural events can attain third place status. At these types of events, consumers obtain a closeness and camaraderie with other attendees which drives their willingness to return, over and above their satisfaction with the event (Jahn, Cornwell, Drengner, & Gaus, 2018). Interestingly, the positive effects disappear, however, with uncomfortable levels of social density (Jahn et al., 2018), suggesting that the social and socially symbolic elements of a servicescape interact and should be considered holistically.

The need for social contact helps to explain why some consumers visit certain retail locations, and in some cases it may become the driving force for their patronage. Johnstone (2012) suggests direct interaction with others isn't even required for camaraderie to develop and consumers to experience the social symbolism of the third place; knowing that they are part of the social atmosphere is enough to encourage consumer loyalty. Some research suggests, however, that there may be some potentially negative consequences for service providers that become third place destinations. Eroglu and Michel (2018) demonstrate that over time customers may lose their sense of interdependent freedom in favored stores and instead begin to feel a sense of obligation which ultimately reduces their patronage.

Servicescape research with emphasis on natural elements

Arnould, Price, and Tierney (1998) were among the first to investigate servicescapes that depend largely on natural rather than built environments. Their investigation of white water rafting operators in the Yampa and Green river canyons, highlights some of the differences between built and natural servicescapes. Specifically, in a natural servicescape, there is limited managerial control of the staging of the site; preserving the site takes precedence over satisfying customer wants, the servicescape is the foreground rather than background of service delivery, and both the customer and service provider are guests in the space (Arnould et al., 1998). The authors suggest that natural servicescapes provide feelings of being outside the normal day-to-day routine and a sense of awe, wonder, and connectedness while simultaneously capturing attention and allowing for introspection and reflection.

There is evidence that some of the positive effects of a purely natural environment can also be injected into more commercial (i.e. built) environments. Biophilic store design (Joye, Willems, Brengman, & Wolf, 2010), for example, is a design strategy that fuses natural forms and elements into the retail environment, which has been found to elicit pleasure and reduce stress in complex store designs (Brengman, Willems, & Joye, 2012). Investigation into the effects of incorporating natural elements into shopping centers finds similar positive impacts, which lead to improved attitudes, behavioral intentions, and loyalty (Rosenbaum, Ramírez, and Camino, 2018). There is some conflicting evidence, however, as to whether these findings are robust across different types of shopping experiences. For example, Rosenbaum, Ramírez, and Camino (2018) find that positive effects hold regardless of whether shoppers patronize the shopping center to browse or to purchase a specific item, or whether they are searching for full price or discounted items. Purani and Kumar (2018), however, suggest that biophilic store designs work better when consumers have hedonic shopping goals in mind.

Electronic servicescape research

Rosenbaum and Massiah (2011) expanded servicescape framework and subsequent work, as well as the introduction of the Pizam and Tasci (2019) experiencescape framework (discussed in the previous section), continued Bitner's (1992) focus on the environment involving face-to-face service exchange. Other frameworks, however, have also been developed to capture digital environmental factors present in electronic exchange. One of the earliest, developed by Eroglu, Machleit, and Davis (2001, p. 179), contains two dimensions based on leanness, "the degree to which the information presented to the online shopper on the screen is directly relevant to his shopping goals." In low task-relevant environments, shoppers are provided with information that is inconsequential to completion of the shopping task; high task-relevant environments, on the other hand, are specifically designed to facilitate and enable completion of the shopping task. For example, vivid graphics, stylized photos of the goods being purchased, and depictions of good users may provide some hedonic benefits, but are largely unimportant to task completion and would therefore be categorized as low task-relevant. The inclusion of purely hedonic elements has been shown to improve flow (a sense of deep involvement that is intrinsically enjoyable), but does little to promote online purchases (Bridges & Florsheim, 2008). Conversely, detailed good descriptions, sizing, and ordering information are important details needed to complete a transaction and therefore are included in a high task-relevant environment. The framework presented by Eroglu et al. (2001) closely followed that set out by Bitner (1992) in that the two dimensions (low task-relevant or high task-relevant) impact consumers' affective and cognitive states, which subsequently influence approach or avoidance responses to the online environment.

Eroglu, Machleit, and Davis' (2003) empirical test of the model confirms the relationship between the online servicescape and consumer internal states and behaviors. It also shows that the effect of the environment is moderated by an individual's involvement and responsiveness to atmospheric elements. Along the same lines, Orth, Lockshin, Spielmann, and Holm (2019) show that the visual information in an online servicescape influences telepresence (the feeling of being within the online environment), which consequently impacts consumer intentions. Subsequent research building from Eroglu, Machleit, and Davis' (2003) model further expands dimensions associated with the online servicescape. For example, Tang and Zhang (2018) investigate task cues (i.e. merchandise description and navigation aids) and aesthetic cues (i.e. visual appearance and layout), which are akin to high task-relevant and low task-relevant dimensions in Eroglu, Machleit, and Davis' (2001) framework. Alongside these dimensions, Tang and Zhang investigate social cues (i.e. social media links, other customers' reviews, and good ratings) in an online experiment and find that all three dimensions positively impact approach responses. Other researchers have also studied the impact of online social cues. For example, Wang, Baker, Wagner, and Wakefield (2007) find that avatars can provide online retailers with a competitive advantage by enhancing the perception of human connection and emotional bonds. Social cues are important regardless of whether the consumer is shopping for hedonic or utilitarian goods (Wakefield, Wakefield, Baker, & Wang, 2011) and are particularly important for online-only retailers, as compared to businesses that operate physical stores (Toufaily, Souiden, & Ladhari, 2013).

A second online servicescape framework was proposed by Harris and Goode (2010); these authors more specifically detail the individual components that make up the environment. Two of three dimensions they suggest closely mirror those in Bitner's (1992) framework. The first, aesthetic appeal, represents online ambient conditions (originality of design, visual appeal, and entertainment value). The second, layout and functionality, refers to the usability, relevance, and organization of the elements within the online servicescape and their facilitation of service goals. Replacing Bitner's (1992) dimension related to signs, symbols, and artifacts is a new dimension related to financial security. According to Harris and Goode (2010, p. 233), this dimension represents "the extent to which consumers perceive the payment processes and general policies of a web site as secure or safe"; empirical tests confirm its importance in influencing consumer trust of a website, and subsequent behavioral intentions.

Additional research based on the Harris and Goode (2010) framework considers the importance and impact of the dimensions across a range of online service offerings. For example, Venkatesh, Chan, and Thong (2012) investigate the importance of usability (akin to layout and function in the Harris and Goode model) and security alongside technical support provision and computer resource requirements in online government services, finding that usability and security are the most important attributes driving adoption and use. Work by Krasonikolakis, Vrechopoulos, Pouloudi, and Dimitriadis (2018) creates a typology of 3-D online store layouts and shows that layout type influences online shopping enjoyment, entertainment, and ease of navigation. The importance of aesthetic appeal is highlighted by Kühn and Petzer (2018) who find visual appeal and perceived usability affect consumers' purchase intentions, website trust, and flow in online retail websites. Aesthetics are also found to be one of the most important drivers for eliciting positive attitudes and eWOM intentions toward a website (Phan, Rivas, & Bat, 2019).

Broadening servicescape to the service ecosystem

In addition to Rosenbaum and Massiah (2011) and Pizam and Tasci (2019) adaptations of Bitner's (1992) servicescape model, other more expansive models can also be useful in providing a frame for the interaction that occurs during a service exchange. These models consider not only additional elements but also additional constituents. As discussed in a previous section, Vargo and Lusch's (2010) service ecosystem includes not only the physical, social, symbolic, and relational dimensions considered in Bitner's (1992), Rosenbaum and Massiah's (2011), and Pizam and Tasci's (2019) models, but also considers related institutions in a wider socio-historic space (Vargo & Lusch, 2010, Figure 1, p. 173).

Akaka and Vargo (2015) provide more details as to what a servicescape might entail within this larger expanse. They note that the time/place component of a service interaction is a critical feature of service experience and, when viewed from the service ecosystem perspective, it can be considered at several levels of aggregation. Take, for example, a festival. At the microlevel, the interactions between the festivalgoers and those hosting and performing at the event are key. The mesolevel would expand the perspective to investigate not only the interactions between individuals, but also their interactions with the physical, natural, and social surroundings. Finally, at the macrolevel, interactions are considered within a wider sociocultural context. For example, social and cultural norms might dictate what type of attire and behavior would be acceptable at a music festival. As the example illustrates, "service encounters and institutional arrangements are embedded within a variety of servicescapes and both are nested within broader service ecosystems" (Akaka & Vargo, 2015, p. 460).

The service ecosystem view has been used to investigate services from a variety of industries. Tsiotsou (2016) applies a service ecosystem perspective to sports marketing, identifying five factors that influence the consumer experience and illustrate the interconnected nature of the physical, social, and symbolic dimensions already discussed. The first, historical meaning, is achieved when the value of a sports tradition has nostalgic meaning or provides a way for the consumer to experience history. An example might be the added value that comes from boxing in the Columbia Gym in Louisville, KY, where Mohammed Ali first learned to box. The second factor identified by Tsiotsou (2016) is tribal logics, whereby consumers belong to particular sports communities (either as players or as fans), which often results in a complex network of ties to overlapping communities. A third factor, rituals and socialization, provides "a vehicle through which individuals can connect their identities to the social and cultural values of the sport subculture" (Tsiotsou, 2016, p. 498). The ritual of US football players showering their coach with coolers full of Gatorade after an important win is an example. The final two factors, value in subcultural context and co-construction/co-destruction of context, highlight the importance of interaction between members of the sports community. According to Tsiotsou (2016, p. 493), the "experience is no longer viewed as purely personal and subjective, but as shared and collective"; this serves to reinforce the co-construction of value and fosters resistance to outside influence.

A service ecosystem perspective is also adopted by Luca et al. (2016), who investigate how coalitions of community members and organizations jointly influence smoking cessation programs. Their study incorporates personal interviews and observation of smoking cessation programs carried out at children's centers and a children's hospital. Findings indicate the service is characterized by a network of actors, including staff members and program participants, interacting with one another and with tangible elements associated with the smoking cessation message (e.g., pamphlets, signage, and promotional materials). The process is further influenced by social connections, or "a spirit of shared purpose" (Luca et al., 2016, p. 1157), and social constructs (e.g., healthcare staff members are in positions of authority). Beirão, Patrício, and Fisk (2017) also applied the service ecosystem perspective to healthcare, looking at how electronic health records support value co-creation in a complex network made up of healthcare professionals and patients. These stakeholders access, configure, combine, and generate new resources using the electronic health records across a variety of service locations. The records also facilitate the ability of healthcare organizations and the government to monitor healthcare service delivery. Finally, the common language, shared norms, and rules defined by governments and healthcare institutions further help to generate value in the use of the electronic health records.

In a retailing and entertainment context, Di Pietro and colleagues (2018) consider how a service ecosystem can scale up to attract new collaborators and customers. The authors identify four key drivers: the creation of value propositions; partnering with new strategic actors; access to new resources and integration practices; and new institutionalized norms and rules. By partnering with new strategic actors, firms gain access to new resources that contribute to the development of new and innovative servicescapes, which reinforce the companies' value propositions. In the case of one retailer studied by Di Pietro and colleagues, this led to themed rooms wherein the consumer could have an immersive experience with the product. In a second business, an educational entertainment provider, partnerships with a technology company resulted in the development of a proprietary system that provided consumers with a fun and engaging experience. In both cases, the servicescape was constructed with careful consideration of the social and cultural contexts in which the firms operated. Broadening the context somewhat, Winkler and Nicholas (2016) apply the ecosystem framework to a study of wine regions in England and the United States. They find that residents and wine producers in each area have strongly held and varying perspectives regarding the service ecosystem. Some have a strong attachment to the current ecosystem and are skeptical of changes (i.e. they possess a place-protective attitude), whereas others are more accepting of changes. Perhaps, not surprisingly, wine producers attach more value to the production capabilities of the ecosystem, whereas residents also value the aesthetic and entertainment value of the wine regions.

Implications for theory and practice

Implications for theory related to servicescape research and its application have already been discussed as they pertain to specific frameworks and research studies in previous sections of this chapter. However, it may be useful to consider how the various revelations and advancements in the area *collectively* impact theory and practice. Two areas seem particularly noteworthy: the increased emphasis on social and cultural features in the servicescape, and the continued migration to a service ecosystem approach.

One overarching implication for theory and practice is increased attention on expanding the servicescape literature to investigate more than just the physical surroundings. Mari and Poggesim (2013), in a review of the servicescape literature, identify four servicescape research trends: virtual servicescape, the 'dark side' of the servicescape, the integration of Bitner's

(1992) model, and advancements in the underlying theory used in the servicescape literature. The authors argue that these trends are largely heterogeneous in content and goals, but most incorporate a social perspective that was neglected in the early servicescape literature. Although early servicescape research did tend to emphasize the physical over the social components, it is worth noting that Bitner's (1992) framework did, in fact, include social interaction. Specifically, Bitner (1992, p. 61) states that service environments should be designed to enhance approach behaviors and encourage "appropriate social interactions" between/ among customers and employees. Research based on Bitner's framework has also included a social and/or cultural component (Arnould & Price, 1993; Hanks et al., 2017; Rosenbaum & Massiah, 2011).

Although social interactions were not completely excluded in earlier work, contemporary servicescape research more explicitly highlights its importance. In both Rosenbaum and Massiah's (2011) and Pizam and Tasci's (2019) work, social and cultural dimensions are now incorporated into the servicescape framework. Studies based on this expanded framework, as discussed previously, begin to build a base showcasing the importance of social and cultural elements in servicescape design. As servicescape literature continues to expand, more studies might bring in research streams which highlight social or cultural influence. For example, consumer culture theory (Arnould & Thompson, 2005) seems to offer a promising complement to servicescape research. Work by Spitzkat and Fuentes (2019) directly references consumer culture theory when exploring frenzied shopping at a temporary retail site. According to these authors, retail servicescapes are not purely technical or material entities, nor purely cultural constructs; instead, "they consist of both material and social elements" (Spitzkat & Fuentes, 2019, p. 199). In studying pop-up sellers located in temporary sites lacking design features common to more conventional retail servicescapes (e.g., changing rooms, fixtures for display of goods), the authors find that the physical components of the servicescape worked together with the temporary nature of the seller to create conditions which impact not only the customers' purchasing behavior, but also they ways in which they interact with one another.

In a slightly broader vein, Visconti (2015) combines consumer culture theory and servicescape research to present an agenda by which commercial spaces can be used to improve marketers' ethnic marketing competitiveness as well as the ethnic group empowerment, self-esteem, and self-efficacy. According to Visconti (2015, p. 78), the servicescape can be viewed as a spatially situated "factory of ethnicity," in which ethnic groups compare dominant ideologies regarding ethnicity to the "more specifically situated meanings and ideologies embedded in a given servicescape." The tailored servicescape then serves as a conduit to build a relationship between the service provider and the ethnic target market. To this end, Visconti (2015) suggests service providers consider the ethnic diversity of a given target market, the compatibility of the service provider's and target market's image, and the meanings that may be assigned to a specific servicescape design. Both Visconti (2015) and Spitzkat and Fuentes (2019) offer examples of how consumer culture theory can work in tandem with servicescape research to better inform servicescape design.

A second, and related, implication for servicescape theory and practice is the continued shift to the more expansive service ecosystem model. Vargo and Lusch's (2010) service ecosystem model and related research have already been discussed in previous sections. One interesting example of work that incorporates this ecosystem perspective to more specifically examine servicescapes is that of Sheng, Simpson, and Siguaw (2017). These authors investigate nested servicescapes whereby the controllable and uncontrollable dimensions of the immediate environment (the "nestscape"), is encompassed by a larger environment (the "surroundscape"), which together define the customer experience. The context for their study was a group of older consumers who leave their permanent homes to winter in the more temperate climate of the Rio Grande Valley in Texas. Specifically, Sheng et al. (2017) investigate the ambient, design, and social dimensions of both the retirement communities in which the respondents lived temporarily (the nestscape) and the larger Rio Grande Valley (the surroundscape). Findings indicate that all three dimensions are important in determining satisfaction with both the nestscape and the surroundscape. Further, the impact of satisfaction with the surroundscape on loyalty intentions is mediated by satisfaction with the nestscape. Sheng et al.'s (2017) nested servicescape model could be applied to any number of service settings. Going forward, more servicescapes might be examined in tandem, rather than in isolation from one another. For example, collegiate athletic facilities could be investigated alongside their respective college campuses (e.g., Ohio Stadium and the Ohio State University campus in the central US), the impact of an individual attraction and its encompassing larger tourist destination could be examined (e.g., Old Faithful and Yellowstone National Park in the western United States), or researchers might reconsider the joint impact of individual theaters and the surrounding theater district (e.g., the Royal Opera House and the West End theater district in London).

Future of servicescape research

In addition to the increased emphasis on the social and cultural components of a servicescape and the shift toward a service ecosystem perspective that might be seen, other under-researched servicescape topics are also important and warrant more research attention. Three of these areas are discussed in this final section of the chapter with specific ideas offered for future research.

Incorporating digital technologies into physical servicescapes

One area that seems poised for investigation is how the digital components common to online servicescapes could be incorporated into physical environments. Poncin and Ben Mimoun (2014) address how two such technologies (i.e. mirrors with augmented reality and interactive game terminals) can be incorporated into a physical store to impact consumer perceptions. Their investigation, conducted in a physical toy store, reveals that the new technologies improve consumer perceptions of the servicescape and result in increased satisfaction and patronage intentions. Lecointre-Erickson, Daucé, and Legohérel's (2018) investigation of the impact of interactive touchscreen window displays results in similar findings; the technology has a significant influence on arousal and expected shopping experience which influences patronage intentions.

Bäckström and Johansson (2017), in their investigation of the current state of retailing, consider how receptive retailers are to enhancing the technological components of their physical stores to provide an experience closer to what might be found online. Despite the potential positive outcomes attributed to incorporating technology, many retailers continue to emphasize more traditional elements (e.g., layout, display, etc.) ahead of cutting-edge technology in their physical stores; consumers also downplay the importance of in-store technology and multichannel retailing (Bäckström & Johansson, 2017). Thus, more research seems warranted to better understand the relationship between traditional servicescape dimensions (e.g., personnel, atmosphere, and layout) and technologies typically associated with online service provision. Going forward it will be important to consider the impact both from the customer as well as the service provider perspectives.

In addition to continued work regarding the technology identified above, future research might consider how other technologies, such as customer reviews, navigation aids, and real-time customization can/should be incorporated into physical servicescapes to produce more positive customer experiences. For example, how would interactive screens displaying customer reviews impact purchasing behavior in physical stores? How could electronic navigation aids (akin to a live site map) be incorporated into a hospital servicescape to improve wayfinding? Researchers may also want to consider how individual differences might impact the outcomes of technology enhancements. In this regard, Mathwick, Wagner, and Unni's (2010) Computer-Mediated Customization Tendency scale (describing individual preferences for designing and interacting with adaptive online environments) might be modified to apply to interacting with technology in a physical servicescape.

Influence of the servicescape on employees

A second area that seems to be somewhat neglected in the servicescape literature is the impact of the servicescape on employee perceptions and behaviors. Although employee reactions are explicitly included in Bitner's (1992) model, and some research (e.g., Arnould & Price, 1993; Fowler & Bridges, 2012) has examined how the servicescape impacts employees, more research is needed. A study by Kok, Mobach, and Omta (2015) suggests that different employees in the servicescape are charged with varying tasks which might require correspondingly different support from the environment. In the higher education context used in their study, the authors find that although the overall perception of the facility design is comparable, the importance of specific dimensions diverges depending on the employee's position and associated tasks. A study by Slosberg, Nejati, Evans, and Nanda (2018) concerning the development of a new children's hospital emergency department and neonatal intensive care unit finds that when staff are involved in the design of the servicescape, overall satisfaction with the building after occupancy is improved.

Building upon this work, future research could consider the impact of servicescape dimensions on employees in different industries, with different lengths of tenure with the service provider, different backgrounds, and/or different job responsibilities. For example, does the servicescape have a different impact on employees in the hospitality or tourism sectors as compared to the financial services sector? Do new employees respond differently or have different needs than more established employees? In service settings where employees have a wide variety of backgrounds, education levels, and socioeconomic status (e.g., a hospital), how much do individual differences impact response to the servicescape? Is the impact different for those with customer contact (e.g., nurses) as compared to those that provide internal services to other employees (e.g., transcriptionists)?

Servicescape dominant services

Finally, a new business format has recently emerged that relies heavily on the impact of the servicescape and presents interesting research opportunities. Businesses using this new format are called "selfie factories" (Pardes, 2017); they are designed with Instagram (and other social media sites) in mind. Part art installation, part roadside attraction, these sites are designed as series of themed photo backdrops for guests. Examples would include the Museum of Ice Cream, Refinery 29's pop-up 29Rooms, and the Color Factory. Each of these venues charge guests up to $85 for a chance to work their way through a series of rooms, each with elaborate sets made to photograph beautifully. For example, at the Museum of Ice Cream, guests get a chance to lounge in a wading pool full of artificial sprinkles while snapping selfies; another room features giant cherries and marshmallow clouds as backdrops. At 29Rooms, the servicescape is designed around a common theme. Themes from previous years have included "Powered by People," "Turn it Into Art," and "Expand your Reality," and rooms have featured everything from hundreds of landline phones hanging from the ceiling to large Chinese lanterns that guests were invited to write on (29rooms.com/about). The Color Factory, designed to be a celebration of color, was originally scheduled to run as a monthlong pop-up; however, given the overwhelmingly positive response the exhibit has since expanded to two permanent locations.

With selfies in mind, the servicescape for these venues must be designed to enhance the photographic potential. In some cases, that means that the ambient conditions in the physical servicescape may be slightly less than ideal in order to photograph better; for example, lights often have a whiter glow rather than warmer tones (Pardes, 2017). One interesting avenue for future research might include determining how much guests are willing to sacrifice in their immediate experience in order to capture the perfect shot. Would guests be willing to suffer uncomfortably cold temperatures, or brighter lights, or touch unpleasant materials in their quest for the best photo? Another avenue for future research might be to determine what compels guests to visit the venues. Although they are presently designed by and for the millennial generation, could selfie factories be designed to attract other target markets? What changes would be necessary? Finally, future researchers might want to consider how the design principles used in the selfie factories could be incorporated into other types of servicescapes. Restaurants, museums, and even natural environments are beginning to consider how well their servicescape photographs, with the thought that better photographs equate to more social media presence (Pardes, 2017). Future research might want to consider how far these more traditional service providers can push the photographic potential of their servicescape before it begins to hurt their core service.

Conclusion

Servicescape research has evolved considerably from Kotler's (1973) conceptualization of atmospherics. Current research has expanded the types of elements making up the service environment to include not only the more traditional ambient and design features, but also natural, technological, social, and cultural components. In addition, instead of simply considering the interaction between individual consumers and service providers, new frameworks take a wider view and consider networks made up of multiple service providers and consumer groups, as well as other pertinent constituents. As noted in previous sections of this chapter, these new and innovative conceptualizations have already been applied in a number of different contexts and industries. However, additional work is still warranted. The frameworks and theories described in this chapter can be applied in a wider array of both traditional (e.g., tourism, retailing, or healthcare) and nontraditional (e.g., selfie factories or subscription/rental services) settings. Additionally, as new trends and technologies become available, the frameworks may need to be expanded or reconfigured to capture modifications to the servicescape. The result, for academics and practitioners alike, will be a more nuanced conceptualization of how elements of the servicescape impact consumer perceptions of, and behaviors toward, a service offering.

References

Akaka, M. A. & Vargo, S. L. (2015). Extending the context of service: From encounters to ecosystems. *Journal of Services Marketing*, 29(6/7), 453–462.

Andersson-Cederholm, E. & Gyimóthy, G. (2010). The service triad: Modelling dialectic tensions in service encounters. *The Service Industries Journal*, 30(2), 265–280.

Arnould, E. J. & Price, L. L. (1993). River magic: Extraordinary experience and the extended service encounter. *Journal of Consumer Research*, 20(1), 24–45.

Arnould, E. J., Price, L. L., & Tierney, P. (1998). Communicative staging of the wilderness servicescape. *The Service Industries Journal*, 18(3), 90–115.

Arnould, E. J. & Thompson, C. (2005). Twenty years of consumer culture theory: Retrospect and prospect. *Advances in Consumer Research*, 32(1), 129–130.

Bäckström, K. & Johansson, U. (2017). An exploration of consumers' experiences in physical stores: Comparing consumers' and retailers' perspectives in past and present time. *International Review of Retail, Distribution and Consumer Research*, 27(3), 241–259.

Baker, J. (1986). The role of the environment in marketing services: The consumer perspective. In J. A. Czepiel, C. A. Congram, & J. Shanahan (Eds.), *The services challenge: Integrating for competitive advantage* (pp. 79–84). Chicago: American Marketing Association.

Beirão, G., Patrício, L., & Fisk, R. P. (2017). Value cocreation in service ecosystems. *Journal of Service Management*, 28(2), 227–249.

Bellizzi, J. A., Crowley, A. E., & Hasty, R. W. (1983). The effects of color in store design. *Journal of Retailing*, 59(1), 21–45.

Bitner, M. J. (1992). Servicescapes: The impact of physical surroundings on customers and employees. *Journal of Marketing*, 56(2), 57–71.

Bogicevic, V., Bujisic, M., Cobanoglu, C., & Feinstein, A. H. (2018). Gender and age preferences of hotel room design. *International Journal of Contemporary Hospitality Management*, 30(2), 874–899.

Bonfanti, A. (2013). Towards an approach to signage management quality (SMQ). *Journal of Services Marketing*, 27(4), 312–321.

Brengman, M., Willems, K., & Joye, Y. (2012). The impact of instore greenery on customers. *Psychology & Marketing*, 29(11), 807–821.

Briand Decré, G. & Pras, B. (2013). Simulating in-store lighting and temperature with visual aids: Methodological propositions and S–O–R effects. *International Review of Retail, Distribution and Consumer Research*, 23(4), 363–393.

Bridges, E. & Florsheim, R. (2008). Hedonic and utilitarian shopping goals: The online experience. *Journal of Business Research*, 61(4), 309–314.

Brocato, E. D., Voorhees, C. M., & Baker, J. (2012). Understanding the influence of cues from other customers in the service experience: A scale development and validation. *Journal of Retailing*, 88(3), 384–398.

Chebat, J. & Michon, R. (2003). Impact of ambient odors on mall shoppers' emotions, cognition, and spending: A test of competitive causal theories. *Journal of Business Research*, 56(7), 529–539.

Childerhouse, P., Luo, W., Basnet, C., Ahn, H. J., Lee, H., & Vossen, G. (2013). Evolution of inter-firm relationships: A study of supplier-logistical services provider-customer triads. *International Journal of Industrial Engineering*, 20(1/2), 126–140.

Curhan, R. C. (1973). Shelf space allocation and profit maximization in mass retailing. *Journal of Marketing*, 37(3), 54–60.

Di Pietro, L., Edvardsson, B., Reynoso, J., Renzi, M. F., Toni, M., & Mugion, R. G. (2018). A scaling up framework for innovative service ecosystems: Lessons from Eataly and KidZania. *Journal of Service Management*, 29(1), 146–175.

Dijkstra, K., Pieterse, M. E., & Pruyn, A. T. H. (2008). Individual differences in reactions towards color in simulated healthcare environments: The role of stimulus screening ability. *Journal of Environmental Psychology*, 28(3), 268–277.

Eisend, M. (2014). Shelf space elasticity: A meta-analysis. *Journal of Retailing*, 90(2), 168–181.

Eroglu, S. & Michel, G. (2018). The dark side of place attachment why do customers avoid their treasured stores? *Journal of Business Research*, 85, 258–270.

Eroglu, S. A., Machleit, K. A., & Davis, L. M. (2003). Empirical testing of a model of online store atmospherics and shopper responses. *Psychology & Marketing*, 20(2), 139–150.

Eroglu, S. A., Machleit, K. A., & Davis, L. M. (2001). Atmospheric qualities of online retailing: A conceptual model and implications. *Journal of Business Research*, 54(2), 177–184.

Ferreira, D. C. S. & Oliveira-Castro, J. M. (2011). Effects of background music on consumer behaviour: Behavioural account of the consumer setting. *The Service Industries Journal*, 31(15), 2571–2585.

Fodness, D. & Murray, B. (2007). Passengers' expectations of airport service quality. *Journal of Services Marketing*, 21(7), 492–506.

Fowler, K. & Bridges, E. (2012). Service environment, provider mood, and provider–customer interaction. *Managing Service Quality*, 22(2), 165–183.

Garlin, F. V. & Owen, K. (2006). Setting the tone with the tune: A meta-analytic review of the effects of background music in retail settings. *Journal of Business Research*, 59, 755–764.

Hanks, L., Line, N., & Kim, W. G. (2017). The impact of the social servicescape, density, and restaurant type on perceptions of interpersonal service quality. *International Journal of Hospitality Management*, 61, 35–44.

Harris, L. C. & Ezeh, C. (2008). Servicescape and loyalty intentions: An empirical investigation. *European Journal of Marketing*, 42(3/4), 390–422.

Harris, L. C. & Goode, M. H. (2010). Online servicescapes, trust, and purchase intentions. *Journal of Services Marketing*, 24(3), 230–243.

Hoehle, H., Aloysius, J. A., Chan, F., & Venkatesh, V. (2018). Customers' tolerance for validation in omnichannel retail stores. *International Journal of Logistics Management*, 29(2), 704–722.

Holmlund, M. (2001). The D&D model: Dimensions and domains of relationship quality perceptions. *The Service Industries Journal*, 21(3), 13–36.

Jahn, S., Cornwell, T. B., Drengner, J., & Gaus, H. (2018). Temporary communitas and willingness to return to events. *Journal of Business Research*, 92, 329–338.

Johnstone, M. L. (2012). The servicescape: The social dimensions of place. *Journal of Marketing Management*, 28(11–12), 1399–1418.

Joye, Y., Willems, K., Brengman, M., & Wolf, K. (2010). The effects of urban greenery on consumer experience: Reviewing the evidence from a restorative perspective. *Urban Forestry & Urban Greening*, 9(1), 57–64.

Kok, H., Mobach, M., & Omta, O. (2015). Facility design consequences of different employees' quality perceptions. *The Service Industries Journal*, 35(3), 152–178.

Kotler, P. (1973). Atmospherics as a marketing tool. *Journal of Retailing*, 49(4), 48–64.

Krasonikolakis, I., Vrechopoulos, A., Pouloudi, A., & Dimitriadis, S. (2018). Store layout effects on consumer behavior in 3D online stores. *European Journal of Marketing*, 52(5/6), 1223–1256.

Kühn, S. W. & Petzer, D. J. (2018). Fostering purchase intentions toward online retailer websites in an emerging market: An S-O-R perspective. *Journal of Internet Commerce*, 17(3), 255–282.

Lecointre-Erickson, D., Daucé, B., & Legohérel, P. (2018). The influence of interactive window displays on expected shopping experience. *International Journal of Retail & Distribution Management*, 46(9), 802–819.

Line, N. D. & Hanks, L. (2019). The social servicescape: Understanding the effects in the full-service hotel industry. *International Journal of Contemporary Hospitality Management*, 31(2), 753–770.

Liu, S. Q., Bogicevic, V., & Mattila, A. S. (2018). Circular vs. angular servicescape: "Shaping" customer response to a fast service encounter pace. *Journal of Business Research*, 89, 47–56.

Luca, N. R., Hibbert, S., & McDonald, R. (2016). Midstream value creation in social marketing. *Journal of Marketing Management*, 32(11–12), 1145–1173.

Lucia-Palacios, L., Pérez-López, R., & Polo-Redondo, Y. (2018). Can social support alleviate stress while shopping in crowded retail environments? *Journal of Business Research*, 90, 141–150.

Maglio, P. P. & Spohrer, J. (2008). Fundamentals of service science. *Journal of the Academy of Marketing Science*, 36(1), 18–20.

Mari, M. & Poggesim, S. (2013). Servicescape cues and customer behavior: A systematic literature review and research agenda. *The Service Industries Journal*, 33(2), 171–199.

Mathwick, C., Wagner, J., & Unni, R. (2010). Computer-mediated customization tendency (CMCT) and the adaptive e-service experience. *Journal of Retailing*, 86(1), 11–21.

Mehrabian, A. & Russell, J. A. (1974). *An approach to environmental psychology*. Cambridge, MA: Massachusetts Institute of Technology.

Mukherjee, A., Pinto, M. B., & Malhotra, N. (2009). Power perceptions and modes of complaining in higher education. *The Service Industries Journal*, 29(11), 1615–1633.

Newman, A. J. (2007). Uncovering dimensionality in the servicescape: Towards legibility. *The Service Industries Journal*, 27(1), 15–28.

Nilsson, E. & Ballantyne, D. (2014). Reexamining the place of servicescape in marketing: A service-dominant logic perspective. *Journal of Services Marketing*, 28(5), 374–379.

Oldenburg, R. (1999). *The great good place*. New York: Marlow.

Orth, U. R., Lockshin, L., Spielmann, N., & Holm, M. (2019). Design antecedents of telepresence in virtual service environments. *Journal of Service Research*, 22(2), 202–218.

Otterbring, T. (2018). Decompression zone deconstructed: Products located at the store entrance do have an impact on sales. *International Journal of Retail & Distribution Management*, 46(11/12), 1108–1116.

Pardes, A. (2017). *Selfie factories: The rise of the made-for-Instagram museum.* Retrieved from: www.wired. com/story/selfie-factories-instagram-museum/ June 6, 2019.

Pham, M. T. (2013). The seven sins of consumer psychology. *Journal of Consumer Psychology*, 23(4), 411–423.

Phan, Q. P. T., Rivas, A. A. A., & Bat, T. (2019). Analyzing electronic word of mouth intention for shopping websites: A means-end chain approach. *Journal of Internet Commerce*, 18(2), 113–140.

Pizam, A. & Tasci, A. D. A. (2019). Experienscape: Expanding the concept of servicescape with a multi-stakeholder and multi-disciplinary approach (invited paper for "luminaries" special issue of *International Journal of Hospitality Management*). *International Journal of Hospitality Management*, 76, 25–37.

Poncin, I. & Ben Mimoun, M. S. (2014). The impact of "e-atmospherics" on physical stores. *Journal of Retailing and Consumer Services*, 21(5), 851–859.

Purani, K. & Kumar, D. S. (2018). Exploring restorative potential of biophilic servicescapes. *Journal of Services Marketing*, 32(4), 414–429.

Rafaeli, A. & Vilnai-Yavetz, I. (2004). Instrumentality, aesthetics, and symbolism of physical artifacts as triggers of emotion. *Theoretical Issues in Ergonomics Science*, 5(1), 91–112.

Rosenbaum, M. S. (2006). Exploring the social supportive role of third places in consumers' lives. *Journal of Service Research*, 9(1), 59–72.

Rosenbaum, M. S. & Massiah, C. (2011). An expanded servicescape perspective. *Journal of Service Management*, 22(4), 471–490.

Rosenbaum, M. S., Ramírez, G. C., & Camino, J. (2018). A dose of nature and shopping: The restorative potential of biophilic lifestyle center designs. *Journal of Retailing and Consumer Services*, 40, 66–73.

Russell, J. A. & Snodgrass, J. (1987). Emotion and the environment. In D. Stokols & I. Altman (Eds.), *Handbook of environmental psychology*, Vol. 1 (pp. 245–281). (New York: John Wiley & Sons, Inc.

Sheng, X., Simpson, P. M., & Siguaw, J. A. (2017). Communities as nested servicescapes. *Journal of Service Research*, 20(2), 171–187.

Slosberg, M., Nejati, A., Evans, J., & Nanda, U. (2018). Transitioning to a new facility: The crucial role of employee engagement. *Journal of Healthcare Management*, 63(1), 63–77.

Spangenberg, E. R., Sprott, D. E., Grohmann, B., & Tracy, D. L. (2006). Gender-congruent ambient scent influences on approach and avoidance behaviors in a retail store. *Journal of Business Research*, 59, 1281–1287.

Spence, C., Puccinelli, N. M., Grewal, D., & Roggeveen, A. L. (2014). Store atmospherics: A multisensory perspective. *Psychology & Marketing*, 31(7), 472–488.

Spitzkat, A. & Fuentes, C. (2019). Here today, gone tomorrow: The organization of temporary retailscapes and the creation of frenzy shopping. *Journal of Retailing and Consumer Services*, 49, 198–207.

Summers, T. A. & Hebert, R. H. (2001). Shedding some light on store atmospherics: Influence of illumination on consumer behavior. *Journal of Business Research*, 54, 145–150.

Surprenant, C. F. & Solomon, M. R. (1987). Predictability and personalization in the service encounter. *Journal of Marketing*, 51(2), 86–96.

Tang, J. & Zhang, P. (2018). The impact of atmospheric cues on consumers' approach and avoidance behavioral intentions in social commerce websites. *Computers in Human Behavior*. doi:10.1016/j. chb.2018.09.038.

Teller, C. & Dennis, C. (2012). The effect of ambient scent on consumers' perception, emotions and behaviour: A critical review. *Journal of Marketing Management*, 28(1–2), 14–36.

Tombs, A. & McColl-Kennedy, J. R. (2003). Social-servicescape conceptual model. *Marketing Theory*, 3(4), 447–475.

Toufaily, E., Souiden, N., & Ladhari, R. (2013). Consumer trust toward retail websites: Comparison between pure click and click-and-brick retailers. *Journal of Retailing and Consumer Services*, 20(6), 538–548.

Tsiotsou, R. H. (2016). A service ecosystem experience-based framework for sport marketing. *The Service Industries Journal*, 36(11–12), 478–509.

Tumbat, G. & Belk, R. W. (2013). Co-construction and performancescapes. *Journal of Consumer Behaviour*, 12(1), 49–59.

Underhill, P. (2008). *Why we buy: The science of shopping.* Updated and rvised for the internet, the global consumer, and beyond. New York: Simon & Schuster.

Vargo, S. & Lusch, R. (2010). From repeat patronage to value co-creation in service ecosystems: A transcending conceptualization of relationship. *Journal of Business Market Management (Springer Science & Business Media B.V.)*, 4(4), 169–179.

Venkatesh, V., Chan, F. K. Y., & Thong, J. Y. L. (2012). Designing e-government services: Key service attributes and citizens' preference structures. *Journal of Operations Management*, 30(1–2), 116–133.

Visconti, L. M. (2015). Emplaced ethnicity: The role of space(s) in ethnic marketing. In A. Jamal, L. Peñaloza, & M. Laroche (Eds.), *The Routledge companion to ethnic marketing* (pp. 69–83). Abingdon, Oxon: Taylor & Francis.

Wakefield, K. L. & Blodgett, J. G. (1996). The effect of the servicescape on customers' behavioral intentions in leisure service settings. *Journal of Services Marketing*, 10(6), 45–61.

Wakefield, R. L., Wakefield, K. L., Baker, J., & Wang, L. C. (2011). How website socialness leads to website use. *European Journal of Information Systems*, 20(1), 118–132.

Wang, J. & Zhou, Y. (2018). Impact of queue configuration on service time: Evidence from a supermarket. *Management Science*, 64(7), 3055–3075.

Wang, L. C., Baker, J., Wagner, J. A., & Wakefield, K. (2007). Can a retail web site be social? *Journal of Marketing*, 71(3), 143–157.

Ward, P., Davies, B. J., & Kooijman, D. (2003). Ambient smell and the retail environment: Relating olfaction research to consumer behavior. *Journal of Business and Management*, 9(3), 289–302.

Winkler, K. J. & Nicholas, K. A. (2016). More than wine: Cultural ecosystem services in vineyard landscapes in England and California. *Ecological Economics*, 124, 86–98.

Yapicioglu, H. & Smith, A. E. (2012). Retail space design considering revenue and adjacencies using a racetrack aisle network. *IIE Transactions*, 44(6), 446–458.

9

Finding the next edge in service innovation

A complex network analysis

Zhen Zhu and Dmitry Zinoviev

Introduction

Network theory has been recognized as a valuable tool, used in research across the natural and social sciences. It offers explanations for social phenomena in a myriad of disciplines, ranging from psychology to economics, communication to political science, and other fields (Borgatti, Mehra, Brass, & Labianca, 2009). One particular type of network – a semantic network that represents relationships among concepts within a knowledge framework – has emerged in recent years in business and management fields. As a potent tool for literature review and knowledge categorization, it often generates novel insights for understanding the trajectories of past knowledge development and reveals directions for future research (Kovacs, 2010).

In the services field, the topic of service innovation (SI) attracts substantial interest among both service researchers and industrial practitioners. After more than four decades of conceptual evolution, SI has entered a multidimensional phase characterized by rapidly expanding components and scope (Carlborg, Kindström, & Kowalkowski, 2014). Meanwhile, the conceptualization of SI, including its domains and its involvement with other concepts in services, remains relatively understudied compared to goods innovation (Ostrom, Parasuraman, Bowen, Patrício, & Voss, 2015). Following the call for a systematic review of the existing knowledge base (Gallouj & Savona, 2009) and inspired by other recent review works on service innovation (e.g., Antons & Breidbach, 2018; Witell, Snyder, Gustafsson, Fombelle, & Kristensson, 2016), this chapter achieves three research purposes. First, it adopts the network analysis method to map the structural status of the SI mindscape in order to detect its inner structure and subdomains. Second, it aims to clarify understanding of the constructs of each subdomain by highlighting critical theoretical concepts, commonly employed research methods, and highly related industrial sectors. Last, this chapter identifies the connections and 'structural holes' among the subdomains (where one node is connected with two other disconnected nodes in the network), revealing potential combinative frontiers for future research in SI.

Methodologically, this chapter follows the guide of network theory (Borgatti & Halgin, 2011; Newman, 2010) in adopting the term 'vector models' from automated network analysis to plot business scholars' interests and foci in SI studies. An output of a semantic analysis is a scale-free complex network that represents the concepts 'communities' (also termed clusters or domains) of the SI field. This is expected to elaborate and clarify the meaning and scope of SI.

The impetus of this chapter is to identify and explicate the differences and distances among SI subdomains, to bring awareness to the need for understanding other subdomains beyond one's own in terms of theoretical concepts, research methodologies, and industrial contexts. This is anticipated to set a foundation for more combinative creations in the future among researchers from different subdomains in the SI field. As a secondary contribution, this chapter illustrates the network analysis procedure and outcomes for conceptual mapping. Thus, the contribution is readily transferrable to other research topics.

This chapter is organized as follows: the network theory is introduced first (especially assumptions regarding use of structural holes for idea generation). This is followed by the details of the network analysis method, which is explained for exploring the structure of the SI field. Next, findings on the detected subdomains, including their features and interconnections, are delineated. This chapter closes with a conceptual framework on SI, which is proposed based on the findings and the implications for future research and contributions of this study.

Networks and network theory

A network consists of a set of actors or nodes that are directly or indirectly connected through a set of ties of a specified type (such as friendship or similarity) (Borgatti & Halgin, 2011). The pattern of ties in a network results in a particular structure, and nodes occupy positions within this network. Much of the theoretical relevance of network analysis stems from characterizing network structures (e.g., inner communities) and node positions (e.g., centrality) and relating these to group and node outcomes. A complex network featuring a heavy or flat tail in the distribution curve for the number of edges per node (i.e., the frequency of ties connecting to each node decreases quickly), a high clustering coefficient, and a clear community structure can reflect real-world complexity, such as in social networks.

A fundamental premise of network theory is its emphasis on structure, including structure shape, position, and structural environment of the nodes in the network. Whereas traditional social studies investigate characteristics of an actor, be it a member of a social network or a theoretical concept in a certain literature, as a function of other characteristics of the same actor (e.g., income as a result of education and gender), network research focuses on one's influence (from and to) and similarity with other actors, in other words, one's position in the network. Common outcomes of network analysis include graph-theoretic features of a network (such as modularity) and overall distribution of ties (such as density and weak ties).

Structural properties of a network can be analyzed by various network measures and metrics, among which centrality, 'betweenness,' and clusters are the most basic and also typical in network research (Newman, 2010, p. 9). Therefore, these are explained here. *Centrality* quantifies how important each node is in a networked system. A simple but useful measure of centrality is *degree*, indicating the number of edges attached to a node. Nodes with unusually high centrality or degree can be marked as hubs, which can exercise disproportionate effect on others despite being few in number. In conceptual maps, such hubs play central roles, often forming significant themes in concept clusters. Another special measure of centrality is *betweenness*; this term refers to the extent to which a node lies on paths between other nodes. Nodes of high betweenness may have considerable influence within an overall network, owing to their unique position in bridging otherwise disparate nodes or groups. Without such bridging nodes, structural holes appear instead. *Clusters* or communities are tightly knit groups within a larger, looser network. For semantic networks, the way a network breaks down into clusters can reveal levels and concepts of a knowledge field that are otherwise hard to conjecture.

Recently, network analysis in the social sciences has developed into a coherent and generalized research paradigm organized around four core features – a focus on the ties that link individual actors (rather than the on attributes of the actors per se), and the heavy use of systematic empirical data, graphic imagery, and mathematical and/or computational models (Freeman, 2004). This chapter engages all four of these features in later sections.

One prominent network theory is concerned with missing ties or structural holes within a network. By definition, a structural hole exists when a focal actor links to a pair of disconnected actors. According to structural hole theory, networks are rift with structural holes, which expose an actor to novel communities, diverse experiences, unique resources, varying preferences, and multiple thought worlds, providing superior opportunities (Burt, 2004). The association between novel ideas and structural holes is crucial to the social capital of brokerage, and the actors who possess the feature of structural holes are considered to be in critical locations to identify future innovations. Meanwhile, a bridge built to mend a structural hole often starts weak, lacking the shared viewpoints and methods to realize or germinate novel ideas. Following these guidelines, this chapter explores major structural holes in the existing network of concepts related to SI and suggests potential combinative ideas for future service research.

In contrast with structural holes, dense networks where members of a community are tightly connected are recognized to have the advantage of carrying out collaborative actions through frequent communications and strong ties that often entail trust, norms of cooperation, and effective exchange of complex knowledge. Such dense clusters are defining features of networks where ties are denser within than between the clusters. Close bonding among members sets the boundary or scope of a community, differentiating the in-group members from the outsiders (Borgatti et al., 2009). For a conceptual network, nodes within the same cluster, be it opinions, keywords, or information, are more homogeneous, forming converging themes. On the negative side, dense networks may not offer novel concepts or ideas, because members have already been widely assimilated and information fully shared (Obstfeld, 2005). This chapter detects dense conceptual clusters and identifies primary themes of each cluster within the SI domain.

Semantic network analysis method

For conceptual mapping, such as in linguistics literature, two major approaches to semantic analysis are identified as broadly defined concepts: ontologies and term vector models (Manning, Raghavan, & Schütze, 2008). An ontology is a form of knowledge representation, usually within a certain domain, that uses a shared vocabulary (Gruber, 1993). An overview of ontology construction techniques is given by Perez-Corona et al. (2012). All of these techniques (e.g., free list, bounded list, and double entrance matrix) require extensive human involvement. On the contrary, term vector models, also known as "vector space models" (Salton, Wong, & Yang, 1975) rely on the availability of previously defined keywords or subject tags that can be automatically harvested and compared for similarity by customized software and programming. An output of a semantic analysis is a small-world semantic network (Steyvers & Tenenbaum, 2005; Zhang, Luo, Xuan, Chen, & Xu, 2014) that represents the term associated with the original concept (in this chapter, 'service innovation') and therefore elaborates and clarifies its meaning. Semantic network analysis (SNA) has also been used to examine concepts, such as differences in national cultures or the evolution of the communication discipline.

Comparing SNA and citation analysis

It is noteworthy that SNA differs from citation analysis in that the latter features the connections among authors (agents) or articles (artifacts), but not associations among the subject tags (the terms). (Please see Figure 9.1.) Although citation analysis has been widely used to track knowledge evolution in research fields, it bears the limitation of potentially overestimating the impact of certain popular or methodological citations that have remote or no conceptual connections to the concept of interest. In addition, because academic journal articles often include dozens of citations each, the network among articles can be unnecessarily dense, reducing the clarity of key association paths. In contrast, each academic article has a limited number of subject terms assigned by the database or journal editors, so the subject tag network has the potential to offer a crisper map of interconnectedness among the concepts. Furthermore, because each subject term is expected to convey the most important ideas in the article, a subject tag network is likely to reveal links among the most substantive meanings around the central concept, enhancing their clarity.

Comparing SNA and content analysis

SNA and content analysis differ both in terms of human labor involvement and processing approach. A typical meta-analysis involves an intensive and laborious content analysis requiring multiple reviewers to independently and manually comb through original verbatims and sort them into often predetermined categories. In contrast, automated SNA does not always require a priori definitions of the categories to be used. Instead, this method allows the use of the natural language of the participants to determine their shared meaning. As a result, threats to reliability or validity due to the coders or categories are not an issue in SNA (Rice & Danowski, 1993).

Another critical difference between SNA and content analysis lies in the object of analysis. First, consider content analysis. Meta-analyses often focus on identifying and classifying the meaning and scope of a particular theoretical concept per se. For instance, Witell et al. (2016)

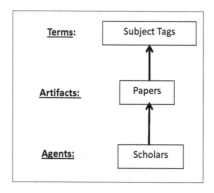

Figure 9.1 Data structure.

identified 84 definitions of SI in 1,301 articles published between 1979 and 2014. Carlborg et al. (2014) reviewed the progression of the SI concept between 1986 and 2010, based on 128 articles published in leading marketing and innovation journals. In contrast, the small-world semantic network represents a conceptual ecosystem in which the central concept resides (Witell et al., 2016). Instead of investigating "what is SI?" directly, SNA investigates "what are the concepts that are studied together with SI within the literature?" or "what concepts are similar to SI?" In this sense, SNA is similar to social network analysis because both are able to provide structure to a network. Semantic networks are analyzed based on shared meaning, whereas social networks are based on communication partners; connections in SNA are formed by the use of overlapping concepts, whereas instances of social interaction constitute social links (Doerfel & Barnett, 1999).

This chapter employs the vector space modeling approach in forming the conceptual network of SI. The SNA approach is expected to augment or complement traditional literature review techniques by providing an alternative but holistic network view.

SNA of SI

To explore the mental space or the mindscape related to 'service innovation,' this chapter applied semantic decomposition (Kovacs, 2010; Salton et al., 1975; Zinoviev, Stefanescu, Swenson, & Fireman, 2013) consisting of two phases: (1) construction of a semantic network associated with the concept in question on the collected corpus or body of information, and (2) extraction of semantic domains to describe the concept. Figure 9.2 depicts the framework of the analytical process used in the chapter. The analysis starts by acquiring SI-related data from academic journal articles; this is followed by selecting analysis terms, calculating similarities between the terms, and clustering the terms based on their similarity into service domains. Last, the topicality is extracted, including key concepts, methods, and related service industries for each domain of SI.

Data sources and acquisition

The importance of SI has been embraced by a broad spectrum of business disciplines, including financial services, management, information systems, hospitality and tourism, public administration, etc. To gather data, the Elton B. Stephens Co. (EBSCO) database Business Source Complete was selected as appropriate, owing to its extensive content and audience coverage that matches with the broad SI theme. For instance, EBSCO offers more than 375 full-text and secondary research databases and provides access to audiences at academic institutions, schools, public libraries, hospitals and medical institutions, corporations, associations, and government institutions. In addition, EBSCO has been previously used as a search engine in social network literature (e.g., Gondal, 2011), which increases confidence in using this data source for SNA.

Figure 9.2 Framework of analytical steps.

Search term selection

The EBSCO database facilitates searches of articles by either keywords or subject terms, instead of only by author names, article titles, or full text (so it is less limited than the Thomson Reuters *Web of Science*). The keywords are suggested by authors, whereas the subject terms are created and applied by editors, professional lexicographers, and subject specialists to fit the scope of the database. This research hypothesizes that subject terms are more objective and authoritative by nature than are keywords, because the latter are likely to be employed as a personal statement of research interest or a marketing tactic to show association to trendy topics and thereby attract readership. Thus, the present analysis uses the subject terms from the selected articles to form semantic networks of SI.

The dataset is built from articles published between 2003 and 2018, retrievable by searching the subject terms "service innovation" or "service" + "innovation." The corpus includes original terms from 2,341 SI-related articles published in 786 scholarly journals, resulting in 4,318 unique subject terms. The number of subject terms per article averages seven (standard deviation = one). Among the included scholarly journals, *Health Affairs* published more than 60 articles related to SI; it ranked the highest on the 'Top 25 Journals' list, followed by *Research Policy*, and *Journal of Business Research* (see Figure 9.3a). At the concept level, the top five most frequently used subject terms – technological innovations, innovations in business, service establishment/merchant wholesalers, customer services, and service industries – each appeared more than 250 times in the overall dataset (see 'Top 25 Subject Terms' in Figure 9.3b). To highlight the major clusters

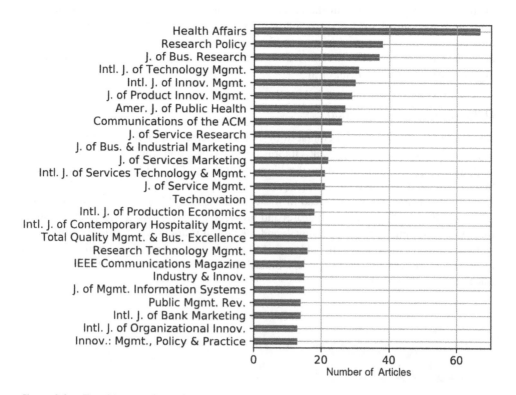

Figure 9.3a Top 25 Journals Publishing in Service Innovation.

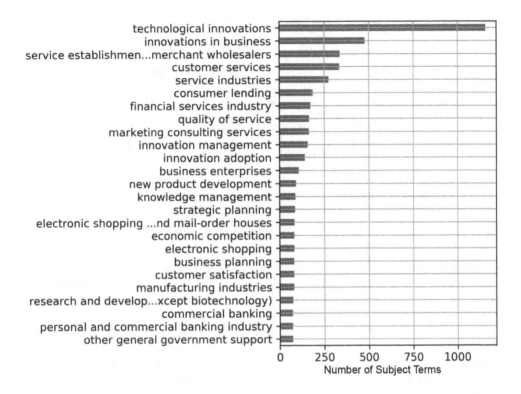

Figure 9.3b Top 25 Subject Terms Related to Service Innovation.

of the network and reduce unwanted noise, 668 terms were retained, each of which appeared at least four times in the original term corpus and was significantly similar to at least one other term (with generalized similarity >.70) in the SNA.

Similarity analysis

Defining similarity among concepts of a semantic network is a critical concern in a large sample literature review. How and why concepts are perceived to be similar (or not) and how they are then categorized or classified has far-reaching impact on cognitive structures. In this context, a research approach to defining similarity among SI-related concepts shapes the conceptualization of the domains in the mindscape of SI. Previous works have primarily depicted similarity by frequency among terms that co-occur in the *same* articles (e.g., Antons & Breidbach, 2018). This chapter, however, adopts the recursive definition of generalized similarities proposed by Kovacs (2010): two terms (such as subject terms) are similar if they are associated with *similar* artifacts (such as articles); two artifacts are similar if they are associated with *similar* terms. This critical departure from previous works is obtained by relaxing a point connection (i.e., same article) to a generalized group or class connection (i.e., any article in a group of similar articles). This approach has been adopted in several recent works in both political science and medical research for SNA (Mu, Goulermas, Korkontzelos, & Ananiadou, 2016; Zhang & Zinoviev, 2018).

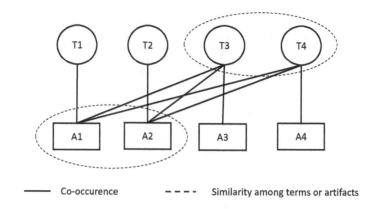

Figure 9.4 Visualized difference between Pearson correlation and generalized similarity.

The main advantage of the generalized similarity over other similarity measures (such as Pearson correlation or cosine distance) is that it allows comparison of terms that are not directly associated with the same artifacts (and vice versa). As visualized in Figure 9.4, the Pearson correlation of two terms (T_1 and T_2) is zero when they are associated only one-to-one with the artifacts (A_1 and A_2), but the generalized similarity is possibly nonzero if A_1 and A_2 are associated through other terms (T_3 and T_4). Along the same line, on the artifact side, A_3 and A_4 are not correlated (using Pearson correlation) but they are likely to be similar when the similarity between T_3 and T_4 through their links with A_1 and A_2 are considered. Through a simulation and two empirical examples, Kovacs (2010) shows that in two-mode data or a bipartite network, the generalized similarity measure magnifies within-group similarities and between-group dissimilarities, illustrating the effectiveness of this approach in detecting otherwise less salient community or domain patterns, particular those muted by sparsity of data. This feature is particularly valuable in detecting emerging or early-stage trends within the overall semantic network.

The software Python is used to process the adjacency matrix of 2,341 artifacts (research articles) and 668 terms (subject terms), from which a two-mode dataset or a bipartite non-directional network is formed. The values of the generalized similarity measures in the matrix range from −1 to 1, where 1 denotes perfect similarity and −1 denotes perfect dissimilarity. Values around 0 indicate independence (or neutrality) between the actors. The detailed description and mathematical illustration of the analytical procedure can be found in Kovacs (2010).

Extracting term clusters

Graphic illustrations of the SNA in this chapter were produced using Gephi – a powerful software package for network visualization and analysis (Bastian, Heymann, & Jacomy, 2009). Overall network size, average degree centrality, density, number of clusters, average clustering coefficient, and modularity coefficient are calculated for the network (see Table 9.1). The outline of the semantic network is plotted in Figure 9.5. Subject terms in the SI field are found to be densely interconnected, with average degree centrality (a count of how many connected neighbors a node has) at 63.7 and average clustering coefficient of the network at a level of .634. Meanwhile, six term communities (clusters in different colors in Figure 9.5) identified from the network graph are considered conceptual domains of the SI

Table 9.1 Network measures of the SI domains

SI Domain Name	# of Nodes	# of Tags	# of Edges	Density
Innovation in Business and Service Strategy	226	5299	7791	0.306
Technology Innovation and Customer Interfaces	114	2937	1902	0.295
Digital Innovations and Financial Services	117	1718	3367	0.496
Transformative Services and Public Services	158	1856	5460	0.44
Service Ecosystem and Knowledge-Based Services	33	547	231	0.438
Agency Services in Cultural and Entertainment Industries	20	107	161	0.847

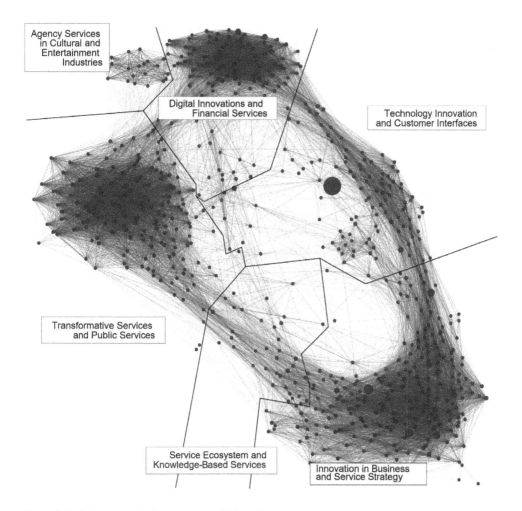

Figure 9.5 Interconnectedness among SI domains.

field (Ottenheimer, 2006). Overall modularity (which measures the ratio of edge densities within clusters to edge densities between clusters) reaches .62, indicating a community structure that shows relatively stronger within-domain connection while allowing certain conceptual similarity between domains of the same field.

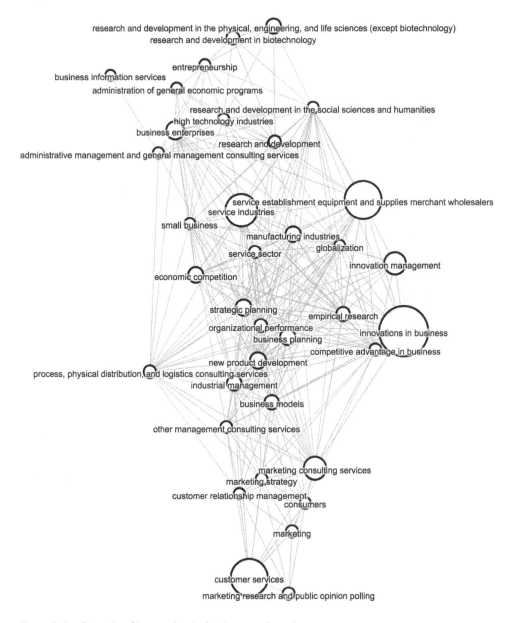

Figure 9.6a Domain of innovation in business and service strategy.

Six SI domains

To label the clusters that emerged, the top 25 most frequent subject terms in each cluster were first listed to identify the common theme among them. The common theme of each cluster was then used to name the conceptual domain. This analysis reveals subject terms reflecting different aspects as compared to the published articles. Most domains (with the exception of Domain 6) consist of three types of subject terms – theoretical concepts, research and analytical methods, and industrial contexts. Thus, unique connections are found between SI concepts and the industrial backdrops in which they are most prominent and therefore also most frequently investigated. To manifest the theory–industry connection, several domain names were labeled with a combination of one critical theoretical theme and one salient practical context. In particular, the six conceptual domains of SI are labeled as: (1) Innovation in Business and Service Strategy, (2) Technology Innovation and Customer Interfaces, (3) Digital Innovation and Financial Services, (4) Transformative Services and Public Services, (5) Service Ecosystem and Knowledge-Based Services, and (6) Agency Services in Cultural and Entertainment Industries. (Graphs of SI domains are provided in Figures 9.6a through 9.6f.) Conceptual properties of each domain are summarized in Table 9.2. Example works in each SI domain are provided in Table 9.3. In the next section, conceptual meanings, featured research contexts, and frequently used research methods of each domain are further elaborated to provide more nuanced understanding of the SI field.

Domain 1: innovation in business and service strategy

The largest conceptual domain in terms of unique subject terms (226), total count of subject terms (5299), and ties between terms (7791) within the SI network relates to both the innovation practices in business as well as service strategies. The first sub-theme in the domain includes 'innovation in business,' 'innovation management,' 'new product development,' and 'R&D.'

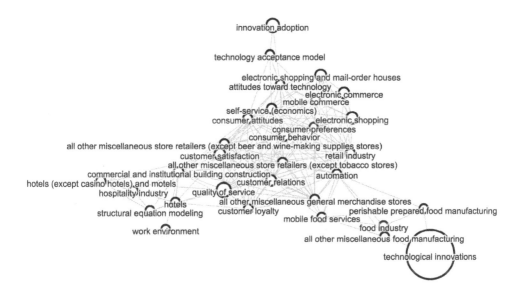

Figure 9.6b Domain of technology innovation and customer interfaces.

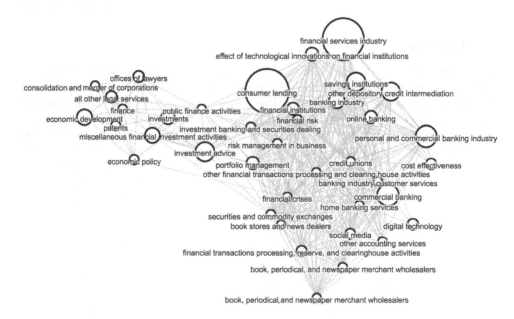

Figure 9.6c Domain of digital innovations and financial services.

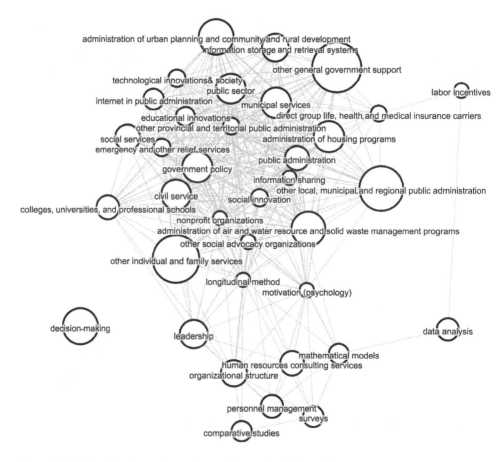

Figure 9.6d Domain of transformative services and public services.

Figure 9.6e Domain of service ecosystem and knowledge-based services.

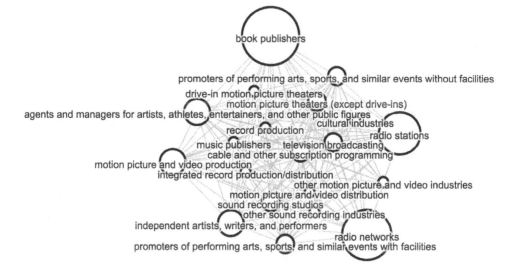

Figure 9.6f Domain of agency services in cultural and entertainment industries.

Table 9.2 Key concepts, research methods, and industries within each SI domain

SI Domain	Key Concepts	Research Methods	Service Industries
Innovation in Business and Service Strategy	• innovation in business • business model • innovation management • strategic planning • new product development • R&D • CRM • outsourcing • knowledge management	• industry research • meta-analysis • regression • conjoint analysis	• consulting • B2B • tourism • high techlogistics
Technology Innovation and Customer Interfaces	• technological innovation • quality of service • innovation adoption • customer satisfaction • customer relationship • self-service • automation	• structural equation modeling • Delphi method • RFIS (Radio Frequency Identification Systems) • statistical sampling • logistic regression analysis	• e-commerce • retailers • hotels • food service • construction • automobile services • internet marketing
Digital Innovations and Financial Services	• digital technology • economic development • technology and society • effect of technology innovation on financial industry • patent	• data mining • big data • data envelopment analysis (DEA) • AI • algorithms • machine learning • grounded theory	• financial services (including online and mobile banking) • legal services • news publishing
Transformative Services and Public Services	• decision-making • leadership • government policy	• data analysis • surveys • mathematical models	• public sector • civil services • education

Service Ecosystem and Knowledge-Based Services

• info storage and retrieve	• comparative studies	• insurance
• org. structure		
• social innovation		
• knowledge management	• qualitative	• support services
• org. change	• quantitative	• office admin. services
• ecosystem services	• multivariate	
• corp. culture	• best practices	
• stakeholders		
• MIS		
• resource management		
• info. architecture		
• cultural	N/A	• publishing
• art		• performing arts
• entertainment		• motion pictures
		• music
		• recording
		• radio station

Table 9.3 Example works in each SI domain

SI Domain	Author(s)	Article Title
Innovation in Business and Service Strategy	Obstfeld, 2005	Social networks, the tertius iungens orientation, and involvement in innovation
	Van Wijk, Jansen, & Lyles, 2008	Inter- and intra-organizational knowledge transfer: a meta-analytic review and assessment of its antecedents and consequences
	Verhoef & Leeflang, 2009	Understanding the marketing department's influence within the firm
	Drejer, 2004	Identifying innovation in surveys of services: a Schumpeterian perspective
	Hipp & Grupp, 2005	Innovation in the service sector: the demand for service-specific innovation measurement concepts and typologies
Technology Innovation and Customer Interfaces	Meuter, Bitner, Ostrom, & Brown, 2005	Choosing among alternative service delivery modes: an investigation of customer trial of self-service technologies
	Dong, Evans, & Zou, 2008	The effects of customer participation in co-created service recovery
	Wunderlich et al., 2012	High tech and high touch: a framework for understanding user attitudes and behaviors related to smart interactive services
	Zhu, Nakata, Sivakumar, & Grewal, 2007	Self-service technology effectiveness: the role of design features and individual traits
	Zhu, Nakata, Sivakumar, & Grewal, 2013	Fix it or leave it? Customer recovery from self-service technology failures
Digital Innovations and Financial Services	Blazevic & Lievens, 2004	Learning during the new financial service innovation process: antecedents and performance effects
	Xue, Hitt, & Chen, 2011	Determinants and outcomes of internet banking adoption
	Forman, 2005	The corporate digital divide: determinants of internet adoption
	Zhu et al., 2007	Self-service technology effectiveness: the role of design features and individual traits
	Gomber, Kauffman, Parker, & Weber, 2018	On the Fintech revolution: interpreting the forces of innovation, disruption, and transformation in financial services
Transformative Services and Public Services	Alves, 2013	Co-creation and innovation in public services
	West, 2004	E-government and the transformation of service delivery and citizen attitudes
	Damanpour, Walker, & Avellaneda, 2009	Combinative effects of innovation types and organizational performance: a longitudinal study of service organizations

(Continued)

Table 9.3 (Cont.)

SI Domain	Author(s)	Article Title
	Osborne & Brown, 2011	Innovation, public policy and public services delivery in the UK: the word that would be king?
	Zhang & Li, 2010	Innovation search of new ventures in a technology cluster: the role of ties with service intermediaries
Service Ecosystem and Knowledge-Based Services	Lusch & Nambisan, 2015	Service innovation: a service-dominant logic perspective
	Agarwal & Selen, 2009	Dynamic capability building in service value networks for achieving service innovation
	Voss & Hsuan, 2009	Service architecture and modularity
	Damanpour et al., 2009	Combinative effects of innovation types and organizational performance: a longitudinal study of service organizations
	Leonardi & Barley, 2008	Materiality and change: challenges to building better theory about technology and organizing
Agency Services in Cultural and Entertainment Industries	Sunley, Pinch, Reimer, & Macmillen, 2008	Innovation in a creative production system: the case of design
	Jantunen, Ellonen, & Johansson, 2012	Beyond appearances: do dynamic capabilities of innovative firms actually differ?
	Olleros, 2007	The power of non-contractual innovation
	Brammer & Galloway, 2007	IEEE transactions on professional communication: looking to the past to discover the present
	Lee, Close, & Love, 2010	How information quality and market turbulence impact convention and visitors bureaus' use of marketing information: insights for destination and event marketing

These sub-themes address the processes and practices of goods and services design and development, mostly at the innovation project level. From these sub-themes, calls for service-specific innovation measures for service sectors emerged. The second sub-theme investigates strategic-level, service-related business model innovation, enlisting subject terms such as 'business model,' 'strategic planning,' 'CRM,' and 'knowledge management' (e.g., Drejer, 2004; Van Wijk et al., 2008). The third sub-theme consists of terms like "customer service," which is seemingly unrelated to innovation in business but detected nevertheless in the domain. One possible explanation for this finding can be traced to the argument of Hipp and Grupp (2005) that human elements, including an employee's individual-level experience and service skills, contribute to organizational knowledge and non-technological components in SI processes. Structurally, the customer service sub-theme bridges Domains 1 and 2 (Technology Innovation and Customer Interfaces), whereas the business model innovation sub-theme links to Domain 5 (Service Ecosystem and Knowledge-Based Services).

Although the themes of 'innovation in business' and 'business model innovation' are widely investigated across many service industries, several service sectors – consulting, business-to-business services, tourism, high tech, and logistics – are among the most typical contexts for empirical examinations in the domain. Meanwhile, industrial research (e.g., Drejer, 2004; Hipp & Grupp, 2005) and meta-analysis (e.g., Van Wijk et al., 2008) are among the frequently used research methods for this domain. In addition, regression analysis and conjoint analysis are commonly employed in new SI design, converging with their traditional roots in the new product development literature.

Domain 2: technology innovation and customer interfaces

The second conceptual domain in SI addresses technology innovations, primarily in traditional consumer-facing service encounters. This domain contains 114 unique subject terms that appear 2,937 times in the corpus and form 1,902 links among the nodes. Possibly because of the broad inclusion of service sectors in the domain, the overall density (.295) of the network is among the lowest across the six conceptual domains. Three themes coexist in the domain. The first centers on technology and innovation adoption concepts, such as technology innovation, innovation adoption, self-service, and automation. Empirical works in the past 15 years have extended further into new technology-based services such as self-service technology, automation, mobile services, and smart interactive services (Meuter et al., 2005; Wunderlich et al., 2012; Zhu et al., 2007). These are based on earlier works, such as the technology readiness concept (Parasuraman, 2000), the technology acceptance model (TAM) model (Davis, Bagozzi, & Warshaw, 1989), and the flow and control theories offered by Hoffman and Novak (1996). The second theme of this domain spans over innovation in an array of high-touch, non-technology-based customer service interfaces as well as some well-documented service concepts, including customer satisfaction, quality of service, customer relationship, service failure and recovery, omni-channel user experience, and relationship management in retailing SIs. Evidence of overlap between the two themes can be found in studies that feature technological failure and recovery in the user experience of computer-mediated SIs (Dong et al., 2008; Zhu et al., 2013).

Technology innovation and customer interface research is found to be connected with digital innovation and financial services (Domain 3) through shared interests in digital services (e.g., e-commerce, mobile technology, and internet marketing) and the TAM. This domain is also linked to the Innovation in Business and Service Strategies Domain through classic concepts such as 'customer service' and 'quality of service.' In addition, a weak link to the Transformative and Public Services Domain is detectable via the 'innovation adoption' concept and other shared analytical methods. One salient feature of the domain is the presence of the super node – 'technology innovation' – which implies an overwhelming emphasis on technology-based SI in this domain. Meanwhile, innovation with regard to human elements (such as employee creativity) or non-technological process innovation is potentially understudied in the consumer service experience literature.

The most commonly used industrial contexts in this research domain include e-commerce, retailing, hotel and food services, construction, automobile services, and internet marketing. Methodologically, the Delphi method, Radio Frequency Identification Systems (RFIS), statistical sampling, structural equation modeling, and logistic regression analysis are often employed for data collection or analysis.

Domain 3: digital innovation and financial services

The third most developed domain addresses innovations, especially those based on information technology and adoption of technology-mediated interfaces in an array of financial services, from consumer lending, saving and checking, investment advising, stock exchange, insurance, to accounting services, to name just a few. This domain contains 117 unique subject terms which appeared 1,718 times in the corpus. Among the subject terms, 3,367 edges were established to form a dense conceptual community, reaching a density level of .496. A wide range of studies and disciplines joined the discourse regarding the adoption of financial innovation and its effect on consumers, financial institutions, and society at large. This domain centers on corporate strategies in developing, adopting, and deploying digital innovations of any kind. For earlier digital technologies, Alvarez and Lippi (2009) employed econometrics methods to model branch distribution and deployment of ATMs to meet consumer money or cash demand; Forman (2005) investigated the corporate digital divide in financial services in early internet adoption decisions. In recent years, more disruptive analytical and operational technologies, such as artificial intelligence (AI), machine learning, and blockchain are embraced under the banner of Fintech to further digitize business and consumer financial solutions (Gomber et al., 2018; Qi & Xiao, 2018). Organizational learning and adaptive capacities appear to be the common theoretical underpinnings of the related studies (e.g., Blazevic & Lievens, 2004; Weigelt & Sarkar, 2012).

Apart from corporate innovation practices and strategies, the second theme, individual consumer adoption attitudes toward and behaviors regarding innovative financial solutions (such as e-commerce payment systems and mobile banking services) are also investigated (e.g., Xue et al., 2011; Zhu et al., 2007). The third theme in this domain looks further into the far-reaching effects of digital innovation in financial services on broader society, often from the economic development and legislation viewpoints. Unique issues such as information transparency strategy, financial inclusion, federal safety nets, and patent protection have attracted attention from researchers in recent publications (e.g., Lumsden, 2018; Oney, 2018). Structurally, the technology and society theme bridges to Domain 4 (Transformative Services and Public Services) and Domain 6 (Agency Services in Cultural and Entertainment Industries), whereas the consumer adoption of digital innovation theme ties to Domain 2 (Technology Innovation and Customer Interfaces).

Publications in this domain expand across multiple disciplines, including business strategy, finance, marketing and consumer behavior, accounting and auditing, and business law. Thus, the research contexts include financial services, related legal services, and news publication industries. It is noteworthy that most of the cutting-edge digital innovations in financial services have been investigated outside of the United States, indicating that European countries, and some emerging countries, are leading digital innovations in financial services thus far. Methodologically, data mining, data envelopment analysis (DEA), and AI algorithms are among the frequently used research methods for this domain. Interestingly, grounded theory qualitative research has also been employed to explore the unknowns of the radical innovations rising in the related service sectors.

Domain 4: transformative services and public services

The fourth SI domain concerns the innovation and design of public services and the transformative value brought about by various service practices. This domain gathers 158 unique subject terms that appear 1,856 times in the dataset and establish 5,460 ties within the domain. A number of public services, such as civil services, education, and insurance provision, have been set as research contexts for studying innovations in the transformative and public services. In terms of methodological approaches, conceptual, analytical (i.e., mathematical modeling), and empirical methods (i.e., surveys and comparative studies) are all found in this service domain.

The first theme addresses a variety of innovation design and adoption issues in government and public services. For example, concepts such as e-government, public service leadership and social innovation within public administration and civil service, information storage and retrieval, and government policy are frequently cited as subject terms for related publications (Alves, 2013; Osborne & Brown, 2011; Scheirer & Dearing, 2011; West, 2004). The second theme of the domain highlights the public, transformative value of services beyond the typical public sectors (Anderson & Ostrom, 2015; Baron et al., 2014; Finsterwalder et al., 2017). For example, Blocker and Barrios (2015) drew from service-dominant logic and structuration theory to conceptualize the transformative value of service design and innovation as a social dimension of value creation that illuminates uplifting changes among individuals and collectives in the marketplace, which differs from the routine or habitual values offered in such services. Researchers in the domain have investigated the impact of holistic value propositions and communal practices on consumer and employee wellbeing (Rosenbaum, 2015), inclusion and accessibility to vulnerable consumers or members of society (Dickson, Darcy, Johns, & Pentifallo, 2016; Rosenbaum et al., 2017), and mitigating inequalities due to poverty (Martin & Hill, 2015).

The network density of this domain reaches .44, indicating a good balance between internal congruency and external connection. Transformative services and public services are found to be conceptually linked to Digital Innovations and Financial Services (Domain 3) through shared concerns about health insurance, government regulation, legal services, and communication of technical information. Meanwhile, transformative services are also loosely connected with Technology Innovation and Customer Interface (Domain 2) through concepts such as work environment and employee well-being. Interestingly, the connection to the Service Ecosystem and Knowledge-Based Services (Domain 5) is mostly driven by shared system thinking and system-level qualitative research methods. In addition, transformative services innovation ties loosely to Agency Services in Cultural and Entertainment Industries (Domain 6). Thus, the Transformative Services and Public Services Domain arises as the most broadly connected domain within the overall SI mindscape, which also reflects the intersectional and cross-disciplinary nature of many works in the domain (Corus & Saatcioglu, 2015).

Domain 5: service ecosystem and knowledge-based services

Two emerging SI domains were identified in the conceptual network. These present significantly fewer nodes, and links among nodes, as compared to other more fully developed domains. The first new domain – namely, Service Ecosystems and Knowledge-Based Services – entails 33 unique subject terms that appear 547 times in the corpus and form 231 edges among each other, reaching a network density of .438. It appears to be spun out of the border area between Transformative Services and Public Services (Domain 4) and Innovation in Business and Service Strategy (Domain 1). Knowledge-Based Services include tasks that require use of detailed processes or technical knowledge. Professional services, such as consulting, healthcare, and software engineering, are typical knowledge-based services.

Despite the small number of subject terms in the domain, the current pool offers a rich set of concepts for theoretical development and practical examination along two themes. One theme focuses on innovations related to system-level infrastructure and resources, such as those in resource management, management information systems, and information architecture (Voss & Hsuan, 2009). Such concepts are especially relevant to value networks in platform-based economies, such as those that many societies are moving toward (Agarwal & Selen, 2009; Lusch & Nambisan, 2015). The other theme of the domain points to human (and hence managerial) issues, such as corporate culture, knowledge management, organizational change, stakeholders, and employee empowerment in service ecosystems. As Blocker and Barrios (2015) point out, because all social and economic actors are resource integrators, the locus of value creation can be broadened beyond a provider–customer dyad and toward a view of service ecosystems. Other stakeholders such as customers, employees, suppliers, and complementors are embraced into the value creation of the service ecosystem. One notable issue, the customer's journey to interact with service delivery network (Tax, McCutcheon, & Wilkinson, 2013), has attracted recent attention in the SI field. The presence of the two-theme structure resembles the social/technological subsystems or information technology/organization pair, as highlighted conceptually by Leonardi and Barley (2008). Structurally, the system-level infrastructure theme closely bridges the domain to Transformative Services and Public Services (Domain 4). Meanwhile, the managerial theme spans toward Innovation in Business and Service Strategy (Domain 1).

Industries such as ecosystem services, logistics, support services, and office administrative services are found in existing publications. Methodologically, more qualitative methods (e.g., best practices and case studies) than quantitative research methods are used in these studies, possibly owing to the difficulty of accessing system-level data in empirical research on service ecosystems, which will continue to be a challenge in future research.

Domain 6: Agency Services in Cultural and Entertainment Industries

Another nascent domain, Agency Services in Cultural and Entertainment Industries, emerges from the present research; this may be the first time this industry appears in a literature review on SI. Among the 20 nodes in the domain, agency decisions and behaviors of agencies, managers, publishers, or promoters of various art and cultural designs and offerings take shape into an identifiable theme (e.g., Scott, 2006; Sunley et al., 2008). Research works on agency emphasize that design emerges from interfaces that synthesize and recombine diverse knowledge so as to produce emergent effects and new designs.

Modular architecture and noncontractual innovation (or open innovation) are found to proliferate in industries, such as visual art and gaming sectors, where uncertainty of pertinent problems and their solution is high and the relevant knowledge is widely dispersed (e.g., Christensen, 2006; Olleros, 2007). This industry may eschew centralized platforms or leader-dominant ecosystems, choosing instead distributed and self-organized innovation processes driven by the desire of many independent agents to exploit some platform potentialities, bringing positive or negative surprises to platform leaders (Cusumano & Gawer, 2002; Iansiti & Levien, 2004). Thus, noncontractual innovation processes not only add conceptual completeness to the understanding of a platform economy, as suggested by Olleros (2007), but also enrich the innovation frameworks for service offerings.

Domain 6 features a high-density structure. Innovation phenomena from motion picture, performing arts, radio network, theater, television broadcasting, and publishing industries are closely interconnected within the domain, reaching a density level of .847. This high similarity (or convergence) among the different creative fields is impressive given the fact that, although they often share a common tendency to focus on ideas and to hold a strong aesthetic component, they differ starkly in relationships with markets, distribution channels, and intellectual property rights. Meanwhile, the high density leaves little room for other concepts outside the domain to set bridges or links. Only two weak outward ties were detected for Domain 6, one connecting to Domain 3 (Digital Innovation and Financial Services) through news publishing topics and the other to Domain 4 (Transformative Services and Public Services) through 'metropolitan areas' and 'transportation' topics. Although no method subject term has been detected in this domain, possibly because it is still in early development, inductive approaches such as case studies and interviews are commonly used in this domain. Meanwhile, its methodological void indicates a promising research opportunity for future studies in the creative service domain.

Recent shifts among domains in SI literature

Over the last 15 years, the SI literature has experienced rapid growth. As shown in Figure 9.8, the annual publication rate increased from below 100 prior to 2007, to more than 150 afterward, with a peak of more than 200 in 2015. Meanwhile, the distribution of publications among the six SI domains shows an uneven and dynamic pattern (see Figure 9.7). The Digital Innovation and Financial Services domain was the most prominent in the early 2000s, appearing in 35% of the publications (about 30). During an expansion of the SI field in the past decade, the number of publications in this domain increased to about 25 annually, but its relative weight reduced to 13% of all publications. In contrast, the weight of Innovation in Business and Service Strategy domain started with 27% in 2003, but increased to 43% during the same time period. The Technology Innovation and Customer Interfaces domain maintained its second place ranking throughout the entire time period investigated. One interesting upward trend in SI research can be identified in the Transformative Services and Public Services domain, whose weight in the SI topic surged from 5% in 2003 to 17% in 2018. Last, the number of publications regarding the Agency Services in Cultural and Entertainment Industries domain remained lower than 2% over this time. (Please see Figure 9.9.)

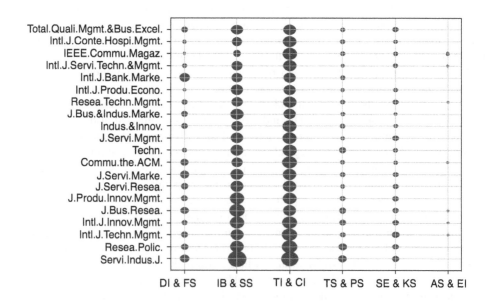

Figure 9.7 Journal publications by SI domains.

Notes: DI & FS denotes 'Digital Innovation and Financial Services'; IB & SS denotes 'Innovation in Business and Service Strategy'; TI & CI denotes 'Technology Innovation and Customer Interfaces'; TS & PS denotes 'Transformative Services and Public Services'; SE & KS denotes 'Service Ecosystem and Knowledge-Based Services'; AS & EI denotes 'Agency Services in Cultural and Entertainment Industries.'

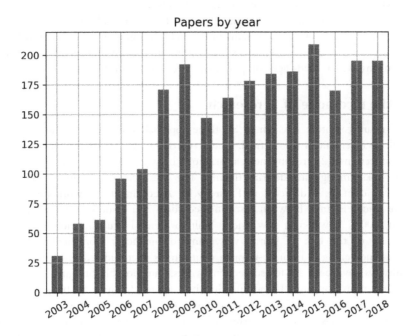

Figure 9.8 SI publications by year from 2003 to 2018.

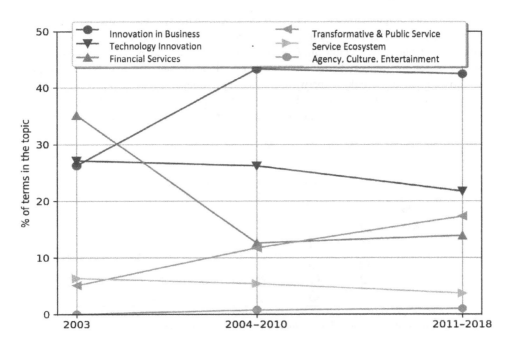

Figure 9.9 Domain evolution from 2003 to 2018.

This investigation into the structure of the SI mindscape provides a novel perspective for mapping the principle thoughts and their related methods and industrial relevance. Beyond the assessment of the developmental status of the field, this graphic approach also helps with visualizing the structural holes (white spaces) within and, more importantly, between conceptual domains, which sheds light on potential directions for future research.

Finding the next edge of SI research

Looking forward to future research in SI, three approaches are proposed to explore novel conceptual advancement in the SI field. These approaches are (1) strengthening loose inter-domain connections; (2) creating new associations between disconnected domains; and (3) thickening links among intra-domain themes. The presence of structural holes and weak links between domains is depicted in Figure 9.10. According to network theory, forming associations and relevance between disconnected ideas is a critical source of combinative ideas (Burt, 2004); however, a new bridge built to mend a structural hole often starts out weak because of the lack of shared viewpoints or methods. Compared to the second approach, strengthening loose inter-domain connections is considered less risky because the initial pathways have been set for subsequent works, thus possibly bringing in low hanging fruit for further investigation. Regarding the third approach, there is still much room for further deepening the conceptual connections within each domain, especially for the rising and nascent SI domains (such as Domains 4, 5, and 6). However, thickening intra-domain links falls outside the scope of this chapter, so it focuses on the first two approaches in the discussion of future research directions.

Weak inter-domain links

Three loose ties among the six SI domains were detected. The first weak link is located between the Technology Innovation and Customer Interfaces Domain and the Transformative Services and Public Services Domain. Currently, the 'innovation adoption' concept and other shared analytical methods are barely pinning the two domains together. Future research questions should invite direct linkages between themes across domains, such as: 'How should transformative value and habitual value be balanced or prioritized in creating public services?' and 'To what extent are performance concepts (such as customer satisfaction and loyalty) applicable

	IB & SS	TI & CI	DI & FS	TS & PS	SE & KS	AS & ES
IB & SS	--					
TI & CI	↵	--				
DI & FS	○	↵	--			
TS & PS	○	⊘	⊘	--		
SE & KS	↵	○	○	↵	--	
AS & ES	○	○	↵	⊘	○	--

Note: ↵ denotes linked, ○ structure holes, and ⊘ weakly linked.

Figure 9.10 Potential structural holes and opportunities for future SI research.

in nonpublic services?' Similarly, 'How can transformative value be mindfully added to the design and delivery of nonpublic services?' In addition, considering the ubiquitous influence of technology innovation, it is appropriate to ask: 'What are the roles that technological innovations can play in advancing transformative value in public services?' These are fascinating linkages to explore between domains.

Another weak tie is found between the Digital Innovations and Financial Services Domain and the Transformative Services and Public Services Domain, mainly bounded through the concept 'technology and society.' Many further investigation questions can be conjectured along the lines of: 'How does digital innovation (such as AI and machine learning) facilitate or inhibit financial inclusion, especially to vulnerable social members or unattractive market segments?' and 'What should be the principle or framework for designing, applying, and assessing such digital innovations to promote the transformative value in public services, be it healthcare, education, telecommunication, or wealth distribution?'

Last, the Transformative Services and Public Services Domain connects with the Agency Services in Cultural and Entertainment Services Domain only through 'metropolitan areas' and 'transportation.' Much more research is needed to investigate the impact of creative innovations on public services and social well-beings and vice versa. In addition, it will be theoretically intriguing to probe: 'How can the distributed innovation model featured in the cultural creation sectors be extended to scattered transformative resources, such as volunteer forces, to achieve broader impact in society?'

As previously argued, early works between these loosely connected domains, though rare or preliminary, have gleaned early evidence on the subjects and tested the interest among the academic audience and practitioners. Thus, this helps to develop future studies that will deepen the conceptual or methodological connections.

Structural holes between domains

Structural holes exist when a focal actor (in this analysis, a central domain) links to a pair of disconnected actors (or two other domains) (Borgatti & Halgin, 2011; Burt, 2004). Mapping of the subject term network reveals seven structural holes, as shown in Figures 9.5 and 9.10. This research found that structural holes are often located surrounding nascent domains (such as the Service Ecosystem and Knowledge-Based Services Domain and the Agency Services in Cultural and Entertainment Services Domain), where conceptual relevance to other domains in the overall network has yet to be proposed or verified. However, structural holes can also exist between mature domains (such as between the Digital Innovations and Financial Services Domain and the Innovation in Business and Service Strategy Domain), implying potentially departing interests, reasoning logics, and even theoretical foundations. The discussion begins with these structural holes, owing to their theoretical significance.

The network graph reveals two substantial structural holes among three mature SI domains (Domain 1, 3, and 4). The Innovation in Business and Service Strategy Domain, being the most populous cluster, has not yet conceptually connected with the Digital Innovations and Financial Service Domain. The puzzling phenomenon is that, although both domains are closely tied to the Technology Innovation and Customer Interfaces Domain, somehow the direct edge between the two is hard to find. It can be speculated that the central reasoning of digital innovations (such as machine learning from big data) is based on bottom-up, inductive pattern search and detection from accumulated huge datasets, whereas strategic thinking in regard to organizational innovation in services relies primarily on top-down planning and managerial functioning. Thus, the two reasoning logics still need to find ways to creatively integrate and complement each other in the theorization and practices of SI. Researchers may investigate: 'What are the mechanism(s) for digital innovations to influence organizational innovations?' and vice versa. For example, 'How can cloud-based technologies and services change the employee–technology relationship and facilitate global virtual collaboration?' This chapter considers the need for integrating the inductive and deductive approaches paramount in SI, indicating a promising direction for future research.

The Innovation in Business and Service Strategy Domain also misses a direct connection to the Transformative Services and Public Services Domain. Because most transformative innovations focus on services to individual citizens or consumers, few researchers have proposed the transformative meaning that a service may provide to another business. For instance, 'Can a business collaborator be the target of transformative service? If so, how?' To better understand the nature of new product development for transformative services, researchers may ask: 'To what extent do sustainable or transformative innovations differ from other innovations in terms of orientation? To what extent should they differ?' For instance, decisions may include the trade-off between customer-centric versus stakeholder-oriented, the organizational learning mechanism (e.g., learning versus unlearning), and performance metrics to be used (e.g., market growth versus well-being versus triple bottom lines). The substantial theoretical and empirical implications of the probes into such strategic-level challenges in innovations of transformative services warrant a critical direction for future SI research.

Apart from structural holes among mature SI domains, new frontiers in SI can be projected around and between the rising and emerging SI domains (such as Domains 5 and 6). This chapter first explores two structural holes around the nascent Service Ecosystem and Knowledge-Based Services Domain, followed by those around the Agency Services in Cultural and Entertainment Services Domain.

As Iansiti and Levien (2004, p. 1) stated, "Strategy is becoming, to an increasing extent, the art of managing assets that one does not own." Building and leveraging ecosystem strengths to address strategic challenges, be they market growth, resource orchestration, or service delivery, is a formidable approach to SI success. Research on ecosystem strengths first needs to embrace digital innovations (Domain 3), where important contemporary developments – including cloud, grid, and web services as well as smart, wearable, and mobile technologies – are involved in such transformations as contractually bound business grids, digital ecosystems, and on-demand and availability-based service level agreements. These service developments build upon and extend established core infrastructure and progressive institutionalization of standards (Chesbrough, Vanhaverbeke, West, 2006). Such digital technology not only increases scale, scope, and reach, but also shapes design and delivery, becoming more central to the structuring of services (Orlikowski & Scott, 2015). It is foreseeable that the combinative ideas between digital innovation and service ecosystem domains will bring about novel service theories and coveted insights into the ever-expanding digital economy.

In relation to technology innovation in customer interfaces (Domain 2), there are significant research opportunities in combining foundational ecosystem or platform theories with customer experience research. For example, one tenet of a service platform delineates its externality or network effect, which occurs when the value of the network or service ecosystem increases whenever other actors (such as additional customers) join the network (Van Alstyne, Parker, & Choudary, 2016). Both positive and negative network effects can influence the consumer service experience. For instance, Amazon Prime delivery service on Black Friday offers positive network effects and therefore attracts more merchandisers offering goods, which justifies denser warehouse deployment for delivery. Thus, negative network effects take place when too many accepted offers need to be delivered in a limited time window, causing delivery failures and customer dissatisfaction. It is important to understand consumer adoption attitudes and behaviors toward ecosystem-based services, including their mental accounting of the positive and negative network effects in service experiences.

Next, the discussion moves to structural holes found around the new SI domain – Agency Services in Cultural and Entertainment Services – in relation to organizational innovation (Domain 1) and customer interfaces (Domain 2). These structural holes invite high-level questions such as: 'How can agency models commonly used in dispersed cultural innovation inform a study in organizational innovation and service process innovation?' Looking at this from the reverse side, 'What relevance and utility do conceptual models and research methods established in mature SI domains bring to the future development of the cultural creation field?' Linking the innovation model in agency industries to customer experience management, comparison can be drawn between the sourcing decisions among agencies in cultural creation fields and crowdsourcing management between a service firm and its customer base. Therefore, 'How is the governance of noncontractual agencies in cultural creation similar to or different from herding crowd-based customer value co-creation?' Answers to such research questions will help to fill the structural holes around the agency service domain.

The Agency Services in Cultural and Entertainment Industries domain can be theoretically and practically connected with the service ecosystem domain. Based on real world observations, many entertainment and cultural service industries rely heavily on innovation ecosystems (e.g., video game developer markets) and distribution platforms (e.g., iTunes music store). Contractual and noncontractual innovations can complement each other and jointly foster the development of these service sectors. Olleros (2007) comments that innovation contracts tend to be over-specified and thus limit solutions availability or opportunities detection. By contrast, networks of noncontractual innovation can more effectively mobilize distributed local knowledge, not only for problem-solving, but also for problem-seeking (Sunley et al., 2008). Investigation into the collaboration or integration mechanisms between the two types of innovation networks will help to shape more open-ended and fertile innovation processes.

Conclusion

This chapter draws from network theory and complex network analysis methods to map the conceptual structure of SI, by detecting critical conceptual domains within the field and delineating related themes, service industry contexts, and related research methods within each domain. Based on the observed connections and missing links (or structural holes) among the conceptual domains, potential directions for future research on SI are pointed out. Hopefully, these will ignite creative and combinative ideas to promote the research work across otherwise disparate domains in the SI field. Methodologically, this chapter demonstrates how automated SNA methods can be applied on large-size literature databases for conceptual mapping in service research.

References

Agarwal, R., & Selen, W. (2009). Dynamic capability building in service value networks for achieving service innovation. *Decision Sciences*, 40(3), 431–475.

Alvarez, F., & Lippi, F. (2009). Financial innovation and the transactions demand for cash. *Econometrica*, 77(2), 363–402.

Alves, H. (2013). Co-Creation and innovation in public services. *Service Industries Journal*, 33(7–8), 671–682.

Anderson, L., & Ostrom, A. L. (2015). Transformative service research: Advancing our knowledge about service and well-being. *Journal of Service Research*, 18(3), 243–249.

Antons, D., & Breidbach, C. F. (2018). Big data, big insights? Advancing service innovation and design with machine learning. *Journal of Service Research*, 21(1), 17–39.

Baron, S., Warnaby, G., & Hunter-Jones, P. (2014), Service(s) Marketing Research. *International Journal of Management Reviews*, 16(2), 150–171.

Bastian, M., Heymann, S., & Jacomy, M. (2009) Gephi: An open source software for exploring and manipulating networks. *Proc. Intl. AAAI Conf. on Weblogs and Social Media*, San Jose, CA, May 2009.

Blazevic, V., & Lievens, A. (2004). Learning during the new financial service innovation process: Antecedents and performance effects. *Journal of Business Research*, 57(4), 374.

Blocker, C. P., & Barrios, A. (2015). The transformative value of a service experience. *Journal of Service Research*, 18(3), 265–283.

Borgatti, S. P., & Halgin, D. S. (2011). On network theory. *Organization Science*, 22(5), 1168–1181.

Borgatti, S. P., Mehra, A., Brass, D. J., & Labianca, G. (2009). Network analysis in the social sciences. *Science*, 323(5916), 892–895.

Brammer, C., & Galloway, R. (2007). IEEE transactions on professional communication: Looking to the past to discover the present. *IEEE Transactions on Professional Communication*, 50(4), 275–279.

Burt, R. S. (2004). Structural holes and good ideas. *American Journal of Sociology*, 110(2), 349–399.

Carlborg, P., Kindström, D., & Kowalkowski, C. (2014). The evolution of service innovation research: A critical review and synthesis. *Service Industries Journal*, 34(5), 373–398.

Chesbrough, H. W., Vanhaverbeke, W., & West, J. (eds.) (2006). *Open innovation: Researching a new paradigm*. Oxford: Oxford University Press.

Christensen, C. M. (2006). The ongoing process of building a theory of disruption. *Journal of Product Innovation Management*, 23(1), 39–55.

Corus, C., & Saatcioglu, B. (2015). An intersectionality framework for transformative services research. *Service Industries Journal*, 35, 415–429.

Cusumano, M. A., & Gawer, A. (2002). The elements of platform leadership. *MIT Sloan Management Review*, 43(3), 51–58.

Damanpour, F., Walker, R. M., & Avellaneda, C. N. (2009). Combinative effects of innovation types and organizational performance: A longitudinal study of service organizations. *Journal of Management Studies*, 46(4), 650–675.

Davis, F. D., Bagozzi, R. P., & Warshaw, P. R. (1989). User acceptance of computer technology: A comparison of two theoretical models. *Management Science*, 35(8), 982–1003.

Dickson, T. J., Darcy, S., Johns, R., & Pentifallo, C. (2016). Inclusive by design: Transformative services and sport-event accessibility. *Service Industries Journal*, 36(11–12), 532–555.

Doerfel, M. L., & Barnett, G. (1999). A semantic network analysis of the International Communication Association. *Human Communication Research*, 25(4), 589–603.

Dong, B., Evans, K. R., & Zou, S. (2008). The effects of customer participation in co-created service recovery. *Journal of the Academy of Marketing Science*, 36(1), 123–137.

Drejer, I. (2004). Identifying innovation in surveys of services: A Schumpeterian perspective. *Research Policy*, 33(3), 551.

Finsterwalder, J., Foote, J., Nicholas, G., Taylor, A., Hepi, M., Baker, V., & Dayal, N. (2017). Conceptual underpinnings for transformative research in a service ecosystems context to resolve social issues: Framework foundations and extensions. *Service Industries Journal*, 37(11–12), 766–782.

Forman, C. (2005). The corporate digital divide: Determinants of Internet Adoption. *Management Science*, 51(4), 641–654.

Freeman, L. C. (2004). *The development of social network analysis: A study in the sociology of science*. Vancouver: Empirical Press.

Gallouj, F., & Savona, M. (2009). Innovation in services: A review of the debate and a research agenda. *Journal of Evolutionary Economics*, 19(2), 149–172.

Gomber, P., Kauffman, R. J., Parker, C., & Weber, B. W. (2018). On the fintech revolution: Interpreting the forces of innovation, disruption, and transformation in financial services. *Journal of Management Information Systems*, 35(1), 220–265.

Gondal, N. (2011). The local and global structure of knowledge production in an emergent research field: An exponential random graph analysis. *Social Networks*, 33(1), 20–30.

Gruber, T. (1993). A translation approach to portable ontology specifications. *Knowledge Acquisition*, 5(2), 199–220.

Hipp, C., & Grupp, H. (2005). Innovation in the service sector: The demand for service-specific innovation measurement concepts and typologies. *Research Policy*, 34(4), 517–535.

Hoffman, D., & Novak, T. P. (1996). Marketing in hypermedia computer-mediated environments: Conceptual foundations. *Journal of Marketing*, 60(July), 50–68.

Iansiti, M., & Levien, R. (2004). Strategy as ecology. *Harvard Business Review*, 82(3), 68–78.

Jantunen, A., Ellonen, H.-K., & Johansson, A. (2012). Beyond appearances: Do dynamic capabilities of innovative firms actually differ? *European Management Journal*, 30(2), 141–155.

Kovacs, B. (2010). A generalized model of relational similarity. *Social Networks*, 32(3), 197–211.

Lee, S., Close, A. G., & Love, C. (2010). How information quality and market turbulence impact convention and visitors bureaus' use of marketing information: Insights for destination and event marketing. *Journal of Convention & Event Tourism*, 11(4), 266–292.

Leonardi, P. M., & Barley, S. R. (2008). Materiality and change: Challenges to building better theory about technology and organizing. *Information and Organization*, 18(3), 159–176.

Lumsden, E. (2018). The future is mobile: Financial inclusion and technological innovation in the emerging world. *Stanford Journal of Law, Business & Finance*, 23(1), 1–44.

Lusch, R., & Nambisan, S. (2015). Service innovation: A service-dominant logic perspective. *MIS Quarterly*, 39(1), 155–175.

Manning, C. D., Raghavan, P., & Schütze, H. (2008). *Introduction to information retrieval.* New York: Cambridge University Press.

Martin, K. D., & Hill, R. P. (2015). Saving and well-being at the base of the pyramid: Implications for transformative financial services delivery. *Journal of Service Research*, 18(3), 405–421.

Meuter, M. L., Bitner, M. J., Ostrom, A. L., & Brown, S. W. (2005). Choosing among alternative service delivery modes: An investigation of customer trial of self-service technologies. *Journal of Marketing*, 69, 61–83.

Mu, T., Goulermas, J., Korkontzelos, I., & Ananiadou, S. (2016). Descriptive document clustering via discriminant learning in a co-embedded space of multilevel similarities. *Journal of the Association for Information Science and Technology*, 67(1), 106–133.

Newman, M. E. J. (2010). *Networks: An introduction.* Oxford, UK: Oxford University Press.

Obstfeld, D. (2005). Social networks, the Tertius Iungens orientation, and involvement in innovation. *Administrative Science Quarterly*, 50(1), 100–130.

Olleros, F. X. (2007). The power of non-contractual innovation. *International Journal of Innovation Management*, 11(1), 93–113.

Oney, C. (2018). Fintech industrial banks and beyond: How banking innovations affect the federal safety net. *Fordham Journal of Corporate & Financial Law*, 23(2), 541–575.

Orlikowski, W. J., & Scott, S. V. (2015). The algorithm and the crowd: Considering the materiality of service innovation. *MIS Quarterly*, 39(1), 201–216.

Osborne, S., & Brown, L. (2011). innovation, public policy and public services delivery in the UK: The word that would be king? *Public Administration*, 89, 1335–1350.

Ostrom, A. L., Parasuraman, A., Bowen, D. E., Patrício, L., & Voss, C. A. (2015). Service research priorities in a rapidly changing context. *Journal of Service Research*, 18(2), 127–159.

Ottenheimer, H. J. (2006). *The Anthropology of Language: An Introduction to Linguistic Anthropology.* Belmont, CA: Thomson, Wadsworth.

Parasuraman, A. (2000). Technology Readiness Index (TRI): A multiple-item scale to measure readiness to embrace new technologies. *Journal of Service Research*, 2, 307–320.

Perez-Corona, N., Hernández-Colín, D., Bustillo-Hernández, C., & Figueroa-Nazuno, J. (2012). Model of natural semantic space for ontologies construction. *International Journal of Combinational Optimization Problems and Informatrics*, 3(2), 93–108.

Qi, Y., & Xiao, J. (2018). Fintech: AI powers financial services to improve people's lives. *Communications of the ACM*, 61(11), 65–69.

Rice, R. E., & Danowski, J. A. (1993). Is it really just like a fancy answering machine? Comparing semantic networks of different types of voice mail users. *The Journal of Business Communication*, 30(4), 369–397.

Rosenbaum, M. S. (2015). Transformative service research: Focus on well-being. *Service Industries Journal*, 35(7–8), 363–367.

Rosenbaum, M., Seger-Guttmann, T., & Giraldo, M. (2017). Commentary: vulnerable consumers in service settings, *Journal of Services Marketing*, 31(4/5), 309–312.

Salton, G., Wong, A., & Yang, C. S. (1975). A vector space model for automatic indexing. *Communications of the ACM*, 18(11), 613–620.

Scheirer, M. A., & Dearing, J. W. (2011). An agenda for research on the sustainability of public health programs. *American Journal of Public Health*, 101(11), 2059–2067.

Scott, A. J. (2006). Creative cities: Conceptual issues and policy questions. *Journal of Urban Affairs*, 29, 1–17.

Steyvers, M., & Tenenbaum, J. (2005). The large-scale structure of semantic networks: Statistical analyses and a model of semantic growth. *Cognitive Science*, 29, 41–78.

Sunley, P., Pinch, S., Reimer, S., & Macmillen, J. (2008). Innovation in a creative production system: The case of design. *Journal of Economic Geography*, 8(5), 675–698.

Tax, S. S., McCutcheon, D., & Wilkinson, I. F. (2013). The Service Delivery Network (SDN): A customer-centric perspective of the customer journey. *Journal of Service Research*, 16(4), 454–470.

Van Alstyne, M., Parker, G. G., & Choudary, S. P. (2016). Pipelines, platforms, and the new rules of strategy. *Harvard Business Review*, 94(4), 54–62.

Van Wijk, R., Jansen, J. J. P., & Lyles, M. A. (2008). Inter- and intra-organizational knowledge transfer: A meta-analytic review and assessment of its antecedents and consequences. *Journal of Management Studies*, 45(4), 830–853.

Verhoef, P. C., & Leeflang, P. S. (2009). Understanding the marketing department's influence within the firm. *Journal of Marketing*, 73(2), 14–37.

Voss, C. A., & Hsuan, J. (2009). Service architecture and modularity. *Decision Sciences*, 40(3), 541–569.

Weigelt, C., & Sarkar, M. B. (2012). Performance implications of outsourcing for technological innovations: Managing the efficiency and adaptability trade-off. *Strategic Management Journal*, 33(2), 189–216.

West, D. M. (2004). E-government and the transformation of service delivery and citizen attitudes. *Public Administration Review*, 64(1), 15–27.

Witell, L., Snyder, H., Gustafsson, A., Fombelle, P., & Kristensson, P. (2016). Defining service innovation: A review and synthesis. *Journal of Business Research*, 69(8), 2863–2872.

Wunderlich, N. V., Wangenheim, F. V., & Bitner, M. J. (2012). High tech and high touch: A framework for understanding user attitudes and behaviors related to smart interactive services. *Journal of Service Research*, 11(1), 3–20.

Xue, M., Hitt, L. M., & Chen, P. (2011). Determinants and outcomes of internet banking adoption. *Management Science*, 57(2), 291–307.

Zhang, S., Luo, X., Xuan, J., Chen, X., & Xu, W. (2014). Discovering small-world in association link networks for association learning. *World Wide Web*, 17(2), 229–254.

Zhang, W., & Zinoviev, D. (2018). How North Korea views China: Quantitative Analysis of Korean Central News Agency Reports. *Korean Journal of Defense Analysis*, 30(3), 377–396.

Zhang, Y., & Li, H. (2010). Innovation search of new ventures in a technology cluster: The role of ties with service intermediaries. *Strategic Management Journal*, 31(1), 88–109.

Zhu, Z., Nakata, C., Sivakumar, K., & Grewal, D. (2013). Fix it or leave it? Customer recovery from self-service technology failures. *Journal of Retailing*, 89(1), 15–29.

Zhu, Z., Nakata, C., Sivakumar, K., & Grewal, D. (2007). Self-service technology effectiveness: the role of design features and individual traits. *Journal of the Academy of Marketing Science*, 35(4), 492–506.

Zinoviev, D., Stefanescu, D., Swenson, L., & Fireman, G. (2013). Semantic networks of interests in online NSSI communities. *Proceeding of the Workshop "Words and Networks,"* Evanston, IL, June 2012.

Part III
Organizing the service business

10

Modeling consumer engagement with front line service providers

Ainsworth Anthony Bailey and Carolyn M. Bonifield

Introduction

Front line service employees play an important role in marketing, given that in many instances they are the proverbial 'face' of their organizations. They perform a number of different functions and consumer interactions with them, therefore, provide the possibility for enhancement of the brand image and reputation (in the case of favorable interactions) or for degradation of the brand (in the case of unfavorable interactions) (Dodd, 2013; Korschun, Bhattacharya, & Swain, 2014). Traditionally, front line employee (FLE) interactions with consumers occurred face-to-face. However, as more and more consumers use social media for customer-to-customer communication as well as customer-to-business communication, another dimension has been added to the traditional in-person front line service employee–consumer interaction. Interactions can now take place online, including via websites and social media platforms. In addition, there are some service providers that deliver services purely online, whereas some service providers deliver their services primarily in-person. In both of these contexts, service employees can utilize social media in their interactions with consumers. As a result, this brings into focus multichannel (offline and online) service delivery and the nature of front line service employee–consumer interactions in both environments. Among the issues that arise are (1) the extent to which front line service employees become involved in customer engagement and customer relationship management (CRM) on behalf of their organizations in multichannel contexts, (2) identifying the factors that enable FLEs to affect customer relationships in multichannel contexts, and (3) the extent to which channel plays a role in moderating relationships between front line service employees and customers of service providers.

This chapter addresses the aforementioned issues. It has as its primary goal an investigation of the role of front line service employees in customer engagement in both online and offline environments. Therefore, it is important to understand who the front line service employees are, the functions they perform in both environments, offline or online, and how they engender customer engagement. Finally, the chapter presents a conceptual model of front line service employee involvement in CRM efforts and consumer engagement. The model focuses on how the nature of the environment (online or offline) in which customer engagement takes place can moderate the impact of front line service employee involvement in CRM efforts on customer engagement outcomes.

The chapter is organized as follows: First, there is a discussion of front line service employees in context, which focuses on their skills, roles, and customer outcomes based on their interactions with customers. This is followed by a discussion of front line service employee delivery of service in both online and offline environments. Next, the role of front line service employees in customer relationship building is explored. To do so, a conceptual model of FLE involvement in CRM is proposed; this highlights the linkages and relationships among front line service employee CRM involvement, front line service employee CRM investment, front line service employee–customer relationship quality, and subsequent customer behavior and intentions. Of particular interest are front line service employee–customer engagement and feedback intentions on the part of customers. The chapter closes with a discussion of practical implications.

Background

Front line service employees in context

FLEs and their role in organizations continues to generate interest and academic research. This may be because they perform a number of functions on behalf of organizations and, oftentimes, they are viewed as the 'ambassadors' of organizations (Korschun et al., 2014; Sok, Sok, Danaher, & Danaher, 2018; Stoneman, 2007). According to Stoneman (2007, p. 20), "people judge the quality of brands and products on the quality of the encounters they have with frontline employees" and "these interactions directly affect sales and brand image." Korschun et al. (2014, p. 20) argue that FLEs are involved in "sensing market demand, disseminating information to customers about company offerings, and delivering value in ways that contribute to customer acquisition and customer loyalty."

Korschun et al. (2014) and Harris, Brown, Mowen, andand Artis (2014) underscore that FLEs play dual social roles, as they serve both organizations and customers, and so develop relationships with both. In particular, Korschun et al. (2014) explore FLE–customer identification and its relationship to customer orientation and job performance. They define FLE–customer identification as

> the extent to which an employee senses a sameness or oneness with the organization's customers ... it reflects the extent to which employees perceive customers to be fellow members of a social category and therefore as relevant to defining their self-concept.
>
> (p. 22)

Their research, conducted among FLEs of a US subsidiary of a Global 500 financial services company, showed that FLE–customer identification enjoys a positive relationship with employee organizational identification and job performance. In addition, employee customer orientation mediates the relationship between employee–customer identification and job performance.

Front line service employee skills

Keh, Ren, Hill, adand Li (2013) found that employee helpfulness plays an important role in influencing customer satisfaction. In the case of emotional competence, or being "capable of perceiving, understanding and regulating customers' emotions," Fernandes, Morgado, and Rodrigues (2018, p. 835) found that emotional competence has a significant impact on post-recovery satisfaction following negative service encounters. Post-recovery satisfaction was measured in terms of trust, word-of-mouth intentions, and intentions to repurchase, and was more pronounced in high-contact customized service contexts. Sahu and Das (2018), identified factors that influence front line service employee ability to manage customer relationships, including knowledge, reliability, attitude, job satisfaction, managing self, efficiency, dependability, and communication. Sok et al. (2018) discuss the importance of FLE creativity and attention to detail in driving their service performance. They contend that FLEs need to be ambidextrous, that is be able to display high levels of both creativity and attention to detail in order to enhance service performance, and this ambidexterity should be encouraged by service managers. Other researchers have identified customer orientation as an important influencer of FLE effectiveness (Harris et al., 2014; Korschun et al., 2014). Recently, Gaucher and Chebat (2019) conducted a study assessing the impact of uncivil customer behavior on FLEs in an offline context. They found that uncivil customer behavior generated anger among retail store employees and, because the employees have to conceal their negative reactions to the uncivil behavior, this eventually leads to emotional exhaustion and deviant behavior.

Front line service employee roles

Research has highlighted that FLEs perform different functions on behalf of service providers. Among the more apparent roles played by FLEs is that of building relationships with customers (Liao & Chuang, 2007; Sok et al., 2018). FLEs are also involved in cross-selling and upselling of goods and services, both in person and remotely (Jasmand, Blazevic, & de Ruyter, 2012; Yu, de Ruyter, Patterson, & Chen, 2018). Tax, Brown, and Chandrashekaran (1998) contend that FLEs also play an important role in complaint handling; Marinova, Singh, and Singh (2018) found that FLEs play an important role in generating customer satisfaction during interactions related to service failure complaints. Interestingly, the latter authors also found that higher levels of front line relational work, or displayed affect, attenuated the positive impact of FLE customer satisfaction problem-solving. Front line service employees are also expected to play a role in maintaining customer relationships (Sahu & Das, 2018). In a survey of front line service employees, Sahu and Das (2018) found that attitude, job satisfaction, and managing self were among factors that facilitated management of customer relationships. Schepers and Nijssen (2018) argue that FLEs are expected to be brand advocates for their service providers, communicating service offerings and benefits to consumers in a favorable manner. Research has also shown that consumers typically pass along feedback to front line service employees with whom they interact (Hu, Parsa, Chen, & Hu, 2016).

Customer outcomes from FLE engagement

There are a number of customer outcomes that are impacted by FLEs, and to which researchers have paid attention. Among the outcomes of FLE efforts are perceptions of service quality and customer satisfaction (Schepers & Nijssen, 2018), customer loyalty (Stock, de Jong, & Zacharias, 2017), generation of customer feedback (Celuch, Robinson, & Walsh, 2015), and customer cooperation and s with FLEs (Zhao, Yan, & Tat Keh, 2018). Sirianni, Bitner, Brown, andandand Mandel (2013) found that the alignment of FLE behavior with a service provider's brand positioning positively influenced overall brand evaluations and customer-based brand equity, particularly for unfamiliar brands.

Celuch et al. (2015), in a study of offline FLEs, found that employee customer-oriented behavior created social benefits for customers, which in turn impacted the customer willingness to provide feedback, defined as general positive and negative feedback as well as thoughts, feelings, and suggestions about the company's goods and services. Zhao et al. (2018) conducted a study among Chinese consumers that had just interacted with FLEs in a retail bank. They found that the employee behavior impacted consumer emotions, which in turn influenced customer cooperation and value creation in service delivery. Tuan (2018) found that in the hospitality sector, employee organizational citizenship behavior (i.e., corporate social responsibility, in this case for the environment) had a positive impact on customer citizenship behavior for the environment.

Front line service employees and service delivery channels

Traditionally, service providers have made their services available to customers through brick-and-mortar channels, necessitating face-to-face interactions between FLEs and customers who utilize the services (Barger & Grandey, 2006). However, service providers increasingly offer their services in online channels and through self-service technologies (Blut, Wang, & Schoefer, 2016; Campbell & Frei, 2010; Parasuraman & Zinkhan, 2002; Zeithaml, Parasuraman, & Malhotra, 2002). This results from efforts to lower service delivery costs and provide more efficient service delivery; in addition, more consumers are using online channels to interact with service providers. This has generated additional research on service delivery modes, including research related to factors that distinguish between consumer perception of traditional service quality and that of e-service quality, or service delivered through electronic means (Zeithaml et al., 2002). Other research focuses on factors that consumers use in their assessment of websites and the quality of service delivered via this medium (Parasuraman & Zinkhan, 2002), and in comparing traditional methods of service delivery (offline) to electronic (online) service delivery (Chakravarthi & Gopal, 2012). In addition, marketers have been examining different ways to deal with the increasing role that technology plays in service delivery, by testing various technologies including online socialization agents (Köhler, Rohm, de Ruyter, & Wetzels, 2011) and mobile shopping assistants (Spreer & Rauschnabel, 2016). Köhler et al. (2011) highlighted the role of online "socialization agents," or online "front line employees" who interact with customers and help them to assess unfamiliar service offerings. These developments indicate that FLEs are beginning to function differently and interact differently with customers depending on the channels in which they are operating.

Whereas services delivered primarily in person have to be accessed in person by consumers, some services delivered online or remotely can be accessed by consumers without personal contact or interaction with FLEs. One issue that arises in offline front line service encounters is that front line service employees can make an assessment of a customer's disposition and can make adjustments in the encounter. For instance, a salesperson can engage in adaptive selling, that is, "the unique ability to adapt sales messages and persuasive arguments by salespeople" (Kaptein, McFarland, & Parvinen, 2018; p. 1038). Kaptein et al. (2018) argue that adaptive selling is difficult in an online context, leading to their proposal of an online customization approach they refer to as "automated adaptive selling." Sugathan, Rossmann, and Ranjan (2018) concluded that perceptions of complaint handling quality influence consumer loyalty and word-of-mouth communication about brands, and that this effect is stronger in social media (online) than in traditional channels (offline).

In traditional face-to-face channels, interactions between FLEs and customers are impacted by affective displays, which can vary in intensity and authenticity (Cheshin, Amit, & van Kleef, 2018; Lechner & Paul, 2019). Such displays can influence outcomes from these front line service employee–customer interactions, including customer loyalty, trust, and satisfaction (Cheshin et al., 2018; Wang et al., 2017). Online channels of service delivery differ from traditional offline channels in one important way when it comes to affective displays: there is a limit on the display of emotions in an online channel, and this impacts front line service employee–customer interactions. Research has also shown that in cases where interpersonal exchanges between front line service employees and customers involve the use of technology, employee rapport plays an important role (Giebelhausen, Robinson, Sirianni, & Brady, 2014). Giebelhausen et al. (2014) found that technology use adversely affects the ability of consumers to react in a desired manner to rapport-building efforts on the part of the front line service employees, due to psychological discomfort on the part of customers. Research has also shown resistance on the part of FLEs to using mobile shopping assistants in their interactions with customers, with "relationship deterioration" being among the three higher-order factors that explain this resistance (Spreer & Rauschnabel, 2016).

As argued earlier in the chapter, front line service employees exercise important functions in service provision and impact customer outcomes. For these reasons, service providers are interested in encouraging FLEs to build relationships with customers. However, some of the above discussion suggests that the ability of front line service employees to build effective relationships with customers depends on the context within which the interactions take place (offline or online). Thus, in seeking to foster FLE–customer relationships, service providers should be mindful of the moderating role of delivery channel in influencing these relationships. The proposed model of front line service employee CRM investment, which is explicated in the following section, takes the delivery channel into account.

Conceptual model

The following section develops a conceptual model of front line service employee CRM investment and its relation to consumer outcomes. The model depicted in Figure 10.1 takes into account the influence of perceived FLE involvement in CRM on customer perceptions of FLE relationship investment. This, in turn, has an impact on customer perceptions of

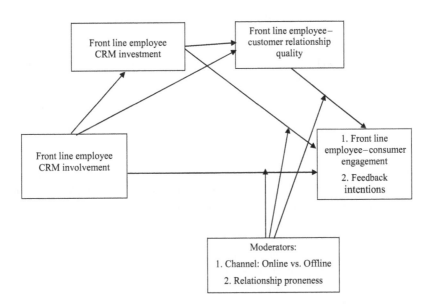

Figure 10.1 Conceptual model of FLE investment in CRM relationships.

employee–customer relationship quality, which generates certain behavioral outcomes on the parts of customers: specifically, they increase engagement and feedback intentions. The model also posits that the service delivery channel – that is, whether interactions and service provision take place online or offline – and consumer relationship proneness play moderating roles in customer outcomes. A discussion of the core constructs in the model and the resulting propositions are presented below.

Perceived FLE involvement in CRM

Although firm recognition of the importance of effective CRM strategies is not new, the need for better CRM is perhaps even more critical now. Forging strong relationships with customers in an increasingly competitive marketplace can give service providers an edge over competitors. Lovelock and Wirtz (2007, p. 619) define CRM as "the overall process of building and maintaining positive and profitable customer relationships through creating values and satisfaction for customers." Thus, the relationship between the company and the customer impacts customer propensity to do business with the firm, both in the present and future.

FLEs are often the face of the firm and, as such, are critical to delivering positive experiences to customers. How customers perceive customer–company interactions are, in large part, determined by FLEs. In recent years, a number of researchers have studied the nature of employee involvement in CRM and, specifically, the impact of employee involvement on customer perceptions. In an effort to explore FLE perspectives on how company–customer interactions might be improved, O'Reilly and Paper (2012) conducted in-depth interviews with FLEs. They found that interactions between FLEs and customers vary in terms of how much knowledge is needed by FLEs to effectively serve customers, and by the routine or nonroutine nature of the interaction. In fact, deteriorating service levels can result from management attempts to standardize the service interface (e.g., through the use of service centers).

In a study of 300 department store customers, Long, Khalafinezhad, Ismail, and Rasid (2013) found that employee behaviors are significantly related to and contribute to both customer satisfaction and loyalty. Specifically, positive relationships between FLEs and customers increase the level of customer satisfaction, and employee behavior significantly affects customer loyalty. Gremler and Gwinner (2008) explored rapport between FLEs and retail customers, finding that retail employees use five categories of behaviors to build rapport with their customers. These include uncommonly attentive behavior, common grounding behavior (e.g., identification of mutual interests), courteous behavior, connecting behavior (developing a connection with the customer), and information sharing behavior (i.e., gathering information to better understand the customer). Guenzi and Pelloni (2004) also studied the impact of interpersonal relationships between FLEs and customers (in a fitness club). Their findings suggest that strong customer-to-employee relationships benefit the service provider by leading to greater customer satisfaction, behavioral loyalty, and loyalty intention.

With the advent of social media, customers can engage with companies in an interactive environment, where both parties can exchange information and build relationships (Colliander, Dahlén, & Modig, 2015; Colliander & Wien, 2013). According to Kumar and Pansari (2016, p. 498), engagement is "the attitude, behavior, the level of connectedness (1) among customers, (2) between customers and employees, and (3) of customers and employees within a firm." In the specific case of employee engagement, Kumar and Pansari (2016, p. 500) state that it "pertains to the level of connectedness of employees with the customers and the attitude and behavior of the employees toward the firm." These researchers found that employee engagement has a positive impact on customer engagement, and that the effect of employee engagement on customer engagement is higher in service industries than in manufacturing.

Sirianni et al. (2013, p. 119) conducted research on the impact of leveraging service encounters involving employees to enhance brand positioning, finding that "branded service encounters, or those in which employee behaviors are aligned with the brand positioning, can significantly influence customer brand responses." Acker, Gröne, Akkad, Pötscher, and Yazbek (2011, p. 4) observe that if companies are to excel in the new environment of social CRM, "they must encourage their marketing, sales and customer service teams to collaborate in responding to social consumers." These authors further argue that investments in employee engagement with social consumers lead to more favorable long-term relationships. Therefore, if consumers perceive that service provider employees are involved in social CRM, perceptions of the service provider's social CRM relationship investment will be enhanced.

FLE–customer relationship investment

De Wulf, Odekerken-Schröder, and Iacobucci (2001, p. 35) define *perceived relationship investment* as a consumer's perception of the extent to which a service provider devotes resources, efforts, and attention in order to maintain or strengthen relationships "with regular customers that do not have outside value and cannot be recovered if these relationships are terminated." This research suggests that different relationship marketing tactics – direct mail, preferential treatment, interpersonal communication, and tangible rewards – affect consumer perceptions of retailer relationship investments differently. Furthermore, De Wulf et al. (2001) found that perceived relationship investments positively affect relationship quality and ultimately behavioral loyalty, and that the effect of perceived relationship investment on relationship quality depends on consumer relationship proneness as well as involvement with the product category.

Drawing on the De Wulf et al. (2001) definition of perceived relationship investment, this chapter proposes a concept of perceived FLE investment in customer relationships. This concept may be described in terms of the extent to which consumers perceive that a FLE has devoted resources, effort, and attention in order to develop and sustain relationships with consumers. This concept suggests that much as consumers can perceive that a service provider invests in building relationships with them, FLEs of the service provider also make efforts to develop and maintain relationships with them.

Perceived FLE involvement in CRM contributes to consumer perceptions regarding the level of FLE CRM investment in developing relationships with them. The more CRM activities in which FLEs are engaged, the higher will be the evaluations of their levels of CRM investment. This discussion leads to the following proposition.

P1. FLE involvement in CRM positively affects consumer perception of FLE CRM investment.

Perceived CRM relationship quality

A number of studies in relationship marketing have explored the construct of relationship quality. For instance, De Wulf et al. (2001, p. 36) studied it as an outcome variable, described as "an overall assessment of the strength of a relationship"; they further noted that relationships higher in quality are those characterized by greater consumer satisfaction, trust in the supplier, and commitment. De Wulf et al. (2001) found that higher perceived levels of relationship investment lead to higher levels of relationship quality, which lead to higher levels of behavioral loyalty. Moreover, they found that higher levels of consumer relationship proneness strengthen the impact of perceived relationship investment on relationship quality

Hennig-Thurau and Klee (1997) viewed relationship quality as a three-dimensional variable, including customer perceptions of service-related quality, trust, and relationship commitment, and postulated that relationship quality moderates the relationship between satisfaction and customer retention. Moliner, Sánchez, Rodriguez, andand Callarisa (2007b) stated that perceived relationship quality is a critical aspect of customers' attitudes toward suppliers, and found that consumer satisfaction is the primary basis for perceived relationship quality. Dant, Weaven, and Baker (2013) examined how certain franchisee personality traits affect perceived relationship quality in a franchisee–franchisor context and found that agreeableness, conscientiousness, and emotional stability positively influenced relationship quality, whereas extraversion negatively affected relationship quality.

Malhotra, Mavondo, Mukherjee, and Hooley (2013) compared FLEs in face-to-face encounters as compared to in call centers for a retail bank in the UK, finding that employees with stronger affective commitment (i.e., they value organizational goals and identify with the service provider) tend to perform better than other employees. Furthermore, their results suggest that the difference between employee groups is greater where face-to-face interactions are involved. In a study of FLEs in the hospitality industry, Slåtten and Mehmetoglu (2011) found that higher levels of employee engagement led to more innovative behaviors. Engagement has been closely linked with higher levels of customer loyalty and stronger business results (Richman, 2006).

The interaction between relationship quality and loyalty has been studied in a variety of settings, including healthcare (Moliner, 2009), tourism (Moliner et al. 2007a, 2007b), and hospitality (Ha & Jang, 2009). Rauyruen and Miller (2007) proposed that, in a business-to-business context, relationship quality comprises trust, commitment, satisfaction, and service quality. They found that all four of these dimensions influence attitudinal loyalty, but that only satisfaction and perceived service quality influence behavioral loyalty (i.e., purchase intentions). Crosby, Evans, and Cowles (1990) advanced a relationship quality model that looked at the nature, antecedents, and consequences of perceived relationship quality. These authors tested their model in the context of the life insurance agent–policyholder relationship and found, among other results, that relationship quality significantly influenced customer expectations of future interaction with the salesperson.

Prior research suggests that there should be a positive relationship between perceptions of FLE–customer relationship investment and perceived FLE–customer relationship quality. For example, in a study of university students, Cho and Auger (2013) found that student perceptions of their academic department's relationship investment positively influenced perceived relationship quality between students and their respective departments. Specifically, perceived relationship investment was positively associated with higher levels of student trust, satisfaction, commitment, and control mutuality (the extent to which both parties perceive they influence one another). Park and Kim (2014) examined online brand communities, finding that consumer perceptions of brand relationship investment are positively influenced by experiential (social and hedonic) and functional (informational and economic) benefits of a brand's social network website. Moreover, these authors found that perceived relationship investment positively affects brand relationship quality and consumer willingness to engage in positive word-of-mouth about the brand's social networking. Popp, Wilson, Horbel, and Woratschek (2016) investigated key drivers of consumer–brand relationships in the context of social networking sites, specifically looking at Facebook brand page loyalty. These authors found that higher levels of perceived relationship investment by the brand led its fans to higher Facebook brand page loyalty. The resulting proposition follows.

P2. Perceived FLE–customer relationship investment has a positive effect on perceived FLE–customer relationship quality.

Outcomes: consumer engagement

Service providers increasingly recognize the positive effects that engaged consumers can have on their organizations. For instance, van Doorn et al. (2010, p. 254) acknowledge that engagement involves considerably more than a customer purchase, stating that "customer engagement behaviors go beyond transactions, and may be specifically defined as a customer's behavioral manifestations that have a brand or firm focus, beyond purchase, resulting from motivational drivers." These authors posit that consumer engagement behaviors include activities such as word-of-mouth activity, recommendations, helping other customers, blogging, and writing reviews. They also propose that there are varying degrees of engagement, which fall on a continuum ranging from very low to intensely high levels.

Pansari and Kumar (2017, p. 295), based on a literature review, define customer engagement as "the mechanics of a customer's value addition to the firm, either through direct or/ and indirect contribution." These authors suggest that direct contributions relate to customer purchases, whereas indirect contributions include factors such as referrals provided by another customer, social media conversations customers have about the brand/company, as well as feedback and suggestions to the brand/company. Malthouse, Haenlein, Skiera, Wege,and and Zhang (2013) highlight the positive effects of "higher levels" of customer engagement with brands/companies, such as writing reviews or designing a product prototype.

The benefits of consumer engagement are apparent in both face-to-face interactions between FLEs and customers and in online contexts. As noted above, customer–service provider engagement offers a number of benefits to firms. For instance, such engagement is a critical dimension of a service provider's social media efforts. Bailey and Ben Mimoun (2016) point out that consumers engage in online word-of-mouth, which has a number of forms such as public posting in social media platforms (e.g., blogs, social network sites), referrals (e.g., tagging, embedding, invitation), ratings and reviews (e.g., on websites such as Amazon.com), and voting for and liking a service.

Recognizing the benefits that engaged consumers can have for a brand, it is in service providers' best interest to increase customer engagement with their companies. Considering the levels of interaction that FLEs typically have with customers, these individuals have substantial potential to affect the level of customer engagement. van Doorn et al. (2010) point out that although the main effects of antecedents of customer engagement behaviors may be apparent (e.g., highly satisfied customers engage in more positive word-of-mouth), it is less obvious how antecedents interact with each other to affect customer engagement behaviors. Ashley, Noble, Donthu,and and Lemon (2011) examined factors that affect customer engagement in relationship marketing efforts, finding that company-controlled factors, which may impact consumer perceptions of both inconvenience and benefits, affect consumer responses to relationship marketing efforts. These authors also found that customer factors including involvement, privacy concerns, and shopping frequency influence customer receptiveness to relational marketing programs.

Cambra-Fierro, Melero-Polo, and Vázquez-Carrasco (2014) explored the role that FLEs play in increasing service customer satisfaction and engagement. These authors found that employees with positive attitudes can increase customer satisfaction, and that this significantly influences the level of customer engagement. They also found a direct relationship between employee attitudes and the level of customer engagement.

P3. Perceived FLE–customer relationship quality will positively influence FLE–customer engagement.

Consumer feedback

There is increasing interest in the service literature regarding consumer provision of feedback to service marketers on their experiences and the performance of service providers. Celuch et al. (2015) point to a number of benefits of feedback to service providers, such as signaling customer satisfaction and indicating consumer perceptions of the service provider. Such feedback, according to these researchers, relates not only to complaining behavior but also to positive feedback about performance; they note that much of the literature on feedback to date has focused on negative feedback. FLEs are crucial in the effective handling of negative feedback such as complaints (e.g., Tax et al., 1998). Furthermore, as the 'face' of the service provider, their role with respect to both the intake and handling of all feedback, both positive and negative, is critical. Qin and Prybutok (2009), in a study of fast-food restaurants, examined relationships among customer service, satisfaction, and behavioral intentions (e.g., saying good things and recommending the restaurant to others), confirming that satisfaction directly influenced behavioral intentions. Abbas, Gao, and Shah (2018) found that customer engagement leads to increased customer word-of-mouth and feedback intentions. Finally, Béal and Sabadie (2018), in research on retail banking customers, found that stronger feelings of psychological ownership (member-owned vs. investor-owned businesses) led to greater commitment to companies and greater voice. The following proposition is based in this stream of literature.

P4. Perceived FLE–customer relationship quality positively influences consumer intentions to provide feedback to the service provider through FLEs.

Moderators

The proposed model identifies two moderators of relationships/links, including the service *delivery channel* and *customer relationship proneness*. One of these moderators is the channel in which FLE–customer interactions take place, or in which the service provider operates (offline or online). This occurs because computer-mediated communication has a different impact on the nature of interactions between consumers and front line service employees than does face-to-face communication (Sengupta, Ray, Trendel, & Vaerenbergh, 2018; Walther & Tidwell, 1995). Although there are oral and physical cues (body language) as well social cues in face-to-face communication, no such cues exist in online settings, and this is likely to influence relationship perceptions. There is evidence from the communication literature that nonverbal communication plays an important role in relationships between parties in an exchange, such as front line service employees and customers (Mehrabian, 1972).

Recently, in a study of the effects of apologies for service failures, Sengupta et al. (2018) investigated whether cultural differences existed among consumers from Western and Eastern cultures when it came to offering apologies for service failures online or offline. These authors found that the same strategies used for apologies in online contexts could not be transferred to offline settings. For instance, in an offline retailing context, consumers from Eastern cultures placed more value on an apology from a manager compared to one from a FLE, in contrast to consumers from Western cultures. The same was not true for an online setting. Research from Bacile, Wolter, Allen, and Xu (2018) also suggests that FLE–customer interaction is likely to be impacted by the channel in which the interaction takes place, given their findings regarding the levels of incivility in online interactions and the impact on service providers when they do not respond to uncivil online behavior.

P5a. Channel modality (offline vs. online) moderates the link between perceived FLE CRM involvement and (i) consumer engagement; (ii) feedback intentions.

P5b. Channel modality moderates the link between perceived FLE– relationship investment and (i) consumer engagement; (ii) feedback intentions.

P5c. Channel modality moderates the link between perceived FLE–customer relationship quality and (i) consumer engagement; (ii) feedback intentions.

Consumer relationship proneness

Prior research supports the idea that some consumers are more *relationship prone* than others (Bendapudi & Berry, 1997; Christy, Oliver, & Penn, 1996). This may vary across categories, that is, consumer proclivity to form relationships with marketers most likely differs depending on the type of service (e.g., retailing as compared to financial services) (e.g., Bendapudi & Berry, 1997). Researchers have studied the impact of this consumer characteristic on a variety of outcome variables and in a number of service settings.

De Wulf et al. (2001) suggest that relationship-prone consumers reciprocate retailer efforts to a greater extent simply because they are more likely to develop relationships. These authors find that higher levels of consumer relationship proneness strengthen the impact of perceived relationship investment on relationship quality, and that consumer relationship proneness has a positive indirect impact on buying behavior. Bloemer, Odekerken-Schröder, and Kestens (2003) study consumer relationship proneness in hairdresser–customer relationships, finding that consumers with higher needs for social affiliation have higher levels of consumer relationship proneness, which results in greater trust in and commitment to the service provider. Bloemer and Odekerken-Schröder (2006) found that relationship-prone bank employees are more likely to exhibit behavioral loyalty in the form of positive word-of-mouth, intention to stay with their current employer, benefit insensitivity (i.e., an employee's tendency to be indifferent about salary and benefits offered by alternative employers), and complaining behavior (i.e., an employee's willingness to express criticism directly to the employer).

Parish and Holloway (2010) found that consumer relationship proneness positively impacts trust and other relationship outcomes, such as customer share of wallet and adherence (the likelihood that a customer will respond favorably to provider requests). These authors also found that as service exchanges move from transactional to relational, consumer relationship proneness has greater influence on commitment and trust. Kim, Kang, and Johnson (2012) confirmed, in a study of apparel store loyalty program members, that more relationship-prone consumers are more likely to resist changing to another loyalty program. More relationship-prone consumers are expected to view FLE CRM involvement, relationship investment, and employee–customer relationship quality more favorably than less relationship-prone consumers. The resulting prediction of the moderating role of consumer relationship proneness is the following.

P6a. Consumer relationship proneness moderates the link between perceived FLE CRM involvement and (i) consumer engagement; (ii) feedback intentions.

P6b. Consumer relationship proneness moderates the link between perceived FLE relationship investment and (i) consumer engagement; (ii) feedback intentions.

P6c. Consumer relationship proneness moderates the link between perceived FLE–customer relationship quality and (i) consumer engagement; (ii) feedback intentions.

Conclusion

This chapter examines front line service providers and develops a testable conceptual model of front line service employee involvement in CRM and the impact of such involvement on desired consumer outcomes, in particular front line service employee–customer engagement and customer feedback intentions. The conceptual model takes into account the influence of perceived FLE involvement in CRM on perceptions of FLE relationship investment. The argument made was that the more consumers perceived that front line service employees engage in different relationship-building activities, the more favorably they view the front line service employee investment in CRM. This, in turn, has an impact on perceptions of employee–customer relationship quality. Higher levels of perceived front line service employee CRM investment are expected to generate more favorable perceived employee–customer relationship quality. Thus, consumers will respond by placing greater value on their interactions and relationships with front line service employees, because the level of investment serves as a positive signal to these customers of the organization's customer care. As a result, customers are expected to engage more with service providers through increased levels of engagement with FLEs. Customers will also be more inclined to provide both negative and positive feedback as well as recommendations for service improvement through the FLEs.

The conceptual model presented in this chapter introduces certain variables that are expected to impact relationships. For instance, front line service employee CRM involvement, front line service employee CRM investment, and front line service employee–customer relationship quality can all influence customer outcomes. The modality of the service – that is, whether front line service employee–customer interactions and service provision take place online or offline – and consumer relationship proneness play moderating roles in the model. The proposed model should be empirically tested, as its validation can add to understanding of the various factors that impact consumer engagement with service providers. As marketers, particularly service providers, struggle to engage and retain consumers, such research can provide them with information on how to maximize their efforts. For example, if customers perceive that they have a better relationship with service providers because of their perception of employee engagement in CRM, then service providers should ensure that they engage employees more in their CRM strategy. However, the context in which interactions take place (offline or online) must be considered, as prior research has shown that the modality of service delivery and interactions can impact perceptions of relationship. In addition, the extent to which consumers want a relationship with service providers should also be explored, in efforts to enhance engagement through FLEs. Survey data could be gathered to assess the dimensionality of constructs in the model, as well as the convergent validity, reliability, and discriminant validity of its constructs. This would be followed by empirical testing of propositions in the conceptual model.

References

Abbas, M., Gao, Y., & Shah, S. (2018). CSR and customer outcomes: The mediating role of customer engagement. *Sustainability*, *10*(11), 4243.

Acker, O., Gröne, F., Akkad, F., Pötscher, F., & Yazbek, R. (2011). Social CRM: How companies can link into the social web of consumers. *Journal of Direct, Data and Digital Marketing Practice*, *13*(1), 3–10.

Ashley, C., Noble, S. M., Donthu, N., & Lemon, K. N. (2011). Why customers won't relate: Obstacles to relationship marketing engagement. *Journal of Business Research*, *64*(7), 749–756.

Bacile, T. J., Wolter, J. S., Allen, A. M., & Xu, P. (2018). The effects of online incivility and consumer-to-consumer interactional justice on complainants, observers, and service providers during social media service recovery. *Journal of Interactive Marketing (Elsevier)*, *44*, 60–81.

Bailey, A. A., & Ben Mimoun, M. S. (2016). Consumer social orientation-based personality and social media use: An exploration among young US consumers. *International Journal of Internet Marketing and Advertising, 10*(1/2), 1–27.

Barger, P. B., & Grandey, A. A. (2006). Service with a smile and encounter satisfaction: Emotional contagion and appraisal mechanisms. *Academy of Management Journal, 49*(6), 1229–1238.

Béal, M., & Sabadie, W. (2018). The impact of customer inclusion in firm governance on customers' commitment and voice behaviors. *Journal of Business Research, 92*, 1–8.

Bendapudi, N., & Berry, L. L. (1997). Customers' motivations for maintaining relationships with service providers. *Journal of Retailing, 73*(1), 15–37.

Bloemer, J., & Odekerken-Schröder, G. (2006). The role of employee relationship proneness in creating employee loyalty. *International Journal of Bank Marketing, 24*(4), 252–264.

Bloemer, J., Odekerken-Schröder, G., & Kestens, L. (2003). The impact of need for social affiliation and consumer relationship proneness on behavioral intentions: An empirical study in a hairdresser's context. *Journal of Retailing and Consumer Services, 10*(4), 231–240.

Blut, M., Wang, C., & Schoefer, K. (2016). Factors influencing the acceptance of self-service technologies. *Journal of Service Research, 19*(4), 396–416.

Cambra-Fierro, J., Melero-Polo, I., & Vázquez-Carrasco, R. (2014). The role of frontline employees in customer engagement. *Revista Española De Investigación De Marketing ESIC, 18*(2), 67–77.

Campbell, D., & Frei, F. (2010). Cost structure, customer profitability, and retention implications of self-service distribution channels: Evidence from customer behavior in an online banking channel. *Management Science, 56*(1), 4–24.

Celuch, K., Robinson, N. M., & Walsh, A. M. (2015). A framework for encouraging retail customer feedback. *Journal of Services Marketing, 29*(4), 280–292.

Chakravarthi, J. S. K., & Gopal, V. (2012). Comparison of traditional and online travel services: A concept note. *IUP Journal of Business Strategy, 9*(1), 45–58.

Cheshin, A., Amit, A., & van Kleef, G. A. (2018). The interpersonal effects of emotion intensity in customer service: Perceived appropriateness and authenticity of attendants' emotional displays shape customer trust and satisfaction. *Organizational Behavior and Human Decision Processes, 144*, 97–111.

Cho, M., & Auger, G. A. (2013). Exploring determinants of relationship quality between students and their academic department: Perceived relationship investment, student empowerment, and student–faculty interaction. *Journalism & Mass Communication Educator, 68*(3), 255–268.

Christy, R., Oliver, G., & Penn, J. (1996). Relationship marketing in consumer markets. *Journal of Marketing Management, 12*(1-3), 175–187.

Colliander, J., Dahlén, M., & Modig, E. (2015). Twitter for two: Investigating the effects of dialogue with customers in social media. *International Journal of Advertising, 34*(2), 181–194.

Colliander, J., & Wien, A. H. (2013). Trash talk rebuffed: Consumers' defense of companies criticized in online communities. *European Journal of Marketing, 47*(10), 1733–1757.

Crosby, L. A., Evans, K. R., & Cowles, D. (1990). Relationship quality in services selling: An interpersonal influence perspective. *Journal of Marketing, 54*(3), 68–81.

Dant, R. P., Weaven, S. K., & Baker, B. L. (2013). Influence of personality traits on perceived relationship quality within a franchisee–franchisor context. *European Journal of Marketing, 47*(1/2), 279–302.

De Wulf, K., Odekerken-Schröder, G., & Iacobucci, D. (2001). Investments in consumer relationships: A cross-country and cross-industry exploration. *Journal of Marketing, 65*(4), 33–50.

Dodd, L. (2013). Corporate reputation and the role of frontline employees. *Strategic Communication Management, 17*(2), 34–36.

Fernandes, T., Morgado, M., & Rodrigues, M. A. (2018). The role of employee emotional competence in service recovery encounters. *Journal of Services Marketing, 32*(7), 835–849.

Gaucher, B., & Chebat, J.-C. (2019). How uncivil customers corrode the relationship between frontline employees and retailers. *Journal of Retailing and Consumer Services, 46*(2019), 1–10.

Giebelhausen, M., Robinson, S. G., Sirianni, N. J., & Brady, M. K. (2014). Touch versus tech: When technology functions as a barrier or a benefit to service encounters. *Journal of Marketing, 78*(4), 113–124.

Gremler, D. D., & Gwinner, K. P. (2008). Rapport-building behaviors used by retail employees. *Journal of Retailing, 84*(3), 308–324.

Guenzi, P., & Pelloni, O. (2004). The impact of interpersonal relationships on customer satisfaction and loyalty to the service provider. *International Journal of Service Industry Management, 15*(4), 365–384.

Ha, J., & Jang, S. S. (2009). Perceived justice in service recovery and behavioral intentions: The role of relationship quality. *International Journal of Hospitality Management, 28*(3), 319–327.

Harris, E. G., Brown, T. J., Mowen, J. C., & Artis, A. (2014). Exploring the role of productivity propensity in frontline employee performance: Its relationship with customer orientation and important outcomes. *Psychology & Marketing*, *31*(3), 171–183.

Hennig-Thurau, T., & Klee, A. (1997). The impact of customer satisfaction and relationship quality on customer retention: A critical reassessment and model development. *Psychology & Marketing*, *14*(8), 737–764.

Hu, H.-H., (Sunny), Parsa, H. G., Chen, C.-T., & Hu, H.-Y. (2016). Factors affecting employee willingness to report customer feedback. *Service Industries Journal*, *36*(1/2), 21–36.

Jasmand, C., Blazevic, V., & de Ruyter, K. (2012). Generating sales while providing service: A study of customer service representatives' ambidextrous behavior. *Journal of Marketing*, *76*(1), 20–37.

Kaptein, M., McFarland, R., & Parvinen, P. (2018). Automated adaptive selling. *European Journal of Marketing*, *52*(5/6), 1037–1059.

Keh, H. T., Ren, R., Hill, S. R., & Li, X. (2013). The beautiful, the cheerful, and the helpful: The effects of service employee attributes on customer satisfaction. *Psychology & Marketing*, *30*(3), 211–226.

Kim, H.-Y., Kang, J.-U. M., & Johnson, K. P. (2012). Effect of consumer relationship proneness on perceived loyalty program attributes and resistance to change. *International Journal of Retail & Distribution Management*, *40*(5), 376–387.

Köhler, C. F., Rohm, A. J., de Ruyter, K., & Wetzels, M. (2011). Return on interactivity: The impact of online agents on newcomer adjustment. *Journal of Marketing*, *75*(2), 93–108.

Korschun, D., Bhattacharya, C. B., & Swain, S. D. (2014). Corporate social responsibility, customer orientation, and the job performance of frontline employees. *Journal of Marketing*, *78*(3), 20–37.

Kumar, V., & Pansari, A. (2016). Competitive advantage through engagement. *Journal of Marketing Research*, *53*(4), 497–514.

Lechner, A. T., & Paul, M. (2019). Is this smile for real? The role of affect and thinking style in customer perceptions of frontline employee emotion authenticity. *Journal of Business Research*, *94*, 195–208.

Liao, H., & Chuang, A. (2007). Transforming service employees and climate: A multilevel multisource examination of transformational leadership in building long-term service relationships. *Journal of Applied Psychology*, *92*(4), 1006–1019.

Long, C. S., Khalafinezhad, R., Ismail, W. K. W., & Rasid, S. Z. A. (2013). Impact of CRM factors on customer satisfaction and loyalty. *Asian Social Science*, *9*(10), 247.

Lovelock, C., & Wirtz, J. (2007). *Services marketing: People, technology, strategy*. Upper Saddle River, NJ: Pearson Prentice Hall.

Malhotra, N., Mavondo, F., Mukherjee, A., & Hooley, G. (2013). Service quality of frontline employees: A profile deviation analysis. *Journal of Business Research*, *66*(9), 1338–1344.

Malthouse, E. C., Haenlein, M., Skiera, B., Wege, E., & Zhang, M. (2013). Managing customer relationships in the social media era: Introducing the social CRM house. *Journal of Interactive Marketing*, *27*(4), 270–280.

Marinova, D., Singh, S. K., & Singh, J. (2018). Frontline problem-solving effectiveness: A dynamic analysis of verbal and nonverbal cues. *Journal of Marketing Research*, *55*(2), 178–192.

Mehrabian, A. (1972). *Nonverbal communication*. New Brunswick, NJ: Transaction.

Moliner, M. A. (2009). Loyalty, perceived value and relationship quality in healthcare services. *Journal of Service Management*, *20*(1), 76–97.

Moliner, M. A., Sánchez, J., Rodriguez, R. M., & Callarisa, L. (2007a). Relationship quality with a travel agency: The influence of the postpurchase perceived value of a tourism package. *Tourism and Hospitality Research*, *7*(3–4), 194–211.

Moliner, M. A., Sánchez, J., Rodriguez, R. M., & Callarisa, L. (2007b). Perceived relationship quality and post-purchase perceived value: An integrative framework. *European Journal of Marketing*, *41*(11/12), 1392–1422.

O'Reilly, K., & Paper, D. (2012). CRM and retail service quality: Front-line employee perspectives. *International Journal of Retail & Distribution Management*, *40*(11), 865–881.

Pansari, A., & Kumar, V. (2017). Customer engagement: The construct, antecedents, and consequences. *Journal of the Academy of Marketing Science*, *45*(3), 294–311.

Parasuraman, A., & Zinkhan, G. M. (2002). Marketing to and serving customers through the internet: An overview and research agenda. *Journal of the Academy of Marketing Science*, *30*(4), 286–295.

Parish, J. T., & Holloway, B. B. (2010). Consumer relationship proneness: A reexamination and extension across service exchanges. *Journal of Services Marketing*, *24*(1), 61–73.

Park, H., & Kim, Y.-K. (2014). The role of social network websites in the consumer–brand relationship. *Journal of Retailing and Consumer Services*, *21*(4), 460–467.

Popp, B., Wilson, B., Horbel, C., & Woratschek, H. (2016). Relationship building through Facebook brand pages: The multifaceted roles of identification, satisfaction, and perceived relationship investment. *Journal of Strategic Marketing, 24*(3–4), 278–294.

Qin, H., & Prybutok, V. R. (2009). Service quality, customer satisfaction, and behavioral intentions in fast-food restaurants. *International Journal of Quality and Service Sciences, 1*(1), 78–95.

Rauyruen, P., & Miller, K. E. (2007). Relationship quality as a predictor of B2B customer loyalty. *Journal of Business Research, 60*(1), 21–31.

Richman, A. (2006). Everyone wants an engaged workforce how can you create it. *Workspan, 49*(1), 36–39.

Sahu, T. L., & Das, R. P. (2018). Factors influencing management of customer relationship of frontline employees in selected service-sector organizations. *International Journal on Customer Relations, 6*(2), 33–40.

Schepers, J., & Nijssen, E. J. (2018). Brand advocacy in the frontline: How does it affect customer satisfaction? *Journal of Service Management, 29*(2), 230–252.

Sengupta, S., Ray, D., Trendel, O., & Vaerenbergh, Y. V. (2018). The effects of apologies for service failures in the global online retail. *International Journal of Electronic Commerce, 22*(3), 419–445.

Sirianni, N. J., Bitner, M. J., Brown, S. W., & Mandel, N. (2013). Branded service encounters: Strategically aligning employee behavior with the brand positioning. *Journal of Marketing, 77*(6), 108–123.

Slåtten, T., & Mehmetoglu, M. (2011). Antecedents and effects of engaged frontline employees: A study from the hospitality industry. *Managing Service Quality, 21*(1), 88–107.

Sok, P., Sok, K. M., Danaher, T. S., & Danaher, P. J. (2018). The complementarity of frontline service employee creativity and attention to detail in service delivery. *Journal of Service Research, 21*(3), 365–378.

Spreer, P., & Rauschnabel, P. A. (2016). Selling with technology: Understanding the resistance to mobile sales assistant use in retailing. *Journal of Personal Selling & Sales Management, 36*(3), 240–263.

Stock, R. M., de Jong, A., & Zacharias, N. A. (2017). Frontline employees' innovative service behavior as key to customer loyalty: Insights into FLEs' resource gain spiral. *Journal of Product Innovation Management, 34*(2), 223–245.

Stoneman, S. (2007). Frontline ambassadors. *Marketing Week, 30*(15), 20–21.

Sugathan, P., Rossmann, A., & Ranjan, K. R. (2018). Toward a conceptualization of perceived complaint handling quality in social media and traditional service channels. *European Journal of Marketing, 52*(5/6), 973–1006.

Tax, S. S., Brown, S. W., & Chandrashekaran, M. (1998). Customer evaluations of service complaint experiences: Implications for relationship marketing. *Journal of Marketing, 62*(2), 60–76.

Tuan, L. T. (2018). Activating tourists' citizenship behavior for the environment: The roles of CSR and frontline employees' citizenship behavior for the environment. *Journal of Sustainable Tourism, 26*(7), 1178–1203.

van Doorn, J., Lemon, K. N., Mittal, V., Nass, S., Pick, D., Pirner, P., & Verhoef, P. C. (2010). Customer engagement behavior: Theoretical foundations and research directions. *Journal of Service Research, 13*(3), 253–266.

Walther, J. B., & Tidwell, L. C. (1995). Nonverbal cues in computer-mediated communication, and the effect of chronemics on relational communication. *Journal of Organizational Computing and Electronic Commerce, 5*(4), 355.

Wang, Z., Singh, S. N., Li, Y. J., Mishra, S., Ambrose, M., & Biernat, M. (2017). Effects of employees' positive affective displays on customer loyalty intentions: An emotions-as-social-information perspective. *Academy of Management Journal, 60*(1), 109–129.

Yu, T., de Ruyter, K., Patterson, P., & Chen, C.-F. (2018). The formation of a cross-selling initiative climate and its interplay with service climate. *European Journal of Marketing, 52*(7/8), 1457–1484.

Zeithaml, V. A., Parasuraman, A., & Malhotra, A. (2002). Service quality delivery through web sites: A critical review of extant knowledge. *Journal of the Academy of Marketing Science, 30*(4), 362–375.

Zhao, Y., Yan, L., & Tat Keh, H. (2018). The effects of employee behaviors on customer participation in the service encounter: The mediating role of customer emotions. *European Journal of Marketing, 52*(5/6), 1203–1222.

11

Front line service providers with two jobs

Antecedents of naturally felt emotions

Gianfranco Walsh and Mario Schaarschmidt

Introduction

The continuing shift in Western and other countries toward service-based economies has stimulated research into the behavior and work conditions of service employees. Yet most service literature assumes that service employees work for only one organization at any given time, even as reality increasingly challenges this assumption. The modern generation of service employees commonly holds multiple service jobs, reflecting the needs of households that have experienced stagnant wages, decreasing real incomes (Savage, 2018), and reduced social welfare expenditures by government agencies (Hamnett, 2014). To make ends meet, many people take second or third jobs, such that in 2015 close to 9 million people employed in the European Union had more than one job (Pouliakas, 2017). Similarly, according to the US Department of Labor (2017), more than 7.5 million US workers hold multiple jobs, many in service sectors. But dual job holding is not only a Western phenomenon: an estimated 40% of Chinese and 30% of Singaporean employees hold a second job (Goh, 2018; Ping, 2016). Following Walsh, Dahling, andanand, Schaarschmidt (2016), this study distinguishes the primary job, which requires the most time and earns the most income, from secondary jobs that provide fewer hours and less supplementary income.[1]

Addressing these labor developments is critical because working two jobs may lead to resource depletion that detrimentally affects employee ability to perform role-prescribed, customer-directed behaviors (Keith & Schafer, 1980; Walsh et al., 2016). As such, so-called 'dual service jobbers' constitute a special group of service employees in terms of the skill set that they require and the demands that they have to deal with. Walsh et al. (2016) argue that meeting the emotional requirements of two service jobs is more demanding and resource depleting than working overtime in one job. In other words, emotional job requirements in many service jobs, which stipulate that employees perform emotional labor when interacting with customers (Groth, Hennig-Thurau, & Walsh, 2009), are more likely to sap the resources of dual than single jobbers.

Prior service research attends closely to the drivers (Cheung and Tang, 2009; Grandey, 2003; Mikolajczak, Menil, & Luminet, 2007) and outcomes of employee emotional labor, in the form of surface and deep acting, and cites its draining effects on employees (Goodwin,

Groth, & Frenkel, 2011; Hochschild, 2012), but it rarely addresses how employees who perform two service jobs (i.e., dual service jobbers), cope with such emotional job demands. Furthermore, extant research does not address (in relation to dual service jobbers) the drivers of an additional emotional labor strategy, which is to offer customers naturally felt emotions (NFE). Webster, Edwards, & Smith, (2018) indicate that dual jobbers (cf. single jobbers) do not necessarily exhibit lower work engagement, organizational citizenship behavior, or job performance, but they may experience higher levels of work–family conflict. Walsh et al. (2016) report that surface acting efforts at the primary and secondary jobs interact to predict levels of emotional exhaustion which mediate the relationship between surface acting (at the primary job) and organizational commitment. However, there is inadequate service research that addresses authentic emotional deployments and antecedents for dual jobbers. Table 11.1 provides a representative, but not exhaustive, sample of studies on antecedents of naturally felt emotions.

Drawing on a framework by Grandey (2003), the present study tests a proposed model and hypotheses (Figure 11.1) among a sample of US-based dual service jobbers. Grandey (2003) investigated the effects of job satisfaction and display rules on two emotional labor strategies, surface acting and deep acting, without including NFE in the model.

This chapter advances existing insights with a framework that distinguishes job satisfaction at the primary job, job satisfaction at the secondary job, display rule commitment, and service emotion rule fairness (SERF) as antecedents of service employees' NFE at the primary

Table 11.1 Selected literature on antecedents of service employees' expression of NFE

Author(s)	Sample	Antecedents of NFE	Findings
Diefendorff, Croyle, & Gosserand (2005)	n=297 US undergraduate students and 179 service employees/survey	Emotional expressivity, extraversion, neuroticism, openness, conscientiousness, agreeableness, self-monitoring, positive display rules, negative display rules, frequency and duration of interaction, routineness	Negative display rules, extraversion positively, agreeableness, and frequency of interaction positively predicted of the expression of NFE
Dahling and Perez (2010)	n=191 US students and non-students/survey	Age, positive affect	Age and positive affect positively predict the expression of NFE
Brach, Walsh, Hennig-Thurau, & Groth (2015)	n=275 customer–employee dyads	Employee-customer orientation	Customer orientation positively predicts the expression of NFE
Cheung and Tang (2010)	n=386 service employees in Hong Kong	Age as well as an age x gender interaction	Neither age nor the age x gender interaction had an effect on NFE
Yagil (2014)	n=41 Israeli supervisors and 164 employee–customer dyads	Trust in the supervisor	Trust in the supervisor relates to authentic emotional displays in service encounters

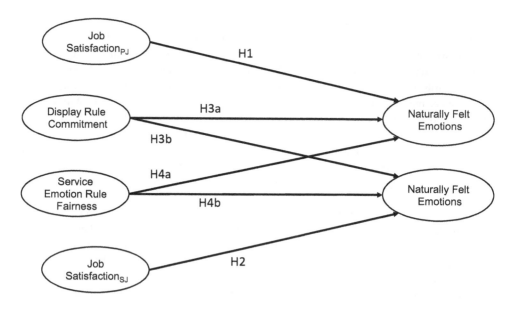

Figure 11.1 Conceptual model.

Note: PJ refers to primary job; SJ refers to secondary job.

and secondary jobs. The focus is on NFE as outcomes because they remain insufficiently researched as a type of emotional labor that differs conceptually from surface or deep acting (Walsh, 2018). Moreover, NFE have not been studied in relation to dual jobbers. But as Walsh et al. (2016) argue, there may be limits to the emotions that a service employee can deploy across two jobs, so dual service jobbers might prefer emotional labor that is less resource depleting than are surface and deep acting.

Background and hypotheses

Front line service employees are the most important factor driving customer satisfaction (Chu, 2002) and, according to Groth and Grandey (2012, p. 208), the "quality of interpersonal interactions between frontline service employees and customers is a critical component of any customer service experience." Being able to provide high-quality interpersonal interactions requires employees to manage and deploy emotions during service transactions. Past service management research has focused on the role of emotions in service deliveries, especially on the role of emotional labor performed by front line service employees. Front line employees are often expected to display certain emotions (e.g., friendliness) and suppress others (e.g., frustration) in their interactions with customers, in order to comply with employer expectations and job requirements. Therefore, front line employees have to engage in "emotional labor," which refers to the "process of regulating both feelings and expressions for the organizational goals" (Grandey, 2000, p. 97). Over the years, emotional labor has received attention in the services literature; much of the research has focused on the concept's dimensionality and its effects on important employee outcomes.

In regard to emotional labor dimensions, surface acting and deep acting represent the principal emotion regulation strategies (or types of emotional labor) available to service employees (Hochschild, 2012). When an employee engages in surface acting, s/he hides felt emotions while at the same time adjusting her/his emotional expression to match normative patterns (Hochschild, 2012). Because surface acting involves pretending emotions one does not really feel, it is sometimes referred to as "faking." Deep acting, on the other hand, requires a concerted effort by the employee to experience desired emotions. When engaged in deep acting, the service employee manipulates her/his emotional state to conform with mandated or expected behaviors (Hochschild, 2012).

Using a dramaturgical perspective, Grandey (2003) examines the effects of job satisfaction and display rules on deep and surface acting, which in turn predict employee stress and performance. Grandey (2003) shows that job satisfaction negatively affects both types of emotional labor, whereas display rules relate positively to deep acting but are not related to surface acting. Display rules prescribe behaviors necessary for effective job performance. Specifically, many service firms have an implicit rule that positive emotions should be displayed and negative emotions should be suppressed (Diefendorff & Richard 2003). In contrast, service scripts include behavioral and/or verbal prescriptions used in service firms as a means of standardizing employees' reactions during their interactions with customers (Nguyen, Groth, Walsh, & Hennig-Thurau, 2014; Walsh, Gouthier, Gremler, & Brach, 2012). Consistent with the notion that emotional labor, as surface acting, depletes personal resources, Grandey (2003) finds that surface acting promotes emotional exhaustion. This chapter builds on Grandey's (2003) framework to posit that job satisfaction in the primary and secondary jobs positively affects NFE in these two job settings. It also anticipates that a service employee's display rule commitment and the degree to which she or he perceives organizational display requirements as fair relate to NFE in the primary and secondary jobs.

Generally, 'job satisfaction' refers to an employee's affective feelings toward a job (Locke & Dunnette, 1976; Spector, 1997); it is a key determinant of employee motivation (Moynihan & Pandey, 2007; Tsai, Yen, Huang, & Huang, 2007), such that employees with high job satisfaction are more likely to engage in behaviors associated with tasks that contribute positively to organizational goals (e.g., Judge & Bono, 2001). However, Grandey (2003) establishes a negative job satisfaction–surface acting link, suggesting that satisfied service employees are less inclined to deploy superficial, inauthentic, and/or fake emotions. The present chapter deduces in turn that satisfied employees likely prefer to act naturally when interacting with customers, in both primary and secondary jobs. This notion gains credence from literature that defines job satisfaction as an employee's pleasurable or positive emotional state, resulting from the appraisal of the job (Locke & Dunnette, 1976). Consistent with this notion, it can be reasoned that dual service jobbers who are satisfied (i.e., experience pleasurable, positive emotional states) display genuine emotions in their interactions with customers.

H1. Job satisfaction in the primary job positively affects NFE in the primary job.
H2. Job satisfaction in the secondary job positively affects NFE in the secondary job.

Many service firms acknowledge the heterogeneous nature of service delivery episodes; every employee and every customer is different. Nonetheless, service firms strive for consistently high levels of service quality and therefore make efforts to ensure such service experiences for customers. They often implement organizational display and/or rules service scripts, in the form of verbal and/or behavioral prescriptions for how front line service employees should interact with customers (Nguyen et al., 2014). Display rules often specify what kind of emotions employees should deploy toward the customer; however, not all service employees embrace such mandated emotions. Rather, service employees differ in their commitments to such display rules and preferred emotional states (e.g., Wang, Liao, Zhan, & Shi, 2011).

The present chapter anticipates that dual service jobbers might be particularly aware and critical of display rules. According to Allen, Pugh, Grandey, anand Groth (2010), display rules impose requirements to regulate emotions, which are effortful and tax personal resources. Similarly, Witt, Andrews, andand Carlson (2004, p. 151) posit that following "display rules may provide sufficient stress to bring on emotional exhaustion for many workers." Therefore, working two service jobs and following two sets of display rules is likely to be more psychologically draining than having only one job. One might therefore surmise that employees who accept that mandated emotion regulation efforts are part of their (primary or secondary) job and are committed to following display rules typically follow mandated emotional displays, in the form of surface or deep acting. In contrast, employees who are less committed to display rules might prefer to express their NFE during customer interactions.

H3. Display rule commitment negatively affects NFE in both (a) primary and (b) secondary jobs.

This line of reasoning suggests that display rules are not universally accepted by front line employees, and that some resent having to follow them. In support of this notion, Grandey and Fisk (2004) argue that, when service employees perceive that emotional display rules reduce their control over their emotions, they perceive insufficient SERF, which may create job-related strain. That is, perceived unfairness leads to diminished performance and less norm-congruent behavior (Blakely, Andrews, & Moorman, 2005; Cohen, Holder-Webb, Sharp, & Pant 2007; O'Neill, Lewis, & Carswell, 2011). This leads to expectations that low SERF is incompatible with displays of mandated emotions. To avoid job strain resulting from following display rules, service employees who regard display requirements as unfair may instead favor less stressful emotional displays, in the form of NFE. In the case of dual jobbers, this argument should hold for both the primary and secondary jobs.

H4. SERF negatively affects NFE in both (a) primary and (b) secondary jobs.

Method

Data collection and sample

Front line service employees holding two jobs in a variety of service industries were surveyed, using an online crowdsourcing service. Similar to other survey services, crowdsourcing services can produce reliable results if configured correctly (Buhrmester, Kwang, & Gosling, 2011; Schaarschmidt, Ivens, Homscheid, & Bilo, 2015). To this end, the US-based crowdsourcing platform Amazon Mechanical Turk was selected; participants who had demonstrated their trustworthiness in prior interactions with that platform were invited to take the survey. In particular, participants were requested who were US residents, had completed at least 1,000 previous survey tasks, and had an approval rating of greater than 95%. The participants received compensation for providing answers, so it is important to control for their attentiveness; therefore, two questions were included that simply provided the instruction: "Please answer the following question with 'disagree'." In addition, gender and age data were gathered twice; respondents who did not give the same answers on both occasions were removed. Finally, considering the specific interest in dual jobbers, respondents were asked twice how many service jobs they currently held. To classify a job as primary or secondary, average work hours per week were used.

Respondents reported that they interacted with customers for an average of 83.0% (SD=17.4%) of their workday in their primary job and 85.2% (SD=18.0%) in their secondary job. The final sample of 492 respondents included 244 women (49.6%). The mean age for the entire sample was 32 years (SD=7.4).

Measures

The survey contained reflective, multi-item measures of job satisfaction, display rule commitment, perceived SERF, and NFE. For constructs that were captured for both the first and second job, respondents were instructed to consider the job in which they worked the most hours as their primary job. In addition, each set of questions started with the stem, "Please answer the following questions in relation to your primary job."

To measure job satisfaction, a subscale of the Michigan Organizational Assessment Questionnaire with three items (Cammann, Fichman, Jenkins, & Klesh, 1983) was used. Display rule commitment was measured with a five-item scale, previously used by Dahling (2017) and Klein, Wesson, Hollenbeck, Wright, andand DeShon (2001). For SERF, a measure adapted from Grandey and Fisk (2004) was relied upon. Finally, the NFE for both jobs was captured with three items based on Gosserand and Diefendorff (2005). For the items that reflect constructs, a Likert response scale ranging from 1 ('strongly disagree') to 7 ('strongly agree') was employed. (All construct scale items appear in Table 11.2.) Respondents were asked about demographic and potential control variables, which included gender, age, and the amount of customer contact (as a percentage of workday) for both the primary and secondary jobs.

Definitions of variables used in the study are as follows:

Job Satisfaction$_{PJ}$ = Job satisfaction at the primary job
Job Satisfaction$_{SJ}$ = Job satisfaction at the secondary job
NFE$_{PJ}$ = NFE at the primary job
NFE$_{SJ}$ = NFE at the secondary job

Results

Measurement validation

Measures were assessed using a confirmatory factor analysis (CFA). All latent variables used in the conceptual model were included in a CFA, conducted with Amos 25 and a maximum-likelihood estimator. The measurement model reveals a good fit with the data (χ^2=542.18; df=215; χ^2/df=2.522; p<.001), based on the comparative fit index (CFI=.96), incremental fit index (IFI=.96), Tucker–Lewis index (TLI=.95), and root mean squared error of approximation (RMSEA=.056). (For the latter assessment, see Hu and Bentler (1999).) Table 11.2 reports regression weights of at least .6 for all indicators, composite reliability values of at least .7, and average variances extracted (AVE) that exceed .5 for all constructs. In support of discriminant validity, all squared covariances are smaller than the related AVE (see Fornell & Larcker, 1981). Table 11.3 displays the correlations and the square root of the AVE on the diagonal.

Table 11.2 Construct scale items, factor loadings, and reliabilities

	Factor loadings (PJ/SJ)	Composite reliability (CR) (PJ/SJ)	AVE (PJ/SJ)
Job satisfaction (adapted from Cammann et al., 1983)		.94/.94	.85/.83
All in all, I am satisfied with my job at COMPANY.	.93/.94		
In general, I don't like my job at COMPANY. (Reverse)	.92/.87		
In general, I like working at COMPANY.	.91/.94		
Display rule commitment (adapted from Dahling, 2017; Klein et al., 2001)		.78	.56
It's hard to take the goal of displaying positive emotions to customers seriously. (Reverse)	.65		
Quite frankly, I don't care if I display positive emotions to others or not. (Reverse)	.82		
I am strongly committed to pursuing the goal of showing positive emotions to customers.	.78		
It wouldn't take much for me to abandon the goal of displaying positive emotions to customers. (Reverse)	.75		
I think that displaying positive emotions to others is a good goal to shoot for.	.73		
SERF (adapted from Grandey & Fisk, 2004)		.76	.56
It seems reasonable for service employees to be told to 'smile' as part of their job.	.82		
It is fair for any employee to be expected to hide negative feelings from customers.	.65		
Smiling at customers even when one is upset seems like a fair request to make of employees.	.83		
It is fair to expect service employees to smile: that is part of what they are paid to do.	.85		
Service employees shouldn't have to pretend they aren't upset at a customer when they really are. (Reverse)	.62		
It seems unfair for service employees to have to smile at customers in addition to everything else. (Reverse)	.70		
NFE (adapted from Gosserand & Diefendorff, 2005)		.89/.93	.73/.82
I express genuine emotions to customers.	.80/.91		
The emotions I show to customers come naturally.	.92/.94		
The emotions I show match what I spontaneously feel.	.84/.87		

Note: "COMPANY" was replaced with the name of the employer that each respondent provided.

Table 11.3 Correlations between key variables.

Variable	1	2	3	4	5	6
1 Job satisfaction (PJ)	(0.92)					
2 Job satisfaction (SJ)	0.15	(0.91)				
3 Display rule commitment	-0.42	-0.33	(0.75)			
4 SERF	0.24	0.14	0.68	(0.75)		
5 NFE (PJ)	0.54	0.25	-0.46	0.19	(0.86)	
6 NFE (SJ)	0.16	0.65	-0.37	0.12	0.54	(0.91)

Note: PJ = primary job, SJ = secondary job

Because a single source of data and the same measurement instrument were used to assess the independent and dependent variables, the results could potentially be affected by common method variance (CMV). To test for this, several recommended procedures (e.g., Podsakoff, MacKenzie, Lee, & Podsakoff, 2003) were implemented. First, Harman's single-factor test with an exploratory factor analysis (without rotation) was conducted in SPSS 25. This resulted in a single factor accounting for only 33.6% of the variance, so no dominant single factor emerged from the data. Second, an unmeasured common latent factor method was used to compare a model that included all of the variables to one in which all of the indicators loaded on a single unmeasured construct. The regression weights of the two models were then compared. Large deviations in regression weights would signal CMV but, in this case, the largest deviation between the two models was $\Delta\gamma = .15$, well within accepted ranges.

Regression results

The hypothesized model (Figure 11.1) was tested using SPSS Amos 25 and a maximum-likelihood estimator (see Figure 11.2). A model with controls (age and gender for both dependent variables; customer contact portion for the respective jobs) fits the data well (χ^2=884.66; df=310; χ^2/df = 2.854; CFI=.93; IFI=.93; TLI=.92; RMSEA=.061). None of the controls yielded significance for a single dependent variable. The antecedents explain NFE in the primary job (R^2_{PJ} =.42) and in the secondary job (R^2_{SJ} = .49) fairly well.

The study findings support H1 and H2, in that job satisfaction relates positively to NFE (H1: β_{PJ}=.40; p<.001; H2: β_{SJ}=.56; p<.001). As predicted in H3(a) and H3(b), negative values were obtained for the paths of display rule commitment to NFE (H3a: β_{PJ}=-.50; p<.001; H3b: β_{SJ}=-.26; p<.001). Finally, the paths from SERF to NFE were significant and negative for both primary and secondary jobs (H4a: β_{PJ} = -.21, p < .001; H4b β_{SJ} = -.37, p < .001), supporting both H4(a) and H4(b).[2]

Discussion

Changes in macroeconomic conditions that influence the well-being and behaviors of service employees command scholarly attention. As people seek out two or more service jobs, it becomes even more critical for service researchers to devote effort to understanding how front line service providers cope with job-related demands. The dual jobber phenomenon

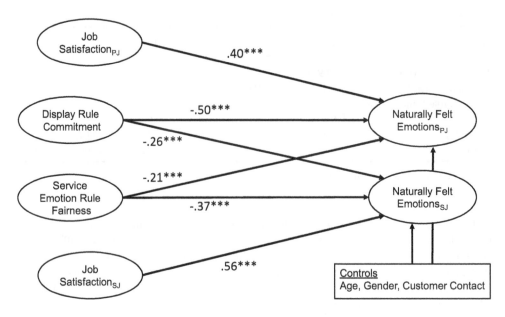

Figure 11.2 Hypothesis test results.

Note: PJ refers to primary job; SJ refers to secondary job.

presents service firms with a potential dilemma: on the one hand, they need to fill positions with front line employees. On the other hand, working multiple jobs is emotionally and cognitively demanding, which could lead to poorer performance by these employees (Ray & Miller, 1994; Sliter & Boyd, 2014). Consequently, service firms need to know how job-related antecedents affect key employee outcomes, such as emotion deployment skills.

The research reported here examines how dual jobbers' job satisfaction, in their primary and secondary jobs, as well as their commitment to display rules and perceptions of SERF, affect their use of NFE in interactions with customers in their primary and secondary jobs. In doing so, this research considers a largely neglected emotional labor strategy as outcome – offering the customer the provider's NFE. The findings indicate that dual jobbers' job satisfaction in the primary job is a positive antecedent of NFE in the primary job, and that job satisfaction in the secondary job is a positive antecedent of NFE in the secondary job. Commitment to display rules negatively predicts NFE in both primary and secondary jobs, though the negative effect appears stronger in relation to the primary job. Perceived SERF also negatively predicts NFE in both primary and secondary jobs. With these findings, this research extends prior studies that explore the emotional labor of dual jobbers more generally (Walsh et al., 2016).

Theoretical implications

Despite the increasing number of dual jobbers in many countries, service research predominantly focuses on single job front line employees. Extant studies on dual job holders also tend to include a general working population (e.g., Bouwhuis et al., 2017), possibly for comparison. In describing emotional labor strategies, most studies investigate deep and surface acting, without addressing NFE (Walsh, 2018). The study presented in this chapter takes the next step in developing service theory by bridging research on dual jobbers and literature pertaining to front line employee emotional labor strategies. Most service jobs require employees to display organizationally desired emotions when interacting with customers, but commitment to organizational display rules and the perceived fairness of such rules negatively affect NFE across service jobs. Job satisfaction instead positively drives NFE in first and second jobs. By identifying positive and negative antecedents of NFE, the present research extends service theory.

Limitations and further research

This study has several limitations that offer avenues for further research. For example, it focused on employees with two service jobs, not those who might hold three or more jobs or employees who work in both service and non-service (e.g., manufacturing) settings. Ongoing studies should assess if the investigated relationships hold across different types of multiple jobbers. Moreover, the present study investigated relationships between job-related antecedents and NFE deployed during the performance of primary and secondary jobs. Although it included some controls, it did not examine boundary conditions of the relationships, which further research could address. Despite these limitations, the results have implications for practice, as described below.

Managerial implications

The present study highlights the need to understand antecedent–outcome relationships for dual jobbers. Job satisfaction is an important construct in its own right, but this study shows that dual jobbers' job satisfaction, in both their primary and secondary jobs, drives their use of NFE during interactions with customers. This finding is good news, in that deploying NFE, rather than engaging in deep or surface acting, is far less resource-depleting or detrimental to the service employee (Walsh, 2018). Firms that hire or already employ dual jobbers know that their employees face cumulative job demands. It is in these employers' interest to nurture and ensure job satisfaction in order to avoid greater resource depletion.

The present findings regarding the effect of display rule commitment and perceived SERF may be of concern to service managers. Dual jobbers who are committed to organizational display rules appear less likely to deploy NFE, which may be acceptable if the firms expect their front line employees to engage in surface or deep acting. However, managers must bear in mind that surface or deep acting is more draining for the employee (Walsh, 2018) and therefore either of these types of acting may not be a preferred emotional labor strategy. Moreover, dual jobbers who perceive low SERF may be reluctant to use their NFE. Service firms have two options in this case: (1) invest in measures designed to explain the usefulness and fairness of display rules, or (2) accept that dual jobbing front line employees will not use NFE. The employee resource depletion and ensuing negative outcomes that result from the latter choice should be taken into consideration.

Notes

1 Some employees may work two part-time service jobs instead of a full-time job. The present study, however, focuses on employees who hold one primary job and one secondary job.
2 We also checked for cross-job influences by introducing two additional paths; one from Job satisfaction$_{PJ}$ to NFE$_{SJ}$ and one from Job satisfaction$_{SJ}$ to NFE$_{PJ}$. The resulting model fits equally well (χ^2 = 880.04, df = 308, χ^2/df = 2.858, CFI = .93, IFI = .93, TLI = .92, and RMSEA = .062), however, none of the paths yielded significance.

References

Allen, J. A., Pugh, S. D., Grandey, A. A., & Groth, M. (2010). Following display rules in good or bad faith? Customer orientation as a moderator of the display rule–emotional labor relationship. *Human Performance*, 23(2), 101–115.

Blakely, G. L., Andrews, M. C., & Moorman, R. H. (2005). The moderating effects of equity sensitivity on the relationship between organizational justice and organizational citizenship behaviors. *Journal of Business and Psychology*, 20(2), 259–273.

Bouwhuis, S., Garde, A. H., Geuskens, G. A., Boot, C. R., Bongers, P. M., & van der Beek, A. J. (2017). The longitudinal association between multiple job holding and long-term sickness absence among Danish employees: An explorative study using register-based data. *International Archives of Occupational and Environmental Health*, 90(8), 799–807.

Brach, S., Walsh, G., Hennig-Thurau, T., & Groth, M. (2015). A dyadic model of customer orientation: Mediation and moderation effects. *British Journal of Management*, 26(2), 292–309.

Buhrmester, M., Kwang, T., & Gosling, S. D. (2011). Amazon's Mechanical Turk: A new source of inexpensive, yet high-quality, data? *Perspectives on Psychological Science*, 6(1), 3–5.

Cammann, C., Fichman, M., Jenkins, G. D., & Klesh, J. (1983). Michigan organizational assessment questionnaire. In S. E. Seashore, E. E. Lawler, P. H. Mirvis, & C. Cammann (Eds.), *Assessing organizational change: A guide to methods, measures, and practices* (pp. 71–138): New York: Wiley-Inter-Science.

Cheung, F. Y. L., & Tang, C. S. K. (2009). The influence of emotional intelligence and affectivity on emotional labor strategies at work. *Journal of Individual Differences*, 30(2), 75–86.

Cheung, F. Y. L., & Tang, C. S. K. (2010). Effects of age, gender, and emotional labor strategies on job outcomes: Moderated mediation analyses. *Applied Psychology: Health and Well-Being*, 2(3), 323–339.

Chu, R. (2002). Stated-importance versus derived-importance customer satisfaction measurement. *Journal of Services Marketing*, 16(4), 285–301.

Cohen, J. R., Holder-Webb, L., Sharp, D. J., & Pant, L. W. (2007). The effects of perceived fairness on opportunistic behavior. *Contemporary Accounting Research*, 24(4), 1119–1138.

Dahling, J. J. (2017). Exhausted, mistreated, or indifferent? Explaining deviance from emotional display rules at work. *European Journal of Work and Organizational Psychology*, 26, 1–12.

Dahling, J. J., & Perez, L. A. (2010). Older worker, different actor? Linking age and emotional labor strategies. *Personality and Individual Differences*, 48(5), 574–578.

Diefendorff, J. M., Croyle, M. H., & Gosserand, R. H. (2005). The dimensionality and antecedents of emotional labor strategies. *Journal of Vocational Behavior*, 66(2), 339–357.

Diefendorff, J. M., & Richard, E. M. (2003). Antecedents and consequences of emotional display rule perceptions. *Journal of Applied Psychology*, 88(2), 284–294.

Fornell, C., & Larcker, D. F. (1981). Evaluating structural equation models with unobservable variables and measurement error. *Journal of Marketing Research*, 18(1), 39–50.

Goh, P. X. (2018). *Is moonlighting illegal in Singapore?* https://singaporelegaladvice.com/moonlighting-illegal-singapore/, accessed 16 November 2018.

Goodwin, R. E., Groth, M., & Frenkel, S. J. (2011). Relationships between emotional labor, job performance, and turnover. *Journal of Vocational Behavior*, 79(2), 538–548.

Gosserand, R. H., & Diefendorff, J. M. (2005). Emotional display rules and emotional labor: The moderating role of commitment. *Journal of Applied Psychology*, 90, 1256–1264.

Grandey, A. A. (2000). Emotional regulation in the workplace: A new way to conceptualize emotional labor. *Journal of Occupational Health Psychology*, 5(1), 95–110.

Grandey, A. A. (2003). When 'the show must go on': Surface acting and deep acting as determinants of emotional exhaustion and peer-rated service delivery. *Academy of Management Journal*, 46(1), 86–96.

Grandey, A. A., & Fisk, G. M. (2004). Display rules and strain in service jobs: What's fairness got to do with it? In Pamela L. Perrewé and Daniel C. Ganster (eds), *Exploring interpersonal dynamics* (pp. 265–293). Bingley, UK: Emerald Group Publishing Limited.

Groth, M., & Grandey, A. (2012). From bad to worse: Negative exchange spirals in employee–customer service interactions. *Organizational Psychology Review*, 2(3), 208–233.

Groth, M., Hennig-Thurau, T., & Walsh, G. (2009). Customer reactions to emotional labor: The roles of employee acting strategies and customer detection accuracy. *Academy of Management Journal*, 52(5), 958–974.

Hamnett, C. (2014). Shrinking the welfare state: The structure, geography and impact of British government benefit cuts. *Transactions of the Institute of British Geographers*, *39*(4), 490–503.

Hochschild, A. R. (2012). *The managed heart: Commercialization of human feeling*. Berkeley: University of California Press.

Hu, L.-T., & Bentler, P. M. (1999). Cutoff criteria for fit indexes in covariance structure analysis: Conventional criteria versus new alternatives. *Structural Equation Modeling: A Multidisciplinary Journal*, *6*(1), 1–55.

Judge, T. A., & Bono, Joyce E. (2001). Relationship of core self-evaluations traits – self-esteem, generalized self-efficacy, locus of control, and emotional stability – with job satisfaction and job performance: A meta-analysis. *Journal of Applied Psychology*, *86*(1), 80–92.

Keith, P. M., & Schafer, R. B. (1980). Role strain and depression in two-job families. *Family Relations*, *29*(4), 483–488.

Klein, H. J., Wesson, M. J., Hollenbeck, J. R., Wright, P. M., & DeShon, R. P. (2001). The assessment of goal commitment: A measurement model meta-analysis. *Organizational Behavior and Human Decision Processes*, *85*, 32–55.

Locke, E. A., & Dunnette, M. D. (1976). The nature and causes of job satisfaction. In M. D. Dunnette (Ed.), *Handbook of industrial and organizational psychology* (pp. 1297–1349): New York: Holt, Rinehart & Winstonlocke.

Mikolajczak, M., Menil, C., & Luminet, O. (2007). Explaining the protective effect of trait emotional intelligence regarding occupational stress: Exploration of emotional labour processes. *Journal of Research in Personality*, *41*(5), 1107–1117.

Moynihan, D. P., & Pandey, S. K. (2007). Finding workable levers over work motivation: Comparing job satisfaction, job involvement, and organizational commitment. *Administration & Society*, *39*(7), 803–832.

Nguyen, H., Groth, M., Walsh, G., & Hennig-Thurau, T. (2014). The impact of service scripts on customer citizenship behavior and the moderating role of employee customer orientation. *Psychology & Marketing*, *31*(12), 1096–1109.

O'Neill, T. A., Lewis, R. J., & Carswell, J. J. (2011). Employee personality, justice perceptions, and the prediction of workplace deviance. *Personality and Individual Differences*, *51*(5), 595–600.

Ping, C. H. (2016). *Internet makes it easier for Chinese to work two jobs*, www.straitstimes.com/asia/east-asia/internet-makes-it-easier-for-chinese-to-work-two-jobs, accessed 15 November 2018.

Podsakoff, P. M., MacKenzie, S. B., Lee, J. Y., & Podsakoff, N. P. (2003). Common method biases in behavioral research: A critical review of the literature and recommended remedies. *Journal of Applied Psychology*, *88*(5), 879–903.

Pouliakas, K. (2017). Multiple job-holding: Career pathway or dire straits? *IZA World of Labor*, *356*, http://hdl.handle.net/10419/162366.

Ray, E. B., & Miller, K. I. (1994). Social support, home/work stress, and burnout: Who can help? *Journal of Applied Behavioral Science*, *30*(3), 357–373.

Savage, M. (2018). Poorest made poorer? Welfare implications of cross-sectional and longitudinal income changes during the Great Recession. *Research in Social Stratification and Mobility*, *53*, 64–76.

Schaarschmidt, M., Ivens, S., Homscheid, D., & Bilo, P. (2015). Crowdsourcing for survey research: Where Amazon Mechanical Turk deviates from conventional survey methods. *Technical Report 1/2015*, University of Koblenz-Landau.

Sliter, M. T., & Boyd, E. M. (2014). Two (or three) is not equal to one: Multiple jobholding as a neglected topic in organizational research. *Journal of Organizational Behavior*, *35*(7), 1042–1046.

Spector, P. E. (1997). *Job satisfaction: Application, assessment, causes, and consequences*. Thousand Oaks: SAGE.

Tsai, P. C. F., Yen, Y. F., Huang, L. C., & Huang, C. (2007). A study on motivating employees' learning commitment in the post-downsizing era: Job satisfaction perspective. *Journal of World Business*, *42*(2), 157–169.

US Department of Labor (2017). *Persons not in the labor force and multiple jobholders by sex, not seasonally adjusted*, www.bls.gov/news.release/empsit.t16.htm.

Walsh, G. (2018). Service employees' naturally felt emotions: Do they matter? *European Management Journal*, doi:10.1016/j.emj.2018.06.008.

Walsh, G., Dahling, J. J., Schaarschmidt, M., & Brach, S. (2016). Surface-acting outcomes among service employees with two jobs: Investigating moderation and mediation effects. *Journal of Service Management*, *27*(4), 534–562.

Walsh, G., Gouthier, M., Gremler, D. D., & Brach, S. (2012). What the eye does not see, the mind cannot reject: Can call center location explain differences in customer evaluations? *International Business Review, 21*(5), 957–967.

Wang, M., Liao, H., Zhan, Y., & Shi, J. (2011). Daily customer mistreatment and employee sabotage against customers: Examining emotion and resource perspectives. *Academy of Management Journal, 54*, 312–334.

Webster, B. D., Edwards, B. D., & Smith, M. B. (2018). Is holding two jobs too much? An examination of dual jobholders. *Journal of Business and Psychology*, doi:10.1007/s10869-018-9540-2.

Witt, L. A., Andrews, M. C., & Carlson, D. S. (2004). When conscientiousness isn't enough: Emotional exhaustion and performance among call center customer service representatives. *Journal of Management, 30*(1), 149–160.

Yagil, D. (2014). Trust in the supervisor and authenticity in service roles. *Journal of Service Management, 25*(3), 411–426.

12

Service process design and management

Steven W. Rayburn, Sidney T. Anderson,
and Kendra Fowler

Introduction

Services impact all facets of human well-being (Sangiorgi, 2011); however, they often fail because they are not grounded in consumer needs and wants (Brown & Wyatt, 2010). Because of this, service providers should rely on design tools that can assist them in meeting customer requirements, a process that necessitates starting with understanding customers (Matthing, Sanden, & Edvardsson, 2004; Patrício & Fisk, 2013; Shostack, 1977, 1984b).

Because it was accepted in the early service literature that organizations managed the entire service experience (Bitner, Ostrom, & Morgan, 2008; Shostack, 1982, 1985), three additional 'Ps' (i.e., tactics) of service marketing – processes, physical evidence, and people – were introduced to better explain what needed to be planned and managed (Booms & Bitner, 1981). 'Processes' are the procedures, actions, and activities needed to produce the service (Booms & Bitner, 1981; Shostack, 1977). These processes include employee actions, front- and back-of-house activities, and interactions among customers, employees, and organizations. 'Physical evidence' is the environment, or characteristics of the location, in which the service is enacted; this is where service interactions among customers, employees, and organizations occur (Booms & Bitner, 1981; Kotler, 1973; Shostack, 1977). The term 'people' refers to service employees who enact the service for and with customers (Booms & Bitner, 1981; Shostack, 1977).

Service design, viewed holistically, provides a structured approach to developing and managing service offerings. Processes, physical evidence, and people, along with service technologies (e.g., co-production, self-service, etc.), are combined to plan service offerings. Service design facilitates the development and management of complex service networks to meet customer needs and wants. Some research suggests that service design should be undertaken with the customer's point of view in mind. This perspective, called 'customer journey design,' describes the procedural course customers will go through (the customer journey) to address their needs (Kuehnl, Jozic, & Homburg, 2019). Although service design and customer journey design include planning for all facets of the customer experience, this chapter specifically focuses on service process design, as the planning for elements related to physical evidence and people are discussed in depth in other chapters.

As examples will later illustrate, service process design is complex and warrants careful consideration if service providers are to deliver services that meet customer requirements.

The chapter is organized as follows. First, it reviews the current state of service process design, calling attention to efforts related to collaborative design and the increased role of technology. Originally, physical presence of both the employee and the customer was assumed in most service processes. However, as more services are provided remotely and via technology, physical presence of neither party can be assumed, further complicating the planning needed to ensure that the service is appropriately designed and managed. Therefore, this chapter contrasts self-service technology (SST) and technology-based self-service (TBSS) with in-person service delivery processes where applicable. A five-stage design process is offered, which service providers may find helpful when planning the process for service provision. Specific tools and techniques that designers can use to better meet customer needs and facilitate the planning and/or evaluation of service processes are suggested for each stage. Finally, the chapter concludes with ideas for future research.

Service process design

"Design exists as a means to a greater end – enhancing human experience, solving complicated problems, and ultimately creating designs that resonate with the audience" (Kolko, 2011, p 39). Service design tools can be used to understand, explain, design, and redesign complex value networks and service ecosystems (Patrício et al., 2018a). This facilitates the introduction of new or renewed services through a human-centered and holistic approach (Patrício, Fisk, Cunha, & Constantine, 2011; Patrício et al., 2018b). As an iterative process, service design includes rounds of conceptualization, research, blueprinting, and user input prior to introducing a service to the consumer (Shostack, 1984b). For example, Airbnb was first conceptualized as a means for two roommates in San Francisco to take advantage of the scarcity of available accommodations for a local design conference. A onetime rental of the founders' own apartment morphed into months of work on a roommate-matching website, before realizing that that service already existed. After refocusing on short-term rentals, the company worked through several unsuccessful launches (aimed at attendees to events including the SXSW music festival and Democratic National Convention), ultimately refining their service to better meet customer needs (Carson, 2016).

As the previous example illustrates, service design is about both problem-setting and problem-solving (Meroni, 2008), and should reflect the market perspective of the service. In other words, it should describe how consumers and other stakeholders perceive the role and function of the service (Shostack, 1977). Hence, service process design is about more than the service outcome; it is about the system and user experiences (Bitner et al., 2008; Brown, 2008). Design turns data and information into processes and systems (Kolko, 2011) and considers how users (both provider and consumer) will react to the system and processes therein (Brown & Martin, 2015). Therefore, service process design should start with an intimate understanding of the customer (Matthing et al., 2004; Trischler, Pervan, Kelly, & Scott, 2018) and a focus on customer experiences (Holopainen, 2010) and expand from there to include the requirements of other stakeholders. Thus, design thinking often moves from the design of services in isolation to the design of service experiences holistically (Kolko, 2011). Continuing with the earlier example, over time Airbnb has made alterations to their service process based on inputs from Airbnb guests, property owners, and municipalities where the service takes place. Changes include instituting a coverage policy to compensate owners for damages and the collection of hotel taxes for the cities that allow Airbnb rentals (Carson, 2016).

Service process design should address the infrastructure that supports the service as well as the needs of the customer, and may best be accomplished using design thinking (Brown & Wyatt, 2010). Design thinking "uses the designer's sensibility and methods to match people's needs with what is technologically feasible and what a viable business strategy can convert into customer value and market opportunity" (Brown, 2008, p. 86). Using design thinking, a service provider upon encountering a circumstance of unmet customer need would search for possible remedies, develop and test possible solutions (often including the potential user in the process), and consider the path to market if any of the possible solutions are to be implemented. In other words, service process design, as viewed through the lens of design thinking, can be thought to emerge from a repetitive process of inspiration, ideation, and implementation (Brown, 2008). Within this framework, designers move from being translators of needs to facilitators of collaborative design processes (Sanders & Stappers, 2008). Often these collaborative initiatives are focused on transforming existing service systems or innovating to identify new potential service systems to fulfill both expressed and unarticulated needs.

Rent the Runway is an example of a service that has undergone several rounds of ideation and implementation. The clothing rental business was conceived in response to consumer desire for both the latest fashion and environmental stewardship. Consumers rent, rather than buy, high-end clothing items, which are then cleaned and mended (if needed) in order to be rented again; thereby giving consumers access to fashionable designer clothing and minimizing waste created when clothing is worn only a limited number of times before being discarded. Originally designed as an e-commerce business whereby customers rented merchandise for onetime use, the company has expanded to also include a subscription service offering ongoing style assistance. Physical locations (either freestanding or within partnering retailers) are also offered where customers can browse, try on, rent, and return merchandise. The addition of a local option, rather than relying on shipping of garments can more closely align with customer environmental goals. Additional enhancements planned for the service process include a doubling of the customer service team, new online tools to help customers manage their accounts, new fulfillment facilities to expedite shipping and returns, and a series of live Twitter 'RTR Town Halls' for customers to share feedback (Baron, 2019). Continuing to reconsider and test how to best meet their customers' needs has allowed Rent the Runway to prosper, reaching a $1 billion valuation in just ten years (Baron, 2019).

Collaborative and transformative service process design

Service process design can be collaborative and interdisciplinary; those individuals affected by problems that design might solve can, and should be, involved in the design of solutions (Meroni, 2008). Design is about change-making and can be strategically used to orient the collective sensibility to a preferred future (Meroni, 2008) thereby facilitating change in organizations and communities (Meroni, 2008; Sangiorgi, 2011). It is imperative to move from designing *for* to designing *with* users (Binder, Brandt, & Gregory, 2008; Kolko, 2011; Matthing et al., 2004; Storey & Larbig, 2018; Trischler et al., 2018). Such an approach to service process design emphasizes working with users and other impacted parties in the design of service processes that offer solutions. For example, Lee (2019) proposes that within the healthcare context, both patients and medical staff are design thinkers who can co-create value through collaboration. To facilitate collaboration, Lee (2019) suggests a new model of healthcare service process design whereby both service workers and patients are encouraged to share their experiences and the needs of both groups are considered in the design.

The key to successfully using design for change is user involvement, power redistribution, building capacity, collaboration, and vision creation (Anderson, Nasr, & Rayburn, 2018; Meroni, 2008; Sanders & Stappers, 2008; Sangiorgi, 2011). Collaborative design can result in novel and potentially beneficial service innovations; it is important for design teams to be composed of multiple stakeholder groups who work together to develop concepts (Trischler et al., 2018). Collaborative, transformative design includes the following elements with a holistic perspective to create a fundamental change: (1) identify the right problem, (2) follow an interdisciplinary approach, (3) use participatory methods, and (4) ensure capacity building within communities impacted by the resulting service systems (Sangiorgi, 2011).

Collaborative design is thought to have the potential to engage and solve many large-scale problems faced in the world (Sanders & Stappers, 2008). For example, as refugee populations worldwide continue to grow, processes must be designed to help the displaced attain basic necessities and traverse the foreign culture and complex systems of education, government, and social aid in their new surroundings. Using the steps outlined by Sangiorgi (2011), service process design would first try to identify the most pressing problems from the refugee perspective, as service users are the primary focus of collaborative design approaches (Patrício et al., 2018a; Trischler et al., 2018). Users, however, are not the only stakeholders, and efforts should be made to consider all perspectives in the design process. Therefore, the needs of the host communities, as well as those of the service workers, should also be considered. The complex, interconnected services needed by refugees require an interdisciplinary and participatory approach to design (steps two and three in Sangiorgi's (2011) model). Design sessions, therefore, should be attended by stakeholders within the host community, as well as three additional groups suggested by Sanders and Stappers (2008): (1) the user of the service, in this case the refugee, who is the 'expert' of their experience and is vital to idea generation and concept development; 2) the researcher, who provides tools and techniques to facilitate idea generation; and 3) the designer who gives form to the ideas presented. In coming together, these groups can help to facilitate the capacity building within communities impacted by the resulting service systems, as suggested by the final step in Sangiorgi's (2011) model.

As mentioned above, designers should include not only customers but also other stakeholders in the design process, prototyping, and refinement of the overall service design (Bitner et al., 2008; Brown & Martin, 2015). One of the key groups of stakeholders that may be consulted is service employees. In the case of in-person services, service design can and should be informed by these employees' perspectives (Sundbo, Sundbo, & Henten, 2015). In these situations, because employees are the service to some consumers (Shostack, 1977), they have an outsized importance to the success of the service; as enactors of the service, they also have an intimate understanding of the impact of processes used to deliver services. Interestingly, there is also evidence that employee perspectives can be helpful even when the service encounter occurs over information and communication networks such as web pages, blogs, or short message services (Sundbo et al., 2015). The increased role of technology and its implications in the design of SST and TBSS is discussed next.

Technology

Technology is increasingly implemented across a wide range of services (Nili, Tate, & Johnstone, 2019). Its use is dramatically altering service encounters and, in some cases, eliminating them altogether (Bitner, Brown, & Meuter, 2000); thereby "challenging the notion that provider-customer interaction is an essential feature of services marketing" (Dabholkar, 2000, p. 103). Technology innovation often drives service innovation (Patrício et al., 2018a; Rust & Huang, 2014) as new practices and processes are designed to take advantage of new technologies. SSTs lead to TBSSs, 'any activity or benefit based on technology which service firms offer so that customers can perform the service, or parts of the service, by themselves without employees' help' (Kim, Kim, Moon, & Chang, 2014).

Technological innovations in the areas of big data, analytics, and artificial intelligence can be used to inform design (Bantau & Rayburn, 2016) by offering the use of real-time behavioral and attitudinal data to refine existing services, expose the need for new services, and, increasingly, assist in the design of innovative services. For example, the sensor, communication, and artificial intelligence technologies already present in many homes may converge in the near future into a platform of services to deliver care as we age (Coughlin, 2019). By combining information obtained from wired appliances and communication systems with artificial intelligence-enabled devices, services can be designed and delivered remotely to help monitor and treat chronic illness, assist in basic home maintenance, and monitor the safety and well-being of aging adults. Service designs that result from technological advances such as these often have substantial benefits to consumers such as customization, improved service recovery, and even spontaneous delight in response to the unprompted and unsolicited actions taken by the service provider (Bitner et al., 2000).

Despite the potential positive outcomes, organizations sometimes misstep and introduce technology-driven interfaces without completely considering customer needs and wants (Patrício et al., 2008a). For example, some consumers may prefer the social aspects of interpersonal interactions (Bitner et al., 2000; Kiely, Beamish, & Armistead, 2004). However, SSTs are rapidly taking the place of many service interactions that were conducted in person in the past (Beatson, Lee, & Coote, 2007). Research indicates that acceptance of TBSS depends on consumer ability and willingness to use the technology (Wang, 2017), as well as the amount of previous experience with the specific SST and service type (Reinders, Frambach, & Kleijnen, 2015). Hence, SSTs may not be suitable for every customer segment, and should be implemented only after careful consideration and research (Beatson et al., 2007).

Care must be taken to make sure that service recovery systems are in place when implementing TBSS, as service failure may occur due to technical errors or issues created by support staff or user mistakes (Nili et al., 2019). For instance, a study of university students, professors, and staff found that when experiencing a problem with the university SST, most individuals used multiple recovery methods whereby they relied on themselves, their peers, or designated SST support staff to remedy the problem (Nili et al., 2019). A study of retail TBSS found that providing speedy recovery of SST failures and a low-anxiety environment in which to use the SST both positively influenced customer satisfaction (Dabholkar & Spaid, 2012). As technology continues to advance, more self-service interactions will be possible (Rust & Huang, 2014). It will be up to service process designers to consider how best to incorporate SSTs and TBSS into service offerings. A comprehensive model depicting customer motivation and behavior in regard to TBSS by Bobbitt and Dabholkar (2001) may be helpful in advancing theory in this area.

Service process design: five stages

This section of the chapter is devoted to identifying the resources, capabilities, and design tools that are available for service process design and discussing how they should be used to better meet customer needs. Using service process design, organizations can identify key resources and capabilities that will both satisfy customer needs and wants and provide the organization with a competitive advantage (Ceric, D'Alessandro, Soutar, & Johnson, 2016). Thus, service process design tools can provide a path to delivering superior customer value and achieving superior organizational performance (Ceric et al., 2016). The following section describes a five-stage process based on Cahn et al. (2016), which can be used to guide service process design. Each stage is explained and applicable tools are suggested that might be valuable in guiding implementation or evaluating results.

Discovery

The first stage is discovery, which emphasizes gathering stories based on firsthand experiences of key stakeholders (Cahn et al., 2016). This preliminary stage of service process design requires taking a human-centered approach to gain a comprehensive understanding of the problem to be solved (Dahl, Chattopadhyay, & Gorn, 1999). Furthermore, it requires understanding customer motivations for use and goals of using the system (Veryzer & Borja de Mozota, 2005). This stage is fundamental to service success, as it encourages designers to forego their assumptions and gain insight into user needs. Customers are viewed as sources of innovation and ideas that can be uncovered using techniques such as depth interviews, focus groups, and other ethnographic techniques which rely on observing users to reveal problems that are either unknown or unarticulated (Rosenthal & Capper, 2006). In addition, customer journey mapping and empathy mapping can be used to gain insight into how users think and feel, and what they hear, see, say, and do while using the service. Each of these techniques is described below.

Depth interviews are one-on-one conversations between a researcher and research respondent. When used in the discovery stage of service process design, the focus of the conversation is often about service encounters. During depth interviews, consumers are asked to tell stories, the analysis of which can illuminate the social and temporal aspects of the service and be used to refine the service organization's understanding of its role in relation to customer value creation (Hansen, 2017). Depth interviews therefore represent a customer-centric approach to gaining customer insights, which can lead to a firm-centric approach to the operationalization of these insights (Hansen, 2017). For example, Jones and Taylor (2018) used depth interviews to investigate consumer response to requests for positive post-purchase evaluations in retail situations. Depth interviews with consumers revealed, through personal stories of service encounters, that the request generally has a negative overall impact and results in negative emotions, perceptions of inequity, and perceptions of injustice (Jones & Taylor, 2018). From a service process design perspective, this would suggest that the practice of asking consumers to positively evaluate the retailer in a post-purchase survey should be left out of the service process, or discontinued if already in place.

Focus groups are a type of group interview in which a researcher facilitates dialogue among a group of consumers in order to gain insights on their needs and experiences. Participants add value to the conversation by asking one another questions and exchanging stories about their personal experiences and points of view (Richard et al., 2018). For example Vakulenko, Hellström, and Hjort (2018) conducted focus groups to explore customer value in relation to parcel lockers which are used for self-service collection and return of goods purchased online. Consumers discussed their needs and experiences with parcel lockers, revealing that four types of value (functional, social, emotional, and financial) can be created; service providers are encouraged to consider how the service process can be designed to best deliver all four (Vakulenko et al., 2018). Although many focus groups are conducted in person, research shows that online focus groups are able to achieve a similar level of quality (measured in terms of the novelty, usefulness, and feasibility of ideas generated) as compared to in-person focus groups (Richard et al., 2018), often at a lower cost.

Ethnographic research uses observational techniques to learn about human cultures, is interpretive in nature, and relies on understanding individual actions in light of the context under study (Kelly & Gibbons, 2008). In the discovery phase of service process design, ethnographic techniques such as consumer immersion studies or shop-alongs can be used to understand not only the way in which the service is used, but also what drives the user to seek out the service to begin with. For example, Elms and Tinson (2012) present an ethnographic case study of a disabled wife/mother shopping for groceries. Her shopping behavior (both in-person and online) is detailed but, perhaps more interestingly, the study finds that although online grocery shopping reduces the impracticalities associated with shopping in-store, the consumer's emotional needs (including her sense of self) are not met when shopping online (Elms & Tinson, 2012). This insight could be used in service process design to improve upon the service offered in both physical grocery stores and online outlets. When conducting ethnographic research, Rosenthal and Capper (2006) make the following recommendations: use multiple tools and techniques for gathering data, be open to new tangents that might be worthy of exploration, probe for insights when surprises occur, synthesize viewpoints of the whole research team, and capture relevant visuals that can be used for explanation and idea generation.

Customer journey mapping is useful in the discovery phase, as it is an effective tool for modeling and visualizing customers' experience across channels and touchpoints from the customers' point of view (Rosenbaum, Otalora, & Ramírez, 2017; Zomerdijk & Voss, 2010). The customer journey map is "a visual depiction of the sequence of events through which customers may interact with a service organization during an entire purchase process" (Rosenbaum et al., 2017, p. 144). As such, the map is based on customer actions, extending to what customers feel and think, and how they behave throughout the journey. One of the key functions of customer journey maps is the ability to identify pain points and gain insights that are gleaned from an understanding of customers' perceptions of their experiences. Not all customer touchpoints are equally important to all customers (Rosenbaum et al., 2017), nor are all customer journeys the same. Thus, customer journey maps must be designed with a specific persona in mind (Zomerdijk & Voss, 2010). This allows service providers to design services that prioritize customer needs and wants.

Empathy mapping approaches the customer journey from a slightly different perspective. As a tool of empathetic design, it explores customer emotions in order to transform customer ideas into appealing solutions; in a manner similar to customer journey mapping, it seeks to reveal points of frustration and to identify what users seek to gain from the service (Mattelmäki, Vaajakallio, & Koskinen, 2014). Discovering this information is crucial, as creating an effective solution requires a deep understanding of the person (i.e., persona) and problem to be solved. The queue for rides at amusement parks is one area where empathic design can be implemented. Take for example, the popular Harry Potter and the Forbidden Journey at Universal. Recognizing that consumers become bored stuck in-line waiting for the ride, designers used an engaging story to move customers along the line, weaving them through a replica of a castle where picture frames come to life and holographic images of Harry Potter actors interact with customers (Tripp, 2013). Empathetic service process design focuses on listening to the emotional and personal responses of potential users (e.g., amusement parks are fun, but waiting in-line is tedious) and considering how the service might be better designed (e.g., maybe the wait in-line itself can become part of the fun) in order to create a satisfying experience (Tripp, 2013).

Interpretation

Using the insights gained during the discovery phase, the primary objective of the 'interpretation' stage is to produce actionable human-centered problem statements that are based on what was learned about user needs and the context in which the service will be delivered. Here, key ideas from the discovery phase are arranged in clusters according to emerging themes (Cahn et al., 2016). Storyboarding is a useful technique to draw out potential problem statements, because it illuminates the issues in an individual's life that the service process is designed to overcome.

A storyboard is a cinematographic method that has been adapted for use in service design. Story-boards are useful because they represent the service through a narrative sequence of pictures or drawings and create a common visual language that people from different backgrounds can 'read' and understand (van der Lelie, 2006). Moreover, the storyboard illustrates the relationships among the users, touchpoints, and employees. Storyboards focus on a persona and tell the story about how the service works; the initial frames introduce the story, the middle frames develop it, and the last frames conclude it. The activity of making storyboards encourages consideration of the situations, atmospheres, feelings, and interactions taking place within the service process (van der Lelie, 2006). For example, Parke, Hunter, and Marck (2015) use storyboards to study relationships between healthcare systems and processes and older patients living with dementia. The researchers find that storyboards are useful in systematically incorporating the views of the patients, whose opinions may have otherwise have been overlooked. Further, the act of storyboarding captures the service process in a way that encourages discussion of less tangible aspects of service delivery (Parke et al., 2015).

Ideation

The third stage of the design process is ideation (Cahn et al., 2016). As the name implies, it is the phase of the process in which designers concentrate on idea generation. Specifically, information gleaned from previous stages is used to generate possible ideas for service provi-sion. The objective of this stage is to develop actionable ideas that could potentially be implemented in later stages. This approach requires a willingness to engage with participants and incorporate their experiences and ideas into the design process for the benefit of both the organization and users. Useful techniques for this stage of service process design include service blueprinting and service experience blueprinting.

Service blueprinting has a long history in service process design (Shostack, 1977, 1982, 1984a, 1984b, 1985) and is based on an explicit understanding of customer needs (Bitner et al., 2008; Patrício et al., 2008a; Patrício et al., 2011; Shostack, 1982). A service blueprint offers a clear and complete diagram of a service process, highlighting 'moments of truth' (contact points) between the customer and the firm (Bitner et al., 2008). It is at these points of contact that the customer experiences the service and an impression of the firm is formed or perhaps changed. For example, Bitner et al. (2008) recounts how service blueprinting helped a trucking and logistics company identify the most important moments of truth (interactions between the clients and the drivers, support service workers, and terminal employees) and design a process to best take advantage of these opportunities to influence client perceptions.

Early service blueprinting typically focused on one aspect of an overall service system (Shostack, 1984a); however, as the scope, interdependencies, and the complexity of services have grown, the approach to service design and blueprinting has evolved to account for ser-vice systems holistically (Sangiorgi, Patrício, & Fisk, 2017). Thus, more current service experience blueprints expand the scope of service design to explicitly integrate multiple ser-vice interactions and identify the optimal service interface for a particular consumer need (Patrício et al., 2008b). This approach recognizes the importance of the interplay between the customer, the service provider, and a wider community; and therefore, recognizes that value can be created individually or collectively and can originate from customer and/or provider actions (Heinonen, Campbell, & Lord Ferguson, 2019).

The service experience blueprint explicitly considers technology and multichannel inter-actions, and introduces a service interface link representing a point in the service encounter where the customer is guided to another interface to enhance the service experience (Patrí-cio, Fisk, Cunha, & Constantine, 2011). Some proponents even suggest replacing human focused interactions with SSTs when possible, so long as consumers are happy with this approach (Patrício, Cunha, & Fisk, 2008a; Patrício et al., 2008a). The steps in service experience blueprinting include: (1) elicitation of requirements based on research into consumer needs and wants, (2) service design for customer/organization interaction at each channel, and (3) service design for interactions across channels to integrate the service system (Patrício et al., 2008b). This approach to service design extends the focus to people, processes, physical evidence, *and* technology (Patrício & Fisk, 2013; Patrício et al., 2011). Interested readers are encouraged to see Patrício et al. (2011) for an example of a service experience blueprint and specifically figure 9 (Patrício et al., 2011, p. 191) which highlights service processes.

Experimentation

The fourth stage of the design process is experimentation (Cahn et al., 2016). This stage is crucial because it reduces the likelihood of failure (Brown & Wyatt, 2010). It is here that the team creates one or more prototypes to investigate the problems that were identified in earlier stages. Prototyping takes intangible insights, ideas, and concepts and makes them tangible and understandable to different stakeholders (Brown, 2008). Using information gleaned from the tools previously discussed (customer journey maps, storyboards, and service experience blueprints), designers create prototypes to explore how well the proposed solutions address the problem. In service prototyping, the designer works as a facilitator, using photos, sounds, and relevant props and technologies that allow customers to visualize and experience the proposed service process (Miettinen & Kuure, 2013).

Once prototypes are constructed, testing can begin. Testing of the prototype should include users of the system to reveal possible system constraints, which allows the design team to address such issues before the actual system is implemented. The key objective of this stage is to provide insight into how users will feel, think, and behave when they interact with the proposed service delivery system. One research tool that might be helpful at this stage is value stream mapping. Value stream mapping is a specific type of process map which identifies steps in the service process that do not add value from the customer's perspective (Sugianto et al., 2015). These non-value-adding steps can be due to needless movement of items or individuals within the service environment, waiting on items or individuals needed to perform the service, service processes that utilize more effort than necessary, or service processes that need to be redone due to error (Sugianto et al., 2015). Once identified, the processes can be refined to eliminate the occurrence of such problems, when feasible.

Evolution

The final step in service process design is evolution, a process which tests, at scale, the most promising service processes revealed during prototyping (Cahn et al., 2016). This step requires an appraisal by the designers, customers, and perhaps even other stakeholders, to assess whether or not the designed process meets the goals or objectives that resulted from the discovery and interpretation stages. As service process design is iterative, designers may elect to return to previous stages and revise their assumptions or collect new information to refine the system until all are confident that the system meets the identified needs.

Different research tools may be utilized to adequately capture the viewpoints of different stakeholder groups. To determine whether front line employees are satisfied with the service process they have to implement and/or customers are getting what they want or expect from the service process, satisfaction surveys can be conducted. Attitude surveys such as

SERVQUAL and e-SERVQUAL would also be helpful in assessing customer reaction to the service process. The SERVQUAL model considers service quality to be multifaceted, made up of dimensions related to tangibles, reliability, responsiveness, assurance, and empathy (Parasuraman, Zeithaml, & Berry, 1985, 1988). This chapter focuses on the service process; therefore, the key dimension in SERVQUAL would be reliability, the "ability to perform the promised service dependably and accurately" (Parasuraman et al., 1988, p. 23), as the other dimensions deal more explicitly with people or physical evidence. The e-SERVQUAL model measures a company's website service performance along areas of efficiency, fulfillment, availability or technical functionality, and security issues, all of which are pertinent to service process design (Parasuraman, Zeithaml, & Malhotra, 2005).

From the designer's or service provider's perspective, alpha or beta testing (running the process in-house or in a customer site) would test whether the process design is accomplishing what the designers intended. Following implementation, service process management can be examined and controlled via auditing. A service audit considers the match between firm competencies and quality standards and allows a service provider to see how to improve the quality of service through the careful consideration of various internal resource parameters and external market factors that act as constraints on meeting the desired levels of customer service for the firm (Armistead, 1989). More specifically, auditing allows service providers to identify areas of the service process in need of improvement, determine which specific elements can be leveraged for maximum return, perform 'what-if' analyses, and ensure that service elements are working synergistically (Reid & Koljonen, 2000). The process can be applied to online service provision as well. In this case, an e-process audit would monitor online applications to detect inconsistencies between actual processes and originally designed functionalities (Huang, Hua, Will, & Wu, 2012).

Future research

This chapter illustrates the complex nature of service process design and suggests a five-stage model with specific tools and techniques for each step that designers can use to better meet customer needs and facilitate the planning and/or evaluation of service processes. This final section of the chapter highlights new research being done in service process design and suggests several potential research topics warranting further consideration.

One of the newest approaches to service process design merges two perspectives, management and interaction design, resulting in an interdisciplinary method – the Management and INteraction Design for Service (MINDS) – to orchestrate complex, technology-infused service systems which enable seamless customer experiences (Teixeira et al., 2017). The MINDS method applies design tools from service marketing, operations management, and interaction design to technology-based services, allowing for consideration of the service concept (i.e., the benefits the service provides), the service system (i.e., the tools that facilitate the production of the benefit), and the service act itself (Teixeira et al., 2017). Initial tests of the MINDS method in entertainment and healthcare contexts were positive, showing how the interdisciplinary integration of design tools helps to make the contribution of technology more visible, facilitates backstage processes, and enables integration with network partners (Teixeira et al., 2017). Additional tests of the model are needed to confirm the benefits of integration and to explore potential disadvantages that might result from the approach.

Another promising area of future research is Service Design for Value Networks (SD4VN) which allows for value co-creating interactions among members of a network (Patrício et al., 2018b). SD4VN involves: (1) problem framing, (2) understanding multiple actors' experiences and interactions, and (3) designing the value network to support the interaction and goal attainment of the various actors in the system (Patrício et al., 2018b). It is an expanded approach to service process design that incorporates many of the research tools previously discussed and considers not only the actions of a single customer–provider interaction, but also the larger context in which the encounter takes place. SD4VN has been applied to a public healthcare system (Patrício et al., 2018b), but the technique needs further testing in other complex service systems (e.g., education, multichannel retailing, travel).

A third new perspective on service process design is offered by Voorhees et al. (2017) who present a framework to guide comprehensive service experience research. These authors divide the design process into three components: (1) pre-core service encounter, (2) core service encounter, and (3) post-core service encounter; they suggest that historically too much emphasis has been paid to the core service encounter while the other areas have been neglected (Voorhees et al., 2017). Extant literature is reviewed and pertinent questions to guide future research are offered in all three areas.

Going forward, research in service process design should also consider how new tools can inform each stage of the process. For example, Iriarte, Hoveskog, Justel, Val, and Halila (2018) suggest that maps, flows, images, and narratives all play an important role in helping providers conceptualize and plan new service value propositions by facilitating structured discussions using a shared vision and common language. Specific tools recommended include empathy maps, customer journey maps, and service blueprints (all of which have been discussed in previous sections of this chapter), as well as synchronic images detailing service outcomes and interaction maps highlighting the relationships among the customers, providers, and partners (Iriarte et al., 2018). Future research could test the approach across a broad spectrum of manufacturers, looking for differences that might arise due to industry or size.

Other research explores how additional technologies can be incorporated into service process design. Pöppel, Finsterwalder, and Laycock (2018), for example, propose that digital film can be used to develop a service experience blueprint that better captures the intricacies of customer–service provider interaction and experience. Bantau and Rayburn (2016) suggest that technologies such as sensors, SSTs using mobile phone applications, artificial intelligence, robotics, and smart products can autonomously collect and analyze data to offer real-time service innovations that will enhance service stakeholder experiences. These types of technologies would be helpful in all five stages of service process design. In the discovery and interpretation stages, sensors could be used to determine behavioral patterns (both in person and online) which might expose unarticulated habits or needs. In the ideation stage, film-based service experience blueprints could be used to convey the service concept. SSTs based on mobile phone applications, artificial intelligence, and robotics would be helpful in the experimentation stage to implement new service offerings and the integration of smart products would allow for close monitoring and fine-tuning in the evolution stage.

References

Anderson, S. T., Nasr, L., & Rayburn, S. W. (2018). Transformative service research and service design: Synergistic effects in healthcare. *The Service Industries Journal, 38*(1–2), 99–113.

Armistead, C. G. (1989). Customer service operations management in service businesses. *The Service Industries Journal, 9*(2), 247–260.

Bantau, G., & Rayburn, S. W. (2016). Advanced information technology: Transforming service innovation and design. *The Service Industries Journal, 36*(13–14), 699–720.

Baron, J. (2019). *Rent the Runway is finally addressing its customer service issues.* Retrieved from: www.forbes.com/sites/jessicabaron/2019/07/01/rent-the-runway-is-finally-addressing-its-customer-service-issues/#40b34f7e112d.

Beatson, A., Lee, N., & Coote, L. V. (2007). Self-service technology and the service encounter. *The Service Industries Journal, 27*(1), 75–89.

Binder, T., Brandt, E., & Gregory, J. (2008). Design participation(-s). *CoDesign*, *4*(1), 1–3.

Bitner, M. J., Brown, S. W., & Meuter, M. L. (2000). Technology infusion in service encounters. *Journal of the Academy of Marketing Science*, *28*(1), 138–149.

Bitner, M. J., Ostrom, A. L., & Morgan, F. N. (2008). Service blueprinting: A technique for service innovation. *California Management Review*, *50*(3), 66–94.

Bobbitt, L. M., & Dabholkar, P. A. (2001). Integrating attitudinal theories to understand and predict use of technology-based self-service. *International Journal of Service Industry Management*, *12* (5), 423–450.

Booms, B. H., & Bitner, M. J. (1981). Marketing strategies and organization structures for service firms. In J. H. Donnelly & W. R. George (Eds.), *Marketing of services* (pp. 47–51). Chicago, IL: American Marketing Association.

Brown, T. (2008). Design thinking. *Harvard Business Review*, *86*(6), 85–92.

Brown, T., & Martin, R. (2015). Design for action. *Harvard Business Review*, *93*(9), 57–64.

Brown, T., & Wyatt, J. (2010). Design thinking for social innovation. *Stanford Social Innovation Review*, *3*(1), 31–35.

Cahn, P. S., Bzowyckyj, A., Collins, L., Dow, A., Goodell, K., Johnson, A. F., Klocko, D., Knab, M., Parker, K., Reeves, S., & Zierler, B. K. (2016). A design thinking approach to evaluating interprofessional education. *Journal of Interprofessional Care*, *30*(3), 378–380.

Carson, B. (2016). *How 3 guys turned renting an air mattress in their apartment into a $25 billion company.* Retrieved from: www.businessinsider.com/how-airbnb-was-founded-a-visual-history-2016-2.

Ceric, A., D'Alessandro, S., Soutar, G., & Johnson, L. (2016). Using blueprinting and benchmarking to identify marketing resources that help create customer value. *Journal of Business Research*, *69*(12), 5653–5661.

Coughlin, J. (2019). *How robots and your smart fridge can keep you out of a nursing home.* Retrieved from: www.marketwatch.com/story/this-new-tech-can-turn-any-home-into-a-retirement-home-2019-05-21.

Dabholkar, P. (2000). Technology in service delivery: Implications for self-service and service support. In T. A. Swartz & D. Iacobucci (Eds.), *Handbook of services marketing and management* (pp. 103–110). Thousand Oaks, CA: Sage.

Dabholkar, P., & Spaid, B. (2012). Service failure and recovery in using technology-based self-service: Effects on user attributions and satisfaction. *The Service Industries Journal*, *32*(9), 1415–1432.

Dahl, D. W., Chattopadhyay, A., & Gorn, G. J. (1999). The use of visual mental imagery in new product design. *Journal of Marketing Research*, *36*(1), 18–28.

Elms, J., & Tinson, J. (2012). Consumer vulnerability and the transformative potential of internet shopping: An exploratory case study. *Journal of Marketing Management*, *28*(11–12), 1354–1376.

Hansen, A. V. (2017). What stories unfold: Empirically grasping value co-creation. *European Business Review*, *29*(1), 2–14.

Heinonen, K., Campbell, C., & Lord Ferguson, S. (2019). Strategies for creating value through individual and collective customer experiences. *Business Horizons*, *62*(1), 95–104.

Holopainen, M. (2010). Exploring service design in the context of architecture. *The Service Industries Journal*, *30*(4), 597–608.

Huang, S.-M., Hua, J.-S., Will, H., & Wu, J.-W. (2012). Metamodeling to control and audit e-commerce web applications. *International Journal of Electronic Commerce*, *17*(1), 83–118.

Iriarte, I., Hoveskog, M., Justel, D., Val, E., & Halila, F. (2018). Service design visualization tools for supporting servitization in a machine tool manufacturer. *Industrial Marketing Management*, *71*, 189–202.

Jones, M. A., & Taylor, V. A. (2018). Marketer requests for positive post-purchase satisfaction evaluations: Consumer depth interview findings. *Journal of Retailing and Consumer Services*, *41*, 218–226.

Kelly, D., & Gibbons, M. (2008). Ethnography: The good, the bad and the ugly. *Journal of Medical Marketing*, *8*(4), 279–285.

Kiely, J., Beamish, N., & Armistead, C. (2004). Scenarios for future service encounters. *The Service Industries Journal*, *24*(3), 131–149.

Kim, T., Kim, M. C., Moon, G., & Chang, K. (2014). Technology-based self-service and its impact on customer productivity. *Services Marketing Quarterly*, *35*(3), 255–269.

Kolko, J. (2011). *Thoughts on interaction design* (2nd ed.). Burlington, MA: Elsevier.

Kotler, P. (1973). Atmospherics as a marketing tool. *Journal of Retailing*, *49*(4), 48–64.

Kuehnl, C., Jozic, D., & Homburg, C. (2019). Effective customer journey design: Consumers' conception, measurement, and consequences. *Journal of the Academy of Marketing Science*, *47*(3), 551–568.

Lee, D. (2019). A model for designing healthcare service based on the patient experience. *International Journal of Healthcare Management, 12*(3), 180–188.

Mattelmäki, T., Vaajakallio, K., & Koskinen, I. (2014). What happened to empathic design? *Design Issues, 30*(1), 67–77.

Matthing, J., Sanden, B., & Edvardsson, B. (2004). New service development: Learning from and with customers. *International Journal of Service Industry Management, 15*(5), 479–498.

Meroni, A. (2008). Strategic design: Where are we now? Reflection around the foundations of a recent discipline. *Strategic Design Research Journal, 1*(1), 31–38.

Miettinen, S., & Kuure, E. (2013). Designing a multi-channel service experience. *Design Management Review, 24*(3), 30–37.

Nili, A., Tate, M., & Johnstone, D. (2019). The process of solving problems with self-service technologies: A study from the user's perspective. *Electronic Commerce Research, 19*(2), 373–407.

Parasuraman, A., Zeithaml, V. A., & Berry, L. L. (1985). A conceptual model of service quality and its implications for future research. *Journal of Marketing, 49*(4), 41–50.

Parasuraman, A., Zeithaml, V. A., & Berry, L. L. (1988). SERVQUAL: A multiple-item scale for measuring consumer perceptions of service quality. *Journal of Retailing, 64*(1), 12–40.

Parasuraman, A., Zeithaml, V. A., & Malhotra, A. (2005). E-S-QUAL: A multiple-item scale for assessing electronic service quality. *Journal of Service Research, 7*(3), 213–233.

Parke, B., Hunter, K. F., & Marck, P. B. (2015). A novel visual method for studying complex health transitions for older people living with dementia. *International Journal of Qualitative Methods, 14*(4), 1–11.

Patrício, L., Cunha, J. F., & Fisk, R. P. (2008a). Requirements engineering for multi-channel services: The SEB method and its application to a multi-channel bank. *Requirements Engineering, 14*(3), 209–227.

Patrício, L., Fisk, R. P., & Cunha, J. F. (2008b). Designing multi-interface service experiences: The service experience blueprint. *Journal of Service Research, 10*(4), 318–334.

Patrício, L., & Fisk, R. P. (2013). Creating new services. In R. P. Fisk, R. Bennett, & L. C. Harris (Eds.), *Serving customers: Global services marketing perspectives* (pp. 185–207). Prahan, Victoria: Tilde University Press.

Patrício, L., Fisk, R. P., Cunha, J. F., & Constantine, L. (2011). Multilevel service design: From customer value constellation to service experience blueprinting. *Journal of Service Research, 14*(2), 180–200.

Patrício, L., Gustafsson, A., & Fisk, R. P. (2018a). Upframing service design and innovation for research impact. *Journal of Service Research, 21*(1), 3–16.

Patrício, L., Pinho, N. F., Teixeira, J. G., & Fisk, R. P. (2018b). Service design for value networks: Enabling value cocreation interactions in healthcare. *Service Science, 10*(1), 76–97.

Pöppel, J., Finsterwalder, J., & Laycock, R. A. (2018). Developing a film-based service experience blueprinting technique. *Journal of Business Research, 85*, 459–466.

Reid, R. A., & Koljonen, E. L. (2000). Operations management audit: Service customer assessment technique for managerially-initiated improvements. *Journal of Professional Services Marketing, 21*(2), 125–148.

Reinders, M., Frambach, R., & Kleijnen, M. (2015). Mandatory use of technology-based self-service: Does expertise help or hurt? *European Journal of Marketing, 49*(1/2), 190–211.

Richard, B., Sivo, S., Orlowski, M., Ford, R., Murphy, J., Boote, D., & Witta, E. (2018). Online focus groups: A valuable alternative for hospitality research? *International Journal of Contemporary Hospitality Management, 30*(11), 3175–3191.

Rosenbaum, M. S., Otalora, M. L., & Ramírez, G. C. (2017). How to create a realistic customer journey map. *Business Horizons, 60*(1), 143–150.

Rosenthal, S. R., & Capper, M. (2006). Ethnographies in the front end: Designing for enhanced customer experiences. *The Journal of Product Innovation Management, 23*(3), 215–237.

Rust, R. T., & Huang, M.-H. (2014). The service revolution and the transformation of marketing science. *Marketing Science, 33*(2), 206–221.

Sanders, E. B. N., & Stappers, P. J. (2008). Co-creation and the new landscapes of design. *CoDesign, 4*(1), 5–18.

Sangiorgi, D. (2011). Transformative services and transformation design. *International Journal of Design, 5*(2), 29–40.

Sangiorgi, D., Patrício, L., & Fisk, R. (2017). Designing for interdependence, participation, and emergence in compex service systems. In D. Sangiorgi & A. Prendiville (Eds.), *Designing for service: Key issues and directions* (pp. 49–64). London, UK: Bloomsbury Academic.

Shostack, G. L. (1977). Breaking free from product marketing. *Journal of Marketing, 41*(2), 73–80.

Shostack, G. L. (1982). How to design a service. *European Journal of Marketing, 16*(1), 49–63.

Shostack, G. L. (1984a). Designing services that deliver. *Harvard Business Review, 62*(10), 133–139.

Shostack, G. L. (1984b). Service design in the operating environment. In W. R. George & C. E. Marshall (Eds.), *Developing new services* (pp. 27–43). Chicago, IL: American Marketing Association.

Shostack, G. L. (1985). Planning the service encounter. In J. A. Czpiel, M. R. Solomon, & C. F. Surprenant (Eds.), *The service encounter: Managing employee/customer interaction in service businesses* (pp. 243–252). Lexington, MA: Lexington Books.

Storey, C., & Larbig, C. (2018). Absorbing customer knowledge: How customer involvement enables service design success. *Journal of Service Research, 21*(1), 101–118.

Sugianto, J. Z., Stewart, B., Ambruzs, J. M., Arista, A., Park, J. Y., Cope-Yokoyama, S., & Luu, H. S. (2015). Applying the principles of lean production to gastrointestinal biopsy handling: From the factory floor to the anatomic pathology laboratory. *Laboratory Medicine, 46*(3), 259–264.

Sundbo, J., Sundbo, D., & Henten, A. (2015). Service encounters as bases for innovation. *The Service Industries Journal, 35*(5), 255–274.

Teixeira, J. G., Patrício, L., Huang, K. H., Fisk, R. P., Nóbrega, L., & Constantine, L. (2017). The MINDS method: Integrating management and interaction design perspectives for service design. *Journal of Service Research, 20*(3), 240–258.

Tripp, C. (2013). No empathy – No service. *Design Management Review, 24*(3), 58–64.

Trischler, J., Pervan, S. J., Kelly, S. J., & Scott, D. R. (2018). The value of codesign: The effect of customer involvement in service design teams. *Journal of Service Research, 21*(1), 75–100.

Vakulenko, Y., Hellström, D., & Hjort, K. (2018). What's in the parcel locker? Exploring customer value in e-commerce last mile delivery. *Journal of Business Research, 88*, 421–427.

van der Lelie, C. (2006). The value of storyboards in the product design process. *Personal and Ubiquitous Computing, 10*(2/3), 159–162.

Veryzer, R. W., & Borja de Mozota, B. (2005). The impact of user-oriented design on new product development: An examination of fundamental relationships. *The Journal of Product Innovation Management, 22*(2), 128–143.

Voorhees, C. M., Walkowiak, T., Fombelle, P. W., Gregoire, Y., Bone, S., Gustafsson, A., & Sousa, R. (2017). Service encounters, experiences and the customer journey: Defining the field and a call to expand our lens. *Journal of Business Research, 79*, 269–280.

Wang, C. (2017). Consumer acceptance of self-service technologies: An ability–willingness model. *International Journal of Market Research, 59*(6), 787–802.

Zomerdijk, L. G., & Voss, C. A. (2010). Service design for experience-centric services. *Journal of Service Research, 13*(1), 67–82.

13

Service supply chain configurations

From agile to efficient value networks

Christoph F. Breidbach, Hendrik Reefke, and Tobias Widmer

Introduction

Service supply chains consist of multiple value co-creating entities that interact and exchange information for mutual benefit (Breidbach et al., 2015a). During the past decade, interest in service supply chain research increased, but work to date largely followed established 'product' (i.e., goods) supply chain research trajectories and themes (Sengupta et al., 2006). Here, service supply chains are perceived as distinct from goods-centric or 'product' supply chains (Ellram et al., 2004), with resulting attempts to transfer insights gained from goods-driven to service supply chains not being particularly successful. This is, in part, because prior service supply chain research focused on service providers only, thereby omitting the role of service customers (see e.g. Akkermans and Vos, 2003). Such limited perspective is problematic because understanding the roles of customers in service is a key decisive factor influencing the performance of service supply chains (Maull et al., 2012). Previous work explicitly or implicitly focused on existing, mature service chains that operate in a steady state (Walsh and Wellman, 2000), and explored the exchange of physical resources between entities within these (Giannakis, 2011). Consequently, it remains unclear how service supply chains can evolve through early stages, and how these processes are coordinated in a strategic fashion. In fact, gaining a better understanding of how any value co-creating activities in service settings can and should be orchestrated recently emerged as a key research priority under the service-dominant logic (S-DL) lens on service more broadly (Vargo and Lusch, 2016), but also within the service science discourse more specifically (Breidbach, Antons, and Salge, 2016). Put differently, it remains unclear how service supply chains can evolve through early stages, and how these processes can and should be coordinated in a strategic fashion to increase the overall performance of the service supply chain itself and the value network at large.

This chapter aims to address the above questions by exploring and outlining distinct strategic pathways in the evolution of service supply chains. Key coordination mechanisms are discussed, with emphasis on how these may change over time as service supply chains seek to move from, for example, an agile configuration to one that is increasingly efficient. This chapter therefore expands the literature on service supply chains by focusing on early-stage service supply chains, and how their emergence can be orchestrated.

The structure is as follows: initially, the chapter provides an overview of extant research related to service supply chains and the management of service supply chain performance aspects. The subsequent section puts forward four potential service supply chain configurations. This is followed by outlining pathways between the configurations, which is illustrated by a practical case example. Finally, the chapter delineates further theoretical and managerial implications stemming from this work and provides an agenda for future research.

Perspectives on service supply chains

Demarcation studies

Three unique schools of thought have defined service supply chains to date. First, *demarcation* scholars differentiate between service- and goods-centric economic exchange, thereby perceiving service supply chains as distinctly different from goods-centric supply chains. Examples for studies following these approaches include the work of Ellram et al. (2004), who investigated purchasing in professional services, Frohlich and Westbrook (2002), who compared online strategies across supply chains in the manufacturing and service sector, and Youngdahl and Loomba (2000), who reviewed the concept of a 'service factory' in global supply chains.

Work following this line of thought typically argues that service supply chains rely on the flow of information rather than physical goods, as is the case in goods supply chains. Information sharing is, in the supply chain literature, typically perceived as key to enhanced coordination, and related to inventory forecasting or production planning (Lee and Whang, 2000; Li, Yan, Wang, and Xia, 2005; Zhao, Xie, and Zhang, 2002). Sampson (2000) extends this understanding and argues that the flow of information in service supply chains is bidirectional, rather than unidirectional, as is the case in goods supply chains where the flow of physical goods follows from supplier to customer, who responds with a unidirectional flow of demand information in return.

The second hallmark of demarcation studies is the understanding that customer interaction, simultaneity of production and consumption, intangibility, perishability, and labour intensity are unique characteristics that define service supply chains (Akkermans and Vos, 2003; Zeithaml, Parasuraman, and Berry, 1985). In this context, the demarcation school further highlights the distinctiveness of the 'human element,' arguing that, in contrast to goods-centric supply chains, service supply chains hold no finished goods inventory, but are constrained by the availability of skilled labour (Anderson et al., 2006; Sengupta et al., 2006). Consequently, human, rather than technology-based decision-making in service supply chains leave the output at each stage of the chain uncertain, and to a degree unpredictable. Service supply chains therefore have to focus on the flexibility of resources and service performance and cash flows, all of which are less relevant in a traditional supply chain that follows a comparably static approach, thus allowing it to be standardized through centralized procedures and controls (Meier and Voelker, 2006; Sengupta et al., 2006). As such, service supply chains are often explored by demarcation scholars in the context of professional services, "such as outsourced engineering and technical services, consulting, financial services such as mortgage and insurance, commercial construction" (Anderson et al., 2006, p. 262; see also Lusch et al., 2010).

Expansion studies

Breidbach et al. (2015a) explain that the *expansion* school of thought advocates that service supply chains enhance "manufacturing organizations' ability to compete" (Youngdahl and Loomba, 2000, p. 329). Although expansion scholars also differentiate between goods and services more generally, an individual service is seen as an extension, 'add-on,' or enhancement of a traditional goods-centric supply chain only. Service supply chains are therefore perceived as an artefact that can help "expand manufacturing organizations' ability to compete beyond traditional measures" which include cost, quality, or flexibility (Youngdahl and Loomba, 2000, p. 329). Meier and Voelker (2006) perceive service supply chains as similar to 'traditional' goods-oriented supply chains, in which a service represents an additional component that is provided by a firm other than the manufacturer controlling the chain. This notion of service as an additional element in a goods-oriented supply chain, is similar to the idea of 'servitisation,' a term initially introduced by Vandermerwe and Rada (1988), to describe the "innovation of an organisation's capabilities and processes to shift from selling products to selling integrated products and services that deliver value" (Baines, Lightfoot, Benedettini, and Kay, 2008, p. 547). Servitisation thereby investigates so-called "Product-Service Systems" (Goedkoop et al., 1999; Neely, 2008) that "create additional value adding capabilities for traditional manufacturers" (Baines et al., 2008, p. 547).

As an example of services value-added, consider offerings that include services which increase competitive advantage, set up entry barriers for competitors, and integrate the customer into the business processes by offering 'bundles' consisting of customer-focused combinations of goods, services, support, self-service, and knowledge (Vandermerwe and Rada, 1988). Conversely, 'productization' describes the process of including physical goods in a service offering, such as traditional broadband providers that include a router or other technologies as part of an internet service subscription. Comparing these two situations results in the convergence of offerings that become indistinguishable combinations of goods and services, which Tukker (2004) defines as a spectrum ranging from mainly good-oriented to mainly service-oriented. However, in this context, Baltacioglu, Ada, Kaplan, Yurt, and Kaplan (2007) argue that 'services' are part of many goods-centric supply chains, which makes it unnecessary to even differentiate between goods-driven and service supply chains, thus rendering expansion studies on service supply chains a somewhat niche area in the wider research discourse.

Service-centric studies

The emergence of S-DL (Vargo and Lusch, 2004, 2008, 2016) led to a reconceptualization of service (singular) as the foundation of economic exchange. This lens implies that a single service supply chain is nested within a larger value network, consisting of multiple economic actors who are connected by information flows (Lusch et al., 2010) and engage with one another in economic exchange, often using ICT-enabled engagement platforms (Breidbach and Brodie, 2016; Breidbach, Brodie, and Hollebeek, 2014). One example of this is the case of the sharing economy (Breidbach and Brodie, 2017). S-DL, therefore, can "serve as a framework for integrating [...]supply chain management practices" (Lusch et al., 2010, p. 19), which implies a considerable shift away from a unidirectional supply chain toward a multidirectional value network, a "dynamic network of customer/supplier partnerships and information flows" (Bovet and Martha, 2000, p. 22), in which social and economic actors interact through institutions and ICT in order to "(1) co-produce service offerings, (2) exchange service offerings, and (3) co-create value" (Lusch et al., 2010, p. 20). The role of a single supply chain in a value network is simply to support a customer's value co-creation processes with value propositions which can be goods- and/or service-based. From this standpoint, the focus of a firm is shifting from selling goods and services, to creating offerings that meet customer needs (Stahel, 2008). However, this also implies that the conceptual boundaries of single service supply chains are difficult to define (Sampson and Spring, 2012). S-DL shifts away from a supplier-centric (e.g. demarcation) approach, to a holistic world-view that includes customers and/or other actors in a dynamic economic exchange (Spohrer et al., 2008). Of course, this viewpoint is fundamentally different from servitisation studies that perceive service as a value generating 'add-on' (Verstrepen et al., 1999) and from goods or 'product'-oriented supply chains, which 'deliver value' to a customer (Baines et al., 2008). Instead, a service-centric lens would argue that a manufactured good and the mechanisms needed to disseminate it to customers as recipients (i.e., via a supply chain), represent a distribution mechanism for service, with its value determined in use by the beneficiary (Michel, Brown, and Gallan, 2008; Vargo and Lusch, 2004; Vargo, Lusch, and Akaka, 2010).

Although it acknowledges prior work in the increasingly important domain of service supply chain research, this chapter ultimately follows suggestions by Lusch et al. (2010) and Sampson and Spring (2012) to define individual service supply chains as distinct components of larger value networks that represent institutionalized configurations of one or multiple service providers engaging with one or multiple service customers for common purposes. This assumption implies that a single service supply chain represents an entire value network in the absence of other actors, but also acknowledges that value networks can consist of multiple service supply chains. This customer-centric focus requires careful planning to ensure adequate capacity and inventory are available for service processes, which are typically personalized for each customer through increased levels of responsiveness in the supply chain (Wu and Yang, 2009). Therefore, there is greater uncertainty (Sengupta et al., 2006), which "makes it more difficult to design and implement effective operational processes ... of the service supply chain" (Field and Meile, 2008, p. 186), thus making service supply chain coordination particularly important, but challenging.

Coordinating and managing service supply chain performance

When viewed through the lens of S-DL, the performance of a service supply chain is contingent on its ability to facilitate the co-creation of value (Spohrer and Maglio, 2010). In fact, S-DL assumes that all economic actors within a service supply chain or larger value network are willing and able to engage in this process (Vargo and Lusch, 2008). However, this may not be the case in every instance. Empirical work has demonstrated that the inherent complexity underpinning many service processes, coupled with the bounded rationality of human economic actors, impedes individuals from engaging in value co-creation (Simon, 1996).

As an example of customer disengagement, Santos and Spring (2015) and Breidbach and Maglio (2016) both found in the context of professional consulting services that customers actively disengage from interactions with their service providers. Today, service research draws a more realistic picture of customers as boundedly rational actors, who may be unable to actively engage in value co-creation processes (Vargo and Lusch, 2016). Consequently, any organization aiming to overcome the challenges associated with customers' bounded rationality must attempt to actively orchestrate and facilitate value co-creation processes (Breidbach et al., 2016). In this context, Vargo and Lusch (2016) recently acknowledged the limitations of the existing theoretical underpinnings of S-DL due to the "absence of a clearly articulated specification of the mechanisms of ... coordination and cooperation involved in the cocreation of value" (Vargo and Lusch, 2016, p. 5), and now argue value co-creation processes need to be "coordinated through actor-generated institutions" (Vargo and Lusch, 2016, p. 18).

Supply chain research touched on the issue of coordination more generally, defining it as "the act of managing interdependencies between activities performed to achieve a goal"

(Malone and Crowston, 1990, p. 357). Others have argued that supply chain coordination and orchestration involve the "determination and design of interface points between stages of the supply chain" (Thomas and Griffin, 1996, p. 13). This is required so that an effective alignment of processes and activities can be achieved, thus resulting in reduced costs and times, and improved customer service processes (Sarmah, Acharya, and Goyal, 2006). The goal of any organization is to improve its offerings without increasing complexity in internal structures (Eloranta and Turunen, 2016). However, within value networks, many inter-firm structures and connections exist, thus increasing complexity, which requires new capabilities to manage the network. For example, complexity-related challenges in network orchestration arise from the supply base and industry structure that become increasingly diverse, changing roles of economic actors, or changes in the structure of markets (Eloranta and Turunen, 2016). However, Eloranta and Turunen (2016) argue that organizations can benefit from complexity by extending the network using platform-based attractors, by gathering innovative combinations of resources and capabilities, by strengthening relational processes and social dependencies, as well as through learning and recognizing the diverse contextual factors of actors.

The body of research from which these ideas are drawn discusses institutionalized coordination mechanisms such as contracts (Selviaridis and Spring, 2010), incentive systems (Li et al., 2005), information technology (IT) and information sharing (Akkermans and Vos, 2003), relational governance mechanisms including joint decision-making (Arshinder and Deshmukh, 2008), and reputation effects (Ching et al., 1996). In contrast, prior research related to service sourcing (Alvarez et al., 2010; Baltacioglu et al., 2007) discussed institutionalized coordination mechanisms as compared to relational governance mechanisms. Although these may be seen as substitutes, they are also seen as complementary by some authors (Baltacioglu et al., 2007). Institutionalized means to coordinate supply chains (e.g. contracts) are easy to implement and they also alleviate risks. Relational mechanisms are more time-consuming, but hold the potential to reduce the need for complicated and costly formal mechanisms, because they are based on trust, commitment, and social norms (Alvarez et al., 2010).

An emerging body of research associated with the coordination of supply chains explores 'network orchestration' as the process of a firm's efforts in assembling and managing inter-organizational networks (Gebauer, Paiola, and Saccani, 2013; Perks, Kowalkowski, Witell, and Gustafsson, 2017). Here, the role of the orchestrator is mutually accepted by all other members in the network, so that the orchestrator is able to purposefully manage the network through deliberate activity (Perks et al., 2017). As such, the orchestrator selects all other actors needed, including logistics providers, or suppliers to address the operational needs of the network as a whole (Gebauer et al., 2013). However, as the number of actors and resources involved in the network increases, the orchestration shifts toward a comparatively decentralized approach that is no longer managed by a single actor, but through the collaborative efforts of all actors involved in the network (Perks et al., 2017).

Yet another approach associated with the coordination of supply chains explores 'value facilitation' as a means of facilitating customer value-creating process in everyday practices (Grönroos, 2008). Firms are seen to provide necessary resources, thus creating a foundation for value emergence. A customer combines these resources with other resources to transform potential sources of value through use. Essentially, the customer creates value, whereas the firm's role is seen as providing customers with the necessary resources to accomplish their goals. As such, the firm needs to understand the customer process and relevant practices to maximize value creation, and the customer needs to understand the firm's business logic and be prepared and willing to conform to its practices (Grönroos and Helle, 2010). With this logic, value is not an outcome at the end of a process, but is created in customer usage throughout the use phase (Nordin and Kowalkowski, 2010). This focus on creating value-in-use no longer relies on the price of a service to measure successful coordination outcomes, but rather on the experiences, logic, and ability to extract value out of resources used (Grönroos and Voima, 2013; Nordin and Kowalkowski, 2010).

Despite these various attempts in the literature, coordination mechanisms in the context of service supply chains represent a topic of interest that remains poorly understood. Breidbach et al. (2015a) explain that initial service supply chain emergence relies on relational, rather than institutionalized, coordination mechanisms. This research extends prior work by Alvarez et al. (2010), with the argument that provider–customer interaction and coordination must be treated as distinct from provider–provider interaction. This raises the question of how institutional and relational coordination mechanisms in a service supply chain evolve after the chain has matured into a steady state.

Service supply chain configurations

Service supply chains are anticipated to evolve over time as they attempt to create new competitive advantages. This chapter specifies that four service supply chain configurations can emerge, each characterized by different states, features, and strategic priorities. The analyzability and novelty of interactions within each service supply chain configuration represent two distinct dimensions, which are largely determined by the availability of resources and the respective ability to use them to co-create a value proposition. Conversely, a lack of available resources hinders the ability of economic actors within a service supply chain to co-create the value proposition. A potential mismatch between available and needed resources can, of course, be offset by acquiring or otherwise obtaining resources from other organizations, thus forming a service supply chain. Figure 13.1 provides an overview of this conceptualization.

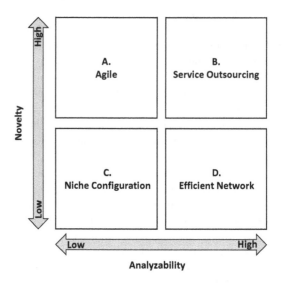

Figure 13.1 Service supply chain configurations.

Agile (A)

Initially, service supply chains are typically in an *Agile* configuration in order to be able to respond to unique customer demands. In this configuration, they can apply innovative solutions to challenges by, for instance, locating additional resources that enable them to achieve their objectives. For example, a professional consulting service typically commences as an agile configuration, working on a 'project' basis. Such projects may require the resolution of a significant service issue, which can be divided into smaller subproblems. Frequently, these subproblems may be new to the service provider, thus requiring new and innovative solutions in order to address customer needs. In some cases, specialists are brought on board to complement the range of human resources available in the consulting firm. Novelty is high; there are low levels of stability. At the same time, analyzability of problems is low. Finding solutions can be challenging and time-consuming. Because such a solution for the customer has not been created before, and there are no experiences or past instances to use as a template, service supply chains may fail to comprehend core requirements, which makes matching of available inputs to requirements more challenging. Furthermore, when inputs are received, it is not always apparent whether or not they meet requirements. In other words, the definitions of requirements are unclear and imprecise, particularly during the early stages in the life of a professional consultancy.

Service outsourcing (B)

In the *Service Outsourcing* configuration, the service supply chain is subjected to a large number of (novel) challenges, but the analyzability is higher. That is, it is easier to identify appropriate types of information and resources required to co-create a service. This means that a central coordinator within the service-providing organization is able to analyse requirements (which cannot be met by resources internally), collect information, and then outsource the work to other firms for either partial support or full completion. The focus is therefore on reliability and control of the processes. Service offerings in which this configuration approach takes place could include routine activities, such as accounting or standard IT services. For example, firms often outsource accounting activities, because these are externalized processes which are well understood and require little supervision once the requirements have been communicated. Hence, such work can be outsourced relatively easily. Even in cases with a high demand for such activities, the analyzability is high, allowing for speedy searches for solutions and transmission of clear requirements to the respective service provider.

Niche configuration (C)

The *Niche Configuration* is characterized by a lower degree of service novelty in comparison to *Service Outsourcing*, which would point to the possibility of developing internal supply chain resources that can deal with routine processes. However, at the same time, the analyzability of service requirements remains low, which may be detrimental to establishing standardized resources. This may be due to not repeating a specific type of task frequently enough to gain required routine experience. Furthermore, sourcing appropriate support (i.e., supply chain partners) with the necessary knowledge may be more difficult due to the lack of analyzability, thus resulting in challenges when trying to overcome exceptions.

Exceptions represent a mismatch between available information and resources on the one hand, and service or customer requirements on the other. The potential for routinizing exceptions over time, as would be the case in an *Efficient Network* configuration, is lower due to continuing variations in certain parts of the overall service requirements. Whilst such services are characterized by complexities due to these characteristics, supply chains in the niche configuration are also likely to encounter fewer unforeseen exceptions overall, due to a lower degree of service novelty. Fewer exceptions generally means that routine operational processes can take place without interruptions. Hence, supply chains in a niche configuration are well advised to develop adequate internal resources to address the majority of routine processes, but are also likely to require a support network where they can access adequate resources on an as-needed basis. Examples in this configuration may include standard services, such as audits or IT solutions, which are marketed in varying contexts (e.g. different geographical locations or industries). The challenges of this configuration are that customers seek a standard solution (lower service novelty) at a lower price point. However, being able to analyse specific customer requirements in varying contexts whilst developing and maintaining the respective support network is likely to be time- and cost-intensive. Hence, supply chains in this quadrant may operate in niche markets.

Efficient network (D)

Efficient Networks are configurations of service supply chains that can run in a stable steady state due to relatively low novelty coupled with high analyzability. Hence, configuring the operations of individual service supply chains that enable effective routinized operations and exchange of resources between individual actors becomes possible as well as desirable. This allows supply chains in this configuration to offer standard service offerings at higher volume and lower price points, driven by a continuing focus on efficient resource usage and process optimization.

Whenever exceptions to standard operating procedures are identified, it is easier to alter behaviour and allocate appropriate resources within the network. This is due to several characteristics of an efficient network. First, standard services are offered in larger quantities, supporting a network of service companies that can provide their specific offerings cost effectively. Second, the high analyzability allows for accurate assessment of service requirements and minimization of exceptions overall. Third, in order to further foster efficiency of the network, operations may be brought in-house to enable maximum control. Or alternatively operations can be allocated permanently to service supply chain partners, thereby extending resource availability in the network. Ultimately, an efficient network configuration may lead to an in-house focus encompassing the bulk of required resources for primarily routine operations. The result is a well-established, stable, and highly integrated service supply chain that resembles a single actor.

Pathways between the configurations

It is important to note that the value propositions within each of the configurations outlined are not static, but are subject to changes during their life cycles. This occurs because service firms are constantly caught in tension between having to engage with customers individually, whilst also maintaining their abilities to execute rapid and efficient service processes. Depending on the type of organization, and the type of service that it provides, the evolutionary pathways between the configurational archetypes outlined may be different. Each of the configurations offers different advantages, ranging from the ability to overcome new and innovative challenges (agile), to providing cost-effective services (efficient), to solving standard challenges in a unique context (niche), or to solving multiple novel problems in an efficient manner (outsourced). To further illustrate these scenarios, the chapter next introduces and discusses the case of a service supply chain transformation in the professional consulting industry.

Practical example: the case of a service supply chain in professional consulting

Professional consulting firms tend to be organized such that individual service supply chains drift toward more efficient configurations over the duration of their lifetimes. For instance, this change might take place through the introduction of new roles, such as service orchestrators (Breidbach et al., 2016), who facilitate resource exchange between other interdependent actors in a value network. The individuals in these new roles must rapidly gain understanding and trust of customers, enabling effective communication.

Based on the service supply chain illustrated by Breidbach et al. (2015a), a practical example of a shift from an agile to an efficient configuration emerges. The professional consulting industry has been established in the literature as an excellent context in which to perform service supply chain research (Anderson et al., 2006; Giannakis, 2011). Consulting depends on effective sharing of information between consultants and customers (Bettencourt et al., 2002), which is a defining characteristic of both service supply chains (Ellram et al., 2004) and larger value networks (Lusch et al., 2010). The service supply chain in the present case consists of three consulting firms and one customer organization. The service goal, which was the preparation of an Infrastructure Asset Management Framework, motivated the supply chain's formation.

Figure 13.2 illustrates that the formation of a service supply chain can be separated into the distinct stages of initiation, probation, and ongoing operation. However, the focus here is on the stages of development (i.e., from supply chain initiation, to an agile configuration, to ongoing efficient operation).

Moving from agility to efficiency

Initiation of the supply chain in the case (example) was triggered by a new market opportunity for the preparation of a national Infrastructure Asset Management Framework.

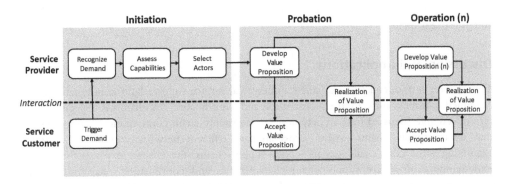

Figure 13.2 A service supply chain from formation to operation.

Because no single company could fulfil all of the service requirements alone, the capabilities of multiple entities had to be combined. The resulting service supply chain partners underwent a subsequent probation stage, which was found to be crucial when building a service supply chain that can be sustained and operated on an ongoing basis. The probation stage can hence be described as the first instance that all actors of this newly formed service supply chain interacted with one another. The case then culminated in ongoing operation, with reconfiguration of the chain being avoided to some extent through relationships between the service supply chain partners and mutual trust. In the last stage ('operation (n)'as illustrated in Figure 13.2), the chain ultimately moved from an agile configuration toward a more efficient network configuration throughout further iterations of service interactions. This transition between service supply chain configurations is depicted in Figure 13.3.

In summary, the initial operation stage of a service supply chain may be described as iterative and dynamic (Lindberg and Nordin, 2008). The value propositions offered become increasingly objectified (Lindberg and Nordin, 2008); in other words, routinized and standardized. As shown in Figure 13.3, the transition from agile to efficient is motivated by factors such as market expansion; thus, there is an increase in service volume as well as repeat business opportunity. Throughout multiple iterations, the service requirements become more predictable for the service providers. The potential for more standardized operations, without the need to source additional resources or members of the chain, can lead to both the potential for cost reductions and quality improvements. These are also improvements that are likely to be demanded by business customers as service offerings mature.

The case service supply chain started with characteristics that allow for good agility, in order to permit more novel and individually customizable services. The network was not fully formed by, but relied on, an emerging pool of resources; therefore, new service partners were sourced as required. These characteristics in combination may influence service interactions as well as outcomes, making such aspects less predictable. Driven by the motivational factors outlined, the chain moved toward a more efficient network through service iterations. As described by Breidbach et al. (2015a), in this transition the importance of institutionalized coordination mechanisms in the service supply chain increased, in order to support a stable network configuration that is well positioned to produce a set of standardized service offerings. Whilst some customizability is always important in professional consulting contexts, the case organization now largely supports this through an established pool of resources and processes. Additional resources can still be brought in, but are less likely to be required within the stabilized network configuration. Because of this transition, agility to respond to novel business opportunities has been replaced by the provision of more standard service offerings characterized by higher levels of dependability and consistent quality.

Discussion and implications

This chapter introduced and explained archetypical service supply chain configurations, and examined possible shifts in their structures and coordination mechanisms. Specifically, it introduced and discussed four archetypical service supply chain configurations, and suggested that service supply chains evolve across an agile/efficient network continuum. Through examining some core challenges in service supply chains, the chapter expands the current understanding of service supply chain characteristics and coordination requirements, and offers possible evolutionary trajectories. This can enhance understanding of how value co-creating activities in service settings should be orchestrated to improve customer experiences.

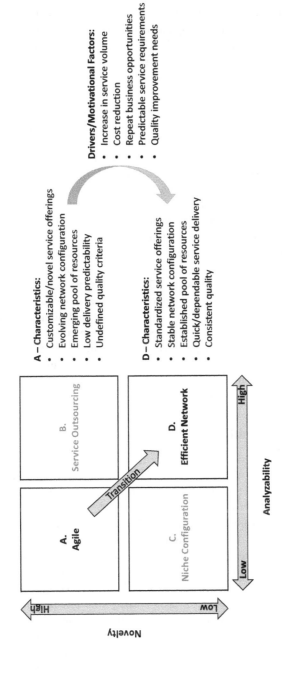

A – Characteristics:
- Customizable/novel service offerings
- Evolving network configuration
- Emerging pool of resources
- Low delivery predictability
- Undefined quality criteria

D – Characteristics:
- Standardized service offerings
- Stable network configuration
- Established pool of resources
- Quick/dependable service delivery
- Consistent quality

Drivers/Motivational Factors:
- Increase in service volume
- Cost reduction
- Repeat business opportunities
- Predictable service requirements
- Quality improvement needs

Figure 13.3 Service supply chain transition: from agile to efficient

This important question represents a key research priority under the S-DL lens more broadly (Vargo and Lusch, 2016), but also within the service science discourse more specifically (Breidbach et al., 2016; Breidbach et al., 2015b).

In addition, this chapter discussed three distinct schools of thought that have previously attempted to conceptualize service supply chains, and put forward a definition that acknowledges service supply chains as distinct components of larger value networks. In the absence of other actors, a single service supply chain thereby represents an entire value network, but this chapter also acknowledges that value networks can consist of multiple service supply chains, explaining that coordination mechanisms of service supply chains remain poorly understood.

The chapter outlined how the practice of coordination has previously been delineated as "the act of managing interdependencies between activities performed to achieve a goal" (Malone and Crowston, 1990, p. 357), with contracts (Selviaridis and Spring, 2010), incentive systems (Li et al., 2005), and IT or information sharing (Akkermans and Vos, 2003) all representing typical examples for institutionalized coordination mechanism. Because the initial service supply chain emergence relies on relational, rather than institutionalized, coordination mechanisms, the chapter discussed joint decision-making (Arshinder and Deshmukh, 2008) and reputation effects (Ching et al., 1996) in this context. It also expanded the current discourse by incorporating 'network orchestration' as the process of a firm's efforts in assembling and managing inter-organizational networks (Gebauer et al., 2013; Perks et al., 2017) and 'value facilitation' as a means of facilitating customer value creating processes in everyday practices (Grönroos, 2008) into the academic debate. As such, future practitioners can use the present work to develop better strategies for managing a changing service supply chain environment, and ultimately understanding how to increase the competitiveness of their operations. In particular, the realization that there are multiple possible service supply chain configurations, and that these can shift over time, may provide greater opportunities in the future. This can occur through different value propositions offered to customers, through individual and customized solutions, or those that utilize service supply chain efficiencies.

Future research opportunities

Ample research opportunities exist for developing theory and practical insights about service supply chains. Despite the fact that the field has seen many useful contributions over the years, applicable models and prescriptive methods are just emerging. This is an important topic, because service supply chain managers need guidelines and prescriptive support in order to guide long-term planning and daily operations of their organizations, and to manage the service experiences of their customers (Breidbach et al., 2015b). Thus, prospective guidelines need to be able to deal with the multifaceted nature of service supply chains, the many systemic emerging interconnections between its respective actors (Pena, Breidbach, and Turpin, 2018), and the trade-offs involved in decision-making processes in increasingly complex sociotechnical environments that will dominate future business processes (Breidbach et al., 2018). Future scholars are encouraged to address the challenges described here.

First, the archetypical service supply chain configurations presented in this chapter should be *empirically* verified. To do this, researchers could deliberately sample cases that fulfil the characteristics outlined in each quadrant. Such multiple case-study approaches have previously been adopted in order to study service systems (Breidbach, Kolb, and Srinivasan, 2013; Breidbach and Maglio, 2016), and could provide rich descriptions and further insights into the area of enquiry. Similarly, scholarly research should investigate performance issues related to each service supply chain configuration. Ultimately, the goal should be to provide managerial insights that go beyond the mere description of a unit of analysis, and enfold suggestions regarding how these individual archetypes can ideally be initiated and managed.

In this context, there are particular opportunities for longitudinal research designs, which may be required to understand the evolution and trajectories of the service supply chain configurations, as well the trajectories between them. This is particularly true from the perspective of service firms that change their strategic positioning, to offer understanding of the motivation for change, and to determine whether the pathways for change identified in this chapter are valid. Prominent future research areas range from new business model development, digitization, sustainability, the sharing economy, or new retail channels to the ethical implications associated with these contexts (Asadi-Someh et al., 2016). Furthermore, developing an understanding of current and future service supply chain actors and their engagement with end customers is of utmost importance.

This chapter highlights a substantial lack of *conceptual* understanding underpinning service supply chains more broadly. With a new-found focus on coordination and value networks, the role of coordination of resources between organizations becomes more important within value networks. Traditionally, planning and coordination of internal resources has been the focus of goods-oriented supply chain research, but this chapter highlights how this narrow firm-centric perspective is no longer applicable in a dynamic environment characterized by changing supply chain configurations. Ultimately, this necessitates the development of new forms of planning and coordination, which take the dynamic requirements in value networks into consideration. In addition, new insights into how customers perceive service supply chains and value networks more generally could improve their alignment overall. This would represent the incorporation of 'service' as more than just a process of 'servitisation' and 'tacking on' service to a goods offering. As Sampson (2012) asserts, what really matters is the 'value' that is the essence of a particular service and the value proposition it offers. Being able to comprehend how customers perceive value through the use of the physical goods in a service supply chain may enable practitioners to develop new interactions and opportunities to create benefits for their customers, fundamentally transforming the overall formation of their businesses.

Finally, there are significant *methodological* opportunities to advance future research about service supply chains. The sources of data available to service supply chain researchers today are substantially different from those even a decade ago. Virtually every interaction, physical movement, or behaviour of actors in service supply chains and value networks can, and is, recorded in one way or another. Examples include: (1) the physical tracking of customers using mobile phone position, (2) images uploaded to social media, and (3) metadata that can provide useful insights about the behaviour of individuals and perception of experiences within a value network (Breidbach et al., 2015a). At the same time, unstructured natural language texts (i.e., recorded complaint calls, patent applications, or government records) can also be analysed (Antons and Breidbach, 2018). The next step for service supply chain research will be to identify which sources of data are available, what questions can be answered, and what methods are needed to do so.

One way to expand the methodological repertoire of service supply chain research would be to initially build on approaches common in other fields, such as experiments, mixed-method designs, or netnographies, all of which are still niche approaches (Breidbach and Ranjanm, 2017). The more significant advancements in service supply chain research will likely stem from the integration of computational methods into the field's discourse. Topic modelling with machine learning (Brust et al., 2017), any type of natural language processing, and simulations with agent-based modelling (Pena et al., 2018), can reveal insights about actors and complex value networks, and enable the researcher to ask entirely new questions, generating unprecedented insights about current and future service supply chains.

References

Akkermans, H. and Vos, B. (2003). Amplification in service supply chains: An exploratory case study from the telecom industry, *Production and Operations Management*. 12(2), 204–223.

Alvarez, G., Pilbeam, C., and Wilding, R. (2010). Nestlé Nespresso AAA sustainable quality program: An investigation into the governance dynamics in a multi-stakeholder supply chain network, *Supply Chain Management*. 15(2), 165–182.

Anderson, E.G., Morrice, D.J., and Lundeen, G. (2006). Stochastic optimal control for staffing and backlog policies in a two-stage customized service supply chain, *Production and Operations Management*. 15(2), 262–278.

Antons, D. and Breidbach, C.F. (2018). Big data, big insights? Advancing service innovation and design with machine learning, *Journal of Service Research*. 21(1), 17–39.

Arshinder, K.A. and Deshmukh, S.G. (2008). Supply chain coordination: Perspectives, empirical studies and research directions, *International Journal of Production Economics*. 115(2), 316–335.

Asadi-Someh, I., Breidbach, C.F. Davern, M., and Shanks, G. (2016). Ethical implications of big data analytics. *Proceedings of the 24th European Conference on Information Systems (ECIS)*, Istanbul, TR, June 2016.

Baines, T.S., Lightfoot, H.W., Benedettini, O., and Kay, J.M. (2008). The servitization of manufacturing, *Journal of Manufacturing Technology Management*. 20(5), 547–567.

Baltacioglu, T., Ada, E., Kaplan, M.D., Yurt, O., and Kaplan, Y.C. (2007). A new framework for service supply chains, *The Service Industries Journal*. 27(2), 105–124.

Bettencourt, L.A., Ostrom, A.L., Brown, S.W., Roundtree, R.I. (2002), Client co-production in knowledge-intensive business services, *California Management Review*. 44(4), 100–128.

Bovet, D. and Martha, J. (2000). *Value nets: Breaking the supply chain to unlock hidden profits*. New York: Wiley & Sons.

Breidbach, C.F., Antons, D., and Salge, T.O. (2016). Seamless service? On the role and impact of service orchestrators in human-centered service systems, *Journal of Service Research*. 19(4), 458–476.

Breidbach, C.F. and Brodie, R.J. (2016). Nature and purpose of engagement platforms. In R.J. Brodie, L. D. Hollebeek, & J. Conduit (Eds.), *Customer engagement: Contemporary issues and challenges* (pp. 124–136). London: Routledge.

Breidbach, C.F. and Brodie, R.J. (2017). Engagement platforms in the sharing economy: Conceptual foundations and research directions, *Journal of Service Theory and Practice*. 27(4), 761–777.

Breidbach, C.F., Brodie, R.J., and Hollebeek L.D. (2014). Beyond virtuality: From engagement platforms to engagement ecosystems, *Managing Service Quality*. 24(6), 592–611.

Breidbach, C.F., Chandler, J. D., and Maglio P.P. (2015b). The duality of second screens: A phenomenological study of multi-platform engagement and service experiences. *Proceedings of the 48th Hawaii International Conference on System Sciences (HICSS)*, 1432–1441.

Breidbach, C.F., Choi, S., Ellway, B.P., Keating, B.W., Kormusheva, K, Kowalkowski, C, Lim, C., and Maglio P.P. (2018). Operating without operations: Where does the firm fit in?, *Journal of Service Management*. 29(5), 809–833.

Breidbach, C.F., Kolb, D.G., and Srinivasan, A. (2013). Connectivity in service systems: Does technology-enablement impact the ability of a service system to co-create value?, *Journal of Service Research*. 16(4), 428–441.

Breidbach, C.F. and Maglio P.P. (2016). Technology-enabled value co-creation: An empirical analysis of actors, resources, and practices, *Industrial Marketing Management*. 56(July), 73–85.

Breidbach, C. F. and Ranjanm, S. (2017). How do fintech service platforms facilitate value co-creation? An analysis of twitter data. *Proceedings of the 38th International Conference on Information Systems (ICIS)*, Seoul, KOR, December 2017.

Breidbach, C.F., Reefke, H., and Wood, L.C. (2015a).Investigating the Formation of Service Supply Chains, *The Service Industries Journal*. 35(1–2), 5–23.

Brust, L., Breidbach, C.F., Antons, D., and Salge T.O. (2017). Service-dominant logic and information systems research: A review and analysis using topic modelling. *Proceedings of the 38th International Conference on Information Systems (ICIS)*, Seoul, KOR, December 2017.

Ching, C., Holsapple, C.W., and Whinston, A.B. (1996). Toward IT support for coordination in network organizations, *Information & Management*. 30(4), 179–199.

Ellram, L.M., Tate, W.L., and Billington, C. (2004). Understanding and managing the services supply chain, *Journal of Supply Chain Management*. 40(4), 17–32.

Eloranta, V. and Turunen, T. (2016). Platforms in service-driven manufacturing: Leveraging complexity by connecting, sharing, and integrating, *Industrial Marketing Management*. 55, 178–186. doi: 10.1016/j.indmarman.2015.10.003.

Field, J.M. and Meile, L.C. (2008). Supplier relations and supply chain performance in financial services processes, *International Journal of Operations & Production Management*. 28(2), 185–206.

Frohlich, M.L. and Westbrook, R. (2002). Arcs of integration: An international study of supply chain strategies, *Journal of Operations Management*. 19(2), 185–200.

Gebauer, H., Paiola, M., and Saccani, N. (2013). Characterizing service networks for moving from products to solutions, *Industrial Marketing Management*. 42(1), 31–46. doi: 10.1016/j.indmarman.2012.11.002.

Giannakis, M. (2011). Conceptualizing and managing service supply chains, *The Service Industries Journal*. 31(11), 1809–1823.

Goedkoop, M., van Halen, C., te Riele, H., and Rommens, P. (1999). Product service-systems, ecological and economic basics, in *Report for Dutch Ministries of Environment (VROM) and Economic Affairs (EZ)*. PRe Consultants: Amersfoort, NL.

Grönroos, C. (2008). Service logic revisited: who creates value? And who co-creates? *European Business Review*. 20, 298–314.

Grönroos, C. and Helle, P. (2010). Adopting a service logic in manufacturing, *Journal of Service Management*. 21, 564–590.

Grönroos, C. and Voima, P. (2013). Critical service logic: Making sense of value creation and co-creation, *Journal of the Academy of Marketing Science*. 41, 133–150.

Lee, H.L., and Whang, S. (2000), Information sharing in a supply chain. *International Journal of Technology Management*. 20(3-4), 373–387.

Li, G., Yan, H., Wang, S., and Xia, Y. (2005). Comparative analysis on value of information sharing in supply chains, *Supply Chain Management: An International Journal*. 10(1), 34–46.

Lindberg, N. and Nordin, F. (2008). From products to services and back again: Towards a new service procurement logic, *Industrial Marketing Management*. 37(3), 292–300.

Lusch, R.F., Vargo, S.L., and Tanniru, M. (2010). Service, value networks and learning, *Journal of the Academy of Marketing Science*. 38(1), 19–31.

Malone, T.W. and Crowston, K. (1990). What is coordination theory and how can it help design cooperative work systems, in *Conference on Computer Supported Cooperative Work*. Los Angeles, California.

Maull, R., Geraldi, J., and Johnston, R. (2012). Service supply chains: A customer perspective, *Journal of Supply Chain Management*. 48(4), 72–86.

Meier, H. and Voelker, O. (2006). Industrial product-service-systems: Typology of service supply chain for IS providing, in *The 41st CIRP Conference on Manufacturing Systems*. New York: Springer.

Michel, S., Brown, S.W., and Gallan, A.S. (2008). An expanded and strategic view of discontinuous innovations: Deploying a service-dominant logic, *Journal of the Academy of Marketing Science*. 36, 54–66.

Neely, A. (2008). Exploring the financial consequences of the servitization of manufacturing, *Operations Management Research*. 1(2), 103–118.

Nordin, F. and Kowalkowski, C. (2010). Solutions offerings: A critical review and reconceptualisation, *Journal of Service Management*. 21, 441–459.

Pena, M.V.T., Breidbach, C.F., and Turpin, A. (2018). Self-organizing service ecosystems: Exploring a new concept for service science. *Proceedings of the Australasian Conference on Information Systems (ACIS)*, Sydney, NSW, December 2018.

Perks, H., Kowalkowski, C., Witell, L., and Gustafsson, A. (2017). Network orchestration for value platform development, *Industrial Marketing Management*. 67(July), 106–121. doi: 10.1016/j.indmarman.2017.08.002.

Sampson, S.E. (2000). Customer-supplier duality and bidirectional supply chains in service organizations, *International Journal of Service Industry Management*. 11(4), 348–364.

Sampson, S.E. (2012), Visualizing service operations, *Journal of Service Research*. 15(2), 182–198.

Sampson, S.E. and Spring, M. (2012). Customer roles in service supply chains and opportunities for innovation, *Journal of Supply Chain Management*. 48(4), 30–50.

Santos, J.B. and Spring, M. (2015). Are knowledge intensive business services really co-produced? Overcoming lack of customer participation in KIBS, *Industrial Marketing Management*. 50(October), 85–96.

Sarmah, S.P., Acharya, D., and Goyal, S.K. (2006). Buyer vendor coordination models in supply chain management, *European Journal of Operational Research*. 175(1), 1–15.

Selviaridis, K. and Spring, M. (2010). The dynamics of business service exchanges: Insights from logistics outsourcing, *Journal of Purchasing and Supply Management*. 16(3), 171–184.

Sengupta, K., Heiser, D.R., and Cook, L.S. (2006). Manufacturing and service supply chain performance: A comparative analysis. *Journal of Supply Chain Management*. 42(4), 4–15.

Simon, H.A. (1996). *The sciences of the artificial*. Cambridge, MA: The MIT Press.

Spohrer, J., Anderson, L.C., Pass, N.J., Ager, T. and Gruhl, D. (2008). Service science, *Journal of Grid Computing*. 6(3), 313–324.

Spohrer, J. and Maglio, P. (2010). Toward a science of service systems: Value and symbols. In P. Maglio, C.A. Kieliszewski, & J. Spohrer (Eds.), *Handbook of service science* (pp. 157–193). Berlin: Springer.

Stahel, W. (2008). The performance economy: Business models for the functional service economy. In K. B. Misra (Eds.), *Handbook of Performability Engineering* (pp.127–138). London: Springer-Verlag.

Thomas, D.J. and Griffin, P.M. (1996). Coordinated supply chain management, *European Journal of Operational Research*. 94(1), 1–15.

Tukker, A. (2004), Eight types of product–service system: Eight ways to sustainability? Experiences from SusProNet, *Business Strategy & the Environment*. 13(4), 246–260.

Vandermerwe, S. and Rada, J. (1988). Servitization of business: Adding value by adding services, *European Management Journal*. 6(4), 314–324.

Vargo, S.L. and Lusch, R.F. (2004). Evolving to a new dominant logic for marketing, *Journal of Marketing*. 68(1), 1–17.

Vargo, S. L. and Lusch, R. F. (2008). From goods to service(s): Divergences and convergences of logic, *Industrial Marketing Management*. 37(3), 254–259.

Vargo, S.L. and Lusch, R.F. (2016). Institutions and axioms: An extension and update of service-dominant logic, *Journal of the Academy of Marketing Science*. 44(1), 5–23.

Vargo, S.L., Lusch, R.F., and Akaka, M.A. (2010). Advancing service science with service-dominant logic. In P. Maglio, C.A. Kieliszewski, & J. Spohrer (Eds.), *Handbook of service science* (pp. 133–156). Berlin: Springer.

Verstrepen, S., Deschoolmeester, D., and van Den Berg, R. (1999). Servitization in the automotive sector: Creating value and competitive advantage through service after sales. In K. Mertins, O. Krause, & B. Schallock (Eds.), *Global production management*, (pp. 538–545). Norwell, MA: Kluwer Academic Publishers.

Walsh, W.E. and Wellman, M.P. (2000). Modeling supply chain formation in multiagent systems. . In A. Moukas, F. Ygge, & C. Sierra (Eds.), *Agent mediated electronic commerce II* (pp. 94–101). Berlin/Heidelberg: Springer.

Wu, W.P., and Yang, H.L. (2009), An empirical investigation of the relationships between moral intensity and ethical decision making in electronic commerce, *International Journal of Organizational Innovation*. 2(2), 195–210.

Youngdahl, W.E. and Loomba, A.P.S. (2000). Service-driven global supply chains, *International Journal of Service Industry Management*. 2000, 11(4), 329–347.

Zeithaml, V.A., Parasuraman, A. and Berry, L. (1985). Problems and strategies in services marketing, *Journal of Marketing*. 49(Spring), 33–46.

Zhao, X., Xie, J., and Zhang, W.J. (2002). The impact of information sharing and ordering coordination on supply chain performance, *Supply Chain Management: An International Journal*. 7(1), 24–40.

14

Strategic pathways to cost-effective service excellence

Jochen Wirtz

Introduction

Strategy research widely holds that it is extremely difficult to combine the supposedly incompatible strategies of differentiation (e.g., through service excellence and continuous innovation) and cost leadership (Porter 1980, 1996). Porter argued that it is not possible to do so for a sustained period because dual strategies entail contradictory investments and organizational processes, and the organization risks being "stuck in the middle." Many strategy experts contend that companies must choose between differentiation (e.g., on service excellence) to combat commoditization or cost leadership, which can be used when it is difficult to command an adequate price premium.

The trade-off between customer satisfaction and productivity has been widely acknowledged in the service marketing and operations management literatures, and it remains a key challenge for organizations to strive for both objectives (Anderson, Fornell, & Rust 1997; Rust & Huang 2012). These two objectives conflict because too strong a focus on productivity (often associated with cost reduction) can reduce customer satisfaction, whereas concentration on customer satisfaction may increase cost, thereby reducing productivity (Rust & Huang 2012).

Research in marketing has confirmed that this is, in fact, a trade-off (Anderson et al. 1997; Rust & Huang 2012; Rust, Moorman, & Dickson 2002), and it has been shown to be more pronounced in services than in goods, especially when front line employees are involved (Anderson et al. 1997; Marinova, Ye, & Singh 2008; Singh 2000). In addition to the intangibility and variability of services that make them difficult to standardize (Chase 1978, 1981; Frei 2006), perceived quality in services frequently depends on customization desired by consumers. High levels of customization are costly because employees typically play a prominent role in service delivery (Anderson et al. 1997). As expressed by Rust and Huang, "increasing service productivity often involves a trade-off, with better service typically requiring more labor intensity, lower productivity, and higher cost" (2012, p. 47).

Few service organizations seem to be capable of pursuing a strategy focused on customer satisfaction and productivity at the same time given that they require "distinctive organizational systems, structure, and cultural underpinnings" (Rust, Moorman, & van Beuningen 2016, p. 156). Therefore, pursuing a dual strategy combining service excellence and high productivity is likely to be a "daunting task" for most organizations (Mittal, Anderson, Sayrak, & Tadikamalla 2005, p. 547).

Although the general belief is that this trade-off holds and that service excellence and cost-effectiveness are in conflict, examples can be proffered in which organizations managed to align high productivity and customer satisfaction. For example, the Vanguard Group, a fund and investment management firm, had the highest American Customer Satisfaction Index (ACSI) scores and also the lowest expense ratio of its industry. Ristorante D'O, a Michelin-starred restaurant, was so productive that it could profitably charge only one-third the amount of typical prices in its competitive set. Finally, the National Library Board of Singapore was one of the globally most innovative libraries, having unparalleled member satisfaction while showing the highest labor productivity of its competitors worldwide (Wirtz & Zeithaml 2018). These organizations exemplified *cost-effective service excellence* (CESE) by combining the purportedly incompatible strategies of service excellence and high productivity. CESE refers to a state in which an organization is simultaneously among the best performers in its competitive set, in terms of both customer satisfaction and productivity (Wirtz & Zeithaml 2018).

This chapter builds on an article by Wirtz and Zeithaml (2018) and integrates and synthesizes the literature in marketing, management, and service operations to explain the strategic pathways by which CESE can be achieved. The potential alignment and conflicts between service excellence and cost-effectiveness are discussed, and potential strategies explore how organizations can mitigate these conflicts. The chapter ends with promising questions for future research.

Service excellence, productivity, and organizational performance

Empirical research on the satisfaction–productivity trade-off

Literature in marketing shows empirically that pursuing a customer satisfaction strategy generally improves financial performance (Anderson et al. 2004, Anderson, Fornell, & Mazvancheryl 2004; Gupta & Zeithaml 2006; Kamakura, Mittal, De Rosa, & Mazzon 2002; Rust, Zahorik, & Keiningham 1995). The services marketing literature uses various terms to describe an organization's focus on delivering customer satisfaction, including revenue emphasis (Rust et al. 2016), customer satisfaction (Anderson et al. 1997; Swaminathan, Groening, Mittal, & Thomaz 2014), and effectiveness (Rust & Huang 2012).

A strategy focused on customer satisfaction results in superior risk-adjusted equity returns (Aksoy, Cooil, Groening, Keiningham, & Yalcin 2008; Fornell, Mithas, Morgeson, & Krishnan 2006). This occurs largely through the positive effects customer satisfaction has on repeat purchase, cross-buying, referrals (Gupta & Zeithaml 2006; Oliver 2010), reduced customer switching (Wirtz et al. 2014), increased attitudinal loyalty, and reduced price sensitivity (Umashankar, Bhagwat, & Kumar 2016; Wirtz, Mattila, & Lwin 2007). A number of studies have shown that the relationships between customer satisfaction and its key outcome variables generally follow a positive linear or inverse S-shaped functional form, which is convex at high levels of customer satisfaction (Kumar, Dalla Pozza, & Ganesh 2013). Keiningham, Aksoy, Williams, and Buoye (2015a) and Keiningham et al. (2015b) showed that the relationship between individual customer-level relative (ranked) customer satisfaction and share-of-wallet follows a Zipfian distribution with sharply increasing share-of-wallet for firms with higher customer satisfaction rankings. As such, it is important for organizations to be at the leading edge in terms of customer satisfaction and service excellence in their respective industries.

The operations management literature shows that increased productivity generally improves business performance through cost reduction (Breyfogle 2003; Crosby 1979; Deming 1986).

The literature uses various terms to describe an organization's focus on productivity, including cost emphasis (Rust et al. 2002, 2016), cost reduction (Mittal et al. 2005), efficiency (Swaminathan et al. 2014), and productivity (Anderson et al. 1997). Productivity is defined throughout this chapter in terms of the output/input ratio (Grönroos & Ojasalo 2004).

Combining the dual foci on customer satisfaction and productivity, service organizations can pursue one of at least three alternative customer satisfaction- and productivity-focused strategies: (1) increase customer satisfaction, (2) increase productivity, and (3) engage in a dual strategy pursuing customer satisfaction and productivity simultaneously. Of the three strategies, empirical evidence suggests that focusing on customer satisfaction has a higher financial return than either focusing on productivity or trying to execute a dual strategy (Rust et al. 2002). Furthermore, the literature distinguishes between organizations that *pursue* a dual strategy and those that *actually achieve it* (Mittal et al. 2005). Empirical findings showed that after organizations successfully achieved a dual strategy they reaped the highest financial returns compared to organizations that focused on either customer satisfaction or productivity alone (Mittal et al. 2005). A dual strategy is clearly desirable but difficult to achieve (Rust et al. 2002).

Root causes of the service excellence and productivity conflict

To achieve CESE, root causes underlying the service excellence–productivity conflict must be addressed. There are three key root causes (Wirtz & Zeithaml 2018), which are detailed in this section.

First, many services are produced through distributed operations with simultaneous production and consumption, as well as customization in real time at the customer interface (e.g., fast-food outlets, hotels, and bank branches can be viewed as mini-factories). Achieving CESE seems particularly difficult for service organizations because having distributed operations makes industrialization, de-skilling, economies of scale, productivity, and quality control difficult to achieve (Chase 1978, 1981).

Second, customer-introduced input, process, and output variability have been identified as key limiting factors in increasing productivity. That is, operations cannot be organized and scheduled at optimum efficiency because customer arrival times, product choices, service preferences, and their capabilities, effort, and involvement in the service process vary (Chase 1978, 1981; Frei 2006). Offering sufficient capacity and process flexibility, employee skills, and supplies 'on demand' and at high quality is challenging and expensive.

Third, customer experience and satisfaction often depend on the additional three Ps of services marketing: people, process, and physical environment (Booms & Bitner 1981). Furthermore, information technology (IT) is frequently required to connect all parts at the customer interface. Therefore, to deliver service excellence, the functions of operations, IT, marketing, and human resources need to be tightly integrated. This integration frequently leads to trade-offs between functional objectives, especially between marketing and operations. These trade-offs are well documented, with marketing typically focusing on service excellence, loyalty, sales, upselling, cross-selling, and market share, whereas operational concerns include unit costs, productivity, and capacity utilization (Lovelock 1992). Striving for CESE must address these three causes of the customer satisfaction–productivity trade-off.

The service excellence, productivity, and profitability triangle

Examining the individual relationships between customer satisfaction and productivity one can see that, all else being equal, higher customer satisfaction improves the bottom line through higher loyalty (Mittal et al. 2005; Rust et al. 1995; Watson, Beck, Henderson, & Palmatier 2015). Similarly, everything else being equal, higher productivity leads to higher profitability through cost reduction (Mittal et al. 2005). However, the relationship between productivity and customer satisfaction is complex because it can be positive, neutral, or negative for a number of reasons.

First, although the relationship between productivity and customer satisfaction can introduce conflict, examples can be proffered where productivity gains and customer satisfaction are aligned. For instance, if customer service processes are redesigned to be leaner, faster, and more convenient by eliminating non-value-adding work steps, then productivity and customer satisfaction improve concurrently (Rust et al. 2016). That is, productivity improvements have a direct positive and relatively immediate effect on profitability through cost reductions, and a positive indirect (and typically delayed) effect through enhanced customer satisfaction (Rust et al. 2016). For example, the United Services Automobile Association (USAA) introduced a popular remote check crediting service Deposit@Home. This service allowed customers to take a picture of a check and upload it with a smartphone to instantly deposit the check without having to either mail it or deliver it in person. This process substituted relatively inexpensive and easy-to-use technology for front line employees and physical check processing. In this case, a positive impact on profitability can be expected through increased productivity and increased customer satisfaction.

Second, some quality improvements may not have any implications for productivity (e.g., improving a front-office process that does not change its cost) and vice versa for improvements in productivity in the back office (e.g., using more efficient back-office operations that do not have implications for customer touch points). Thus, there is only a positive effect on profitability of such customer satisfaction or productivity improvements. That is, not all quality and productivity improvements necessarily involve trade-offs.

Third, and in contrast to the prior discussion, if productivity improvements result in changes in the service experience that customers find sufficiently poor (e.g., replacing a human agent in a customer contact center with an interactive voice response system to reduce head count, increasing group sizes in a child care center, or reducing the frequency of trains to increase load factors), then a trade-off is to be expected. This means that these productivity improvements have a positive direct effect on profitability, but also a negative indirect effect through reduced customer satisfaction. If the cost savings from productivity enhancements are more than offset by revenue and contribution losses through decreased satisfaction, the net effect is negative (c.f., Rust & Huang 2012).

Service quality improvements often result in lower productivity owing to "better service typically requiring more labor intensity, lower productivity, and higher cost" (Rust & Huang 2012, p. 47). This trade-off is common in service organizations (Rust & Huang 2012). That is, investments in quality can only have a positive financial return if the financial benefits resulting from increased satisfaction exceed the costs of achieving the higher quality level (Rust et al. 1995).

In summary, the relationship between productivity and customer satisfaction enhancements can be positive, neutral, or negative. If it is neutral or positive, the net effect on profitability is positive. If productivity and quality improvements are in conflict, the net effect on profitability depends on the relative strengths of the effects on profitability. This microlevel perspective offers a more differentiated view of the empirical findings related to the productivity–customer satisfaction trade-off. In particular, it shows that customer satisfaction and productivity are often positively aligned or do not affect each other, whereas the trade-off relates only to those situations where there is direct conflict. The remainder of this chapter provides guidance on how to mitigate such conflicts.

Framework for strategic pathways to achieve CESE

The following sections discuss and synthesize relevant streams of the marketing, management, and operations literature that relate to the constructs service productivity, excellence, and profitability. Two main streams of literature are particularly relevant. The first, on organizational ambidexterity, is rooted in the management literature and explores how organizations can simultaneously pursue and integrate different, often conflicting, objectives. The second stream is based on the operations management literature, and tackles the root causes of low productivity in service operations, offering potential solutions. Integration of the literature suggests three specific pathways organizations can pursue to achieve CESE: dual culture strategy, operations management approach, and the focused service factory strategy (Wirtz & Zeithaml 2018).

The pathways to CESE are illustrated in the following sections with case examples drawn from Wirtz and Zeithaml (2018). These examples were among the leading organizations in their respective industries in both service excellence and productivity. Wirtz and Zeithaml (2018) coded each organization on use of the key CESE strategies, and they serve as illustrations in the following sections. Figure 14.1 synthesizes the coding into core strategies and observed combinations; Figure 14.2 provides an overview of the three core strategies available to organizations that want to achieve CESE. The remainder of this chapter describes these approaches in the context of their respective literatures.

Dual culture strategy

The dual culture strategy uses organizational ambidexterity to drive the deployment of generic productivity strategies and tools to the extreme. At the same time, this strategy is exceedingly customer-centric and also focuses on service excellence.

Organizations	Dual Culture Strategy	Operations Management Approaches	Focused Service Factory
Singapore Airlines, Ristorante D'O	●	○	○
National Library Board Singapore, Google, USAA	○	●	○
Shouldice Hospital, JetBlue	○	○	●
Vanguard, Amazon	●	●	○
Narayana Health	●	○	●

Use of Strategies/Tools: ● Extensive ○ Little/Not at all

Figure 14.1 Observed constellations of CESE strategies.

Notes: Coding is relative to the respective industry in which an organization operates. This table is based on case analyses reported in Wirtz and Zeithaml (2018).

Culture for Service Excellence

Dual Culture Strategy	Operation Management Approaches to Reduce Process Variability			Focused Service Factory
	Buffering & Front-office Minus	Modularization of Service	Self-service Technology (SST)	
No/little change in customer interface	**Reduces real time responsiveness & flexibility**	**Reduces customer choice**	**Reduces customer contact**	**Offers a highly standardized service**
> Focuses the entire organization on CESE through leadership ambidexterity and contextual ambidexterity. Structural ambidexterity can play a supporting role > Requires a credible rationale for employees to subscribe to a dual culture strategy > Extreme use of generic productivity strategies and tools to achieve the same output with less input, incl.: • Cost control • Train and motivate employees to do things faster, better, and more efficiently • Better capacity utilization (better matching of supply and demand) • Customer service process redesign; (Lean) Six Sigma; • Use of systems and technology (e.g., biometrics) • Outsourcing of non-core activities • Tiering of service to better allocate resources	> Isolates the back office through separating and buffering activities in the front and back office > Industrializes the back office > Shifts activities from the inefficient front office to the back office > Uses: • Plant-within-a-plant and buffering of two separately focused operations: front office focuses on customer satisfaction and sales; back office focuses on productivity and low error rate • Systems and technology to industrialize the back-office	> Reduces customer input into the service process to reduce variability > Is enabled by modularization of services and their features > Uses: • Reduced process divergence and complexity • Hard product and service level choices • Systems and technology to industrialize the front office	> Reduces customer contact in the service production system > Uses: • SSTs that replace customer interactions with front line employees • Tight customer scripts • Service robots (in physical and virtual form) and AI	> Standardizes and industrializes service offerings and their delivery processes > Uses: • Standardized product offering with few standard options and little flexibility and customization • Standardized and industrialized service processes also in the front office • Tight selection of customer segments whose needs fit the service model precisely • Standardized customer input into the service process through tight customer scripts
	Operations management approaches require careful consideration of target customers' needs and wants. i.e., customers have to be satisfied with changes in customer interface and options offered.			
	Can be pursed in combination with a dual culture strategy			Can be pursed in combination with a dual culture strategy
Case examples: Singapore Airlines; Ristorante D'O	National Library Board Singapore's book lockers and drops	Google's stand-alone products	USSA; Vanguard; chat bots	Shouldice Hospital; Narayana Health; JetBlue; fintechs

Figure 14.2 Three strategic approaches to achieving CESE.

Note: Adapted from Wirtz and Zeithaml (2018) (see note 1).

Organizational ambidexterity

In management, the pursuit of conflicting organizational goals has been studied in the ambidexterity literature. 'Ambidexterity' describes how organizations are able to simultaneously pursue courses of action along different, often conflicting dimensions. Robust findings link organizational ambidexterity to improved financial performance (O'Reilly & Tushman 2013). Dimensions that have been studied include exploitation (e.g., enhancing cash flows through fine-tuning of current operations), exploration (e.g., R&D to develop a new generation of breakthrough products), incremental versus radical innovation, continuous versus radical change, and efficient versus flexible organizational structure (for a review, see Raisch & Birkinshaw 2008). However, cost-effectiveness versus service excellence has not yet been examined in the management literature, and this is the focus of this section.

To be ambidextrous, organizations must resolve internal conflicts for resources as well as shift demands in their task environments. Although earlier studies viewed these trade-offs as insurmountable, more recent research has presented three organizational approaches to support ambidexterity (Benner & Tushman 2003; Raisch & Birkinshaw 2008). First, *leadership ambidexterity* can enable organizations to manage conflicting demands (Lubatkin, Simsek, Ling, & Veiga 2006; Smith & Tushman 2005). Paradoxical senior management frames lead to a "both/and logic" rather than an "either/or logic" (Collins & Porras 1994, pp. 43–45; Smith, Lewis, & Tushman 2016). This view enables positive conflict and allows leaders to embrace rather than avoid contradictions (Smith & Tushman 2005). Leaders then play a critical role in putting the systems in place that allow supportive contexts for ambidexterity to emerge; they focus and energize the organization on these key ideas, role model the desired ambidextrous behaviors, and reinforce them with rewards and recognition (Gibson & Birkinshaw 2004).

Second, *contextual ambidexterity* involves achieving alignment and adaptability by pushing the integration of conflicting goals to the individual employee (Gibson & Birkinshaw 2004, p. 209). Individual-level behavior is then shaped by the context (i.e., systems, processes, and beliefs), which is designed to enable and encourage individuals to exercise their own judgment in dealing with conflicting demands (Gibson & Birkinshaw 2004). Third, *structural ambidexterity* involves separating organizational units to allow units with different competencies to address inconsistent demands (Benner & Tushman 2003; Gibson & Birkinshaw 2004).

Wirtz and Zeithaml (2018) advanced the idea that an organization's simultaneous focus on service excellence and cost-effectiveness is akin to other potentially conflicting goals studied in the organizational ambidexterity literature. Specifically, and as discussed next, they found that leadership ambidexterity and contextual ambidexterity were both pursued in all dual culture organizations examined; however, structural ambidexterity, which arguably received the most attention in the management literature, featured least prominently.

Dual culture focused on service excellence and cost-effectiveness

Wirtz and Zeithaml (2018) used the lenses of leadership, contextual, and structural ambidexterity, to examine how ten case organizations achieved CESE. All ten organizations focused on service excellence, but only five pursued dual culture strategies, in which they consciously drove foci on both service excellence and productivity. The literature uses various terms similar to 'dual culture strategy,' including "dual strategy," "dual emphasis" (Mittal et al. 2005; Rust et al. 2016; Swaminathan et al. 2014), and "simultaneous attempts to increase both customer satisfaction and productivity" (Anderson et al. 1997). In this chapter, the term 'dual culture strategy' is used throughout.

The roles and interplay of three types of ambidexterity

Leadership ambidexterity, the first dual culture approach, requires that *leaders* push and even rally their organizations to pursue the dual culture, which is typically done through internal communications, training, and incentives (Gibson & Birkinshaw 2004). For example, Jeff Bezos, the CEO of Amazon, was known to put the needs of customers first; he was infamous for becoming enraged upon receiving customer complaints, requiring that anxious employees find solutions immediately. At the same time, he role modelled and communicated frugality on anything that did not touch the customer (Stone 2013, pp. 330–331). "Customer obsession" and "frugality" were core values at Amazon (Stone 2013, p. 88). John Bogle, the founder and former CEO of Vanguard, emphasized the organization's strategy to "provide the highest quality of investor services, at the *lowest possible cost* [sic]" (Bogle 2002, p. 138). Vanguard emphasized frugality even when recruiting, by looking for team members who "understand and sympathize with the need for frugality" (Heskett, Sasser, & Schlesinger 2015, p. 77).

Dr. Devi Shetty, founder and chairman of Narayana Health, stated, "The notion that 'if you want quality, you have to pay for it' went out the window a long time ago at Narayana Health" (Global Health and Travel 2014, p. 44). Senior employees received daily text messages detailing the previous day's expenses, to drive cost-consciousness and motivate team members to generate cost saving and process improvement ideas (Anand 2009; Govindarajan & Ramamurti 2013). Chef Davide Oldani, founder and head chef of Ristorante D'O, was passionate about keeping prices low, in order to make the Michelin-starred restaurant accessible to a broad audience; he constantly communicated this to his team (Cheshes 2015; Nobel 2013).

As a final example, Singapore Airlines' leadership, internal communications, and training continuously emphasize that profit is a function both of service excellence (which drives the loyalty of demanding business travelers, its core target segment) and costs (the other side of the profit equation). To reinforce that message, Singapore Airlines offered bonuses to all employees depending on the airline's profitability, but also cut base pay by as much as 20% when it had losses. The result was a culture that became exceedingly customer-centric and that internalized the idea that anything that touched the customer must be consistent with Singapore Airlines' premium positioning. On the other hand, everything behind the scenes was subject to extreme cost control, with employees focusing intensely on managing costs and improving productivity (Heracleous & Wirtz 2010, 2014).

Contextual ambidexterity is apparent in many of the dual culture strategy organizations; it governs employee thinking and decision-making about when to focus on service excellence, when to emphasize cost-effectiveness, and ideally, how to integrate both objectives synergistically. Often, both objectives are aligned and can be pursued simultaneously, but sometimes trade-offs have to be made. Employees need to know how to make such decisions, and an internalized dual culture provides this governance mechanism. Using Singapore Airlines as an example again, Krug Grande Cuvée and Dom Pérignon were served in first class. To minimize costs, cabin crews offered whichever bottle was open unless a passenger specifically requested the other brand. No cost was considered too small to reduce (Heracleous & Wirtz 2010, 2014).

Narayana Health had an intense focus on surgery quality and success rates. However, its surgeons constantly compared and generated ideas across their network on how to cut costs, such as through the routine reuse of medical devices that were sold as single-use goods. For example, the $160 steel clamps that were employed during open-heart surgeries were sterilized and reused up to 80 times (Govindarajan & Ramamurti 2013).

Similar observations can be made at Amazon and Vanguard, where trade-off decisions were pushed to decision makers to integrate the conflicting objectives. As stated in Amazon's leadership principles: "Frugality – We try not to spend money on things that don't matter to customers. Frugality breeds resourcefulness, self-sufficiency and invention" (Stone 2013, p. 330). As these examples show, leadership and contextual ambidexterity seem to go hand in hand.

Structural ambidexterity can play a supporting role in achieving CESE. For example, Singapore Airlines invested heavily in a centralized innovation department, a separate unit that developed its next industry-leading inflight service products (Heracleous & Wirtz 2010; Tuzovic, Wirtz, & Heracleous 2018).

In summary, organizational ambidexterity can help to implement a CESE strategy. The mechanisms for achieving organizational ambidexterity (i.e., leadership, contextual, and structural ambidexterities) allow firms to simultaneously achieve service excellence and cost-effectiveness.

CESE-specific departures from the ambidexterity literature

Wirtz and Zeithaml (2018) observed three interesting differences in the CESE context from the traditional ambidexterity literature in management. First, it seems that all departments (albeit with different emphases) must be involved in supporting a dual culture, which differs from the traditional view of structural ambidexterity in the management literature (c.f., Gibson & Birkinshaw 2004). For example, Singapore Airlines' centralized innovation department not only focused on service and inflight product innovation but also rigorously emphasized costs. When the company launched the widest business class seat in the industry, it was designed in a way that 'wowed' travelers: the seat could be flipped over and turned into a flat bed with a duvet and bigger pillows. Because the 'flipping' was done manually, the number of heavy and engineering-intensive motors in a seat was reduced and provided significant savings in fuel, repair and maintenance, and purchase costs (Heracleous & Wirtz 2010; Tuzovic et al. 2018).

Although not completely separated structurally, dual culture organizations typically distinguish between the customer-facing front office and the back office. The front office is generally more focused on customer and service excellence than is the back office. Even at Singapore Airlines, the cost squeeze was less intense when related to inflight service excellence and cabin crew, who had extensive training, reasonable travel allowances, and expensive uniforms. In the back office, Singapore Airlines drove distributed innovation throughout the organization. As the departments were largely not customer-facing, their foci tended to be on cutting labor and other costs. But again, potential customer impact was always considered, so that service excellence would not be compromised (Heracleous & Wirtz 2010; Tuzovic et al. 2018). The front and back offices were both customer-centric and cost-conscious at the same time, and the cost and service excellence foci differed only in degree and not in substance. In sum, although structural ambidexterity can have a supporting role, it is unlikely to be a key enabler for CESE.

The focus on service excellence, although difficult to achieve, is a corporate mission that is more attractive to employees than one focusing on cost cutting and frugality. It is easier to establish buy-in from employees for the former, perhaps because they feel pride in being associated with an excellent organization (Gouthier & Rhein 2011). However, when asked to be cost-effective at the same time, employees tend to find this mission difficult to accept. That is, high productivity and cost-effectiveness combined with customer centricity can put a strain on employees. For example, in spite of Amazon's top

ACSI ratings, it did not appear anywhere on the lists of best companies to work for and was even accused of achieving its high level of productivity by squeezing employees (Nocera 2015).

In the organizations described in Wirtz & Zeithaml (2018), employee strain was mitigated by emphasizing various rationales for expecting cost-effectiveness and service excellence at the same time, to obtain employee buy-in. Examples included a mission to provide the best customer value (Amazon), appreciation that employees are working for members (Vanguard), making Michelin-starred food affordable (Ristorante D'O), and supporting a charitable cause (Narayana Health). It seems that a dual culture strategy requires a strong rationale for employees to accept that cost-effectiveness is critical, in addition to providing service excellence. That is, employees seem to need a credible 'rallying cry' to be willing to subscribe to a dual culture strategy.

In summary, it is apparent that CESE permeates the entire organization and is more complex than the typical exploration and exploitation conflict studied in management. Furthermore, the finding that leadership ambidexterity was present in all dual culture organizations studied by Wirtz and Zeithaml (2018) is consistent with work by Rust et al. (2016), who found that firms that are successful in their cost emphases tend to have it pushed down from the top. To accomplish the dual goals, senior management must build a culture of cost-consciousness and intense service excellence simultaneously (Anderson et al. 2004; Mittal et al. 2005).

Dual culture as driver of generic productivity strategies and tools

The operations management literature distinguishes between actual and potential efficiencies at a given level of variability. It identifies variability in terms of input (e.g., customer arrival patterns), process (e.g., customer process preferences), and output (e.g., customer requests) as the key factors that determine the potential level of efficiency (Chase 1978, 1981). Service organizations that want to improve efficiency can reduce the gap between their actual and potential levels of efficiency at the current level of variability (Wirtz & Zeithaml 2018). Generic productivity strategies and tools for implementing them include cost control, waste reduction, training and motivation of employees (to do things faster, better, and cheaper), improved capacity utilization, redesign of customer service processes (Breyfogle 2003; Crosby 1979; Deming 1986; Wirtz 2018), outsourcing of noncore activities (Wirtz, Tuzovic, & Ehret 2015), and service tiering to allocate resources to more important customers (Frei 2006).

These strategies keep the current business model unchanged and adopt best practices to achieve the same output – a largely unchanged customer experience – with less input. However, the service operations management literature is not typically concerned specifically with service excellence, and generic productivity strategies in themselves do not necessarily lead to service excellence. Therefore, a culture of service excellence is also required. Integrating these two literatures, it can be argued that a dual culture strategy allows organizations to drive generic productivity tools to the extreme (Heracleous & Wirtz 2010, 2014), such that employees focus on closing the gap between potential and actual efficiencies while maintaining service excellence.

Dual culture organizations must be masters of using generic productivity strategies and tools to cut costs and boost productivity, while managing for service excellence. All five of the case organizations studied by Wirtz and Zeithaml (2018) that pursued a dual culture examined every aspect of their operations to reduce costs, and used the full gamut of management, operations, and technology tools to boost productivity. For example, Ristorante D'O examined every aspect of its restaurant operations to reduce costs. It introduced multitasking (with the chefs serving the food so they did not have to employ waiters), leading to a significant reduction in labor costs. It chose glasses and plates that withstand breakage to reduce replacement costs. It located in a low rent area (situated 20 km away from the city, where rent was estimated to be half of that for restaurants in the center of Milan) and ran at a 100% capacity utilization for one lunch and two dinner shifts to reduce unit costs rather than having only one dinner seating, as is typical for Michelin-starred restaurants (Nobel 2013; Pisano, Di Fiore, Corsi, & Farri 2013).

In summary, dual culture strategy refers to organizations that achieved CESE through ambidexterity (i.e., leadership, contextual, and structural ambidexterity), making both service excellence and productivity integral parts of the organizational culture. A dual culture strategy enables organizations to deploy generic productivity strategies and tools to the extreme, and to minimize the gap between actual and potential efficiencies at an excellent level of service at a given level of process variability.

An additional observation is that organizations can increase their potential efficiencies by reducing process variability. This allows organizations to deploy specialization and industrialization tools (Frei 2006; Levitt 1972, 1976). The resulting interplay between closing the gap (between actual and potential levels of efficiencies) at a given level of uncertainty, and increasing the level of potential efficiency through variability reduction is synthesized in Figure 14.3. The next section explores how variability can be reduced to increase the potential level of efficiency.

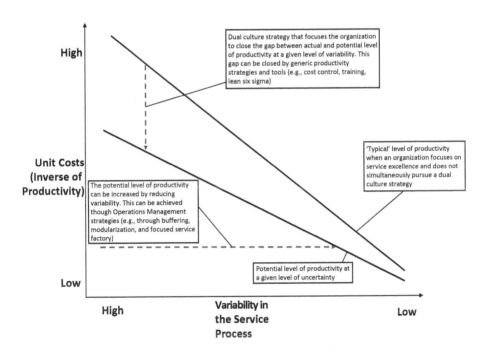

Figure 14.3 Productivity as a function of process variability; constant high level of service excellence.

Operations management approaches to reducing process variability

Much of the service operations management literature centers on how organizations can increase their levels of efficiency by reducing customer-induced variability. The term "customer-induced uncertainty" was used in early service operations research to discuss efficiency-related challenges in service organizations (Chase 1981). More recent work uses the term "variability" (e.g., in arrival times and service requests) (Frei 2006), although in marketing, variability typically relates to customization (e.g., Anderson et al. 1997). For simplicity, this chapter refers to customer-induced uncertainty, variability, and customization as 'customer-induced variability.'

From a cost-effectiveness point of view, approaches to reducing customer-induced variability require a reduction in process flexibility that involves changes both in customer behavior (e.g., giving customers a tighter script, which makes them an integral part of the service process) and customer choice (e.g., offering modular options rather than full customization). The key approaches advanced in the literature are: (1) isolating and industrializing the back office, and shifting activities from the expensive front office to the mechanized back office (Chase 1981), (2) modularizing service through reduced customer choice (Chase 1978; Frei 2006; Shostack 1987), and (3) deploying self-service technologies (SSTs) (Meuter, Bitner, Ostrom, & Brown 2005; Meuter, Ostrom, Roundtree, & Bitner 2000). Such strategies reduce process variability and, therefore, potential conflicts between productivity and service excellence. The three approaches to reducing customer-induced variability are discussed next.

First, low customer contact systems are easier to industrialize (Chase 1978, 1981), and decoupling and buffering the 'technical core' (i.e., back office) from the front office allows higher productivity in the back office, as it can operate without customer-induced variability (Chase 1981). Firms can then operate the back office in a much more cost-effective manner by deploying technology and systems, leading to a reduction of fluctuations in capacity utilization. The back office can focus on productivity and process quality, and the front office can focus on customer satisfaction and sales. This 'plant-within-a plant' approach generally results in overall higher productivity and better service quality. However, decoupling can affect the customer experience, as buffered activities move from real-time interactions between the front line and customers, to offline transactions executed by the industrialized back office.

Second, a buffered and reduced front office can be further simplified (and variability lowered) by reducing customer choice, interaction flexibility, and contact in the front office through modularization of service, allowing an increased deployment of systems and technology in the front office (Chase 1978, 1981; Frei 2006). Furthermore, reducing complexity (i.e., number and intricacy of the steps involved) and divergence (i.e., executional latitude customers and employees have available) can reduce variability and lead to uniformity enabling higher productivity, but doing so also reduces customization and customer choice (Shostack 1987).

Finally, when processes and products have been modularized and have low complexity, the deployment of SSTs, robotics, and artificial intelligence (AI) becomes easier. These technologies provide opportunities for increasing service productivity (Frei 2006; Meuter et al. 2005; Meuter et al. 2000; Wirtz et al. 2018). However, deploying such technologies and systems, including web- and app-based services and approaches to co-creation, can have a significant impact on the customer experience and require careful management of customer behavior (Collier & Sherrell 2010; Lovelock & Young 1979; Meuter et al. 2005; Wunderlich, Wangenheim, & Bitner 2012).

Although in theory these three approaches could be pursued in isolation, they tend to build on one another. For example, the National Library Board of Singapore had extensive physical customer–organization contact. Buffering front-office activities from the back office (e.g., book drops, RFID-enabled dropping of books into Singapore Post mailboxes, auto-sorting systems, and robot-assisted shelf-reading) all helped to reduce waiting times, improved availability of titles, and enhanced convenience. Modularizing the service (e.g., payment was accepted only through a low-fee cashless system) enabled the pervasive deployment of SSTs. The National Library Board's heavy focus on SSTs resulted in constant experimentation and innovation (e.g., with app-delivered services, digital services, and self-service reservation systems via lockers), and it became a globally leading library in terms of SST deployment (Menkhoff & Wirtz 2018).

Vanguard too decoupled its customer-service processes, modularized them, and then moved them to self-service platforms. It had no branches and relied almost entirely on the internet, apps, phone, and mail to interact with its customers. The result was that the typical Vanguard client required little direct contact with the organization (Heskett et al. 2015, p. 78). Even personal interactions were augmented through technology. For example, its Personal Advisor Service used analytics to match a client's investment strategy with his/her financial goals, which dramatically reduced the time needed to serve a client while enhancing advisory quality (Sunderam, Viceira, & Ciechanover 2016).

Amazon reduced its front office to a minimum. Its business model was built on use of the internet, with a pervasive use of SSTs (e.g., search, selection, payment, account management, and reviews) facilitated by modular services (i.e., highly structured processes with a few, clear options) and powerful analytics (e.g., for making recommendations). It had an almost completely buffered and industrialized back office that could run highly efficient fulfilment services (McGee, Agnew, & Hook 2017; Peters 2006; Stone 2013).

In summary, three key operations management-based approaches increase efficiencies by reducing customer-induced process variability and the related conflicts between productivity and service excellence. Unlike a dual culture approach, operations management-based approaches require changes in the customer interface and tend to reduce customer choice, interaction flexibility, and contact. Finally, the three operations management-based approaches create a natural flow of steps from (1) isolating and industrializing the back office, and shifting activities from the expensive front to the mechanized back office, to (2) modularizing service, and to (3) using SSTs, robots, and AI, whereby each step eases the implementation of the next and leads the approaches to be used in tandem (see Figure 14.4).

Focused service factory strategy

It is typically more costly to satisfy heterogeneous than homogeneous customer preferences (Fornell 1992). One way to drastically increase productivity and customer satisfaction simultaneously is to tailor a single solution to meet the exact needs of a specific segment. This approach draws from the focused factory, which typically delivers a single product to a homogeneous segment (Skinner 1974). Simplicity, repetition, homogeneity, and experience in a focused factory breed competence and the "focused factory will out produce, undersell, and quickly gain competitive advantage over the complex factory" (Skinner 1974, p. 116). A focused factory is even more effective in a service context, with its distributed operations, customer-induced variability, and need for functional integration.

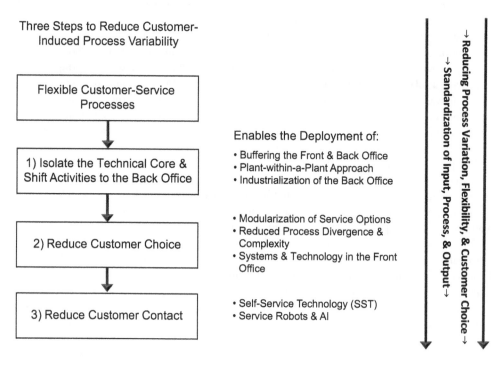

Three Steps to Reduce Customer-Induced Process Variability

Flexible Customer-Service Processes

Enables the Deployment of:

1) Isolate the Technical Core & Shift Activities to the Back Office

• Buffering the Front & Back Office
• Plant-within-a-Plant Approach
• Industrialization of the Back Office

2) Reduce Customer Choice

• Modularization of Service Options
• Reduced Process Divergence & Complexity
• Systems & Technology in the Front Office

3) Reduce Customer Contact

• Self-Service Technology (SST)
• Service Robots & AI

↓ Reducing Process Variation, Flexibility, & Customer Choice↓
↓ Standardization of Input, Process, & Output↓

Figure 14.4 Operations management approaches for achieving CESE.

Levitt (1972, 1976) extended the idea of the focused factory to high-volume services delivered through highly predictable systems that allow industrialization of services through planned, controlled, and automated processes. Tightly integrated hard, soft, and hybrid technologies together replaced labor and reduced its skill requirements, leading to high levels of productivity and consistency in quality. That is, "everything is built integrally into the machine itself, into the technology of the system" (Levitt 1972, p. 46).

For example, Narayana Health focused on cardiac surgeries. It operated a focused service factory and, compared to general hospitals, pursued a highly targeted business model. Narayana Health's focus enabled it to concentrate on surgery quality and innovation (e.g., it pioneered "beating open heart surgery") (Global Health and Travel 2014). Centralization of surgeries in a few hospitals (with larger facilities) allowed concentrated utilization and low unit costs, and drove learning and innovation. The volume of similar surgeries enabled detailed analyses and continuous improvement. Doctors received comparative performance data for 22 hospitals, including their own, encouraging them to share best practices. The high volume enabled Narayana to drive a hard bargain, especially for equipment and consumables (Global Health and Travel 2014; Govindarajan & Ramamurti 2013).

Another example of a focused service factory company is JetBlue, which offers low-cost, high-quality, operationally simple, point-to-point airline service. Its focused operations are supported by a young fleet of limited aircraft types, resulting in low maintenance costs. The airline also operates longer-haul overnight flights to increase aircraft utilization. Its operating model results in low cost per seat mile but delivers higher quality service than full-service airlines and other low-cost carriers (Harris & Lenox 2015; Trefis Team 2015). Finally, many app-based and online services follow a focused service model, whereby they offer highly standardized and tightly designed solutions to narrowly defined customer segments. Examples include fintechs that address specific financial needs (e.g., travel insurance and international money transfer).

In summary, the focused service factory serves the largely homogeneous needs of a tightly defined target segment. The resulting low variability in its operations enables these organizations to achieve both service excellence and high productivity.

Summary and discussion

This chapter discussed three strategic pathways to CESE as outlined in the conceptual framework shown in Figure 14.2.

The first pathway is an organizational strategy called 'dual culture strategy.' It focuses the entire organization on the simultaneous pursuit of service excellence and productivity. The dual culture strategy aims to provide high levels of service (including costly customization) at top quality and low cost. The service offering is wide, processes are not highly structured or standardized, and customer service is flexible and customized. This type of full service is typically expensive and inefficient to deliver. The dual culture strategy is akin to ambidextrous organizational approaches in the management literature (Raisch & Birkinshaw 2008) with a focus on leadership ambidexterity (Smith et al. 2016; Smith & Tushman 2005) and contextual ambidexterity (Gibson & Birkinshaw 2004).

The organizations that successfully achieve a dual culture strategy combine an intense focus on costs with equally passionate customer centricity and focus on service excellence. Specifically, they show an extreme deployment of generic productivity strategies and tools that allow them to minimize the gap between actual and potential efficiencies in a given service operation, while delivering service excellence. Such strategies push customer satisfaction and productivity toward best practice and the organizations have cultures that drive employees to integrate customer satisfaction and productivity when there are conflicts. Furthermore, the dual culture approach requires a rationale employees can buy into, as it seems counterintuitive to offer great service externally, but be stingy internally. Being cost conscious (especially on employee salaries and benefits) must be sold effectively to employees.

The second strategy, the operations management approach, addresses the root causes of inefficiencies in service processes through operations management approaches that reduce customer-induced variability and thereby reduce potential conflicts between productivity and service excellence. This approach deploys a combination of operations management tools that are used to reduce process variability so that systems and technologies can be increasingly deployed to deliver CESE. The tools include (1) isolating and industrializing the back office and reducing the front office by shifting activities to the industrialized back office, (2) modularization of service, and (3) using SSTs, robotics, and AI. Unlike dual culture approaches, operations management approaches typically require some degree of change in the customer interface.

The third strategy is a focused service factory that achieves CESE through a highly specialized operation, typically delivering a single type of service to a highly focused customer segment. The focused service factory features tightly defined and industrialized service processes targeted at a highly homogeneous customer base. As a result, it delivers reliably exactly what its target customers want. It also reduces customer-induced variability to a minimum – customers tend to receive a single, highly standardized, and excellent service offering.

Implementation of CESE strategies

Of the three core strategies, the dual culture strategy seems the hardest to execute. Service excellence is a natural focus of service employees (Gouthier & Rhein 2011), but cost-effectiveness is a harder sell to them. A dual culture approach requires that senior management has a convincing narrative as to why a cost focus is necessary. Senior management must drive cultures of cost-consciousness and service excellence simultaneously, which is difficult (Mittal et al. 2005). However, intensifying competition and cost pressures increasingly push organizations to seek new ways to increase efficiencies while maintaining high levels of quality. There is a palpable shift across many industries toward best practices, which typically involve a rigorous application of generic productivity strategies; a dual culture strategy may be a promising approach to moving actual efficiency levels closer to their potential.

As organizations pursue an operations management or focused service factory strategy, the systems and technology can increasingly hardwire productivity and cost-effectiveness into the business model, and employees can focus on service excellence without having to focus so heavily on costs and incremental productivity gains. This makes operations management approaches and focused service factory strategies easier to implement than dual culture strategies.

Combining CESE strategies

Conceptually, one could expect the three CESE strategies to be used in a modular manner that allows a mixing and matching of tools, while placing different degrees of emphasis on each, depending on the industry context and organizational objectives. However, examining Figure 14.1 suggests that the three core strategies can each stand alone. It is also possible for the operations management approaches and the focused service factory strategy to be combined with a dual focus strategy (Wirtz & Zeithaml 2018).

It is noteworthy that none of the configurations show a combined operations management and focused service strategy approach. Perhaps the operations management and focused service strategy both deliver a reduction in customer-induced variability so that their combination would not result in substantial sufficient incremental productivity gains. For example, organizations such as Google and Amazon have such highly standardized processes that pursuing the focused service factory strategy may not add substantial efficiency gains through a reduction in customer-induced variability.

The incremental productivity gains a dual culture strategy can offer seem to be reduced in organizations that have already implemented either the operations management approaches or the focused service factory strategy, as compared to organizations that do not pursue either of these two strategies. A full service business model, such as that of Ristorante D'O, must painstakingly identify and implement efficiency gains and cost savings in all its operations. In contrast, an organization that follows the focused service factory strategy already has dramatic cost savings from the business model itself, and the incremental savings of a dual culture tend to be small (see Figure 14.3). For example, Google was well known for its positive treatment of employees, offering high pay, free meals, sports facilities, and even massages (Groysberg, Thomas, Wagonfeld 2011; Schmidt & Rosenberg 2014, pp. 125–127). However, whether Google's employees enjoyed free massages and meals did not much affect the cost per transaction. This intense focus on scalable SSTs allowed it to be generous to its comparatively small number of employees, virtually all of whom were involved in the creation of new services rather than in providing customer service.

However, if several players pursue a focused service factory strategy, an additional dual culture strategy may be required to achieve cost leadership. For example, when Southwest Airlines was the only low-cost carrier in the passenger air travel market, it had by far the lowest operating cost in its competitive set (Lovelock 1994, pp. 78–84). As more players entered the low-cost carrier market, the benchmark shifted, and greater cost discipline was needed in order to be the most efficient player, leading back to a dual culture strategy.

Customer-induced variability as a strategic decision

The level of variability allowed in customer service processes and the resulting business model is a strategic decision. If a business model keeps variability high, it requires an extraordinary effort to achieve CESE largely through leadership ambidexterity and contextual ambidexterity to successfully execute a dual culture strategy. It is possible that variability can be reduced either on the process side through operations management approaches, or on the customer input side through the focused service factory strategy. These alternatives imply very different business models with different value propositions and customer segments.

Even within a given business model, service organizations need to be intensely aware of the cost implications of providing options, flexibility, customization, and added products and features to their customers. Complexity and variability grow exponentially and thereby reduce the level of potential productivity, while making it more difficult to deliver excellence (Shostack 1987). Therefore, it is an important strategic decision how much variability a business model should contain.

The focused service factory model offers many interesting business opportunities in both the offline and online worlds. Focused service factories typically combine smart processes and new technologies that provide tailored solutions for well-defined problems and narrowly defined customer segments (Frei 2006; Levitt 1972, 1976). For example, in healthcare, Narayana Health decided against building a general hospital that intertwined many service processes and patient segments, and therefore would have been incredibly complex and expensive without the same quality output (Global Health and Travel 2014; Govindarajan & Ramamurti 2013). The principle is simple – a specialist who only delivers a single product to a single segment will be better and have lower costs than the generalist who must cater to a wide range of customer needs.

The industrialization of service

The service sector appears to be at an inflection point with regard to productivity gains and service industrialization, similar to the industrial revolution in manufacturing that started in the 18th century (Wirtz & Zeithaml 2018). Rapidly developing technologies that become better, smarter, smaller, and cheaper are transforming virtually all service sectors. Especially exciting are the opportunities offered by developments in robotics, AI, big data, analytics, the Internet of Things, geo tagging, virtual reality, speech recognition, and biometrics. These technologies will lead to a wide range of service innovations that have the potential to dramatically improve the customer experience, service quality, and productivity simultaneously. What happened in information processing services through websites, apps, and mobile technologies seems ready to happen next for people and possession processing services; self-driving cars, drone-delivery, and largely robot-staffed hotels and restaurants will only be the beginning of this revolution.

Robot- and AI-delivered service is likely to show unprecedented economies of scale and scope as the bulk of the costs are incurred in their development. Physical robots cost a fraction of adding head count, and virtual robots can be deployed at negligible incremental costs. For example, a holograph-based humanoid robot providing service at an information counter will require only low-cost components (e.g., a projector, speaker, camera, and microphone), and fully virtual robots (e.g., voice-based chat bots) have already nearly zero incremental costs (Wirtz et al. 2018).

In summary, the frameworks discussed in this chapter offer strategic lenses through which new services can be viewed. In particular, similar to the shift that started in the industrial revolution from craftsmen to mass production, an accelerated shift in the service sector toward modular, SST, robotics, AI and focused service factory-based business models is likely to occur. As in manufacturing, the craftsman-equivalent will continue to offer a viable business model, but at a high price point. The mass market for many services is likely to shift to operations management approaches and focused service factory strategies with a rapidly increasing deployment of service robots and AI (Wirtz et al. 2018; Wirtz & Zeithaml 2018).

Further research

Because there is little research on CESE, this chapter is based/builds on Wirtz and Zeithaml's (2018) article (see note 1) and aims to be a next step in the development of a robust body of knowledge. There is a wealth of further research opportunities linked to studying a broader set of service organizations that achieved CESE. A stronger cross-fertilization and integration of the literature on customer satisfaction, service quality, and service excellence, the management literature on organizational ambidexterity, and the operations management literature on service productivity are needed. Table 14.1 highlights a number of suggestions for further research on the questions surrounding the simultaneous pursuit of service excellence and productivity.

Table 14.1 Research questions related to the integration of service excellence and productivity

Future research topics	Research questions
Financial outperformance of CESE strategies	• Organizations that successfully achieve a dual strategy reap the highest long-term financial return compared to organizations that focus on either customer satisfaction or productivity alone (Mittal et al. 2005). However, those that pursue but not achieve CESE underperform, and it is not clear what explains this underperformance. One hypothesis is that achieving CESE is more difficult than a strategy focusing on either customer satisfaction or productivity and that therefore more organizations fail to achieve their goals.
The satisfaction– productivity trade-off	• It would be interesting to measure the presence of the three root causes of the satisfaction–productivity trade-off across service organizations and link them to organizational performance. That is, do firms that handle these root causes well also perform better in terms of customer satisfaction, productivity, and financial performance?
	• There is little research that explores under what conditions customer satisfaction and productivity conflict are positively aligned, or are independent of each other. A better understanding is needed of what determines the relationship between these two variables.

(Continued)

Table 14.1 (Cont.)

Additional pathways to CESE	• It would be interesting to explore whether there are other pathways in addition to the three identified by Wirtz and Zeithaml (2018) to CESE. For example, would a stronger innovation culture and a resulting deeper adoption of technology (e.g., robotics and AI) compared to industry also allow the successful pursuit of a CESE strategy?
Drivers and barriers of CESE implementation	• Wirtz and Zeithaml (2018) explored organizations that successfully implemented a CESE strategy. However, it would also be of interest to examine organizations that pursued but did not succeed in achieving CESE. This would help to identify the potential drivers and barriers of CESE success and the interplay of the three CESE strategies.
Implementing a CESE strategy	• Current research explored successful organizations that pursued a CESE strategy but remains silent on how an organization can embark on a journey toward CESE. Research is needed to explore how the knowledge of change management in general (Kotter 1995) and driving rapid service improvements in particular (Wirtz & Kaufman 2016a, 2016b) can be applied to CESE
CESE culture and organizational ambidexterity	• The ambidexterity literature has examined the pursuit of conflicting organizational goals along a number of variables but cost-effectiveness versus service excellence has not been studied yet. It seems worthwhile examining these goals in the context of the ambidexterity literature, including its measurement and antecedents.
	• Further research seems warranted to explore whether the relative importance of leadership, contextual, and structural ambidexterity is a function of the service organization-specific root causes of the customer satisfaction–productivity trade-off.
	• Research is needed to better understand how the different types of ambidexterity can be successfully infused into an organization's culture and climate. For example, how can supportive contexts for ambidexterity emerge, and focus and energize the organization on CESE? How important are reward and recognition systems, and leaders' role modelling of the desired ambidextrous behaviors? Is leadership ambidexterity a necessary but not sufficient condition for achieving contextual and structural ambidexterity in service organizations with their cross-functional integration needs? How can individual employees be enabled and encouraged to exercise their judgment in successfully dealing with conflicting demands?
Leadership, contextual, and structural ambidexterity	• Empirical research is needed to confirm the observation by Wirtz and Zeithaml (2018) that all departments including those with an exploration focus had a service excellence and a productivity focus at the same time, and whether this observation is driven by the nature of services and the related root causes of the service excellence–productivity trade-off.
	• Empirical research is needed to validate the Wirtz and Zeithaml (2018) case observation that dual culture organizations distinguish between the customer-facing front office and the back office, and that the cost and service excellence foci differ only in

(*Continued*)

Table 14.1 (Cont.)

		degree and not in substance. One can hypothesize that the closer a unit is to customers, the stronger the focus will be on service excellence.
	•	The observation that employees need a credible 'rallying cry' to be willing to subscribe to a dual culture strategy and that cost-consciousness needs to be 'sold' to employees to gain their buy-in (Wirtz & Zeithaml 2018) warrants empirical testing. Future research is needed to explore when, why, and how employees buy into a CESE strategy.
Components of operations management approaches	•	Empirical research is needed to explore whether the three operations management approaches are mostly used together and build on one another, or whether they can also be used in isolation and/or with differing levels of intensity. For example, people processing services may require a much tighter approach to reducing process variability than information processing services. Here, robotics and AI may potentially offer new ways to use these operations management approaches. Unlike front line employees who would have to be trained for many different types of services, such training is fully scalable for AI (Wirtz et al. 2018).
Relative advantage of a focused service factory	•	The potential outperformance of the focused service factory seems to be higher for people and physical possession processing services such as hospitals, restaurants, and car repair workshops as it is more expensive to deal with customer-induced variability in these contexts. Here, distributed capabilities and facilities limit productivity potential and the focused service factory seems to be able to offer much more significant cost savings and quality advantages over a service operation with a wider scope. In contrast, information processing services may offer more possibilities to deal with customer-induced uncertainty as AI will increasingly be able to deal with such issues. For example, a call center 'manned' by voice-based chat bots will be able to deal with a much wider range of questions and transactions compared to a call center manned by people (Wirtz et al. 2018). Further research is needed to understand better which of the CESE strategies suit best for certain service characteristics.

In summary, this chapter aims to help academics and practitioners alike to better understand the potential approaches to a CESE strategy and to encourage more research in this area. A large number of references are provided to assist those who wish to engage in further reading.

Note

1 This chapter is based on and extends the article by Jochen Wirtz and Valarie Zeithaml (2018), "Cost-Effective Service Excellence," *Journal of the Academy of Marketing Science* 46 (1), 59–80. This article is available for download at https://link.springer.com/article/10.1007/s11747-017-0560-7/, and all parts of it can be copied, distributed, and reprinted freely under the terms of the Creative Commons Attribution 4.0 International License and the Creative Commons license at https://creativecommons.org/licenses/by/4.0/.

References

Aksoy, L., Cooil B., Groening C., Keiningham T. L., & Yalcin A.. (2008). The Long-Term Stock Market Valuation of Customer Satisfaction. *Journal of Marketing* 72 (4), 105–122.

American Customer Satisfaction Index (ACSI). (2017). www.theacustomer satisfactioni.org accessed April 15, 2017.

Anand, G. (2009). The Henry Ford of heart surgery. *Wall Street Journal* Eastern Edition, published 11/21/2009, 254(122), A1, A12.

Anderson, E. W., Fornell C., & Mazvancheryl S. K.. (2004). Customer Satisfaction and Shareholder Value. *Journal of Marketing* 68 (4), 172–185.

Anderson, E. W., Fornell C., & Rust R. T.. (1997). Customer Satisfaction, Productivity, and Profitability: Differences between Goods and Services. *Marketing Science* 16 (2), 129–145.

Benner, M. J., & Tushman M. L.. (2003). Exploitation, Exploration, and Process Management: The Productivity Dilemma Revisited. *Academy of Management Review* 28 (2), 238–256.

Bogle, J. C. (2002). *Character counts: The creation and building of The Vanguard Group.* New York: McGraw-Hill.

Booms, B. H., & Bitner M. J. (1981). Marketing strategies and organization structures for service firms. In J. H. Donnelly & W. R. George (Eds.), *Marketing of services* (pp. 47–51).Chicago, IL: American Marketing Association.

Breyfogle, F. W. (2003). *Implementing six sigma.* Hoboken, NJ: John Wiley & Sons.

Chase, R. B. (1978). Where Does the Customer Fit in a Service Operation? *Harvard Business Review* 56 (6), 137–142.

Chase, R. B. (1981). The Customer Contact Approach to Services: Theoretical Bases and Practical Extensions. *Operations Research* 29 (4), 698–706.

Cheshes, J. (2015). Davide Oldani of D'O restaurant expands his empire: After taking things slow with his affordable, michelin-Star eatery outside Milan, the chef is opening new locations this summer. *Wall Street Journal* (Online), retrieved from http://libproxy1.nus.edu.sg/login?url=http://search.proquest.com.libproxy1.nus.edu.sg/docview/1667372596?accountid=13876 accessed March 22, 2017.

Collier, J. E., & Sherrell D. L.. (2010). Examining the Influence of Control and Convenience in a Self-Service Setting. *Journal of the Academy of Marketing Science* 38 (4), 490–509.

Collins, J. C., & Porras J. I.. (1994). *Built to last: Successful habits of visionary companies.* New York: HarperCollins.

Crosby, P. B. (1979). *Quality Is free.* New York: McGraw-Hill.

Deming, E. W. (1986). *Out of the crisis.* Boston, MA: MIT Center for Advanced Engineering Study.

Fornell, C. (1992). A National Customer Satisfaction Barometer: The Swedish Experience. *Journal of Marketing* 56 (1), 6–21.

Fornell, C., Mithas S., Morgeson III F. V., & KrishnanM. S.. (2006). Customer Satisfaction and Stock Prices: High Returns, Low Risk. *Journal of Marketing* 70 (1), 3–14.

Frei, F. X. (2006). Breaking the Trade-Off between Efficiency and Service. *Harvard Business Review* 84 (11), 93–101.

Gibson, C. B., & Birkinshaw J.. (2004). The Antecedents, Consequences, and Mediating Role of Organizational Ambidexterity. *Academy of Management Journal* 47 (2), 209–226.

Global Health and Travel. (2014). Dr. Devi Shetty: Maverick, Crusader, and Caregiver. 40–46.

Gouthier, M. H. J., & Rhein M.. (2011). Organizational Pride and Its Positive Effects on Employee Behavior. *Journal of Service Management* 22 (5), 633–649.

Govindarajan, V., & Ramamurti R.. (2013). Delivering World-Class Health Care, Affordably. *Harvard Business Review* 91 (11), 117–122.

Grönroos, C., & Ojasalo K.. (2004). Service Productivity: Towards a Conceptualization of the Transformation of Inputs into Economic Results in Services. *Journal of Business Research* 57 (4), 414–423.

Groysberg, B., Thomas D. D., & WagonfeldA. B.. (2011). *Keeping Google 'Googley.'* Boston, MA: Harvard Business School Publishing.

Gupta, S., & ZeithamlV. (2006). Customer Metrics and Their Impact on Financial Performance. *Marketing Science* 25 (6), 718–739.

Harris, J.D., & Lenox, M.J. (2015), The Battle for Logan Airport: JetBlue Airways versus American Airlines, Case #UV6980, Charlottesville, VA, Darden Business Publishing, The University of Virginia.

Heracleous, L., & Wirtz J.. (2010). Singapore Airlines' Balancing Act: Asia's Premier Carrier Successfully Executes a Dual Strategy: It Offers World-Class Service and Is a Cost Leader. *Harvard Business Review* 88 (7/8), 145–149.

Heracleous, L., & Wirtz J.. (2014). Singapore Airlines: Achieving Sustainable Advantage Through Mastering Paradox. *Journal of Applied Behavioral Science* 50 (2), 150–170.

Heskett, J. L., Sasser W. E., Jr., & SchlesingerL. A.. (2015). *What great service leaders know & do*. Oakland, CA: Berrett-Koehler Publishers.

Kamakura, W. A., Mittal V., De Rosa F., & Mazzon J. A.. (2002). Assessing the Service Profit Chain. *Marketing Science* 21 (3), 294–317.

Keiningham, T. L., Aksoy L., Williams L., & Buoye A.. (2015a). *The wallet allocation ruse: Winning the battle for share*. Hoboken, NJ: John Wiley & Sons.

Keiningham, T. L., Cooil B., Malthouse E. C., Buoye A., AksoyL., De KeyserA., & Larivière B. (2015b). Perceptions are Relative: An Examination of the Relationship between Relative Satisfaction Metrics and Share of Wallet. *Journal of Service Management* 26 (1), 2–43.

Kotter, J. P. (1995). Leading Change: Why Transformation Efforts Fail. *Harvard Business Review* 73 (2), 59–67.

Kumar, V., Dalla Pozza I., & GaneshJ.. (2013). Revisiting the Satisfaction–Loyalty Relationship: Empirical Generalizations and Directions for Future Research. *Journal of Retailing* 89 (3), 246–262.

Levitt, T. (1972). Production-Line Approach to Service. *Harvard Business Review* 50 (5), 41–52.

Levitt, T. (1976). The Industrialization of Service. *Harvard Business Review* 54 (5), 63–74.

Lovelock, C. H. (1992). The search for synergy: What marketers need to know about service operations." In C. H. Lovelock (Ed.), *Managing services: Marketing, operations, and human resources* (pp. 392–405).Englewood Cliffs, NJ: Prentice Hall.

Lovelock, C. H. (1994). *Product plus: How product + service = competitive advantage*. New York: McGraw-Hill.

Lovelock, C., & Young R. F.. (1979). Look to Consumers to Increase Productivity. *Harvard Business Review* 3 (1979), 168–178.

Lubatkin, M. H., Simsek Z., Ling Y., & Veiga J. F.. (2006). Ambidexterity and Performance in Small- to Medium-Sized Firms: The Pivotal Role of Top Management Team Behavioral Integration. *Journal of Management* 32 (5), 646–672.

Marinova, D., Ye J., & Singh J.. (2008). Do Frontline Mechanisms Matter? Impact of Quality and Productivity Orientations on Unit Revenue, Efficiency, and Customer Satisfaction. *Journal of Marketing* 72 (2), 28–45.

McGee, P., Agnew H., & Hook L.. (2017). Amazon's no-checkout store threatens death of the cashier. *Financial Times*, www.ft.com/content/e89f5c3e-bd55-11e6-8b45-b8b81dd5d080 accessed March 25, 2017.

Menkhoff, T., & Wirtz J.. (2018). National Library Board Singapore: World-class service through innovation and people centricity. In J. Wirtz & C. Lovelock (Eds.), *Services marketing: People, technology, strategy*. (8th Edition). Instructor Resources.https://www.researchgate.net/publication/326587122_National_Library_Board_Singapore_World-Class_Service_through_Innovation_and_People_Centricity

Meuter, M. L., Bitner M. J., Ostrom A. L., & BrownS. W.. (2005). Choosing among Alternative Service Delivery Modes: An Investigation of Customer Trial of Self-Service Technologies. *Journal of Marketing* 69 (2), 61–83.

Meuter, M. L., Ostrom A. L., Roundtree R. I., & BitnerM. J. (2000). Self-Service Technologies: Understanding Customer Satisfaction with Technology-Based Service Encounters. *Journal of Marketing* 64 (3), 50–64.

Mittal, V., Anderson E. W., Sayrak A., & Tadikamalla P.. (2005). Dual Emphasis and the Long-Term Financial Impact of Customer Satisfaction. *Marketing Science* 24 (4), 544–555.

Nocera, J. (2015). The Amazon way. *New York Times*. August 21, 2015, in Section A, 17.

Oliver, R. L. (2010). *Satisfaction: A behavioral perspective on the consumer*. Armonk, NY: M.E. Sharpe.

O'Reilly, C. A., III, & Tushman M. L.. (2013). Organizational Ambidexterity: Past, Present, and Future. *Academy of Management Perspectives* 27 (4), 324–338.

Peters, K. (2006). Amazon, which stresses self-service, is tops in customer service survey, internet retailer. www.digitalcommerce360.com/2006/11/03/amazon-which-stresses-self-service-is-tops-in-customer-service accessed March 25, 2017.

Pisano, G., Di Fiore A., Corsi E., & Farri E. (2013). *Chef Davide Oldani and Ristorante D'O*. Boston, MA: Harvard Business School Publishing, HBS. No. 9-613-080.

Nobel, C. (2013). D'O: Making a Michelin-Starred Restaurant Affordable. HBS Working Knowledge; see: https://hbswk.hbs.edu/item/do-making-a-michelin-starred-restaurant-affordable. I have also marked in the text where Pisano should be replaced by Nobel.

Porter, M. E. (1980). *Competitive advantage: Creating and sustaining superior performance*. New York: Free Press.

Porter, M. E. (1996). What Is Strategy? *Harvard Business Review* 74 (6), 61–78.

Raisch, S., & Birkinshaw J. (2008). Organizational Ambidexterity: Antecedents, Outcomes, and Moderators. *Journal of Management* 34 (3), 375–409.

Rust, R. T., & Huang M. H. (2012). Optimizing Service Productivity. *Journal of Marketing* 76 (March), 47–66.

Rust, R. T., Moorman C., & DicksonP. R. (2002). Getting Return on Quality: Revenue Expansion, Cost Reduction, or Both? *Journal of Marketing* 66 (4), 7–24.

Rust, R. T., MoormanC., & van Beuningen J. (2016). Quality Mental Model Convergence and Business Performance. *International Journal of Research in Marketing* 33 (1), 155–171.

Rust, R. T., Zahorik A. J., & Keiningham T. L.. (1995). Return on Quality (ROQ): Making Service Quality Financially Accountable. *Journal of Marketing* 59 (April), 58–70.

Schmidt, E., & Rosenberg J.. (2014). *How Google works*. London: John Murray.

Shostack, L. G. (1987). Service Positioning through Structural Change. *Journal of Marketing* 51 (1), 34–43.

Singh, J. (2000). Performance Productivity and Quality of Frontline Employees in Service Organizations. *Journal of Marketing* 64 (2), 15–34.

Skinner, Wickham. 1974. "The Focused Service Factory." *Harvard Business Review* 52 (3), 113–121.

Smith, W. K., Lewis M. W., & Tushman M. L.. (2016). 'Both/And' Leadership: Don't Worry So Much about Being Consistent. *Harvard Business Review* 94 (5), 62–70.

Smith, W. K., & Tushman M. L. (2005). Managing Strategic Contradictions: A Top Management Model for Managing Innovation Streams. *Organization Science* 16 (5), 522–536.

Stone, B. (2013). *The everything store: Jeff Bezos and the age of Amazon*. New York: Little, Brown and Company.

Sunderam, A., Viceira L., & Ciechanover A.. (2016). The Vanguard Group, Inc. in 2015: Celebrating 40. Boston, MA: Harvard Business School Publishing.

Swaminathan, V., Groening C., MittalV., & ThomazF. (2014). How Achieving the Dual Goal of Customer Satisfaction and Efficiency in Mergers Affects a Firm's Long-Term Financial Performance. *Journal of Service Research* 17 (2), 182–194.

Trefis Team. (2015). A closer look at JetBlue's strategy. *Forbes*, www.forbes.com/sites/greatspeculations/2015/10/15/a-closer-look-at-jetblues-strategy/print accessed March 28, 2017.

Tuzovic, S., Wirtz J., & Heracleous L.. (2018). How Do Innovators Stay Innovative? A Longitudinal Case Analysis. *Journal of Services Marketing* 32 (1), 34–45.

Umashankar, N., Bhagwat Y., & KumarV. (2016). Do Loyal Customers Really Pay More for Services? *Journal of the Academy of Marketing Science* 22 (2), 99–113.

Watson, G. F., IV, Beck J. T., Henderson C. M., & Palmatier R. W. (2015). Building, Measuring, and Profiting from Customer Loyalty. *Journal of the Academy of Marketing Science* 43 (6), 790–825.

Wirtz, J. (2018). *Service quality and productivity management*. Winning in Service Markets Series Vol. 12. Hackensack, NJ: World Scientific.

Wirtz, J., & Kaufman R.. (2016a). Revolutionizing Customer Service. *Harvard Business Review* 94 (4), 26–27.

Wirtz, J., & Kaufman R. (2016b). LUX: Staging a service revolution in a resort chain. In J. Wirtz & C. Lovelock (Eds.), *Services marketing: People, technology, strategy* (8th Edition) 728–743. Hackensack, NJ: World Scientific.

Wirtz, J., Mattila A. S., & Lwin M. O. (2007). How Effective Are Loyalty Reward Programs in Driving Share of Wallet? *Journal of Service Research* 9 (4), 327–334.

Wirtz, J., Patterson P., Kunz W., Gruber T., Lu V. N., Paluch S., & Martins A. (2018). Brave New World: Service Robots in the Frontline. *Journal of Service Management* 29 (5), 907–931.

Wirtz, J., Xiao P., Chiang J., and Malhotra N. (2014), Contrasting Switching Intent and Switching Behavior in Contractual Service Settings, Journal of Retailing, 90 (4), 463–480.

Wirtz, J., Tuzovic S., & Ehret M. (2015). Global Business Services Increasing Specialization and Integration of the World Economy as Drivers of Economic Growth. *Journal of Service Management* 26 (4), 565–587.

Wirtz, J. & Zeithaml V. (2018). Cost-Effective Service Excellence. *Journal of the Academy of Marketing Science* 46 (1), 59–80. This article is distributed under the terms of the Creative Commons Attribution 4.0 International License, see https://link.springer.com/article/10.1007/s11747-017-0560-7 and the Creative Commons license at https://creativecommons.org/licenses/by/4.0/.

Wunderlich, N. V., Wangenheim F. V., & Bitner M. J. (2012). High Tech and High Touch: A Framework for Understanding User Attitudes and Behaviors Related to Smart Interactive Services. *Journal of Service Research* 16 (1), 3–20.

Part IV
Service design, delivery, and customer engagement

15

Service digitization and the provider-to-customer handoff

Eileen Bridges, Charles F. Hofacker, and
Chi Kin (Bennett) Yim

Introduction

It may be argued that, in an active and increasingly specialized economy, busy consumers increasingly engage service workers to complete tasks for which they do not have time; these tasks typically require physical labor (e.g., yard work or meal preparation). On the other hand, digital technology allows many information-based (i.e., intangible) service tasks to be completed more quickly and easily, whether by service employees or by the customer directly. Therefore, completion of the latter type of task tends to migrate in the opposite direction, from service employees to consumers. For example, in the past, medical doctor schedules were kept in physical form, such that patients who wanted to make an appointment would have to either call the office or visit in person. This function is now often handled using a self-service technology (SST). However, other aspects of a medical visit may not yet be available in a virtual form. For instance, medical doctors typically require patients to visit the office in person in order to receive a diagnosis and/or prescription. Therefore, it is possible that additional tasks involved in a medical visit could be virtualized in the future; in fact, some physicians are already offering online visits for more common and benign ailments, and prescriptions are being sent electronically for fulfillment.

Other information-based service processes are already largely digitized. For instance, tasks such as investigating travel options, making reservations, handling purchase of tickets, checking in, and obtaining virtual boarding passes or room keys may be completed entirely by a customer using SSTs. Thus, these customers engage in technology-based self-service (TBSS), according to Dabholkar (1996). Some service processes have partially migrated to consumers, with tasks such as placing an order for groceries or clothing utilizing SSTs; however, the remainder of the process (which requires physical labor) continues to be completed by service providers, including packaging and delivery of items. The present chapter considers the set of all service processes executed in the economy that do not require physical labor. Some subset of the tasks involved in these processes is performed by service employees and another subset of these tasks, formerly executed by employees, is performed by customers using SSTs. During a particular period of time, some elements of the former subset (i.e., tasks performed by employees) migrate into the latter subset (i.e., performed by customers). The purpose of this chapter is to better understand which service processes tend to migrate from service providers to customers, when, and why.

To organize thought regarding which current employee processes are already or will be digitized and then operated directly by customers, service processes may be described as either *physical* (e.g., baggage handling) or *informational* (e.g., providing flight information) categories. These two categories reflect "tangible" and "intangible" core service processes, as defined by Lovelock (1983). Among informational processes, Lovelock (1983) identified "mental stimulus processing" as acting upon a person, and "information processing" as acting upon a possession. Another way of viewing informational processes is to identify them as either: (1) those enabled by digital storage and communication (e.g., providing account balances) or (2) those enabled by digital computation and processing (e.g., investment advice). The latter elements may be sub-divided into sensing/signal processing (e.g., voice recognition) and higher-order cognition/symbolic processing (e.g., artificial intelligence (AI)). This chapter takes as its domain the full range of informational service processes, and describes the process by which they are moved into SSTs.

A particular service encounter may require many tasks that include both tangible and intangible elements, and operate on either people or their possessions. This chapter proposes that a firm's decision to digitize a particular informational task in a service process depends, in addition to social and cultural considerations, on technical aspects such as the labor costs involved in carrying out the task manually, the number of states required to digitally model the task, and the number of times the task must be repeated (Hilbert 2014a, b). Perhaps more importantly, if the newly digitized task is to be carried out by consumers, issues such as sensory needs, relationship preferences, synchronization requirements, and needs for identification and control must also be considered in making the decision to virtualize for customer use (Overby 2008).

In summary, the focus of this chapter is on informational service processes and tasks which can be digitized; the goal is to examine which individual tasks and complete processes are likely to migrate to SST form, and how customer and firm adoption considerations affect this migration. To narrow the focus of the chapter, the assumption is made that processes and/or tasks which are handed off to customers have been virtualized prior to making the handoff. Therefore, there are two situations to consider: (1) the process is currently handled by employees in person, but is digitized to hand off to customers, and (2) the process has already been digitized for employees and is handed off to customers using similar technology. From the firm's point of view, situation (1) is more complex, because the service process must first be digitized; situation (2) might be viewed as simpler because the technology is already available and may require only minor modification for customer use. From the customer point of view, it does not matter whether the firm faces situation (1) or (2); customers are presumed to adopt a digitized version of the service task or process and to begin using TBSS at the time of the handoff. Therefore, it is equally important in both situations for the firm to understand and consider potential customer reactions before deciding to hand off the service process to customers in the form of an SST.

The *conceptual development* section begins by providing background on adoption of SSTs to position this chapter within the relevant research streams. Next, it looks at the customer point of view, including elements that may encourage or discourage use of an SST. It continues by considering this topic from the firm's point of view, examining literature that relates to development of new SSTs as well as trial and continuing use of existing SSTs. Next, it goes into firm considerations when making a decision to invest in an SST, as well as customer decisions regarding use of SSTs. Background regarding how a firm might decide when to invest in digitizing a service process, and when to hand it off to customers for their direct use is also described. The chapter continues with some qualitative predictions regarding service processes that will be handled by customers using digital technology, based on the conceptual framework that is developed.

Conceptual development

The SST lifecycle

For the first half-century of their existence, telephone calls required operator assistance. Beginning in 1951, long distance calls could be self-dialed, and it would be humorous to refer to placing a call as an "SST." (Even use of the word 'dialed' is long out of date!) This observation illustrates how successful SSTs follow an evolutionary process that begins with a digitizable innovation and finishes with ubiquity (Brodie, Winklhofer, Coviello, & Johnston 2007; Hennig-Thurau et al. 2010). Thus, the spread of a successful digital innovation follows a sort of diffusion process, penetrating the population at an increasing rate (Parasuraman 2000) until virtually all potential customers have adopted (i.e., the innovation reaches ubiquity, as illustrated in Figure 15.1). At this point, the service process is no longer considered an SST, because it is perceived as always performed by customers, and is no longer compared to a provider-performed service.

Of course, in some cases an innovation fails and the related SST does not reach ubiquity; this possibility is also shown in Figure 15.1. Another possibility is that a particular innovation is replaced by some superior SST that comes along later. For instance, it is not yet known whether a sufficient number of consumers will adopt device-driven home security/operation systems to permit these products to continue in their present forms. If an insufficient number of consumers adopt, it would become too expensive to continue updating software and delivering these digital products; consequently, those brands already on the market might fade away. Alternatively, the present device-driven technology might be replaced by some more advanced technological breakthrough.

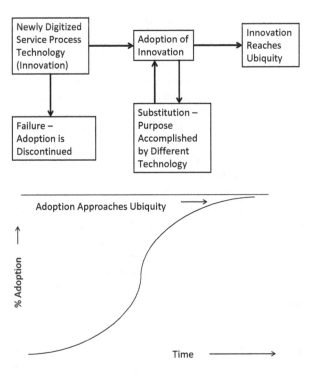

Figure 15.1 Dynamic process of adoption of SST.

Although possibly transparent to the user, a new digital technology could potentially accomplish the same purpose more conveniently and/or at lower cost. In this example, the current digitized service process for home security/operation would not reach ubiquity.

As mentioned above, the goal of this chapter is to identify the set of service tasks now performed by employees (either in person or using a virtual interface) that will migrate to SSTs in the near future, and to better understand the reasons behind firm decisions to migrate. Although the approach taken in this chapter is more descriptive than prescriptive, it is clear that understanding the decision to introduce new SSTs is quite important. Ceteris paribus, as the number of service employees declines, productivity increases. On the other hand, as SSTs emerge and productivity increases, corresponding sectors of the economy will suffer downturns in employment. (Aside from these societal level phenomena, predicting future adoption patterns for SSTs would be useful in identifying service investment opportunities.) More germane to the present purpose is the fact that within larger firms, the marketing and IT functions are most involved in developing and managing SSTs and have an inherent interest in understanding their evolution (Bridges & Hofacker 2016). Both disciplines would benefit from a positive theory that anticipates the SST cycle illustrated in Figure 15.1 and facilitates strategic thinking. For academics in business disciplines, this positive theory suggests important future research topics, and perhaps even cycles of research categories.

To review, the goal for this chapter is to address the following question: of all the informational service tasks and processes that are currently performed by employees, which will soon be performed by customers with the help of information technology? The literature review continues below with a more detailed look at the customer and provider points of view on service process digitization.

Service innovation and the customer point of view

There are substantial streams of research focused on service innovation leading to new SSTs as well as on factors that enhance customer adoption of these SSTs. For instance, Meuter, Bitner, Ostrom, and Brown (2005) distinguish between characteristics of the innovation and characteristics of the consumer, and use both to understand and predict consumer trial of an SST. There is also some extant literature on ubiquitous SSTs, describing the state that follows in the wake of near-universal customer adoption, as pictured in Figure 15.1 (see e.g., Hennig-Thurau et al. 2010). However, there is very little in the literature on continuing use of SSTs; for a notable exception, see the work of Prins, Verhoef, and Franses (2009). Of course, continuing use is typically related to customer satisfaction, and there is a growing literature on customer satisfaction with SSTs.

From the literature on service innovation, Brohman et al. (2009) make use of service dominant logic to better understand the evolution of SSTs, and go on to identify and test several principles that assist firms in improving the design of SSTs. Later work by Ordanini, Parasuraman, and Rubera (2014) takes a closer look at the specific needs of customers who wish to deal with service providers in an online environment. Such digitized service processes invite the customer to participate in value co-creation experiences (Prahalad & Ramaswamy 2004). An early means of assessing a customer's willingness to do so was provided by the "Technology Readiness Index" (TRI) proposed by Parasuraman (2000). This instrument allows measurement of the challenges and frustrations faced by customers who move from receiving personal service to using SSTs. Matthing, Kristensson, Gustafsson, and Parasuraman (2006) tested the instrument among a sample of consumers, finding that it successfully identifies innovative customers who are highly creative and willing to adopt new technology. The effects of each of the dimensions of the TRI instrument (innovativeness, optimism, discomfort, and insecurity) were confirmed as predictors of acceptance, adoption, and usage of internet-related technologies by Lam, Chiang, and Parasuraman (2008). Parasuraman and Colby (2015) improved and updated the TRI scale by reducing the total number of items required, revising retained items for relevance (i.e., appropriateness for current technologies), and including new items to enhance the scale's usefulness.

Some of the issues that affect customer adoption of TBSS relate to convenience (Berry, Seiders, & Grewal 2002) and other improvements in the service encounter experience, often based on use of SSTs (Bitner, Brown, & Meuter 2000). To assess this, Dabholkar (1996) conducted a qualitative, interview-based study of key characteristics of TBSS options, finding that required time, effort, and complexity of a digitized service process, reliability and accuracy of the outcome, and overall enjoyment influence customer perceptions of service quality. In addition, Dabholkar (1996, p. 35) mentions that control is "quite relevant for evaluating technology-based self-service options," even though its importance is not clearly supported in the study.

Several authors observe that the general attitude of customers toward technology as well as situational influences can impact their likelihood of adopting TBSS (Bobbitt & Dabholkar 2001; Dabholkar 1996; Dabholkar & Bagozzi 2002; Parasuraman 2000). Furthermore, customers who desire human interaction tend to have lower likelihood than others of selecting TBSS (Bobbitt & Dabholkar 2001; Dabholkar & Bagozzi 2002; Forman & Sriram 1991); these customers are more likely to select an option that offers in-person service. Bobbitt and Dabholkar (2001) argue that a unifying theory is needed to describe how customer attitudes can be used to predict adoption of TBSS. In particular (p.424), they specify that "consumers are more likely to use technology-based self-service if it offers them a sense of control, and if they do not have to wait to use it."

Specific influences on adoption of a TBSS are offered by Dabholkar and Bagozzi (2002), who observe that not only do individual characteristics such as novelty seeking, technology self-efficacy, and low need for personal interaction enhance adoption of technology, but situational factors such as waiting time and anxiety may also. Dabholkar, Bobbitt, and Lee (2003) find that consumer differences, situational influences, and attributes of the technology are all reasons that consumers do or do not adopt use of a TBSS. Other researchers suggest that customer adoption of e-services depends on such drivers as organizational reputation, relative advantage, and perceived risk (DeRuyter, Wetzels, & Kleijnen 2001).

In regard to customer satisfaction, which relates directly to continuing use of SSTs, Meuter, Ostrom, Roundtree, and Bitner (2000) examine categories of critical incidents and customer satisfaction with SSTs. Their results indicate customers will choose TBSS if it offers benefits over personal service and helps in difficult situations. Pires, Stanton, and Rita (2006) find that customers are empowered and receive greater control when using TBSS; because they have the power to choose among more available options, loyal customers are increasingly valuable to firms. Similarly, Prahalad and Ramaswamy (2004) observe that customer value is created by a personalized customer experience; thus, the interaction between firm and customer both creates and extracts value.

To ascertain customer levels of satisfaction with TBSS (specifically websites), Parasuraman, Zeithaml, and Malhotra (2005) developed the "E-S-Qual" scale, which measures customer perceptions of efficiency, fulfillment, system availability, and privacy. These authors also briefly considered service recovery in an online environment, but very small incidences of failure led to insufficient numbers of respondents to complete the analysis. Customer satisfaction with use of SST has been investigated in specific categories of online services, including retailing (Wolfinbarger & Gilly 2003) and business-to-business services (Pujari 2004). Efficiency, reliability, and security are found to be very important to customer satisfaction, and service recovery is also a crucial issue. Other authors that looked at service recovery in TBSS situations include Dabholkar and Spaid (2012), who found that dissatisfaction owing to technology failure can be mitigated by interpersonal interaction with an employee, but that this in itself increases negative attributions to the technology. In a related study, Reinders, Dabholkar, and Frambach (2008) observed that involuntarily moving customers from a full service situation into one where the service personnel are replaced by TBSS can result in negative customer attitudes.

In summary, customers are more likely to welcome an SST when it offers improved convenience, perceptions of control, and an overall better user experience. In addition, consumers who have low need for personal interaction and are comfortable with technology are more likely to adopt TBSS. They prefer a process that reduces time and effort requirements and is less complex; the service should also be enjoyable to use (possibly offering novelty) and provide a reliable and accurate outcome.

Service innovation and the firm point of view

From the service firm's point of view, SST introductions are not always rosy (Bendapudi & Leone 2003; Brady, Saren, & Tzokas 2002). However, implementation of SSTs can be strategically transforming and should be carefully considered (Brodie et al. 2007). In fact, Brodie et al. (2007, p. 3) observed "a positive relationship between the intensity of e-Business adoption and firm performance." This section of the chapter follows up by describing literature on topics that relate to pros and cons of transferring a service process to the customer in the form of an SST, from the firm point of view.

Some of the issues that must be considered in replacing customer–provider interactions with technology-based interfaces are addressed by Overby (2008). According to Overby (2008), process virtualization theory (PVT) identifies four inhibitors that negatively impact the virtualizability of service processes from the firm's point of view: sensory requirements, relationship requirements, synchronism (i.e., immediate results) requirements, and identification and control (i.e., process involvement) requirements. Given these inhibitors that can reduce the appropriateness of SSTs for particular service tasks or processes, firms may need to provide more personal interfaces; these would allow customers to use their five senses to evaluate products and/or would facilitate interpersonal relationships for customers that prefer in-person service to technology-based interaction. Furthermore, specific timing requirements and/or the need for identification or other process inputs may affect the choice of interface.

As part of transforming service processes from provider-operated to customer-operated SSTs, it is important to identify design and functionality to maximize the increase in usage with respect to potential usage (Piccoli, Brohman, Watson, & Parasuraman 2004). Piccoli et al. (2004) developed a taxonomy that describes customer needs amenable to online fulfillment and studied the evolution of website design accordingly, noting areas for potential improvement. These authors observed that change occurs quickly, soon after a firm adopts TBSS, and slows as the technology matures, consistent with the shape of a diffusion curve approaching ubiquity. Boyer, Hallowell, and Roth (2002) provided a detailed case study illustrating this type of successful introduction of TBSS, its adoption by customers, and subsequent retention. Another article that studies managing and improving e-service quality from the firm point of view is that by Field, Heim, and Sinha (2004). These authors developed a process model for an e-service system, and examined it at the component level to identify areas where quality improvements were needed. Finally, Bauer, Falk, and Hammerschmidt (2006) examined a specific example of such an e-service system, identifying five quality dimensions critical to online shopping, including functionality/design, enjoyment, process, reliability, and responsiveness.

Returning to the idea that it is not always appropriate for a firm to adopt SSTs or encourage their customers to engage in TBSS, Åkesson and Edvardsson (2008) identified five categories of change required when certain government services move online, including the service encounter/process, customers as co-creators/sole producers of services, efficiency, integration, and complexity. (The latter issue is discussed further in a later section of this chapter.) Barnes, Hinton, and Mieczkowska (2004) also urge caution, following their observation that a move to e-commerce can result in conflicts between the technology adopted and the management of operations. In other words, the technology may be inconsistent with the overall business strategy, which may require changes to the technology and/or redesign of operations.

Combining firm and customer points of view: co-production and the service blueprint

When considering whether to move a service process from the firm to customer use of TBSS, Chan, Yim, and Lam (2010) observed that customer participation can help and/or harm co-creation of value. This occurs due to the combination of improvements in customization and control for customers as well as additional effort required to obtain it. Building on this background, Yim, Chan, and Lam (2012) examined how customer participation in co-creation of value can be enjoyable, resulting in increased satisfaction. Mende, Scott, Bitner, and Ostrom (2017) looked at the opposite extreme: they considered what happens when co-production is allocated to customers, in situations where they may not wish to assume the burden, and/or are ill-equipped to do so. Subsequently, they evaluated customer response to the allocated workload, finding that it may require additional organizational support, and may or may not improve customer satisfaction, depending on individual differences. Finally, Rust and Huang (2014) examined how firms respond to nearly ubiquitous customer use of communication technology, finding that service becomes more personalized through use of increasingly sophisticated analytics. Huang and Rust (2018) built on this background to enhance understanding of how this technological change leads to new definitions of work in services. Specifically, AI first replaces more analytical service provider tasks; as it improves, it is expected to begin to replace more intuitive and empathetic skills as well. Thus, as AI improves more sophisticated service tasks increasingly become candidates for migration.

Another way of looking at what occurs as technology permits customers to perform more service processes for themselves is to represent the changes in a stylized service blueprint, shown in Figure 15.2. In this example, tasks that move into the customer domain are relocated to positions above the line of interaction, showing that customers assume tasks previously performed by service providers. This idea was pioneered by Letheren, Russell-Bennett, and Mulcahy (2018). It is also of interest where the tasks are taken from when this occurs. Some of the tasks taken on by customers might be those previously completed directly by front line employees: such tasks, which were previously just below the line of interaction (and typically visible to customers), can be more physical tasks involving tangible service processes, which are modified as such for compatibility with self-service. However, despite the presence of counterexamples, it is more common for informational tasks to be taken on by customers following a migration to TBSS. Such tasks, typically those which were previously below the line of internal interaction (i.e., embedded well within the firm and hidden from the viewpoint of the customer), often include those that were already digitized for employee use, which tend to be easier to migrate to TBSS than those which have not yet been virtualized.

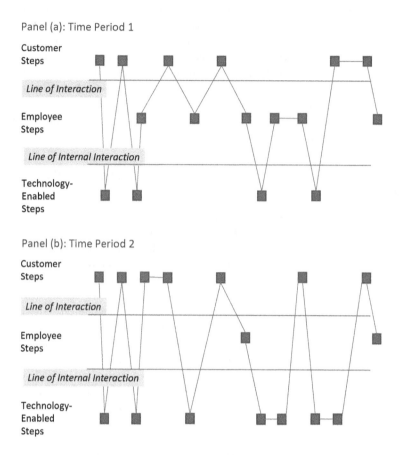

Figure 15.2 Changes in a service blueprint as customers take over tasks using SSTs.

Figure 15.2 shows lines of interaction and internal interaction that separate tasks assigned to customers, employees, and technology. Between panels (a) and (b) in the figure, these lines move such that more tasks are performed digitally by customers, whereas fewer tasks are performed by employees. In panel (a) of Figure 15.2, Time Period 1 is illustrated with a specific mixture of tasks or steps in the service process performed by employees, by customers, and by technology. In panel (b), the mixture has shifted, because in Time Period 2 some tasks previously executed by employees are executed by customers using TBSS, which may be based on a new SST or perhaps a more powerful version of a previous SST.

Campbell, Maglio, and Davis (2011, p. 184) suggest five steps involved in shifting the service boundary between provider and customer:

(1) defining value from the customer's perspective; (2) mapping the current service boundary between provider and customer so that their respective activities are clearly laid out; (3) mapping the proposed boundary shift in which opportunities for shifting the boundary are identified and analyzed; (4) identifying the resources that are required by both the service provider and its customers to co-create value at the new boundary position; and (5) executing the service boundary shift, putting the proposed shifts into practice.

The service digitization decision

This section develops an organizational scheme linking the application of digital technology to development of SSTs. Also included is a description of how complexity underlies decisions regarding SST development.

Service process evolution

Evolution of digitized SSTs represents a subcategory of service process evolution; the more general case is illustrated in Figure 15.3. New SSTs emerge in the upper right-hand corner; this is followed by service employee processes being digitized or replaced by technology, and customers beginning to take over tasks that are digitized through TBSS. In some luxury examples, employees take over a task previously performed by digital technology; for example, a high-end hotel might have a personal assistant help a high value guest, allowing them to skip the kiosk and receive personal, human attention.

The allocation problem

One way for a firm to consider the issues involved in making the decision to digitize a particular service process and hand it off to customers for direct use is called the 'allocation problem,' because it is concerned with allocating tasks between machines and humans. The idea in the allocation literature is to assign tasks to humans and machines based on what 'Men Are Best At' and what 'Machines Are Best At,' otherwise known as the 'MABA-MABA' approach. Much of this literature is rooted in 'Fitts' list'; among other tasks, Fitts (1951, p. 10) listed "reasoning inductively," "improvising," and "using flexible procedures" as things that humans do relatively better, whereas "responding quickly to control signals" and "applying great force smoothly and precisely" were tasks listed as better suited to machines. A more recent analysis was done for the service sector by Huang and Rust (2018), who focused on four categories of abilities (mechanical, analytical, intuitive, and empathetic) that are required to perform tasks. AI is viewed as taking

Task Now Performed by:

Task Previously Performed by:	Employee	Customer	Technology
Employee		Self-Service	Automation
Customer	New Service		New e-Service
Technology	Luxury Service	TBSS	

Figure 15.3 Categorization of service evolution paths.

over these types of tasks sequentially, beginning with those requiring mechanical abilities. Thus, these findings are consistent with those of Fitts, in that both view the decision (whether to assign a task to humans or technology) from the perspective of the abilities required to perform the task.

An organizational scheme for making SST development decisions

For the present purposes, it is useful to categorize service tasks and processes based on some information-theoretic notions. This section recommends an organizational scheme for SST design based on three basic types of information system capabilities, and on subcategories of those three capabilities. The three fundamental informational capabilities include data storage, communication, and computation/analysis, as described by Hilbert and López (2011). Changes to digital SST capabilities can be classified into these three groups, providing a clear picture of how SSTs evolve over time. In the following discussion, storage and communication are combined for simplicity.

Storage and communication

To date, most SSTs have been enabled by improvements in firm abilities to store or communicate digital information. The long distance dialing SST mentioned at the beginning of the *conceptual development* emerged when firms created a way for customers to communicate the desired number directly to the switchboard. SSTs based on storage and communication capabilities can be thought of as 'pass-through' SSTs, because the firm passes access or information through to the customer and thereby substitutes customer cognitive and physical processes for (more costly) employee processes. For example, online banking became possible when financial institutions developed ways to provide stored customer financial data over the internet. Online travel sites and airline self-booking became possible when firms learned to communicate stored flight data across the internet and present it appropriately to the customer. In offline retailing, some stores use digital technology to offer self-service checkout, providing customers with direct access to the information systems that underlie point-of-purchase technology such as cash registers, scales, and so forth. Online retailing goes a step further, offering customers pass-through access to see and command firm inventory and fulfillment systems. In this and similar cases, the customer acquires 'read' access, and even 'write' capability, to stored information that was previously accessible only to employees.

Another example of SSTs is based on changes in the retailing of information products. For instance, iTunes is implemented as an SST whereby music is sold directly to the customer, who then gets access to the raw data file. This abrupt change in the supply chain for music provides an example of the disruption that can be created when electronic channels are run directly from corporate storage to the consumer, allowing transfer of music, video, or books. To anticipate where new SSTs in this category might be expected, it is reasonable to look for economic sectors that still require a firm employee to access information or information systems. For instance, an airline or the post office might require employee intervention for access to lost baggage or lost package information, respectively. Other examples might include providing private, identity-related access to healthcare data or educational materials.

Computation

Compared to storage and communication, there are fewer examples of computation or processing extant in the current economy; however, improvements in computational speed, developments in AI, and the recent appearance of 'born digital' firms imply that new developments may accelerate the pending disruption of service workplaces and markets. For the purpose of this chapter, computation is further split into two categories: signal processing and symbolic processing, the latter of which tends to emulate higher-order cognitive processes.

Signal processing

This section discusses human sensory processes and how they are incorporated into technology-based service provision. One type of sensory process encompasses balance, equilibrioception, and the vestibular, which are senses capable of receiving gravity, body movement, angular momentum, or acceleration information. Similar sensors are now routinely built into handheld devices that can modify the orientation of a screen depending on the angle at which it is held. Developments in this area are driving improved robotic walking gaits through outside or inside spaces. Newer industrial robots have integrated vision systems based on detection of electromagnetic radiation, allowing them to recognize objects in different orientations. Visual signal processing is at the heart of automated systems' abilities to read analog documents and convert them to text. Developments in automated driving, such as those being made by Google, foretell important changes to the transportation sector. Improvements in machine hearing have been rapid in recent years, leading to new forms and increased use of telephonic SSTs. These systems are becoming more capable and developments are changing the nature of the input to other SST systems, such as Apple's Siri interface. Although these developments are automated, as opposed to being used by customers in the form of TBSS, the technologies involved may eventually address some of the concerns expressed by Overby (2008), in that they allow service processes having more sensory requirements to potentially be virtualized.

Although not as far along at present, new developments might be anticipated in the senses of touch, pain perception, temperature, taste, smell, echolocation, detection of polarized light, electrical current, and pressure (Clark 2013). In these examples, capabilities are apparent that are not always analogous to human capabilities. For example, long wavelength infrared detectors might notice customers in a store before a clerk does.

Symbolic processing and the meaning of complexity

As mentioned above, the second type of computation is symbolic processing, which takes place at a higher level of abstraction than does signal processing, because it uses symbols to represent information. Here, it is necessary to broach the management of SST complexity, the resulting programming cost, and the representation of such complex information in the context of the firm's decision-making. Because of the difficulties involved in symbolic processing, it is important to comprehend the meaning of complexity.

The present usage of the term 'complexity' is consistent with Shostack's notion, which is "the number and intricacy of the steps required to perform" a service process (Shostack 1987, p. 35). Shostack (1987, p. 36) also refers to "divergence," or the "executional latitude stemming from the judgment and decisions of the individual performing the service." Thus, divergence represents the amounts of flexibility and customization potential that are present. It is clear that divergence produces additional (hidden or stored) states in the blueprint, such as table lookup processes whereby the provider finds a good match between a customer's taste and product feature combinations, which lead to greater complexity. (Thus, divergence is a service blueprint term used to indicate the presence of multiple possible states, which are not explicitly drawn.) However, note that complexity may occur without divergence, whereas increased divergence leads to increased complexity.

Another reason for considering the complexity involved in digitizing service processes and offering additional SSTs is proposed by Benedettini, Swink, and Neely (2017, p. 114), who argue that supporting more complex services can result in "loss of focus, complexity of coordination and potential increase in … uncertainty." This can impact customers and, consequently, it is important to verify trade-offs between the value to customers of additional services (such as SSTs) and their costs in terms of both investment and risk in making the decision to digitize. Issues to consider include resource consistency and cash flow synergy over time, alongside any improvements that can be obtained in product positioning and customer satisfaction.

Complexity may also be considered from the customer point of view. Customers prefer not to deal with increases in complexity (Rogers 1983), so if changes to a service (such as digitizing it and offering SSTs) result in greater complexity for the customer, this could make the service unattractive and actually reduce adoption. Therefore, in making the decision to digitize a service process, firms must consider any additional costs to the customer as well as their own costs. Considering the service blueprint in Figure 15.2, the discussion about complexity must evaluate the whole service, not just the part that is on the customer side of the line of interaction. Depending on how the digitization is done, it is possible that complexity for the customer may decrease even though there is more complexity overall (which must be dealt with by the firm). For instance, if switching several tasks from personal handling to use of digital technology by the employee does not involve the customer (i.e., these tasks are invisible from the customer point of view), this may increase complexity for the employee while complexity for the customer might stay the same or even decline. However, it is important to note that the complexity of digitizing those steps can influence the cost of virtualizing the service process, because the firm must then figure out how to turn the steps into an algorithm.

Firms may wish to consider which type(s) of programming complexity will be involved in digitizing a particular service process; these may be due to execution time, execution (memory) space, and/or program size required. Program size complexity may be most important to making the decision regarding shifting from personal service to an SST, because this investment must be borne by the firm up front. Because time and memory are less expensive in digital form than in human form, it is anticipated that, after the programming work is done, the investment can begin to pay for itself.

Digitizing a service process and the SST development decision

Clearly it is more difficult to create SSTs by digitizing complex service processes as compared to simple service processes. As mentioned earlier, the number of states required by a service blueprint can be used as a rough measure of the complexity of that service. One advantage of this measure is that the number of states is closely tied to the cost of programming required to digitize the service process (Binmore & Samuelson 1992). Thus, a given service process is more amenable to digitization when it will be repeated a large number of times as compared to a onetime event: it is not worth investing in the technology if it won't be used repeatedly. In effect, there is a trade-off between costly lack of elegance or parsimony of the algorithm, and savings based on the number of times the algorithm will be repeated on behalf of the firm. However, the cost of producing elegant software can be reduced through design techniques such as recursion, modularity, and reusability. If a firm has accumulated software objects that employ such techniques and the know-how to utilize them, it may be easier to justify a more elegant digital approach. The presence of open-source software may also appear to offer opportunities to reduce cost; however, this also incurs added risk, owing to the fact that it is not adequately tested for firms that wish to utilize it as part of a product. Typically, such firms will need to invest in both customizing and testing the software; this is particularly true for unique and/or divergent service processes. One additional concern with regard to this approach is that the number of program steps required to implement a service process cannot be known in advance (Chaitin 1975; Sipser 2006).

Anticipating applications of technology

This section uses the framework described qualitatively in the previous sections to link information and choices regarding application of technology to development of SSTs. In particular, the chapter focuses on SSTs that are digitized service tasks or processes performed by customers; these tasks and processes were previously performed by employees, in either in-person or digitized forms. Thus, as new SSTs emerge, customers take over technology-based performance of informational tasks and processes previously carried out by service employees. Viewed as such, this evolution to SSTs represents a subcategory of service process evolution. This is true for two reasons. First, instead of evolving to SSTs, service processes may instead evolve into being 'automated,' which implies having no active human intervention; therefore, automated tasks are different from SSTs, which inherently require active customer participation. Second, in yet another type of evolution, service processes may move from being completed by employees to being completed by customers in person, particularly if they require physical tasks rather than informational tasks. This chapter considers only those informational service tasks and processes performed by employees that transition to being performed by customers using SSTs. Furthermore, the scope of the chapter is limited to SSTs for informational processes that are implemented using digital technology. In this situation, the term 'TBSS' is used to clarify that customers serve themselves using digitized or technology-based service processes.

Technology usage by the customer

Before considering a firm's decision regarding movement of service tasks or processes to SSTs, this section provides additional detail on consumer acceptance and value placed on availability of digital self-service. Specifically, the chapter focuses on informational service processes carried out by consumers in virtual form, regardless of whether they were previously handled by service employees digitally or in person. Therefore, an evaluation of a particular task for its SST potential can be facilitated by better understanding customer needs and desires within this scope.

Success of online services, such as retailing, indicates that consumers would like to be able to obtain information, evaluate products, and place orders online. However, they may not believe that they will be able to accomplish the full range of tasks in a service process virtually. For instance, Overby (2008) indicates that consumers may require a human interface when they need to use their five senses to evaluate products and/or when they wish to interact in person with a front line service provider. In addition, specific timing requirements and/or the need for identification or other process inputs may affect consumer preference for a human or virtual interface. Bobbitt and Dabholkar (2001) provide consistent results, observing that online services may be selected over in-person services due to perceptions of waiting time (i.e., synchronism), fun, and ease of use (i.e., process involvement). In addition, Dabholkar (1996) found that consumers prefer an interface offering greater ease of use, enjoyment, and control, all of which are increasingly available virtually. Consistent with this, Moon, Kim, Choi, and Sung (2013) observed that online shoppers can meet needs for personal interaction by engaging socially with an avatar. This is particularly true as a virtual interface becomes more anthropomorphic (i.e., human-like), according to Moon (2000).

In a different type of study focusing on consumer preference for SSTs in evaluating and controlling electricity usage, Russell-Bennett et al. (2017) found that customers prefer to use an interface that offers greater functional value, ease of use, convenience of on-demand availability, fun, and reward programs. In summary, consumers wish to obtain value, but they do not want to deal with added complexity to obtain it; they also want ease of use and convenience. Thus, across a range of industries, consumers have been found to prefer an SST when it offers functional value (i.e., ability to accomplish tasks, convenience, and ease of use), hedonic value (i.e., fun and enjoyment), and control, without increasing the difficulty of use.

In summary, from the consumer point of view, a virtual interface or SST is preferred when it is not necessary to use five senses to evaluate products, when a personal relationship is not needed, if specific timing requirements are important, and when greater control is perceived over the process and/or outcome. Furthermore, not only do consumers want functionality, convenience, and control, they want these advantages without incurring costs (such as increased complexity or difficulty of use), and they want additional fun and enjoyment. Thus, there is a high bar to overcome when converting informational tasks previously performed by service employees into SSTs.

Technology development by the firm

Predictions regarding future task and process migration

Which service processes and tasks currently performed by employees are firms more likely to migrate to SSTs? The characteristics and variables that drive these decisions may be small and seemingly minor, such as issues related to specific difficulties of creating the software for an SST, or as large as overarching concerns of senior executives, possibly related to external issues, or to the size and scope of the conversion project. It is important to work through the anticipated computational (and especially symbolic) processing aspects of the service process that will need to be implemented in digital form to create the SST. Perhaps, even more importantly, qualitative comments should be obtained regarding how to assess influences on migration of informational service processes from employees to customer-interfacing SSTs. Current innovations in AI focus on perception, reasoning, and inference. Therefore, a new wave of digitized processes is anticipated that will disrupt the service sector, as many informational tasks (e.g., computationally difficult verbal tasks) are moved to SSTs. This section contains thoughts related to these topics.

Identifying tasks to digitize

The allocation literature reflects on whether tasks should be automated or handled in person; one potentially useful contribution in this literature is Fitts' (1951) list. Specifically, this list suggests that tasks requiring inductive reasoning, flexible procedures, and use of improvisation and judgment are better allocated to humans, whereas tasks requiring response to control signals, performance of repetitive tasks, and use of deductive reasoning are best handled by machines. Therefore, because the focus of this chapter is on which tasks can be handed off to customers in a digitized form for use in TBSS, this literature is helpful. It can assist in advising firms as to which service tasks (and entire processes) previously performed by employees will add the most value and successfully migrate to SSTs. Those tasks made available through TBSS will include non-repetitive tasks requiring the ability to be flexible and think quickly, using inductive reasoning and judgment, because they will be operated by customers. On the other hand, repetitive tasks that require response to control signals and deductive reasoning may be digitized in order to be automated.

As mentioned earlier, PVT (Overby 2008) recommends that firms considering virtualizing service tasks or processes identify the potential impact of sensory, relationship, synchronism, and identification/control requirements. If customers will be able to use their five senses to evaluate products, form interpersonal relationships, meet specific timing requirements, and provide identity and/or other process inputs as needed, then the task(s) may be candidates for digitizing and providing in SST form. Because of innovations in AI, it is becoming possible to address an increasing array of sensory requirements, so it is anticipated that more service tasks and processes should be candidates for virtualization. The changing trade-off will increasingly rely on having good potential for signal processing capacity improvements, which will make them attractive to migrate to SSTs. AI is also expected to facilitate an increased ability to meet requirements related to relationships, timing, and identification/control, which will allow additional tasks to migrate to SSTs.

Considerations related to creating software for task digitization

The decision to virtualize an informational service process to obtain an SST for use by customers is not a simple decision. After considering the needs of the customers and the costs and benefits to the firm, it is also important to evaluate its potential for representation (i.e., the ability to present relevant information in a virtual form), reach (i.e., the ability to serve customers across time and space), and monitoring capability (i.e., the ability to authenticate participants and track activity), according to Overby (2008).

Because of the need to develop software representing service tasks and processes, the firm must commit to and then manage these projects, including such mundane aspects as tracking progress, collating modules for repeated use, and observing change over time in the tasks taken on by outsourced software companies (or in-house programming departments). Because of modularity, software has become an asset that can be deployed in the front and/ or back offices. Thus, there is a mix of administrative and production costs involved in developing and using software, which change as task complexity increases. Firms must assess the costs of complexity that accrue in production of software, and use this information in making subsequent digitization decisions. For this reason, Pekkarinen and Ulkuniemi (2008) observe that some organizational aspects of services themselves are increasingly similar to organizing software projects (even to the terminology such as 'modularity').

Specific issues meriting consideration in future research that investigates firm choice (as to when to introduce an SST to replace an employee–customer interaction) include the following.

1   The more times the same employee action will be repeated, the better the prospects for conversion to an SST. The 'same action' refers to actions that share identical service blueprint tasks or processes. An action might be repeated within-customer, as in the case that the customer's preferences might lead to a similar action, or between-customer, as in the case that there is modest or no heterogeneity of customer preferences.
2   The higher the labor cost per service process, the better the prospects for digitizing and converting to TBSS. Specifically, assuming that labor markets are reasonably efficient, firms pay employees when they cannot practically replace them with digitized customer interfaces. The higher the unit labor cost, the more motivated the firm is to try to replace each employee with less expensive software.
3   Because programming costs are typically related to the complexity of the service task or process, the simpler that is, the better the opportunity for digitizing. The number of

service blueprint activities that describe the task or process can be used as a rough guideline for judging the complexity of the interaction.

In summary, issues related to a firm's decision to build the software for migrating informational tasks from being carried out by employees to being offered in digitized SST form fall into three categories. First, the task type must be evaluated, because more routine tasks need not be handled by either employees or customers and may be automated. If a particular task is not fully automated (i.e., it requires human input), then it may be a candidate to move from (in-person or digital) employee effort to SST form, to be handled virtually by customers using TBSS. Second, the task should be evaluated to determine whether or not it will be possible to meet sensory, relationship, synchronism, and identification/control requirements if it is digitized. Finally, it will be important to assess whether the task can be digitized cost-effectively. This means evaluating how frequently the task is repeated, the cost of using employees to handle the task, and programming costs, which are related to task complexity.

Conclusion

This chapter, informed by literature and offering a qualitative framework for firm decision-making, develops a basis for thought regarding which informational service tasks and processes will migrate from employee handling to customer handling. Two situations are within the scope of the chapter. The first is a task or process that is performed by employees in person, and is digitized to hand off to customers in a virtual format. The second type of task or process has already been digitized for employee use; therefore, fewer changes are required to hand off to customers in the form of SSTs. By offering the service tasks to customers to carry out using TBSS, it is important to note that the tasks are not being automated: automation refers to tasks that are performed without human intervention. Thus, the chapter offers some thoughts on future investments in SSTs and conversion decisions that allow TBSS.

Consumers are increasingly willing to use SSTs to carry out their own informational service processes. For instance, airport kiosks for self-check-in, ATMs for self-service financial transactions, and online restaurant reservations all require that the consumer adds (primarily) digital input to a specific virtual service system. The general category of e-tail self-service technology substitutes consumer labor for front line service provider labor. Thinking about websites like WebMD and TurboTax makes it clear that technology can already, at least to some degree, substitute for professional services as well. Online financial calculators, calendars that remind the user of important meetings, and book recommendation systems are other examples of digitized services. Mobile devices offer electronic payment (making the bank teller redundant) and travel mapping (making a guide redundant). In fact, a mobile mapping service, as used with a GPS device or smartphone, is technically a new e-service, because the role of guide is particular to the tourism context, and travel routing is useful in a variety of contexts.

The focus in this chapter is on information-based services; the primary goal is to assess which types of these services are most likely to move from provider delivery to consumer effort, implemented via SSTs. Several characteristics have been identified that appear to increase the desirability of a particular service to move to TBSS in the near future. The chapter also details issues from both the customer and firm points of view to assess the decision from both sides. From the consumer point of view, use of TBSS is more attractive if it is not necessary to use the five senses to evaluate products, when a personal relationship is not needed, if specific timing requirements are important, and when greater personal control is perceived. Thus, consumers want greater functionality and convenience, without having to deal with increased complexity or difficulty of use.

From the firm point of view, some of the concerns are similar. For instance, for an informational service process to be made available to customers using an SST, it must be evaluated to ensure that it will be possible to meet sensory, relationship, synchronism, and identification/control requirements. In addition, firms must determine that the task can be digitized cost-effectively, which involves assessing how frequently the task is repeated, the cost of using employees rather than customers to handle the task, and programming costs (which are related to task complexity).

Predicting future adoption potential of SSTs would be useful in identifying investment opportunities for service businesses. However, more germane to the present purpose is the fact that within firms the marketing and IT functions are most involved in developing and managing SSTs and have an inherent interest in understanding their evolution (Bridges & Hofacker 2016). Both disciplines can benefit from a positive theory that anticipates the SST cycle as illustrated in Figure 15.3 and which therefore facilitates strategic thinking. For academics in business disciplines, the positive theory suggested in this chapter provides important future research topics, and perhaps even cycles of research categories.

This chapter has described a qualitative framework to evaluate which informational service tasks and processes that are currently performed by service employees (either in person or using a virtual interface) will soon be performed by customers with the help of information technology. A number of issues have been identified that are pertinent to firm decisions to move these tasks into TBSS contexts. Future research should address creation of metrics to assess the qualitative issues that are identified here. In addition, it would be helpful to better understand consumer preferences regarding features as well as situational usage of virtual and in-person interfaces.

References

Åkesson, M. & Edvardsson, B. (2008). "Effects of e-Government on Service Design as Perceived by Employees," *Managing Service Quality*, 18(5), 457–478.

Barnes, D., Hinton, M. & Mieczkowska, S. (2004). "The Strategic Management of Operations in E-Business," *Production Planning & Control*, 15(5), 484–494.

Bauer, H. H., Falk, T. & Hammerschmidt, M. (2006). "EeeTransQual: A Transaction Process-Based Approach for Capturing Service Quality in Online Shopping", *Journal of Business Research*, 59(7), 866–875.

Bendapudi, N. & Leone, R. P. (2003). "Psychological Implications of Customer Participation in Co-Production," *Journal of Marketing*, 67(1), 14–28.

Benedettini, O., Swink, M. & Neely, A. (2017). "Examining the Influence of Service Additions on Manufacturing Firms' Bankruptcy Likelihood," *Industrial Marketing Management*, 60, 112–125.

Berry, L. L., Seiders, K. & Grewal, D. (2002). "Understanding Service Convenience," *Journal of Marketing*, 66(3), 1–17.

Binmore, Kenneth G. & Samuelson, L. (1992). "Evolutionary Stability in Repeated Games Played by Finite Automata," *Journal of Economic Theory*, 57(2), 278–305.

Bitner, M. J., Brown, S. W. & Meuter, M. L. (2000). "Technology Infusion in Service Encounters," *Journal of the Academy of Marketing Science*, 28(1), 138–149.

Bobbitt, M. L., & Dabholkar, P. A. (2001). "Integrating Attitudinal Theories to Understand and Predict Use of Technology-Based Self-Service: The Internet as an Illustration," *International Journal of Service Industry Management*, 12(5), 423–450.

Boyer, K. K., Hallowell, R. & Roth, A. V. (2002). "E-services: Operating Strategy: A Case Study and a Method for Analyzing Operational Benefits," *Journal of Operations Management*, 20(2), 175–188.

Brady, M., Saren, M. & Tzokas, N. (2002). "Integrating Information Technology into Marketing Practice: The IT Reality of Contemporary Marketing Practice," *Journal of Marketing Management*, 18(5–6), 555–577.

Bridges, E., & Hofacker, C. F. (2016). "Service Marketing and Adoption of Promotional Technology: A Qualitative Study," *Service Science*, 8(4), 368–385.

Brodie, R. J., Winklhofer, H. M., Coviello, N. E. & Johnston, W. J. (2007). "Is E-Marketing Coming of Age? An Examination of the Penetration of E-Marketing and Firm Performance," *Journal of Interactive Marketing*, 21(1), 3–31.

Brohman, K. M., Piccoli, K., Martin, P., Zulkernine, F., Parasuraman, A., & Watson, R. T. (2009). "A Design Theory Approach to Building Strategic Network-Based Customer Service Systems," *Decision Sciences*, 40(3), 403–430.

Campbell, C. S, Maglio, P. P., & Davis, M. M. (2011). "From Self-Service to Super-Service: A Resource Mapping Framework for Co-Creating Value by Shifting the Boundary between Provider and Customer," *Information Systems and E-Business Management*, 9(2), 173–191.

Chaitin, G. J. (1975). "A Theory of Program Size Formally Identical to Information Theory," *Journal of the Association for Computing Machinery*, 22(3), 329–340.

Chan, K. W., Yim, C. K., & Lam, S. S. K. (2010). "Is Customer Participation in Value Creation a Double-Edged Sword? Evidence from Professional Financial Services across Cultures," *Journal of Marketing*, 74(3), 48–64.

Clark, L. (2013). Study: Echolocation algorithm maps cathedral in 3D to the millimetre," *Wired Magazine*, visited at www.wired.co.uk/article/echolocation-app, last visited October 30, 2018.

Dabholkar, P. A. (1996). "Consumer Evaluations of New Technology-Based Self-Service Options: An Investigation of Alternative Models of Service Quality," *International Journal of Research in Marketing*, 13(1), 29–51.

Dabholkar, P. A. & Spaid, B. I. (2012). "Service Failure and Recovery in Using Technology-Based Self-Service: Effects on User Attributions and Satisfaction," *Service Industries Journal*, 32(9), 1415–1432.

Dabholkar, P. A., Bobbitt, L. M., & Lee, E-J. (2003). "Understanding Consumer Motivation and Behavior Related to Self-scanning in Retailing: Implications for Strategy and Research on Technology-Based Self-Service," *International Journal of Service Industry Management*, 14(1), 59–95.

Dabholkar, P. A., & Bagozzi, R. P. (2002). "An Attitudinal Model of Technology-Based Self-Service: Moderating Effects of Consumer Traits and Situational Factors," *Journal of the Academy of Marketing Science*, 30(3), 184–201.

DeRuyter, K., Wetzels, M., & Kleijnen, M. (2001). "Customer Adoption of E-Service: An Experimental Study," *International Journal of Service Industry Management*, 12(2), 184–207.

Field, J. M., Heim, G. R., & Sinha, K. K. (2004). "Managing Quality in the e-Service System: Development and Application of a Process Model," *Production and Operations Management*, 13(4), 291–306.

Fitts, P. M. (1951). *Human engineering for an effective air-navigation and traffic-control system*. Washington, DC: National Research Council.

Forman, A. M., & Sriram, V. (1991). "The De-Personalization of Retailing: Its Impact on the 'Lonely' Consumer," *Journal of Retailing*, 67(2), 226–243.

Hennig-Thurau, T., Malthouse, E. C., Friege, C., Gensler, S., Lobschat, L., Rangaswamy, A., & Skiera, B. (2010). "The Impact of New Media on Customer Relationships," *Journal of Service Research*, 13(3), 311–330.

Hilbert, M. (2014a). "Technological Information Inequality as an Incessantly Moving Target: The Redistribution of Information and Communication Capacities Between 1986 and 2010," *Journal of the Association for Information Science & Technology*, 65(4), 821–835.

Hilbert, M. (2014b). "How Much of the Global Information and Communication Explosion Is Driven by More, and How Much by Better Technology?" *Journal of the Association for Information Science & Technology*, 65(4), 856–861.

Hilbert, M. & López, P. (2011). "The World's Technological Capacity to Store, Communicate, and Compute Information," *Science*, 6018, 692–693.

Huang, M-H., & Rust, R. T. (2018). "Artificial Intelligence in Service," *Journal of Service Research*, 21(2), 155–172.

Lam, S. Y., Chiang, J., & Parasuraman, A. (2008). "The Effects of the Dimensions of Technology Readiness on Technology Acceptance: An Empirical Analysis," *Journal of Interactive Marketing*, 22(4), 19–39.

Letheren, K., Russell-Bennett, R. & Mulcahy, R. (2018). Making the invisible, visible: Humanised technology for low-contact services, Paper presented at *Frontiers in Service*, Austin, TX, September 6-9, 2018.

Lovelock, C. H. (1983). "Classifying Services to Gain Strategic Marketing Insights," *Journal of Marketing*, 47(3), 9–20.

Matthing, J., Kristensson, P. Gustafsson, A. & Parasuraman, A. (2006). "Developing Successful Technology-Based Services: The Issue of Identifying and Involving Innovative Users," *Journal of Services Marketing*, 20(5), 288–297.

Mende, M., Scott, M. L. Bitner, M. J., & Ostrom, A. L. (2017). "Activating Consumers for Better Service Coproduction Outcomes Through Eustress: The Interplay of Firm-Assigned Workload, Service Literacy, and Organizational Support," *Journal of Public Policy & Marketing*, 36(1), 137–155.

Meuter, M. L., Bitner, M. J. Ostrom, A. L., & Brown, S. W. (2005). "Choosing among Alternative Service Delivery Modes: An Investigation of Customer Trial of Self-Service Technologies," *Journal of Marketing*, 69(2), 61–83.

Meuter, M. L., Ostrom, A. L. Roundtree. R. I., & Bitner, M. J. (2000). "Self-Service Technologies: Understanding Customer Satisfaction with Technology-Based Service Encounters," *Journal of Marketing*, 64(3), 50–64.

Moon, J. H., Kim, E., Choi, S. M., & Sung, Y. (2013). "Keep the Social in Social Media: The Role of Social Interaction in Avatar-Based Virtual Shopping," *Journal of Interactive Advertising*, 13(1), 14–26.

Moon, Y. (2000). "Intimate Exchanges: Using Computers to Elicit Self-Disclosure from Consumers," *Journal of Consumer Research*, 26(4), 323–339.

Ordanini, A., Parasuraman, A., & Rubera, R. (2014). "When the Recipe Is More Important Than the Ingredients: A Qualitative Comparative Analysis (QCA) of Service Innovation Configurations," *Journal of Service Research*, 17(2), 134–149.

Overby, E. (2008). "Process Virtualization Theory and the Impact of Information Technology," *Organization Science*, 19(2), 277–291.

Parasuraman, A. (2000). "Technology Readiness Index (TRI): A Multiple-Item Scale to Measure Readiness to Embrace New Technologies," *Journal of Service Research*, 2(4), 307–320.

Parasuraman, A. & Colby, C. L. (2015). "An Updated and Streamlined Technology Readiness Index: TRI 2.0," *Journal of Service Research*, 18(1), 59–74.

Parasuraman, A., Zeithaml, V. A., & Malhotra, A. (2005). "A Multiple-Item Scale for Assessing Electronic Service Quality," *Journal of Service Research*, 7(3), 213–233.

Pekkarinen, S. & Ulkuniemi, P. (2008). "Modularity in Developing Business Services by Platform Approach," *International Journal of Logistics Management*, 19(1), 84–103.

Piccoli, G., Brohman, M. K., Watson, R. T. & Parasuraman, A. (2004). "Net-Based Customer Service Systems: Evolution and Revolution in Web Site Functionalities," *Decision Sciences*, 35(3), 423–455.

Pires, G. D., Stanton, J. & Rita, P. (2006). "Commentary: The Internet, Consumer Empowerment, and Marketing Strategies," *European Journal of Marketing*, 40(9/10), 936–949.

Prahalad, C. K. & Ramaswamy, V. (2004). "Co-Creation Experiences: The Next Practice in Value Creation," *Journal of Interactive Marketing*, 18(3), 6–14.

Prins, R., Verhoef, P. C. & Franses, P. H. (2009). "The Impact of Adoption Timing on New Service Usage and Early Disadoption," *International Journal of Research in Marketing*, 26(4), 304–313.

Pujari, D. (2004). "Self-Service with a Smile? Self-Service Technology (SST) Encounters among Canadian Business-to-Business," *International Journal of Service Industry Management*, 15(2), 200–219.

Reinders, M. J., Dabholkar, P. A., & Frambach, R. T. (2008). "Consequences of Forcing Consumers to Use Technology-Based Self-Service," *Journal of Service Research*, 11(2), 107–123.

Rogers, E. M. (1983). *Diffusion of innovations*. New York: Free Press.

Russell-Bennett, R., Mulcahy, R., McAndrew, R., Letheren, K., Swinton, T., Ossington, R., & Horrocks, N. (2017). Taking advantage of electricity pricing signals in the digital age: Householders have their say. A summary report, Brisbane: Queensland University of Technology, 1–98.

Rust, R. T. & Huang, M-H. (2014). "The Service Revolution and the Transformation of Marketing Science," *Marketing Science*, 33(2), 206–221.

Shostack, L. G. (1987). "Service Positioning through Structural Change," *Journal of Marketing*, 51(1), 34–43.

Sipser, M. (2006). *Introduction to the theory of computation* (Second ed.). Boston, MA: Thomson Course Technology.

Wolfinbarger, M. & Gilly, M. C. (2003). "EEeTailQ: Dimensionalizing, Measuring and Predicting Etail Quality," *Journal of Retailing*, 79(3), 183–198.

Yim, C. K., Chan, K. W., & Lam, S. S. K. (2012). "Do Customers and Employees Enjoy Service Participation? Synergistic Effects of Self- and Other-Efficacy," *Journal of Marketing*, 76(6), 121–140.

16

Managing customer performance in services

*Enrico Secchi, Uzay Damali, David McCutcheon,
and Stephen S. Tax*

Introduction

Customers assume a variety of roles in service delivery systems, from mostly passive recipients to providers of work, prompting the use of the term "partial employee" (Halbesleben & Buckley, 2004; Hsieh, Yen, & Chin, 2004; Mustak, Jaakkola, Halinen, & Kaartemo, 2016; Scherer, Wünderlich, & von Wangenheim, 2015). Different roles demand different forms of performance encompassing a variety of skills, resources, and motivational levels. For example, a customer role would be relatively simple in the context of a barber shop, where the requirements are to communicate the desired service and to be present for a short time while the service provider performs the task. Conversely, customer roles can be highly complex, as is the case with many healthcare services, where patients and medical providers jointly diagnose a condition and decide on a treatment plan that requires patient compliance. Such a treatment regimen often involves an extensive set of tasks over a long period of time to achieve the desired outcome.

In many cases, customer performance is strategic (Tax, Colgate, & Bowen, 2006). Customer actions impact their own experiences, frequently affect the satisfaction of other consumers, and contribute (positively or negatively) to firm productivity (Mustak et al., 2016). Thus, customer performance may be a central component of a firm's competitive advantage. Regardless of whether customer roles are large or small, how well they are carried out is of concern to the service provider; improving customer performance is often central to firm success.

Service research provides extensive evidence of effective customer performance, including reducing costs and improving service quality (Merlo, Eisingerich, & Auh, 2014; Mustak et al., 2016). Cost reduction stems largely from transferring operational activities from the service provider to the customer. Savings are achieved by transferring tasks from paid employees to unpaid customers (Lovelock & Young, 1979; Xie, Bagozzi, & Troye, 2008). Effective customer performance then focuses on the speed and efficiency (in part reflected by the absence of errors) with which these activities are carried out.

Service quality improvements may also arise from different factors, such as customer motivation to meet expectations by acquiring the needed skills or capabilities to effectively perform the service. Higher perceived quality may result from increased customization, stemming from customer abilities to shape the service delivery process to match individual preferences (Jaakkola, Helkkula, & Aarikka-Stenroos, 2015; McColl-Kennedy, Hogan, Witell, & Snyder, 2017; Mustak et al., 2016; Prahalad & Ramaswamy, 2004). Furthermore, many customers seek higher involvement in service delivery and are motivated to perform well as a way to shape their own unique experiences. Active participation in service creation can elicit feelings of belonging and accomplishment that augment customer perceived value (Jaakkola et al., 2015; Karmarkar & Karmarkar, 2014).

Clearly, negative impacts can result from poor customer performance. A recent *New York Times* article points to staggering costs in the US healthcare system due to patients' failure to take prescribed medications; this leads to an estimated 100,000 deaths annually and accounts for 10% of hospitalizations (Brody, 2017). Increased strain on hospital capacity produced by these unnecessary hospitalizations results in adverse effects for other potential patients. As with other scenarios, poor customer performance may affect the underperforming (or 'misperforming') customers themselves (i.e., the patients), other customers (i.e., other patients forced to wait longer for treatment), or the service system (i.e., the hospital).

This leads to the question of how organizations can best manage customer performance to ensure that service outcomes meet the expectations of customers as well as service firms. This chapter advances a model of antecedents of customer performance rooted in extant service marketing and service operations management research. More specifically, it identifies seven broad categories of practices that organizations can adopt to improve customer performance. All of these practices act by improving customer ability and motivation, and can be subsumed under the following categories: (1) task design, (2) customer learning, (3) customer selection, (4) multichannel strategies, (5) customer incentives, (6) gamification, and (7) employee adaptiveness. The next section provides a brief review of the literature on customer participation. This is followed by a discussion of the proposed model and each type of recommended practice in detail. The chapter concludes by reviewing the implications of the proposed model.

Customer participation

The study of customer participation has a long history in service management research. Although customer participation was initially regarded as a distinctive characteristic of services (Chase, 1981; Eiglier & Langeard, 1977; Grönroos, 1978; Sasser, Olsen, & Wyckoff, 1978; Shostack, 1977), more recently it has been suggested that all offerings require customer participation in order to generate value (Lusch & Vargo, 2006; Vargo & Lusch, 2004, 2008, 2016). Customers are often required to perform tasks instrumental to service outcomes. For instance, as mentioned above in the context of healthcare services, effective patient participation contributes to improved patient health (Damali, Miller, Fredendall, Moore, & Dye, 2016; McColl-Kennedy et al., 2017; Sweeney, Danaher, & McColl-Kennedy, 2015). As an example within healthcare, patients diagnosed with diabetes are expected to plan their meals and monitor blood glucose levels; lack of effective performance of these tasks can result in complications and more frequent hospital visits.

Early service management research outlined potential downsides that customer participation can present to operational performance (Berry, 1980; Chase, 1981; Dong, Sivakumar, Evans, & Zou, 2014; Field, Ritzman, Safizadeh, & Downing, 2006; Plé & Cáceres, 2010). This stream of research focused on reducing the variability introduced by customers; specifically, it (1) provided means of isolating the service's technical core from exogenous disturbances (Chase & Tansik, 1983; Metters & Vargas, 2000) or (2) created focused operations to reduce the potential variability in the system (Levitt, 1972; Van Dierdonck & Brandt, 1988). Although such approaches can be extremely useful, they assume that a service provider's processes and technologies are the primary source of value creation. The customer is seen as passive recipient and/or a source of uncertainty and inefficiency. Owing to increasing use of business models that rely on customer productive inputs (e.g., implementation of self-service technologies(SSTs)), management and marketing researchers developed more nuanced conceptualizations of the critical role of customers in value creation (Jaakkola et al., 2015).

Recently, a growing body of research has shown potential benefits of increasing the amount of customer participation in service systems (Dong, Evans, & Zou, 2008; Dong et al., 2014; Merlo et al., 2014; Mustak et al., 2016). The terms 'co-production' and 'co-creation of value' are frequently used to frame customer participation in positive terms. Although these terms have often been used interchangeably to describe customer performance within the service delivery system, some distinctions have also been identified (Bitner, Faranda, Hubbert, & Zeithaml, 1997; Lusch & Vargo, 2006). Notably, co-creation of value typically refers to customers acting in a partnership role, supplying the service provider with insights and intellectual contributions (Prahalad & Ramaswamy, 2004; Vargo & Lusch, 2008). Co-production is more closely associated with customers acting as a productive resource (e.g., using SSTs), often replacing employees in performing tasks needed to create the service experience (Bitner et al., 1997; Field, Xue, & Hitt, 2012; Lovelock & Young, 1979). This chapter encompasses both definitions, as well as other situations in which customer participation has a significant influence on service outcomes. Therefore, it refers to the more general concept of customer *participation*, defined as "provision of inputs, including effort, time, knowledge, or other resources related to service production and delivery" (Mustak et al., 2016, p. 250). Services that require a significant amount of customer participation may need to manage and incentivize customer performance, as it has an important effect on service outcomes. The next section introduces a model of the antecedents of customer performance, based on extant customer participation literature.

Model of customer performance

Managing customer performance entails recognizing that customers come with individual sets of skills, motivations, and expectations, each of which influences both ability and willingness to perform the tasks required for positive service outcomes (both for the customer and the provider). Moreover, customers vary in terms of their relevant attribute mix, which can lead to substantial variation in service outcomes. In the words of Sampson and Froehle (2006, p. 334), "heterogeneity in processing and outcome is primarily caused by heterogeneity in process inputs, specifically customer inputs."

Building on this insight, this chapter develops a conceptualization of the challenges of managing customer participation. For ease of exposition, the abstraction is made that a customer's attributes which determine performance can be represented in a linear form, where each customer possesses a particular amount of each specific skill, knowledge, or motivation level. Although this abstraction may fail to capture some complexities, it is a useful starting point to derive basic principles. Figure 16.1 illustrates a hypothetical distribution of customer attributes in a population of customers potentially engaging with a service. The curve could be used to represent the distribution of motivation, and the area under the curve would then represent the likelihood that a randomly selected customer has less than a specified level of motivation required to actively participate in service delivery.

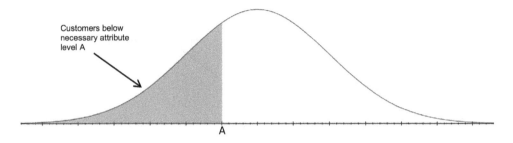

Figure 16.1 Distribution of customer attributes.

In this example, if the required level of motivation to successfully perform a service task is denoted by A, then the shaded area represents the probability that a random customer will not be willing to perform the task (alternatively, this may be viewed as the proportion of customers that lack the required motivation). The same form of representation can be used for customer skills and knowledge. Thus, *customer attributes* denote motivation, skills, knowledge, or any other characteristic of customers that can influence their performance. If the probability of failure is deemed too high, the service firm can intervene in three ways: (1) by acting on the customers, such that the distribution of attributes changes; (2) by acting on the service characteristics, reducing the participation requirements of service process; or (3) by acting on the service delivery system to increase its flexibility, to accommodate customers possessing different attribute levels.

Interventions of the first kind would work by increasing the average level of attributes among customers (see Figure 16.2) and/or by reducing the variability in attributes (see Figure 16.3). For example, customer motivation could be enhanced by persuading unwilling customers that they would extract a higher utility from the service if they more fully participated, and/or by changing the effort required (e.g., allowing for after-hours cash withdrawal from ATMs). Similarly, a service provider could reduce the variability in customer skills by providing appropriate training (e.g., nurses can show patients how to inject their own medications). Such interventions, by increasing the distribution mean or reducing its variance, result in a lower probability that customers will lack the required attributes to perform the necessary service delivery tasks.

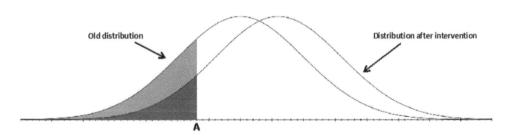

Figure 16.2 Effect of shifting the mean of attributes.

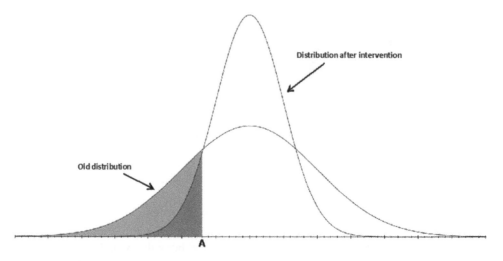

Figure 16.3 Effect of reducing variance of attributes.

The second type of intervention entails simplifying the service process, such that customer attribute requirements are reduced. Figure 16.4 illustrates this type of intervention, wherein the level of attributes required to complete the service process is lowered from A to A'. The outcome of this type of intervention is analogous to that of increasing customer attributes; the amount of motivation, skills, or knowledge possessed by the customer population increases relative to the requirements of the service, thereby reducing the probability of failure.

The third type of intervention works by either intervening to compensate for a customer's lack of motivation (e.g., when bank employees help unwilling customers to fill out a form), or by creating separate channels for customers with differing levels of motivation. Such practices result in outcomes similar to the one illustrated in Figure 16.4 however, an important difference is that customers that are able and willing to perform the task requiring higher attributes can do so (they do not require employee intervention, or they can self-select into a 'high attributes' channel).

Figure 16.5 shows the proposed model of customer performance antecedents. This model posits that seven categories of practices support aligning the required motivation and ability

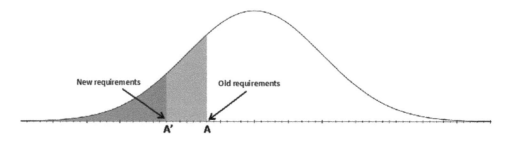

Figure 16.4 Effect of reducing service performance requirements.

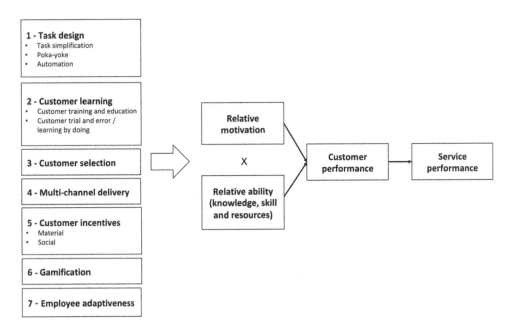

Figure 16.5 Antecedents of customer performance.

of customers with the service requirements to perform their roles effectively. The goal of these practices is to reduce the probability of failure to perform (depicted in Figure 16.1 and in the subsequent figures). Some of the practices have a larger effect on knowledge and skills, whereas others primarily affect motivation. It is important to note that disparate customer attributes interact and may reinforce or weaken each other. Moreover, the effects of the practices described here are not always linear, and can interact in unexpected ways. The last part of this section discusses each practice in greater detail.

Task design

To improve customer performance, service firms often change design elements of the tasks that their customers need to perform. Better task design may require lower levels of skills or motivation from customers. The research on customer participation identifies three primary ways in which this can be achieved: (1) task simplification, (2) 'poka-yokes' or mistake proofing, and (3) automation/SSTs. These practices are explained in the following three sub-sections, respectively.

Task simplification

Service customers are expected to perform a variety of tasks. For example, customers at a restaurant might make reservations, arrive on time, place their order, eat, and pay. Given their experience with performing this role and the similarity across contexts, these tasks are usually simple and straightforward. Other services may require substantially greater customer effort. For example, a client of a financial planner may be required to develop a budget, track expenditures, and forecast future financial needs. If tasks are perceived to be too difficult, clients may not be capable or motivated to maintain compliance, which can result in ineffective financial performance.

One available practice to improve customer performance is to simplify the task, making do with the attributes that most customers already possess. The goal of task simplification is primarily to reduce the threshold point for failure, as illustrated in Figure 16.4. Task simplification does not change the shape of the distributions of either ability or motivation, but it reduces the threshold for what constitutes adequate customer performance.

The theoretical basis for task simplification practices can be found in the theory of lean operations. Improvements to obtain lean operations date back to post-World War II Japan when its industry had limited resources; therefore, Japanese manufacturers developed operational practices that reduced employee failure through task design. Toyota Motor Company, one of the leaders in this endeavor, created the foundation for lean manufacturing, which gradually became their competitive advantage in the global automotive market. In 1978, the senior manager of Toyota, Taiichi Ohno, published *Toyota Production System* (TPS) that explained the lean practices used on Toyota's shop floor (Ohno, 1988). In the early 1980s, US manufacturers were introduced to TPS; however, several years passed before they realized its potential and began to apply it to improve production systems. Although TPS involves a wide variety of strategies, the term 'Just-in-Time' (JIT) replaced TPS in the late 1980s. The term "lean" was first used by Krafcik (1988); Womack, Jones, and Roos (1990), in *The Machine that Changed the World*, popularized the term as a replacement for JIT. Although lean approaches were developed for manufacturing, their application to services is becoming increasingly common (Bowen & Youngdahl, 1998; Malmbrandt & Åhlström, 2013). Documented applications range from airlines (Bowen & Youngdahl, 1998), to schools (Åhlström, 2005), to hospitals (Allway & Corbett, 2002).

Furniture retailer IKEA provides an excellent example of how the above-described task simplification concept can be applied to customer participation. The company is known for the simplicity of its designs and assembly processes: customer participation requirements can be as simple as those for building a bookcase in a living room or as complex as installing a kitchenette in a basement suite. Because IKEA designers understand that reducing complexity of the assembly process is critical for the success of the product, they put significant effort into simplifying the process so that customers are less likely to fail. However, IKEA can only simplify these tasks to a limited extent. They can simplify the construction of a bookcase—by limiting the number of tools needed and designing pre-fitted interlocking parts—to the point where the assembly task is so robust that almost anyone, without using specialized tools, can easily assemble an IKEA bookcase. However, IKEA cannot simplify a kitchen installation process as much without losing important details; for instance, customers may need to do some plumbing and electrical work. Therefore, IKEA can incur substantial risk by simplifying the process too much, as customers might be exposed to health and safety hazards. The task simplification strategy may need to give way to other approaches, such as offering customers additional installation services or training/education to supplement the design process.

Mistake proofing (poka-yokes)

From the lean manufacturing tradition spring two other commonly used task design practices that can improve customer performance. Poka-yokes are the subject of this subsection; this term describes designing a delivery system that does not allow for mistakes. Jidoka (or process automation) is the subject of the next subsection.

Mistake proofing, or poka-yoke, is the implementation of design features that make it impossible for an error to occur, or make the error immediately obvious once it has occurred. Chase and Stewart (1994) were the first to investigate the role of poka-yokes in services, identifying many different examples of mistake-proofing practices in various service operations. They describe an automotive service into which poka-yokes were integrated by the identification of fail-points; they then designed innovative solutions to eliminate errors. For example, customer failure to realize a car was due for service was recognized as a common problem, which was then managed through the use of reminders via post or phone. Similarly, many professional service providers send reminders to clients so they will not miss upcoming appointments.

Mistake-proofing reminders may also be used to assist service providers: for instance, to avoid an unnoticed customer arrival, a business may install a bell at the door. A considerable amount of research has documented many other uses of poka-yokes in services to reduce incidences of poor task performance (Kellogg, Youngdahl, & Bowen, 1997). Other examples of poka-yokes include airlines sending flight reminders, and banks implementing ATM systems in which customer cards must be retrieved before money is dispensed (to avoid customers forgetting their cards). It should be noted that the overuse of poka-yokes may result in the frustration of some customers, who might seek a less standardized process to avoid the fail-safe routine (Stuart & Tax, 1996).

Automation and SSTs (Jidoka)

SSTs are the technological interfaces that allow customers to produce services without the direct involvement of service employees. SSTs are replacing many face-to-face service interactions, with the intention to make service transactions more accurate, convenient, and expedient (Bateson, 1985; Blut, Wang, & Schoefer, 2016; Campbell & Frei, 2010; Meuter, Ostrom, Roundtree, & Bitner, 2000; Scherer et al., 2015). Widespread diffusion of internet-enabled service delivery allows customers to access more services with greater flexibility, through increasingly customizable self-service options that enhance motivation to participate (Meuter, Bitner, Ostrom, & Brown, 2005). The use of technology-based self-service (TBSS) can increase customer satisfaction by providing a more customized experience while at the same time increasing efficiency of the service delivery process (Dabholkar, 1996; Froehle & Roth, 2004). Although such technologies can reduce the level of skills and knowledge required for the customer to perform adequately in the service (Figure 16.4), they might also have a detrimental effect on customer motivation to engage with the service by reducing face-to-face contacts. Furthermore, extant research shows that lack of customer technology readiness and/or self-efficacy can represent substantial barriers to adoption of technology (Liljander, Gillberg, Gummerus, & van Riel, 2006). The practices discussed in the next section can effectively be used to increase customer knowledge and self-efficacy.

Customer learning

Although task redesign can reduce the incidence of service failures by lowering customer requirements, it does not affect ability or willingness of customers to do the work. To act on customer skills and knowledge, service organizations often encourage customers to go through a learning process. Practices to foster customer learning in services can be classified into two categories: service providers can implement training programs, thereby increasing customer ability and motivation to perform the tasks, or they can create systems in which customers can learn by engaging with the service, through trial and error (Bell, Auh, & Eisingerich, 2017; Damali et al., 2016).

Customer training and education

Customer training and education (CTE) is defined as "planned service practices that increase a customer's knowledge, ability and motivation to perform service tasks in order to improve customers' performance" (Damali et al., 2016, p. 80). CTE results in customers performing service tasks effectively, by increasing their average level of skills and knowledge as shown in Figure 16.2, and/or by reducing the disparity among them as shown in Figure 16.3 (Bell et al., 2017; Damali et al., 2016). In other words, when a service provides effective CTE, average customer performance increases and the standard deviation of customer performance decreases.

It is important that service designers understand that customers use a service to obtain its core benefit, not to receive training. For example, a cable television customer purchases the service for the functions it performs to enhance enjoyment, not to gain the knowledge or skill in programming recordings or accessing streaming services. The process of obtaining CTE should be easy for customers and support their success in gaining the benefits sought from an ongoing subscription; such benefits must outweigh the costs associated with any CTE, or the firm risks losing the customer.

In some services, notably healthcare, the benefits of CTE are dramatic compared to the costs of not offering CTE: for instance, failure to effectively manage a chronic condition may result in such negative outcomes as reduced quality of life and increased financial expenses. In addition to personal costs, if patients fail to manage their conditions, health costs to the public may increase. Therefore, hospitals are required to provide training and education to their patients. For example, patients suffering from diabetes receive training on how to manage their diet, how to check their blood sugar levels, and how to inject insulin if necessary.

In addition to calculating costs and benefits of CTE to the service firm, costs and benefits should also be calculated from the customer perspective. Costs of CTE to customers may include their time and any other costs they might have to be subjected to: for instance, customers may need to pay for rental equipment if they wish to learn how to rock climb. Because customers purchase services for the anticipated benefits, and not necessarily to learn how to perform tasks, service firms need to communicate that service benefits only accrue to those who are able to perform the tasks effectively. Furthermore, there are potential risks involved in missing necessary education/training. This means that customers need to understand the benefits of CTE before they invest time and effort in the educational process.

From a service firm's perspective, costs and benefits can be evaluated using the "Cost of Quality" model (Crosby, 1979; Rust, Zahorik, & Keiningham, 1995; Schiffauerova & Thomson, 2006). There are two components to the costs related to offering CTE: one is prevention and the other is failure. The decision to provide CTE is a prevention cost. Service firms need to calculate the amount of resources to allocate (e.g., spending on printed materials and employee time to deliver the education and training); this will depend on the anticipated cost of a failure. Although the cost of CTE is generally clear, the benefits (such as avoiding failure) are uncertain.

An effective design of CTE requires addressing two questions: (1) the content or type of knowledge to be delivered through CTE; and (2) the media to be used to deliver the CTE. Three types of knowledge need to be communicated in a CTE program (Bowen, 1986; Damali et al., 2016):

- Know-what: what is the role of customer and what is expected? Customers need to realize that they may have an extended role in the service system.
- Know-how: how can the customer accomplish these tasks?

- Know-why: why do these tasks need to be performed effectively (include an explanation of monetary and nonmonetary benefits)?

In addition to the knowledge content to be communicated, the type(s) of media used to deliver the CTE need to be determined. Three common methods of CTE include face-to-face interaction, written documentation, and online materials. Face-to-face media can take many forms, from employee to individual customer interactions, employees delivering to groups of customers (group training), and customer-to-customer interactions. Providing documents for customers to read, either in printed or electronic form, in their own time represents a less rich form of media. Other formats such as online, video, and audio offer intermediate levels of media richness.

Customer trial and error, learning by doing and observations of other customers

As an alternative to CTE, customers can learn how to participate in a service using trial and error. For example, the NikeiD website empowers and enables customers to design their own shoes (Sorescu, Frambach, Singh, Rangaswamy, & Bridges, 2011). This retailer allows the customers to freely experiment and learn from the system, rather than offering a structured learning platform. Indeed, for many customers that use such 'product configurator' technologies, experimenting with the system is part of the experience, and reaching the desired outcome can increase satisfaction and brand loyalty (Franke, Schreier, & Kaiser, 2010). As people purchase more products that require them to engage in digital or physical assembly or installation, they become more familiar with typical procedures involved and can graduate to more complex versions. YouTube now provides a vast array of videos that train customers in how to prepare complex meals, hang television screens, and do many other activities. This type of self-learning is increasingly becoming the preferred way of a substantial segment of the population to learn and develop new capabilities.

Communities can serve a similar function. Customers may initially rely on friends to support them in completing tasks in which they have little experience, such as loading new programs onto computers. Service firms can support these communities; for instance, software companies create online spaces where customers can discuss and inform each other, effectively taking on a customer support role. Firms can create incentives by both enhancing the status of individual customers in the community and by offering additional benefits, such as discounts or early releases. Although customers might be used to receiving training or socialization from other customers (both offline and online), and learning by doing may be more common for SSTs, CTE is appropriate for more complex services, such as healthcare.

Customer selection

Although service providers might wish to provide service to all potential customers, some groups of customers are more risky to service firms, and hence less valuable. The distribution of motivation, skills, and knowledge in the population of potential customers is usually multimodal; that is, it can be subdivided into groups characterized by different distribution parameters (Konuş, Verhoef, & Neslin, 2008; Verhoef, Kannan, & Inman, 2015). The participation of the subgroups that do not have the required attributes to receive service may result in inefficient and ineffective behaviors. Poor customer performance may have substantial negative impact when it harms the experience of other customers, and/or reduces firm productivity. Therefore, one possible answer for the service firm is to restrict access to customers that have the required attributes (Tax et al., 2006).

As an example, Mayo Clinic has successfully adopted this strategy by creating a highly efficient 'focused factory' for qualifying cardiac surgery patients, who are screened based on the complexity of their cases (Cook et al., 2014). Similarly, some golf courses only allow players to tee off early in the morning if they have demonstrated that they can finish the round in under four hours. This restricted access ensures a pace of play demanded by an important customer segment, and also ensures that tee-off time reservations are kept. Thus ensuring that customers are productive is an important aspect of service strategy and competitive advantage (Tax et al., 2006). By focusing on a narrow customer segment, a service organization can both increase the average level of customer attributes and also reduce variability among those in its customer population (Figures 16.2 and 16.3).

Multichannel strategy

Another means that service organizations use to accommodate a wider variety of customer motivation and skill levels is to make a number of service delivery channels available (Xue, Hitt, & Harker, 2007). Such a service design allows customers to select the channel that matches their preferences and abilities. For instance, one movie theatre customer may prefer to purchase tickets online in advance of a show, whereas another might use a kiosk at the theatre or purchase through a box office staffed by theatre employees. The advantages of multichannel service delivery are many; they include increased levels of customization, cost savings arising from customer use of self-service channels, and the potential for service innovations arising from the addition of new service delivery modalities as well as the interplay of multiple channels (Campbell & Frei, 2010; van Birgelen, de Jong, & de Ruyter, 2006; Xue et al., 2007).

In the context of the framework introduced in this chapter, allowing customers to self-select into the most appropriate channel would help to better match customer motivation and skill levels to channel characteristics, thereby reducing failures. For example, an online channel might require higher skill levels and resources than a telephone channel; customers that possess adequate skills may choose to perform their transactions through the online channel, whereas customers who don't have the skills will use either a phone or in-person option (Konuş et al., 2008). Therefore, comparing the curves within each channel (Figure 16.1) is anticipated to result in similar probabilities of failure. Because online channels are typically less costly to operate than in-person channels, a service is expected to benefit from having more customers use the online channel. However, the probability of failure can be limited by offering the phone channel to customers with lower skills. An example of such a multichannel service delivery system occurs at banks, which responded early to availability of new technologies by offering online services (Huete & Roth, 1988; Xue, Hitt, & Chen, 2011). Contrary to some expectations, however, most banks have not eliminated preexisting self-service (ATMs, phone banking) or in-person (branch offices) service delivery channels. Retaining this configuration of options may address the variability of customer skills and motivations within each channel, resulting in optimal efficiency (Xue et al., 2007).

Providing a greater range of choices to customers in regard to channel options can present challenges and costs for the service organization. In particular, it has been shown that satisfaction in one channel can negatively influence satisfaction in another channel (van Birgelen et al., 2006). Furthermore, highly skilled customers use multiple channels in ways that are better for them, but not necessarily more efficient for the service provider (Xue et al., 2007). Customer use of multiple channels might go beyond sub-optimal use of one firm's channels to the concomitant use of multiple channels of competing services (Verhoef, Neslin, & Vroomen, 2007). For example, a customer might gather information through the website of one company and then purchase through the retail store of a different company. This behavior is referred to as 'cross-channel free-riding'; it can have a significant impact on a firm's bottom line (Chiu, Hsieh, Hsieh, Roan, & Tseng, 2011). Although some results show that these risks can be mitigated by seamlessly integrating different channels (Bendoly, Blocher, Bretthauer, Krishnan, & Venkataramanan, 2005), design of systems that mitigate these risks is a continuing challenge.

Customer incentives and penalties

Service organizations can increase the motivations of customers to behave in specific ways by providing incentives to encourage certain behaviors or by introducing penalties which incur a cost for inappropriate performance. The literature related to use of such incentives in prosocial contexts is particularly relevant (Ariely, Bracha, & Meier, 2009; Osterhus, 1997). The most common type of incentive/penalty is monetary, often in the form of discounts or fines, but social incentives—in the form of a social pressure from other customers to behave according to a shared norm—can play an important role in eliciting the required behavior.

Monetary incentives

Financial incentives are often used when productivity is the central aspect of customer performance that a firm is trying to manage. For example, incentives are used to migrate customers to less costly channels when airlines offer lower rates to online customers as compared to those making phone reservations. Although multichannels are often used to retain customers who prefer particular higher cost channels, incentives may be implemented in an attempt to migrate them to more efficient options (Ansari, Mela, & Neslin, 2008).

In the framework this chapter presents, customer incentives affect motivation to perform required tasks and reduce the probability of service failure (see Figure 16.2). As an example, some car insurers offer discounts for drivers who agree to participate in driving classes, creating an incentive that motivates customers to acquire higher skill levels. Another option that many insurers offer is to install remote monitoring on a car in exchange for a lower premium. This directly links insurance rates to the driver's behavior, creating a deterrent for unwanted behaviors. As another example, service firms often price self-service options (such as ATMs and self-service gas stations) at lower rates than the equivalent full service options.

Penalties may be used in cases where firm and customer goals are misaligned and in situations where customers may engage in opportunistic behavior (Tax, Kim, & Nair, 2013a). For instance, no-show penalties may be used to manage customer conduct and reduce the impact when appointments are missed. Late cancellation fees are particularly important in industries (e.g., airlines or cruise lines) characterized as having limited capacity and high per-unit cost, along with reservation systems that are critical for yield management. Penalties can change customer behavior: having penalties in place for late payment encourages customers to pay on time. Restocking fees were introduced by retailers, in part to reduce the practice of 'renting,' wherein a customer purchases a product (e.g., a television right before the Super Bowl or a prom dress immediately prior to the prom), and then returns it a few days later after using it for the event.

It is important that customers perceive penalties to be imposed through fair procedures and that the amount of penalties is in line with the cost to the firm of inappropriate customer actions; otherwise, customer defection and negative word of mouth may occur (Tax et al., 2013a). Customer penalties must be strong enough to reduce negative behaviors; if not, such penalties may be misinterpreted and exacerbate them. Gneezy and Rustichini (2000) provide a striking example in a field experiment, in which they introduced a fine for parents who were late in picking up their children from day care. They hoped the fine would reduce this problematic behavior, which forced workers to stay after their shifts ended. However, because the fine was perceived to be small, parents perceived it as a fee that they were more than willing to incur in order to receive additional services, which led to an increase in the number of late pickups. Paying the fine also reduced the anxiety and/or feelings of guilt that parents faced for making employees stay late.

Social incentives: customer socialization and citizenship behaviors

Social norms and expectations can play an important role in shaping customer behaviors. Often customers possess the knowledge and skills required by a service, but have little motivation to exhibit the desired behaviors. For example, in a fast-food restaurant, cleaning the table and separating the recyclables can require extra effort. By creating a shared social norm among customers, some reluctant customers might be induced to comply through social pressure and perhaps shaming (Temerak, Winklhofer, & Hibbert, 2018).

In the framework described in this chapter, social incentives may provide results similar to those offered by CTE, but through influencing customer motivation to perform the required tasks. An example is offered by the pressure put on golfers by players that come after them. When a group of more experienced players follows a less experienced group, they are likely to catch up and be forced to wait for the next hole. The social system put in place by golf clubs creates the expectation that slower players will allow faster groups to 'play through' if the wait becomes too long (Tax et al., 2006). Social pressure can also result in customer engagement behaviors, such as when weight loss clients participate in peer groups to share their experiences and tips to create better service experiences for other members (Damali et al., 2016; van Doorn et al., 2010).

Gamification

In a quest to increase customer motivation to perform required service delivery roles, service organizations are increasingly introducing game-like features into service delivery processes (Robson, Plangger, Kietzmann, McCarthy, & Pitt, 2014). The "application of game design principles in non-gaming contexts" is referred to as *gamification* (Robson, Plangger, Kietzmann, McCarthy, & Pitt, 2015, p. 411). The goal of gamification is to use lessons learned by game designers and implement them in service delivery systems to increase customer motivation to either perform specific tasks or acquire new skills. In the present framework, gamification shifts the normal distribution curve for motivation to the right, thereby reducing the probability of a service failure (Figure 16.2).

Examples of gamification can be found in several industries. Many power companies use intelligent sensors to allow homeowners to compare their energy use to that of their neighbors and share the results on social platforms (Robson et al., 2015). This opportunity for comparison creates incentives to adopt behaviors that reduce energy consumption. Gamification is also used to increase acceptance of policies that would not normally be welcome, such as differential pricing. For instance, some pubs adopt 'drink exchange' systems that allow them to price beverages based on demand, incentivizing customers to purchase items that are not being consumed, leading to both increased yields for the pub and a more entertaining atmosphere for customers. Online reviews for places like the Brew Exchange in

Austin, Texas emphasize the 'fun' aspect of fluctuating prices. Some of these bars even ring a bell when the market crashes, generating a race to get to the drinks first, before prices start climbing again.

Hammedi, Leclercq, and Riel (2017) describe two cases of gamification in healthcare: the introduction of Wii Fit technology in the physical rehabilitation of patients, and the use of tablet computers to facilitate treatment of children. These authors found that both utilitarian and experiential expected outcomes are important drivers of willingness to engage in games. They also found that the outcomes of gamification, in terms both of engagement and clinical results, are significantly influenced by the role expectations of the participants, which are usually a function of demographic variables. In the face of uncertainty surrounding the outcomes of gamification, it should be noted that gamification might require commitments in terms of both design and financial resources. Offering a gamified experience can backfire on the company and create negative emotions in customers, such as sadness over losing a game, or feelings of inadequacy (Harwood & Garry, 2015; Robson et al., 2015).

Employee adaptiveness

Rather than trying to increase customer ability and/or motivation, or reducing the overall requirements of service delivery processes, service organizations can develop protocols for intervening in situations where customers appear unable or unwilling to perform the necessary tasks. The abilities of service employees to change behavior based on the contingent needs of the moment has been referred to as "employee adaptiveness" (Gwinner, Bitner, Brown, & Kumar, 2005) and "service improvisation competence" (Secchi, Roth, & Verma, 2019).

Secchi et al. (2019, p. 1329) proposed that successful service companies possess a specific Service Improvisation Competence (Serv-IC), defined as "the systemic ability of a service firm's employees to deviate from established service delivery processes and routines to respond in a timely manner to unforeseen events using available resources." The development of such competence can create a band of acceptable performance around the required skill level, whereby employees possess abilities and resources to intervene when customer skills are not up to required tasks, or when customers are taking advantage of the system. For example, airline employees are trained to identify and intervene in situations when a passenger is having trouble checking in through self-check-in kiosks. The creation of a Serv-IC is not a trivial undertaking, but it is the result of a consistent set of service delivery system design choices. The design of a physical and/or virtual servicescape (Bitner, 1990, 1992), human resource management practices, process design, and information management must be aligned to enable and empower employees to act.

The service system has to be designed to provide: (1) transparency—employees have to be able to assess the status of important variables in a system to quickly identify any potential problem, and (2) availability of resources—employees need easy access to a wide enough range of resources to be able to perform appropriate corrective actions when needed. For example, many casinos have developed systems in which the check-in clerk can immediately access preferences and other data regarding repeat customers. This information can be used to craft a unique experience for a customer. Furthermore, human resource practices play an important part in developing Serv-IC: hiring and training practices should be aimed at selecting employees with strong customer orientations who are willing to develop deep knowledge of the way the service system operates (Morgan, Rapp, Richey, & Ellinger, 2014). Information sharing among different parts of the service system (such as front and back office) plays an important part in the ability of employees to successfully intervene

315

during service delivery. Sharing the appropriate information in a timely manner can help both in terms of identifying situations where an intervention is warranted, and notifying other parts of the service delivery system that a deviation has occurred, thereby minimizing the potential disruption (Vera & Crossan, 2005).

Finally, service delivery processes must be designed to be flexible. Research on organizational improvisation has shown that effective improvisation relies on clear and well-defined processes coupled with the empowerment of employees to deviate from them when necessary (John, Grove, & Fisk, 2006; Secchi, Roth, & Verma, 2016). The design of detailed and flexible service routines is one of the most difficult aspects of fostering service improvisation and, consequently, if done well, can lead to substantial competitive advantage in managing customer participation.

In a probabilistic conceptualization of customer performance, improvisation can be used as a means of selectively reducing the levels of customer skill, knowledge, and motivation required to perform a service (Figure 16.4). This implies that the requirements need not be lowered for all customers, because the system is capable of adapting to each individual situation. Many grocery stores have responded to customers that run into problems with self-checkout terminals by strategically positioning an employee to monitor customers in the check-out process and intervene as needed. Although this makes it possible to reduce the total number of employees and still allows customers to use the self-service option, the store could use improvisation to minimize the negative impact slow customers have on themselves, the store's operations, and other customers.

Conclusion and future research opportunities

This chapter provides an overview of factors that influence customer performance in service delivery systems. It argues that, given the increase in self-service, technology mediated, and generally co-produced services, the adequacy of customer motivation, skills, and knowledge becomes of paramount importance to service organizations. The chapter discusses a set of practices that can reduce the probability of failure due to customer lack of required attributes.

Starting from minimal assumptions regarding the distribution of attributes relevant to customer performance in the population, this chapter suggests that possible interventions fall into three main categories. The first category impacts the shape and position of the distribution by increasing customer capabilities along a target attribute or reducing the variance in the population. Such practices as customer training increase the level of customer skills and knowledge, and the provision of incentives can increase the level of motivation. The second category acts on service design, making the tasks at hand simpler or lowering the required motivation, resulting in an increase in the proportion of customers that are willing and able to participate in service delivery. The use of poka-yokes and automation are included in this category. Finally, service providers can find ways to segment customers based on their attributes and channel them into more or less participative service delivery processes. Thus, the service creates subgroups that possess the required attributes for a defined level of customer participation. Customer selection, multichannel strategies, and employee adaptiveness fall into this category.

The potential for combining interventions offers the opportunity to develop uniquely tailored management strategies for participative services. Indeed, some of these practices can reinforce each other. For example, incentives can be used to encourage customers to engage in training. Similarly, automation can be used to encourage customers to self-select into the most appropriate channel; gamification options can be delivered to less motivated customers by empowered and enabled employees.

This chapter also highlights some of the possible downsides of customer participation performance practices. Much of the extant literature takes the view that shifting work to customers yields positive results, although some have challenged the ubiquity of this outcome (Jaakkola et al., 2015; Mustak et al., 2016). Overestimating the likely benefit of shifting tasks to customers could lead to disappointment for both the customer and the firm. An important avenue for future research concerns better understanding the set of risks associated with transferring additional responsibilities to customers or significantly changing the roles they play in the service. In addition, understanding how to mitigate such risks is of particular value to managers.

One question to consider in future research in this domain is whether changes in customer roles lead to significant customer defection. If so, a companion question would be how to best combat that decision. Developing a better understanding of how customers decide whether or not to take on new roles or find a provider who does not require the change would make a valuable contribution to the customer participation literature. From the customer perspective, altering their roles may be seen as an innovation. The diffusion of innovations literature is a useful starting point for developing mitigation strategies and formulating approaches to encourage adoption of the new role (Rogers, 2003).

Multichannel strategies can be used by savvy customers to obtain benefits that could incur unanticipated costs to the service provider (Hitt & Frei, 2002). When customers possess elevated knowledge of how a system works, they can find a way to use it to personal advantage (Fisk et al., 2010; Shang, Ghosh, & Galbreth, 2017).

The issues discussed in this chapter can be significantly extended by considering the complex web of relationships that characterize many modern services. The service literature has recognized the need to view the customer journey as one delivered by a network, as opposed to a dyadic exchange between firm and customer (Tax, McCutcheon, & Wilkinson, 2013b). Increasingly, this means that customer participation includes establishing a set of providers who will be part of their network for a "job" that needs to be performed (Bettencourt & Ulwick, 2008). Firms who had a central role and a strong relationship with customers may find themselves viewed increasingly as a commodity, whereas others may achieve more dominant positions. For instance, this is seen in the travel industry, where airlines, hotels, and third party providers such as Travelocity all compete to be the central node in the customer network. Research is needed to better understand how customers go about putting together networks and how they decide which partners will take on primary roles and which will be viewed as commodities. For firms, this may mean adding new capabilities to assist customers in putting together and dealing with network partners.

In summary, this chapter offers a useful framework for practitioners and delineates a map of current knowledge that can be used to identify novel and interesting research questions.

References

Åhlström, P. (2005). Lean service operations: Translating lean production principles to service operations. *International Journal of Services Technology and Management, 5*(5-6), 545–564.

Allway, M., & Corbett, S. (2002). Shifting to lean service: Stealing a page from manufacturers' playbooks. *Journal of Organizational Excellence, 21*(2), 45.

Ansari, A., Mela, C. F., & Neslin, S. A. (2008). Customer channel migration. *Journal of Marketing Research, 45*(1), 60–76.

Ariely, D., Bracha, A., & Meier, S. (2009). Doing good or doing well? Image motivation and monetary incentives in behaving prosocially. *American Economic Review, 99*(1), 544–555.

Bateson, J. E. (1985). Self-service consumer: An exploratory study. *Journal of Retailing, 61*(3), 49–76.

Bell, S. J., Auh, S., & Eisingerich, A. B. (2017). Unraveling the customer education paradox: When, and how, should firms educate their customers? *Journal of Service Research, 20*(3), 306–321.

Bendoly, E., Blocher, J. D., Bretthauer, K. M., Krishnan, S., & Venkataramanan, M. A. (2005). Online/in-store integration and customer retention. *Journal of Service Research, 7*(4), 313–327.

Berry, L. L. (1980). Services marketing is different. *Business Week, 30*(3), 24–39.

Bettencourt, L. A., & Ulwick, A. W. (2008). The customer-centered innovation map. *Harvard Business Review, 86*(5), 109–130.

Bitner, M. J. (1990). Evaluating service encounters: The effects of physical surroundings and employee responses. *Journal of Marketing, 54*(2), 69–82.

Bitner, M. J. (1992). Servicescapes: The impact of physical surroundings on customers and employees. *Journal of Marketing, 56*(2), 57–71.

Bitner, M. J., Faranda, W. T., Hubbert, A. R., & Zeithaml, V. A. (1997). Customer contributions and roles in service delivery. *International Journal of Service Industry Management, 8*(3), 193–205.

Blut, M., Wang, C., & Schoefer, K. (2016). Factors influencing the acceptance of self-service technologies: A meta-analysis. *Journal of Service Research, 19*(4), 396–416.

Bowen, D. E. (1986). Managing customers as human resources in service organizations. *Human Resource Management, 25*(3), 371–383.

Bowen, D. E., & Youngdahl, W. E. (1998). "Lean" service: In defense of a production-line approach. *International Journal of Service Industry Management, 9*(3), 207–225.

Brody, J. E. (2017, 2018 November 22). The cost of not taking your medicine. *The New York Times.* Retrieved from www.nytimes.com/2017/04/17/well/the-cost-of-not-taking-your-medicine.html.

Campbell, D., & Frei, F. (2010). Cost structure, customer profitability, and retention implications of self-service distribution channels: Evidence from customer behavior in an online banking channel. *Management Science, 56*(1), 4–24.

Chase, R. B. (1981). The customer contact approach to services: Theoretical bases and practical extensions. *Operations Research, 29*(4), 698–706.

Chase, R. B., & Stewart, D. M. (1994). Make your service fail-safe. *Sloan Management Review, 35*(3), 35–44.

Chase, R. B., & Tansik, D. A. (1983). The customer contact model for organization design. *Management Science, 29*(9), 1037–1050.

Chiu, H.-C., Hsieh, J.-K., Hsieh, Y.-C., Roan, J., & Tseng, K.-J. (2011). The challenge for multichannel services: Cross-channel free-riding behavior. *Electronic Commerce Research and Applications, 10*(2), 268–277.

Cook, D., Thompson, J. E., Habermann, E. B., Visscher, S. L., Dearani, J. A., Roger, V. L., & Borah, B. J. (2014). From "solution shop" model to "focused factory" in hospital surgery: Increasing care value and predictability. *Health Affairs, 33*(5), 746–755.

Crosby, P. B. (1979). *Quality is free: The art of making quality certain.* New York, NY: New American Library.

Dabholkar, P. A. (1996). Consumer evaluations of new technology-based self-service options: An investigation of alternative models of service quality. *International Journal of Research in Marketing, 13*(1), 29–51.

Damali, U., Miller, J. L., Fredendall, L. D., Moore, D., & Dye, C. J. (2016). Co-creating value using customer training and education in a healthcare service design. *Journal of Operations Management, 47–48,* 80–97.

Dong, B., Evans, K. R., & Zou, S. (2008). The effects of customer participation in co-created service recovery. *Journal of the Academy of Marketing Science, 36*(1), 123–137.

Dong, B., Sivakumar, K., Evans, K. R., & Zou, S. (2014). Effect of customer participation on service outcomes: The moderating role of participation readiness. *Journal of Service Research, 18*(2), 160–176.

Eiglier, P., & Langeard, E. (1977). A new approach to service marketing. In P. Eiglier & E. Langeard (Eds.), *Marketing consumer services: New insights* (pp. 77–115). Cambridge, MA: Marketing Science Institute.

Field, J. M., Ritzman, L. P., Safizadeh, M. H., & Downing, C. E. (2006). Uncertainty reduction approaches, uncertainty coping approaches, and process performance in financial services. *Decision Sciences, 37*(2), 149–175.

Field, J. M., Xue, M., & Hitt, L. M. (2012). Learning by customers as co-producers in financial services: An empirical study of the effects of learning channels and customer characteristics. *Operations Management Research, 5*(1–2), 43–56.

Fisk, R., Grove, S., Harris, L. C., Keeffe, D. A., Daunt, K. L., Russell-Bennett, R., & Wirtz, J. (2010). Customers behaving badly: A state of the art review, research agenda and implications for practitioners. *Journal of Services Marketing*, *24*(6), 417–429.

Franke, N., Schreier, M., & Kaiser, U. (2010). The "i designed it myself" effect in mass customization. *Management Science*, *56*(1), 125–140.

Froehle, C. M., & Roth, A. V. (2004). New measurement scales for evaluating perceptions of the technology-mediated customer service experience. *Journal of Operations Management*, *22*(1), 1–21.

Gneezy, U., & Rustichini, A. (2000). A fine is a price. *The Journal of Legal Studies*, *29*(1), 1–17.

Grönroos, C. (1978). A service-orientated approach to marketing of services. *European Journal of Marketing*, *12*(8), 588–601.

Gwinner, K. P., Bitner, M. J., Brown, S. W., & Kumar, A. (2005). Service customization through employee adaptiveness. *Journal of Service Research*, *8*(2), 131–148.

Halbesleben, J. R. B., & Buckley, M. R. (2004). Managing customers as employees of the firm: New challenges for human resources management. *Personnel Review*, *33*(3), 351–372.

Hammedi, W., Leclercq, T., & Riel, A. C. R. (2017). The use of gamification mechanics to increase employee and user engagement in participative healthcare services: A study of two cases. *Journal of Service Management*, *28*(4), 640–661.

Harwood, T., & Garry, T. (2015). An investigation into gamification as a customer engagement experience environment. *Journal of Services Marketing*, *29*(6/7), 533–546.

Hitt, L. M., & Frei, F. X. (2002). Do better customers utilize electronic distribution channels? The case of pc banking. *Management Science*, *48*(6), 732–748.

Hsieh, A.-T., Yen, C.-H., & Chin, K.-C. (2004). Participative customers as partial employees and service provider workload. *International Journal of Service Industry Management*, *15*(2), 187–199.

Huete, L. M., & Roth, A. V. (1988). The industrialization and span of retail banks' delivery systems. *International Journal of Operations &Production Management*, *8*(3), 46–66.

Jaakkola, E., Helkkula, A., & Aarikka-Stenroos, L. (2015). Service experience co-creation: Conceptualization, implications, and future research directions. *Journal of Service Management*, *26*(2), 182–205.

John, J., Grove, S. J., & Fisk, R. P. (2006). Improvisation in service performances: Lessons from jazz. *Managing Service Quality*, *16*(3), 247–268.

Karmarkar, U. S., & Karmarkar, U. R. (2014). Customer experience and service design. In E. Baglieri & U. S. Karmarkar (Eds.), *Managing consumer services: Factory or theater?* (pp. 109–130). Heidelberg, Germany: Springer International.

Kellogg, D. L., Youngdahl, W. E., & Bowen, D. E. (1997). On the relationship between customer participation and satisfaction: Two frameworks. *International Journal of Service Industry Management*, *8*(3), 206–219.

Konuş, U., Verhoef, P. C., & Neslin, S. A. (2008). Multichannel shopper segments and their covariates. *Journal of Retailing*, *84*(4), 398–413.

Krafcik, J. F. (1988). Triumph of the lean production system. *Sloan Management Review*, *30*(1), 41–52.

Levitt, T. (1972). Production-line approach to service. *Harvard Business Review*, *50*(5), 41–52.

Liljander, V., Gillberg, F., Gummerus, J., & van Riel, A. (2006). Technology readiness and the evaluation and adoption of self-service technologies. *Journal of Retailing and Consumer Services*, *13*(3), 177–191.

Lovelock, C. H., & Young, R. F. (1979). Look to consumers to increase productivity. *Harvard Business Review*, *57*(3), 168–178.

Lusch, R. F., & Vargo, S. L. (2006). Service-dominant logic: Reactions, reflections and refinements. *Marketing Theory*, *6*(3), 281–288.

Malmbrandt, M., & Åhlström, P. (2013). An instrument for assessing Lean service adoption. *International Journal of Operations & Production Management*, *33*(9), 1131–1165.

McColl-Kennedy, J. R., Hogan, S. J., Witell, L., & Snyder, H. (2017). Cocreative customer practices: Effects of health care customer value cocreation practices on well-being. *Journal of Business Research*, *28*(1), 2–33.

Merlo, O., Eisingerich, A. B., & Auh, S. (2014). Why customer participation matters. *MIT Sloan Management Review*, *55*(2), 81.

Metters, R., & Vargas, V. (2000). Organizing work in service firms. *Business Horizons*, *43*(4), 23–32.

Meuter, M. L., Bitner, M. J., Ostrom, A. L., & Brown, S. W. (2005). Choosing among alternative service delivery modes: An investigation of customer trial of self-service technologies. *Journal of Marketing*, *69*(2), 61–83.

Meuter, M. L., Ostrom, A. L., Roundtree, R. I., & Bitner, M. J. (2000). Self-service technologies: Understanding customer satisfaction with technology-based service encounters. *Journal of Marketing, 64*(3), 50–64.

Morgan, T. R., Rapp, A., Richey, R. G., & Ellinger, A. E. (2014). Marketing culture to service climate: The influence of employee control and flexibility. *Journal of Services Marketing, 28*(6), 498–508.

Mustak, M., Jaakkola, E., Halinen, A., & Kaartemo, V. (2016). Customer participation management: Developing a comprehensive framework and a research agenda. *Journal of Service Management, 27*(3), 250–275.

Ohno, T. (1988). *Toyota production system: Beyond large-scale production.* New York, NY: Productivity Press.

Osterhus, T. L. (1997). Pro-social consumer influence strategies: When and how do they work? *Journal of Marketing, 61*(4), 16.

Plé, L., & Cáceres, R. C. (2010). Not always co-creation: Introducing interactional co-destruction of value in service-dominant logic. *Journal of Services Marketing, 24*(6), 430–437.

Prahalad, C. K., & Ramaswamy, V. (2004). Co-creating unique value with customers. *Strategy &Leadership, 32*(3), 4–9.

Robson, K., Plangger, K., Kietzmann, J., McCarthy, I., & Pitt, L. (2014). Understanding gamification of consumer experiences. *Advances in Consumer Research, 42*, 352–356.

Robson, K., Plangger, K., Kietzmann, J., McCarthy, I., & Pitt, L. (2015). Is it all a game? Understanding the principles of gamification. *Business Horizons, 58*(4), 411–420.

Rogers, E. M. (2003). *The diffusion of innovation* (5th ed.). New York, NY: Free Press.

Rust, R. T., Zahorik, A. J., & Keiningham, T. L. (1995). Return on quality (roq): Making service quality financially accountable. *Journal of Marketing, 59*(2), 58–70.

Sampson, S. E., & Froehle, C. M. (2006). Foundations and implications of a proposed unified services theory. *Production & Operations Management, 15*(2), 329–343.

Sasser, W. E., Olsen, R. P., & Wyckoff, D. D. (1978). *Management of service operations: Text, cases, and readings.* Boston, MA: Allyn and Bacon.

Scherer, A., Wünderlich, N., & von Wangenheim, F. (2015). The value of self-service: Long-term effects of technology-based self-service usage on customer retention. *MIS Quarterly, 39*(1), 177–200.

Schiffauerova, A., & Thomson, V. (2006). A review of research on cost of quality models and best practices. *International Journal of Quality & Reliability Management, 23*(6), 647–669.

Secchi, E., Roth, A., & Verma, R. (2016). The role of service improvisation in improving hotel customer satisfaction. *Cornell Hospitality Report, 16*(1), 2–11.

Secchi, E., Roth, A. V., & Verma, R. (2019). The impact of service improvisation competence on customer satisfaction: Evidence from the hospitality industry. *Production and Operations Management.*

Shang, G., Ghosh, B. P., & Galbreth, M. R. (2017). Optimal retail return policies with wardrobing. *Production and Operations Management, 26*(7), 1315–1332.

Shostack, G. L. (1977). Breaking free from product marketing. *Journal of Marketing, 41*(2), 73–80.

Sorescu, A., Frambach, R. T., Singh, J., Rangaswamy, A., & Bridges, C. (2011). Innovations in retail business models. *Journal of Retailing, 87*(1), S3–S16.

Stuart, I. F., & Tax, S. S. (1996). Planning for service quality: An integrative approach. *International Journal of Service Industry Management, 7*(4), 58–77.

Sweeney, J. C., Danaher, T. S., & McColl-Kennedy, J. R. (2015). Customer effort in value cocreation activities: Improving quality of life and behavioral intentions of health care customers. *Journal of Service Research, 18*(3), 318–335.

Tax, S. S., Colgate, M., & Bowen, D. E. (2006). How to prevent your customers from failing. *MIT Sloan Management Review, 47*(3), 30–38.

Tax, S. S., Kim, Y. S., & Nair, S. (2013a). Getting the right payoff from customer penalty fees. *Business Horizons, 56*(3), 377–386.

Tax, S. S., McCutcheon, D., & Wilkinson, I. F. (2013b). The service delivery network (SDN) a customer-centric perspective of the customer journey. *Journal of Service Research, 16*(4), 454–470.

Temerak, M. S., Winklhofer, H., & Hibbert, S. A. (2018). Facilitating customer adherence to complex services through multi-interface interactions: The case of a weight loss service. *Journal of Business Research, 88*, 265–276.

van Birgelen, M., de Jong, A., & de Ruyter, K. (2006). Multi-channel service retailing: The effects of channel performance satisfaction on behavioral intentions. *Journal of Retailing, 82*(4), 367–377.

Van Dierdonck, R., & Brandt, G. (1988). The focused factory in service industry. *International Journal of Operations & Production Management*, 8(3), 31–38.

van Doorn, J., Lemon, K. N., Mittal, V., Nass, S., Pick, D., Pirner, P., & Verhoef, P. C. (2010). Customer engagement behavior: Theoretical foundations and research directions. *Journal of Service Research*, 13(3), 253–266.

Vargo, S. L., & Lusch, R. F. (2004). Evolving to a new dominant logic for marketing. *Journal of Marketing*, 68(1), 1–17.

Vargo, S. L., & Lusch, R. F. (2008). Service-dominant logic: Continuing the evolution. *Journal of the Academy of Marketing Science*, 36(1), 1–10.

Vargo, S. L., & Lusch, R. F. (2016). Institutions and axioms: An extension and update of service-dominant logic. *Journal of the Academy of Marketing Science*, 44(1), 5–23.

Vera, D., & Crossan, M. (2005). Improvisation and innovative performance in teams. *Organization Science*, 16(3), 203–224.

Verhoef, P. C., Kannan, P. K., & Inman, J. (2015). From multi-channel retailing to omni-channel retailing: Introduction to the special issue on multi-channel retailing. *Journal of Retailing*, 91(2), 174–181.

Verhoef, P. C., Neslin, S. A., & Vroomen, B. (2007). Multichannel customer management: Understanding the research-shopper phenomenon. *International Journal of Research in Marketing*, 24(2), 129–148.

Womack, J. P., Jones, D. T., & Roos, D. (1990). *The machine that changed the world*. New York, NY: Rawson Associates.

Xie, C., Bagozzi, R. P., & Troye, S. V. (2008). Trying to prosume: Toward a theory of consumers as co-creators of value. *Journal of the Academy of Marketing Science*, 36(1), 109–122.

Xue, M., Hitt, L. M., & Chen, P.-Y. (2011). Determinants and outcomes of internet banking adoption. *Management Science*, 57(2), 291–307.

Xue, M., Hitt, L. M., & Harker, P. T. (2007). Customer efficiency, channel usage, and firm performance in retail banking. *Manufacturing & Service Operations Management*, 9(4), 535–558.

17

Value co-creation and its meaning for customers

Andrew S. Gallan and Josephine Go Jefferies

Introduction

Service-dominant logic (S-DL) has ushered in a new way of thinking about service interactions, integration of customer and provider resources, and the co-creation of value (Vargo & Lusch, 2004). Indeed, nothing is more central to S-DL thinking, marketing theory, and service provision than the concept of value. What is *of value* to a customer? What does a particular customer *value* in her life? What goals does a customer have when engaging with a service organization? How might a hierarchy of goals influence her behaviour prior to, during, and after the service interaction? What resources and capabilities does a customer need to bring to a service interaction in order to co-create the type of value that she is looking for? These questions are important to consider in order to fully understand value co-creation in services.

This chapter examines the concept of value co-creation from a customer perspective. It draws on current debates from the marketing literature to consider the implications of the S-DL Axiom 4: value is always uniquely and phenomenologically determined by its beneficiaries in light of Axiom 5: value co-creation is coordinated through actor-generated institutions and institutional arrangements (Vargo & Lusch, 2016). This chapter begins by defining value co-creation, and then reviews the literature to describe its antecedents and consequences and explain implications for customers.

S-DL advocates that value is not created *for* customers, but rather that value is co-created *with* customers and in systems. It moves from viewing consumption and production as separate activities, and eschews the term *consumer*, because nothing is consumed. Rather, resources are utilized to co-create value for various actors in a service ecosystem, which is defined as "a relatively self-contained, self-adjusting system of resource-integrating actors connected by shared institutional arrangements and mutual value creation through service exchange" (Lusch & Vargo, 2014, p. 158). The implications of this way of thinking include more sustainable, ethical, and transformative manners of regarding and interacting with customers.

It is widely accepted that value co-creation is underpinned by processes of resource integration to realize meaningful value for customers (Arnould, Price, & Malshe, 2006). Value is determined differently by different actors (Helkkula, Kelleher, & Pihlström, 2012) and can depend on the effort required of customers in order to integrate resources effectively (Hibbert, Winklhofer, & Temerak, 2012). Focusing on resources and capabilities in value co-creation is analytically useful for identifying the role that mundane, yet considerable, barriers and facilitators play by affecting integration. Understanding how a customer's situation affects access to the resources required for service outcomes to be realized, and how resources themselves have different weights and meanings to different customers (Chandler & Vargo, 2011; Ng, 2014) is important for improving service processes.

Drawing on service scholarship in a business-to-business (B2B) context, this chapter explains the meaning of value co-creation from a customer perspective by applying the concept of "resourceness" to the customer context, thereby affecting their experience of designed service processes (Koskela-Huotari & Vargo, 2016; Peters, 2016). This approach is useful for explaining how differences between provider and customer perceptions of value potentially create barriers to value co-creation (Helkkula et al., 2012) that can be addressed through innovation.

The concept of value co-creation

To begin, the concept of 'service' must be differentiated from 'services': "Service is a perspective on value creation rather than a category of market offerings" (Edvardsson, Gustafsson, & Roos, 2005, p. 118). Service is defined as "the application of specialized competences (knowledge and skills), through deeds, processes, and performances for the benefit of another entity or the entity itself" (Lusch & Vargo, 2006, p. 283).

> Adopting service as a logic for business has profound consequences for how value is created for customers and for the roles of suppliers and customers in value creation. Furthermore, it has equally profound consequences for how marketing should be understood and managed.
>
> *(Grönroos, 2008a, p. 270)*

Value co-creation is a central concept in S-DL and contextualizes the emergence of customer value within service systems. It involves customers in processes of resource integration by network actors within the context of wider service systems for benefits to emerge (Vargo & Lusch, 2004, 2008, 2016). McColl-Kennedy and Cheung (2018) provide an extensive analysis of the developments of value co-creation, explaining conceptual confusions and contributions from multiple disciplines to the conceptualization of value and its emergence. Value co-creation develops from customer participation in the co-production of value (Normann & Ramírez, 1993; Prahalad & Ramaswamy, 2002, 2004), variously describing "value-in-use" (Vargo & Lusch, 2008), "value-in-context" (Akaka, Vargo, & Schau, 2015; Chandler & Vargo, 2011), and "value-in-social context" (Edvardsson, Tronvoll, & Gruber, 2011). This advances an experiential view of customer value (Helkkula et al., 2012; Holbrook & Hirschman, 1982) as "always uniquely and phenomenologically determined by the beneficiary" (Vargo & Lusch, 2008, p. 7). S-DL's synthesized form of value is created when the customer's well-being improves in some way (Vargo, Maglio, & Akaka, 2008), which has enabled transformative service researchers to focus upon determinants of well-being in relation to value co-creation processes (Anderson et al., 2013; Ostrom, Mathras, & Anderson, 2014).

What is value?

Although many definitions of value have been advanced, it is important to note that value is determined by customers first. "Value is perceived by customers in their internal processes and in interactions with suppliers or service providers when consuming or making use of services, goods, information, personal contacts, recovery and other elements of ongoing relationships" (Grönroos, 2000, p. 140). Is the customer "better off" after engaging in service (Grönroos, 2011)? Indeed, Vargo and Lusch (2008, p. 4) state: "We have always considered value to be phenomenologically determined." Because of this, and because value is "influenced by previous and anticipated service experiences" (Helkkula et al., 2012, p. 59), it is unique to customers, settings, and circumstances. Furthermore, value is "an ongoing, interactive circular process of individual and collective customer sense making, as opposed to a linear, cognitive process restricted to isolated service encounters" (Helkkula et al., 2012, p. 59).

In a seminal article that first defined value from a customer's point of view, value was construed as being customer-specific, related to customer goals, and emanating from use. However, it was restricted to goods use, not the larger context of service (singular) that S-DL advanced later: "Customer value is a customer's perceived preference for an evaluation of those product attributes, attribute performances, and consequences arising from use that facilitate (or block) achieving the customer's goals and purposes in use situations" (Woodruff, 1997, p. 141). Focusing on the importance of perceived utility of product attributes is consistent with a goods-dominant logic (G-DL), which takes a goods-manufacturing view of value as primarily added to raw materials through a firm's processing activities. Whereas G-DL considers the firm as the focal actor in the creation of value, S-DL argues that value is co-created through a firm's interactions with customers (Vargo & Lusch, 2004).

Here a note of caution is appropriate: care must be taken when assessing the definition of customer value, as this term can often be used to connote the (financial) value of a customer to a firm (e.g., Slater & Narver, 2000). In the definition advanced by Woodruff, customer value is defined differently: value is perceived and subjectively determined in relation to a customer's desired goal or purpose. Customer value and customer perceived value are the most common terms for these two distinct constructs.

Financial value is one small and specific aspect of value. It is equivalent to money, and to make this distinction clear, the use of the term 'worth' (to denote economic worth to customers) is important for facilitating exchange, and is related to value but is not fully equal to a complete definition of value (Ng, 2014). Thus, financial value has a specific meaning that should not be equated with a holistic definition of value. Often, businesses are driven by revenues and profits, resulting in financial value; however, this is only one small aspect of what is important to customers (as well as to organizations and employees). In fact, "there are two sides to value creation, viz. value for the customer and financial value for the firm" (Grönroos, 2011, p. 281).

In this chapter, the concept of value is assessed from a customer point of view, with the understanding that financial value cannot be optimized without co-creation of value with customers (Vargo & Lusch, 2008). This is not to say that the pursuit of financial value to firms is irrelevant to customers. Indeed, customers can simultaneously be direct beneficiaries in the firms they purchase from and also benefit indirectly as stakeholders from the corporate taxes payable on profits. However, it is important to understand that the things customers do to improve their well-being are affected by economic and non-economic determinants of value. For example, the concept of "balanced centricity" (Gummesson, 2008) that further developed a dyadic view of value co-creation, suggests that firm and customer value are intertwined. Recently it was suggested that this means taking care to calculate the net economic value that is generated for firms and customers so that it also fairly accounts for the non-economic costs borne by customers (i.e., the emotional, physical, and psychological costs that customers must integrate) in order to co-create value for themselves and others (Ng, 2014). It is important to be aware that different disciplines eschew this view, instead sticking to a definition of value as economic value. This is not what is reviewed here. This chapter examines value co-creation as a multi-actor process of generating outcomes that are valuable to each actor, including but not limited to addressing needs and wants, making progress toward or achieving goals, and producing emotional, physical, social, and other types of well-being.

There has been much developmental work to define value relationally. Value-in-exchange is viewed as embedded in matter through production, as value-added, not as the provision of a service (Vargo & Lusch, 2004). In this perspective, value is determined by the producer. Value-in-use is a foundational concept of value co-creation. "Value-in-use means that value for the user is created or emerges during usage, which is a process of which the customer as user is in charge" (Grönroos, 2011, p. 287). Value-in-use is determined by the customer and depends on context and the customer's current and past experiences (Heinonen et al., 2010). Value-in-context (Chandler & Vargo, 2011) and value-in-cultural-context (Akaka, Schau, & Vargo, 2013) emerged to reflect the realization that value must be understood in the context of the customer's domain, along with associated resources and other actors . Current perspectives of holistic value as relational and dynamic subscribe to an understanding that resources-in-context are mutable, that is, they have the potential to become necessary for value co-creation to occur (Löbler, 2013). This property of resources becoming critical to value co-creation underpins the concept of 'resourceness,' which describes the relational properties of resources that are mutually valued by service beneficiaries (Koskela-Huotari & Vargo, 2016; Mele et al., 2018; Peters, 2012; Peters, 2016).

Resourceness emanates from a B2B context, where tangible and intangible resources shared between businesses become more or less important during different stages of collaboration. For example, tacit knowledge about pre-existing trading arrangements can become more important (acquires resourceness) during the early phase of contract negotiations and become less important as interactions become routine practices. Resourceness is relevant to service interactions, as providers need to understand the resource constraints experienced by their customers (and employees) that are likely to interfere with realizing envisaged value co-creation. Why does this matter to customers? Resourceness of their skills, attitudes, and personal and social resources can affect the ease or difficulty they experience when trying to co-create value through service interactions.

What is value co-creation?

Stated simply, S-D logic considers "that *value is created* when a service or a good is *used* by customers or other actors" (Skålén, 2016, p. 11, italics in original). Additionally, the term 'co-creation' by itself is meaningless; what is being co-created? It is important to specify exactly what is being co-created. In this chapter, the focus is on the concept of co-creation of value, or *value co-creation*. Value is created through customer processes, and is customer-driven (Grönroos & Gummerus, 2014).

Generally speaking, services can be co-designed and co-produced by various actors in a system, with the potential for value to be co-created. Co-design is an approach that involves customers in collaborative design processes intended to utilize their expertise in their own experiences (Dietrich, Trischler, Schuster, & Rundle-Thiele, 2017). Co-design helps "users to articulate … precisely and realistically which benefits to aim for and to match these benefits to the goals of a service design project" to realize customer perceived value (Steen, Manschot, & Koning, 2011). Co-designing a service means that an organization and its customers have inputs into how the service will be enacted; that is, everyone involved in producing the service and everyone who may benefit from it have a say in how it will go.

Co-production represents "the joint activities of the firm and the customer in the creation of firm output," whereas value co-creation represents "collaborative, customer-specific value creation … closely aligned with 'value-in-use'" (Vargo, 2008, p. 211). Lusch and Vargo (2006, p. 284) specify that the second component of cocreation is what might more correctly be called co-production. It involves the participation in the creation of the core offering itself. It can occur through shared inventiveness, co-design, or shared production of related goods, and can occur with customers and any other partners in the value network.

Moreover, they state that "because both 'cocreation of value' and 'co-production' make the consumer endogenous, they are both different from the production concepts associated with G-D logic" (Lusch & Vargo, 2006, p. 284).

Other uses of the term 'co-creation' include the term 'service co-creation,' conceptualized as "a process comprising value potential, resource integration, and resource modification" (Hilton, Hughes, & Chalcraft, 2012, p. 1504). This perspective supports the idea that "value, being a personal evaluative judgement cannot be co-created; rather, it is realized by actors as an outcome of service co-creation" (Hilton et al., 2012, p. 1504). Another investigation of co-creation of services positions this term with the concept of service co-production (Oertzen, Odekerken-Schröder, Brax, & Mager, 2018). A more accepted view of value co-creation relies on the understanding that service interactions provide opportunities for value (including but not limited to financial value) to be realized by multiple actors. Thus, the term value co-creation is consistent with S-DL definitions.

Value can be co-created when customers, service providers, and other potential service ecosystem actors converge in a "joint sphere" where providers and customers interact to integrate resources to co-produce a service (Grönroos & Voima, 2013). It has long been argued that managers focus on the value creation activities that occur in the joint sphere, so that service-for-service exchange ensures the realization of benefits to providers and customers. However, recent scholarship encourages a holistic view of customer experience and the meaning of value – moving away from provider-led, partial views of value-creating resources and activities. As the determination of value is highly dependent on the context of value-in-use (Helkkula, Dube, & Arnould, 2018), understanding the process of value co-creation is concerned not only with focusing on those critical experiences of direct interaction that occur across service touchpoint(s), but also along customer journeys that directly and indirectly influence value creation. This entails considering how service experiences are informed by the mundane realities that customers bring and that influence services (McColl-Kennedy et al., 2015) in pre-, during-, and post-interaction stages to facilitate access to appropriate resources during these various stages in order that value co-creation can succeed (Voorhees et al., 2017). Customer views of value are influenced by situation, social networks, context, and various other factors that are deemed to be important to the customer (Chandler & Vargo, 2011). Indeed, social systems and service ecosystems interact to create interdependencies that impact how customers are capable of co-creating value (Skålén, 2016).

These interdependencies between actors interacting across multiple contexts indicate that value co-creation has been advanced as a multidimensional construct. This is because the interactions between focal actors and service touchpoints are linked in the trajectory of customer experience. For example, Randall, Gravier, and Prybutok (2011) discuss three potential dimensions of value co-creation, namely connection, trust, and commitment. They suggest that ensuring the right level of involvement when provider and customer roles converge during the process of value co-creation is important for establishing positive experiences. Commitment rooted in emotional attachment affects potential for building an enduring, mutually beneficial relationship and increases the likelihood of future interactions. Greater convergence between providers and customers and their resources is influenced by a sense of connection, trust, and commitment to move beyond a transactional relationship toward a more enduring value co-creation relationship.

Thus, building and maintaining lasting and mutually beneficial relationships involves looking beyond the joint sphere's core service interaction, to consider the factors that enhance the customer service experience across all touchpoints, including those touchpoints that indirectly affect the core service from the customer sphere (Bolton, Gustafsson, McColl-Kennedy, Sirianni, & Tse, 2014) and target resources to manage them effectively. This means there is greater scope to consider how resources can be managed strategically to affect various points of the service experience that extend beyond the joint sphere (Voorhees et al., 2017) and affect value co-creation. For example, investing in communication targeting influential actors in the customer sphere can affect the pre-, during-, and post-service experiences to improve value co-creation. As social, physical, and technological dimensions converge in the future, managing these elements and their interactions will be critical for service companies to optimize value co-creation with customers (Bolton et al., 2018).

Gustafsson et al. (2012) empirically identified four dimensions of communication as potential dimensions of value co-creation within an innovation context: frequency, direction, modality, and content. These authors suggest that innovation results in value for customers through focusing on customer needs and conceptualizing the customer role in innovation as one that communicates future needs. Aligning innovation processes with customers' envisaged value-in-context allows innovation design to be grounded in value co-creation. Researching value co-creation therefore requires expanded consideration of customer value-in-context as it relates to various interdependencies (e.g., temporal, technological, organizational, and societal) between core service experiences and adjacent encounters that involve the past, present, and future interactions (Voorhees et al., 2017).

Value co-destruction

Although value can be co-created, it can also be destroyed through interactions that generate adverse consequences (Plé & Cáceres, 2010). This can be a result of the fact that "resource integration is carried out in such a way that the customer's perceived value is continuously reduced the longer the interaction goes on" (Skålén, 2016, p. 121). From a conservation of resources (COR) view, value co-destruction emanates from the misuse of customer resources (Smith, 2013). "Loss 'cycles' or 'spirals' develop impacting negatively on well-being" (Smith, 2013, p. 1889), which can be termed "value destruction-through-misuse" (Plé & Cáceres, 2010, p. 430). A research challenge is to establish whether, and in which contexts, the S-DL axiom (Vargo & Lusch, 2016) that customers always co-create value – and withal when they *always fail* to co-create value – reflects a normative strategy rather than value co-creation processes in practice (Gummesson, Lusch, & Vargo, 2010; Winklhofer, Palmer, & Brodie, 2007). Indeed, the ethics of expecting customers to always co-create value have been questioned, especially when asymmetrical processes and access to resources lead to systematic exploitation of customers (Cova & Dalli, 2009). The benign aspect of the S-DL value co-creation concept has been seen as part of a shift in marketing thought that advocates for ensuring the emergence of customer value (Martínez-Cañas, Ruiz-Palomino, Linuesa-Langreo, & Blázquez-Resino, 2016) through its increased consideration of a customer's direct involvement in generating firm value (Arvidsson, 2008; Grönroos, 2012). In a further twist, a different view of value co-creation is captured by a customer-dominant logic (C-DL), which purports to avoid a provider-dominant perspective that is inherent in both G-DL and S-DL (Heinonen et al., 2010). The implication of C-DL is that it challenges service providers to examine their level of control in value co-creation, and the scope of customer experiences in order to make their offer relevant to customer needs.

Addressing incongruity between customer and firm value is critical when it potentially leads customers to fail to co-create value. Realignment strategies focus on addressing resource integration necessary for value co-creation. This can be through the enactment of collaborative practices that involve addressing a perceived misfit or mismatch between firm and customer perspectives, so that customers and providers enact practices in a similar way in order that one or both parties are better off. Alignment involves compliance, interpretation, and orientation as strategies to avoid failure to co-create value (Skålén, Pace, & Cova, 2015). Compliance means procedural alignment, interpretation refers to alignment in understandings, and orientation suggests alignment between engagements, or "the emotionally charged purposes and goals that participants associate with a practice" (Skålén et al., 2015, p. 612). An example occurs when an interaction is perceived to be dishonestly motivated to exploit the other party, resulting in disagreement and one party feeling worse off as a result of interacting (i.e., failing to co-create value). Through communication to clarify the orientation of the practice, the engagement can be set right between disparate actors resulting in co-creation of mutual, if distinct, value-in-context. It is further suggested that firms "re-evaluate and re-design value propositions in line with organisational capabilities and customers' resource needs" (Smith, 2013, p. 1889).

Value co-creation literature

There is too much extant research on value co-creation to summarize all of it, even in table form. A Google Scholar search using the term "value co-creation" yields over 27,000 results (as of January 2019). For results of a scholarly literature review on value co-creation as of 2016, based on 149 papers, see Ranjan and Read (2016). The present chapter references articles that represent a wide view of perspectives on value co-creation, with the intent to provide the reader key with citations that may offer an opportunity to explore specific areas in more detail.

S-DL and service logic

The concept of value co-creation has origins in S-DL (Vargo & Lusch, 2004) and service logic, a Nordic perspective (e.g., Grönroos & Voima, 2013). These two streams of literature both offer important contributors to fully comprehending the construct of value co-creation. Indeed, the similarities between the two are more important than the differences in how they view value co-creation. For example, they agree upon the centrality of value co-creation by firm and non-firm actors to explain service. S-DL is concerned with conceptualizing a broad, all-encompassing view of value co-creation as occurring through interactions of a network of linked actors, directly and indirectly influencing the value co-creation processes (Vargo & Lusch, 2016). The service logic perspective is more grounded, emphasizing a specific locus of interactions between firms and customers. This joint sphere is where interactions occur and are visible to managers, whose concern should be to ensure that value is created for customers and firms (Grönroos & Voima, 2013). Perhaps the biggest difference in viewpoints is that the Nordic school views value co-creation as a more specific activity than does S-DL: "Value creation refers to customers' creation of value-in-use; co-creation is a function of interaction" (Grönroos & Voima, 2013, p. 133). Thus, value co-creation can be defined as "the joint actions by a customer (or another beneficiary) and a service provider during their direct interactions" (Grönroos, 2012, p. 1520).

Sometimes a customer engages in a service interaction to achieve a goal, and the experience is secondary to the outcome (e.g., having their clothes dry-cleaned). Other times, the service experience is the goal, and thus is the sole driver of value co-creation (e.g., attending a concert).

A service ecosystem view of value co-creation

A dyadic perspective of value co-creation between a service provider and a customer has given way to a networked or systems view, which argues that services are most often delivered in complex contexts involving multiple actors. Lusch and Vargo state that "value creation is a process of integrating and transforming resources, which requires interaction and implies networks" (2006, p. 285). A service system is "a configuration of resources (including people, information, and technology) connected to other systems by value propositions" (Vargo et al., 2008, p. 145). Service systems can contribute significantly to enhanced value co-creation, yet are also complex and require sophisticated mechanisms in order to facilitate value co-creation (Vargo & Akaka, 2012).

Within marketing theory, the conceptualization of value co-creation continues to evolve through extensive examination of resource integration processes and emergent outcomes in different contexts. The study of contexts includes the immediate service context as well as the wider social context in which it is embedded (Giesler & Fischer, 2017; Humphreys, 2010; Vargo & Lusch, 2016). Multiple contexts can be conceptualized as a service ecosystem, defined as a "relatively self-contained, self-adjusting system of resource-integrating actors connected by shared institutional arrangements and mutual value creation through service exchange" (Vargo & Lusch, 2014, p. 240). Recent literature suggests that a service ecosystem's self-adjusting structures reflect and reinforce the interests and well-being of certain actors over others (Bone, Christensen, & Williams, 2014; Mele et al., 2018). Understanding service ecosystem dynamics and their effects on success or failure to co-create value is fundamentally important to Transformative Service Research (TSR) (Ostrom et al., 2014), and explains growing interest in the study of emergent associations, collaborations, and social platforms that enable ecosystem transformation to facilitate or constrain value co-creation by disadvantaged actors (Anderson et al., 2016; Ben Lataifa, Edvardsson, & Tronvoll, 2016; Edvardsson, Kleinaltenkamp, Tronvoll, McHugh, & Windahl, 2014).

In service ecosystems, "value is a systemic property (i.e., an order parameter) that emerges from micro–macro links in service ecosystems" (Meynardt, Chandler, & Strathoff, 2016, p. 2981). Thus, value is co-created at the ecosystem level and results from many-to-many service exchange. For example, Best, Moffett, Hannibal, and McAdam (2018) consider how value emerges from interactions among networks of non-governmental organizations (NGOs), where outcomes of value differ between multiple actors. In health care, ecosystems exist to serve patients' health and well-being needs, yet various actors view value in disparate ways (Black & Gallan, 2015). For value to be co-created optimally, the ecosystem needs to stay focused on the core service of health care professionals and patients focusing on patient needs. When this occurs, the ecosystem is fuelled by the value that each patient experiences. An ecosystem view highlights dimensions of value co-existing and competing within an interactive network. Therefore, ecosystem perspectives of value are characterized by complex interdependencies between contexts that link disparate actors (Best et al., 2018). This is consistent with theories of value co-creation focusing on contextual characteristics influencing access to key resources required for value co-creation (Edvardsson, Skålén, & Tronvoll, 2012).

An ecosystem perspective integrates earlier work that develops, refines, and distinguishes value co-creation from related concepts, such as value creation and co-production. Having expanded from a focus on the dyadic relationships between service providers and customers to consider multiple actors in a system, the recognition of the role of institutional arrangements brings one back to the notion of interactions between actors with potentially dissimilar interests and practices for determining value. For example, a dyadic view suggests that value creation and c are generally understood to be provider-led in orientation (Chathoth, Altinay, Harrington, Okumus, & Chan, 2013). In contrast, value co-creation is characterized by the idea of balanced centricity between provider and customer in relation to the processes and outcomes of service-for-service exchange (Gummesson, 2008). Although value co-creation has since developed to consider multiple actors, it is underpinned by a normative understanding that alignment between firm and customer value determination is critical, and therefore relevant actors should aim to understand how system actors determine value (Helkkula et al., 2012).

Antecedents of value co-creation

SYSTEM-LEVEL FACTORS

Consistent with the previous section on service ecosystems, service research has moved from firm-centric value-adding toward a dyadic focus between a customer and a firm, and expanded further to recognize a disparate and interconnected system of actors that influence the value co-creation processes. Actors, also referred to as beneficiaries (Vargo & Lusch, 2016), are understood to include networked human, organizational, technological, and institutional entities. This is consistent with, and supported by, a view of "value constellations" advanced by Normann and Ramírez (1993).

Technology has enhanced information access and has enabled communities to emerge that expand the number of factors that may impact value co-creation (Prahalad & Ramaswamy, 2004). At the same time, it is important to remember that technology embedded within sociotechnical systems exerts its own demands on users because the technology must be used in particular ways in order to function (Go Jefferies, Bishop, & Hibbert, 2019). Thus, the design of technology interfaces can be seen as informed by value systems interacting with others and may involve trade-offs (Go Jefferies et al., 2019). Consider the use of digital surveillance to track the global movements of asthma attacks, and how this information may be useful for resourcing health systems and providing evidence for air pollution regulation (although these surveillance systems also involve automated retrieval of personal data at scale from mobile apps) (Kenner, 2016). Service networks can serve to enhance and transform individual well-being and health, and this example shows that there are distinct forms of customer value at play (Black & Gallan, 2015).

Increasingly, system-level factors are examined through the lens of institutional theory, which takes a macro level view of behavioural determinants to explain the interactions that exist at multiple levels within and outside organizations and the social contexts in which they operate to highlight possible motivations for and against change (Beirão, Patrício, & Fisk, 2017; Edvardsson et al., 2014; Kleinaltenkamp, Corsaro, & Sebastiani, 2018). Empirical research has shown that the following factors enable value co-creation in service ecosystems: resource access, resource sharing, resource recombination, resource monitoring, and governance/institutions generation (Beirão et al., 2017). Institutional arrangements are understood to affect the availability of resources and play a part in determining their value (their resourceness), and this influences the customer experience (Edvardsson et al., 2014; Pareigis, Echeverri, & Edvardsson, 2012). Karpen, Bove, and Lukas (2012, p. 25) defined a firm's individuated interaction capability as "an organization's ability to understand the resource integration process, contexts and desired outcomes of individual customers and other value network partners." These conditions are necessary antecedents of value co-creation because of its reliance on resource integration among all actors involved.

INDIVIDUAL-LEVEL FACTORS

Whereas system-level perspectives provide a sociologically informed view of the relevant social structures with which actors interact, a marketing perspective has long assumed that customers have agency to behave unpredictably in their pursuit of value as they perceive it. This is not to say that the actions of individuals exist in isolation; rather, it emphasizes that individuals may be embedded in cultural contexts that may determine value differently (Akaka et al., 2013). Returning to the resources that are integrated in order for value to be co-created, these can include the configuration of capabilities, knowledge, attitudes, willingness, affective state, etc., that affect the experience of the service interaction. Emotions can have a significant impact on customer ability to fully engage in service co-production and value co-creation (McColl-Kennedy et al., 2017a), and can significantly influence subsequent customer-specific outcomes (Gallan, Jarvis, Brown, & Bitner, 2013). Additionally, social structures, systems, roles, positions, and interactions can have a profound effect on value co-creation (Edvardsson et al., 2011). Just as value is experientially determined, individual-level factors that are antecedents of value co-creation are individual in the sense that they are phenomenologically determined by the interpretation of events to make meaning in the customer life-world. This system of meaning-making may reflect, and even overlap with, other meaning-making systems (e.g., how firms determine value, or the ways health care professionals or public health officials conceptualize positive health outcomes) but equally, it may not, potentially leading to contradiction, tension, and frustration, especially if there is a lack of alternative providers with whom to co-create value (Anderson et al., 2016). An integrative framework has identified the following customer prerequisites for value co-creation: involvement, engagement, and participation (Oertzen et al., 2018). The importance of disparate value systems coming together in value co-creation underpins the need for certain customer attitudes and actions to be fostered.

How might service processes encourage individual-level factors to emerge at the right time, and thereby acquire the resourceness needed to co-create value? One way might be to consider the intrinsic motivations of individuals using Maslow's (1943) hierarchy of needs, a psychological theory of motivation to explain individual responses and actions, and to test for them using experimental methods. According to Maslow's framework, after the needs for physiological well-being and safety are satisfied, individuals are motivated by the pursuit of senses of love/belonging, esteem, and self-actualization. These higher level needs may be understood in terms of pursuit of hedonic (pleasure) or eudaimonic (virtue) value co-creation (Ryan & Deci, 2001). Of course, the realization of individual aspirations is contingent on many factors, including timely access to the right resources.

Access to necessary resources may be withheld for various reasons. For example, in health care services, the satisfaction of an individual patient's wish for treatment will be affected by the clinical evidence base, the bureaucratic processes that makes treatment covered by the healthcare plan, and the availability of a clinician. For this reason, social-psychological approaches, especially those informed by social constructionism (Gergen, 1991, 1994, 1999, 2018) may provide further insight, as they consider the roles of intrinsic and extrinsic motivations to understand consumer behaviour in terms of relational entanglements. Given that service interactions and technological interfaces involve external cues to encourage certain customer interactions over others (Löbler & Lusch, 2014; Pareigis et al., 2012), this approach can inform understanding of value co-creation practices (e.g., to produce financial or hedonic value) achieving legitimacy despite their failure to satisfy higher level needs (e.g., by co-creating eudaimonic value).

The topic returns to the sociological study of processes that become legitimized at the system level as practices and provide extrinsic motivations that guide interactions. Increasingly, service researchers recognize that the future of understanding and improving value co-creation requires system-level approaches that integrate individual-level factors (Carr, Sangiorgi, Büscher, Junginger, & Cooper, 2011; Patrício, Fisk, Falcão e Cunha, & Cunha, 2008; Patrício, Gustafsson, & Fisk, 2018; Sangiorgi, Patrício, & Fisk, 2017).

The process of value co-creation

The process of value co-creation, including resource integration, service interaction, and resolution of dual-sided knowledge asymmetry, is discussed in this section. These components are important because they provide a more detailed and nuanced view of what customers and service providers do in order to facilitate value co-creation.

RESOURCE INTEGRATION

Operand resources (tangible goods as vehicles for operant resources) and operant resources (intangible knowledge and skills) must be integrated in order for value to emerge (Skålén, 2016; Vargo & Lusch, 2004). S-DL advocates a view of "value creation through resource integration" (Lusch & Vargo, 2006, p. 284). "One of the distinguishing features of S-DL, in contrast to G-D logic, is the former's treatment of all customers, employees, and organizations as operant resources, which are endogenous to both the exchange and value-creation processes" (Lusch & Vargo, 2006, p. 285).

In a detailed view of resource integration (a fundamental consideration in value co-creation), the concepts of heteropathic and homopathic resource integration were developed to explain how relationships within a service ecosystem affect the quality of resources that are available (Peters, 2016). Heteropathic resource integration connotes an emergent relationship among resources in a service ecosystem, in which the value that emerges from the given resources is enhanced by the interactions. By contrast, homopathic resource integration indicates summative relations among resources. "It is the new emergent properties that result from heteropathic resource integration that become an important factor in enhancing resourceness and thus value co-creation" (Peters, 2016, p. 2999). This work develops from studying B2B resource integration, through business partnerships and alliances bringing different resources together. With reference to B2C (business-to-consumer) contexts, emergent heteropathic relationships are interesting because they allow scope for atypical resources and divergent processes and practices to come together in order that value co-creation can occur, even if the determination of value is not agreed upon by system actors as legitimate or desirable. A growing literature considers how and why system actors' value co-creation processes shape service systems (Baker, Storbacka, & Brodie, 2019; Dolbec & Fischer, 2015; Go Jefferies et al., 2019; Vargo et al., 2017).

"Value is created in use when customers integrate their own resources with the resources of others and the value propositions of companies" (Skålén, 2016, p. 47). Value propositions play a fundamental role in service systems, as they link actors in meaningful ways (Chandler & Lusch, 2015). Service systems play a part in determining customer access to resources, such as when, how, and how much of a necessary resource is required to realize value propositions. An example occurs when airport management introduces self-service ticket kiosks to save time and costs, and limits the number of customer service support agents working during off-peak travel times (Reinders, Dabholkar, & Frambach, 2008). Focusing on ensuring customer value frequently requires cultural change so that customers can co-create the value they expect (Sharma & Conduit, 2016) in exchange for the effort they contribute.

Customer effort, therefore, is a necessary resource. For example, in health care, value co-creation can be realized through varying levels of customer participation, termed "Effort in Value Cocreation Activities" (EVCA) (Sweeney, Danaher, & McColl-Kennedy, 2015). This represents "a hierarchy of activities representing varying levels of customer effort from complying with basic requirements (less effort and easier tasks) to extensive decision making (more effort and more difficult tasks)" (Sweeney et al., 2015, p. 318). These activities take place "within the customer's service network that extends well beyond the customer-firm dyad to include other market-facing as well as public and private resources" (Sweeney et al., 2015, p. 318). Moreover, EVCA is linked to transformative outcomes, including quality of life and behavioural intentions.

Payne, Storbacka, and Frow (2008) systematically developed a process-based value co-creation framework consisting of three main components: (1) customer value-creating processes; (2) supplier value-creating processes; and, (3) encounter processes. Their model included critical components previously not made explicit, including customer emotions and firm metrics and measures, which further developed theory and practice of service design. Process-based value co-creation perspectives are useful for highlighting the critical resources required for customer participation in order that interactions are productive. Harmonizing the management of customer-based resources (e.g., emotions), using firm-based value-creating processes to measure their effects on productivity, therefore ties together customer interests and firm competitiveness. By elaborating the managerial implications of value co-creation, the literature draws together the resource-based view of firm and the basis of customer value co-creation to achieve subjective goals and life projects (Arnould et al., 2006).

KNOWLEDGE ASYMMETRY AND RESOURCE INTEGRATION

In order for value co-creation to be fully realized, customers, service providers, and other eco-system actors need to be adept at integrating various resources. "Knowledge sharing is the basic operant resource that comprises sharing consumers' knowledge, ideas, and creativity" (Ranjan & Read, 2016, p. 292). Knowledge asymmetry is not one-sided, however. In a dyadic situation, both the service provider and the customer have knowledge, expertise, and skills that must be shared with the other; additionally, each has the responsibility of integrating these resources in order to co-create value. For example, in health care services,

> Value emanates from an enhanced ability of customers to integrate provider resources in value-creating activities. Thus, value cocreation requires resolution of dual-sided information asymmetry, where the provider (physician) has technical (clinical) knowledge, and the customer (patient) has personal knowledge. A challenge, therefore, is to synthesize capabilities and knowledge to optimize designs, processes, plans, and outcomes. This requires both customer learning and organizational learning, as value cocreation occurs through knowledge transfer, resource integration, and learning across entities in a network. In health care, patients may provide perspective on issues such as tolerance for risk, knowledge of disease state and possible treatments, and preference for treatment. Physician communication with patients conveys critical clinical information, views on treatment alternatives, and additional resources for the patient. In order for value to be fully realized, knowledge transfer should occur as seamlessly as possible among entities in the network, such that patient and provider obtain the critical information from diverse sources necessary to completely address health-related issues.
>
> (Black & Gallan, 2015, p. 830)

VALUE CO-CREATION PRACTICES

In an effort to better understand value co-creation, it is important to appreciate the practices that customers use in attempting to achieve their goals. Designed processes often highlight differences in understanding and approaches to interactions that suggest there are basic assumptions, beliefs, and habits that are taken for granted, also known as social practices (Hagberg & Kjellberg, 2010; Kjellberg & Helgesson, 2006, 2007), that can interfere with the implementation of processes including the evaluation of outcomes. By studying customer practices in the context of characteristic service processes, the design of service processes can better accommodate customer preferences and consider their implications on resources needed to co-create the desired value. For example, research in the context of health care has identified different customer value co-creation practice styles linked to quality of life: team management, insular controlling, partnering, pragmatic adapting, and passive compliance (McColl-Kennedy, Vargo, Dagger, Sweeney, & van Kasteren, 2012). Co-creative customer practices in health care demonstrate that engagement in co-productive activities leads to value co-creation as well-being (McColl-Kennedy, Hogan, Witell, & Snyder, 2017b). "Interestingly, activities requiring change can have a negative effect on well-being, except in psychological illness, where the opposite is true" (McColl-Kennedy et al., 2017b, p. 55). Therefore, when value propositions require customers to participate in activities by devoting significant efforts (e.g., to change their lifestyles, beliefs, and behaviours) in order to realize value, there is a greater likelihood that value co-creation processes will not succeed as envisioned. This is illustrated by the practical difficulties experienced in trying to realize value propositions in an extended consumer journey (Gallan et al., 2019; Nakata et al., 2018). For instance, in health care services, it is recommended that provider-designed service processes minimize the effort required of patients, to reduce the "burden of treatment" (May et al., 2014).

The implications of this focus should be considered for integrating practices from one service context to another, as it relates to misalignment and realignment strategies to improve value co-creation (Skålén et al., 2015), as discussed above. Research in public transportation revealed five interaction value practices: informing, greeting, delivering, charging, and helping (Echeverri & Skålén, 2011). Their importance to customer experience confirms the notion that value is "intersubjectively assessed by actors" (Echeverri & Skålén, 2011, p. 351).

Social practices, therefore, play an important role in the perception of value and resource requirements to realize value propositions offered. For example, Ballantyne and Varey (2006) propose the roles of communicating, relating, and knowing in value co-creation. "These three overarching concepts are considered fundamental for the success of most joint collaborative activities as they provide the structural support for the actions of the interacting customers and employees, improve the coordination of their actions and intensify their cooperation" (Neghina, Caniëls, Bloemer, & van Birgelen, 2015, p. 228). Neghina et al. (2015) distinguished six types of collaborative joint actions that can be combined to create a more comprehensive value co-creation concept: individualizing, relating, ethical, empowering, developmental, and concerted actions. Furthermore, "co-ideation, co-valuation, co-design, co-testing, and co-launching are classified as regenerative co-creation, while the specific co-creation forms of co-production and co-consumption are recognized as operative co-creation" (Oertzen et al., 2018, p. 641).

OUTCOMES OF VALUE CO-CREATION

Outcomes of value co-creation, or forms of value (goal attainment, well-being, quality of life, self-esteem, etc.), are hard to understand and categorize because they encompass every form of value that humans may desire. Often service organizations don't know what an individual customer values until someone asks – and even then, customers may not know what they desire.

In a study of B2B relationships and the establishment of cross-functional teams, value co-creation was measured as financial outcomes, which is highly inconsistent with an S-DL view and the view advanced here. Three phases of relationships were found to impact value co-creation: joint crafting of value propositions, value actualization, and value determination (Lambert & Enz, 2012).

Customers must participate in service interactions in various ways in order for value to be co-created.

> Customer participation (CP) enhances customer's economic value attainment and strengthens the relational bond between customer and employees, but it also increases employees' job stress and hampers their job satisfaction. Moreover, the effects of CP on value creation depend on the cultural values of both customers and service employees.
>
> *(Chan, Yim, & Lam, 2010, p. 48)*

In sum, although individual customers may conceive of value very differently from one another, value may be best understood as goal attainment or progress toward it, including well-being, quality of life, and other broad concepts that encapsulate customer views of value.

MEASURES OF VALUE CO-CREATION

Measures of value co-creation are nascent, and are not yet well vetted in empirical work. Thus, their theoretical contributions are not yet substantial. One enormous challenge to this type of work is to capture a notion that is context-specific, subjective, and ever-changing. Nonetheless, it is critical to include these efforts in order to better understand a particular vein of research and to keep an eye on further efforts in this area.

A value-in-context measure has been advanced as the "value-in-context of resource integrating activities" (ValConRIA) model (Löbler & Hahn, 2013). Created and validated in various contexts (using a laptop, smoking, using a smartphone, and using Facebook), this model finds five different realms of experience, or dimensions, in three orientations: Self-Oriented (I (-Me)]), Object-Oriented (I-It and It-I) and Social-Oriented (I-You and You-I). This scale purports to measure value of resource-integrating activities as experienced by customers. The authors suggest that "practitioners can use the measurement process to identify value their customers co-create" (Löbler & Hahn, 2013, p. 256).

Another attempt at developing a value co-creation measure found two primary dimensions of co-production and value-in-use (Ranjan & Read, 2016). In this work, co-production includes knowledge, equity, and interaction, whereas value-in-use includes experience, personalization, and relationship elements. Subsequently, a value co-creation instrument was developed and tested which included two main dimensions (co-production and value-in-use) with six total sub-elements (knowledge, equity, and interaction in co-production, and experience, personalization, and relationship in value-in-use). The authors find support for their model, with value co-creation leading to satisfaction.

These two models have quite different approaches and results. Although the former provides an empirical development of conceptual elements of value-in-context, the latter leaves one wondering if a measurement model is possible for value co-creation, given its definition and fugacious nature. Moreover, neither effort explicitly included tying customers' notions of value to *what* they value, what their goals are, and whether either was accomplished.

Implications and future research directions for value co-creation

Implications for service management

What customers aim to accomplish, and how that fits with their life goals, sense of well-being, and overall sense of value in their lives, is important to organizations, as value can only be co-created. Thus, there is no firm value-creating activity that is done in isolation. Capabilities and expertise can only be leveraged into value propositions, which are invitations for customers to engage with an organization through resource integration. Only when these conditions are fulfilled can value be co-created. When firms understand this, they see customers as partners rather than assets; as individuals, rather than belonging to a segment; as individuals who have varying resources and capabilities, including personal ecosystems. This inevitably leads service providers to recognize that to capture value they must first co-create value. "Adopting a service logic makes it possible for firms to get involved with their customers' value-generating processes, and the market offering is expanded to including firm-customer interactions" (Grönroos, 2008b, p. 298). This perspective is aligned with business ethics, and recognizes and upholds the notion of human dignity, an important consideration in the provision of services.

How then can firms create innovations that are meaningful to customers and provide a positive return on investment? When managing innovations to enhance value co-creation, firms must realize that

> discontinuous innovation can arise by changing any of the customer roles of users, buyers and payers on the first dimension. On the second dimension, the firm changes its value creation by embedding operant resources into objects, by changing the integrators of resources, and by reconfiguring value constellations.
>
> *(Michel, Brown, & Gallan, 2008, p. 54)*

In order to facilitate innovation volume and radicalness, firms can collaborate with customers, assume a customer orientation, and collaborate with customer-contact employees (Ordanini & Parasuraman, 2011).

Companies must account for collective and relational customer goals when designing solutions. Specifically, organizations should recognize that customers may display certain network integration processes: offerings assembled around prioritized goals, alternate participation, concurrent participation, and offerings assembled around separate conditions (Epp & Price, 2011). As a result, firms should shape solutions around customer network identity goals and constraints.

Because customers need to integrate resources in order to co-create value, they must acquire the skills and abilities necessary to engage in these activities. "Supporting customer learning, then, is a pressing new challenge for firms that recognize customers engage in resource integration in the course of their value-creating processes" (Hibbert et al., 2012, p. 247). Service organizations and providers must also learn to enhance customer resource integration in order to fully co-create value.

> A recursive process of organizational learning and knowledge management places continual emphasis on knowledge as the fundamental source of competitive advantage. In other words, by starting with the customer's processes, a supplier can design its own processes to align with those of its customers.
>
> *(Payne et al., 2008, p. 88)*

This framework identifies the following opportunities for co-creating value with customers: opportunities provided by technological breakthroughs, opportunities provided by changes in industry logics, and opportunities provided by changes in customer preferences and lifestyles. Service organizations should focus on identifying and exploiting these opportunities to enhance value co-creation with their customers.

Service design can play a significant part in developing services that enhance value co-creation: "contextual and holistic understandings of user experiences can inform value propositions that better fit users' value-in-use" (Yu & Sangiorgi, 2018, p. 40). Additionally, co-designing with customers and prototyping enhances value co-creation through aligning resources and better support capabilities for value co-creation (Yu & Sangiorgi, 2018). Service managers must use extant research to better understand how to motivate both customers and employees to engage in resource integration in order to optimize value co-creation (Oertzen et al., 2018).

Customer engagement and value co-creation

When customers make progress toward goals, and are integral in co-creating value for themselves, they may be *engaged* with a service, a provider, and/or an organization. Engagement can align connections and dispositions within a service system, and thus functions as a critical component in value co-creation (Chandler & Lusch, 2015). As a result, customer engagement behaviours (CEBs), which are beyond the scope of transactions, may be considered an outcome and an element of value co-creation. These behaviours may manifest as positive word of mouth (WOM), recommendations, or referrals (van Doorn et al., 2010). CEBs may also be attempts made by the customer to co-create value with various actors in his network. Firms may enhance CEBs by understanding and managing the contexts in which customers engage with their offerings as well as with actors in a service ecosystem. "Through inducing broader resource integration, CEB makes value co-creation a system-level process" (Jaakola & Alexander, 2014, p. 247). As a result, firms should explore and enhance customer resources and capabilities with an eye toward optimizing value co-creation for all involved actors.

Encouraging the application and implementation of value co-creation as an approach (Sharma & Conduit, 2016) requires continually innovating services (Ng & Vargo, 2018) to minimize the risk that customers fail to co-create value (Skålén et al., 2015). Responding proactively to change processes that result in prolonged periods of value co-destruction (Echeverri & Skålén, 2011; Plé & Cáceres, 2010) can be difficult because they often involve culture change (Sharma & Conduit, 2016). A change of approach to facilitate customer value co-creation is necessary to prioritize experiential customer value that may conflict with and fundamentally challenge institutionally embedded practices (Edvardsson et al., 2014) that characterize service systems and affect resource integration (Frow, McColl-Kennedy, & Payne, 2016; Vargo & Lusch, 2016). One solution is to implement system-wide redesign that focuses on the service experience for multiple actors (Patrício, Fisk, Falcão E Cunha, & Constantine, 2011) to address key processes of resource integration that they engage in across multiple interfaces and system levels (Beirão et al., 2017; Pinho, Beirão, Patrício, & Fisk, 2014; Rayport & Jaworski, 2004). Often a complicated undertaking, scholars suggest that multiple actors collaborate in the co-design of service systems (Patrício et al., 2011), although it is typically service designers that are tasked with designing the interfaces experienced by customers (Kurtmollaiev, Fjuk, Pedersen, Clatworthy, & Kvale, 2018; Yu & Sangiorgi, 2018). Additionally, to mitigate a self-serving bias in which customer satisfaction depends on customer participation, service organizations should provide their customers a choice as to whether to participate (Bendapudi & Leone, 2003).

Future research directions

As value co-creation is a rich and important concept, it begets a number of interesting future research directions. Although not an exhaustive list, some suggestions relate to TSR as well as to human dignity and the co-creation of human value, which are discussed in this section.

TSR focuses on well-being, quality of life, and other customer aspirations that transcend business outcomes (Anderson et al., 2013). This includes a many-to-many approach:

> A conceptual framework provides a big-picture view of how the interaction between service entities (e.g., individual service employees, service processes or offerings, organizations) and consumer entities (e.g., individuals, collectives such as families or communities, the ecosystem) influences the well-being outcomes of both.
>
> *(Anderson et al., 2013, p. 1203)*

It is important that future research extends value co-creation in networks to elements of customers' and other actors' senses of value, including individual and community well-being (Black & Gallan, 2015; Gallan et al., 2019). As the TSR literature grows, it will broaden and strengthen the notion of value co-creation beyond traditional outcomes, such as perceived service quality and customer satisfaction. Future research on quality of life, well-being, and ecosystem views of value co-creation are rich areas for consideration. Moreover, tying micro- to meso- and macro-interpretations of value is an important step in integrating service, marketing, and other streams of research (Gallan et al., 2019).

Co-creation of human value is based on respect for human dignity. The implications of thinking about value co-creation over value-in-exchange include a more sustainable, ethical, and transformative way of regarding and interacting with customers. Understanding and engaging customer views of value leads to a more disciplined respect for the dignity of the individual. Additionally, this philosophy begets a more holistic view of value that subsumes themes consistent with collaborative capitalism (Cova, Dalli, & Zwick, 2011), corporate social responsibility (Ramaswamy, 2009), and other related themes. As such, understanding how service interactions and experiences impact customer self-esteem and sense of whether their human dignity has been respected will undoubtedly lead to new service design and management practices.

References

Akaka, M. A., H. J. Schau, and S. L. Vargo (2013). "The Co-Creation of Value-in-Cultural-Context," in *Consumer Culture Theory* (Research in Consumer Behavior, Russell W. Belk and Linda L. Price and Lisa Peñaloza, eds., Vol. 15. West Yorkshire, UK: Emerald Group Publishing Limited, 265–84.

Akaka, M. A., S. L. Vargo, & H. J. Schau (2015). "The Context of Experience," *Journal of Service Management*, Vol. 26 No. 2, 206–223.

Anderson, L., A. L. Ostrom, C. Corus, R. P. Fisk, A. S. Gallan, M. Giraldo, M. Mende, M. Mulder, S. W. Rayburn, M. S. Rosenbaum, K. Shirahada, & J. D. Williams (2013). "Transformative Service Research: An Agenda for the Future," *Journal of Business Research*, Vol. 66 No. 8, 1203–1210.

Anderson, L., J. Spanjol, J. Go Jefferies, A. L. Ostrom, C. Nations Baker, S. A. Bone, H. Downey, M. Mende, & J. M. Rapp (2016). "Responsibility and Well-Being: Resource Integration under Responsibilization in Expert Services," *Journal of Public Policy & Marketing*, Vol. 35 No. 2, 262–279.

Arnould,E., L. L. Price, & Malshe, A. (2006). Toward a cultural resource-based theory of the customer. In R. F. Lusch & S. L. Vargo (Eds.), *The service-dominant logic of marketing: Dialog, debate, and directions* (pp. 91–104). Armonk, NY: M.E. Sharp.

Arvidsson, A. (2008). "The Ethical Economy of Customer Coproduction," *Journal of Macromarketing*, Vol. 28 No. 4, 326–338.

Baker, J. J., K. Storbacka, and R. J. Brodie (2018). "Markets Changing, Changing Markets: Institutional Work as Market Shaping," *Marketing Theory*, Vol. In Press No. https://doi.org/10.1177%2F1470593118809799 pp. 301–328.

Ballantyne, D. & R. J. Varey (2006). "Creating Value-in-Use through Marketing Interaction: The Exchange Logic of Relating, Communicating and Knowing," *Marketing Theory*, Vol. 6 No. 3, 335–348.

Beirão, G., L. Patrício, & R. P. Fisk (2017). "Value Cocreation in Service Ecosystems: Investigating Health Care at the Micro, Meso, and Macro Levels," *Journal of Service Management*, Vol. 28 No. 2, 227–249.

Ben Lataifa, S., B. Edvardsson, & B. Tronvoll (2016). "The Role of Social Platforms in Transforming Service Ecosystems," *Journal of Business Research*, Vol. 69 No. 5, 1933–1938.

Bendapudi, N. & R. P. Leone (2003). "Psychological Implications of Customer Participation in Co-Production," *Journal of Marketing*, Vol. 67 No. 1, 14–28.

Best, B., S. Moffett, C. Hannibal, & R. McAdam (2018). "Examining Networked NGO Services: Reconceptualising Value Co-Creation," *International Journal of Operations & Production Management*, Vol. 38 No. 7, 1540–1561.

Black, H. G. & A. S. Gallan (2015). "Transformative Service Networks: Cocreated Value as Well-Being," *The Service Industries Journal*, Vol. 35 No. 15–16, 826–845.

Bolton, R. N., A. Gustafsson, J. R. McColl-Kennedy, N. J. Sirianni, & D. K. Tse (2014). "Small Details that Make Big Differences: A Radical Approach to Consumption Experience as a Firm's Differentiating Strategy," *Journal of Service Management*, Vol. 25 No. 2, 253–274.

Bolton, R. N., J. R. McColl-Kennedy, L. Cheung, A. S. Gallan, C. Orsingher, L. Witell, & M. Zaki (2018). "Customer Experience Challenges: Bringing Together Digital, Physical and Social Realms," *Journal of Service Management*, Vol. 29 No. 5, 776–808.

Bone, S. A., G. L. Christensen, & J. D. Williams (2014). "Rejected, Shackled, and Alone: The Impact of Systemic Restricted Choice on Minority Consumers' Construction of Self," *Journal of Consumer Research*, Vol. 41 No. 2, 451–474.

Carr, V. L., D. Sangiorgi, M. Büscher, S. Junginger, and R. Cooper (2011). "Integrating Evidence-Based Design and Experience-Based Approaches in Healthcare Service Design," *Health Environments Research & Design Journal*, Vol. 4 No. 4, pp. 12–33.

Chan, K. W., C. K. B. Yim, & S. S. K. Lam (2010). "Is Customer Participation in Value Creation a Double-Edged Sword? Evidence from Professional Financial Services across Cultures," *Journal of Marketing*, Vol. 74 No. 2, 48–64.

Chandler, J. D. & R. F. Lusch (2015). "Service Systems: A Broadened Framework and Research Agenda on Value Propositions, Engagement, and Service Experience," *Journal of Service Research*, Vol. 18 No. 1, 6–22.

Chandler, J. D. & S. L. Vargo (2011). "Contextualization and Value-in-Context: How Context Frames Exchange," *Marketing Theory*, Vol. 11 No. 1, 35–49.

Chathoth, P., L. Altinay, R. J. Harrington, F. Okumus, & E. S. W. Chan (2013). "Co-Production versus Co-Creation: A Process Based Continuum in the Hotel Service Context," *International Journal of Hospitality Management*, Vol. 32 No. 1, 11–20.

Cova, B. & D. Dalli (2009). "Working Consumers: The Next Step in Marketing Theory?" *Marketing Theory*, Vol. 9 No. 3, 315–339.

Cova, B., D. Dalli, & D. Zwick (2011). "Critical Perspectives on Consumers' Role as 'Producers': Broadening the Debate on Value Co-Creation in Marketing Processes," *Marketing Theory*, Vol. 11 No. 3, 231–241.

Dietrich, T., J. Trischler, L. Schuster, & S. Rundle-Thiele (2017). "Co-Designing Services with Vulnerable Consumers," *Journal of Service Theory and Practice*, Vol. 27 No. 3, 663–688.

Dolbec, P.-Y. and E. Fischer (2015). "Refashioning a Field? Connected Consumers and Institutional Dynamics in Markets," *Journal of Consumer Research*, Vol. 41 No. 6, pp. 1447–1468.

Echeverri, P. & P. Skålén (2011). "Co-Creation and Co-Destruction: A Practice-Theory Based Study of Interactive Value Formation," *Marketing Theory*, Vol. 11 No. 3, 351–373.

Edvardsson, B., A. Gustafsson, & I. Roos (2005). "Service Portraits in Service Research: A Critical Review," *International Journal of Service Industry Management*, Vol. 16 No. 1, 107–121.

Edvardsson, B., M. Kleinaltenkamp, B. Tronvoll, P. McHugh, & C. Windahl (2014). "Institutional Logics Matter When Coordinating Resource Integration," *Marketing Theory*, Vol. 14 No. 3, 291–309.

Edvardsson, B., Skålén, P., & Tronvoll, B. (2012). Service systems as a foundation for resource integration and value co-creation. InS. L. Vargo & R. F. Lusch (Eds.), *Review of marketing research: Toward a better understanding of the role of value in markets and Marketing*, Vol. 9 (pp. 79–126). Bingley, UK: Emerald Group Publishing Limited.

Edvardsson, B., B. Tronvoll, & T. Gruber (2011). "Expanding Understanding of Service Exchange and Value Co-Creation: A Social Construction Approach," *Journal of the Academy of Marketing Science*, Vol. 39 No. 2, 327–339.

Epp, A. M. & L. L. Price (2011). "Designing Solutions around Customer Network Identity Goals," *Journal of Marketing*, Vol. 75 No. 2, 36–54.

Frow, P., J. R. McColl-Kennedy, & A. F. Payne (2016). "Co-Creation Practices: Their Role in Shaping a Health Care Ecosystem," *Industrial Marketing Management*, Vol. 56 July, 24–39.

Gallan, A. S., C. B. Jarvis, S. W. Brown, & M. J. Bitner (2013). "Customer Positivity and Participation in Services: An Empirical Test in a Health Care Context," *Journal of the Academy of Marketing Science*, Vol. 41 No. 3, 338–356.

Gallan, A. S., M.-K. T. Barakshina, B. Figueiredo, J. Go Jefferies, J. Gollnhofer, S.Hibbert, N. Luca, S. Roy, J. Spanjol,& H. Winklhofer (2019). "Transforming Community Well-Being through Patients' Lived Experiences," *Journal of Business Research*, Vol. 100 July, 376–391.

Gergen, K. J. (1991). *The Saturated Self: Dilemmas of Identity in Contemporary Life*. New York: Basic Books.

Gergen, K. J. (1994). *Realities and Relationships: Soundings in Social Construction*. Boston: Harvard University Press.

Gergen, K. J. (1999). *An Invitation to Social Construction* (2nd ed.). New York: SAGE Publications Ltd.

Gergen, K. J. (2018). "Social Psychology as Social Construction: The Emerging Vision," Swarthmore College, Vol. https://www.swarthmore.edu/kenneth-gergen/social-psychology-social-construction-emerging-vision No. October 31, 2018.

Giesler, M. & E. Fischer (2017). "Market System Dynamics," *Marketing Theory*, Vol. 17 No. 1, 3–8.

Go Jefferies, J., S. Bishop, & S. Hibbert (2019). "Service Innovation through Resource Integration: An Empirical Examination of Co-Created Value Using Telehealth Services," *Public Policy and Administration*, https://doi.org/10.1177/0952076718822715.

Grönroos, C. (2000). *Service management and marketing: A customer relationship approach*. Chichester: John Wiley.

Grönroos, Christian (2008a). "Adopting a service business logic in relational business-to-business marketing: value creation, interaction and joint value co-creation," *Otago Forum 2* (2008) – Academic Papers, Paper No. 15, pp. 269–287.

Grönroos, C. (2008b). "Service Logic Revisited: Who Creates Value? And Who Co-Creates?" *European Business Review*, Vol. 20 No. 4, 298–314.

Grönroos, C. (2011). "Value Co-Creation in Service Logic: A Critical Analysis," *Marketing Theory*, Vol. 11 No. 3, 279–301.

Grönroos, C. (2012). "Conceptualising Value Co-Creation: A Journey to the 1970s and Back to the Future," *Journal of Marketing Management*, Vol. 28 No. 13–14, 1520–1534.

Grönroos, C. & J. Gummerus (2014). "The Service Revolution and Its Marketing Implications: Service Logic vs Service-Dominant Logic," *Managing Service Quality*, Vol. 24 No. 3, 206–229.

Grönroos, C. & P. Voima (2013). "Critical Service Logic: Making Sense of Value Creation and Co-Creation," *Journal of the Academy of Marketing Science*, Vol. 41 No. 2, 133–150.

Gummesson, E. (2008). "Extending the Service-Dominant Logic: From Customer Centricity to Balanced Centricity," *Journal of the Academy of Marketing Science*, Vol. 36 No. 1, 15–17.

Gummesson, E., R. F. Lusch, & S. L. Vargo (2010). "Transitioning from Service Management to Service-Dominant Logic: Observations and Recommendations," *International Journal of Quality and Service Sciences*, Vol. 2 No. 1, 8–22.

Gustafsson, A., P. Kristensson, and L. Witell (2012). "Customer Cocreation in Service Innovation: A Matter of Communication," *Journal of Service Management*, Vol. 23 No. 3, pp. 311–27.

Hagberg, J. & H. Kjellberg (2010). "Who Performs Marketing? Dimensions of Agential Variation in Market Practice," *Industrial Marketing Management*, Vol. 39 No. 6, 1028–1037.

Heinonen, K., T. Strandvik, K.-J. Mickelsson, B. Edvardsson, E. Sundström, & P. Andersson (2010). "A Customer-Dominant Logic of Service," *Journal of Service Management*, Vol. 21 No. 4, 531–548.

Helkkula, A., A. Dube, & Arnould, E. J. (2018). The contextual nature of value and value cocreation. In S. L.Vargo & R. F. Lusch (Eds.),. In *The SAGE handbook of service-dominant logic* (pp. 118—132). Thousand Oaks, CA: SAGE Publications Ltd.

Helkkula, A., C. Kelleher, & M. Pihlström (2012). "Characterizing Value as an Experience: Implications for Service Researchers and Managers," *Journal of Service Research*, Vol. 15 No. 1, 59–75.

Hibbert, S., H. Winklhofer, & M. S. Temerak (2012). "Customers as Resource Integrators: Toward a Model of Customer Learning," *Journal of Service Research*, Vol. 15 No. 3, 247–261.

Hilton, T., T. Hughes, & D. Chalcraft (2012). "Service Co-Creation and Value Realisation," *Journal of Marketing Management*, Vol. 28 No. 13–14, 1504–1519.

Holbrook, M. B. & E. C. Hirschman (1982). "The Experiential Aspects of Consumption: Consumer Fantasies, Feelings, and Fun," *Journal of Consumer Research*, Vol. 9 No. 2, 132–140.

Humphreys, A. (2010). "Megamarketing: The Creation of Markets as a Social Process," *Journal of Marketing*, Vol. 74 No. 2, 1–19.

Jaakola, E. & M. Alexander (2014). "The Role of Customer Engagement Behavior in Value Co-Creation: A Service System Perspective," *Journal of Service Research*, Vol. 17 No. 3, 247–261.

Karpen, I. O., L. L. Bove, & B. A. Lukas (2012). "Linking Service-Dominant Logic and Strategic Business Practice: A Conceptual Model of A Service-Dominant Orientation," *Journal of Service Research*, Vol. 15 No. 1, 21–38.

Kenner, A. (2016). "Asthma on the Move: How Mobile Apps Remediate Risk for Disease Management," *Health, Risk & Society*, Vol. 17 No. 7-8, pp. 510–29.

Kjellberg, H. & C.-F. Helgesson (2006). "Multiple Versions of Markets: Multiplicity and Performativity in Market Practice," *Industrial Marketing Management*, Vol. 35 No. 2006, 839–855.

Kjellberg, H. & C.-F. Helgesson (2007). "On the Nature of Markets and Their Practices," *Marketing Theory*, Vol. 7 No. 2, 137–162.

Kleinaltenkamp, M., D. Corsaro, and R. Sebastiani (2018). "The Role of Proto-Institutions within the Change of Service Ecosystems," *Journal of Service Theory and Practice*, Vol. 28 No. 5, pp. 609–35.

Koskela-Huotari, K. & S. L. Vargo (2016). "Institutions as Resource Context," *Journal of Service Theory and Practice*, Vol. 26 No. 2, 163–178.

Kurtmollaiev, S., A. Fjuk, P. E. Pedersen, S. Clatworthy, & K. Kvale (2018). "Organizational Transformation through Service Design: The Institutional Logics Perspective," *Journal of Service Research*, Vol. 21 No. 1, 59–74.

Lambert, D. M. & M. G. Enz (2012). "Managing and Measuring Value Co-Creation in Business-to-Business Relationships," *Journal of Marketing Management*, Vol. 28 No. 13–14, 1588–1625.

Löbler, H. (2013). "Service-Dominant Networks: An Evolution from the Service-Dominant Logic Perspective," *Journal of Service Management*, Vol. 24 No. 4, pp. 420–34.

Löbler, H. & Hahn, M. (2013). Measuring value-in-context from a service-dominant logic's perspective. In N. K. Malhotra (Ed.),.In *Review of marketing research*, Vol. 10 (pp. 255–282). Bingley, UK: Emerald Group Publishing Limited.

Löbler, H. and R. F. Lusch (2014). "Signs and Practices as Resources in IT-Related Service Innovation," *Service Science*, Vol. 6 No. 3, pp. 1–16.

Lusch, R. F. & S. L. Vargo (2006). "Service-Dominant Logic: Reactions, Reflections and Refinements," *Marketing Theory*, Vol. 6 No. 3, 281–288.

Lusch, R. F. and S. L. Vargo (2014). *Service-Dominant Logic: Premises, Perspectives, Possibilities*. Cambridge, UK: Cambridge University Press.

Martínez-Cañas, R., P. Ruiz-Palomino, J. Linuesa-Langreo, & J. J. Blázquez-Resino (2016). "Consumer Participation in Co-Creation: An Enlightening Model of Causes and Effects Based on Ethical Values and Transcendent Motives," *Frontiers in Psychology*, Vol. 7. DOI: 10.3389/fpsyg.2016.00793.

Maslow, A.H. (1943). "A theory of human motivation." *Psychological review*, 50(4), 370–396.

May, C. R., D. T. Eton, K. Boehmer, K. Gallacher, K. Hunt, S. MacDonald, F. S. Mair, C. M. May, V. M. Montori, A. Richardson, A. E. Rogers, & N. Shippee (2014). "Rethinking the Patient: Using Burden of Treatment Theory to Understand the Changing Dynamics of Illness," *BMC Health Services Research*, Vol. 14. DOI: https://doi.org/10.1186/1472-6963-14-281.

McColl-Kennedy, J. R. & Cheung, L. (2018). Value co-creation: Conceptualizations, origins, and developments. In R. F. Lusch S. L. Vargo (Eds.),. *SAGE handbook of service-dominant logic*. Thousand Oaks, CA: SAGE Publications Ltd. Available at: http://onlinelibrary.wiley.com/doi/10.1002/9781444316568.wiem05055/full.

McColl-Kennedy, J. R., T. S. Danaher, A. S. Gallan, C. Orsingher, L. Lervik-Olsen, & R. Verma (2017a). "How Do You Feel Today? Managing Patient Emotions during Health Care Experiences to Enhance Well-Being," *Journal of Business Research*, Vol. 79 October, 247–259.

McColl-Kennedy, J. R., A. Gustafsson, E. Jaakkola, P. Klaus, Z. J. Radnor, H. Perks, & M. Friman (2015). "Fresh Perspectives on Customer Experience," *Journal of Services Marketing*, Vol. 29 No. 6–7, 430–435.

McColl-Kennedy, J. R., S. J. Hogan, L. Witell, & H. Snyder (2017b). "Cocreative Customer Practices: Effects of Health Care Customer Value Cocreation Practices on Well-Being," *Journal of Business Research*, Vol. 70 January, 55–66.

McColl-Kennedy, J. R., S. L. Vargo, T. S. Dagger, J. C. Sweeney, & Y. van Kasteren (2012). "Health Care Customer Value Cocreation Practice Styles," *Journal of Service Research*, Vol. 15 No. 4, 270–289.

Mele, C., S. Nenonen, J. Pels, K. Storbacka, A. Nariswari, & V. Kaartemo (2018). "Shaping Service Ecosystems: Exploring the Dark Side of Agency," *Journal of Service Management*, Vol. 29 No. 4, 521–545.

Meynardt, T., J. D. Chandler, & P. Strathoff (2016). "Systemic Principles of Value Co-Creation: Synergetics of Value and Service Systems," *Journal of Business Research*, Vol. 69 No. 8, 2981–2989.

Michel, S., S. W. Brown, & A. S. Gallan (2008). "An Expanded and Strategic View of Discontinuous Innovations: Deploying a Service-Dominant Logic," *Journal of the Academy of Marketing Science*, Vol. 36 No. 1, 54–66.

Nakata, C., E. Izberk-Bilgin, L. Sharp, J. Spanjol, A. S. Cui, S. Y. Crawford, and Y. Xiao (2018). "Chronic Illness Medication Compliance: A Liminal and Contextual Consumer Journey," *Journal of the Academy of Marketing Science*, Vol. 47 No. 2, pp. 192–215.

Neghina, C., M. C. J. Caniëls, J. M. M. Bloemer, & M. J. H. van Birgelen (2015). "Value Cocreation in Service Interactions: Dimensions and Antecedents," *Marketing Theory*, Vol. 15 No. 2, 221–242.

Ng, I. C. L. (2014). *Value & worth: Creating new markets in the digital economy*. Cambridge: Cambridge University Press.

Ng, I. C. L. & S. L. Vargo (2018). "Service-Dominant (S-D) Logic, Service Ecosystems and Institutions: Bridging Theory and Practice," *Journal of Service Management*, Vol. 29 No. 4, 518–520.

Normann, R. & R. Ramírez (1993). "From Value Chain to Value Constellation: Designing Interactive Strategy," *Harvard Business Review*, Vol. 71 No. 4, 65–77.

Oertzen, A.-S., G. Odekerken-Schröder, S. A. Brax, & B. Mager (2018). "Co-Creating Services: Conceptual Clarification, Forms and Outcomes," *Journal of Service Management*, Vol. 29 No. 4, 641–679.

Ordanini, A. & A. Parasuraman (2011). "Service Innovation Viewed through a Service-Dominant Logic Lens: A Conceptual Framework and Empirical Analysis," *Journal of Service Research*, Vol. 14 No. 1, 3–23.

Ostrom, A. L., Mathras, D. & Anderson, L. (2014). Transformative service research: An emerging subfield focused on service and well-being. In R. T. RustM. H. Huang (Eds.), *Handbook of service marketing research* (pp. 557–579). Northampton, MA: Edward Elgar Publishing.

Pareigis, J., P. Echeverri, and B. Edvardsson (2012). "Exploring Internal Mechanisms Forming Customer Servicescape Experiences," *Journal of Service Management*, Vol. 23 No. 5, pp. 677–95.

Patrício, L., R. P. Fisk, and J. Falcão e Cunha (2008). "Designing Multi-Interface Service Experiences: The Service Experience Blueprint," *Journal of Service Research*, Vol. 10 No. 4, pp. 318–34.

Patrício, L., R. P. Fisk, J. Falcão E Cunha, & L. Constantine (2011). "Multilevel Service Design: From Customer Value Constellation to Service Experience Blueprinting," *Journal of Service Research*, Vol. 14 No. 2, 180–200.

Patrício, L., A. Gustafsson, and R. P. Fisk (2018). "Upframing Service Design and Innovation for Research Impact," *Journal of Service Research*, Vol. 21 No. 1, pp. 3–16.

Payne, A. F., K. Storbacka, & P. Frow (2008). "Managing the Co-Creation of Value," *Journal of the Academy of Marketing Science*, Vol. 36 No. 1, 83–96.

Peters, L. D. (2012), "The Role of the Knowledgeable Customer in Business Network Learning, Value Creation, and Innovation," in *Special Issue – Toward a Better Understanding of the Role of Value in Markets and Marketing* (Review of Marketing Research), Stephen L Vargo and Robert F. Lusch, eds., Vol. 9. Bingley, West Yorkshire: Emerald Group Publishing Limited, 127–69.

Peters, L. D. (2016). "Heteropathic versus Homopathic Resource Integration and Value Co-Creation in Service Ecosystems," *Journal of Business Research*, Vol. 69 No. 8, 2999–3007.

Pinho, N., G. Beirão, L. Patrício, & R. P. Fisk (2014). "Understanding Value Co-Creation in Complex Services with Many Actors," *Journal of Service Management*, Vol. 25 No. 4, 470–493.

Plé, L. & R. C. Cáceres (2010). "Not Always Co-Creation: Introducing Interactional Co-Destruction of Value in Service-Dominant Logic," *Journal of Services Marketing*, Vol. 24 No. 6, 430–437.

Prahalad, C. K. & V. Ramaswamy (2002). "The Co-Creation Connection," *Strategy and Business*, Vol. 27, 1–12.

Prahalad, C. K. & V. Ramaswamy (2004). "Co-Creating Unique Value with Customers," *Strategy & Leadership*, Vol. 32 No. 3, 4–9.

Ramaswamy, V. (2009). "Co-Creation of Value: Towards an Expanded Paradigm of Value Creation," *Marketing Review St. Gallen*, Vol. 26 No. 6, 11–17.

Randall, W. S., M. J. Gravier, & V. R. Prybutok (2011). "Connection, Trust, and Commitment: Dimensions of Co-Creation," *Journal of Strategic Marketing*, Vol. 19 No. 1, 3–24.

Ranjan, K. R. & S. Read (2016). "Value Co-Creation: Concept and Measurement," *Journal of the Academy of Marketing Science*, Vol. 44 No. 3, 290–315.

Rayport, J. F. & B. J. Jaworski (2004). "Best Face Forward," *Harvard Business Review*, Vol. 82 No. 12, 47–52.

Reinders, M. J., P. A. Dabholkar, & R. T. Frambach (2008). "Consequences of Forcing Consumers to Use Technology-Based Self-Service," *Journal of Service Research*, Vol. 11 No. 2, 107–123.

Ryan, R. M. and E. L. Deci (2001). "On Happiness and Human Potentials: A Review of Research on Hedonic and Eudaimonic Well-Being," *Annual Review of Psychology*, Vol. 52 No. February 2001, pp. 141–66.

Sharma, S. & J. Conduit (2016). "Cocreation Culture in Health Care Organizations," *Journal of Service Research*, Vol. 19 No. 4, 438–457.

Sangiorgi, D., L. Patrício, and R. P. Fisk (2017). "Designing for Interdependence – Participation and Emergence in Complex Service Systems," in *Designing for Service: Key Issues and New Directions*, Daniela Sangiorgi and Alison Prendiville, eds. London: Bloomsbury Academic, 49–64.

Skålén, P. (2016). *Service Logic*. Lund: Studentlitteratur.

Skålén, P., S. Pace, & B. Cova (2015). "Firm-Brand Community Value Co-Creation as Alignment of Practices," *European Journal of Marketing*, Vol. 49 No. 3–4, 596–620.

Slater, S. F. & J. C. Narver (2000). "Intelligence Generation and Superior Customer Value," *Journal of the Academy of Marketing Science*, Vol. 28 No. 1, 120–127.

Smith, A. M. (2013). "The Value Co-Destruction Process: A Customer Resource Perspective," *European Journal of Marketing*, Vol. 47 No. 11/12, 1889–1909.

Steen, M., M. Manschot, & N. Koning (2011). "Benefits of Co-Design in Service Design Projects," *International Journal of Design*, Vol. 5 No. 2, 53–60.

Sweeney, J. C., T. S. Danaher, & J. R. McColl-Kennedy (2015). "Customer Effort in Value Cocreation Activities: Improving Quality of Life and Behavioral Intentions of Health Care Customers," *Journal of Service Research*, Vol. 18 No. 3, 318–335.

van Doorn, J., K. N. Lemon, V. Mittal, S. Nass, D. Pick, P. Pirner, & P. C. Verhoef (2010). "Customer Engagement Behavior: Theoretical Foundations and Research Directions," *Journal of Service Research*, Vol. 13 No. 3, 253–266.

Vargo, S. L. (2008). "Customer Integration and Value Creation: Paradigmatic Traps and Perspectives," *Journal of Service Research*, Vol. 11 No. 2, 211–215.

Vargo, S. L. & M. A. Akaka (2012). "Value Cocreation and Service Systems (Re)Formation: A Service Ecosystems View," *Service Science*, Vol. 4 No. 3, 207–217.

Vargo, S. L., K. Koskela-Huotari, S. Baron, B. Edvardsson, J. Reynoso, and M. Colurcio (2017). "A Systems Perspective on Markets — Toward a Research Agenda," *Journal of Business Research*, Vol. 79 No. October, pp. 260–68.

Vargo, S. L. & R. F. Lusch (2004). "Evolving to a New Dominant Logic for Marketing," *Journal of Marketing*, Vol. 68 No. 1, 1–17.

Vargo, S. L. & R. F. Lusch (2008). "Service-Dominant Logic: Continuing the Evolution," *Journal of the Academy of Marketing Science*, Vol. 36 No. 1, 1–10.

Vargo, S. L. & R. F. Lusch (2014). "Inversions of Service-Dominant Logic," *Marketing Theory*, Vol. 14 No. 3, 239–248.

Vargo, S. L. & R. F. Lusch (2016). "Institutions and Axioms: An Extension and Update of Service-Dominant Logic," *Journal of the Academy of Marketing Science*, Vol. 44 No. 1, 5–23.

Vargo, S. L., P. P. Maglio, & M. A. Akaka (2008). "On Value and Value Co-Creation: A Service Systems and Service Logic Perspective," *European Management Journal*, Vol. 26 No. 3, 145–152.

Voorhees, C. M., P. W. Fombelle, Y. Gregoire, S. A. Bone, A. Gustafsson, R. Sousa, & T. Walkowiak (2017). "Service Encounters, Experiences and the Customer Journey: Defining the Field and a Call to Expand Our Lens," *Journal of Business Research*, Vol. 79 October, 269–280.

Winklhofer, H., R. Palmer, & R. Brodie (2007). "Researching the Service Dominant Logic: Normative Perspective versus Practice," *Australasian Marketing Journal*, Vol. 15 No. 1, 76–83.

Woodruff, R. B. (1997). "Customer Value: The Next Source of Competitive Advantage," *Journal of the Academy of Marketing Science*, Vol. 25 No. 2, 139–153.

Yu, E. & D. Sangiorgi (2018). "Service Design as an Approach to Implement the Value Cocreation Perspective in New Service Development," *Journal of Service Research*, Vol. 21 No. 1, 40–58.

18

Resource integration and co-creation

A customer journey approach

Cátia Jesus and Helena Alves

Introduction

Resource integration (RI) is a key dimension of value co-creation, but has been insufficiently explored, applied, or articulated (Baron & Warnaby, 2011; Edvardsson, Skålén, & Tronvoll, 2012). The present chapter enhances understanding with regard to the role of consumers as integrators of resources in the co-creation process, seeking to understand factors that explain their direction, disposition, and involvement in co-production and interaction with organizations (Bolton & Saxena-Iyer, 2009; Dong, Evans, & Zou, 2008; van Doorn et al., 2010).

To fill this gap, this chapter addresses RI in a context of all the direct and indirect interactions involved in the consumer value co-creation process between actors and occurrences at a cultural event, thereby providing new insights and research scenarios regarding events. By giving priority to the experiential and processual aspects of the service (Edvardsson, Gustafsson, & Roos, 2005; Folstad & Kvale, 2018; Ostrom, Parasuraman, & Bowen, 2015), this chapter uses the customer journey (CJ) map as a methodological technique contributing to a more innovative, detailed, and applicable approach. In other words, it provides a less abstract approach to the topic, highlighting the importance and detailed understanding of consumer resources use at events.

This chapter aims for detailed understanding of what types of resources consumers integrate throughout their *CJs*, how they are integrated, and how this influences their experiences at a particular event. It examines how consumers interact with the multiple actors and then mobilize, adapt, and integrate different resources (both operand and operant) over the phases of their experience (pre-purchase, purchase and post-purchase). It also considers the essential elements and touchpoints at which consumers integrate their resources in the co-creation process. Understanding these phenomena helps organizations to produce better results regarding innovation and consumer satisfaction.

The chapter is structured in five sections: following this introduction, the second section presents a brief review of the literature on key topics. The third section deals with the research methodology, focusing on the methodological procedures of CJ mapping. The fourth section presents and discusses the results, and the final section presents the main conclusions, implications, and limitations of the study.

Value co-creation and RI

Vargo and Lusch (2016) showed value creation to be a process of integrating and transforming resources that requires interaction and networks, with this being the fundamental basis of exchange. With the evolution of service-dominant logic (S-DL), *value-in-use* stands out, recognized as the result for the actors or a goal to achieve through the service. The application of resources, including competencies, skills, and knowledge, can make changes that have value for another, according to Macdonald, Wilson, Martinez, and Toossi (2011) and Grönroos (2011). Therefore, value can represent various forms and meanings for actors. Depending on the context, it can mean, for instance, "cheaper," "more personalized," "more convenient," "more information," "quicker," or "a good choice" (Campbell, Maglio, & Davis, 2011). In an economy dominated by service, the participation of actors and processes integrated in value creation is considered essential (Grönroos & Voima, 2013; Williams, 2012). Furthermore, *value-in-use* is always contextual and gives the necessary meaning to the exchange process (Ballantyne & Varey, 2008; Vargo, Maglio, & Akaka, 2008). The growing interest in the phenomenological aspects of the service experience, wherein all experiences are unique and dependent on context (Akaka, Vargo, & Lusch, 2013), gave rise to the need to create a wider, more dynamic, realistic, and holistic perspective of value creation (Vargo & Lusch, 2016). Therefore, this chapter suggests that *value-in-context* and highlighted elements of context are decisive for actors' effective value creation.

The literature demonstrates that RI is essential for value creation. The RI focus on forming interactive value relates to the actors and all their integration actions and activities (McColl-Kennedy, Vargo, Dagger, Sweeney, & Kasteren, 2012; Peters et al., 2014). RI is a continuous process, through which consumers implement resources and commit themselves to a set of activities that create value directly or facilitate their consumption and use (Hibbert, Winklhofer, & Temerak, 2012). This integrative process does not depend only on the juxtaposition of resources, but rather requires the aggregation and combination of resources that result in contextual configurations (Edvardsson, Tronvoll, & Gruber, 2011; Lusch & Vargo, 2014). *Integration* refers to the incorporation of an actor's resources in the social and cultural processes of other actors, allowing them to become members of a network. Thus, value co-creation occurs through RI, according to expectations, needs, and capacities of the actors (Gummesson & Mele, 2010).

Integration can take three forms: *(a) complementarity* – resources complement each other, and as such should be incorporated appropriately to add what is needed to form a whole; *(b) redundancy* – through sharing redundant information, actors are able to facilitate the transfer of tacit knowledge, which contributes to co-operation and integration of common knowledge and other resources; and *(c) mixing* – actors can have similar and different resources, requiring both redundancy and complementarity. Zhang (2014) mentions the existence of two types of actors' RI: the dominant integration of external resources – a process in which actors depend more on other actors than on their own resources – and the dominant integration of internal resources – in which actors need their own resources above all. In all of these situations, resources, processes, and results are combined aiming to co-create value (Hibbert et al., 2012).

According to Grönroos and Helle (2010) and Andreu et al. (2010), *correspondence* can be interpreted as the agreement or adjustment between resources, activities, and processes, contributing to potential value, which is at the heart of RI. The principle of correspondence is based on the creation of joint value for resource integrators, which does not occur simply as propositions and co-production of value, but as co-creation of benefits for the various actors (Nenonen & Storbacka, 2010; Pels, Möller, & Saren, 2009).

The nature of actors' resources

According to Kleinaltenkamp (2015), the resources integrated by actors are tangible and intangible characteristics of the focal and other actors which are accessible at the moment of deciding to incorporate resources; they are used by actors in order to achieve intended goals relating to integration processes. Therefore, it is not imperative for actors to have ownership of resources, their ability to use or access them being sufficient (Kleinaltenkamp et al., 2012; Wittkowski, Moeller, & Wirtz, 2013). Whether products, knowledge, or competencies, Vargo and Lusch (2004, p. 2) claim that "resources *are* not, they *become,*" acquiring that status if they are able to contribute to a system's improved or increased viability (Vargo et al., 2008) or even an entity's viability (Akaka, Vargo, & Lusch, 2012). Therefore, a resource effectively becomes a resource according to the context of its use: it may be useless for some actors in certain contexts but crucial for other actors in other contexts (Frery, Lecocq, & Warnier, 2015). Resources have the potential to be produced or used by actors allowing/promoting RI; they can also impact value co-creation (Aal, Pietro, Edvardsson, Renzi, & Mugion, 2016; Edvardsson & Tronvoll, 2013). Therefore, the narrow view of resources is not considered as it is linked only to supply; instead, this chapter concentrates on facilitators of the service ecosystem, including information, knowledge, values, skills, physical products, brands, experimental laboratories, and natural resources. Chandler and Vargo (2011), Kleinaltenkamp (2015), and Plé (2016) characterize resources as valuable, because they are central to S-DL and intrinsic and inherent to actors.

One premise of S-DL states that actors are resource integrators aiming to co-create value (Arnould, Price, & Malshe, 2006; Vargo & Lusch, 2008). As such, Altinay, Sigala, and Waligo (2016) defended the existence of operant resources – which act on other resources – and operand resources – which are tangible resources that are put into practice. Rodie and Kleine (2000) divided resources into mental, emotional, and physical categories; Hobfoll (2002) highlighted that an individual's resources can include material, conditional (social status), personal (self-esteem and self-efficacy), and social resources; also underlining the existence of 'energies' (time, money, knowledge) as resources with no intrinsic value but of value in acquiring other resources. In turn, Arnould et al. (2006) classified operant resources into physical resources (physical and mental resources such as energy, strength, and emotion), social resources (family and commercial relationships and brand or consumer communities), or cultural resources (knowledge and aptitudes, as well as life experiences, histories, and imagination).

The consumer who actively engages in a number of roles over a life cycle, and in different social contexts at the same time, develops a number of life projects and describes a narrative that varies in terms of complexity, according to Arnould et al. (2006). These authors also underline the existence of *operand resources* that are tangible resources, particularly regarding culturally formed economic resources (rents, inherited wealth, coupons, vouchers, and credits) and raw material/goods, which the consumer can allocate to perform certain behaviours (including social roles or life projects). These resources include a complement of material objects that vary in terms of quantity and quality; they can be objects acquired in commercial exchanges, gifts, inherited possessions, or found/created objects. Subject to legal restrictions and social norms, customers have the right to allocate those objects and places. Therefore, the quantity and quality of operand resources affect the exchange behaviour between actors.

The accessibility to a resource depends on how, when, and where a service can be provided (Akaka et al., 2012). These authors associate this concept with the dependency of the relationship that allows the application of resources at appropriate times; this requires awareness of potential resources and understanding of how they can be accessed. However, the possession of large amounts of resources doesn't mean that the actors have the skills or abilities to integrate them and obtain value. Therefore, Lusch and Vargo (2014) identify the concept of "resourceness" as the quality and the realization of potential resources obtained through processes of evaluation and transformation. In short, RI occurs in complex and dynamic actor-to-actor (A2A) environments, in which actors seek to be effective and efficient in creating and integrating such resources in order to improve the viability of their relevant ecosystems. In this way, increasing viability depends on increasing density (through the creation of new tangible and intangible resources), on more learning and innovation (through the creation of knowledge and development of new skills), and on greater accessibility (through access and transformation of potential resources into realized resources).

Kleinaltenkamp (2015) distinguished between intellectual inputs such as actors' capacities to receive, process, and deliver relevant information for the creation and use of a service. Emotional inputs describe actors' affective willingness to collaborate and deal with situations, so that the creation and use of a service occurs, but physical inputs require actors' presence, time, and physical stamina. These are influenced by their lifestyles, levels of education, and individual personality characteristics. Rodie and Kleine (2000) and Baron and Harris (2008) showed that the level of inputs varies according to actors' involvement/performance. Plé, Lecocq, and Angot (2010) joined behavioural (interpersonal interaction), temporal (time spent), and financial resources with relational inputs, highlighting that in exchange actors receive benefits that vary according to the value of expenditures. Edvardsson and Tronvoll (2013) distinguished between human and non-human resources. The former represent aspects strictly related to the actors involved (communication, objectives, competencies, and status) and their contributions to the development of structures. Non-human resources are also incorporated into service structures and social systems.

Underlying S-DL is a focus on operant resources, because these resources produce desired effects (Brodie, Hollebeek, Juric, & Ilic, 2011; Vargo & Lusch, 2004). Operant resources are mostly invisible and intangible, allowing actors to multiply the value of natural resources and the creation of additional operant resources (Vargo & Lusch, 2004). Edvardsson et al. (2011) highlighted these as dynamic and likely to change, unlike operand resources which are inert. Operant resources are linked to cultural schemes consisting of generalized procedures applied in disseminating social life (Gidden, 1984). This is because they are essential to activating operand resources and obtaining strategic benefits; thus, they allow for value propositions (Karpen, Bove, & Lukas, 2012; Vargo & Lusch, 2016). Many authors have considered operand and operant resources separately; however, this distinction, which suggests the superiority of operant resources, has been questioned by several authors, as described below.

Peñaloza and Mish (2011) claimed that the borders between operand and operant resources are less and less well defined. In the same way that operand resources are not only material consumer goods, operant resources are not limited to representing actors' interests and competencies (Peñaloza & Mish, 2011; Yngfalk, 2013). These authors emphasized that operant resources can simultaneously serve as operand resources. For example, community supporters develop their lifestyles and create identities by being part of a community, and the meanings that are created by being part of that community can be seen as operant resources. At the same time, clubs and sponsors make use of the supporters (e.g., for marketing purposes). Hence, supporters' engagement can also be treated as an operand resource (Yngfalk, 2013). The challenge is theorizing RI by multiple agents, as one's operant resources become operand for others (Peñaloza & Mish, 2011).

As such, the nature of a resource is relative and dynamic, evolving according to when and how it is perceived (Plé, 2016). Despite this distinction falling short of the context of its use, and various calls for research on the specific nature, types of resources, and contextual uses, the majority of authors adopt a separation of operant and operand resources (Arnould et al., 2006; Baron & Harris, 2008; Edvardsson, Kleinaltenkamp, Tronvoll, McHugh, & Windahl, 2014; Kleinaltenkamp et al., 2012; Lusch & Vargo, 2014; Ng & Smith, 2012). However, the mere presence of resources does not imply integration *per se* (Lusch & Vargo, 2014; Peters, 2016). It is when *resourceness* is recognized and put into practice that potential resources become real; this justifies the importance of RI. This chapter assumes that actors activate both operant and operand resources, with the purpose of pursuing projects/roles.

Resource integrators: consumer roles

RI is a key mechanism in value creation and a process that is exclusive to each actor (Gummesson & Mele, 2010; Mele & Polese, 2011). As such, RI efforts provide fundamental contributions to value creation (Chen, Drennan, & Andrews, 2012). However, with little grounding in the literature, some authors consider both RI and consumer efforts as actors' specific investments in order to achieve their objectives, highlighting the active role of actors as a central question in service research (Hibbert et al., 2012).

In S-DL, value is linked to the meaning of *value-in-use*, wherein the role of producers and consumers is not distinct, meaning that value is always co-created, jointly and reciprocally, in the interactions between providers and beneficiaries resulting from RI and application of competencies (Vargo et al., 2008). Human beings emerge in the nucleus of RI and the value creation process, where they behave as cultural and social actors (Taillard, Peters, Pels, & Mele, 2016). Thus, both organizations and consumers are considered resource integrators, together with other economic agents (Edvardsson et al., 2014; McColl-Kennedy, Vargo, Dagger, & Sweeney, 2009; Merz, He, & Vargo, 2009; Vargo & Lusch, 2008, 2011). Each actor can apply and/or use available resources, with the (direct or indirect) multidirectional interaction being expected to contribute to creating reciprocal benefits and values (Gummesson & Mele, 2010; Plé & Cáceres, 2010).

Kleinaltenkamp et al. (2012) and Aal et al. (2016) stress the importance of actors holding appropriate resources and sharing them with others, through collaborative and integrative processes. Thus, resource integrators are actors (organizations and individuals) with agency, who use operant resources to act on operand resources during the RI process. Actors transform and integrate acquired resources and micro-specialized competencies in value propositions (Edvardsson et al., 2014; Grönroos & Voima, 2013; Gummesson & Mele, 2010; Lusch, Vargo, & Tanniru, 2010). Actors prefer a density of resources to increase the viability of their systems and, for that reason, they integrate resources, co-create value, and assess value phenomenologically from their perspectives and contexts (Lusch & Vargo, 2014; McColl-Kennedy et al., 2012).

Consumers possess a great variety of operant resources they can use and integrate in co-operative relations with organizations to satisfy their needs and fulfil projects (Arnould et al., 2006). As such, they have been recognized by the wealth of personal resources they actively use in value creation and by the resulting unpredictability of the process (Arnould et al., 2006; Baron & Harris, 2008; Rodie & Kleine, 2000). Consumers are active entities able to co-develop and personalize their relations with other customers and suppliers. To do so, they adopt a diversity of roles, and performance depends on the capacity of other actors, in terms of abilities, skills, and competencies, to add new resources and use the available resources efficiently and effectively (Nuttavuthisit, 2010; Payne, Storbacka, & Frow, 2008). Thus, each actor performs distinct and dynamic social roles that serve as exchange resources in seeking socially desirable positions and in obtaining new resources within value networks (Akaka & Chandler, 2011; Edvardsson et al., 2011; Frow et al., 2014; Hibbert et al., 2012). Arnould et al. (2006) emphasized that consumers actively perform multiple roles, during their life cycles and in society, at the same time as engaging in diverse projects. By contributing their knowledge and efforts, consumers can be defined as a fundamental operant resource, or as a productive resource that integrates the production process (Baron & Harris, 2008; Prahalad & Ramaswamy, 2004; Vargo & Lusch, 2004).

The perspective that has dominated in *provider-centric literature* must be more comprehensive, because the roles of the actors may be marked as open-ended and an inherently relational discovery, highlighting the need to approach value propositions for a set of actors as *propositions of reciprocal value* (Truong, Simmons, & Palmer, 2012). Thus, the commonly adopted classifications used to describe exchange relationships differentiated by the nature of the business should be unified (Lusch & Vargo, 2014). This makes sense because all beneficiaries of service exchanges are actors having dual roles as both provider and beneficiary, for service exchanges occurring in an A2A environment. According to Grönroos and Voima (2013), in an A2A relationship, a single, generic actor can be described as an initiator or provider of the service. However, Ekman, Raggio, and Thompson (2016) consider that actors can take on the role of both provider and beneficiary.

The actor who becomes involved in developing a service, to provide a new value proposition, has the function of *initiator*. The initiator begins with an invitation to co-create; after the service is developed, the actor supplying value is a *provider* and the actor receiving value is a *beneficiary*. After a generic actor's initial invitation, there is heterogeneity among actors that are involved in various behaviours, as they take on distinct co-creation functions in the process of defining the value proposition. Thus, actors can simultaneously portray distinct roles that swing, unconsciously, between being active and passive (Edvardsson et al., 2011; Ekman et al., 2016). Over time, the actors involved can discover new ways of using a service, and thereby understand new forms of value; they may be satisfied with their understanding of the current level of value, or they may understand that the service no longer corresponds to their advanced level of knowledge or need (Truong et al., 2012). Due to changing roles, actors' level of involvement can also vary over time, and it is possible that inactive actors who decline/accept the invitation to co-create may opt not to participate going forward (Chandler & Lusch, 2015; Ekman et al., 2016; Jaakkola & Alexander, 2014).

A consumer's investments (i.e., skills, time, money, psychological efforts) are essential to co-creation activities (Hoyer, Rajesh, Dorotic, Krafft, & Siddharth, 2010). Although the literature on consumer effort is still relatively limited, many authors have identified efforts spent by the consumer to obtain a service as physical, mental, and/or financial (Söderlund & Sagfossen, 2017; Sweeney, Dagger, & McColl-Kennedy, 2015). Furthermore, these efforts are defined in terms of the consumer's perception; specifically, efforts are positively associated with the consumer's global assessment of the object. (This assumes that the consumer's great effort in relation to an object is a sign of its importance, usefulness, temptation, attractiveness, and value.) Therefore, the assumption that effort is positively related to perceived value is extremely relevant for Söderlund and Sagfossen (2017), who also demonstrate its positive impact on global assessment, such as consumer satisfaction. The opposite view – *aversion to effort* – is also described in the literature, because consumers prefer to minimize the effort involved in information processing, especially for purchases of convenience products (Berry et al., 2002; Srivastava & Kaul, 2014). According to Sweeney et al. (2015), most consumers prefer activities involving low levels of effort, because effort has a negative impact and can result in a less pleasant, more tiring, and more frustrating activity.

From the point of view of service ecosystems, RI is stimulated by actors' efforts to create value in a particular context. Value co-creation depends on actors' capacity to access, adapt, and integrate resources, always considering the influence of the context (Akaka et al., 2012). Access to resources is obtained through developing exchange relationships, which provide a variety of resources for actors to adapt to specific contexts as well as to integrate within a broader social context. This results in unique experiences in developing new meanings and norms, contributing once again to the social context with the derived value. Thus, social context shows the importance of operant resources, as well as actors' skills in accessing, adapting, and integrating these resources.

Actors not only have access to value propositions, but should know how to adapt and integrate them. They should focus on seeking out resources that are advantageous, which allow the development of learning and adaptation processes so that meaningful relationships are sustained and maintained through economic and social exchanges (Frow et al., 2014; Hilton, Hughes, & Chalcraft, 2012). Because RI efforts allow the construction of something different, resulting in the creation of innovations and solving major problems (Lusch & Spohrer, 2012), exchanges are implemented to improve the context and value of all actors, highlighting the RI process as continuous and dynamic.

In a service ecosystem, exchanges take place because no actor possesses all the resources necessary to act in isolation (Akaka et al., 2012; Frow et al., 2014; Plé & Cáceres, 2010; Skalén, Gummerus, Koskull, & Magnusson, 2015; Vargo & Lusch, 2011). When confronted with insufficient personal resources, actors take advantage of other actors' resources to create and obtain value (Baron & Harris, 2008). The resource activation process can be more effective when consumers are in some way connected to each other, contributing success-fully to immersion in active experiences.

CJ maps

According to the literature, CJ mapping is a visual method, oriented toward a process that conceptualizes and structures consumer experiences (CEs) (Folstad & Kvale, 2018; Nenonen et al., 2008). CJs can be described in various ways, from an involved story about a customer's interaction with a service, to a brief set of touchpoints and interactions between service providers and customers. Zomerdijk and Voss (2010) characterized this method as including the activities and events related to the service provision but from the customer perspective. Folstad and Kvale (2018) related it to the process through which the consumer passes to reach a specific objective, involving one or more actors. CJ maps are used, there-fore, to "reflect thought patterns, considerations, processes, paths and experiences that indi-viduals enjoy in their life" (Nenonen et al., 2008, p. 49). That is, they allow understanding of how customers behave and feel; they identify motivations or attitudes along the journey, and they consider consumer mental models, the flow of interactions, and different touch-points (Zomerdijk & Voss, 2010). Therefore, the CJ map is a systematic and schematic rep-resentation that, through diverse contact episodes, facilitates understanding and profiling the consumer experience (CE) (Hagen & Bron, 2014; Nenonen et al., 2008). Such experiences are formed based on perceptions of all moments of contact with the various actors on a given journey, and do not refer exclusively to the interactions and points of contact during the service encounter, but also to the entire value co-creation process before, during, and after (Folstad & Kvale, 2018; Lemon & Verhoef, 2016; Wolny & Charoensuksai, 2014).

The consumer journey

Consumers make continuous efforts to satisfy specific needs and desires. However, the majority of individuals do not have sufficient resources to fully achieve the desired results, and therefore need to engage with other specific actors and processes (Keyser, Lemon, Klaus, & Keiningham, 2015). Thus, consumers obtain the multiple options necessary to achieve desired results (Huang & Zhang, 2013; Srivastava & Kaul, 2014). Therefore, the CE can be understood as the journey consumers are willing to make together with other actors, over time and various points of contact (Lemon & Verhoef, 2016; Stein & Ramaseshan, 2016).

Carù and Cova (2008) mention that the consumption experience is no longer limited to some pre- and post-purchase activities; instead, it is a diverse set of activities influencing consumers' decisions and future actions. Arnould et al. (2006) state that all interactions with marketing objects could result in experiences, classifying these *'consumption interactions'* into four stages: *(a) anticipated consumption experiences*, including seeking information, planning, desires, and fantasies; *(b) purchase experiences* relating to choices, decisions, payment, atmospheres/environments, and service encounters; *(c) basic consumption experiences* considering sensorial experiences, satisfaction/dissatisfaction reactions, and transformations; and *(d) memorable and nostalgic consumption experiences*, which are related to reliving past and nostalgic experiences through memory or other mementos.

Early research in management and marketing concentrated on the first two phases of the CE – consumption expectation and purchase experience (Schmitt & Zarantonello, 2013). However, over the past two decades, interest in how consumers experience and remember their interactions has increased considerably, highlighting the importance and relevance of the CE. In this context, most authors consider the CE as a dynamic, interactive experience, which flows through the pre-purchase, purchase, and post-purchase processes (Puccinelli et al., 2009; Rosenbaum, Otalora, & Ramírez, 2017; Schmitt, 2009). Keyser et al. (2015) also utilize a cyclical process of three phases, but the stages are called anticipation, realization, and reflection. For the purposes of this chapter, the former terminology was chosen.

- Pre-purchase phase: pre-purchase is the first phase of the service process; it involves aspects of the consumer's interaction with the brand, attributes, and environments before the purchase occurs, and it refers to the CE before entering the service encounter (Lemon & Verhoef, 2016; Rosenbaum et al., 2017). The traditional marketing literature considers this first stage to include the recognition of needs/objectives, search, impulses, considerations, and reflections that indicate the consumer's choices and preferences for a specific path (Keyser et al., 2015; Pieters, Hans, & Doug, 1995). Thus, consumers select a set of actors to contribute to achieving the desired results (Chandler & Lusch, 2015).

  This phase is assessed based on a consumer's available resources and willingness to buy, in relation to the past, present, and future (Anderson, Håkan, & Johanson, 1994; Helkkula, Kelleher, & Pihlström, 2012). Such assessments can be challenging, because customers have access to only a limited number of options for comparison, so they may use simple heuristics to make their choices (Bettman, Luce, & Payne, 1998; Dar-Nimrod, Rawn, Lehman, & Schwartz, 2009). Therefore, they are led by a 'minimum threshold of acceptability' that results from satisfaction or emotions, as opposed to deliberate and conscious reasoning about the various existing options (Bagozzi, Gopinath, & Nyer, 1999; Schwartz et al., 2002). The intensity and level of conscious perception through which this process occurs depend on the prominence of the service exchange and context in which the consumer is immersed (Keyser et al., 2015).

- Purchase phase: the second stage has received significant attention in the consumer behaviour and service literatures, and highlights consumer interactions with the brand and the environment during the purchase event (Keyser et al., 2015; Lemon & Verhoef, 2016; Rosenbaum et al., 2017). Following reflection and a choice, the process to achieve objectives begins and consumers engage actively in a series of events whereby each event or action becomes a specific experience and consequently contributes to the result of the immediate service encounter. Chandler and Lusch (2015) characterize the purchase phase as the specific and immediate experience of events occurring as the result of a customer's involvement in a service exchange. This involvement acquires various intensities over the journey, because it depends on determination in relation to a given objective, the occurrence of other interfering factors/forces and, above all, the consumer's hedonic desires (Andajani, 2015; Brodie et al., 2011; Higgins & Scholer, 2009; Sansone & Thoman, 2006).

  Hirschman and Holbrook (1982) show that customer preferences are not only based on the functional characteristics of goods or services, but on their symbolic elements. Because of this, there is a hedonic view of consumption, which gives special relevance to personal differences between individuals, including factors that influence motivating emotions and fantasies. Ahtola (1985) pointed out that utilitarian aspects of consumption refer to the usefulness and perceived value of a product and the consumer's prudence when purchasing, whereas hedonic aspects relate to the pleasure felt or anticipated from the purchase. It is of note that, despite the differences identified, the division into purely utilitarian or hedonic motives becomes difficult, because nearly all consumption situations involve both. In summary, the CE during the purchase phase depends on the consumer's resources, the conditions in which the event occurs, and the dynamic flow between previous and subsequent events (Keyser et al., 2015).

- Post-purchase phase: the third stage involves consumer interactions with a service brand and its environment after a purchase is completed; therefore, this stage covers post-purchase aspects of the CE (Lemon & Verhoef, 2016; Rosenbaum et al., 2017). Each event is marked by an individual reflection or judgement about the real value obtained (Keyser et al., 2015; Vargo & Lusch, 2008). According to Higgins and Scholer (2009), it is possible to distinguish between consumer value that arises from the purchase process and that from the final state or outcome. Process value is based on the activities experienced that go toward fulfilling objectives. The final state value reflects the nature and experience of the outcome.

  Huang and Zhang (2013) emphasized that difficulties in fulfilling a purchase objective can result in a negative value for the process, but also in a negative reflection on the value of the outcome, bringing consequences for both CE and future involvements. Keyser et al. (2015) warned that the intensity and conscious perceptions of value depend on consumers, their situations, and progress while pursuing an objective. Consequently, some events/actions may have low impact on the process value and the result value, but others may contribute to positive and significant reflections on CE.

Methodology

To provide an example using CJ mapping, a specific event was chosen for study: this was the Óbidos Christmas Town (ÓCT[1]) event. The goals were to understand, describe, and portray in detail the experience, RI, and co-creation processes of consumers at this event. Using an exploratory, interpretative, and descriptive approach, the intention was to identify how and what resources are integrated by consumers and understand how and when the co-creation process occurs over the stages of an event. As consumers sequentially narrated all of the events and activities they experienced during the purchase process, they were able to freely express thoughts, opinions, wishes, attitudes, and expectations (Nenonen et al., 2008). These were then used to create the CJ map. This research technique is valuable and increasingly necessary, because it contributes to inductive research regarding CE in real life situations, and allows development of ideas from patterns obtained.

Data collection and selection processes

Considering the exploratory nature of this qualitative research, it was decided to hold semi-structured interviews with consumers who had attended the event in December of 2016. The interviews were adapted and structured into four distinct parts: (1) pre-purchase phase, (2) purchase phase during the event, (3) post-purchase phase, and (4) information about the interviewee. It is important that the interview questions served only as a check-list in collecting data about the various topics of the three purchase phases, because it was considered more pertinent for interviewees to guide the dialogue toward the specific directions of their experience and RI. Thus, interviewers did not strictly follow the open-ended questions forming the interview guide. This approach emphasized participants' free expression and allowed flexibility. Thus, the interviews can be described as in-depth, but adjusted to the nature of consumers and the specific context of the event, contributing to more detailed insights and assessments of the phenomena in question.

One of the greatest challenges of this method concerns the interviewer's understanding of the resulting content, specifically, how it is understood and what it really means to the interviewee. To reduce the impact of mental frameworks on the interviewer's perceptions, especially in the most ambiguous situations, there was an attempt to validate the responses by asking interviewees to elaborate slightly on their points of view. This approach allowed immediate confirmation of the content obtained. With the consent of those involved, the interviews were audio-recorded. This solution allowed for better interview flow, better capture of details, and facilitated transcription, coding, and analysis.

According to DiCicco-Bloom and Crabtree (2006), the sample should share critical similarities related to the research question. Thus, the selection of interviewees should be established based on an interactive process of intentional sampling. Because participants were required only to have attended the 2016 OCT event, they were selected with the support of a personal contact network. Because the CJ mapping method does not require a large sample, interviews were held until reaching information redundancy (i.e., the "*saturation point*") suggested by experts such as Glaser and Strauss (1967). This was accomplished with 18 consumer interviews.

Analysis and interpretation of data

The data were treated and analysed (using *NVivo 11 Plus* software) based on the stated objectives, which allowed the data to be categorized. According to DiCicco-Bloom and Crabtree (2006), this is an editing approach whereby researchers check and identify segments of text to organize content and recognize patterns. Excerpts from the interviews were grouped according to types of resources used throughout the various phases and stages of the purchase process, generating important insights into RI and consumer co-creation processes.

As mentioned above, the instrument used to analyse and discuss the results was the *CJ map*. Although many platforms allow the download of templates for construction of the CJ map, none was found to be suitable for the research. Therefore, construction of the schemes oriented to CEs at cultural events was carried out by the authors, based on the existing

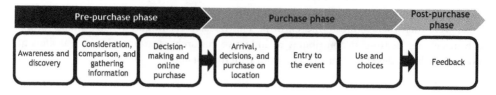

Figure 18.1 Phases and stages used in the research.

literature. The first step was to construct a diagram demonstrating the path typically followed by a customer when involved in the service process. The majority of previous authors seem to consider the experience a dynamic, interactive process, flowing from pre-purchase to purchase and post-purchase (Barwitz & Maas, 2016; Chandler & Lusch, 2015; Keyser et al., 2015; Lemon & Verhoef, 2016; Puccinelli et al., 2009; Rosenbaum et al., 2017). The present research included the three purchase phases, divided into seven more specific stages, as shown in Figure 18.1. An oriented scheme describing the consumer's experience allows representation of different contacts characterizing a consumer's interaction with the event.

Consumer journey maps can take different forms, but must contain certain key elements. This chapter includes:

- Consumer motivations/objectives: what incentivizes consumers to pass to the next stages/phases? What are the objectives?
- Consumer thoughts/expectations: what do customers think about the various stages? What are their primary expectations?
- Consumer activities: what are the primary activities consumers perform over the various stages/phases?
- Recommendations: what improvements do consumers consider important in the various stages/phases? At what level are they important?
- **CE**: to convey visually the interaction with the service and the emotions felt over the CJ, the Hagen and Bron (2014) emotional curve was applied, using three icons:

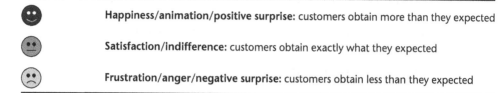

Happiness/animation/positive surprise: customers obtain more than they expected

Satisfaction/indifference: customers obtain exactly what they expected

Frustration/anger/negative surprise: customers obtain less than they expected

Results

Sample characterization

In order to achieve the objectives of this qualitative research, eighteen in-depth interviews were conducted with consumers who attended the 11th annual OCT event. Table 18.1 presents information about the sample.

Table 18.1 Sample information

Nº	Gender	Age group	Marital status	Academic qualifications	Professional situation	Already visited?
1	Male	[35–49]	Married	Master's degree	Employee	Yes
2	Female	[35–49]	Married	Master's degree	Employee	Yes
3	Female	[25–34]	Single	First degree	Employee	No
4	Female	[25–34]	Single	Secondary education	Student	No
5	Female	[35–49]	Married	First degree	Employee	Yes
6	Female	[25–34]	Married	Secondary education	Unemployed	Yes
7	Male	[35–49]	Married	First degree	Employee	Yes
8	Female	[18–24]	Single	Secondary education	Student	No
9	Male	[25–34]	Single	First degree	Unemployed	No
10	Male	[25–34]	Single	Master's degree	Employee	No
11	Female	[50–64]	Married	Secondary education	Employee	No
12	Male	[50–64]	Married	Secondary education	Employee	No
13	Female	[25–34]	Married	Master's degree	Employee	Yes
14	Female	[25–34]	Married	First degree	Employee	No
15	Male	[25–34]	Single	Master's degree	Employee	No
16	Male	[35–49]	Married	First degree	Employee	No
17	Female	[18–24]	Single	Secondary education	Student	Yes
18	Female	[35–49]	Single	Secondary education	Unemployed	No

RI and co-creation processes

The information obtained from the interviewees confirmed the relevance of seven stages over the three phases of the purchase process. The pre-purchase phase was formed of three stages, including: *(1) Awareness and discovery, (2) Consideration, comparison, and search/collection of information,* and *(3) Decision-making and online purchase.* There were also three stages included in the purchase phase: *(1) Arrival/decisions and purchase on location, (2) Entry to the ground,* and *(3) Use and choices during the event.* The *'feedback'* stage alone formed the post-purchase phase. To obtain a better understanding of consumers' RI and co-creation processes, data from the various phases and stages of the purchase process were analysed.

Pre-purchase phase

Social resources (family/commercial relationships or brand communities) were important in the *'awareness and discovery'* stage of the event. The relationships and communication among actors were essential in consumer discovery and decision-making. Here, sharing of experiences and information are the basis of learning for and during the value-creation process, as described by Gummesson and Mele (2010). The incorporation of friends, family, and acquaintance resources was crucial in the interviewees' process. Allied to these resources is the power of social networks and advertising. Most of the interviewees said they gained *"knowledge through Facebook,"* but some highlighted the event's communicative elements, above all regarding *"the media they have used over the years."* Thus, loyalty marketing is seen to involve co-creation with the consumer (Prahalad & Ramaswamy, 2004). Through advertising and promotions, the organization persuades consumers and creates emotional involvement in the co-production.

The importance of **cultural resources** was found to be shared by two moments: memories of past experiences and use of consumer knowledge and capabilities. Consumers who were already familiar with the event resorted to their memories of past experiences to participate once again: "*as the previous experience was pleasant, we wanted to repeat it.*" Therefore, consistent with Payne et al. (2008), experience of the past relationship led to consumer learning. Consumer cognition is an extremely important resource, because it focuses on processing information related to activities that are in the memory. In that context, consumers are willing and able to assess the benefits and sacrifices of maintaining a relationship with the service, confirming that cognitive processes are important in interpreting and assimilating experiences.

Highlighted in the "*consideration, comparison, and seeking/gathering information*" stage are consumer **cultural resources**, which depend on capacities, skills, and knowledge. Nearly all of the interviewees were concerned about obtaining up-to-date information, advantageous solutions, and the opinions of people they did not know. In seeking information, consumers sought to clarify the requirements of the service and satisfy cognitive needs: "*I looked for information on the internet, I consider myself an expert at looking for special offers.*" According to Yi and Gong (2013), looking for information is pertinent to consumers for two reasons:

1) To reduce uncertainty, and thereby be able to understand and control the co-creation environment/context: "*this year I thought about going to the Perlim event* [an identical event that takes place in the north of the country at the same time], *but after looking it up on the internet we ended up abandoning the idea*" (this statement reveals the consumer's proactiveness in seeking information, i.e., actors seek, compare, and consider various possibilities).
2) To master the role of value co-creator, becoming more integrated into the value co-creation process:

> *I paid attention to the discounts announced on the event's website. I looked there more than once and got tickets at a discount; I think it was 30%. But later I contacted BOL* [i.e., the online ticket office] *to find out if entry was limited to the date printed on the tickets. The answer came quickly and was positive, which is always good!* (this statement reveals initiative in seeking clarification, acting in anticipation according to circumstances).

Information can be obtained directly from the organization or from other consumers (directly or indirectly): "*I read other people's comments because that gives an idea of what you'll find and their reactions ... they persuaded me to try it.*" This scenario ties in with the three forces identified by Prahalad and Ramaswamy (2004) leading to value co-creation: omnipresent connectivity, convergence of new technology, and globalization of information, allowing actors to remain interlinked.

At the "*decision-making and online purchase*" stage, consumer **cultural resources** gain greater prominence. Some interviewees demonstrated their aptitudes/skills with new technology, resulting in the purchase of admission tickets online: "*I'm a fan of this type of online purchase. I managed to buy the tickets for half price on Black Friday.*" Consumers who, because of their family groups, always seek more beneficial solutions, became actively involved in the process. In this context, the consumer is a co-producer, which reduces costs and increases satisfaction and loyalty (Prahalad & Ramaswamy, 2004). According to Nuttavuthisit (2010), consumers extend their involvement with the organization to acquire value for themselves, in terms of lower costs, greater suitability, speed, or convenience. Thus, *"participation for oneself"* is related to consumers seeking a better match with their needs and desires. In this case, the interviewees were able to reduce costs (time and energy) with economic rewards, thereby obtaining psychological benefits of satisfaction and confidence in their ability to co-create value for themselves (Nuttavuthisit, 2010).

Consumer **physical resources** relate to the amounts of energy expended in buying tickets online and in seeking information over the various stages. Equally important are the **operand resources** consumers possess or can access. Economic resources were found, through discount coupons and vouchers, but the existence of, and need for, tangible materials can also be helpful for consumers to actively perform the role of co-creators. For instance, they needed computers, mobile phones, or other personal electronic devices. Table 18.2 summarizes co-creation resources and processes included in the pre-purchase phase.

Table 18.2 Contextual elements, consumer resources, and co-creation processes in the pre-purchase phase

	PRE-PURCHASE		
STAGE	*SURROUNDING CONTEXT*	*CONSUMER RESOURCES*	*CO-CREATION PROCESSES*
1. Awareness and discovery	Communicational elements	Physical and operand	Consumers use the operand resources at their disposal to access the unidirectional messages of the event organization. These messages will activate the physical resources of consumers who put energy and excitement into the search for more information about the event
	Elements of inter-action between consumers	Physical and social	Most consumers share with friends, family, and other people their intention to participate in the event (some consumers are aware of the event through friends/family). In this way they activate their social resources and begin to share information. This sharing of information between actors through relations and communication is an essential resource for the learning basis of the consumer's value co-creation and their subsequent integration of resources
2. Consideration, comparison, and seeking/gathering information	Communicative elements	Cultural, physical, and operand	In this stage, the consumer's processing of information allows assessment of the benefits and sacrifices of the co-creation processes. For this, consumers put energy and efforts

(Continued)

Table 18.2 (Cont.)

STAGE	SURROUNDING CONTEXT	CONSUMER RESOURCES	CO-CREATION PROCESSES
			PRE-PURCHASE
			into obtaining information. They also activate their cultural resources at the level of cognition and their individual capacities
	Technological elements	Cultural, Physical, and operand	Consumers' capacities, skills, and knowledge can reduce the uncertainty, increase control of the co-creation environment and let them master their role as co-creator and integrator of resources. Consumers turn to operand resources to obtain the desired economic benefits, through discounts and vouchers
3. Decision-making and online purchase	Functional elements, communicative elements, and technological elements	Cultural, Physical, and operand	Functional elements are elements of great importance and should be present for the positive integration of consumer resources. Consumers' involvement makes them a co-producer which allows better adaptation to their needs and demands. They obtain psychological benefits and trust their co-creation processes and capacities. Consumers use operand resources, through various electronic devices, to achieve their concrete goals

Purchase phase

The "*arrival, decisions, and purchase on-site*" stage showed great differences between interviewees. Some consumers revealed technological competencies and skills, purchasing admission tickets in advance, but this did not happen with other consumers, who acquired tickets on the event day without any discount. The differences are notable for consumers (without children) who do not utilize technological elements but prefer elements of context and employee–consumer interaction. Emerging as determinant factors of purchase on-site are: certain limitations regarding new technology (including online purchases), lack of trust in the ticket platform, and even a lack of knowledge about these practices at the event. In this case, the elements of employee–customer interaction acquire an essential role: "*I don't have much faith in machines and technology; I prefer to be in direct contact with people.*" However, this does not always have the desired effect/result: "*for the time you've got to wait I think the employees could, or rather, should be nicer to people*" or "*the employees could be faster … there was an enormous queue.*" Standing out is their preference for **commercial social resources** to satisfy their fundamental objective. Value co-creation in a service context occurs in a social environment, and as such it is necessary for consumers to resort to social resources, which require courtesy, friendliness, and respect between the different actors (Yi & Gong, 2013). If the actors are in a more pleasant and positive social environment, they will naturally engage more easily in the value co-creation process (Lengnick-Hall, Claycomb, & Inks, 2000).

The results of the "*entry to the ground*" stage did not demonstrate great differences between interviewees, who resorted to **physical resources**, specifically energy and emotions, and **social resources**, specifically relations with employees. Most interviewees said that "*entry to the ground was relatively fast*" underlining that "*things move at a good pace,*" especially for those buying tickets online. Allied to this factor is employees' attitudes, which seem not to have pleased some interviewees: "*the staff in charge of security and entry to the ground don't give any information and were even rather unpleasant.*" This statement shows once more the relevance of elements of the employee–customer interaction, demonstrating that perceptions and interpretations of actors' behaviour can change consumer expectations, with a potentially negative influence on the co-creation experience.

According to Karpen et al. (2012), a company's capacity to improve its social and emotional links with consumers and other partners in the value network is considered essential. This is true because that dimension represents actions destined to establish or improve the social and emotional connection that actors greatly appreciate and assess during the service interaction (Neghina, Caniëls, Bloemer, & Birgelen, 2015). The social relations and contexts of the interactions are essential matters for consumers. Joint actions can understand and explore similarities between actors, share common interests, adopt perspectives, and/or establish a personal bond that creates a mutual basis for comprehension, representing an important process of value co-creation that generates social and emotional value during interaction at the event (Neghina et al., 2015).

Consumers seem not to disregard functional and decorative elements. One interviewee highlighted: "*entry is over uneven ground, in poor condition due to the rain of the last few days, which is unsuitable for small children and even less so for prams*"; giving great importance to the physical conditions in the ground. Decorative and thematic efforts were also aspects referred to by most of the interviewees:

> I liked looking at the walls with a medieval feel, but the most fantastic thing was immediately meeting some unforgettable characters from our childhood … We were approached right away by Puss in Boots who really looked the part … I loved it all!

Consumers underlined the importance of those feelings: "*I liked right away feeling all activity and smells!,*" resorting also to memories: "*I began to feel all that magic and emotion I had felt in previous years. From the moment you enter the ground you enter into the spirit of things and make the most of it.*"

The third stage designated '*use and choices during the event*' is the most complex, because it refers to actual consumer participation and experiences, particularly in sensorial, emotional, relational, behavioural, and cognitive terms. The information obtained from the interviewees revealed great differences between them, with implications regarding the principal touchpoints. However, consumers value, use, and integrate all of their operant and operand resources. The results are analysed by resource type:

- Physical resources: these resources are extremely important during the service purchase phase, when actors use their energies and forces to benefit from the event. Consumers with children were found to be the most active throughout the event and the various attractions: "*I seemed like a big child myself. I went on the ice and buoy with my children. We saw two and a half shows … and basically went wherever we wanted, which in fact was just about everywhere (laughter).*" Consumers' active participation is possible due to the attractions on the ground, and for these interviewees "*the entertainment options are vast, and the shows are also very varied.*" However, they consider elements of the process, such as waiting times, as influencing their experience throughout the event. In these circumstances, actors willing to participate in the activities activate and employ greater physical resources (especially effort) than actors who do not wait; with consumer physical and mental differences being visible.

Despite the positive scenario, in general the interviewees without children and couples consider the event "*very targeted at children*" highlighting that "*for adults that can't participate in most of the entertainment, it ends up being a little boring … the event is designed to captivate children, who certainly seem to make the most of it and have a magical day.*" Thus, some dissatisfaction is shown by these interviewees who say: "*I didn't participate actively.*" A consumer stated:

> as it had rained recently the main attractions (that is, the only ones adults could go on) were closed … not to mention that I also wanted to go on the wheel, when I realized it was for children. My thought was: but why didn't we go to Lisbon Wonderland?
>
> *[an event that takes place in Lisbon].*

With this statement, the consumer showed she was alert to new things appearing in the media and regrets the decision/choice made, because the experience did not live up to expectations; confirming that the absence of process elements, regarding attractions/ activities, harms the experience of the consumer. One interviewee considered that "*even the activities for children are commonplace. I haven't seen big differences over time, apart from being extremely expensive.*" This highlights two important elements influencing actors' choices and decisions: the novelty factor and the price factor. Various studies have suggested that dynamic effects of the CE occur due to consumer personal characteristics; consumers change over time and may react differently after repeated experiences with a particular good or service (Lemon & Verhoef, 2016). Although some consumers develop relationships with brands that have lasting effects, others constantly demand more extraordinary experiences.Consumer emotions emerge as a very important resource and are constantly mentioned. In general, consumers consider that "*the Town is totally transformed. There is magic and joy everywhere, heightened by all the scenarios and structures created. Everything is thought out in detail and this is conveyed to the people.*" That is, "*it's a very nice, welcoming event targeted at family enjoyment*" with a "*perfect atmosphere and a real Christmas spirit that delights everyone with the decoration and animation.*" These statements demonstrate that atmospheric stimuli, through the organization's scene-setting and decoration, influence consumer emotional states, stimulating their participation (Puccinelli et al., 2009). Schmitt (2009) argues that more than the value of the brand, consumers seek something distinctive that can provide attractive experiences, something that arouses the senses and touches their hearts, something that excites or engages them, something real and authentic.The absence of those moments contributes to actors' dissatisfaction and can even harm the whole experience:

I was bothered that I couldn't let my little son see Santa Claus, but the queue would have taken hours! It's one of the most important highlights of the experience! I don't think you can go to the Christmas Town and not see Santa Claus, but that's what happened, and I was a bit disappointed.

Similarly, a consumer underlined: *"I admit I didn't feel the most positive and expected emotions. Perhaps my physical illness influenced this, and together with a cloudy sky ... even worse!,"* adding: *"I was very disappointed."* This statement recognizes that the external, dynamic environment influenced the experience significantly. The idea that external environments (externalities) can act as influencing drivers of CE has been defended by Verhoef et al. (2009) and by Lemon and Verhoef (2016). In this specific case, bad weather diminished the value of an open-air event, influencing the purchase value of the service. Another consumer emphasized: *"it bothered me a lot having to have lunch inside the room of the show. I wasn't at all satisfied. The restaurant space is tiny."* Besides the dissatisfaction, capacities were found to be contextualized within cultural models and transposed to new contexts when necessary, consistent with Arnould et al. (2006). In general, consumers consider that *"everything's fine as long as people go with the idea of enjoying themselves"* with clear implications for actor emotional states: *"I felt like a child again ... I was happy, in a good mood and lively all day. Without realizing it, we spent almost a whole day there!"* The emotions triggered also contributed to future memories: *"it was really good. I was reliving moments and creating others. The joy of our little one was contagious!"* As experiential consumption is based on emotional, contextual, and symbolic aspects, the value of the consumption experience includes feelings, enjoyment, and fantasy (Payne et al., 2008). So, feelings/emotions influence consumer attitudes and their RI.

- Social resources: as observed above, social resources are common among actors. An interviewee who attended the event with friends admitted that *"the first stop was for the typical group photograph ... we were approached by the event's official photographers, who in fact were very nice, and took the opportunity to mark our presence,"* indicating the importance of memories about the service experience and the influence that elements of the employee–consumer interaction might exert on the consumer's purchase decisions and experience. This situation was found throughout the event with the service provided by the various employees, who generally speaking were considered *"professional and friendly."* The exception was revealed by older interviewees who considered there was *"poor service and attitude to the consumer."* Thus, employee characteristics were found to be important and to indicate the quality of the service (Baker, Parasuraman, rewal, & Voss, 2002).

  The interpersonal nature of the interaction between employees and visitors contributes to satisfaction in an event experience and to developing the consumer co-creation processes (Puccinelli et al., 2009; Verhoef et al., 2009). The statement of one consumer draws attention to the shortcomings in, and/or absence of, communicative elements between staff and consumers: *"not having a single traditional restaurant within the grounds is a negative aspect, but at least they could inform people at the entrance that they can leave and come in again with a stamp, but nobody gives that information."* The consumer said she was very annoyed about the situation and went to the organization to share what she considers a recommendation for other actors: *"I went to the ticket office, explained what had happened and advised them to pass on the information to the other visitors."* The consumer co-operated with the event organization to benefit others.

This idea is consistent with the quadrant of *'participation for others'* of Nuttavuthisit (2010), in which customers interact with the organization for the benefit of other actors. Value creation by consumers is intended to share their experiences and influence other actors' purchase decisions. Consumer involvement in co-creation is related to sharing consumption experiences, which provides a source of information so that the organization can reorganize its goods/service portfolio (Kristensson et al., 2008). Furthermore, it allows other consumers to integrate a cognitive process to form appreciations and judgements based on those experiences.

The interactivity and professionalism of those performing character roles were also elements referred to by all interviewees: *"we interacted with the driver and Santa Claus' reindeer on the joy train; in fact, I think it was one of our most enjoyable moments. It was very good to see and experience,"* highlighting that *"the characters are professional, they're at ease in the role, with the public, and are very extroverted ... that interactivity is very positive. We loved it."*

Consumer–consumer interaction also played a crucial role in the CE and RI. One interviewee said:

> *there was one show I would like to have seen very much, the one about ghosts, which took place in the mythical house where the whole true story happened, but as my family don't like tales of the supernatural, I ended up not going.*

This statement demonstrates the influence of other consumers' resources in the focal consumer's decision and behaviour. The idea that customers act on resources produced by the company (led by the company or other actors) to fulfil, retrieve, or create favourite cultural structures is not always confirmed and in their absence there is some dissatisfaction (Arnould et al., 2006).

- Cultural resources: this stage is related to forming experiences in which the organization builds contexts and the consumer is part of them; specifically, the consumer is involved, but the context is directed by the organization (Prahalad & Ramaswamy, 2004). The specialized animation, through characters that move about the ground, is an element that contributes to creating an atmosphere and experience for consumers: *"I interacted with almost all of them. They're very funny, friendly and professional. They delight everyone ... without them it would be difficult for people to let their imagination run loose and enter into the spirit."* In this connection, a consumer admitted: *"I felt I was living the tales of my childhood and those of my children. I admit I was surprised by the characterisation and interpretation; they were fantastic and contributed right away to exceeding my expectations."* The statement indicates that consumers with greater cultural resources (in terms of knowledge, stories, and imagination) gain greater satisfaction from the experience. That is, someone who does not know the characters and the underlying story will not understand the context of the event and will not contribute with such favourable resources and co-creation processes for other actors.

The interviewees who had visited the event in previous years had great knowledge of the event's format: *"above all, my children wanted to see Santa Claus and as I knew the queue would grow throughout the day we went there right away."* This type of thinking was shared by the other consumers because the main factor in their decisions and choices throughout the event was the queues for the activities/attractions and the respective waiting times, which also contributed to others' discontent: "*there are queues everywhere ... it's a big problem,*" to the extent of admitting "*I began to feel a bit stressed ... at that time there were still queues for all the activities!*" Despite this, consumers are prepared to put up with the wait for the sake of the experience: "*that didn't prevent my children from going on what they liked most.*" Actors' experiences depend on the context, and vary according to socio-cultural configurations (Arnould et al., 2006).

• Operand resources: in this stage, consumers resort primarily to their economic resources to be able to use the goods and services provided by the event. All of the interviewees commented on the price of the various activities/attractions, considering them "*excessive*" and "*above average.*" A consumer stated that: "*entry to the ice rink and train was included in the BOL pack, but I still had to pay for the climbing, abseiling, roundabout ... and everything twice and when it wasn't only once,*" considering that: "*it would be great to pay for entry to the ground and then not pay anything else for the most captivating attractions for children.*"

It is important to underline the link between actors' physical resources and operand resources. This type of event requires this analogy, because consumer participation means some monetary sacrifices, with a proportional relationship: the greater the participation, the greater consumer monetary sacrifices. It is also important to highlight that the amount of operand resources affects the consumer exchange behaviour with the organization (Arnould et al., 2006). As a rule, consumers consider that "*there are lots of stalls with a great variety*" showing the power of sensory reactions in the consumers' experience:

> there are lots of nice little things that are tempting. I wasn't immune to the smell of the crepes and I had to try them. My children wanted the hot chocolate ... and they got to keep some very nice mugs of the castle;

pointing out the importance of atmospheric and process elements in the CE and RI.

Operant and operand resources were therefore found to be all related and reflect consumers' individual capacities in the context, where they are faced with different socially interactive and dynamic capacities. Table 18.3 presents consumer resources and co-creation processes in this stage of the purchase.

Post-purchase phase

The information obtained showed that, in a phase subsequent to actually using the service, consumers use and value **social resources** when sharing the experience in conversations with family and friends (in a word-of-mouth context) but also in making recommendations for improvements to the event's organizers. It is essential for consumers to share information, so that they can convey details of their experiences to other consumers as well as conveying information to actors about what displeased them most during the experience (e.g., consumers were clearly dissatisfied with the prices set by the event's organizers). These examples of sharing form and provide a service that goes toward exclusive and specific needs of consumers, as argued by Yi and Gong (2013).

Cultural resources are also valued, through sharing the experience and respective photographs on social media and other virtual platforms: "*I've already posted photos on Facebook (it's an addiction) ... and I'm going to devote a whole post to the Óbidos Christmas Town event in*

Table 18.3 Contextual elements, consumer resources, and co-creation processes in the purchase phase

	PURCHASE DURING THE EVENT		
STAGE	SURROUNDING CONTEXT	CONSUMER RESOURCES	CO-CREATION PROCESSES
1. Arrival/decisions and purchase on location	Elements of interaction with staff and communicative elements	Social and cultural	The arrival at the event requires activation of all different resources by consumers. At this stage, social resources predominate because there is a direct interaction with employees. The existence of positive relational aspects between actors means bigger and better co-creation processes by the consumer
2. Entry to the event enclosure	Elements of interaction with staff, process and communicative elements	Physical and social	In this stage, consumers use their physical resources (energy and tolerance) and social resources to enter the event. Social resources predominate again and consumers' capacity to improve their social and emotional bonds with other actors is considered essential. That dimension represents actions destined to form or enhance a social and emotional connection between actors during the interaction
3. Use and choices during the event	Elements of interaction with the service, process, and atmospheric elements	Physical	During the event, physical resources predominate. Consumers' physical skills are contextualized within cultural models and transposed to the context (the existence of all the contextual elements of this stage translates into greater activation of physical resources, i.e., greater participation and emotion on the part of consumers)
	Elements of interaction between consumers, elements of interaction with staff and communicative elements	Social	The relations and social contexts of the interactions are fundamental questions. Joint actions can include and explore similarities between actors, share mutual interests, adopt perspectives, or form a personal bond that creates a mutual basis of understanding between actors; meaning important co-creation processes that generate social and emotional value during interaction at the event

(Continued)

Table 18.3 (Cont.)

		PURCHASE DURING THE EVENT	
STAGE	*SURROUNDING CONTEXT*	*CONSUMER RESOURCES*	*CO-CREATION PROCESSES*
	Atmospheric, process elements and elements of interaction with staff	Cultural	Consumers' experiences depend on the context and vary according to socio-cultural configurations. Consumers with higher cultural resources contribute with more and better co-creation processes during the event
	Process elements and elements of interaction with the service	Operand	Consumers turn mainly to their economic resources to be able to use goods and services. The amount of these resources affects the consumer's exchange behaviour with the organization: the greater the resources, the greater the co-creation process behaviour

my travel blog." **Physical resources** are used because they do not mind spending energy and efforts on sharing information and spreading appreciation, which are generally favourable, with other actors. So, the last stage of the purchase process – *'feedback'* – concerns actors' recommendations, repeated participation, and sharing of photos. The results confirm that the **operand resources** consumers own or have available are crucial for spreading their experiences. Therefore, just as in the pre-purchase phase, consumers resort to computers or other electronic devices to share information. Table 18.4 presents a summary of the results.

Conclusions and implications

The results of the qualitative study reveal the existence of certain elements as essential for actors to activate, use, and integrate the different types of resources they own, whether operant (cultural, physical, and social) or operand (monetary resources and tangible goods). All of the direct and indirect interactions with actors, and occurrences at the event, resulted in the integration of resources and fundamental processes of value co-creation. However, the importance of the different resources varied over the purchase stages.

Consumers make various continuous efforts (from cognitive, physical, and psychological efforts to monetary ones) to satisfy specific needs and desires. As mentioned in the literature review, consumers do not possess sufficient resources to achieve the desired results over the three phases of purchase, and therefore it is necessary for them to engage with other specific actors and processes in experiencing the OCT event. Aggregating and combining other actors' resources resulted in contextual configurations that contributed to consumer satisfaction, concluding that integration is closely linked to incorporating an actor's resources in the social and cultural process of other actors (Edvardsson et al., 2011; Lusch & Vargo, 2014). Consumer (operant and operand) resources are all related and reflect actors' individual

Table 18.4 Contextual elements, consumer resources, and co-creation processes in the post-purchase phase

	POST-PURCHASE		
STAGE	*SURROUNDING CONTEXT*	*CONSUMER RESOURCES*	*CO-CREATION PROCESSES*
1. Feedback	Elements of interaction between consumers, with actors/organization and technological elements	Social	The share of information by consumers is essential for them to be able to convey details about their experience to other consumers of the event, and be able to convey information to actors or collaborators about what displeased them most during the experience
	Process and technological elements	Cultural	When sharing the experience and respective photographs on social networks and other virtual platforms
	Technological elements	Physical	Invest energy and effort in sharing information with other actors and in spreading opinions about the event
	Technological elements	Operand	Resorting to operational resources, through various electronic devices, to achieve objectives (especially the sharing of experiences and photographs)

knowledge and capacities in a given context when faced with various socially interactive and dynamic capacities, with clear implications for co-creation and RI processes.

This chapter contributed to S-DL literature by detailing understanding of the resources consumers integrate and the respective value co-creation processes followed over the various phases and stages of the CE, using a cultural event as an example (Tables 18.2, 18.3, and 18.4). Thus, this chapter contributes by applying a detailed qualitative approach to CJ mapping.

Event organizers should always consider actors' experiences as a whole. That is, they should bear in mind the three purchase phases, but above all pay attention to each stage included in each purchase phase. The information obtained from the interviewees confirmed the relevance of seven stages in the context of cultural events. The initial pre-purchase phase is formed of three stages: *(1) awareness and discovery of the event, (2) consideration, comparison, and seeking/gathering information,* and *(3) decision-making and online purchase.* The purchase phase at the event itself should also be formed of three stages, noting the importance of the third stage: *(1) arrival, decisions, and purchase on-site; (2) entry to the ground,* and *(3) uses and choices at the event.* The final post-purchase phase is formed of only one stage designated as *feedback.*

Through these specific stages, consumers activate, adapt, and use different resources according to their motivations and specific objectives. That is, the importance of the various resources was found to vary over the experience, the circumstances, and the different moments lived by consumers; it is important to note that these vary from consumer to consumer. For each specific stage, event organizers must consider the characteristics of the consumers attending the event and provide the elements they appreciate so as to satisfy their expectations and needs. In the case of the OCT event, and considering the information provided by the interviewees, four *personas* were identified, having different aims and behaviours concerning RI: *(1) friends, (2) couples, (3) families with children,* and *(4) families without children.* These categories represent *personas,*[2] which, although fictitious, attempt to represent an archetype of consumer groups based on their interactions with the event.

The most obvious difference was found at the moment of buying admission tickets, where the *'friends'* and *'family with children'* personas purchased in advance using the ticket platform and benefited from significant discounts, whereas the *'couple'* and *'family without children'* personas acquired tickets at the entrance to the ground, had to cope with queuing, and did not get any discount, because they preferred to interact with other actors to using new technology. The *'friends'* and *'family with children'* personas demonstrated their skills and became actively involved in the process, highlighting the use of their cultural (knowledge and skills) and physical (energy and effort) resources, thus requiring communication and process elements of the organization with regard to online ticket platforms and social networks. The *'couple'* and *'family without children'* personas activated primarily their social resources, due to their technological limitations and preferences for elements of interaction with employees (requiring relational aspects such as courtesy, friendliness, and respect shown by staff).

Participation throughout the event was another notable difference between the *personas.* The *'friends'* and *'family with children'* personas showed themselves to be participative and active by nature (having children in the group also contributed to this aspect), whereas the *'couple'* and *'family without children'* personas showed the opposite. These examples can alert event organizers to the differences between consumers and their resources throughout their experiences at the event. It is extremely important for companies to focus on analysing their consumer groups and providing the elements they value most. This way, consumers can consequently activate and use their respective resources in favourable co-creation processes, increasing their satisfaction and loyalty.

Regarding limitations, it is important to mention the great interpretative requirements, which became a complex and potentially imprecise task due to the crossing of themes and selection of the primary focus. (Of course, this is always true of qualitative research.) Even so, all of the resources were identified and coded in categories supported by the existing literature. The sample was a quota sample from the target market, and because the event was targeting families, primarily those with children, the results should be considered bearing all of these factors in mind.

Notes

1 ÓCT is an event taking place annually in the town of Óbidos in Portugal. It runs during the month of December in the open air outside a castle, which is a setting with unique characteristics. It is visited by people of different ages from the entire country.

2 *Persona* is a semi-fictional profile representing a company's ideal customer. These profiles are created to help the business understand who customers are and what they need, allowing more focused marketing strategies. In this research, there are four *persona:* 'friends' when attending the event with friends; 'couple' attending the event with the partner, spouse, boy/girlfriend; 'family with children' when attending the event with relations including at least one child no older than 12; and 'family without children' when attending the event with relations but without children.

References

Aal, K., Pietro, L., Edvardsson, B., Renzi, M. & Mugion, R. (2016). Innovation in service ecosystems: an empirical study of the integration of values, brands, service systems and experience rooms. *Journal of Service Management*, 27(4), 619–651.

Ahtola, O. T. (1985). Hedonic and utilitarian aspects of consumer behavior: an attitudinal perspective. *Advances in Consumer Research*, 12(1), 7–10.

Akaka, M. & Chandler, J. (2011). Roles as resources: a social roles perspective of change in value networks. *Marketing Theory*, 11(3), 243–260.

Akaka, M., Vargo, S. & Lusch, R. (2012). An exploration of networks in value cocreation: a service-ecosystems view. *Review of Marketing Research*, 9(1), 13–50.

Akaka, M., Vargo, S. & Lusch, R. (2013). The complexity of context: a service ecosystems approach for international marketing. *Journal of Marketing Research*, 21, 4.

Altinay, L., Sigala, M. & Waligo, V. (2016). Social value creation through tourism enterprise. *Tourism Management*, 54, 404–417.

Andajani, E. (2015). Understanding customer experience management in retailing. *Procedia: Social and Behavioral Sciences*, 211, 629–633.

Anderson, J., Håkan, H. & Johanson, J. (1994). Dyadic business relationships within a business network context. *Journal of Marketing*, 58(4), 1–15.

Andreu, L., Sanchez, I. & Mele, C. (2010). Value co-creation between retailers and consumers: an application to the furniture market. *Journal of Retailing and Consumer Services*, 217, 241–250.

Arnould, J., Price, L. & Malshe, A. (2006). Toward a cultural resource-based theory of the customer. In R. F. Lusch & S. L. Vargo (Eds.), *The New Dominant Logic in Marketing* Armonk, NY: M. E. Sharpe (pp. 91–104).

Bagozzi, R., Gopinath, M. & Nyer, P. (1999). The role of emotions in marketing. *Journal of the Academy of Marketing Science*, 27(2), 184–206.

Baker, J., Parasuraman, A., Grewal, D. & Voss, G. (2002). The influence of multiple store environment cues on perceived merchandise value and patronage intentions. *Journal of Marketing*, 66(2), 120–141.

Ballantyne, D. & Varey, R. (2008). The service-dominant logic and the future of marketing. *Journal of the Academy of Marketing Science*, 36(1), 11–24.

Baron, S. & Harris, K. (2008). Consumers as resource integrators. *Journal of Marketing Management*, 24(1–2), 113–130.

Baron, S. & Warnaby, G. (2011). Individual customers' use and integration of resources: empirical findings and organizational implications in the context of value co-creation. *Industrial Marketing Management*, 40, 211–218.

Barwitz, N. & Maas, P. (2016). Value creation in a multichannel world understanding the customer journey. *6th Global Innovation and Knowledge Academy Conference (GIKA)* – Valencia, Spain.

Berry, L., Carbone, L. & Haeckel, S. (2002). Managing the total customer experience. *MIT Sloan Management Review*, 43(3), 85–89.

Bettman, R., Luce, M. & Payne, J. (1998). Constructive consumer choice processes. *Journal of Consumer Research*, 25(3), 187–217.

Bolton, R. & Saxena-Iyer, S. (2009). Interactive services: a framework, synthesis and research directions. *Journal of Interactive Marketing*, 23(1), 91–104.

Brodie, R., Hollebeek, L., Juric, B. & Ilic, A. (2011). Customer engagement: conceptual domain, fundamental propositions, and implications for research. *Journal of Service Research*, 14(3), 252–271.

Campbell, C., Maglio, P. & Davis, M. (2011). From self-service to super-service: a resource mapping framework for co-creating value by shifting the boundary between provider and customer. *Information Systems and e-Business Management*, 9(2), 173–191.

Carù, A. & Cova, B. (2008). Small versus big stories in framing consumption experiences. *Qualitative Market Research: An International Journal*, 11(2), 166–176.

Chandler, J. & Lusch, R. (2015). Service systems: a broadened framework and research agenda on value propositions, engagement and service experience. *Journal of Service Research*, 18(1), 6–22.

Chandler, J. & Vargo, S. (2011). Contextualization and value-in-context: how context frames exchange. *Marketing Theory*, 11(1), 35–49.

Chen, T., Drennan, J. & Andrews, L. (2012). Experience sharing. *Journal of Marketing Management*, 28(13–14), 1535–1552.

Dar-Nimrod, I., Rawn, C., Lehman, D. & Schwartz, B. (2009). The maximization paradox: the costs of seeking alternatives. *Personality and Individual Differences*, 46(5-6), 631–635.

DiCicco-Bloom, B. & Crabtree, B. (2006). The qualitative research interview. *Medical Education*, 40(4), 314–321.

Dong, B., Evans, R. & Zou, S. (2008). The effects of customer participation in co-created service recovery. *Journal of the Academy of Marketing Science*, 36(1), 123–137.

Edvardsson, B., Gustafsson, A. & Roos, I. (2005). Service portraits in service research: a critical review. *International Journal of Service Industry Management*, 16(1), 107–121.

Edvardsson, B., Kleinaltenkamp, M., Tronvoll, B., McHugh, P. & Windahl, P. (2014). Institutional logics matter when coordinating resource integration. *Marketing Theory*, 14(3), 291–309, 10.1177/1470593114534343.

Edvardsson, B., Skålén, P. & Tronvoll, B. (2012). Service systems as a foundation for resource integration and value co-Creation. *Review of Marketing Research*, 9(1), 79–126.

Edvardsson, B. & Tronvoll, B. (2013). A new conceptualization of service innovation grounded in S-D logic and service systems. *International Journal of Quality and Service Sciences*, 5(1), 19–31.

Edvardsson, B., Tronvoll, B. & Gruber, T. (2011). Expanding understanding of service exchange and value co-creation: a social construction approach. *Journal of the Academy of Marketing Science*, 39(2), 327–339.

Ekman, P., Raggio, R. & Thompson, S. (2016). Service network value co-creation: defining the roles of the generic actor. *Industrial Marketing Management*, 56, 51–62.

Folstad, A. & Kvale, K. (2018). Customer journeys: a systematic literature review. *Journal of Service Theory and Practice*, https://doi.org/10.1108/JSTP-11-2014-0261.

Frery, F., Lecocq, X. & Warnier, V. (2015). Competing with ordinary resources. *MIT Sloan Management Review*, 56(3), 69–77.

Frow, P., McColl-Kennedy, J., Hilton, T., Davidson, A., Payne, A. & Brozovic, D. (2014). Value propositions: a service ecosystems perspective. *Marketing Theory*, 14(3), 327–351, https://doi.org/10.1177/1470593114534346.

Gidden, A. (1984). *The constitution of society*. Berkeley, CA: University of California Press.

Glaser, B. & Strauss, A. (1967). *The discovery of grounded theory: Strategies for qualitative research*. New York: Aldine Publishing Company.

Grönroos, C. (2011). Value co-creation in service logic: a critical analysis. *Marketing Theory*, 11(1), 279–301.

Grönroos, C. & Helle, P. (2010). Adopting a service logic in manufacturing: conceptual foundation and metrics for mutual value creation. *Journal of Service Management*, 21, 5.

Grönroos, C. & Voima, P. (2013). Critical service logic: making sense of value creation and co-creation. *Journal of the Academy of Marketing Science*, 41(3), 133–150.

Gummesson, E. & Mele, C. (2010). Marketing as value co-creation through network interaction and resource integration. *Journal of Business Market Management*, 4(4), 181–198, 10.1007/s12087-010-0044-2.

Hagen, M. & Bron, P. (2014). Enhancing the experience of the train journey: changing the focus from satisfaction to emotional experience of customers. *Transportation Research Procedia*, 1, 253–263, 10.1016/j.trpro.2014.07.025.

Helkkula, A., Kelleher, C. & Pihlström, M. (2012). Characterizing value as an experience: implications for service researchers and managers. *Journal of Service Research*, 15(1), 59–75.

Hibbert, S., Winklhofer, H. & Temerak, M. (2012). Customers as resource integrators: toward a model of customer learning. *Journal of Service Research*, 15(3), 247–261.

Higgins, T. & Scholer, A. (2009). Engaging the consumer: the science and art of the value creation process. *Journal of Consumer Psychology*, 19(2), 100–114.

Hilton, T., Hughes, T. & Chalcraft, D. (2012). Service co-creation and value realization. *Journal of Marketing Management*, 28(13–14), 1504–1519.

Hirschman, E. & Holbrook, M. (1982). Hedonic consumption: emerging concepts, methods and propositions. *Journal of Marketing*, 46, 92–101.

Hobfoll, S. (2002). Social and psychological resources and adaptation. *Review of General Psychology*, 6(4), 307–324.

Hoyer, W., Rajesh, C., Dorotic, M., Krafft, M. & Siddharth, S. (2010). Consumer cocreation in new product development. *Journal of Service Research*, 13(3), 283–296.

Huang, S. & Zhang, Y. (2013). All roads lead to Rome: the impact of multiple attainment means on motivation. *Journal of Personality and Social Psychology*, 104(2), 236–248.

Jaakkola, E. & Alexander, M. (2014). The role of customer engagement behavior in value co-creation: a service system perspective. *Journal of Service Research*, 17(3), 1–15.

Karpen, I., Bove, L. & Lukas, B. (2012). Linking service-dominant logic and strategic business practice: a conceptual model of a service-dominant orientation. *Journal of Service Research*, 86(12), 50–59.

Keyser, A., Lemon, K., Klaus, P. & Keiningham, T. (2015). A framework for understanding and managing the customer experience. *Marketing Science Institute Working Paper Series*.

Kleinaltenkamp, M. (2015). Value creation and customer effort: the impact of customer value concepts. *The Nordic School, Service Marketing and Management for the Future, Hanken, CERS*, 283–294.

Kleinaltenkamp, M., Brodie, J., Frow, P., Hughes, T., Peters, D. & Woratschek, H. (2012). Resource integration. *Marketing Theory*, 12(2), 201–205.

Kristensson, P., Matthing, J. & Johansson, N. (2008). Key strategies for the successful involvement of customers in the co-creation of new technology-based services. *Journal of Service Management*, 19(4), 475–491.

Lemon, K. & Verhoef, P. (2016). Understanding customer experience throughout the customer journey. *Journal of Marketing*, 80(6), 69–96.

Lengnick-Hall, C., Claycomb, V. & Inks, W. (2000). From recipient to contributor: examining customer roles and experienced outcomes. *European Journal of Marketing*, 34, 359–383.

Lusch, R. & Spohrer, J. (2012). Evolving service for a complex, resilient, and sustainable world. *Journal of Marketing Management*, 28(13–14), 1491–1503.

Lusch, R. & Vargo, L. (2014). *Service-dominant logic: Premises, perspectives, possibilities*. Cambridge: Cambridge University Press.

Lusch, R., Vargo, L. & Tanniru, M. (2010). Service, value networks and learning. *Journal of the Academy of Marketing Science*, 38(1), 19–31.

Macdonald, K., Wilson, H., Martinez, V. & Toossi, A. (2011). Assessing value-in-use: a conceptual framework and exploratory study. *Industrial Marketing Management*, 40(5), 671–682.

McColl-Kennedy, J., Vargo, S., Dagger, T. & Sweeney, J. (2009). Customers as resource integrators: styles of customer co-creation. Paper presented at The 2009 Naples Forum on Services. Italy: 16–19.

McColl-Kennedy, J., Vargo, S., Dagger, T., Sweeney, J. & Kasteren, Y. (2012). Health care customer value cocreation practice styles. *Journal of Service Research*, 15(4), 370–389.

Mele, C. & Polese, F. (2010). Key dimensions of service systems in value-creating networks. In *The science of service systems* (pp. 37–60). Springer.

Merz, M., He, Y. & Vargo, L. (2009). The evolving brand logic: a service dominant logic perspective. *Journal of the Academy of Marketing Science*, 37(3), 328–344.

Neghina, C., Caniëls, M., Bloemer, J. & Birgelen, M. (2015). Value cocreation in service interactions: dimensions and antecedents. *Marketing Theory*, 15(2), 221–242.

Nenonen, S., Rasila, H., Junnonen, J-M. & Kärnä, S. (2008). Customer journey – a method to investigate user experience. In *European Facility Management Conference 10.-11.6.2008*, Manchester, UK, 54–63.

Nenonen, S. & Storbacka, K. (2010). Business models design: conceptualizing networked value co-creation. *International Journal of Quality and Service Sciences*, 2(1), 43–59.

Ng, I. C. L. & Smith, L. A. (2012). An integrative framework of value. *Review of Marketing Research*, 9(1), 207–243.

Nuttavuthisit, K. (2010). If you can't beat them, let them join: the development of strategies to foster consumers' co-creative practices. *Business Horizons*, 53(3), 315–324.

Ostrom, L., Parasuraman, A. & Bowen, E. (2015). Service research priorities in a rapidly changing context. *Journal of Service Research*, 18(2), 127–159.

Payne, F., Storbacka, K. & Frow, P. (2008). Managing the co-creation of value. *Journal of the Academy of Marketing Science*, 36(1), 83–96.

Pels, J., Möller, K. & Saren, M. (2009). Do you really understand business marketing? Getting beyond the RM and BM matrimony. *Journal of Business and Industrial Marketing*, 24(5/6), 322–336.

Peñaloza, L. & Mish, J. (2011). The nature and processes of market co-creation in triple bottom line firms: leveraging insights from consumer culture theory and service dominant logic. *Marketing Theory*, 11(1), 9–34.

Peters, D., Löbler, H., Brodie, J., Breidbach, F., Hollebeek, D., Smith, D. & Varey, J. (2014). Theorizing about resource integration through service-dominant logic. *Marketing Theory*, 14(3), 249–268.

Peters, L. (2016). Heteropathic versus homopathic resource integration and value co-creation in service ecosystems. *Journal of Business Research*, 69, 2999–3007.

Pieters, R., Hans, B. & Doug, A. (1995). A means-end chain approach to consumer goal structures. *International Journal of Research in Marketing*, 12, 227–244.

Plé, L. (2016). Studying customers' resource integration by service employees in interactional value co-creation. *Journal of Services Marketing*, 30(2), 152–164.

Plé, L. & Cáceres, R. (2010). Not always co-creation: introducing interactional co-destruction of value in service-dominant logic. *Journal of Services Marketing*, 24, 6.

Plé, L., Lecocq, X. & Angot, J. (2010). Customer-integrated business models: a theoretical framework. *M@n@gement*, 13(4), 226–265.

Prahalad, C. & Ramaswamy, V. (2004). *The future of competition: Co-creating unique value with customers*. Boston, MA: Harvard Business School Press.

Puccinelli, N., Goodstein, R., Grewal, D., Price, R., Raghubir, P. & Stewart, D. (2009). Customer experience management in retailing: understanding the buying process. *Journal of Retailing*, 85(1), 15–30.

Rodie, A. & Kleine, S. (2000). Consumer participation in services production and delivery. In Swartz, T. & Iacobucci, D. (Eds.), *Handbook of services marketing and management*. Thousand Oaks, CA: Sage, 111–126.

Rosenbaum, M., Otalora, M. & Ramírez, G. C. (2017). How to create a realistic customer journey map. *Business Horizons*, 60(1), 143–150.

Sansone, C. & Thoman, D. (2006). Maintaining activity engagement: individual differences in the process of self-regulating motivation. *Journal of Personality*, 74(6), 1697–1720.

Schmitt, B. (2009). The concept of brand experience. *Journal of Brand Management*, 16, 7.

Schmitt, B. & Zarantonello, L. (2013). Consumer experience and experiential marketing: a critical review. *Review of Marketing Research*, 10, 25–61.

Schwartz, B., Ward, A., Monterosso, J., Lyubomirsky, S., White, K. & Lehman, D. (2002). Maximizing versus satisficing: happiness is a matter of choice. *Journal of Personality and Social Psychology*, 83(5), 1178–1197.

Skalén, P., Gummerus, J., Koskull, C. & Magnusson, P. (2015). Exploring value propositions and service innovation: a service-dominant logic study. *Journal of the Academy of Marketing Science*, 43(2), 137–158.

Söderlund, M & Sagfossen, S. (2017). The consumer experience: the impact of supplier effort and consumer effort on customer satisfaction. *Journal of Retailing and Consumer Services*, 39, 219–229, http://dx.doi.org/10.1016/j.jretconser.2017.08.019.

Srivastava, M. & Kaul, D. (2014). Social interaction, convenience and customer satisfaction: the mediating effect of customer experience. *Journal of Retailing and Consumer Services*, 21, 1028–1037, http://dx.doi.org/10.1016/j.jretconser.2014.04.007.

Stein, A. & Ramaseshan, B. (2016). Towards the identification of customer experience touch point elements. *Journal of Retailing and Consumer Services*, 30, 8–19.

Sweeney, J., Dagger, T. & McColl-Kennedy, J. (2015). Customer effort in value cocreation activities: improving quality of life and behavioral intentions of health care customers. *Journal of Service Research*, 18(3), 318–335.

Taillard, M., Peters, L., Pels, J. & Mele, C. (2016). The role of shared intentions in the emergence of service ecosystems. *Journal of Business Research*, 69, 2972–2980.

Truong, Y., Simmons, G. & Palmer, M. (2012). Reciprocal value propositions in practice: constraints in digital markets. *Industrial Marketing Management*, 41(1), 197–206.

van Doorn, J., Lemon, K., Mittal, V., Nass, S., Pick, D., Pirner, P. & Verhoef, P. (2010). Customer engagement behavior: theoretical foundations and research directions. *Journal of Service Research*, 13(3), 253–266.

Vargo, S. & Lusch, R. (2004). Evolving to a new dominant logic. *Journal of Marketing*, 68(1), 1–17.

Vargo, S. & Lusch, R. (2008). Why service? *Journal of the Academy of Marketing Science*, 36(1), 25–38.

Vargo, S. & Lusch, R. (2011). It's all B2B and beyond: toward a systems perspective of the market. *Industrial Marketing Management*, 40(2), 181–187.

Vargo, S. & Lusch, R. (2016). Institutions and axioms: an extension and update of service-dominant logic. *Journal of the Academy of Marketing Science*, 44(1), 5–23.

Vargo, S., Maglio, P. & Akaka, M. (2008). On value and value co- creation: a service systems and service logic perspective. *European Management Journal*, 26(3), 145–152.

Verhoef, P., Lemon, K., Parasuraman, A., Roggeveen, A., Tsiros, M. & Schlesinger, L. (2009). Customer experience creation: determinants, dynamics and management strategies. *Journal of Retailing*, 85(1), 31–41.

Williams, J. (2012). The logical structure of the service-dominant logic of marketing. *Marketing Theory*, 12(4), 471–483.

Wittkowski, K., Moeller, S. & Wirtz, J. (2013). Firms' intentions to use nonownership services. *Journal of Service Research*, 16(2), 171–185.

Wolny, J. & Charoensuksai, N. (2014). Mapping customer journeys in multichannel decision-making. *Journal of Direct, Data and Digital Marketing Practice*, 15, 317–326.

Yi, Y. & Gong, T. (2013). Customer value co-creation behavior: scale development and validation. *Journal of Business Research*, 66, 1279–1284.

Yngfalk, A. (2013). It's not us, it's them!' Rethinking value cocreation among multiple actors. *Journal of Marketing Management*, 29(9–10), 1163–1181.

Zhang, J. (2014). Customer resource integration: antecedents and its impact on intent to co-create value. 11th *International Conference on Service Systems and Service Management*, June 25-27, Beijing, China, 1–5, doi: 10.1109/ICSSSM.2014.6874023.

Zomerdijk, G. & Voss, A. (2010). Service design for experience-centric services. *Journal of Service Research*, 13(1), 67–82.

19

Social media and customer engagement

Rodoula H. Tsiotsou

Introduction

Internet users now comprise over half of the world's population, having reached 3.6 billion in 2017 (Meeker, 2018). The internet assists firms in generating value-added experiences for customers and in improving the efficiency of their services offered around the world. The personal and collective data gathered on the internet improves consumer engagement and provides better customer experiences that drive business growth and lead to the development of new services. For example, in real time, consumers can navigate online (e.g. Google Maps), order transportation (e.g. Uber), share social stories (e.g. Snap Map), and obtain local news (e.g. Facebook social groups) and entertainment (e.g. live streaming of a concert).

In addition to the internet, social media obtained significant growth over the last decade. According to Statista (2018), there were 2.46 billion social media users worldwide in 2017, and this number is expected to reach three billion by 2021. Facebook is the most popular social media platform, with 2.07 billion active monthly users, followed by Instagram (800 million active monthly users), LinkedIn (500 million active monthly users), Twitter (330 million active monthly users), Pinterest (200 million active monthly users), and Snapchat (178 million active monthly users) (Statista, 2018).

Social media are "a group of Internet-based applications that build on the ideological and technological foundations of Web 2.0, and allow the creation and exchange of User Generated Content" (Kaplan & Haenlein, 2010, p. 61). There is considerable diversity across types of social media, which encompass formats such as blogs, social networking sites (SNSs), and content communities. For example, Facebook is an SNS, Twitter is a microblogging application, and YouTube is a content community. SNSs are applications that allow users to connect with each other by creating their personal profiles, and inviting friends, family members, acquaintances, and colleagues to connect to their networks; they can share information, ideas, pictures, and videos, and send instant messages and emails (Kaplan & Haenlein, 2010).

Microblogging is a real-time information network, which limits the size (number of words) of each post and encourages a faster mode of communication. Microblogging is the most important and visible field of Web 2.0 technologies due to its light, fast, and easy form of communication that is enabled by instant messages, email, mobile phones, and the internet. It is a frequently updated website consisting of data entries arranged in reverse chronological order (Walker, 2005); it is about posting updates, ideas, or simply quick notifications (McFedries, 2007). There are three types of microblogging: information sharing (followed by many), information seeking (following many), and friendship relationships (following and followed by the same people) (Java, Finin, Song, & Tseng, 2007). Content communities refer to applications where users can share online multimedia material (e.g. videos or photos).

Social media are beneficial because they not only satisfy the needs, desires, and interests of customers, but also support interactivity for promotion and provide market intelligence to businesses. Due to tremendous social media growth, many companies are trying to connect themselves (and/or their brands) with customers via these platforms. Investments in social media advertising worldwide reached $32 billion in 2017 and are expected to reach $48 billion in 2021 (Statista, 2018). Social media provide great opportunities for businesses to reach and engage target customers based on their demographics, interests, desires, and previous behaviors. Social media are becoming customer engagement and brand building tools and, therefore, are now part of the promotional tactics of businesses. Social media enable customers to more efficiently discover and purchase products. A recent study showed that 76% of U.S. customers have purchased a product they saw in a brand's social media post, whereas 50% said that user-generated content (UGC) (e.g. pictures, comments from other users) would make them more likely to buy products through a brand's social media channel (Shelly, 2017).

Social media provide platforms where customers engage in various forms of behaviors (e.g. writing a review, expressing their opinions, and sharing their experiences) and interactions with other customers. Customers might be active (e.g. evaluating service performance, posting comments and material, or reposting others' comments and material), or they might be passive consumers of social media content (e.g. viewing other customers' evaluations, viewing comments and material, or observing the conversations of others) (Munzel & Kunz, 2014; Pagani, Hofacker, & Goldsmith, 2011; Tsiotsou, 2016).

Social media have changed customer behavior in many ways. Nowadays, the majority of social media customers use their apps via their smartphones; 78% of social media time is spent on mobile devices (Lella & Lipsman, 2017). Moreover, customer service is no longer private between a customer and a customer service representative. Sprout Social (2017) found that 46% of a sample of 1,000 customers have 'called out' or complained about a business on social media, whereas 55% of them call out to get a resolution or response. In the same study, 81% of respondents stated that social media have increased accountability for business by uncovering unfair treatment (80%), giving customers power (75%), and encouraging transparency (70%). Only 8% of customers would stay silent if they saw an inappropriate behavior from a brand. In the past, customers felt helpless to complain about business practices, but with social media available, they have a platform to share their experiences and solicit the help of others to petition for resolution or even restitution. The user-friendliness and popularity of social media have led to significant increases in customer engagement with businesses, which in turn results in large amounts of UGC.

Although the significance of customer engagement has been acknowledged in the literature, there are still several gaps regarding why customers engage online with goods and services; also of interest is identifying the consequences of their engagement. Moreover, the majority of available research sheds light on certain aspects of customer engagement and does not provide a holistic approach. This chapter seeks to address these gaps through developing a comprehensive theoretical framework of customer engagement in social media. Thus, the purpose of this chapter is to identify key elements and forms of customer engagement in social media and propose a conceptual framework that explains the drivers (why) and outcomes of the construct as well as the types of engagement (active and/or passive engagement). The proposed framework provides future research directions and managerial implications.

Customer engagement in social media: a proposed conceptual framework

According to Brodie, Hollebeek, Juric, andand Ilic (2011), customer engagement can be considered a multidimensional concept, reflecting a psychological state that takes place as a result of interactive customer experiences with focal points within service relationships. A more recent definition of customer engagement views it as a "psychologically based willingness to invest in the undertaking of focal interactions with particular engagement objects" (Hollebeek, Conduit, & Brodie, 2016, p. 393). Customer engagement with an online community refers to the customer's degree of motivation to participate actively in social media group-related activities (Algesheimer, Dholakia, & Herrmann, 2005). It can be measured based on tweets in Twitter, status updates in Facebook, videos on YouTube, or customer-generated reviews and advertisements. It has been observed that customer engagement consists of three dimensions, namely: cognitive, emotional, and behavioral (Algesheimer, Dholakia, & Herrmann, 2005; Brodie et al., 2011; Patterson, Yu, & De Ruyter, 2006). Cognitive engagement refers to the overall focused mental activity, involving attention and absorption. Affective engagement involves enthusiasm and enjoyment with regard to a focal object, whereas behavioral engagement denotes the active manifestations of the concept, including sharing, reviewing, learning, recommending, and endorsing behaviors (Dessart, 2017).

Several theoretical frameworks have been proposed in the literature, which examine the antecedents and consequences of customer engagement in social media (Dessart, 2017; Wirtz et al., 2013). Wirtz et al. (2013) proposed a model of customer engagement in online brand communities (OBC) that includes three drivers of OBC engagement, which are brand-related drivers (brand identification and brand symbolic function), social drivers (social benefits and social identity), and functional drivers (functional benefits, uncertainty avoidance, information quality, and monetary and explicit normative incentives). These are moderated by product, customer, and situational factors. In their model, they divide the outcomes of OBC engagement into customer- and organization- related outcomes. This model is conceptually sound and should be empirically tested. Dessart (2017) has also proposed a conceptual model of social media engagement including individual factors (e.g. online interaction propensity, attitude toward participation, and product involvement) as antecedents of community and brand engagement and brand relationship outcomes such as brand trust, brand commitment, and brand loyalty. The author tested the model empirically, and although some of her hypotheses were not confirmed, her study offers the important finding that community engagement is the strongest predictor of brand engagement (indicating the significant explanatory power of community participation in brand engagement) (Dessart, 2017). Kumar et al. (2010) proposed the concept of customer engagement value that includes both value deriving from transactions and value from non-transactional behavior such as customer referral value, customer influence value, and customer knowledge value. They further argue that ignoring customer engagement may lead to an underestimation or overvaluation of customers.

The proposed conceptual framework is a synthesis of the available literature, which incorporates the major concepts involved as antecedents and outcomes of customer engagement in social media, while it encompasses the theoretical foundation of current research findings. Specifically, it builds on community brand engagement frameworks and combines some of the recommended antecedents (motives) and relational outcomes (Dessart, 2017; Wirtz et al., 2013). Moreover, it distinguishes engagement into different types such as passive versus active as has been previously proposed in the literature (Munzel & Kunz, 2014; Pagani, Hofacker, & Goldsmith, 2011; Tsiotsou, 2016).

Antecedents of customer engagement

"Individuals engage in many practices in their day-to-day activities, and enactments of routinized practices vary with each individual's goals, skills, context, and other practices in which they engage" (Barrett, Davidson, Prabhu, & Vargo, 2015, p. 144). Uses and Gratifications Theory supports the idea that technology (in this case social media) users are active, self-aware, and goal directed (Katz, Blumler, & Gurevitch, 1973). Social media customers link their need gratification with specific social media alternatives to satisfy their needs. Their psychological and social needs include the strengthening or weakening of connection with family, friends, and the world through human–media interactions (Katz et al., 1973). In other words, customers' motives to satisfy their psychological and social needs determine the degree of their engagement behavior. A motive is an inner desire to actively fulfill a need or want (Deci & Ryan, 1985). According to Pervin (1983), such motives constitute combinations of cognitive, affective, and behavioral processes that organize and regulate behavior. Different engagement behaviors are driven by various motives (Brodie et al., 2011). Thus, customer motivations influence the level at which a person is active or passive.

A number of antecedents (motives and concepts) have been found in the literature to explain customer engagement in social media. Social, entertainment, and information are the most commonly found motives of social media engagement (Courtois, Mechant, De Marez, & Verleye, 2009; Heinonen, 2011; Park, Kee, & Valenzuela, 2009; Shao, 2009). In addition, Park et al. (2009) identified self-status seeking; community development, self-actualization, and self-expression have been also proposed as motives of social media engagement (Courtois et al., 2009; Shao, 2009). Krishnamurthy and Dou (2008) categorized social media engagement motives into two main groups: rational motives (knowledge-sharing and advocacy) and emotional motives (social connection and self-expression).

More recently, social media engagement has been found to be determined by personality traits (Marbach, Lages, & Nunan, 2016; Pagani et al., 2011), brand/product involvement (Dessart, 2017; Hollebeek, Glynn, & Brodie, 2014), need to reduce information search and perceived risk (Brodie, Ilic, Juric, & Hollebeek, 2013), flow, interactivity, and telepresence (Mollen & Wilson, 2010), trust (Brodie et al., 2011), and attitudes toward the community and online interaction propensity (Dessart, 2017). Bolton et al. (2013) proposed a number of antecedents to the use of social media by Gen Y (people born between 1981 and 1995). They have categorized these drivers into environmental and individual factors. Environmental factors affecting social media use include economic, technological, cultural, and political/legal variables. Individual factors include socioeconomic status, personal values/preferences, age/life cycle stage (stable factors), goals, emotions, and social norms (dynamic factors). In this chapter, intrinsic (personal and social motives) and extrinsic factors (social environment) are proposed as antecedents of social media engagement (Figure 19.1).

Intrinsic factors

Personal motives

Social media are sources of information that assist their members in dealing with various problems while providing social support that can help in reducing isolation and dealing with difficulties and stressful situations (Zhu, Woo, Porter, & Brzezinski, 2013). Several motives that satisfy specific needs through participation in social media have been reported in the literature. For instance, the need for activity (Marbach et al., 2016), the need for arousal (Marbach et al., 2016), the need for learning, and altruism (Marbach et al., 2016) have been found to motivate individuals to join social media platforms. Thus, customers may join an

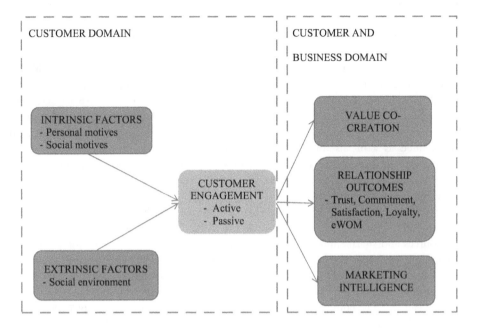

Figure 19.1 Conceptual framework for customer engagement in social media.

OBC to obtain information and reviews from other customers and keep up-to-date and informed with the latest products and offers (Heinonen, 2011; Marbach et al., 2016). Moreover, they might provide feedback or exhibit word-of-mouth behavior in order to help other customers (Heinonen, 2011; Marbach et al., 2016).

Customers may seek experiential value (Mathwick, 2002; Nambisan & Baron, 2009; Nonnecke, Andrews, & Preece, 2006) in their engagements with social media, such as relaxation and fun (Dholakia, Bagozzi, & Klein Pearo, 2004). Based on 57 customer diaries, Heinonen (2011) identified four dimensions of entertainment motives, such as escaping from the real world and relaxing, becoming inspired, mood management (looking for encouragement), self-expression (self-articulation and self-promotion), and entertaining oneself. A recent study by Khan (2017) showed that entertainment motives are not drivers of all forms of engagement behavior. His findings showed that entertainment motives can lead to like, dislike, and sharing videos on YouTube, but not to making comments or uploading videos. However, entertainment seeking has been found to be a strong predictor of viewing videos and reading comments (Khan, 2017). In summary, entertainment is an important motive for participating in social media platforms: it influences social media interactivity and can affect the decision to use social media.

Social motives

The mission of social media marketing is often to create networks of customers in order to assist them in developing relationships such as friendships, professional liaisons, and romantic connections (Chen, 2011; Daugherty, Eastin, & Bright, 2008; Kaplan & Haenlein, 2010;

Marwick, 2015). Social media enable customers to connect with other members of a virtual community and thus satisfy their needs for belonging and community (Heinonen, 2011). Social integration is an important motivator of social media consumption, because it satisfies customer need for belonging and provides the opportunity to increase interpersonal connections (Daugherty et al., 2008). Customers who are active in social media are more likely to feel more connected to other members of a social media group, and gratify their social needs (Chen, 2011). Brown, Broderick, and Lee (2007, p. 2) find that an online social network or online community can act as a "social proxy for individual identification." In other words, individuals behave as themselves in social media and therefore social media communities could be used as a means for their identification. Social media provide information and social support and become an integral part of social and consumption behavior (Wellman et al., 1996). Thus, virtual communities provide the opportunity to members to maintain and develop online relationships.

Research on the topic has been focused on the strength of the online relationships developed over time (Brown et al., 2007; Zhao & Lu, 2012). Social capital, expressed as information resources and social support systems, seems to be a significant motive for participating and engaging in social media that lead to commitment to the community (Mathwick, Wiertz, & de Ruyter, 2008). Customers join online consumption communities such as brand communities in social media not only for the entertainment value, but also for their purposive value. Thus, consumption communities offer brand information, provide solutions to customers' problems, and assist them in making purchase decisions (Dholakia et al., 2004); they might also be another point of socialization with their 'real' friends.

Extrinsic factors

Social environment

The social environment might exert pressure on the customer and can be a factor influencing customer engagement in social media. In sociology, social influence and social selection have been proposed as the two social forces of behavior. Social influence leads customers to adopt behaviors exhibited by those they interact with offline and/or online (Friedkin, 1998). In this vein, customers might participate or upload brand-related content because other people do. When customers see that others have uploaded pictures showing their favored brands or products, they might be stimulated or feel obligated to do the same (Muntinga, Moorman, & Smit, 2011). Social selection (Friedkin, 1998) refers to the tendency people have to form relationships with others who are already similar to them. The two forces of social influence and selection are both seen in a wide range of social settings: people decide to adopt activities (social media use and engagement) based on the activities of the people they interact with (reference groups), and people simultaneously form new interactions as a result of their existing activities (social media use and engagement).

In marketing, friends are often considered a reference group whose perspective an individual takes in forming values, beliefs, attitudes, opinions, and overt behaviors (Sirgy, Rahtz, & Dias, 2014). Research highlights how social networks and friend/peer pressure play a key role in the social media adoption process. In a study conducted by Quan-Haase and Young (2010), 85% of student respondents reported that their primary motivation for joining Facebook was that "a friend suggested it." Once a person has joined, he or she feels obliged to communicate with his or her friends over Facebook and even to suggest it to others. Thus, participation in online communities might require the approval of 'real' friends. The second motivation, indicated by 49% of the respondents, was "everyone I know is on Facebook." Facebook is very popular among peers; nowadays, it is fashionable and a social trend to be a member of it and to be part of the friend/peer group. Not adopting Facebook would mean being excluded from such a network of friendship connections.

Friends, family, colleagues, and peers might constitute reference groups. Reference groups influence customer behavior by setting levels of aspiration and offering cues regarding the lifestyle and related purchasing behaviors customers should exhibit. Moreover, reference groups assist in defining the acceptable goods or services for displaying those aspirations – the kinds of clothing, or brand communities, for example, deemed appropriate for a member of the group (Bourne, 1957). Nowadays, reference groups can exist in both physical and digital environments. For example, when the values and norms of a consumption community are accepted and approved by customers' friends, then customers might be motivated to become engaged or more engaged in the group. Therefore, the approval of customer behavior by others (e.g. friends, peers, and colleagues) who are important in their lives influences their degree of engagement with the consumption group (Tsiotsou, 2016). However, previous research cautions that the impact of the reference group is not equally important in all stages and types of decision-making or across social groups (Chattalas and Harper, 2007).

Customer engagement in social media

Social media are gigantic ecosystems including complex networks of relationships with multiple social nets, levels, and types of interactions. Social media engagement differs among customers based on their ties to the focal object (e.g. brand or brand community). Therefore, different typologies of customer engagement in social media have been proposed in the literature. Some divide it into two types, including engagement with the brand/corporate brand, and engagement with the brand community members (Dessart, 2017). Some others categorize based on the intensity level such as active versus passive engagement (Tsiotsou, 2016) or high and low engagement (Malthouse, Haenlein, Skiera, Wege, & Zhang, 2013; Muntinga et al., 2011). Others combine positive and negative engagement with low and high engagement, and view the result as a continuum of discrete behaviors (Dolan, Conduit, Fahy, & Goodman, 2015). In this chapter, customer engagement is distinguished into two types: active or passive engagement. Following, each type of engagement is discussed.

Active engagement

Social media are considered as an effective means to establish relationships with customers and promote positive word of mouth (Algesheimer et al., 2005). Brand communities in social media involve multiple participants at different stages, with some actively engaged and others simply observing interactions among their members (Libai, Muller, & Peres, 2010). However, these communities might not be very effective without customer engagement. "Community engagement suggests that members are interested in helping other members, participating in joint activities, and otherwise acting volitionally in ways that the community endorses and that enhance its value for themselves and others" (Algesheimer, et al., 2005, p. 21).

As previously mentioned, customer engagement with social media can be active or passive. Active customer engagement might include learning, sharing, advocating, socializing, co-developing (Brodie et al., 2013), and co-creating (Dolan et al., 2015). Customers might engage with a brand or brand community by contributing to existing content on the brand's social media page. For example, customers might indicate their preferences/emotional reactions to a new packaging of the brand on Facebook or Instagram. Thus, customers inter-act with the focal brand and give feedback to the firm and to other members of the brand community.

When customers show positive emotional reactions and/or share content, they endorse the focal brand, which might increase the likelihood of friends becoming engaged with it (Chu, 2011). Co-creators act as co-developers of the content on the social media brand page, through the initiation of positive, active contributions and subsequent interaction with the brand and with other group members. These members create various forms of content in order to disseminate their resources, knowledge, and experiences to the focal firm and other customers (Brodie et al., 2013; Jaakkola & Alexander, 2014). Activities engaged in by co-creators reflect interactive creation behaviors by not only the customers but also by the firm. Thus, firms/brands might benefit from active customer engagement by collecting data and analyzing it in order to improve their products or develop new ones. For example, Ford Motor Company studied social media customer behavior and found that 80% of potential customers favored the hands-free tailgate (Nash, 2014). Customers were talking about the liftgate, why they wanted it, what kind of cars they had, and other wished-for features. Thus, the company decided to build a hands-free liftgate that has proven to be a selling point with customers (Nash, 2014).

Passive engagement

Active customer engagement may be considered a social behavior because it involves social interactions (Cohen, 2004; Heider, 1958), whereas passive engagement is regarded as para-social behavior because it is a one-sided interaction (Auter & Palmgreen, 2000; Horton & Wohl, 1956; Tsiotsou, 2015, 2016). In the social media context, social relationships can be viewed as the sum of social interactions that are based on reciprocity between a customer and his/her online 'friends,' whereas para-social relationships are one-sided relationships in which a customer is aware of the activities of other customers but not vice versa (Baek, Bae, & Jang, 2013).

Para-social customer behavior has recently attracted research attention in the online envir-onment and specifically in relation to social media (Ballantine & Martin, 2005; Munzel & Kunz, 2014; Pagani et al., 2011; Tsiotsou, 2015, 2016). The terms 'passive use,' 'passive par-ticipation,' 'dormancy,' or 'lurking' are often used to describe the behaviors of individuals who only consume the content produced by other social media group members while main-taining anonymity (Brodie et al., 2013; Colliander & Dahlen, 2011; Men & Tsai, 2013; Pagani et al., 2011). Para-social behavior has been studied in connection with blogs (Collian-der & Dahlen, 2011), sports (Sun & Wu, 2012), political candidacies (Thorson & Rodgers, 2006), avatars (Jin, 2010), and SNSs (Tsiotsou, 2015, 2016). One study examined corporate pages in social media and showed that Chinese customers' para-social interaction with a social media corporate representative was high and exhibited a significant positive influence on public engagement (Men & Tsai, 2013). Recently, Tsiotsou (2016) showed that customer para-social relationships, expressed as group identification and problem-solving, precede social relationships expressed as social group active engagement and reference group accept-ance. These, in turn, lead to relationships with the social media group, reflected as trust and loyalty. However, this author's findings need to be confirmed by future studies in order to clarify the relationship between active and passive social media engagement. Moreover, an issue that is important and requires further investigation is to understand when passive engagement becomes active engagement and vice versa. The moment at which para-social interactions become normal social interactions remains a "gray area" (Giles, 2002).

Consequences of customer engagement

Social media communities are powerful tools for building long-term relationships with customers. They do this by encouraging customers to engage with their brands, both by interacting directly with each other (van Doorn et al., 2010; Verhoef, Reinartz, & Krafft, 2010) and by participating in brand communities (Libai et al., 2010), which in turn can increase brand equity and customer lifetime value.

Relationship outcomes

Research shows that customer engagement in a social media community is related to significant outcomes such as trust, satisfaction, value, commitment, and loyalty (Brodie et al., 2011; Casalo, Flavian, & Guinaliu, 2007; van Doorn et al., 2010; Vivek, Beatty, & Morgan, 2012). Casalo et al. (2007) studied (software) consumption communities and found that active customer participation and interactions with other members in the communities influence not only their community trust, as has been previously demonstrated (Brodie et al., 2013), but also their trust in the brand around which the community is developed. Moreover, the literature indicates that customer engagement in brand communities has a significant effect on brand loyalty (Brodie et al., 2013; Casalo et al., 2007; McAlexander, Schouten, & Koenig, 2002; Muniz & O'Guinn, 2001).

The positive relationship between active customer engagement and loyalty to the brand community has been shown in both offline and online environments (Brodie et al., 2013; Casalo et al., 2007; McAlexander et al., 2002; Muniz & O'Guinn, 2001; Tsiotsou, 2016). Casalo et al. (2007) confirmed that increased engagement in community activities exerts a positive influence on brand loyalty. Customers with strong intentions to engage in frequent social media use are more likely to behave in accordance with their intentions and to exhibit behavioral loyalty to the social media group (Baker & White, 2010). Dessart (2017) examined the relationship between customer engagement and brand relationship outcomes and found that customer engagement can have a direct impact on brand trust and commitment, and an indirect influence, through brand commitment, on brand loyalty outcomes in social media contexts. Thus, customers engaged in social media groups develop trust in the brand, and give the brand the opportunity to be assured of its quality as a relationship partner (Hollebeek, 2011).

If a brand behaves in a way that enables customers to satisfactorily engage with it, desire to engage grows over time, and trust is most likely to develop. If brands provide attractive and persuasive content to learn from and share, this keeps customer attention and entertains them through their actions on social media (Malhotra, Malhotra, & See, 2012). Furthermore, it enables customers to be engaged consistently over time; therefore, customers are more likely to develop brand trust (Marzocchi, Morandin, & Bergami, 2013), and to increase their commitment and desire to maintain relationships with the brand (Jang, Olfman, Ko, Koh, & Kim, 2008). Gummerus, Liljander, Weman, andand Pihlström (2012) have supported the influence of customer engagement on loyalty; however, these authors suggest that a relationship is mediated through entertainment benefits. Moreover, their research findings showed the impact of customer engagement on satisfaction being partially mediated by social benefits and entertainment benefits.

Hollebeek et al. (2014) examined the influence of the three dimensions of customer brand engagement (CBE) in social media, which they called "cognitive processing," "affection," and "activation" of customer "self-brand connection" – the authors report a positive relationship. Moreover, they report that among the three CBE dimensions, "affection" had the greatest impact on self-brand connection. Furthermore, they showed that the three dimensions of CBE do not exert the same effect on brand usage intent. Specifically, although they found customer brand-related "affection" and "activation" in specific customer-brand interactions to have a similar significant effect on "brand usage intent," the customer level of "cognitive processing" had no significant effect.

Value co-creation

Social media represents a platform where value is co-created by customers/actors contributing, retrieving, sharing, and exploring content with other actors (customers or company representatives). Co-created value refers to the mutual benefits that both firms and customers derive from sharing in joint activities. Value can be seen as a jointly created phenomenon emerging through interaction (Vargo & Lusch, 2008). If a customer is highly engaged, he/she will derive intrinsic and extrinsic value from the focus of the engagement (Vivek et al., 2012) and thus the intensity of engagement will influence the depth of the value created. Therefore, the more engaged a customer is in a focal object (e.g. brand, brand community), the more value can be created (Hollebeek et al., 2014). The literature suggests that different types of value emerge as a result of engagement, including: social value, play, efficiency, excellence, aesthetic value, and altruistic value (Marbach et al., 2016).

Marketing intelligence

Social media are a potential source for companies to gather market intelligence. "Social media is an essential component of the next-generation business intelligence platform" (Zeng, Chen, Lusch, & Li, 2010, p. 14); this is true for new product development and design, as well as for customer relationship management. Companies monitor social media to collect relevant information concerning marketing of their offerings (Bolton et al., 2013). The advantage of social media customer engagement is that it provides market intelligence at no, or minimum, cost. Thus, social media customer engagement serves as a collection and dissemination point for customer insights. What distinguishes it from traditional marketing intelligence is that most of it is voluntary, unsolicited, unguided, unfiltered, and outside traditional marketers' capacity to obtain or control.

Social media analytics can be used to develop and evaluate informatics tools to gather, control, analyze, and visualize social media data in order to make the best possible market decisions. For example, Nielsen's BuzzMetrics BrandPulse and BrandPulse Insight are two market intelligence tools on the internet. BrandPulse tracks and measures the volume of consumer-generated media about a particular brand, whereas BrandPulse Insight analyzes data daily from public areas of the internet, and especially blogs, to find out about customer trends, opinion shifts, marketplace predictions, and what customers are talking about and in what context.

Social media exist primarily as platforms that allow customers to communicate directly with other customers, without necessitating the interference of companies or marketers who are trying to capture their attention. Most importantly, social media customer engagement plays a growing role in shaping customer purchase behavior, especially as customers increasingly place their buying power and trust in other customers, rather than in other forms of media and traditional marketing communications.

Social media intelligence aims to derive actionable information from social media in context-rich application settings, develop corresponding decision-making or decision-aiding frameworks, and provide architectural designs and solution frameworks for existing and new applications that can benefit from the 'wisdom of crowds' through the Web.

(Zeng et al., 2010, p. 15)

Customer engagement in social media has been linked to increased sales. For example, Manchanda, Packard, and Pattabhiramaiah (2011) reported that customers who joined a brand community increased their online purchases by 37% and their offline purchases by 9%. However, this relationship needs further investigation to be confirmed.

Epilogue

Social media started as entertainment devices; however, they have evolved into powerful marketing tools. Although their primary purpose was to connect people, social media now play a major role in connecting marketers with customers, and customers with other customers. Moreover, social media enable customers to gather information, actively contribute to the creation of new ideas and concepts, while also facilitating and enhancing the relationships developed between a brand and its customers. Marketing via social media is on the rise, because social media have become important in the business world and show great potential for further development (e.g., use of video product presentation and increased sales).

Gaining a better understanding of why and how customers engage with brands in social media has become important to firms all over the world. Social media customer engagement relates to significant marketing activities, ranging from customer complaint handling to new product development. Yet, despite the substantial investment marketers have made in various forms of social media, many of these communities present low engagement levels. This chapter delves into a large number of possible drivers of social media customer engagement and highlights the most important ones. Specifically, it is proposed that customer intrinsic factors, such as individual and social motives, and extrinsic factors (reference groups) affect customer engagement behaviors. Thus, customer engagement may affect marketing metrics such as customer satisfaction, trust, loyalty, and value, which subsequently should affect firm value (e.g. Lehmann 2004). Companies could also gather important marketing intelligence through customer engagement data, which could assist them in developing prediction models and making better decisions. This chapter analyses types of customer engagement, passive and active, and how these two types of engagement complement each other.

The proposed framework can assist managers of social media communities in gaining a better understanding of customer behavior in social media by revealing the antecedents of customer engagement, and what they should expect when customers are passively or actively engaged. Consequently, businesses will be able to better segment their customers through a more detailed understanding of the motives of those who engage in specific communities. Because engagement constitutes the main area of customer input in social media, business strategies in these platforms should be associated with facilitating engagement. In the proposed model, information search/consumption is a motive that drives customer engagement in social media. Companies should offer different information to be accessed by any customer, in order to attract new customers and to increase the contribution/engagement of existing customers.

Social motives are another area that companies need to take into account when designing their social media tactics. These are very important because they might lead to an increased number of engaged customers. Companies should encourage customers to raise questions, share opinions and experiences, initiate discussions about different daily topics, and introduce multiplayer games. Such activities can enable interactions among customers, and between the company and its customers, as well as increase interest in the company and its brands. Moreover, companies should initiate tactics related to activities that will satisfy customers' entertainment motives. Videos and games can be used for this purpose and should be easy to use and free of charge to appeal to larger customer groups.

Through having a better understanding of the role of customer engagement, firms can apply knowledge to make their social media communities more effective. Managers are increasingly concerned with how to enhance the engagement level of their customers, to develop favorable customer experiences and increase value co-creation. Such experiences are critical in maintaining long-term relationships between a brand and its customers. Customer relationship management remains a key marketing priority (Verhoef et al., 2010); it has the potential to develop attractive social media communities, which is important because they build more effective platforms for customer co-creation.

Future studies are needed to test the proposed framework through qualitative and large-scale quantitative research into driving factors of customer engagement, their impact on active and passive engagement, and related outcomes in various social media contexts. Other possible drivers of customer engagement should also be examined. For example, personality traits and economic and political factors might also have an impact on customer engagement. Moreover, how and when passive customer engagement in social media becomes active engagement needs further investigation. More research is also needed on the outcomes of customer engagement in social media, such as company profits and sales, new product development/performance, customer retention/switching behavior, customer lifetime value, and traditional media communications' effectiveness. Finally, the types and uses of market intelligence that businesses gather from social media customer engagement is another research avenue.

References

Algesheimer, R., Dholakia, U., & Herrmann, A. (2005). The social influence of brand community: evidence from European car clubs. *Journal of Marketing*, 69, 19–34.

Auter, P. J., & Palmgreen, P. (2000). Development and validation of a parasocial interaction measure: the audience-persona interaction scale. *Communication Research Report*, 17(1), 79–89.

Baek, Y. M., Bae, Y., & Jang, H. (2013). Social and parasocial relationships on social network sites and their differential relationships with users' psychological well-being. *Cyberpsychology, Behavior, and Social Networking*, 16(7), 512–517.

Baker, R. K., & White, K. M. (2010). Predicting adolescents' use of social networking sites from an extended theory of planned behaviour perspective. *Computers in Human Behavior*, 26(6), 1591–1597.

Ballantine, P. W., & Martin, B. A. S. (2005). Forming parasocial relationships in online communities. *Advances in Consumer Research*, 32, 197–201.

Barrett, M., Davidson, E., Prabhu, J., & Vargo, S. L. (2015). Service innovation in the digital age: key contributions and future directions. *MIS Quarterly*, 39(1), 135–154.

Bolton, R. N., Parasuraman, A., Hoefnagels, A., Migchels, N., Kabadayi, S., Gruber, T., Loureiro, Y. K., & Solnet, D. (2013). Understanding Generation Y and their use of social media: a review and research agenda. *Journal of Service Management*, 24(3), 245–267.

Bourne, F. S. (1957). Group influence in marketing and public relations. In R. Likert & S. P. Hayes (Eds.), *Some applications of behavioral research* (pp. 207–255). Paris: UNESCO.

Brodie, R. J., Hollebeek, L. D., Juric, B., & Ilic, A. (2011). Customer engagement: conceptual domain, fundamental propositions, and implications for research. *Journal of Service Research*, 14(3), 252–271.

Brodie, R. J., Ilic, A., Juric, B., & Hollebeek, L. (2013). Consumer engagement in a virtual brand community: an exploratory analysis. *Journal of Business Research*, 66(1), 105–114. doi:10.1016/j.jbusres.2011.07.029.

Brown, J., Broderick, A. J., & Lee, N. (2007). Word of mouth communication within online communities: conceptualizing the online social network. *Journal of Interactive Marketing*, 21(3, summer), 1–20.

Casalo, L., Flavian, C., & Guinaliu, M. (2007). The impact of participation in virtual brand communities on consumer trust and loyalty. *Online Information Review*, 1(6), 775–792.

Chattalas, M., & Harper, H. (2007), Navigating a hybrid cultural identity: Hispanic teenagers' fashion consumption influences. Journal of Consumer Marketing 24(6), 351–357.

Chen, G. M. (2011). Tweet this: a uses and gratifications perspective on how active Twitter use gratifies a need to connect with others. *Computers in Human Behavior*, 27(2), 755–762.

Chu, S.-C. (2011). Viral advertising in social media: participation in Facebook groups and responses among college-aged users. *Journal of Interactive Advertising*, 12, 30–43.

Cohen, S. (2004). Social relationships and health. *American Psychologist*, 59, 676–684.

Colliander, J., & Dahlen, M. (2011). Following the fashionable friend: the power of social media. Weighing publicity effectiveness of blogs versus online magazines. *Journal of Advertising Research*, 51(1), 313–320.

Courtois, C., Mechant, P., De Marez, L., & Verleye, G. (2009). Gratifications and seeding behavior of online adolescents. *Journal of Computer-Mediated Communication*, 15, 109–137.

Daugherty, T., Eastin, M., & Bright, L. (2008). Exploring consumer motivations for creating user-generated content. *Journal of Interactive Advertising*, 8(2), 1–24.

Deci, E. L., & Ryan, R. M. (1985). *Intrinsic motivation and self-determination in human behavior.* New York: Plenum.

Dessart, L. (2017). Social media engagement: a model of antecedents and relational outcomes. *Journal of Marketing Management*, 33(5–6), 375–399.

Dholakia, U. M., Bagozzi, R. P., & Klein Pearo, L. (2004). A social influence model of consumer participation in network- and small-group-based virtual communities. *International Journal of Research in Marketing*, 21(3), 241–263.

Dolan, R., Conduit, J., Fahy, J., & Goodman, S. (2015). Social media engagement behaviour: a uses and gratifications perspective. *Journal of Strategic Marketing*. doi:10.1080/0965254X.2015.1095222.

Friedkin, N. E. (1998). *A structural theory of social influence.* Cambridge, UK: Cambridge University Press.

Gummerus, J., Liljander, V., Weman, E., & Pihlström, M. (2012). Customer engagement in a Facebook brand community. *Management Research Review*, 35(9), 857–877. doi:10.1108/01409171211256578.

Giles, D.C. (2002) Parasocial Interaction: A Review of the Literature and a Model for Future Research, Mediapsychology. 4, 279–305.

Heider, F. (1958). *The psychology of interpersonal relations.* New York: Psychology Press.

Heinonen, K. (2011). Consumer activity in social media: managerial approaches to consumers' social media behavior. *Journal of Consumer Behaviour*, 10(6), 356–364.

Hollebeek, L. D. (2011). Demystifying customer brand engagement: Exploring the loyalty nexus. Journal of Marketing Management, 27(7-8), 785–807.

Hollebeek, L. D., Conduit, J., & Brodie, R. J. (2016). Strategic drivers, anticipated and unanticipated outcomes of customer engagement. *Journal of Marketing Management*, 32(5–6), 393–398.

Hollebeek, L. D., Glynn, M. S., & Brodie, R. J. (2014). Consumer brand engagement in social media: conceptualization, scale development and validation. *Journal of Interactive Marketing*, 28(2), 149–165.

Horton, D., & Wohl, R. R. (1956). Mass communication and para-social interaction: observations on intimacy at a distance. *Psychiatry*, 19(3), 215–229.

Jaakkola, E., & Alexander, M. (2014). The Role of Customer Engagement Behavior in Value Co-Creation: A Service System Perspective. Journal of Service Research, 17(3), 247–261.

Jang, H., Olfman, L., Ko, I., Koh, J., & Kim, K. (2008). The influence of on-line brand community characteristics on community commitment and brand loyalty. *International Journal of Electronic Commerce*, 12(3), 57–80.

Java, A., Finin, T., Song, X., & Tseng, B. (2007). Why we Twitter: understanding microblogging usage and communities. Proceedings of the Joint 9th WEBKDD and 1st SNA-KDD Workshop 2007.

Jin, S.-A.-A. (2010). "I feel more connected to the physically ideal mini me than the mirror-image mini me": theoretical implications of the "malleable self" for speculations on the effects of avatar creation on avatar–self connection in Wii. *Cyberpsychology, Behavior, and Social Networking*, 13, 567.

Kaplan, A. M., & Haenlein, M. (2010). Users of the world, unite! The challenges and opportunities of social media. *Business Horizons*, 53, 59–68.

Katz, E., Blumler, J. G., & Gurevitch, M. (1973). Uses and gratifications research. *Public Opinion Quarterly*, 37(4), 509–523.

Khan, M. L. (2017). Social media engagement: what motivates user participation and consumption on YouTube? *Computers in Human Behavior*, 66, 236–247.

Krishnamurthy, S., & Dou, W. (2008). Advertising with user-generated content: a framework and research agenda. *Journal of Interactive Advertising*, 8(2), 1–7.

Kumar, V., Aksoy, L., Donkers, B., Venkatesan, R., Wiesel, T., & Tillmanns, S. (2010). Undervalued or overvalued customers: capturing total customer engagement value. *Journal of Service Research*, 13(3), 297–310.

Lehmann, D.R. (2004). Metrics for Making Marketing Matter. Journal of Marketing, 68(4), 73–75.

Lella, A., & Lipsman, A. (2017). The 2017 U.S. mobile app report. Available at: www.comscore.com/Insights/Presentations-and-Whitepapers/2017/The-2017-US-Mobile-App-Report.

Libai, B., Muller, E., & Peres, R. (2010), *Source of social value in word of mouth programs*. MSI working paper 10–103. Cambridge, MA: Marketing Science Institute.

Malhotra, A., Malhotra, C. K., & See, A. (2012). How to create brand engagement on Facebook. *MIT Sloan Management Review*, 54(2), 18–20.

Malthouse, E. C., Haenlein, M., Skiera, B., Wege, E., & Zhang, M. (2013). Managing customer relationships in the social media era: introducing the social CRM house. *Journal of Interactive Marketing*, 27(4), 270–280.

Manchanda, P., Packard, G., & Pattabhiramaiah, A. (2011). *Social dollars: the economic impact of customer participation in firm-sponsored online community*. MSI report 11-115. Cambridge, MA: Marketing Science Institute.

Marbach, J., Lages, C. R., & Nunan, D. (2016). Who are you and what do you value? Investigating the role of personality traits and customer-perceived value in online customer engagement. *Journal of Marketing Management*, 32(5–6), 502–525. doi:10.1080/0267257x.2015.1128472.

Marwick, A. E. (2015). Instafame: luxury selfies in the attention economy. *Public Culture*, 27(1), 137–160.

Marzocchi, G., Morandin, G., & Bergami, M. (2013). Brand communities: loyal to the community or the brand? *European Journal of Marketing*, 47(1/2), 93–114.

Mathwick, C., Wiertz, C., & de Ruyter, K. (2008). Social capital production in a virtual P3 community. *Journal of Consumer Research*, 34, 832–849.

Mathwick, C. (2002). Understanding the on-line consumer: a typology of on-line relational norms and behavior. *Journal of Interactive Marketing*, 16(1), 40–55.

McAlexander, J. H., Schouten, J. W., & Koenig, H. F. (2002). Building brand community. *Journal of Marketing*, 66(1), 38–54.

McFedries, P. (2007). All a-Twitter. *IEEE Spectrum*, 44(10), 84.

Meeker, M. (2018). *Internet trends report 2018. Kleiner Perkins*. Available at: www.kleinerperkins.com/perspectives/internet-trends-report-2018.

Men, L. R., & Tsai, W.-H. S. (2013). Beyond liking or following: understanding public engagement on social networking sites in China. *Public Relations Review*, 39(1), 13–22.

Mollen, A., & Wilson, H. (2010). Engagement, telepresence and interactivity in online consumer experience: reconciling scholastic and managerial perspectives. *Journal of Business Research*, 63(9–10), 919–925. doi:10.1016/j.jbusres.2009.05.014.

Muniz, A. M., Jr., & O'Guinn, T. C. (2001). Brand community. *Journal of Consumer Research*, 27(4), 412–432.

Muntinga, D. G., Moorman, M., & Smit, E. G. (2011). Introducing COBRAs. *International Journal of Advertising*, 30(1), 13–46.

Munzel, A., & Kunz, W. (2014). Creators, multipliers, and lurkers: who contributes and who benefits at online review sites. *Journal of Service Management*, 25(1), 49–74.

Nambisan, S., & Baron, R. A. (2009). Virtual customer environments: texting a model of voluntary participation in value co-creation activities. *Journal of Product Innovation Management*, 26, 388–406.

Nash, K. S. (2014). *How social media can influence high-stakes business decisions*. Available at: www.cio.com/article/2686973/social-media/how-social-media-can-influence-high-stakes-business-decisions.html.

Nonnecke, B., Andrews, D., & Preece, J. (2006). Non-public and public online community participation: needs, attitudes and behavior. *Electronic Commerce Research*, 6(1), 7–20.

Pagani, M., Hofacker, C., & Goldsmith, R. (2011). The influence of personality on active and passive use of social networking sites. *Psychology & Marketing*, 28(5), 441–456.

Park, N., Kee, K. F., & Valenzuela, S. (2009). Being immersed in social networking environment: Facebook groups, uses and gratifications, and social outcomes. *CyberPsychology & Behavior*, 12(6), 729–733.

Patterson, P., Yu, T., & De Ruyter, K. (2006). *Understanding customer engagement in services*. Paper presented at the Australia–New Zealand Marketing Academy Conference: Advancing Theory, Maintaining Relevance, Proceedings, Brisbane, Australia.

Pervin, L. A. (1983). The stasis and flow of behavior: toward a theory of goals. In M. M. Page (Ed.), *Personality: Current Theory and Research (Nebraska Symposium on Motivation)* (Vol. 30, pp. 1–53). Lincoln, NE: University of Nebraska Press.

Quan-Haase, A., & Young, A. L. (2010). Uses and gratifications of social media: a comparison of Facebook and instant messaging. *Bulletin of Science, Technology & Society*, 30(5), 350–3861.

Shao, G. (2009). Understanding the appeal of user-generated media: a uses and gratification perspective. *Internet Research*, 19(1), 7–25.

Shelly, J. (2017). 2017 *Curalate consumer survey: social content is the new storefront* (November 15, 2017). Available at: www.curalate.com/blog/social-media-content-survey/.

Sirgy, M. J., Rahtz, D. R., & Dias, L. P. (2014). *Consumer behavior today*, v. 1.0. eISBN: 978-1-4533-6314-0. Available at: http://catalog.flatworldknowledge.com/catalog/editions/sirgy-consumer-behavior-today-1-0. Accessed on January 21, 2018.

Sprout Social. (2017). *Call-out culture: people, brands & the social media power struggle*. Available at: https://sproutsocial.com/insights/data/q3-2017/.

Statista. (2018). *Social media marketing: Statistics & facts*. Available at: www.statista.com/topics/1538/social-media-marketing/.

Sun, T., & Wu, G. (2012). The influence of personality traits on parasocial relationship with sports celebrities: a hierarchical approach. *Journal of Consumer Behaviour*, 11(2), 136–146.

Thorson, K. S., & Rodgers, S. (2006). Relationships between blogs as eWOM and interactivity, perceived interactivity, and parasocial interaction. *Journal of Interactive Advertising*, 6(2), 34–44.

Tsiotsou, R. H. (2015). The role of social and parasocial relationships on social networking sites loyalty. *Computers in Human Behavior*, 48, 401–414.

Tsiotsou, R. H. (2016). The social aspects of consumption as predictors of consumer loyalty: online vs. offline services. *Journal of Service Management*, 27(2), 91–116.

van Doorn, J., Lemon, K. N., Mittal, V., Nass, S., Pick, D., Pirner, P., & Verhoef, P. C. (2010). Customer engagement behavior: theoretical foundations and research directions. *Journal of Service Research*, 13(3), 253–266.

Vargo, S. L., & Lusch, R. F. (2008). Service-dominant logic: continuing the evolution. *Journal of the Academy of Marketing Science*, 36(Spring), 1–10.

Verhoef, P. C., Reinartz, W. J., & Krafft, M. (2010). Customer engagement as a new perspective in customer management. *Journal of Service Research*, 13(3), 247–252.

Vivek, S. D., Beatty, S. E., & Morgan, R. M. (2012). Customer engagement: exploring customer relationships beyond purchase. *Journal of Marketing Theory and Practice*, 20(2), 122–146.

Walker, J. (2005). Weblogs: learning in public. *On the Horizon*, 13(2), 112–118.

Wellman, B., Salaff, J., Dimitrova, D., Garton, L., Gulia, M., & Haythornthwaite, C. (1996). Computer networks as social networks: collaborative work, telework, and virtual community. *Annual Review of Sociology*, 22, 213–238.

Wirtz, J., Den Ambtman, A., Bloemer, J., Horváth, C., Ramaseshan, B., van de Klundert, J., Canli, Z. G., & Kandampully, J. (2013). Managing brands and customer engagement in online brand communities. *Journal of Service Management*, 24(3), 223–244. doi:10.1108/09564231311326978.

Zeng, D., Chen, H., Lusch, R., & Li, S.-H. (2010). Social media analytics. *IEEE Intelligent Systems*, 25(6), 13–16.

Zhao, L. & Lu, Y. (2012). Enhancing perceived interactivity through network externalities: An empirical study on micro-blogging service satisfaction and continuance intention. Decision Support Systems 53(4), 825–834.

Zhu, X., Woo, S. E., Porter, C., & Brzezinski, M. (2013). Pathways to happiness: from personality to social networks and perceived support. *Social Networks*, 35(3), 382–393.

Part V
Ethics, responsibility, and culture

20

Executive ethical decisions initiating organizational culture and values[1]

Eileen Bridges

Introduction

Ethics come into play when decisions determine which entities benefit, and which suffer (Abela & Murphy, 2008; Doh & Quigley, 2014; Micewski & Troy, 2007; Rest, 1986). Entities that may be affected in organizational ethical decisions include individuals, groups (e.g. employees, or members of a market segment), an entire potential market, or even society as a whole. Such decisions are of greatest interest when resources are scarce and cannot be allocated in such a way that everyone benefits. They also hold greater importance in services than in manufacturing industries, because there is a "need to provide a consistent high-quality customer experience across all the brand–customer interactions and touch-points" (Sierra, Iglesias, Markovic, & Singh, 2017, p. 661). Furthermore, according to Sierra et al. (2017), there is a dearth of research regarding ethical decisions in services as compared to goods industries. The goal of the present research is to explore how high-ranking executives in service organizations make ethical decisions that drive culture and values within the organization, and to develop testable propositions based on the findings.

This chapter begins with a Conceptual Development section, reviewing relevant literature particularly in ethical decision-making and services. The Method section describes the qualitative research approach, the executive interviewees, and steps in data coding and analysis. Detailed analyses of the in-depth interviews are reported in the Results section, where emergent themes are identified. The Discussion section draws together the results, by suggesting testable propositions regarding ethical decision-making by service executives. Finally, the Conclusion recapitulates the research contribution, which fills a gap in academic theory by identifying two groups of service executives that approach ethical decisions differently; these differences are identified in the resulting propositions.

Conceptual development

Layers of ethical decision-making

As mentioned in the Introduction, ethical decisions made on behalf of organizations can impact different entities, ranging from a single individual to all of society. Figure 20.1 provides an interpretation of how previous literature has addressed ethical decisions, showing the locus of affected groups.

The outermost circle in the Figure 20.1 could be named the **'actualization layer.'** This type of organizational decision, typically called 'corporate social responsibility' (CSR), relates to the social ramifications of organizational decisions and affects everyone in society. Although often approved at the executive level, others at lower levels in an organization may select causes and make recommendations for contributions. There is a substantial CSR literature regarding decisions by firms to contribute to society as a whole, both to improve society directly, and to enhance the organization.

Some of the early literature attempts to define CSR; for instance, Brown and Dacin (1997) state that being socially responsible means benefitting society's welfare. It turns out that CSR has been defined in many ways: in a literature review covering 1980–2003, Dahlsrud (2008) finds 37 definitions of CSR, and reduces them through emergent coding to five dimensions, including (p. 6) three "categories of impact" (environmental, social, and economic) and two areas of "concern" (stakeholder and legal requirements). However, the author observes that none of the resulting dimensions actually define CSR. Sen and Bhattacharya (2001, p. 226) comment:

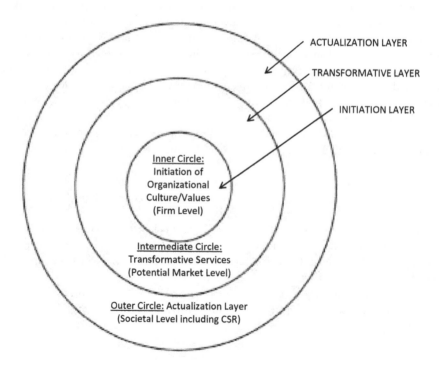

Figure 20.1 Layers of impact in organizations' ethical decision-making.

Although CSR is inextricably linked to corporate ethics, it is a more inclusive conceptualization of companies' responsibility to society at large that encompasses their more specific ethical responsibilities to abide by a set of moral principles or values in conducting business.

Engaging in CSR can also enhance firm financial value (Malik, 2015). Furthermore, Collins (2000) finds that firms having better social performance also have better financial performance, even though firms that invest more in CSR are actually less likely to avoid taxes than are other firms (Lanis & Richardson, 2015). Laczniak and Murphy (2012) reinforce the observation that firms should focus on society and not exclusively on stakeholders when making societal-level ethical decisions.

Ethical decisions regarding CSR influence society as a whole, and therefore the outermost circle in Figure 20.1 depicts decisions that are beyond the scope of the current research. The two remaining circles in Figure 20.1 relate to other entities where ethical decisions may have more focused impact, including on specific stakeholders such as the potential market, the organization, the profession, and the individual (Bergadaà, 2004). Because ethical decisions made at different levels may be influenced by cultural norms, it is important to address different layers of decision-making (shown in Figure 20.1) separately (Srnka, 2004). The intermediate circle in Figure 20.1 includes ethical decisions described by Collins (2000), who observed that ethical firms should do more to increase well-being among the potential market, a topic that is very timely and also vigorously addressed in a stream of service literature called 'transformative service research' (TSR). This literature gives a name to the '**transformative layer**,' pictured in the intermediate circle in Figure 20.1, which relates to impact of organizational ethical decisions on the potential market.

In the transformative layer (Figure 20.1), an organization's ethical decisions are focused on its own potential market. Although the total number of entities affected might be smaller than in society as a whole, each is of greater importance to the organization. TSR is promising because its primary goal is to improve the well-being of those in the potential market (Anderson et al., 2013). Ethical decisions in the transformative layer are often made by marketing managers, owing to their direct responsibility for customers and potential customers. Such decisions are complicated by the fact that the interaction between service providers and customers has changed in the past couple of decades, from traditional interpersonal service encounters involving one customer and one service provider, to new formats that include technology infusion and customer empowerment, and multi-actor service systems offering value co-creation (Bowen, 2016; Ostrom, Parasuraman, Bowen, Patrício, & Voss, 2015). Thus, it has become more difficult to make and implement the tough choices required in ethical decisions affecting the potential market, because identifying the entities that benefit and those that suffer has become more complex.

Another stream of service literature that relates to decisions affecting the potential market, and therefore to the intermediate circle in Figure 20.1, is the literature on co-creation of value. Because of increasing complexity in the relationships between front line people, service process design, and the customer experience, the literature describing co-creation of value has grown substantially. According to Grönroos and Gummerus (2014), when previously separate service provider and customer processes come together to form a single collaborative process during interactions, a platform for co-creation of value develops. The premise of co-creation is that the firm is no longer the sole designer of value; instead, customers take active roles in the creation of value for themselves and cooperate with companies and other organizations to do so. Mutually beneficial relationships are achieved when all relevant actors are enabled to be creative collaborators in the value co-creation process. Personalized interactions between the company and customers, as well as between customers, become the loci of value creation (Grönroos & Gummerus, 2014; Vargo & Lusch, 2004).

In addition to literature on co-creation, there have been some other important recent developments in TSR literature that inform transformative ethical decisions (in the intermediate circle in Figure 20.1). For instance, Yagil and Shultz (2017) address the difficulties involved in preparing front line service providers to make appropriate ethical decisions when dealing with customers. In the transformative layer, this is particularly important when dealing with vulnerable groups among the potential market, who may require special attention from service providers (Brenkert, 1998). However, vulnerable groups may be deemed less profitable to the firm and sink to the bottom of the priority list for service (Homburg, Droll, & Totzek, 2008; Zeithaml, Rust, & Lemon, 2001). This leads to complicated ethical decisions, particularly in such services as healthcare and finance, where concern for the vulnerable means paying attention to the fragility of potential customers such as children, the elderly, immigrants, refugees, and the poor (Rendtorff, 2009). These types of ethical decisions, which affect primarily those in the potential market, occur in the intermediate circle in Figure 20.1, the transformative layer. Ethical decisions regarding TSR impact primarily the potential market, and therefore the intermediate circle in Figure 20.1 depicts decisions that are beyond the scope of the current research.

Organizational culture and values are initiated in the inner circle (in Figure 20.1), so it is named the '**initiation layer**.' The initiation layer sets the tone for high-level ethical decisions that influence organizational culture and values, directly impacting those within the organization. (Of course, culture and values are also felt outside the organization.) Previous literature in business ethics has examined some predictors that go into generic ethical decisions, and there are models available that combine these predictors to surmise decision outcomes (see the next section). However, there is a dearth of qualitative literature that develops understanding of such decisions from the decision maker's human perspective. This research gap is particularly important because of the direct impact of high-level ethical decisions on people, especially front line service providers who interact personally with customers. Understanding decision-making in the initiation layer is the focus of the present research.

There are very few studies that examine specifically how executives make ethical decisions, particularly those affecting people within their own organizations. However, a recent study by Witt and Stahl (2016) addresses how leaders' values and orientations affect their decisions relative to various stakeholders, including employees. In case studies of two organizations, Bowen (2002, p. 272) asked executives three questions about ethics, including:

(1) what is your organization's view of ethics and the importance accorded ethical training and codes of ethics by the CEO and dominant coalition?
(2) When do ethics enter the issues management decision-making process?
(3) Do you think one philosophical approach (materialism, utilitarianism, or deontology) is superior to the others for decision-making in issues management, and which approach do you primarily use?

The responses to these questions were used to describe how ethical decisions are made in each of the two organizations. As Bowen (2002, p. 273) observes, it is "notoriously difficult to gain access to corporate elites." Perhaps this is the reason there are so few such studies available in the literature.

Another way of accessing organizations' normative ethical philosophies (including deontology and utilitarian teleology) involves studying their organizational ethics statements (Hoover & Pepper, 2015); these authors call for additional research on how firms communicate their values to employees. Doh and Quigley (2014) characterize leadership behaviors as either psychological (i.e. need realization) or knowledge-based, which appear related to the ethical philosophies (deontology and teleology). These authors observe that knowledge can be assessed, whereas psychological state cannot, and they call for research on how leaders making ethical decisions can be better understood. They also mention the importance of comprehending the nature of the legacy that a leader wishes to leave. Other researchers calling for additional related studies include Kaposy, Brunger, Maddalena, and Singleton (2016), who state that work is needed on the use of ethical decision-making frameworks, and Valentine and Hollingworth (2015), who examine relationships between coordinated decision-making, communication of business strategy, and employee perceptions of corporate ethical values.

In summary, it is important to enhance understanding of how service executives make ethical decisions in the initiation layer (Figure 20.1), where the primary impact is on others within the organization. This gap is addressed in the present research, which focuses on ethical decisions made by executives, especially those that define organizational culture and values, influencing others within the organization. A grounded theory methodology was selected because the goal is to develop new theory grounded in data from the field: specifically, this theory is based on the views of executive respondents and improves understanding of the information they use and how they make ethical decisions.

Influences on organizational ethical decision-making

The previous section used a new 'concentric circles' model to outline the locus of impact of various ethical decisions in services, and to briefly review literature streams related to each of the three layers (circles). It showed that whereas decisions that impact potential customers and broader constituencies are well covered in the literature, there is a gap in the inner circle, which focuses on executive decisions that primarily impact employees. Although the previous section identified this understudied area, it did not detail published research that examines specifically how such organizational ethical decisions are made. Therefore, this section provides an overview of factors that previous research in business ethics suggests can influence individuals making ethical decisions, as well as descriptions of decision models incorporating these factors.

Organizational decision makers are influenced by their personal characteristics and moral philosophies (Beu, Buckley, & Harvey, 2003; Collins, 2000; Detert, Treviño, & Sweitzer, 2008; Fritzsche, 1995; Hansen, 1992; Hunt & Vitell, 1986; Marta, Singhapakdi, & Kraft, 2008; Robertson, 2008; Singhapakdi, Rao, & Vitell, 1996; Srnka, 2004). Personal characteristics that are evaluated in this literature include gender, age, occupation, culture, and values. There are two personal moral philosophies that the literature indicates must be considered: the first is a *deontology*, which holds that decisions are inherently right or wrong, depending on the decision-making *process* used. The second is a *teleology*, which focuses on the *outcomes* of decisions. Teleologies can be egoist (doing what is best for the individual) or utilitarian (doing the greatest good for the greatest number of people). Hansen (1992, pp. 523–525) provides a helpful summary of moral philosophies, concluding that deontology and utilitarian teleology are most common in the business ethics literature. Ethical decision makers also take into account the organizational mission, values, culture, and financial goals (Craft, 2013; Marta et al., 2012; Vitell, Rallapalli, & Singhapakdi, 1993; Wyld & Jones, 1997); furthermore, Abela and Murphy

(2008) observed that there are tensions because economics cannot be neglected in favor of ethics.

Executive decision makers can both build and be influenced by organizational culture; this culture seems to develop in a circular pattern as executives make decisions and observe the results. Deal and Kennedy (2000) provide a seminal approach to defining corporate culture and identifying the crucial relationships between organizational values and strategic decisions; they define corporate culture as (p. iv): "deep-seated traditions and widely accepted and shared beliefs" that govern organizations. Deal and Kennedy (2000) identify some elements of this culture as the business environment, values, rites and rituals, and cultural network. They observe that top management drives organizational culture; some leaders are viewed as 'heroes' who personify organizational values, have an ethic of creation, and inspire employees with their entrepreneurial spirit. Furthermore, Deal and Kennedy (2000) describe patterns of leadership that are based on the degree of control the leader maintains, how much change they believe is desirable (and at what rate), and on their attitude toward risk.

Other authors that describe corporate culture observe that organizations can move either toward an atmosphere of greater entrepreneurialism, which is more flexible and adaptable, but less controllable by the executives choosing to move in that direction, or toward a more paternalistic atmosphere, which requires high levels of buy-in to existing norms in order to obtain desired corporate outcomes (Fleming, 2005; Hatch, 2011; Price & Whiteley, 2014). Some researchers even find that corporate culture may cause employees to compromise their personal morals when making tough decisions, particularly if there are no sanctions for unethical behavior (Hunt & Vitell, 1986; Kennedy & Lawton, 1993; Sims & Brinkmann, 2003). However, Vitell et al. (1993) offer a contrasting opinion: surveying marketing professionals, they examined relationships between decision-making norms, organizational ethical culture (measured using a scale based on the *American Marketing Association Code of Ethics*), and personal moral philosophy (characterized as either a deontology or a teleology). Their findings indicate that personal moral codes have a greater impact on ethical decisions than do organizational ethics. Based on these contrasting observations, there is a need to better understand how personal and organizational characteristics influence executives' ethical decision-making.

Early researchers in business ethics presented a number of conceptual models describing how personal characteristics and organizational factors are taken into account in ethical decision-making (Ferrell & Gresham, 1985; Treviño, 1986; Treviño & Youngblood, 1990). For instance, Treviño (1986) offered a conceptual discussion of how personal moral philosophy enters into managerial decision-making. In an extension of the previous paper, Treviño and Youngblood (1990) tested the influence of moral development and locus of control on ethical decision-making in an experimental study of MBA students. Ferrell and Gresham (1985) developed an integrated conceptual framework including both individual and organizational influences on managers' ethical decisions. The individual factors considered could be described as knowledge, personal moral philosophy, and cultural values; the organizational factors included other people, corporate policies, and professional codes. Experimental studies and field tests were recommended in future research.

Later models offered greater complexity, incorporating internal or external conflict, or decisions based on reasoning versus intuition (McDevitt, Giapponi, & Tromley, 2007; Woiceshyn, 2011). However, the majority of these models did not use primary research (either qualitative or quantitative) to identify or improve understanding of decision drivers or to test propositions. Expressing the need to better understand actual ethical decisions, Whittier,

Williams, and Dewett (2006), in a focused review, assessed the prescriptive value of ethical decision-making models. Tenbrunsel and Smith-Crowe (2008) built a model of ethical decision-making based on reviewed articles, but closed their analysis with more questions than answers. Among them is: "what is ethical?" an important question they did not answer. Perhaps the most convincing evidence of the need for additional research into how service executives make ethical decisions comes from a recent literature review by Ferrell, Ferrell, and Sawayda (2015, p. 58). Following their detailed and insightful commentary on this literature, they observe: "there may be an ethical divide between marketing scholars who develop models and marketing practitioners who manage ethics in organizations" and "more insights are needed about how to link knowledge to practice." This is an important contribution to the present study.

Method

The goal of this research was to enhance understanding of how service executives make ethical decisions that impact employees directly and customers indirectly, thereby defining organizational culture and values. Because this topic is exploratory, it was necessary to utilize a qualitative methodology (McDaniel & Gates, 1998). A grounded theory approach was selected because it is appropriate for developing new theory in a natural setting, through open-ended interviews that focus on participants' perspectives. As noted by Bryman (2012, p. 387), "grounded theory is not a theory – it is an approach to generation of theory out of data" from the field. The data that are gathered are the verbatim statements of the respondents' views; according to Strauss and Corbin (1990, p. 23), "a grounded theory is one that is inductively derived ... one begins with an area of study and what is relevant to that area is allowed to emerge." Using analysis methods that include inductive and deductive logic, involving reflective and interpretive thought, "the research findings constitute a theoretical formulation of the reality under investigation" (Strauss & Corbin, 1990, p. 24). Thus, in the present research, new theory was generated through studying process, action, and/or interaction in the views of respondents, and the findings are presented in a series of testable propositions.

Sample design

It is important to select a sample that is from the target population, although in qualitative research the sample is typically not representative of this population and therefore findings are not immediately generalizable (Bryman, 2012; Corbin & Strauss, 2008; Gordon & Langmaid, 1988; McDaniel & Gates, 1998; Strauss & Corbin, 1990). Because the goal of the present research was to better understand how senior executives in service organizations make ethical decisions, which inherently influence people within the organization and thereby also customers, respondents were recruited from the highest possible organizational levels. Owing to the relationship between the sample and the research question, it was appropriate to use purposive sampling (rather than convenience sampling) to recruit service executives from the highest echelons of their organizations, including CEOs and senior vice presidents (Bryman, 2012). When members of the target population are extremely difficult to find and/or obtain for participation, it is also appropriate to augment the sample using snowball sampling (Bryman, 2012; McDaniel & Gates, 1998), and this was done.

Because executives typically make decisions alone, it was important to perform individual interviews rather than group interviews, to capture aspects of individual decision-making

(Bristol & Fern, 2003). Furthermore, individual interviews can more effectively elicit insights than can group interviews (Griffin & Hauser, 1993; Wooten & Reed, 2000). In summary, executives interviewed in the present research were recruited using a combination of purposive sampling and snowball sampling and were asked to participate in individual interviews, in order to generate the data required to develop grounded theory.

Sample selection

As mentioned above, in the present research the population of interest was high-level executives in service organizations. It was desirable to have a sample that, although small, is as diverse as possible under the circumstances (Lindlof & Taylor, 2002); this is consistent with representing a number of different types of services among the members of the sample to gain a variety of viewpoints.

A member of the research team was able to meet with each respondent in person prior to the interview, to request participation. As a result of this personalized recruiting, 12 high-level service executives agreed to participate in interviews that were described as being "to improve understanding of managerial decision making." All of the individuals who participated are responsible for making decisions related to the organizational image and the customer experience; some of these decisions are ethical, in that they determine which individuals or groups receive more desirable treatment and which do not. The executives' tenure in their current organizations ranged from two to 37 years; the average was 15 years. Thus, the selected individuals are very senior in their careers, sure of who they are, and clear as to the goals they have that drive organizational culture and values.

Each respondent was told that the interview would take about an hour (in fact, the interviews ranged from 51 to 76 minutes). Prior to beginning the interview, each respondent gave verbal permission to record the interview, and all interviews were recorded in full. In addition, confidentiality of identity was promised unless the respondent was willing to be named in an acknowledgment upon publication. Details regarding individual participants are provided in Table 20.1. Additional information describing the recruitment process for each member of the sample will be provided by the author upon request.

Design of the interview guide

The focus of the research was on how service executives make ethical decisions, which are those that determine which individuals and/or groups benefit, and which suffer. In particular, the present research examines such decisions when they impact employees directly and customers indirectly, consistent with the initiation layer (inner circle) in Figure 20.1. Interviewees were told that they would be asked about their approach to decision-making; this includes what influences their decisions as well as how they use available information to make them.

The interview guide was developed based on relevant literature, which is discussed in the Conceptual Development section, as recommended by Corbin and Strauss (2008) and by Strauss and Corbin (1990). This is also consistent with the stipulation of Bryman (2012, p. 385) that "the research questions will be prompted and stimulated by the literature." Thus, the topics were drawn from those used in ethical decision-making models, including personal background, both cultural and social, and organizational culture and policies. Furthermore, the interview guide was semi-structured, to allow for follow-up questions and

Table 20.1 Details about the executives interviewed

ID	Title	Years w/Org.	Functional Area	Firm Information
R1	Vice President	6 (est.)	Franchisee relations	Service subsidiary of large consumer goods manufacturer
R2	Vice President	15 (est.)	Operations	Large consumer service organization
R3	Director/CEO	16	Business communications	Large service firm
R4	President	19	Marketing	Well-known international advertising agency
R5	Executive VP	9	Supply chain	Major home goods retailer
R6	Director/VP	11	Account management	International online learning tools
R7	Senior VP	19	Marketing	High-growth regional airport
R8	President/CEO	37	Management	National consumer membership organization
R9	Chief Marketing Officer	2	Marketing	National business liability insurance firm
R10	Senior VP	29	Management, corporate banking	Top-ten US-based bank
R11	President	4	Management/ marketing	Large regional charitable foundation
R12	Director	4	Customer experience	Large international retailer

other customization (Bryman, 2012; Gordon & Langmaid, 1988). The topics ranged from descriptive questions about personal background to more difficult questions requiring more thought; as the interviews progressed, inquiry moved from general to specific.

As recommended by McDaniel and Gates (1998), the interview guide began with warm-up topics, including background information such as the family of origin and home life, followed by questions about decision-making and recent decision examples. Personal ethical philosophy was not mentioned until as late as possible in the interview, to reduce the potential for executives being sensitized and limiting their responses. (This modification was made because an early interviewee seemed to be uncomfortable with the terminology.) As such, minor adjustments were made to the interview guide, so that data could be collected on other decision-making topics first. This offered an added advantage, in that answers to all of the other questions could be obtained without any potential bias due to suggestive terminology. An outline of the resulting interview guide is provided in Table 20.2. In addition to the questions listed in the table, because of the semi-structured design, follow-up was conducted wherever appropriate during interviews.

Conducting the interviews

Following the initial in-person meeting with each respondent, six of the interviews were conducted in person and six via skype. Thus, all of the interviews were conducted privately

Table 20.2 Key elements of discussion guide

I WARM-UP/BACKGROUND INFORMATION

Describe your personal cultural identity, social identity, and social style.

What attracted you to your organization initially? How long have you been there and in which position(s)? What are your goals in your job (both personal and professional)?

What is the organization's mission? What does the organization value? Does your organization have a particular culture? How does this fit (or not fit) with what you perceive as your job goals?

II DECISION-MAKING IN THE CURRENT POSITION

What kinds of decisions are you called on to make on a regular basis as part of your job? How would you describe those that are most <u>important</u>? What organizational context/situation do you find most <u>challenging</u> with respect to making decisions? What are some of the things that signal to you that a decision is going to be difficult?

How would you describe your decision-making style? Would you say it is more analytical or intuitive?

What factors do you regularly consider in decision-making? Are answers to your decisions typically fuzzy? Or, do you think that there is usually a right or a wrong answer?

III RECENT DECISION EXAMPLES

Describe a decision you made recently (within the last six months) that you believe was successful.

Describe a recent decision you made that you believe was unsuccessful.

Ask about other recent decisions that clarify the decision-making style.

IV TOPICS RELATED TO ETHICAL DECISIONS

How would you describe your personal moral philosophy?

What do you believe constitutes <u>ethical</u> decision-making?

Describe the process you use when faced with an ethical decision. Do you turn to anyone for guidance when faced with an ethical decision? If so, whom and for what reasons?

In what ways do you find it most challenging to communicate with your subordinates, peers, and superiors about ethical issues?

---

with the individual executive decision maker, which, as mentioned above, has been found to generate the most open and accurate possible responses. The first three interviews were conducted by an assistant; the remaining nine interviews were conducted by the principal investigator. Detailed discussion following the first three interviews resulted in some minor changes to the interview guide and the decision was made to have all remaining interviews conducted by one interviewer, to reduce the potential for interviewer bias (Lincoln & Guba, 1985; Strauss & Corbin, 1990). All interviews were recorded with the permission of the interviewee, and all interviews were transcribed verbatim by the principal investigator within

24 hours of completion; this is consistent with the recommendation of Silverman (2010) to complete the transcript as soon as possible following the interview. This procedure mitigated any sources of bias because the work was done immediately and all transcriptions were completed by the same person. This transcription process resulted in a high level of data familiarity over numerous readings of the transcripts, and copious notes were taken which were examined to identify emerging themes. Thus, data collection and analysis took place concurrently, with memo writing and comparison of ideas to refine emerging theory, as recommended by Strauss and Corbin (1990), Charmaz (2014), and Corbin and Strauss (2008).

Coding the data

As mentioned above, all of the interviews were transcribed verbatim by the principal investigator to maximize familiarity with the material; this was done immediately following completion of each interview. The transcription process was conducted manually, so that each line of each interview was listened to several times in repetition. Following transcription, each interview was reviewed for correctness and detail. The transcribed results were then analyzed using *open coding*, performed by both the principal investigator and an assistant, to identify major categories of information. As stated by Strauss and Corbin (1990, p. 61), "open coding is the process of breaking down, examining, comparing, conceptualizing, and categorizing data." Verbatim remarks were coded using various colored highlighters to clarify the initial categories to which each was assigned, as recommended by Strauss and Corbin (1990). This analysis proceeded carefully, to allow time to determine how to look at the data to yield insights and to begin to conceptualize the interpretation (Lindlof & Taylor, 2002). As the interviews occurred and were transcribed, the data and the coded results were compared to begin to observe relationships, and the categories were updated as necessary (Lindlof & Taylor, 2002). Eventually, the total number of categories levelled out as the last few interviews were completed and coded. Thus, the results of this stage, as noted by Strauss and Corbin (1990, p. 254), were "the basic building block of any grounded theory … a set of concepts grounded in the data."

The themes resulting from open coding included categories of potential decision drivers, as well as decision processes and outcomes in both successful and unsuccessful decisions, among others. The method used for open coding and the categories that resulted are consistent with the recommendations of a number of experts (Charmaz, 2014; Corbin & Strauss, 2008; Creswell, 2013; Gallicano, 2013; Strauss & Corbin, 1990).

Following completion of open coding, *axial coding* was performed to identify relationships; according to Strauss and Corbin (1990, p. 96), "axial coding is a set of procedures whereby data are put back together in new ways after open coding, by making connections between categories." Thus, causal conditions (i.e. factors leading to a core phenomenon), strategies (actions taken in response to a core phenomenon), intervening conditions (i.e. situational factors that influence the strategies), and consequences (outcomes of the strategies) are linked using Creswell's (2013, p. 86) scheme. During axial coding, it was helpful to prepare notes, memos, and diagrams to track thoughts and ideas that began to emerge. Strauss and Corbin (1990) recommend at this stage to look for key differences that add density and variation to theory. According to Lindlof and Taylor (2002), these dimensions of variation provide the key to identifying emerging constructs; such observations can lead to heightened confidence in the findings. The method of axial coding used in the present research is consistent with the recommendations of a number of experts, including Corbin and Strauss (2008), Lindlof and Taylor (2002), and Strauss and Corbin (1990).

The dimensions and relationships identified in axial coding are next subjected to *selective coding*, which, according to Strauss and Corbin (1990, p. 116), "is the process of selecting the core category, systematically relating it to other categories, validating those relationships, and filling in categories that need further refinement or development." Thus, the story to be told emerges in connection with the core category, which is the central theme around which the other categories are integrated. Strauss and Corbin (1990) state that it is like axial coding, but at a higher, more abstract level. By identifying such patterns, the researcher can identify the conditions under which different results occur; these are called "patterned differences" (Strauss & Corbin, 1990, p. 132). According to Corbin and Strauss (2008, p. 261), "patterns emerged from data, but had to be recognized by the researcher." Several, more intricate diagrams were found to be useful at this stage in the data analysis to visualize the emerging patterns. The process used for selective coding is consistent with the recommendations of a number of experts, including Corbin and Strauss (2008), Creswell (2013), and Strauss and Corbin (1990).

In summary, the procedures described in this section were carried out for open, axial, and selective coding; this led to interpretable findings grounded in the interview data. The Results section begins by discussing issues related to sample size, reliability, validity, and generalizability relative to the present research; it then describes some aspects of coding and provides detailed examples of findings.

Results

This section begins by discussing issues related to sample size, reliability, validity, and generalizability, which emerged as the research was conducted. Afterward, it describes details of coding outcomes, starting with themes that resulted from open coding, in which major categories of information were identified. It then presents the results of axial coding, in which relationships began to emerge between the constructs that were identified, through careful memos and thoughtful diagrams. Finally, it sets the stage for the outcome of selective coding, through which the findings of the research were identified in terms of testable propositions to be further examined in future research.

Sample size

It is more difficult to determine the appropriate sample size in a qualitative study, such as this grounded theory research, than it is in quantitative research where a representative sample can be selected, and necessary sample size can be calculated based on the population standard deviation along measures of interest. One way of deciding that a sample is sufficiently large in qualitative research is to consider whether additional data collection is likely to reveal any new information. For instance, Bryman (2012, p. 421) says to continue sampling "until no new or relevant data seem to be emerging"; this point is reiterated on page 568, where he says to stop sampling when "new data are no longer illuminating the concept." Similarly, Lindlof and Taylor (2002) recommend that sampling be discontinued when conceptual returns diminish and the researcher is no longer surprised. Strauss and Corbin (1990) suggest looking for differences within the collected data that add density and variation to theory. In the present research, the last couple of interviews were interesting and consistent, but did not provide as many new ideas or additional variation as did earlier interviews; therefore, these judgment-based methods of assessing sample size indicate that the 12 completed interviews were sufficient.

A number of researchers have corroborated that relatively small sample sizes may be adequate, particularly in studies that require in-depth interviews with respondents that are difficult to obtain, using arguments related to data sufficiency. For instance, Bowen (2002,

p. 273) affirmed that a total of six executive interviews across two organizations were adequate to obtain useful findings in qualitative research. Similarly, Lindlof and Taylor (2002, p. 129) stated that "projects that study hard-to-find participants are more justified in having smaller samples."

In another approach to data sufficiency arguments, several researchers have measured the number of ideas generated by a small number of interviews as compared to a maximum possible number of ideas resulting from a much larger number of interviews. For instance, Griffin and Hauser (1993) found that ten respondents to in-depth interviews typically generate over 90% of all possible ideas (based on 230 customer needs observed in an extensive study). In a similar example, Bryman (2012, p. 426) reports on an empirical study measuring the number of interviews required to achieve theoretical saturation, finding that 12 completed interviews generated 92% of all the codes found in 60 interviews. Thus, 12 interviews were shown to provide thematic exhaustion and adequate variability within the data, without over-sampling. The results of these studies indicate that 12 executive interviews can credibly provide sufficient data for developing grounded theory.

Reliability

The in-depth interviews used in grounded theory research represent events that cannot be repeated or replicated; any new interview will necessarily be different, owing to different people involved, different settings, and/or different temporal qualities. Therefore, traditional definitions of reliability, which are typically based on replicability and/or consistency, cannot be applied. In fact, Lindlof and Taylor (2002, p. 238) assert that reliability is not a consideration in grounded theory research, because such work is not repeatable. Bryman (2012, p. 405) concurs, observing that "it is almost impossible to conduct a true replication." However, Strauss and Corbin (1990, p. 250) observe that, although a grounded theory study is not replicable or reproducible, a different investigator might and should be able to come up with the same theory in a new study. This suggests that correctly conducted studies, although not replicable, could provide support for similar Research Propositions that might be applicable with other people, in different settings and at later times.

Another way to look at reliability in a grounded theory study is to assess whether different observers of the same data reach similar conclusions as to what the data are saying. This is consistent with Bryman's (2012) note that reliability in a qualitative study may be measured based on interobserver consistency. Therefore, as a second way of assessing reliability, it is important to consider how two different coders react to the same verbatim interview transcripts. In the present research, comparison of the coded material resulted in approximately 92% initial agreement; following this initial coding, discussion was used to clarify and resolve discrepancies. The outcome of this coding and discussion provides additional corroboration of reliability, which is consistent with Lindlof and Taylor's (2002) assertion that team coding should be used to increase reliability. Therefore, the present research is reliable in that the study was correctly conducted and that two different coders had very high agreement after the initial coding was complete.

Validity

Validity in qualitative research assures that "you are observing, identifying, or measuring what you say you are," according to Bryman (2012, pp. 389–390). One way of assessing validity, therefore, is to look at the results, to see whether or not they appear to be true.

Gordon and Langmaid (1988, p. x) support seeking apparent truthfulness, noting that one type of validity that can be observed following a qualitative study is "face validity, when viewed against a complete backdrop." Another type of assessment, similar to face validity, is offered by Lindlof and Taylor (2002), who state that a sense of heightened confidence in the results is a test of credibility. Furthermore, these authors recommend evaluating whether the reporting is accurate, because they believe that validity is indicated by trustworthiness and credibility. Similar to Lindlof and Taylor (2002), Lincoln and Guba (1985) propose that, instead of using either reliability or validity, qualitative research results should be assessed using trustworthiness and authenticity.

In addition to the abovementioned indicators of validity, Bryman (2012) suggests that respondents may be asked to validate the research results: a copy of the draft manuscript may be sent to them for confirmation of accuracy. Similarly, Lindlof and Taylor (2002) recommend checking validity by taking the findings back to the field (providing the whole text) to determine whether the participants recognize them as true and accurate. This was carried out in the present research; the entire text of the draft manuscript was sent to nine of the 12 interviewees (the others could not be reached). Of the nine receiving the draft, five responded positively and four did not reply. This indicates that there were no negative responses, which would have alerted the researcher to validity issues; furthermore, five recipients found the results interesting enough to read and take action to support the findings.

One additional way of looking at validity is offered by Strauss and Corbin (1990, p. 132), who comment that "validating one's theory against the data completes its grounding"; this is restated on page 138 as: "make statements of relationship and validate the statements with the data." Therefore, it is important to go back to the data to complete the loop, after the findings (i.e. testable Research Propositions) are available. This was also done in the present study.

Generalizability

As mentioned earlier, it is important to select a sample that is from the target population, although in qualitative research the sample is typically not representative of this population and therefore findings are not immediately generalizable. Some researchers are willing to be slightly more flexible, stating that findings may be generalized, but only back to the conditions of the original study (Strauss & Corbin, 1990, p. 251). This is more true in situations where the original study used a relatively homogeneous sample in a rather narrow domain than it is when sampling attempted to bring in greater diversity. Finally, Bryman (2012, p. 406) points out that interviewees, as members of the sample, "are not meant to be representative of a population"; he adds that findings "generalize to theory rather than to populations." This is certainly consistent with the goals of the present research.

Results of open coding

An important theme that results from open coding relates to respondents' personal moral philosophies, which reflect what they believe constitutes an ethical approach to decision-making. Respondent comments were grouped into process-oriented descriptions reflecting deontologies, and outcome-oriented descriptions reflecting utilitarian teleologies. None of the executives described a personal moral philosophy that might be characterized as either 'egoist teleology' or 'relativism,' so these are not considered further. Such omissions appear to be fairly common in the business ethics literature (e.g. Bergadaà, 2004; Vitell et al., 1993) and this research is consistent, which is appropriate because it focuses on high-level executive interviewees who did not express self-centered philosophies, and need not consider the actions of their peers in making ethical decisions.

A process orientation is identified by a procedure that is followed to make an ethical decision, so the following comments tend to reflect deontological perspectives:

- *Be honest and truthful and transparent.* (R7)
- *You know what's right and wrong. It's the Golden Rule and how you treat people: you don't lie, you don't cheat, and you don't steal.* (R10)
- *The main core is truthfulness … you can't over-promise and under-deliver.* (R6)
- *It is a personal kind of morality and integrity, being a good person and a good citizen.* (R1)
- *It is about considering an issue from a wide variety of perspectives, balancing a lot of different interests in reaching your course. In a situation that raises a direct ethical question, you're faced with finding your own North Star.* (R11)

An outcome orientation is identified by importance placed on the results of an ethical decision, so the following comments tend to reflect teleological perspectives:

- *(Ethical) decisions consider impacts that cause either good or harm.* (R12)
- *Be lawful and do no harm, and overall, help enrich people's lives for the better.* (R4)
- *(Ethical) decisions are made contemplating all of the impacts, to all people, society, and the environment.* (R5)
- *You are dealing with what the government, your stakeholders, and your associates believe is ethical. It depends on who you prioritize.* (R9)
- *(It means) setting any personal self-interest aside and doing what's best for whoever it's going to affect.* (R8)

All of these quotes (and nearby verbatims within the interviews) reflect that the executive interviewees believe an ethical decision is one in which the decision maker tries to do good. However, those that focus on the process refer to *how* the decision maker goes about doing good, whereas those that focus on the outcome reflect *who* reaps the benefits and costs of a particular decision. Thus, those comments on the earlier list are suggestive of a deontological moral philosophy, whereas those on the latter list are indicative of a teleological moral philosophy.

Individual background and values

Key themes mentioned in regard to *individual culture* and *social identity* include characteristics of the family of origin (e.g. attitudes and beliefs, working status, international experience), personal interests (e.g. technology) that began in childhood, and attitude toward/readiness for work. Interviewees described their *social styles* as warm, open-minded, collaborative, and optimistic. In general, the interviewees respect communication, transparency, and getting the job done. Some interviewees expressed an appreciation of others who are different (especially in terms of culture or socioeconomic status) and what these individuals have to contribute. The idea that in some situations the interviewee feels more intense and in others more relaxed was mentioned; a similar theme was described in terms of kindness still being present when firmness and tough calls are required. Through the discussions of individual culture, social identity, and social style, a picture of an effective leader (and ethical decision maker) began to emerge.

Another category of themes resulting from open coding describes *personal values*, a central phenomenon of this research. Ideas expressed relate to (a) how to treat others – being helpful, kind, truthful, respectful, empathetic, and compassionate emerge – and (b) clarity of decision-making. Ideas that came through repeatedly include service orientation, giving back, empathy, reaching out to others, persistence to overcome obstacles, and not being intimidated by new situations. For some executives, there are clear right and wrong paths, but for others, there are not; in the latter case, ethical decisions are based on outcome-related values. These differences relate to the individual's personal moral philosophy, as described above. The identification of themes related to the executives' personal characteristics is based on the data detailed in Table 20.3, which contains specific quotations from the interview transcripts.

Table 20.3 Individual background descriptors used in open coding

Part 1: Culture & Social Identity

I was raised in a very large family; we were always encouraged to <u>help others</u>. My upbringing was one of <u>being of service</u>. (R8)

I was fortunate enough to grow up in a family that was <u>very positive</u>, so I'm traditionally a very "cup-half-full" in life. I feel very blessed every day for the things that I have been able to experience, achieve, and accomplish in my life, and recognize they're a result of not just myself, but other people. I grew up in a family that was very <u>committed to giving back</u>. My parents travelled internationally and exposed us to <u>different cultures and lifestyles and different socioeconomic conditions</u>, and that shaped my view of things. (R9)

I'm conscientious of other people's opinions and feelings; I have a lot of <u>empathy and flexibility</u>. My parents are very <u>conservative-type people</u>, but I've always reached out or leaned towards <u>people that were different than me, either culturally or socioeconomically</u>, and I enjoy getting different perspectives, seeing different things, and trying to <u>understand different cultures</u>. (R6)

This whole idea of <u>being driven</u> is really important. I think it really comes from my blue collar roots. I was never spoon-fed when I was younger; I always had to <u>work hard</u>, even putting myself through school. That has created a <u>vivaciousness and an ability to get things done</u> despite obstacles. (R7)

I thought it was very normal that my <u>mom worked</u>. And my <u>dad worked</u>. Just very middle class growing up. A lot of <u>formality</u> at my house, a lot of big <u>emphasis on manners</u>, always dinner at home, always dinner together, despite working. Formality in table settings, formality in dress, formality in diction. I wasn't allowed to say the word "yeah" – I had to say "yes". I never had to worry about not knowing how to use my cutlery – this comes into play when I take clients out to lunch and to dinner. <u>I'm not intimidated by much</u>. (R10)

My ability to reserve judgment and <u>be open and make people comfortable</u> to come out of their shells and contribute in some way are a really critical piece of my leadership style. This traces back to my parents: I definitely have a <u>strong work ethic</u> and I'm a very "roll-up-my-sleeves" type of person. I oversee plenty of things, but I also still like to get my hands dirty. And I also think that somehow contributes to the culture of <u>"everybody has something to contribute."</u> (R11)

I think I've always been curious. On our team, we actually have a list of "brand attributes" that we want to be known for. The most important are <u>empathy, curiosity, tenaciousness, and the engineering mindset</u>, where creative people that want to build great things for our customer work best. I grew up really poor, and I always looked for ways to <u>find solutions to things, to alleviate poverty</u> in our own lives as a family. So, I'm always trying to build things. (R12)

I had a talent for how to <u>use technology</u> ... I thrive in an environment I can work to control. (R5)

(Continued)

Table 20.3 (Cont.)

Part 2: Social Style

I am <u>collaborative</u>; I value the <u>importance of listening</u>. I am really about "we and not me". (R4)

My colleagues would describe me as a friend. I am <u>welcoming, warm</u>; if there is somebody new into our ranks, I call and welcome them and let them know that I am <u>available</u>. I just want to be a part of the <u>equation for everybody's success</u> ... I reach out to folks, to my peers. (R8)

I am <u>warm, open-minded, and receptive to lots of different ideas</u>. I'm probably more of a <u>strategic-type</u> worker than a detail worker, although I can do the detail stuff. I choose not to, when I can avoid it. And, I am <u>optimistic</u>: I feel like we can do good things in a lot of the areas where we're working. (R11)

I have a completely different style than what is the norm here. I am <u>very optimistic</u>, and I try to inject a lot of fun – it's a very serious place. Up until about a year before I came here, the men were required to wear suit and tie, very formal, very finance-driven. The idea of (<u>more informality</u>) was kind of an anathema to the culture, so I've slowly introduced things, and people have responded really well to that. Also, <u>I am called in as an expert</u>. Whenever there is a new, big system being brought in, I am always involved, so, I hopefully have a <u>balance between expertise and a pretty relaxed approach</u>. (R12)

I'm intense when I need to be, but at other times I'm very relaxed. I try not to overwhelm people. I think <u>I'm an intense / easygoing type of person</u>. Some days it is very intense and other days, you know, I was just telling a colleague not to sweat the small stuff, not to become very anxious. There are some things that can't be changed and some things that can, and you just have to work for it. (R6)

I <u>encourage communication</u>, so the more we have dialog the better. Sometimes people call me a "<u>kindly dictator</u>". I'm not unbending but if I say something has to go, I'm not going to be a pushover. (R3)

I am <u>direct</u>, in the sense that my feedback is not cluttered with other objectives. I am <u>strategic</u>: I typically look at the decisions that we're making today, and how they will affect 2, 3, 4, 5, steps into the future. I am <u>friendly</u>; socially, I can get along with, make conversation with, and I truly <u>care about the success of everyone in the organization</u>. I'm <u>open for constructive feedback</u> and criticism. (R9)

I've coined an expression called "<u>polite but firm</u>", which kind of captures my personal and professional style. I'm what I like to call a Type A-light. I definitely have an opinion and a willingness to talk about things, but I typically want to sit back and try to <u>understand first and be diplomatic</u>. (R1)

I am <u>extremely direct, extremely transparent</u>; I value <u>clear and concise communication</u> and have a penchant for getting things started. I have a <u>high sense of urgency</u> and I tend to be somebody that has to do ... and takes value and pride in getting started and getting things moving. (R2)

<u>I know how to get things done</u>; I'm not shy. I sometimes ask the simple questions, but nobody has thought of them. I always say "great idea. Who's going to do it?" or "Great idea; alright, put your name down for that one." And I hold them accountable. (R10)

I have a big personality; I'm very <u>driven, creative, enthusiastic, and energetic</u>. (R7)

<u>I painted a pretty compelling vision</u> and was able to work with the leadership here to line everybody up to that vision. I was a shock to the system in terms of the level of change that I was ready to lead. (R5)

Part 3: Personal Values

<u>Treat people well</u>. You're only here for a short period of time – why should anybody have to go through more angst in a lifetime than is necessary? I think we're all here to help each other through it, and I think a key to that is treating people well. (R8)

Make sure that, <u>if you tell somebody that you're going to do something, you do it</u>. <u>Be truthful, and treat others with the respect</u> that you would want to be treated with. (R6)

(Continued)

Table 20.3 (Cont.)

It's always helping others, _treating others by the golden rule, treating others respectfully_ and lending a hand. I really root everything in kindness. I think if people are kind to one another and have some sense of empathy, thinking through what's important to the other person, usually the best outcome happens. (R12)

Treat other people the way you want to be treated, and respect them the way that you would want to be respected. I try to give people the benefit of the doubt, because what people do is easy to see, why people do it, not always very clear. Sometimes it's hard for people to determine the difference between what is right and what is wrong. I want to walk away from a choice feeling that I put out into the world something that will add value, something that will constantly give back. (R9)

"Everyone has their story" – everybody is going through a million things that are completely unknown to me, and I try to bear that in mind because it affects everything that goes on around us. Also, _"progress, not perfection"_ – we are all works in progress, and you need to value what people are bringing in the moment they're bringing it. Even if it's not exactly what you thought the right answer was, it probably is advancing the conversation materially. (R11)

I was raised in a Catholic family that valued a sense of moral virtue, doing the right thing, and being empathic, so I try to be _responsible, empathic, and compassionate in the way that I treat others_. (R4)

I believe in doing the right thing, and in _ensuring that we treat everyone fairly and with respect_. (R5)

I hope it's _on the straight and narrow_. That's such a huge element in one's life. I remember when I was a teller and I had thousands upon thousands of dollars around me. I never thought it was mine; I would never, ever think of taking that. You're dealing with people's livelihoods; to me that's a huge responsibility, and morally and ethically, you don't cross that line. (R10)

You live and die by the performance of your unit. Getting the right people off the blocks in the race means _coaching and developing_ them. The hardest thing is, oftentimes, we are handed a decision that is the lesser of two evils, and that might kill a situation that seems very black and white. (R2)

If I think something's wrong, I should say something. I've seen things that I thought were wrong and I've always spoken up about it. (R3)

(I value) integrity, as well as legal principles, _being a good person and a good citizen_. (R1)

I would put myself more at "value" over "cheap" – that's more where my personal standards would lie. _(I value) integrity, that there is a personal sense of integrity_. (R7)

Organizational characteristics and values

Open coding of information related to the organization's *mission and values* resulted in themes that include integrity, maintaining relationships, being proactive, diligent, creative, entrepreneurial, and open to communication, diversity, and teamwork. The *organizational culture* was described in one of two ways, as either "feeling like a family" or as welcoming diversity and cross-cultural experience. Because these two descriptions do not appear together in the same interview, and none of the organizations studied clearly exhibit both, the two may be incompatible. In particular, organizations that have a family-like culture are also described by interviewees as rather paternalistic, with narrowly defined acceptable behaviors. This may occur because of a strong desire to carry out the wishes of a founder; such organizations are also described by interviewees as having strict governance. On the other hand, organizations that are described by interviewees as more welcoming of diversity and international experience are also described as more flexible and accepting of a wider range of behaviors. Interviewees described the latter group of organizations as respectful, welcoming, passionate, and based on trust, empathy, and acceptance. Finally, organizational culture was thought by interviewees to include both a strong work ethic and an acceptable level of risk-taking; some interviewees mentioned taking risks and "reaching for the stars." The identification of themes related to organizational characteristics and values is based on the data detailed in Table 20.4, which contains specific quotations from the interview transcripts.

—

Table 20.4 Organizational descriptors used in open coding

Part 1: Mission & Values

We are very results-oriented; one of the key results is "how are we doing by our Customers, and what are they telling us?" (R8)

The Company is client-focused; Customers are the boss. Everyone in this organization is trying to do the right thing for the customer. And we celebrate that as a group and, for the most part, people feel rewarded in their jobs every day. (R9)

People that have been with this company the longest are driven individuals Everyone's very different; you have Type As, Type Bs, Type Cs, but all are working towards a single goal, making the company the best company that it can be. (R6)

Integrity is huge. Treatment of others is really primary. We care about the customer. (R10)

Values include tactful customer service, entrepreneurial spirit, doing the right thing, and building relationships with each other. (R5)

The Company values its roots, it values its connection to community, and it values its people. We've nurtured a family atmosphere here where people take care of one another. We also value our ability to get things done at very low cost. (R7)

Our values are around proactive shaping of solutions and bringing together of different people, as opposed to just responding to something. Being proactive has taken a really predominant place in our culture and it really ties back to the founder, who was not about waiting around for things to evolve around him, but seeking out. (R11)

We value creativity ... we value collaborative people and diversity of talent. (R4)

The biggest thing that comes to mind is the ability to have a face-to-face conversation with anybody up and down the chain about what's important, which always starts with the customer. There's an etiquette and a politeness here, rooted in a humble nature, and that could be good and bad, right? Everything "values" could have strength and weakness associated with it. (R12)

We value guest/stakeholder value creation and satisfaction and humility. (R2)

One of our core values is diversity and understanding culture, that others are going to behave differently even within the US. So, we have been allowed to develop our own culture, and it's been really important not to have to implement some of the ways people behave in New York; that just wouldn't fly and I would have employee retention issues. There are 10 different values; some of them are "quality is number 1" (tied in to what kind of service we provide our clients), "teamwork" (a huge one), "diversity," and "financial responsibility." There are also some looser ones like "integrity" and "results." (R3)

Part 2: Organizational Culture

This place is very affirming, going back to the idea of family. There's a culture of respect: we respect the job that everybody does here, whether it's cleaning the building or making strategic decisions about our future. We take pride in the place. (R7)

(Continued)

Table 20.4 (Cont.)

It sort of *feels like a family*, but also, in a lot of ways it doesn't feel like a family. The organization is very *welcoming* when new people come. Business decisions are made with clarity, everybody is *accountable and responsible*; everybody earns the job that they have. Decisions get made fast: ideas come in, we try them, there's a lot of tolerance for *"try something, and if you're going to fail, fail quick."* (R9)

We are *passionate about creative ideas*, have a *very strong work ethic*, and do things that have never been done before. We challenge ourselves to bring *breakthrough creativity* into the marketplace. We "reach for the stars," we always *agitate to improve*, we have curiosity to ask "are we asking the right question, can we *dig deeper to get better insight*, can this work be better?" (R4)

We all *work hard*; fortunately, it doesn't feel like work a lot of the time because it's really *energizing, good stuff* and we go out of our way to *have a lot of fun while doing it*. The *work ethic* is something that is very strongly a part of our culture, as well as *diligence and thoroughness*. (R11)

We *really work hard*, but, at the same time, it is expected that there's *work-life balance*. There were 400 of us that had 25 years or more with the company, wonderful lunch, catered in. We recognized the incoming new members and then everybody else that has 30, 35, 40, 45 years of service. (R10)

We are absolutely fastidious about welcoming customers (as though into our homes); we have monthly mystery shops where a third party comes in and evaluates how we are doing in delivering guest *hospitality, quality, convenience, and pleasantness* of our staff. (R2)

We're a brand based on *trust* and that drives a lot of the culture of the organization. We always make sure that we're putting our *best foot forward*, that there aren't things going on that would bring shame or disparage the brand in any way. The organization is a good employer – the key to our staff taking care of the customers is that they know they are being taken care of, as well. (R8)

We talk about *empathy*. They're listening. There's a true *caring and compassion*, and I think this translates throughout the organization. (R12)

It's having all these *different individuals, different cultures, different past experiences, under one roof* – it's interesting having all this *uniqueness* in an organization. The Company values *individualism*, they appreciate *risk-takers*, they embrace *multi-culturalism*, potentially different ways of thinking. (R6)

We incorporate *focus, accountability, continuous improvement, excellence, and service mentality, and of course the foundation of all that is integrity*. Those aren't just randomly thrown-out cultural variables; they are core values that we're all aligned on. (R1)

The Company has a penchant for *solving big problems*; there's *nothing that we can't do if we line everybody up behind it*. (R5)

Decision-making styles

Two additional topics that need to be considered in regard to executive decision-making are (1) whether decision makers typically take an analytical or intuitive approach, and (2) whether they believe there is usually a clear right or wrong answer. Regarding the approach to decision-making, interviewees often began by saying they consider both quantitative data-based and qualitative feeling-based factors in making a decision. However, they tended to then focus on one or the other, justifying this through its importance. Examples of responses exhibiting a more analytical approach to decision-making include:

- *I'm much more analytical; I can't have enough data. I also know there are areas where intuition is the best model to use in the decision making process. When there is not data sufficiency or any data at all, the fastest path is intuition and experience. That's the prime example of an 80/20 rule: mostly data, mostly analysis. (R12)*
- *I love numbers, and I love to have my facts in order, and I say all the time: "The devil is in the detail." If you do not pay attention to detail, you will get burned. The analytics are important, because sometimes there are just so many opinions without any facts. I have to say I'm a blend, but I won't go with my gut until I look at the facts. (R10)*
- *I access both parts of my brain. I'm very big into being logical, but I'm also open-minded enough to consult other people. Sometimes, you just have to go with your gut, but I do tend to rely more on the analytical (side). (R3)*
- *I think you have to have both. The analytics are definitely critical. The intuition can come into play (when) you are making decisions about things that you never decided before or (where) there is not a measurement. So, you are forced to use your intuition. You have to rely on both. You can't just rely on one. (R9)*
- *I am a pretty good balance of both. I am analytical for sure, but I do rely on intuition. (R5)*

Examples of responses exhibiting a more intuitive approach to decision-making include:

- *I'm definitely a hybrid on that one. I ask a jillion questions (because) I really want to understand something deeply before making a decision. I'm aware, but not entirely driven by, the intuitive side. I bring both of those to decisions. (R11)*
- *I am definitely more intuitive, but with strong analytical backup. I honestly don't like to make decisions that are not data-driven, however, sometimes it's just that gut. (R7)*
- *I think you have to strike a balance in any decision, bringing in both. If it's sort of a tossup, I go with the feel more than the numbers. (R8)*
- *(I'm) intuitive. I go with my gut. (R6)*

The above responses can be used to identify two groups of interviewees, those who prefer more quantitative information and those who prefer more qualitative information in decision-making. As a way to obtain additional evidence of personal moral philosophies, interviewees were asked whether they believe there is usually a clear right or wrong answer when making an ethical decision. Some executives exhibited greater concern than others about the process of evaluating an ethical decision; in open coding, these comments were categorized as deontological. Responses that indicated belief in a clear right or wrong answer and/or showed greater concern about outcomes were classified as teleological. Examples of responses exhibiting a more process-oriented (deontological) approach to decision-making include:

- *I don't know if there's ever any truly right or wrong answer. Everyone wants the 100% answer, but I struggle with it personally. (R12)*
- *I think there is usually not a clear right and wrong answer. (R5)*
- *I believe almost everything is in the gray. Occasionally, something comes along that is just so obviously such a clear winner or such an all-alarms-blazing loser that I can feel like that one's black and white. But for the vast majority, particularly decisions where we're working in some of these intractable issues and really complex spaces, it's gray. Rarely is something just 100% versus 0%. (R11)*

Examples of responses exhibiting a more outcome-oriented (teleological) approach to decision-making include:

- *The right answer ultimately surfaces and, by the time it does, it's pretty evident. I don't do a lot of second guessing of decisions. There is value to looking in the rear-view mirror, but it's more important to be looking forward.* (R8)
- *There's right and there's wrong.* (R10)
- *There are some (decisions) that are clearly right and wrong, and there are some that are in the gray area. And even within the gray area, there are levels of gray.* (R7)

Respondents were also asked about the fit between their personal and professional goals and their organizations' objectives. Most likely because all interviewees were senior executives, having high levels of involvement with and commitment to their organizations, all of them expressed high levels of person-organization fit. This is quite consistent with an observation that the interviewees spoke with equal ease about their personal backgrounds and about their organizations.

Successful and unsuccessful decisions

Each interviewee was asked to describe in detail one very successful and one very unsuccessful decision that they had made recently. This was done in order to better understand the criteria that they use to define success as well as to get rich descriptions of their decision-making processes, as recommended by Hoffman, Crandall, and Shadbolt (1998). One interesting theme that was revealed during open coding of this information was the functional areas into which the successful and unsuccessful decisions would fall: interviewees tended to identify decisions related to people or to technology as most salient. Among the decisions chosen as successful, many of the interviewees described topics related to human resources (HR) and partner relationships (people), and a few described adoption of new technology. Among the decisions chosen as unsuccessful, many were related to HR and partner relationships, and a few to technology-based promotional activities. Thus, interviewees believe it is important to consider people in making executive decisions, both directly and in terms of their use of technology. Executives apparently realize that their decisions drive culture and values for the entire organization. Based on this emergent finding that highlights the relationship between personal interaction and the perceived success of decisions, the intersection of people policies and ethical decision-making must be carefully considered.

Results of axial coding

In axial coding, themes identified in open coding are studied to see how they might interact. Therefore, this section includes discussion of themes related to personal moral philosophy, background (culture, social style, and values), organizational characteristics (mission/values and culture), and decision-making style. These categories of data seem to be related to successful and unsuccessful decisions, use of analytical and intuitive decision inputs, and criteria used to evaluate decision outcomes.

Executive interviewees having a strong outcome orientation were often those whose organizations have a clear founder-derived or family-like culture and a high perceived external focus in their organizational values. (This could potentially be explained by the selection processes used by organizations to hire people into leadership positions.) These interviewees described successful decisions as related to people and unsuccessful decisions as related to other elements of the marketing mix (typically based on technology, e.g. promotional activities or customer interface software). They expressed a high need to use analytical or metric data in decision-making, both as an input and in assessing outcomes. For unsuccessful outcomes, these types of data may be used to justify a poor choice, by shifting the blame away from the decision maker and toward the measures instead.

Interviewees having a strong process orientation tended to be those whose organizations place greater value on diversity and international experience; they also seem to have a perceived internal focus in their organizational values. (These relationships were not as clear-cut as the corresponding relationships for interviewees categorized as having an outcome orientation, as described in the previous paragraph.) This group of interviewees described both successful and unsuccessful decisions as related to people. They typically mentioned a mix of analytical and intuitive decision inputs; successful outcomes seem to be evaluated intuitively, whereas unsuccessful outcomes are based on a mix of assessments. It appears that, with unsuccessful outcomes, these interviewees feel a need to use analytical tools or metrics to better understand what went wrong.

As mentioned above, in both the successful and unsuccessful decisions identified as salient, there was a focus on ethical decisions made with regard to people, especially front line service providers, which is an important emergent theme that relates executive decision-making to organizational culture and values. Furthermore, this relationship appears to exist for executives having both process and outcome orientations. Such decisions are considered ethical decisions because of their direct impact on people, determining who wins and who loses; in the present research, the focus is on those within the organization.

In the Discussion section which follows, selective coding moves the research results to a higher, more abstract level, in which observed interrelationships between themes from open and axial coding of the interview data are described. These results point toward propositions for further research, which represent the outcomes of the present qualitative research using a grounded theory methodology. Following the propositions is additional discussion of how the research results relate to the conceptual development and, in particular, to the concentric circles model provided in Figure 20.1.

Discussion

This section begins by detailing the Research Propositions that are the outcome of the study. After doing this, it links the layers of ethical decisions described in the Conceptual Development (see Figure 20.1) and the research findings.

Several interesting relationships emerge, as the results of axial coding are subjected to selective coding; these relationships are described in the Research Propositions, below. The results in the present research are consistent with those in previous research that find an impact of personal characteristics and moral philosophy on ethical decision-making, as described in the Conceptual Development section. Also consistent are findings that suggest organizational values and culture may influence executive decision-making. The link between personal backgrounds and organizational cultures apparently offers excellent person-organization fit, possibly because the executives rank so highly in their organizations that they are instrumental in defining the corporate culture. However, much of what emerges from the axial and selective coding is new and offers a distinctive contribution to the literature. In particular, the present executive interviewees seem to align into two groups, based on their descriptions of personal background, decision-making style, and organizational culture. These groups are related to the core category resulting from open coding, the personal moral philosophy on which ethical decisions depend (see Table 20.5).

Research Propositions resulting from selective coding of the present results offer a contribution beyond previous research: they address new relationships that emerged during axial coding between the themes obtained in open coding. For instance, after grouping the executives based on the reported decision-making style, each executive's personal moral philosophy appears to be related to organizational culture. This apparent group membership

Table 20.5 Results of axial coding

Open Coding Categories	Apparent Deontological Approach to Decisions	Apparent Teleological Approach to Decisions
Personal Characteristics	service orientation, giving back, empathy, persistence, not intimidated by change	service orientation, giving back, empathy, persistence, not intimidated by change
Personal Social Style	warm, open-minded, collaborative, optimistic	warm, open-minded, collaborative, optimistic
Personal Values	remain honest, truthful, and transparent	consider impacts and time frames, prioritize results
Personal Decision-Making Style	mix of analytical and intuitive considerations	tend toward more analytical considerations
Personal Assessment of Decision Outcomes	usually there is not a clear right or wrong answer	the right answer ultimately surfaces
Organization's Desired Employee Characteristics	maintain relationships, proactive, diligent, creative, entrepreneurial, team players	maintain relationships, proactive, diligent, creative, entrepreneurial, team players
Organizational Values	communication, transparency, getting the job done, valuing individual differences	communication, transparency, getting the job done, conforming to expectations
Organizational Culture	welcoming of diversity, flexible, accepting of a wider range of behaviors, more risk-taking	paternalistic, narrowly defined acceptable behaviors, feels like a family, less risk-taking
Organizational Assessment of Decision Outcomes	successful outcomes are evaluated intuitively and most often relate to people; unsuccessful outcomes are evaluated both intuitively and analytically and most often relate to people	successful outcomes are evaluated analytically and tend to relate to people; unsuccessful outcomes are evaluated analytically and tend to relate to technology

relates the tendency to focus on process (deontology) versus outcome (teleology) to the specific types of assessments used in evaluating ethical choices. Therefore, Proposition 1 looks at the relationship between personal moral philosophy and use of intuitive versus analytical assessments of decision options. Organizational values may also potentially impact ethical decision-making: for instance, corporate culture appears to relate to which types of executives are attracted and retained at high levels in an organization (see Proposition 4). In particular, organizations with strong family-like cultures are more likely to be led by executives exhibiting outcome-oriented personal moral philosophies (teleologies), whereas organizations having greater diversity and appreciation of cross-cultural experience are more likely to be led by executives exhibiting process-oriented personal moral philosophies (deontologies). All of the propositions relate to the executive's personal moral philosophy, which is a central phenomenon of this research.

Proposition 1 describes how an executive's personal moral philosophy might influence the types of information considered in ethical decision-making.

P1a: executives holding outcome-oriented personal moral philosophies (teleologies) tend to make greater use of analytical measures than intuition in decision-making.

P1b: executives holding process-oriented personal moral philosophies (deontologies) tend to make use of both intuitive and analytical assessments in decision-making.

Proposition 2 describes how an organization's values, and particularly whether they are focused externally (on customers) or internally (on employees), relate to the moral philosophies of successful executives who drive such organizational values.

P2a: executives exhibiting outcome-oriented personal moral philosophies (teleologies) are more likely to be leaders in organizations having high external focus in values.

P2b: executives exhibiting process-oriented personal moral philosophies (deontologies) are more likely to be leaders in organizations having high internal focus in values.

Proposition 3 brings out the importance of people in service-providing organizations. In particular, an executive's personal moral philosophy can potentially impact the types of decisions considered successful and unsuccessful.

P3a: executives holding outcome-oriented personal moral philosophies (teleologies) tend to find that successful decisions are about people, whereas unsuccessful decisions tend to be about other elements (e.g. technology).

P3b: executives holding process-oriented personal moral philosophies (deontologies) tend to find that both successful and unsuccessful decisions are about people.

Proposition 4 describes how different organizational cultures might attract and foster the success of executives holding different moral philosophies.

P4a: executives in organizations having strong family-like cultures are more likely to exhibit outcome-oriented personal moral philosophies (teleologies).

P4b: executives in organizations having greater diversity and appreciation of cross-cultural experience are more likely to exhibit process-oriented personal moral philosophies (deontologies).

Proposition 5 ties together Propositions 1 and 4 by considering how organizational culture might impact the use of analytical and intuitive inputs to ethical decision-making. In particular, the amount of perceived autonomy that executives have in decision-making appears to be related to organizational characteristics, and to the personal moral philosophies of typical executives in each type of organization (see Proposition 4). This, in turn, appears to be related to different use of potential decision inputs (see Proposition 1). This may occur because executives in organizations having greater diversity perceive less need to justify their choices.

P5a: executives in organizations with strong family-like cultures tend to hold outcome-oriented personal moral philosophies (teleologies) and to make use of primarily analytical decision inputs (i.e. metrics).

P5b: executives in organizations placing greater value on diversity tend to hold process-oriented personal moral philosophies (deontologies) and to use a blend of decision inputs, including both intuition and metrics.

Proposition 6 considers how executives' personal moral philosophies might impact assessment of ethical decision outcomes. Executives having more teleological personal ethical codes do not appear to make use of intuition in evaluating unsuccessful outcomes. As mentioned earlier, this may be related to the importance of outcomes and/or a need to shift blame onto the metrics. Executives holding more deontological moral codes tend to use a range of assessments for unsuccessful outcomes, which may reflect greater desire to find the true reasons behind undesirable results.

P6a: executives holding outcome-oriented personal moral philosophies (teleologies) tend to evaluate successful outcomes intuitively, but unsuccessful outcomes analytically.

P6b: executives holding process-oriented personal moral philosophies (deontologies) tend to evaluate successful outcomes intuitively; with unsuccessful outcomes they use a blend of assessments.

The Research Propositions are shown visually in Figure 20.2. Note that the arrows connecting the personal moral philosophy to the organizational culture are bidirectional, because there appears to be an interactive pattern in which each can affect the other.

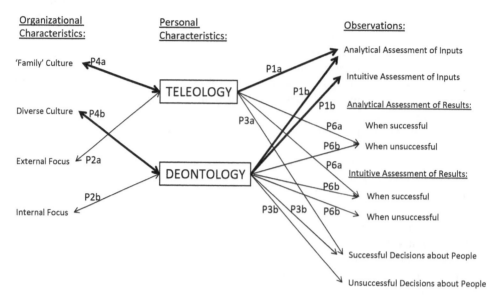

Figure 20.2 Relationships between themes, shown by proposition number.

Note: P5 combines P1 and P4 to result in the bold paths

Looking back at the concentric circles model introduced in the Conceptual Development (see Figure 20.1), facilitates review of the contributions in the present research. In particular, the outer circle or actualization layer depicts ethical decisions that influence society as a whole (e.g. CSR decisions). The intermediate circle or transformative layer depicts ethical decisions that influence the potential market, including current customers (e.g. TSR and other decisions affecting vulnerable customers). The present research is focused in the inner circle or initiation layer; ethical decisions in this circle are made by high-level executives and initiate culture and values within the organization. There are two relevant differences between the layers presented: first, decisions in each layer affect different groups of people and, second, the extent of each of these three groups is very different. Decisions in the actualization layer affect all of society, so the impact is very broad but also very thin. Decisions in the transformative layer affect everyone in the potential market, so the group is smaller, but the decisions are more impactful, both to the affected people and to the organization. Finally, decisions in the initiation layer directly affect people within the organization and have a very strong impact on this group. Such ethical decisions made by executives within the initiation layer are understudied and can greatly influence employees who, in turn, have the power to determine the success or failure of the organization. Therefore, the present research offers an important contribution by improving understanding of how successful executives make and evaluate ethical decisions that initiate organizational culture and values.

The findings suggest that executives making ethical decisions use different inputs depending on their personal moral philosophies: those that are outcome-oriented use analytical measures and focus on external evaluation, whereas those that are process-oriented use both intuitive and analytical tools and focus on internal evaluation. Both groups appear to have greater concern about the impact on people when they make unsuccessful decisions, but those that are outcome-oriented focus on other elements, such as technology, when a decision is successful. Organizational culture appears to affect, and be affected by, the executive's personal moral philosophy: outcome-oriented decision makers are associated with strong family-like cultures, whereas process-oriented executives are affiliated with organizations offering greater diversity and appreciation of cross-cultural experience. Finally, both groups of executives tend to evaluate successful outcomes intuitively; those holding outcome-oriented personal moral philosophies assess unsuccessful outcomes analytically, whereas those that hold process-oriented personal moral philosophies use a blend of assessments in case of an unsuccessful outcome.

These observations can lead to new connections in the service literature, in part because ethical decisions taking place in the initiation layer can have ramifications for service delivery. For instance, the literature review mentions customer co-creation of value, which is a very current research topic in the intermediate layer, owing to the increasing importance of customer participation in creation of services. This literature suggests that mutually beneficial relationships are achieved when personalized interactions between a company and its customers become the loci of value creation (Grönroos & Gummerus, 2014; Grönroos & Ravald, 2011; Grönroos & Voima, 2013; Vargo & Lusch, 2004). Co-creation of value can be said to have been addressed much earlier in literature related to the initiation layer, because value co-creation has been going on for a very long time between employees, under the name of teamwork. Decisions made by an executive in the initiation layer that affect how employees are motivated to work together, such as investment in training programs or compensation plans, may offer useful advice to others currently working to enhance customer value co-creation. Thus, there may be secondary benefits to improved understanding of high-level ethical decisions, owing to the implications for the intermediate and outer layers in Figure 20.1. It is also of note that literature focusing on the actualization layer does not yet appear to address co-creation of value; this may be an interesting opportunity for future research. In summary, developments in co-creation of value point to the importance of better understanding how executives make ethical decisions that affect employees, because co-creation activities have already moved from the initiation layer outward and other topics might do so as well. For instance, related topics such as (1) the role of leaders in creating an ethical organizational climate, or (2) links between ethics, HR, and organizational success are critical and may also exhibit outward-moving patterns. The present research contributes to understanding in these areas, particularly how executive ethical decisions directly impact employees, and therefore indirectly influence customers, suggesting that more guidance on people-oriented decision-making is needed in marketing theory and practice.

As mentioned above, ethical decisions within the initiation layer may have the greatest impact, owing to their focus upon the most narrowly defined layer. Such decisions may also have the greatest impact upon the decision maker, as executives are responsible for culture and values within their organizations. Interviewees expressed positive attitudes toward service, giving back, empathy, reaching out to others, persistence to overcome obstacles, and not being intimidated by new situations. They apparently hold long-term goals and can clearly articulate a vision for the future. Some described "building a legacy" – painting a picture with words of what they were developing to outlast themselves. The organization's culture and values are a key part of an executive's legacy, and the present research suggests that this legacy is critically important to the successful high-level executives interviewed. This is substantiated in the interview data: early in the interviews, executives talked freely about their childhoods, values in the family of origin, and formative experiences. They shared stories about their career paths, including the key choices that led them to where they are today. Most of them described their contributions in some detail, and with pride.

Nearly all envisioned a specific legacy that they wanted to leave to their organizations. It was during these free-flowing conversations that the organizational culture was typically described, and often it was related back to the respondent's early years during which their values were formed.

A final topic that is briefly addressed in the present research is how cultural norms influence an ethical decision. In the actualization layer, all of society is affected, and cultural norms vary widely. In the transformative layer, the potential market is not as broad as all of society, but may still involve a variety of cultural norms. In the initiation layer, the organizational culture applies, so the range of cultural norms is much narrower. Because corporate culture is determined interactively by high-level executives who make ethical decisions directly affecting those within the organization and then observe their decisions in action before making adjustments, it is important to better understand how they make such decisions.

Conclusion

The present research develops understanding of how successful service executives consider and use different types of information and evaluative processes to make decisions that initiate organizational culture and values. Based on the findings from in-depth interviews with 12 high-level service executives, personal moral philosophy is a core phenomenon; other influences on ethical decisions include both individual and organizational cultures and values. Six propositions for future research are developed in this grounded theory research. Briefly, the Research Propositions suggest that personal moral philosophies drive selection of decision inputs and use of information, influence outcome assessment, and affect both organizational culture and its impact on ethical decisions. (The Research Propositions are presented verbally in the Discussion section, and described visually in Figure 20.2.)

The grounded theory methodology was selected, in part, to allow interviewees to describe in their own words how they incorporate different types of information when making ethical decisions. Respondents were asked about their individual family background and culture, social identity, social style, and personal moral philosophy; they also described how they perceive their organizations, including mission, values, and culture. They identified decisions that they found important, challenging, successful, and unsuccessful, and elucidated vignettes describing specific successful and unsuccessful recent decisions. They provided details about their comfort levels with and use of different ways of thinking, such as analytical or intuitive, and described any metrics or other assessments they found particularly helpful. Finally, they defined an 'ethical decision' in their own words and described, in general, the steps they would follow to make such a decision. Analysis of the resulting executive interview data relied on standard qualitative methods recommended by a number of authors (detailed in the Method section) for research leading to grounded theory.

From the qualitative data analysis, two groups of executives emerged; these groups appear to differ based on whether their personal moral philosophies are outcome-oriented (teleologies) or process-oriented (deontologies). Interviewees align with one of these two groups in a manner consistent with their organizational cultures. Specifically, in organizations with strong family-like cultures, executives tend to be teleologists; they are outcome-oriented and report greater use of analytical inputs in decision-making and in evaluation of unsuccessful decision outcomes. These executives may need to justify their decisions using quantitative information because they feel that there are strict expectations of executive decision outcomes in their organizations. If so, this may result in disregard of some available information, particularly intuitive information that might assess unexpressed feelings; such an oversight could potentially lead to less successful decisions and less positive customer results. The stated importance of making good choices may be the reason that members of this group report unsuccessful decisions that focus on technology rather than on people: perhaps in choices perceived as less crucial, it is easier to face a lack of success. The second group of executives includes those from organizations that value diversity as well as international and/ or cross-cultural experience. These executives tend to be deontologists; they are process-oriented and report greater use of a blend of intuitive and analytical assessments in decision-making and in evaluation of unsuccessful decision outcomes.

Limitations

This study is not without limitations. All of the interviewees were chosen because they are quite successful executives at the highest levels in successful service organizations. Thus, the Research Propositions may not be applicable to executives who are personally unsuccessful or leading poorly performing organizations. Interviews conducted among such executives would most likely exhibit greater variation, not only along the lines of personal and organizational characteristics, but also in terms of person-organization fit. Other types of diversity are also lacking from the sample owing to its small size. For instance, it was not also possible to recruit either for greater international diversity (e.g. currently working in various countries) or for less diversity (e.g. all from the same service industry), so choices had to be made for reasons of feasibility. This is a limitation that could be relaxed in future, larger-scale studies.

Another limitation of the present study is that it is inherently cross-sectional: busy executives could not be asked to engage in more than one in-depth interview. Therefore, longitudinal data is lacking and the findings must rely on interviewee reports of changes occurring over time (e.g. outcomes of successful and unsuccessful decisions). Perceptions and actual changes over time might differ. A qualitative, longitudinal study of similar high-level service executives would be helpful in discerning this. However, it may be of even greater benefit to perform a quantitative study using a representative sample, to assess whether or not the propositions developed herein have external validity among a broader population.

Future research

The six Research Propositions developed in the present study are testable in future research. Specifically, they might be used to design a quantitative study in which questionnaire responses measure the impacts of various factors on ethical decisions by a larger, representative sample of executives. Another potentially useful future research direction would be to further develop the concepts and relationships identified in the present study through additional qualitative research, possibly a longitudinal study which would allow an assessment of how responses change over time and through different environmental conditions.

Another interesting direction for future research would be to investigate how the findings in the present study (i.e. the Research Propositions) might be extended across the two layers in Figure 20.1 that are outside the scope of the present research. Specifically, it would be helpful to assess whether personal characteristics of decision makers or their organizational cultures influence decisions in the intermediate layer that directly impact the potential market and/or if this occurs in the outer layer, where decisions impact all of society.

How cultural norms influence an ethical decision is another topic that is briefly addressed in the present research; the influence of cultural norms could be investigated specifically for applicability in different layers of Figure 20.1. It was mentioned above that cultural norms would be expected to be most variable in the activation layer, where decisions impact all of society, less variable in the transformative layer, where decisions impact the potential market, and least variable in the initiation layer, where the applicable cultural norms are those of the organization. Thus, it would be valuable in future research to develop an understanding of how cultural norms themselves, as well as their variability, might influence ethical decisions.

In the present research, interviewees felt that the most important and most difficult decisions involve people; service operations and technology-related decisions were also mentioned as being difficult. The results of these types of decisions are quite visible to customers, especially in services, because of the high levels of both personal and technology-based interaction that often occur. Therefore, it could be interesting to investigate whether this is also true in other layers shown in Figure 20.1. In particular, there may be differences between process–oriented ethical decision makers (who tend to be affiliated with internally focused organizations) and outcome–oriented decision makers (who tend to be affiliated with externally focused organizations) in terms of how they view the importance of people in creating the face of the organization and of considering intangibles such as intuition in evaluating ethical decisions. Such differences may lead to differences in decision-making in each layer of the concentric circles in Figure 20.1. These topics should be considered in future research.

Contributions

Prior research in ethical decision-making is primarily focused in the actualization layer where CSR decisions are made, or in the transformative layer where the well-being of all potential customers is considered (refer to Figure 20.1). The present research is focused in the inner circle, the initiation layer, where high-level executives make crucial ethical decisions that define organizational culture and values and directly impact employees. Compared to the outer and middle circles, the initiation layer is underrepresented in academic research and in practical understanding. Therefore, this research makes an important contribution by providing findings from personal interviews with high-level executives in successful service firms, to clarify the processes they use and outcomes they consider when making such critical decisions that affect people within their own organizations. Results are presented in the form of testable propositions that describe relationships between constructs that drive ethical decisions (refer to the Discussion section and/or Figure 20.2 for details). Based on personal characteristics, organizational values, and decision-making styles, the executive interviewees apparently belong to one of two groups, aligned with either deontological or teleological personal moral philosophies, respectively. Differences that define group membership emerge in open and axial coding of the interview data (refer to Table 20.5 for details). The relationships between observed constructs are new, relevant, and worthy of study in future empirical research. This should be undertaken to clarify how ethical decisions that initiate organizational culture and values are made by successful service executives. Should the findings be upheld in a quantitative study, the results will be applicable in organizational ethical decision-making.

In summary, this research gathered rich descriptions of service executives' personal characteristics, including culture, social identity, social style, and personal moral philosophy, which have been shown in previous literature to influence ethical business decisions. Information about organizational culture, mission, and values, which can also influence executive decision-making, was also obtained. Interviewees held either deontological (process-based) or teleological (outcome-based) personal moral philosophies; their organizations can be grouped into those that have more family-like, externally focused cultures and those that exhibit more diverse, international cultures featuring an internal focus in decision-making. There appears to be a relationship between these characteristics, which is included in the Research Propositions that result from the present study. Furthermore, personal and organizational characteristics appear to be related to an executive's tendency to use analytical or intuitive assessments, both of decision inputs and outcomes. All of these findings are detailed in the Research Propositions, which are presented in the Discussion section and summarized visually in Figure 20.2; these are the outcome of this grounded theory qualitative research.

Note

1 This chapter was originally published as follows:Bridges E. (2018) Executive ethical decisions initiating organizational culture and values. *Journal of Service Theory and Practice* 28(5): 576–608.

References

Abela, A.V., & Murphy, P.E. (2008). Marketing with integrity: ethics and the service-dominant logic for marketing. *Journal of the Academy of Marketing Science*, 36(1): 39–53.

Anderson L., Ostrom A.L., Corus C., Fisk R.P., Gallan A.S., Giraldo M., Mende M., Mulder M., Rayburn S.W., Rosenbaum M.S., Shirahada K., Williams J.D. (2013) Transformative service research: an agenda for the future. *Journal of Business Research* 66(8): 1203–1210.

Bergadaà M. (2004) Évolution de l'épistémè économique et sociale: proposition d'un cadre de morale, de déontologie, d'éthique et de responsabilité pour le marketer. *Recherche et Applications en Marketing* 19(1): 55–72.

Beu D.S., Buckley M.R., Harvey M.G. (2003) Ethical decision-making: a multidimensional construct. *Business Ethics: A European Review* 12(1): 88–107.

Bowen D.E. (2016) The changing role of employees in service theory and practice: an interdisciplinary view. *Human Resource Management Review* 26(1): 4–13.

Bowen S.A. (2002) Elite executives in issues management: the role of ethical paradigms in decision-making. *Journal of Public Affairs* 2(4): 270–283.

Brenkert G.G. (1998) Marketing and the vulnerable. *Business Ethics Quarterly* 8(1): 7–20.

Bristol T., Fern E.F. (2003) The effects of interaction on consumers' attitudes in focus groups. *Psychology & Marketing* 20(5): 433–454.

Brown T.J., Dacin P.A. (1997) The company and the product: corporate associations and consumer product responses. *Journal of Marketing* 61(1): 68–84.

Bryman, A. (2012.) *Social research methods*,4th edition.Oxford, UK: Oxford University Press.

Charmaz K. (2014) *Constructing grounded theory*, 2nd edition. London: SAGE Publications.

Collins D. (2000) The quest to improve the human condition: the first 1,500 articles published in *Journal of Business Ethics*. *Journal of Business Ethics* 26(1): 1–73.

Corbin J., Strauss A. (2008) *Basics of qualitative research: Techniques and procedures for developing grounded theory*, 3rd edition. Thousand Oaks, CA: SAGE Publications.

Craft J.L. (2013) A review of the empirical ethical decision-making literature: 2004–2011. *Journal of Business Ethics* 117(2): 221–259.

Creswell J.W. (2013) *Qualitative inquiry & research design: Choosing among five approaches*. Thousand Oaks, CA: SAGE Publications.

Dahlsrud A. (2008) How corporate social responsibility is defined: an analysis of 37 definitions. *Corporate Social Responsibility and Environmental Management* 15(1): 1–13.

Deal T.E., Kennedy A.A. (2000) *Corporate cultures: The rites and rituals of corporate life...* Cambridge, MA: Perseus Publishing: Persues Pubishing.

Detert J.R., Treviño L.K., Sweitzer V.L. (2008) Moral disengagement in ethical decision-making: a study of antecedents and outcomes. *Journal of Applied Psychology* 93(2): 374–391.

Doh J.P., Quigley N.R. (2014) Responsible leadership and stakeholder management: influence pathways and organizational outcomes. *Academy of Management Perspectives* 28(3): 255–274.

Ferrell O.C., Ferrell L., Sawayda J. (2015) A review of ethical decision-making models in marketing. In A. Nill (Ed.),((ed.) *Handbook of marketing ethics* (pp. 38–60). Cheltenham, UK: Edward Elgar Publishing.

Ferrell O.C., Gresham L.G. (1985) A contingency framework for understanding ethical decision-making in marketing. *Journal of Marketing* 49(3): 87–96.

Fleming P. (2005) 'Kindergarten cop': paternalism and resistance in a high-commitment workplace. *Journal of Management Studies* 42(7): 1469–1489.

Fritzsche D.J. (1995) Personal values: potential keys to ethical decision-making. *Journal of Business Ethics* 14(11): 909–922.

Gallicano T.D. (2013) Relationship management with the millennial generation of public relations agency employees. *Public Relations Review* 39(3): 222–225.

Gordon W., Langmaid R. (1988) *Qualitative market research*. Aldershot, UK: Gower Publishing Company Limited.

Griffin A., Hauser J. (1993) The voice of the customer. *Marketing Science* 12(1): 1–27.

Grönroos C., Gummerus J. (2014) The service revolution and its marketing implications: service logic vs service-dominant logic. *Managing Service Quality* 24(3): 206–229.

Grönroos C., Ravald A. (2011) Service as business logic: implications for value creation and marketing. *Journal of Service Management* 22(1): 5–22.

Grönroos C., Voima P. (2013) Critical service logic: making sense of value creation and co-creation. *Journal of the Academy of Marketing Science* 41(2): 133–150.

Hansen R.S. (1992) A multidimensional scale for measuring business ethics: a purification and refinement. *Journal of Business Ethics* 11(7): 523–534.

Hatch M.J. (2011) Material and meaning in the dynamic of organizational culture and identity with implications for the leadership of organizational change. In N. Ashkanasy, C. Wilderom, M. Peterson (Eds.),(EDs *The handbook of organizational culture and climate*, 2nd (pp. 341–358). editionThousand Oaks, CA: SAGE Publications.

Hoffman R.R., Crandall B., Shadbolt N. (1998) Use of the critical decision method to elicit expert knowledge: a case study in the methodology of cognitive task analysis. *Human Factors* 40(2): 254–276.

Homburg C., Droll M., Totzek D. (2008) Customer prioritization: does it pay off, and how should it be implemented? *Journal of Marketing* 72(5): 110–130.

Hoover K.F., Pepper M.B. (2015) How did they say that? Ethics statements and normative frameworks at best companies to work for. *Journal of Business Ethics* 131(3): 605–617.

Hunt S.D., Vitell S. (1986) A general theory of marketing ethics. *Journal of Macromarketing* 6(1): 5–16.

Kaposy C., Brunger F., Maddalena V., Singleton R. (2016) The use of ethics decision-making frameworks by Canadian ethics consultants: a qualitative study. *Bioethics* 30(8): 636–642.

Kennedy E.J., Lawton L. (1993) Ethics and services marketing. *Journal of Business Ethics* 12(10): 785–795.

Laczniak G.R., Murphy P.E. (2012) Stakeholder theory and marketing: moving from a firm-centric to a societal perspective. *Journal of Public Policy & Marketing* 31(2): 284–292.

Lanis R., Richardson G. (2015) Is corporate social responsibility performance associated with tax avoidance? *Journal of Business Ethics* 127(2): 439–457.

Lincoln Y.S., Guba E. (1985) *Naturalistic inquiry*. Beverly Hills, CA: SAGE Publications.

Lindlof T.R., Taylor B.C. (2002) *Qualitative communication research methods*, 2nd edition. Thousand Oaks, CA: SAGE Publications.

Malik M. (2015) Value-enhancing capabilities of CSR: a brief review of contemporary literature. *Journal of Business Ethics* 127(2): 419–438.

Marta J., Singhapakdi A., Kraft K. (2008) Personal characteristics underlying ethical decisions in marketing situations: a survey of small business managers. *Journal of Small Business Management* 46(4): 589–606.

Marta J., Singhapakdi A., Lee D.J., Burnaz S., Topcu Y.I., Atakan M.S., Ozkaracalar T. (2012) The effects of corporate ethical values and personal moral philosophies on ethical intentions in selling situations: evidence from Turkish, Thai, and American businesspeople. *Journal of Business Ethics* 106(2): 229–241.

McDaniel C., Gates R. (1998) *Marketing research essentials*, 2nd edition. Cincinnati, OH: South-Western College Publishing.

McDevitt R., Giapponi C., Tromley C. (2007) A model of ethical decision-making: the integration of process and content. *Journal of Business Ethics* 73(2): 219–229.

Micewski E.R., Troy C. (2007) Business ethics: deontologically revisited. *Journal of Business Ethics* 72(1): 17–25.

Ostrom A., Parasuraman P., Bowen D.E., Patrício L., Voss C. (2015) Service research priorities in a rapidly changing context. *Journal of Service Research* 18(2): 127–159.

Price C., Whiteley A. (2014) Corporate culture and employee identity: cooption or commitment through contestation? *Journal of Change Management* 14(2): 210–235.

Rendtorff J.D. (2009) Basic ethical principles applied to service industries. *Service Industries Journal* 29 (1–2): 9–19.

Rest J.R. (1986) *Moral development: Advances in research and theory.* New York:. New York: Praeger.

Robertson C.J. (2008) An analysis of 10 years of business ethics research in strategic management journal: 1996–2005. *Journal of Business Ethics* 80(4): 745–753.

Sen S., Bhattacharya C.B. (2001) Does doing good always lead to doing better? Consumer reactions to corporate social responsibility. *Journal of Marketing Research* 38(2): 225–243.

Sierra V., Iglesias O., Markovic S., Singh J.J. (2017) Does ethical image build equity in corporate services brands? The influence of customer perceived ethicality on affect, perceived quality, and equity. *Journal of Business Ethics* 144(3): 661–676.

Silverman D. (2010) *Doing qualitative research: A practical handbook*, 3rd London: edition. SAGE Publications.

Sims R.R., Brinkmann J. (2003) Enron ethics (or: culture matters more than codes). *Journal of Business Ethics* 45(3): 243–256.

Singhapakdi A., Rao C.P., Vitell S.J. (1996) Ethical decision-making: an investigation of services marketing professionals. *Journal of Business Ethics* 15(6): 635–644.

Srnka K.J. (2004) Culture's role in marketers' ethical decision-making: an integrated theoretical framework. *Academy of Marketing Science Review* 8(3): 1–32.

Strauss A., Corbin J. (1990) *Basics of qualitative research: Grounded theory procedures and techniques.* Newbury Park, CA: SAGE Publications.

Tenbrunsel A.E., Smith-Crowe K. (2008) Ethical decision-making: where we've been and where we're going. *Academy of Management Annals* 2(1): 545–607.

Treviño L.K. (1986) Ethical decision-making in organizations: a person-situation interactionist model. *Academy of Management Review* 11(3): 601–617.

Treviño L.K., Youngblood S.A. (1990) Bad apples in bad barrels: a causal analysis of ethical decision-making behavior. *Journal of Applied Psychology* 75(4): 378–385.

Valentine S., Hollingworth D. (2015) Communication of organizational strategy and coordinated decision-making as catalysts for enhanced perceptions of corporate ethical values in a financial services company. *Employee Responsibilities and Rights Journal* 27(3): 213–229.

Vargo S.L., Lusch R.F. (2004) Evolving to a new dominant logic for marketing. *Journal of Marketing* 68 (1): 1–17.

Vitell S.J., Rallapalli K.C., Singhapakdi A. (1993) Marketing norms: the influence of personal moral philosophies and organizational ethical culture. *Journal of the Academy of Marketing Science* 21(4): 331–337.

Whittier N.C., Williams S., Dewett T.C. (2006) Evaluating ethical decision-making models: a review and application. *Society and Business Review* 1(3): 235–247.

Witt M.A., Stahl G.K. (2016) Foundations of responsible leadership: Asian versus Western executive responsibility orientations toward key stakeholders. *Journal of Business Ethics* 136(3): 623–638.

Woiceshyn J. (2011) A model for ethical decision-making in business: reasoning, intuition, and rational moral principles. *Journal of Business Ethics* 104(3): 311–323.

Wooten D.B., Reed A. (2000) A conceptual overview of the self-presentational concerns and response tendencies of focus group participants. *Journal of Consumer Psychology* 9(3): 141–153.

Wyld D.C., Jones C.A. (1997) Importance of context: the ethical work climate construct and models of ethical decision-making: an agenda for research. *Journal of Business Ethics* 16(4): 465–472.

Yagil D., Shultz T. (2017) Service with a conscience: moral dilemmas in customer service roles. *Journal of Service Theory and Practice* 27(3): 689–711.

Zeithaml V.A., Rust R.T., Lemon K.N. (2001) The customer pyramid: creating and serving profitable customers. *California Management Review* 43(4): 118–142.

21

Transformative service research

Thoughts, perspectives, and research directions

Mark S. Rosenbaum, Karen Edwards, Germán Contreras Ramírez, and John Grady

Introduction

The origin of the transformative service research (TSR) movement stems from consumer research, specifically a presidential address given by David Glen Mick at an *Association for Consumer Research* conference in 2006. At that time, Mick (2006) publicly questioned the efficacy of consumer research and its impact on enhancing consumer welfare, as well as the abilities of academics to engage in research that truly matters. Given these exposed voids in consumer research and the seeming inability of this research to make a difference in the health and well-being of most consumers, Mick encouraged the formation of the transformative consumer research (TCR) movement, which is essentially a paradigm that engages in meaningful and impactful research investigations.

TCR encourages consumer researchers to engage in "investigations that are framed by a fundamental problem or opportunity and that strive to respect, uphold, and improve life in relation to the myriad conditions, demands, potentialities, and effects of consumption" (Mick, 2006, p. 2). In general, TCR promotes research investigation into issues, such as poverty and addiction, that affect consumer welfare and social justice, and considers the vulnerability of at-risk populations in consumption settings. Notably, the TCR movement inspired a group of researchers in the service domain to consider engaging in investigations that promote consumer, communal, or global welfare via services, service delivery, or service processes. This field of study became known as the TSR movement (Anderson et al., 2013; Rosenbaum et al., 2011a).

TSR encourages researchers to investigate matters that may ultimately lead to improving the human condition by "creating uplifting changes and improvements in the well-being of individuals (consumers and employees), families, social networks, communities, cities, nations, collectives, and ecosystems" (Rosenbaum et al., 2011a, p. 3). It is worth noting here that TSR encourages research that impacts the lives of consumers and employees in both commercial and nonprofit service settings (Blocker & Barrios, 2015; Rahman & Björk, 2016). Consistent with Mick's (2006) expressed frustrations regarding the lack of impact that years of consumer research had on resultant outcomes, the early TSR pioneers were adamant that researchers' understanding of services, service providers, and service systems may not only be relevant to managers and to promoting managerially relevant outcomes (such as future behavioral intentions, satisfaction, and loyalty), but also to promoting well-being. Indeed, TSR encourages researchers to analyze extant theories and frameworks in the service discipline from new perspectives; these may include understanding how the theories and frameworks may apply (perhaps with modification) when considering the lives and experiences of previously overlooked consumers in the marketplace (e.g., Anderson et al., 2013). Such consumers include those with physical, social, and cognitive disabilities, financial vulnerabilities, or aging issues (Rosenbaum, Seger-Guttmann, & Giraldo, 2017a; Sanchez-Barrios, Giraldo, Khalik, & Manjarres, 2015). Given this theoretical research challenge, it is not surprising that transformative service remains a key research priority among service marketing research scholars and practitioners (Ostrom et al., 2010, 2015).

TSR in the service domain

Service marketing is a relatively new disciplinary field, emerging in the 1980s as a response to the rapidly expanding global service economies (Fisk, 2009). Thus, it is not surprising that service researchers sought to build a foundational theoretical core by examining a "general consumer" and by analyzing consumer subsets based upon common demographic factors, such as gender, race, marital status, age, educational credentials, and so forth. These early investigatory research endeavors resulted in the creation of extant foundational theories and frameworks (e.g., Servuction Model, SERVQUAL, Servicescape, etc.) (Hoffman & Bateson, 2017; Zeithaml, Bitner, & Gremler, 2013). However, many of these early investigations overlooked how services, service providers, and service systems can enhance the lives and experiences of consumers who enter the marketplace with biophysical (e.g., physical disabilities) or psychosocial characteristics (e.g., mental disabilities) that make them vulnerable to receiving diminished value in the marketplace (Emerson & Hatton, 2008; Fisk et al., 2016; Rahman & Björk, 2016).

For example, recent investigations are bringing to light previously under-researched themes, such as exploring the effect of service in high-risk health care settings on afflicted consumers' physical, emotional, and financial well-being (Zayer, Otnes, & Fischer, 2015); exposing the fact that many consumers lack financial literacy to fully comprehend concepts such as credit terms and credit scores (Mende & Doorn, 2015); or discussing challenges that may emerge when service providers' religious values clash with serving lesbian, gay, bisexual, transgender, and queer (LGBTQ) customers (Minton et al., 2017).

Along these lines, surprisingly few studies in service research have explored how consumers respond to working with service providers who possess physical disabilities, such as deafness. Indeed, the few empirical studies that do exist regarding the way consumers respond to deaf or hard of hearing service providers are primary limited to the hospitality industry or to vocational research (Rosenbaum, Baniya, & Seger-Guttmann, 2017b). Despite research which shows that consumers enjoy patronizing service providers who have visible physical disabilities, only 18.7% of persons with a disability are currently employed, compared to the employment-population ratio of 65.7% for those without a disability (U.S. Department of Labor, 2017).

On the one hand, service researchers have generated a plethora of investigations that focus on improving service delivery and quality, and on mastering managerially relevant outcomes, such as satisfaction, loyalty, and word-of-mouth. On the other hand, despite the years of creating foundational theories and frameworks, the reality is that many services foster exclusion, as some groups of consumers lack access to services and encounter systemic bias and discrimination during service exchanges (Fisk et al., 2018). Indeed, leading service researchers recently coined the term "service inclusion" (Fisk et al., 2018, p. 842) to denote a managerial orientation that strives to provide customers (e.g., consumers, clients, patrons, citizens, patients, and guests) with fair access to service, fair treatment during service, and fair opportunities to exit a service. One of the first steps in fostering service inclusiveness is for service organizations to consider how vulnerable consumers experience their services, including their service providers and service systems.

Defining and understanding vulnerable consumers

Through the Americans with Disabilities Act (ADA) (www.ada.gov) and the Federal Trade Commission, the U.S. government strives to ensure that all consumers are able to receive the same value when they engage in marketplace exchanges. Specifically, consumer protection laws were intended to create marketplaces that respect consumer welfare by leveling a potentially uneven playing field between businesses and consumers (Browne, Clapp, Kubasek, & Biksacky, 2015). Similarly, the ADA (see Pub. L. No. 101–336, §2, 104 Stat. 328, 1990) was enacted, in part, to alleviate consumer frustration with lack of access to the marketplace (Baker, Gentry, & Rittenburg, 2005; Baker & Kaufman-Scarborough, 2001). More specifically, Title III (see 42 U.S.C. § 12,181) of the ADA prohibits discrimination against individuals with disabilities in major life activities, including their engagement in the marketplace and other public accommodations, and mandates that service establishments must provide appropriate physical access to individuals with disabilities. Thus, it is worth noting here that the ADA focuses entirely on marketplace value in terms of providing vulnerable consumers with access to physical building structures as well as full access to goods and services, in order for these consumers to have "full enjoyment" of service offerings. All of the aforementioned ADA requirements are architectural design elements as opposed to more general elements that might ensure that all consumers realize value in terms of receiving the same levels of service quality from front line employees.

Despite ADA legislation, conditions at many marketplaces still lead to vulnerability, making some consumers highly susceptible to receiving less than the maximum level of value that is inherent in exchange activities. Thus, it is important to consider what characteristics in service environments will likely result in consumer vulnerability. For example, vulnerable consumers are often at risk for experiencing service failures when they use drive-thru services in fast-food restaurants because of difficulties hearing the employee's voice through the speaker or reading signage (NPD Group, 2012).

Brenkert (1998) argued that, although all consumers are vulnerable in terms of having the potential of being harmed in some way by malfeasant marketing practices, some groups of consumers might be particularly vulnerable in the marketplace because of specific biophysical or psychosocial characteristics that affect their ability to realize maximum value, or any value at all, during service exchanges (Baker et al., 2005; Edwards, Rosenbaum, Brosdahl, & Hughes, 2018; Shultz & Holbrook, 2009). Stigmatizing biophysical traits include blindness/visual impediments, deafness/hearing impairment, elderliness, physical mobility disabilities, recovery issues, spinal cord injuries, and so forth. Psychosocial characteristics that might be stigmatizing include mental illness/mental health issues, autism/developmental disabilities, recovery issues, below-average income, or education. Whether physical, mental, or social, such limiting characteristics and society's response to them are beyond the control of an individual, and can lead to receipt of inferior service quality (Baker et al., 2005; Brenkert, 1998; Dunnett, Hamilton, & Piacentini, 2016).

In contrast to stigmatizing conditions, Baker et al. (2005) defined vulnerable consumers as consumers who enter the marketplace with conditions that put them at a disadvantage in terms of receiving optimal consumption experiences; this refers specifically to a lack of free-dom of choice. Jafari, Dunnett, Hamilton, and Downey (2013) built upon the work of Baker et al. (2005) by suggesting that any consumer who feels uncomfortable or powerless in a service setting due to having a physical, mental, or social characteristic (see also Saatcio-glu & Corus, 2016) may be vulnerable to receiving diminished levels of service quality from front line employees. Indeed, Shi, Jing, Yang, and Nguyen (2017) posited that consumer vulnerability stems from any human condition that makes consumers susceptible to market-place practices which result in receipt of inferior service quality or encourage purchase of harmful products.

Recognizing that external perceptions involve assumptions about the experiences of another person or group and may lead to erroneous conclusions and responses, Baker et al. (2005, p. 129) cautioned that "it is actual vulnerability that should be addressed by public policy makers and marketers." Actual vulnerability is said to be associated with individual characteristics (e.g., age, physical or cognitive disability), personal state (e.g., grief, transition, severe stress), and/or external conditions, whether ongoing or temporary (Pechmann et al., 2011). In contrast, perceived vulnerability involves widespread perception that a group of consumers is at risk, even if members of that group do not agree (Baker et al., 2005). It is important to note that some at-risk consumers might not recognize that they have market-place disadvantages; consequently, when external perceptions of vulnerability do not align with self-perceptions, questions may arise as to whether interventions are necessary or appro-priate (Pechmann et al., 2011). For example, consumers who speak with a Spanish accent may rebuke a service provider who assumes that that they want to converse in Spanish.

As previously discussed, service research has traditionally investigated the marketplace experiences of broad consumer groups, but only recently explored how vulnerable con-sumers experience services (Dunnett et al., 2016). Indeed, it is the contention of this chapter that the marketplace experiences, behaviors, and needs of broad consumer groups cannot be presumed to extend to specific vulnerable consumer segments, including those who enter the marketplace with biophysical characteristics or psychosocial characteristics that make them susceptible to receiving diminished levels of value compared to other consumers in the consumption setting. This chapter suggests that foundational theories and frameworks in ser-vice marketing do not accurately represent the consumption experiences of vulnerable consumers.

In the following sections, this chapter turns attention to highlighting key biophysical and psychosocial characteristics that result in service vulnerabilities for a significant number of consumers. These examples are offered to encourage research that expands upon current ser-vice theories and frameworks, to deliver optimal consumption experiences to all consumers in an equal manner.

Physical disabilities

The U.S. Census Bureau reports that nearly 40 million Americans (12.5% of non-institutionalized civilians) live with one or more physical disabilities (Bialik, 2017). These disabilities include hearing loss and deafness, vison loss and blindness, and conditions that affect human mobility. In addition, over 133 million consumers suffer from chronic health conditions (e.g., heart disease, cancer, type 2 diabetes, obesity, arthritis) that may limit their access to the marketplace (National Health Council, 2014). Both physical disabilities and chronic health conditions negatively affect consumer ability to navigate through, and within, built consumption settings (e.g., Hughes & Baskin, 2014; Kaufman-Scarborough, 1999;

Lahmann, 2010; Smithers, 2014); this brings into question how consumers might assess the quality of built environments or servicescapes (Bitner, 1992).

Baker (2006) posits that inhibiting access to the physical marketplace represses, devalues, and unnecessarily segregates consumers with physical disabilities. This point is valid, and the actions and inactions of service providers often exacerbate the issue. For example, despite advances in technology and alternative ordering methods, 42% of deaf and hearing-impaired people that frequent fast-food restaurants avoid using drive-thru lanes because of communication barriers (Inclusion Solutions, 2004). Similarly, although more than half of all U.S. drivers with disabilities use their vehicles daily, most of these drivers are unable to receive appropriate service at gasoline stations, as most are unable to use the self-service pump and payment processes required to refuel their vehicles (Inclusion Solutions, 2002). These and other access barriers for people with disabilities and chronic health conditions might be alleviated, or even eliminated, through alternative service processes and/or servicescape designs (Edwards et al., 2018).

Beyond the physical challenges of navigating a service environment, consumers with physical impairments often report that employees tend to ignore them or treat them rudely (Berg, 2015). Many visually impaired or blind consumers attest that service employees are often rude and unhelpful, making them reluctant to seek assistance (Kulyukin & Kutiyanawala, 2010). Consumers with hearing loss and deafness report that service providers seem uncomfortable around, and often avoid, interacting with them in the marketplace, contributing to a sense that they are ostracized (Center for Hearing and Communication, 2018). In a particularly egregious case, a deaf customer was scolded by a quick-serve employee for ordering via the drive-thru lane using a paper-and-pencil method of communication (a reasonable accommodation under the circumstances), slowing the lane's flow of traffic. The same woman attempted to use the drive-thru service at a different quick-serve location, but was refused service and subsequently ignored by employees inside the building. The lawsuit that ensued was settled with prejudice against the restaurant (*Cirrincione v. Taco Bell Corp.*, 2016).

Aging issues

The United Nations recently predicted that life expectancy in North America will increase from 79 years to 83 years or more by 2050 (United Nations, 2017). By that time, people over 60 years of age will make up an unprecedented 28% of North America's population (United Nations, 2017). Aging issues pose unique challenges to service providers, especially to health care, as chronic conditions are a primary cause of disability for older persons, with arthritis, hypertension, heart disease, and hearing loss accounting for approximately 60% of the occurrences (Cox, 2016). Notably, four out of five Americans 65 years or older have at least one chronic condition, and many experience multiple health disorders (Cox, 2016). Beyond these chronic and health conditions, older-aged adults are also susceptible to experiencing mental issues and challenges (e.g., loneliness and depression), which often ensue as a result of chronic disease, retirement, or empty-nest syndrome. Finally, older-aged adults are at elevated risk of dementia and Alzheimer's disease (Cox, 2016). Not surprisingly, elderliness is often associated with vulnerability in the marketplace.

Baker, Hunt, and Rittenburg (2007) hold that consumers must be afforded the knowledge, skills, and freedom in the marketplace to obtain their objectives. In the case of older-aged and elderly consumers, marketers are realizing the great extent to which visually impaired older-aged adults appreciate clearly legible signage within servicescapes (Ford, Trott, & Simms, 2016). Marketers also need to understand how arthritis or rheumatism (the most common chronic disease among older-aged and elderly adults) impacts a consumer's journey through a consumption setting (Hootman, Helmick, & Brady, 2012). Indeed, the aging process often results in the personal loss of muscle mass and strength by as much as 40% or more (Keller & Engelhardt, 2013). Unfortunately, servicescape designers do not fully comprehend how the loss of strength influences a consumer's mobility and ability to navigate service environments; additional research is clearly needed to determine how best to incorporate this knowledge into relevant educational programs.

Although researchers may call for service processes that facilitate freedom and autonomy for all consumers in all service settings, in some instances this request may be beyond the reasonable purview of many service providers. For example, more than five million older Americans suffer from chronic memory loss or experience mild cognitive impairments, in addition to other previously discussed issues associated with aging (Alzheimer's Association, 2017). Among other difficulties, consumers with short-term memory loss may have trouble finding the right words to use when interacting with service employees; they might become disoriented or get lost in unfamiliar settings, become confused when looking for entrances, exits, and restrooms in public spaces, and/or become easily frustrated with impatient service personnel (Wooten et al., 2016). Although purposeful servicescape design and appropriate training for service employees can aid in lessening these negative outcomes, they may not be sufficient to eliminate all barriers that stop consumers from obtaining the full value of a marketplace transaction.

Despite the issues that tend to diminish their marketplace experiences, research suggests that marketing to the growing base of elderly consumers requires an approach that communicates "the triumphs rather than the traumas of maturity" (Swimberghe, Darrat, Beal, & Astakhova, 2018, p. 177). Where brands are framed as promoting vitality and wellness, elderly consumers respond more positively (Swimberghe et al., 2018). Recent findings show that a consumer's awareness of aging may foster anticipatory self-perceived vulnerability, even where a negative consumption experience has not yet occurred (Ford et al., 2016). Therefore, it stands to reason that enhancing self-efficacy and accessibility in service contexts to the extent possible could lead to healthier self-esteem and emotional well-being among the aging.

Presently, in-depth studies exploring consumer vulnerability among the elderly are limited (Ford et al., 2016). Because people age in complex ways, researchers have begun to view aging as a multidimensional process and to address related vulnerabilities in terms of more than just chronological age (Ford et al., 2016; Griffiths & Harmon, 2011). Experts on aging recognize the importance of providing enabling environments, goods, and services to empower older people to experience maximum health and well-being (Madrid International Plan of Action, 2002). Accordingly, researchers and practitioners have ample opportunities to develop creative and meaningful ways to transform services to accommodate the best interests of this burgeoning population of consumers.

Mental impairments

More than six million people in the United States have an intellectual disability that limits their cognitive functioning and skills, including communication, social skills, and self-care skills (Special Olympics, 2018). With an intelligence quotient (IQ) below 75, these consumers are characterized by "significant limitations both in intellectual functioning (reasoning, learning, problem solving) and in adaptive behavior" associated with everyday social and practical situations (American Association of Intellectual and Developmental Disabilities,

2018, p. 1). Accordingly, consumers with intellectual disabilities are widely regarded as vulnerable in the marketplace and other service settings, including health care (Havercamp & Scott, 2015).

Approximately 42.5 million adults in the United States suffer from other mental health conditions, such as depression, anxiety, bipolar disorder, schizophrenia, obsessive/compulsive disorder, and post-traumatic stress disorder (National Alliance on Mental Illness, 2018). Such conditions may affect a consumer's ability to comfortably navigate unfamiliar settings, interact effectively with service personnel and other consumers, or restrain compulsive purchasing behaviors (Edwards et al., 2018; Rosenbaum & Kuntze, 2005). An even greater number of people (estimated to be between 15% to 20% of Americans, see U.S. Department of Health and Human Services, 2018) have a learning disability (see also Learning Disabilities Association of America, 2018). Although shopping is deemed the most regular social activity among consumers with learning disabilities (Emerson & Hatton, 2008), they are particularly vulnerable in the marketplace due to difficulties understanding credit and extended payment options (Learning Disabilities Association of America, 2018), calculating pricing schemes, managing personal finances (Abbott & McConkey, 2006), and comprehending complex verbiage on store signage and other informational materials (Cotterill et al., 2015).

People with intellectual disabilities regularly experience negative reactions from others (e.g., staring and avoidance), which trigger an internal sense that they are unwelcome when they are immersed in marketplace environments like shopping malls, transit systems, and public walkways (Wilton, Schormans, & Marquis, 2018). Consumers with mental impairments often confront negativity from other shoppers and service providers, which results in feelings of frustration and marginalization (Cotterill et al., 2015). Ironically, research shows that, despite an increased propensity among these consumers to also suffer disabling physical conditions, some health care providers are often unwilling or unable to properly serve patients with intellectual disabilities (Benassi, 2011; Lennox, Diggens, & Ugoni, 2000).

Service exclusion

Although the previously discussed biophysical and psychosocial characteristics often result in consumers experiencing decreased value in both physical and virtual marketplaces, it is worth noting that the manner in which services are delivered can cause consumers to experience feelings of exclusion. This may be due to unfairness on the part of service providers or other customers present in a service setting. Furthermore, although service providers or other customers may not be explicit regarding their intentions toward people with disabilities in consumer settings, both employees and customers may employ subtle discriminatory tactics, such as negative glances. In addition, front line employees may use inadvertent missteps to slow the pace of a service delivery (Rosenbaum & Montoya, 2007). All of these actions prevent accommodating all consumers fairly and equitably (Edwards et al., 2018; Kaufman-Scarborough, 1999, 2000). Consider the groundbreaking study by Ayres (1991), which demonstrated that, despite federal law forbidding it, intentional discriminatory actions in services can cause some consumers to be vulnerable. The author investigated auto dealerships, finding that they consistently provided less preferential pricing and service levels to females and African-American consumers compared to white male consumers. In a more recent auditing study, social scientists found similar results when they monitored for unlawful discrimination in employment and other contexts (Cherry & Bendick, 2018).

Not all service quality failures that render some consumers vulnerable to diminished transactional value are intentional or even unlawful. Often, service providers are ill-informed of best practices in serving consumers with varying biophysical or psychosocial characteristics, or their businesses have legitimate barriers to physical access that cannot be mitigated (Edwards et al., 2018). The press frequently exposes service failures involving consumers with disabilities, such as airlines losing or damaging wheelchair equipment, leaving customers stranded, or mishandling the needs of customers with physical limitations in other ways (Burke & Welbes, 2018). This has often led to high-profile and costly litigation against major retailers within the United States (Harrilchak, 2018). Proactive steps taken by service providers can ameliorate marketplace vulnerability: for example, a Chicago-area retailer has installed a commercially available bell-call system that alerts staff in stores when a customer outside needs assistance entering the building (Tan, 2016). The same retailer provides training for all employees, enabling them to better interact with individuals with disabilities.

Exclusion and marginalization may result due to inadequate servicescape design (Staeheli & Mitchell, 2006). Although a service environment may meet the standards of applicable law (including the ADA and its regulations), it still might not serve the needs of some consumers, rendering them vulnerable to receiving less transactional value from the service. Identifying this apparent paradox early in the history of the ADA, Kaufman-Scarborough (1999) deduced that reasonable access for people with disabilities would depend heavily upon service providers interpreting the requirements of the law through the lens of consumer experience. For example, under applicable ADA regulations, many small businesses need only make accessibility improvements that are "readily achievable" (New England ADA Center, 2018); that is, they are easily accomplishable improvements that can be carried out without much difficulty or expense. Consequently, many small businesses may be technically in compliance with the law but practically inaccessible to some consumers with vulnerabilities, such as those with intellectual limitations or obesity.

Service inclusion

According to inclusion advocate Jonathan Stearn (2015, p. 66), consumer "vulnerability cannot simply be seen as consumers' failure to engage with the market when markets are failing to engage with consumers." Indeed, Saatcioglu and Corus (2016, p. 243) observed that "the marketplace is not a very welcoming environment for many consumers who are already in disadvantaged positions." The concept of 'social inclusion,' as used in the social sciences, is broadly concerned with the activities, relationships, and environments that make up the social lives of disabled and otherwise vulnerable people (Simplican, Leader, Kosciulek, & Leahy, 2015). Social inclusion incorporates the ability to benefit from services such as leisure activities, retail consumption, and cultural events (Simplican et al., 2015). With respect to service marketing, researchers (e.g., Baker et al., 2005; Commuri & Ekici, 2008) agree that the situational nature of consumer vulnerability necessitates involvement from service providers and policy makers.

As previously discussed, researchers recently coined the term "service inclusion" (Fisk et al., 2018; Stearn, 2015) to denote services, service providers, and service systems that offer consumers fairness in terms of access, treatment, and opportunities to enter/exit. Saatcioglu and Corus (2016) suggest that all social spaces (not only consumption settings) have the capacity to deliver liberation, empowerment, and social justice to vulnerable groups. This is particularly true when policy makers, businesses, consumers, and communities work collaboratively.

Promoting social justice and consumer well-being through welcoming and accessible servicescapes and front line employees, not only provides life-changing opportunities for consumers with vulnerabilities, but its residual effects also stand to financially benefit service organizations. A case can now be made that providing good service to vulnerable consumers not only makes business sense, but also helps to fulfill corporate social responsibility goals which serve a broader audience (Bridges, 2018). People with disabilities represent more than $200 billion in discretionary spending, constituting a substantial market (Brault, 2012). With 35% of U.S. households reportedly having at least one member with a disability (Nielsen, 2016), it is the position of this chapter that service-based organizations must hasten to develop and adopt inclusive business practices and design standards. Notably, market research studies show that consumers with disabilities often become repeat customers of businesses with which they can interact comfortably (U.S. Department of Justice, 2011). In fact, research by a travel industry advocacy group found that although American adults with disabilities spent $17.3 billion annually on their own travel (Open Doors, 2015), spending would be higher if accessible facilities and inclusive services were widely available.

Expanding understanding of vulnerable consumers

The negative effects of consumer marginalization and exclusion are well documented (Adkin & Ozanne, 2005; Jafari et al., 2013). When disabled or otherwise vulnerable adults are excluded or marginalized within service settings, their sense of self and social value erodes (Elms & Tinson, 2012). Yet, research also reveals the positive effects of service inclusion for vulnerable consumers (Lombe & Sherraden, 2008). For example, the act of shopping offers opportunities for people with intellectual disabilities to interact with those who are not disabled, providing valuable social interaction and entertainment (Wiesel & Bigby, 2016).

Compared to some other consumer segments (e.g., those identified by gender, race, or income), relatively little is known about how consumers with physical disabilities, mental impairments, and elderliness can realize the full value potential that is inherent within a service exchange. There is little doubt that where access to a physical service environment is limited, consumers with vulnerabilities may not experience the full value of the transaction at hand. Notably, Baker et al. (2007) found that consumers with disabilities deemed a service environment to be welcoming or unwelcoming based primarily on the treatment that they received from service personnel, rather than solely from factors in the physical setting. Even where service organizations provide appropriate access to public accommodations, some consumers with vulnerabilities may remain limited by other factors, such as discrimination and inferior service from front line employees (Rosenbaum & Montoya, 2007). Simplican et al. (2015) acknowledged that more research is needed to understand how specific organizations and settings either facilitate or constrain inclusion for people with disabilities.

Service researchers have only begun to consider frameworks and measurements needed to improve the well-being of individuals having characteristics that leave them vulnerable in the marketplace and society in general. Because existing models in service research (e.g., satisfaction/ loyalty, service quality, service failure and recovery, servicescapes, relationship marketing; see Zeithaml et al., 2013) were not developed with inclusiveness as an objective, key foundational questions must be addressed for meaningful advancement of the TSR research paradigm. In particular, transformative service researchers are encouraged to address the following questions:

- What, if any, current research frameworks from service industries are generalizable to groups of consumers with vulnerabilities, such as those with physical disabilities, mental impairments, aging, and other at-risk people?
- How might existing frameworks be adapted for investigation into the needs of these groups?
- How can 'uplifting change' and 'improvements in well-being' be reliably measured and analyzed?
- Are self-reported well-being indicators and defined quality of life indicators equally reliable (see Huppert & So, 2013 for mental indicators; Diener et al., 2010 for social well-being scales; Yao, Zheng, & Fan, 2015 for quality of life indicators)?
- Are different models needed to measure and analyze positive outcomes for individuals, groups, and society at large?
- Would applicable measurements differ based on categories of vulnerabilities?
- What differences exist across various service contexts (e.g., health care, retailing, financial services, and government services)?
- How might technology and the internet provide vulnerable consumers fuller access to the marketplace and its services?
- How can community well-being be enhanced via transformative design efforts (e.g., introduction of greenery in urban areas, public spaces, governmental buildings, development of urban farms, and so forth)?
- How can transformative services impact communities of traditionally vulnerable consumers? For example, to what extent can "dementia villages" enhance their residents' well-being (Chrysikou, Tziraki, & Buhalis, 2018). What type of housing and retirement services will lesbian, gay, bisexual, and transgender seniors require (Sullivan, 2014)?

Outside of the marketing discipline, researchers in the sport, entertainment, and leisure management disciplines are also realizing apparent shortcomings in investigations of how their services influence participant (e.g., fan, guest, or member) well-being. For example, a study by Doyle, Filo, Lock, Funk, and McDonald (2016) recently used positive psychological techniques to study the benefits of consumer engagement and social interactions in the context of Australian football. In a similar vein, researchers within the sport management domain are beginning to investigate how their services (i.e., spectatorship at sporting events) influence fan welfare in terms of promoting subjective well-being, life satisfaction, emotional support, and team identification (Inoue, Sato, Filo, Du, & Funk, 2017). These studies show promise as a developing body of literature, identified here as transformative sport service research (TSSR), which demonstrates that consuming sport as either a participant or spectator has both physical and social benefits, especially if the experience is inclusive. This is particularly salient when considering the needs of people with myriad vulnerabilities, including consumers with disabilities and the aging population, and their right to partake in sports, entertainment, and leisure services in a manner that is offered to all consumers (Yantzi, Young, & Mckeever, 2010).

Table 21.1 provides a framework to assist future researchers with understanding the vulnerable groups that are under-researched in the service domain; it shows foundational service theories for frameworks that can be explored, as well as key research questions that promote service inclusion (see Fisk et al., 2018). Although Table 21.1 may not include all vulnerable consumer groups that researchers could explore, by addressing the needs of any of these groups, service researchers will contribute to the betterment of individual lives and societal well-being.

Table 21.1 Moving forward to service inclusion

Vulnerable consumer group(s)	Service theory or framework to update	Key questions to explore:
Blind/visually impaired	Customer journey mapping	Enable opportunities:
Deafness/hard of hearing	Relationship marketing	• Design to eliminate physical and social barriers
Developmental disabilities	Satisfaction/loyalty	
Mental illness/mental health issues	Service failure and recovery	• How to train employees
Older-aged and the elderly	Service perceptions/ expectations	Offering choices:
		• Use of technology in the service process
Physical disabilities	Service quality	
Recovery issues	Servuction	Relieve suffering:
Spinal cord/head injuries	Value co-creation/co-destruction	• Identify service design elements that are pain points
		• –Service blueprinting
		Foster happiness:
		• Identify service design elements that are key to helping consumer obtain their consumption goals

Exploring TSR from other perspectives

Social support

In addition to engaging in TSR investigations by exploring previously under-researched consumer groups, service researchers may also wish to focus on investigations that consider well-being, or other related health outcomes, as dependent variables. For example, many contemporary TSR studies have drawn upon environmental psychology, psychology (Bloom, 1990; Rosenbaum, 2006), sociology (Oldenburg, 1999; Oldenburg & Brissett, 1982), public health (Frumkin, 2003), consumer research (Debenedetti, Oppewal, & Arsel, 2014), and cultural geography (Relph, 1976; Seamon, 2015) to explore the evocative and transformative health role that places (both physical and virtual) can assume in consumers' lives and personal experiences (Rosenbaum, Kelleher, Friman, Kristensson, & Scherer, 2017c; Sherry, 2000).

On the one hand, some commercial and nonprofit physical and virtual settings exist to help consumers satisfy their utilitarian needs; on the other hand, some exist to help consumers satisfy needs beyond goods consumption, such as needs for human support, often in the form of emotional support, companionship, or instrumental support (e.g., assistance with transportation; Rosenbaum, 2006). Indeed, the Mayo Clinic (2018) suggests that the social support that people obtain from close friends, family, and peers helps them battle the negative symptoms associated with chronic illness, stress, isolation, and/or loneliness. Additionally, service researchers have shown that people suffering from stigmatizing diseases (such as hepatitis B) can also receive life-enhancing social support from a virtual community that helps them obtain a sense of community and belonging (Yao et al., 2015).

It is worth noting here that social support is most effective in helping people confront the potentially pathogenic effects of stressful events when they have a perceived support deficit

(Cohen & Wills, 1985). That is, if a person is integrated into a social supportive network, and does not perceive having any supportive deficits, then he or she may respond negatively to socially supportive overtures from others, such as service providers, who want to form close relationships with clients (Surprenant & Solomon, 1987). Indeed, a person's psychological stress may even increase if a different type of support is provided than what the recipient wishes to receive (Thoits, 1986). For instance, a newly diagnosed cancer patient who desires emotional support from an oncologist and instead receives a plethora of informational support (e.g., brochures) may leave the doctor's office confused and stressed. Indeed, according to the matching hypothesis (Cohen & Wills, 1985), social support is most effective to a person when he or she can counterbalance a perceived social support deficit (e.g., companionship) by obtaining the resource from another social entity (see Rosenbaum, 2006).

Given that people may obtain cathartic social support resources (for instrumental, emotional, and companionship purposes) in commercial establishments (e.g., cafés, barbershops; Oldenburg, 1999) and nonprofit service settings (e.g., cancer resource centers; Glover, 2008, 2018), it is not surprising that researchers have recently observed consumer ability to obtain social support from profound person–place bonds, or place attachments (Rosenbaum et al., 2017b). Place attachment is conceptualized as "an emotional bond between an individual (or a community) and a specific location. This bond is based on an accumulation of physical, social, historical and cultural meanings that become associated with the place through time and experience" (Debenedetti et al., 2014, p. 905); it may also be based upon the transformative role that places, physical or virtual, often assume in promoting consumer well-being.

Service researchers are encouraged to look beyond the physical characteristics of a built environment (Bitner, 1992) and its geographical coordinates to fully understand the role that physical or virtual consumption settings often assume in promoting well-being. For example, Relph (1976) encourages researchers to explore how and why people sense deep connections to a place, like feelings of being at home—feelings that Relph (1976, p. 55) conceptualizes as "existential insideness." Relph (1976, p. 51) considers the opposite of existential insideness as "existential outsideness," or feelings of strangeness and alienation. Interestingly, although service researchers have explored consumer responses that result in approach or avoidance, understanding concepts such as place insideness and outsideness, as they apply to commercial and nonprofit service settings, may provide researchers with novel insights into person–place relationships. Perhaps it is now understandable why Sherry (2000) observes that a consumer's ability to cultivate a sense of place has implications for his or her life that are more profound than those associated with the improved design and delivery of servicescapes.

Attention restoration theory

The discussion thus far suggests that places (e.g., coffeehouses, taverns, or cancer resource centers) provide opportunities for consumers to maintain commercially based friendships that promote human well-being via the exchange of socially supportive resources (Cowen, 1982; Rosenbaum, 2006). However, research shows that there are other places that promote human well-being that is not necessarily due to the presence of people but, rather, to the presence of natural elements, such as greenery and water displays (Brengman, Willems, & Joye, 2012; Joye, Willems, Brengman, & Wolf, 2010; Rosenbaum, Ramírez, & Matos, 2018b; Tifferet & Vilnai-Yavetz, 2017).

Over a century ago, James (1892; see also Kaplan, 2001) observed that people use two types of attention when they respond to environmental stimuli: involuntary or voluntary.

James speculated that involuntary attention is reflexive, enables people to be in a passive state, and requires little effort or will to remain in an attentive state. In contrast, voluntary attention enables people to focus on unpleasant but nonetheless important stimuli, such as concentrating on work despite being interrupted, or caring for a sick loved one. Voluntary attention requires use of an internal mechanism and corresponding resources that may become depleted over time, resulting in directed attention fatigue (Kaplan, 1995). Although the symptoms associated with directed attention fatigue can be extreme, Attention Restoration Theory (ART) posits that people possess an innate means to recover from it and to regain their ability to focus on unpleasant stimuli in the future—by spending time in natural settings, including green areas, beaches, parks, and so forth. In other words, ART postulates that natural settings are archetypical restorative environments. The reason is, that when people are immersed in restorative environments such as natural areas, they use involuntary attention, thus helping them heal from the fatigue caused by demands requiring voluntary or directed attention (Berman, Jonides, & Kaplan, 2008; Kaplan & Kaplan, 1989).

Voluntary attention is believed to be integral to mental health, enabling a person to engage in self-regulation (i.e., self-control) and to successfully execute functioning tasks, such as the ability to undertake work- and/or school-related activities (Kaplan & Berman, 2010). Interestingly, ART suggests that a person's ability to engage in voluntary attention requires the use of an internal mechanism that becomes fatigued over time leading to 'mental exhaustion,' or 'burnout'; symptoms including irritability, depression, stress, inability to concentrate, and even aggression (Kaplan, 2001).

According to ART, environments with certain features have restorative qualities that may help people recover from directed attention fatigue. Environmental psychologists have shown that restorative environments should have four characteristics: fascination, a sense of being away, extent, and compatibility (Felsten, 2009; Ivarsson & Hagerhall, 2008; Kaplan, 1995; Pasini, Berto, Brondino, Hall, & Ortner, 2014; Shu & Ma, 2018). *Fascination* refers to environmental stimuli that have engaging qualities and do not require mental effort to absorb. A *sense of being away* refers to people's feelings that they are 'in another place' from their everyday locale, whether actual or imaginary. *Extent* offers people the feeling of being in a place large enough that no boundaries are evident. Last, *compatibility* refers to how well the content of a specific environment supports the needs and inclinations of the user.

Although environmental psychologists have focused on exploring the restorative potential of natural settings on human well-being, over a quarter-century ago Kaplan (1995) speculated that consumption settings requiring the involuntary attention of their users, such as shopping centers, museums, or zoos, would be idyllic places in which people could remedy symptoms associated with mental fatigue. In a similar vein, service researchers have begun to show the restorative potential of enclosed shopping malls and open-air lifestyle centers that incorporate greenery into their shopping areas (Purani & Kumar, 2018; Rosenbaum, Otalora, & Ramírez, 2016; Rosenbaum, Ramírez, & Camino, 2018a). Indeed, research (Rosenbaum et al., 2011b; Rosenbaum & Wong, 2015) suggests that any built environment, or servicescape, that contains these four key characteristics (fascination, being away, extent, and compatibility) is likely to ameliorate symptoms associated with mental fatigue and its consequential symptoms.

Conclusion

The purpose of this chapter was to help readers understand the TSR paradigm with the hope that future researchers will continue to develop it. Although the authors have put forth several avenues of pioneering research for further exploration, any future research in the TSR movement that aims to improve the human condition is encouraged. Services, service settings, and service processes each have the potential to profoundly transform the human experience; indeed, for the betterment or to the detriment of individuals, communities, and even the world.

References

Abbott, S., & McConkey, R. (2006). The barriers to social inclusion as perceived by people with intellectual disabilities. *Journal of Intellectual Disabilities, 10*(3), 275–287.

Adkin, N.R., & Ozanne, J.L. (2005). The low literate consumer. *Journal of Consumer Research, 32*(1), 93–105.

Alzheimer's Association. (2017). Alzheimer's disease facts and figures. Retrieved from www.alz.org/documents_custom/2017-facts-and-figures.pdf.

American Association of Intellectual and Developmental Disabilities. (2018). Definition of intellectual disability. Retrieved from http://aaidd.org/intellectual-disability/definition.

Americans with Disabilities Act of 1990, Pub. L. No. 101–336, 104 Stat. 328. (1990).

Anderson, L., Ostrom, A.L., Corus, C., Fisk, R.P., Gallan, A.S., Giraldo, M., ... Williams, J.D. (2013). Transformative service research: An agenda for the future. *Journal of Business Research, 66*(8), 1203–1210.

Ayres, I. (1991). Fair driving: Gender and race discrimination in retail car negotiations. *Harvard Law Review, 104*(4), 817–872.

Baker, S.M. (2006). Consumer normalcy: Understanding the value of shopping through narratives of consumers with visual impairments. *Journal of Retailing, 82*(1), 37–50.

Baker, S.M., Gentry, J.W., & Rittenburg, T.L. (2005). Building understanding of the domain of consumer vulnerability. *Journal of Macromarketing, 25*(2), 128–139.

Baker, S.M., Hunt, D.M., & Rittenburg, T.L. (2007). Consumer vulnerability as a shared experience: Tornado recovery process in Wright, Wyoming. *Journal of Public Policy & Marketing, 26*(1), 6–19.

Baker, S.M., & Kaufman-Scarborough, C. (2001). Marketing and public accommodation: A retrospective on Title III of the Americans with Disabilities Act. *Journal of Public Policy & Marketing, 20*(2), 297–304.

Benassi, P. (2011). The intellectually disabled patient: Are they forgotten in medical training? *McMaster University Medical Journal, 8*, 68–70.

Berg, L. (2015). Consumer vulnerability: Are older people more vulnerable as consumers than others? *International Journal of Consumer Studies, 39*(4), 284–293.

Berman, M.G., Jonides, J., & Kaplan, S. (2008). The cognitive benefits of interacting with nature. *Psychological Science, 19*(12), 1207–1212.

Bialik, K. (2017). 7 facts about Americans with disabilities. *Pew Research Center.* Retrieved from www.pewresearch.org/fact-tank/2017/07/27/7-facts-about-americans-with-disabilities/.

Bitner, M.J. (1992). Servicescapes: The impact of physical surroundings on customers and employees. *Journal of Marketing, 56*(2), 57–71.

Blocker, C.P., & Barrios, A. (2015). The transformative value of a service experience. *Journal of Service Research, 18*(3), 265–283.

Bloom, J.R. (1990). The relationship of social support and health. *Social Science & Medicine, 30*(5), 635–637.

Brault, M. (2012). Americans with disabilities: 2010. *U.S. Census Bureau.* Retrieved from www2.census.gov/library/publications/2012/demo/p70-131.pdf.

Brengman, M., Willems, K., & Joye, Y. (2012). The impact of in-store greenery on customers. *Psychology & Marketing, 29*(11), 807–821.

Brenkert, G. (1998). Marketing and the vulnerable. *Business Ethics Quarterly, Ruffin Series, 1*, 7–20.

Bridges, E. (2018). Executive ethical decisions initiating organizational culture and values. *Journal of Service Theory and Practice, 28*(5), 576–608.

Browne, M.N., Clapp, K.B., Kubasek, N.K., & Biksacky, L. (2015). Protecting consumers from themselves: Consumer law and the vulnerable consumer. *Drake Law Review, 63*(1), 157–191.

Burke, P., & Welbes, J. (2018). Minneapolis–St. Paul International Airport: Instilling a culture of accessibility for people with disabilities that goes above and beyond requirements. *Journal of Airport Management, 12*(2), 198–206.

Center for Hearing and Communication. (2018). Statistics and facts about hearing loss. Retrieved from http://chchearing.org/facts-about-hearing-loss/.

Cherry, F., & Bendick, M. (2018). Making it count: Discrimination auditing and the activist scholar tradition. In S. Gaddis (Ed.), *Audit studies: Behind the scenes with theory, method, and nuance.* Methods Series. (pp. 45–62). New York: Springer.

Chrysikou, E., Tziraki, C., & Buhalis, D. (2018). Architectural hybrids for living across the lifespan: Lessons from dementia. *The Service Industries Journal, 38*(1/2), 4–26.

Cirrincione v. Taco Bell Corp. (2016), No. 33-0001 (D.N.J., filed July 13).

Cohen, S., & Wills, T.A. (1985). Stress, social support, and the buffering hypothesis. *Psychological Bulletin, 98*(2), 310–357.

Commuri, S., & Ekici, E. (2008). An enlargement of the notion of consumer vulnerability. *Journal of Macromarketing, 28*(2), 183–186.

Cotterill, D., Wolverson, C., Bell, A., Boothe, M., Bradshaw, A., Norat, S., ... Thompson, R. (2015). Shopping experiences of people with learning disabilities. *Learning Disability Practice, 18*(8), 16–20.

Cowen, E. (1982). Help is where you find it: Four informal helping groups. *American Psychologist, 37*(4), 385–395.

Cox, H. (2016). *Later life: The realities of aging*, 6th ed. New York: Routledge.

Debenedetti, A., Oppewal, H., & Arsel, Z. (2014). Place attachment in commercial settings: A gift economy perspective. *Journal of Consumer Research, 40*(5), 904–923.

Diener, E., Wirtz, D., Tov, W., Kim-Prieto, C., Choi, D.W., Oishi, S., & Biswas-Diener, R. (2010). New well-being measures: Short scales to assess flourishing and positive and negative feelings. *Social Indicators Research, 97*(2), 143–156.

Doyle, J.P., Filo, K., Lock, D., Funk, D.C., & McDonald, H. (2016). Exploring PERMA in spectator sport: Applying positive psychology to examine the individual-level benefits of sport consumption. *Sport Management Review, 19*(5), 506–519.

Dunnett, S., Hamilton, K., & Piacentini, M. (2016). Consumer vulnerability: Introduction to the special issue, *Journal of Marketing Management, 32*(3/4), 207–210.

Edwards, K., Rosenbaum, M., Brosdahl, D., & Hughes, P. (2018). Designing retail spaces for inclusion. *Journal of Retailing and Consumer Services, 44*, 182–190.

Elms, J., & Tinson, J. (2012). Consumer vulnerability and the transformative potential of internet shopping: An exploratory case study. *Journal of Marketing Management, 28*(11/12), 1354–1376.

Emerson, E., & Hatton, C. (2008). Self-reported well-being of women and men with intellectual disabilities in England. *American Journal on Mental Retardation, 113*(2), 143–155.

Felsten, G. (2009). Where to take a study break on the college campus: An attention restoration theory perspective. *Journal of Environmental Psychology, 29*(1), 160–167.

Fisk, R.P. (2009). A customer liberation manifesto. *Service Science, 1*(3), 139–141.

Fisk, R.P., Anderson, L., Bowen, D.E., Gruber, T., Ostrom, A., Patrício, L., Reynoso, J., & Sebastiani, R. (2016). Billions of impoverished people deserve to be better served: A call to action for the service research community. *Journal of Service Management, 27*(16), 43–55.

Fisk, R.P., Dean, A., Alkire, L., Joubert, A., Previte, J., Robertson, N., & Rosenbaum, M.S. (2018). Design for service inclusion: Creating inclusive service systems by 2050. *Journal of Service Management, 29*(5), 834–858.

Ford, N., Trott, P., & Simms, C. (2016). Exploring the impact of packaging interactions on quality of life among older consumers. *Journal of Marketing Management, 32*(3/4), 275–312.

Frumkin, H. (2003). Healthy places: Exploring the evidence. *American Journal of Public Health, 93*(9), 1451–1456.

Glover, T.D. (2008). A third place in the everyday lives of people living with cancer: Functions of Gilda's Club of Greater Toronto. *Health & Place, 15*(1), 97–106.

Glover, T.D. (2018). All the lonely people: Social isolation and the promise and pitfalls of leisure. *Leisure Sciences, 40*(1/2), 25–35.

Griffiths, M.A., & Harmon, T.R. (2011). Aging consumer vulnerabilities influencing factors of acquiescence to informed consent. *Journal of Consumer Affairs, 45*(3), 445–466.

Harrilchak, M. (2018). ADA website lawsuits a growing problem for retailers. Retrieved from https://nrf.com/blog/ada-website-lawsuits-growing-problem-retailers.

Havercamp, S.M., & Scott, H.M. (2015). National health surveillance of adults with disabilities, adults with intellectual and developmental disabilities, and adults with no disabilities. *Disability and Health Journal, 8*(2), 165–172.

Hoffman, D.K., & Bateson, J.E.G. (2017). *Services marketing: Concepts, strategies, & cases*. Boston, MA: Cengage.

Hootman, J.M., Helmick, C.G., & Brady, T.J. (2012). A public health approach to addressing arthritis in older adults: The most common cause of disability. *American Journal of Public Health, 102*(3), 426–433.

Hughes, P., & Baskin, M. (2014). People with disabilities: Community engagement report. Retrieved from www.inclusionsolutions.com/wp-content/uploads/2016/10/IS-Connect-RochesterMN-2014-FINAL.pdf.

Huppert, F.A., & So, T.T. (2013). Flourishing across Europe: Application of a new conceptual framework for defining well-being. *Social Indicators Research, 110*(3), 837–861.

Inclusion Solutions. (2002). *Pump access survey: The state of refueling assistance for drivers with disabilities.* Chicago, IL: Inclusion Solutions.

Inclusion Solutions. (2004). *The state of drive-thru dining access and assistance for customers who are deaf or hard of hearing.* Chicago, IL: Inclusion Solutions.

Inoue, Y., Sato, M., Filo, K., Du, J., & Funk, D.C. (2017). Sport spectatorship and life satisfaction: A multicountry investigation. *Journal of Sport Management, 31*(4), 419–432.

Ivarsson, T.C., & Hagerhall, C.M. (2008). The perceived restorativeness of gardens: Assessing the restorativeness of a mixed built and natural scene type. *Urban Forestry & Urban Greening, 7*(2), 107–118.

Jafari, A., Dunnett, S., Hamilton, K., & Downey, H. (2013). Exploring research vulnerability: Contexts, complications, and conceptualization. *Journal of Marketing Management, 29*(9/10), 1182–1200.

James, W. (1892). *Psychology: The briefer course*. New York: Holt.

Joye, Y., Willems, K., Brengman, M., & Wolf, K. (2010). The effects of urban greenery on consumer experience: Reviewing the evidence from a restorative perspective. *Urban Forestry & Urban Greening, 9*(1), 57–64.

Kaplan, R., & Kaplan, S. (1989). *The experience of nature: A psychological perspective*. New York: Cambridge University Press.

Kaplan, S. (1995). The restorative benefits of nature: Toward an integrative framework. *Journal of Environmental Psychology, 15*(3), 169–182.

Kaplan, S. (2001). Mediation, restoration, and the management of mental fatigue. *Environment and Behavior, 33*(4), 480–506.

Kaplan, S., & Berman, M.G. (2010). Directed attention as a common resource for executive functioning and self-regulation. *Perspectives on Psychological Science, 5*(1), 143–157.

Kaufman-Scarborough, C. (1999). Reasonable access for mobility-disabled persons is more than widening the door. *Journal of Retailing, 75*(4), 479–508.

Kaufman-Scarborough, C. (2000). Seeing through the eyes of the color-deficient shopper: Consumer issues for public policy. *Journal of Consumer Policy, 23*(4), 461–492.

Keller, K., & Engelhardt, M. (2013). Strength and muscle mass loss with aging process: Age and strength loss. *Muscles, Ligaments and Tendons Journal, 3*(4), 346–350.

Kulyukin, V.A., & Kutiyanawala, A. (2010). Accessible shopping systems for blind and visually impaired individuals: Design requirements and the state of the art. *The Open Rehabilitation Journal, 3*(1), 158–168.

Lahmann, S. (2010). Disability 101: Accessibility in grocery stores. Retrieved from www.summitdaily.com/news/disability-101-accessibility-in-grocery-stores/.

Learning Disabilities Association of America. (2018). New to LD. Retrieved from https://ldaamerica.org/.

Lennox, G., Diggens, J., & Ugoni, N. (2000). Health care for people with an intellectual disability: General practitioners' attitudes, and provision of care. *Journal of Intellectual Developmental Disability, 25*(2), 127–133.

Lombe, M., & Sherraden, M. (2008). Inclusion in the policy process: An agenda for participation of the marginalized. *Journal of Policy Practice, 7*(2/3), 199–213.

Madrid International Plan of Action. (2002). Political Declaration and Madrid International Plan of Action on Ageing. Retrieved from www.un.org/en/events/pastevents/pdfs/Madrid_plan.pdf.

Mayo Clinic. (2018). Social support: Tap this tool to beat stress. Retrieved from www.mayoclinic.org/healthy-lifestyle/stress-management/in-depth/social-support/art-20044445.

Mende, M., & van Doorn, J. (2015). Coproduction of transformative services as a pathway to improved consumer well-being findings from a longitudinal study on financial counseling. *Journal of Service Research, 18*(3), 351–368.

Mick, D.G. (2006). Presidential address: Meaning and mattering through transformative consumer research. In C. Pechmann, & L. Price (Eds.), *Advances in consumer research* (Vol. 33, pp. 1–4). Duluth, MN: Association for Consumer Research.

Minton, E.A., Cabano, F., Gardner, M., Mathras, D., Elliot, E., & Mandel, N. (2017). LGBTQ and religious identity conflict in service settings. *Journal of Services Marketing, 31*(4/5), 351–361

National Alliance on Mental Illness. (2018). Mental health by the numbers. Retrieved from www.nami. org/learn-more/mental-health-by-the-numbers.

National Health Council. (2014). About chronic diseases. Retrieved from www.nationalhealthcouncil. org/sites/default/files/NHC_Files/Pdf_Files/AboutChronicDisease.pdf.

New England ADA Center. (2018). What is program accessibility? Retrieved from www.adachecklist. org/about.html.

Nielsen. (2016). Reaching prevalent, diverse consumers with disabilities. Retrieved from www.nielsen. com/us/en/insights/reports/2016/reaching-prevalent-diverse-consumers-with-disabilities.html.

NPD Group. (2012). Drive-thru windows still put the fast in fast food restaurants. Retrieved from www. npd.com/wps/portal/npd/us/news/press-releases/pr_120530a/.

Oldenburg, R. (1999). *The great good place: Cafés, coffee shops, bookstores, bars, hair salons, and other hangouts at the heart of community.* Philadelphia, PA: Perseus Books.

Oldenburg, R., & Brissett, D. (1982). The third place. *Qualitative Sociology, 5*(4), 265–284.

Open Doors Organization. (2015). 2015 market study. Retrieved from http://opendoorsnfp.org/market-studies/2015-market-study/.

Ostrom, A.L., Bitner, M.J., Brown, S.W., Burkhard, K.A., Goul, M., Smith-Daniels, V., … Rabino-vich, E. (2010). Moving forward and making a difference: Research priorities for the science of service. *Journal of Service Research, 13*(1), 4–36.

Ostrom, A.L., Parasuraman, A., Bowen, D.E., Patrício, L., Voss, C.A., & Lemon, K. (2015). Service research priorities in a rapidly changing context. *Journal of Service Research, 18*(2), 127–159.

Pasini, M., Berto, R., Brondino, M., Hall, R., & Ortner, C. (2014). How to measure the restorative quality of environments: The PRS-11. *Procedia: Social and Behavioral Sciences, 159*, 293–297.

Pechmann, C., Moore, E.S., Andreasen, A.R., Connell, P.M., Freeman, D., Gardner, M.P., & Soster, R. L. (2011). Navigating the central tensions in research on at-risk consumers: Challenges and opportunities. *Journal of Public Policy & Marketing, 30*(1), 23–30.

Purani, K., & Kumar, D.S. (2018). Exploring restorative potential of biophilic servicescapes. *Journal of Services Marketing, 32*(4), 414–429.

Rahman, A., & Björk, P. (2016). Transformative service: Leveraging future progresses through an inclusive approach, *Proceedings of the 14th International Research Conference in Service Management*, La Londe les Maures, France.

Relph, E. (1976). *Place and placelessness.* London: Pion.

Rosenbaum, M.S. (2006). Exploring the social supportive role of third places in consumers' lives. *Journal of Service Research, 9*(1), 59–72.

Rosenbaum, M.S., Baniya, R., & Seger-Guttmann, T. (2017b). Customer responses towards disabled frontline employees. *International Journal of Retail & Distribution Management, 45*(4), 385–403.

Rosenbaum, M.S., Corus, C., Ostrom, A.L., Anderson, L., Fisk, R.P., Gallan, A.S., … Williams, J.D. (2011a). Conceptualisation and aspirations of transformative service research. *Journal of Research for Consumers, 19*, 1–6.

Rosenbaum, M.S., Kelleher, C., Friman, M., Kristensson, P., & Scherer, A. (2017c). Re-placing place in marketing: A resource-exchange place perspective. *Journal of Business Research, 79*(October), 281–289.

Rosenbaum, M.S., & Kuntze, R. (2005). Looking good at the retailer's expense: Investigating unethical retail disposition behavior among compulsive shoppers. *Journal of Retailing and Consumer Services, 12*(3), 217–225.

Rosenbaum, M.S., & Montoya, D. (2007). Am I welcome here? Exploring how ethnic consumers assess their place identity. *Journal of Business Research, 60*(3), 206–214.

Rosenbaum, M.S., Otalora, M.L., & Ramírez, G.C. (2016). The restorative potential of shopping malls. *Journal of Retailing and Consumer Services, 31*, 157–165.

Rosenbaum, M.S., Ramírez, G.C., & Camino, J.R. (2018a). A dose of nature and shopping: The restorative potential of biophilic lifestyle center designs. *Journal of Retailing and Consumer Services, 38*, 66–73.

Rosenbaum, M.S., Ramírez, G.C., & Matos, N. (2018b). A neuroscientific perspective of consumer responses to retail greenery. *The Service Industries Journal.* Retrieved from www.tandfonline.com/doi/abs/10.1080/02642069.2018.1487406.

Rosenbaum, M.S., Seger-Guttmann, T., & Giraldo, M. (2017a). Commentary: Vulnerable consumers in service settings. *Journal of Services Marketing*, *31*(4/5), 309–312.

Rosenbaum, M.S., Sweeney, J., & Smallwood, J. (2011b). Restorative cancer resource center servicescapes. *Managing Service Quality: An International Journal*, *21*(6), 599–616.

Rosenbaum, M.S., & Wong, I.A. (2015). When gambling is healthy: The restorative potential of casinos. *Journal of Services Marketing*, *29*(6/7), 622–633

Saatcioglu, B., & Corus, C. (2016). Exploring spatial vulnerability: Inequality and agency formulations in social space, *Journal of Marketing Management*, *32*(3/4), 230–251.

Sanchez-Barrios, L.J., Giraldo, M., Khalik, M., & Manjarres, R. (2015). Services for the underserved: Unintended well-being. *The Service Industries Journal*, *35*(15/16), 883–897.

Seamon, D. (2015). Understanding place holistically: Cities, synergistic relationality, and space syntax. *Journal of Space Syntax*, *6*(1), 19–33.

Sherry, J.F., Jr. (2000). Place, technology, and representation. *Journal of Consumer Research*, *27*(2), 273–278.

Shi, H.Y., Jing, F.J., Yang, Y., & Nguyen, B. (2017). The concept of consumer vulnerability: Scale development and validation. *International Journal of Consumer Studies*, *41*(6), 769–777.

Shu, S., & Ma, H. (2018). The restorative environmental sounds perceived by children. *Journal of Environmental Psychology*, *60*, 72–80.

Shultz, C.J., & Holbrook, M.B. (2009). The paradoxical relationships between marketing and vulnerability. *Journal of Public Policy & Marketing*, *28*(1), 124–127.

Simplican, S., Leader, G., Kosciulek, J., & Leahy, M. (2015). Defining social inclusion of people with intellectual and developmental disabilities: An ecological model of social networks and community participation. *Research in Developmental Disabilities*, *38*, 18–29.

Smithers, R. (2014). Disabled shoppers deterred by difficult high street experience. *The Guardian*. Retrieved from www.theguardian.com/money/2014/jan/14/disabled-shoppers-deterred-high-street-shop-online.

Special Olympics. (2018). What is intellectual disability? Retrieved from www.specialolympics.org/Sections/Who_We_Are/What_Is_Intellectual_Disability.aspx.

Staeheli, L., & Mitchell, D. (2006). USA's destiny? Regulating space and creating community in American shopping malls. *Urban Studies*, *43*(5/6), 977–992.

Stearn, J. (2015). Consumer vulnerability is market failure. In K. Hamilton, S. Dunnett, & M. Piacentini (Eds.), *Consumer vulnerability: Conditions, contexts and characteristics* (pp. 66–76). London: Routledge.

Sullivan, K.M. (2014). Acceptance in the domestic environment: The experience of senior housing for lesbian, gay, bisexual, and transgender seniors. *Journal of Gerontological Social Work*, *57*(2–4), 235–250.

Surprenant, C.F., & Solomon, M.R. (1987). Predictability and personalization in the service encounter. *Journal of Marketing*, *51*(2), 86–96.

Swimberghe, K., Darrat, M.A., Beal, B.D., & Astakhova, M. (2018). Examining a psychological sense of brand community in elderly consumers. *Journal of Business Research*, *82*(January), 172–178.

Tan, S.W. (2016). Freshii welcomes all customers with open doors. *Medill Reports Chicago*. Retrieved from http://news.medill.northwestern.edu/chicago/freshii-welcomes-all-customers-with-open-doors/.

Thoits, P.A. (1986). Social support as coping assistance. *Journal of Consulting and Clinical Psychology*, *54*(4), 416–423

Tifferet, S., & Vilnai-Yavetz, I. (2017). Phytophilia and service atmospherics: The effect of indoor plants on consumers. *Environment and Behavior*, *49*(7), 814–844.

United Nations. (2017). World population prospects: 2017 revision. Retrieved from https://esa.un.org/unpd/wpp/Publications/Files/WPP2017_KeyFindings.pdf.

United States Department of Health and Human Services. (2018). How many people are affected/at risk for learning disabilities? Retrieved from www.nichd.nih.gov/health/topics/learning/conditioninfo/risk.

United States Department of Justice. (2011). ADA update: A primer for small business. Retrieved from www.ada.gov/regs2010/smallbusiness/smallbusprimer2010.htm.

United States Department of Labor. (2017). Persons with a disability: Labor force characteristics summary. Retrieved from www.bls.gov/news.release/disabl.nr0.htm.

Wiesel, I., & Bigby, C. (2016). Mainstream, inclusionary, and convivial places: Locating encounters between people with and without intellectual disabilities. *Geographical Review*, *106*(2), 201–214

Wilton, R., Schormans, A.F., & Marquis, N. (2018). Shopping, social inclusion and the urban geographies of people with intellectual disability. *Social & Cultural Geography*, *19*(2), 230–252.

Wooten, J., Chandaria, K., Graty, C., Newby, C., Harkin, S., & Gascoigne, A. (2016). Becoming a dementia-friendly retailer: A practical guide. *Alzheimer's Society*. Retrieved from www.alzheimers.org.uk/sites/default/files/migrate/downloads/dementia_friendly_retail_guide.pdf.

Yantzi, N.M., Young, N.L., & Mckeever, P. (2010). The suitability of school playgrounds for physically disabled children. *Children's Geographies*, *8*(1), 65–78.

Yao, T., Zheng, Q., & Fan, X. (2015). The impact of online social support on patients' quality of life and the moderating role of social exclusion. *Journal of Service Research*, *18*(3), 369–383.

Zayer, L.T., Otnes, C.C., & Fischer, E.M. (2015). The nature and implications of consumers' experiential framings of failure in high-risk service contexts. *Journal of Service Research*, *18*(3), 303–317.

Zeithaml, V.A., Bitner, M.J., & Gremler, D.D. (2013). *Services Marketing: Integrating Customer Focus Across the Firm*, 6th edition, McGraw-Hill Education, New York.

22

Green services and the quest for sustainable environment

Chasing a holy grail

Michael J. Dorsch, William E. Kilbourne, and Stephen J. Grove

Introduction

Service organizations, and businesses in general, are increasing their efforts to develop business practices that are less harmful to the natural environment (Heiskanen & Jalas 2003; Wong, Wong, & Boon-itt 2013). Although business-related efforts to enhance environmental sustainability, including green marketing practices, seem to be a recent phenomenon, calls for accountable environmental business and marketing strategies date back five decades (Kassarjian 1971; Kinnear, Taylor, & Ahmed 1974; Polonsky 2011). The increased importance of green marketing initiatives began during the late 1980s (Brown 1996) and achieved substantial visibility in the 1990s (Harrison 1993; Sheth & Parvartiyar 1995). Nevertheless, available evidence indicates that green marketing initiatives (Peattie & Crane 2005) and other environmental impact assessment programs in general (Jay, Jones, Slinn & Wood 2007; Morgan 2012) have not achieved full potential. Consequently, the continued and widespread environmental degradation facing current and future generations (Anderson 2014; Kotler 2011; Ottman 2011) is prompting renewed calls for businesses, including service organizations, to address environmental sustainability (e.g., Chan et al. 2016; Kassinis & Soteriou 2003; Kotler 2011; Shrivastava 1995; Wong et al. 2013).

Examining the environmental sustainability efforts of service organizations is especially important because the service sector is the primary driver of economic growth in many societies (CIA 2018). Current estimates suggest that service activities account for nearly 80% of the gross domestic product (GDP) in the United States (CIA 2018) and 80% of the nation's labor force (Lee & Mather 2008). Furthermore, over 50% of the average annual family budget can be traced to service expenditures (US Census Bureau 2012). Nevertheless, when discussions of environmental consciousness and green marketing issues are raised, the focus is usually confined to the manufacturing sector (Wong et al. 2013). This is unfortunate, as service consumption accounts for approximately 65% of a person's carbon footprint (Carbon Footprint Ltd 2012). Thus, there is a need to gain a deeper understanding of the role of services in achieving environmental sustainability (Grove, Fisk, Pickett, & Kangun 1996; Makower 2006).

To date, a majority of the green marketing literature takes a micro-level perspective (Polonsky 2011), including examining how service organizations can gain a competitive advantage by becoming more r (Heiskanen & Jalas 2003; Wong et al. 2013). Moreover, the natural-resource based view (N-RBV) theory is typically used to understand how companies, including service organizations, can achieve competitive advantages by engaging in environmentally sustainable economic activity (Hart 1995; Hart & Dowell 2011; Kassinis & Soteriou 2003; Wong et al. 2013). Specifically, the N-RBV view of the firm advocates the development of three strategic capabilities to facilitate environmentally sustainable economic actions, including: (1) pollution prevention, (2) product stewardship, which focuses on minimizing production and operations impact on the natural environment, and (3) sustainable development, which focuses on minimizing the environmental burden resulting from firm growth and development (Hart 1995; Hart & Dowell 2011). The pollution prevention and product stewardship capabilities address a company's efforts to reduce pollution throughout the product value chain (i.e., product design, development, production, and disposition of used products). In contrast, a company's sustainable development capability seeks to reduce environmental damage in two ways. First, it encourages the company to pursue production processes that can be maintained indefinitely; and, second, it engages in efforts to increase the economic benefits to lesser developed countries (Hart & Dowell 2011). Nevertheless, most applications of the N-RBV address pollution reduction capability and examine the circumstances under which improving environmental performance (i.e., pollution reduction) enhances or detracts from short-term financial performance (Hart & Dowell 2011). Although the N-RBV tends to be company specific, concerns about environmental impact are expanding beyond outputs of a focal business to an entire industry (Kirk 1995). Therefore, limiting this investigation into environmental sustainability issues to a micro-level perspective results in an incomplete understanding; environmental sustainability is considered to be a macro-level issue (Polonsky 2011).

From a macro-level perspective, the demand for services is influenced, in part, by population size. Worldwide growth of the human population combined with increasing affluence raises a concern that activities required to provide basic amenities, even with green initiatives, might not be ecologically sustainable using current technologies and production methods (Hart 1995). Furthermore, even though individual service operations tend to utilize small amounts of nonrenewable resources and produce small amounts of pollution, an entire service industry's accumulated use of nonrenewable resources and pollution creation (considered from a global perspective) contributes substantially to environmental degradation (Kirk 1995). Thus, for the past quarter-century, organizations have been challenged to change their business practices in fundamental ways or risk irreversible damage to the planet's essential ecological systems (Hart 1995). In fact, environmentalism was identified as one of the major issues to address during the new millennium (Thiele 1999), and green marketing has moved beyond being simply a familiar buzzword to a strategic imperative that embraces the notion of environmental well-being (Porter & Reinhardt 2007). Correspondingly, achieving environmental sustainability on the part of business requires transformations at both the macro- and micro-levels (Kotler 2011; Polonsky 2011). Moreover, green service management must be considered a necessity for survival (Gummesson 1994), and the environmental impact of service industries is expected to come under increasing scrutiny (Brown 1996; Makower 2006).

This chapter explores how micro- and macro-level factors together shape the extent to which services, individually and collectively, contribute effectively to environmental sustainability. To accomplish this purpose, the chapter begins by describing the green service concept and identifying important challenges of achieving environmental sustainability. Next, micro-level factors that impact green services are examined, and greenprinting (Patrício, Fisk, & Grove 2009) is proposed as an environmental management practice that service organizations can use to help them achieve environmental sustainability. The chapter continues by describing macro-level factors that influence the extent and rate to which the service sector can contribute to environmental sustainability. Finally, it concludes by providing directions for continued research into green service practices.

Green services and the challenges of achieving environmental sustainability

The relationship between green services and environmental sustainability

Environmental sustainability, green marketing, and green services are broad concepts that have been defined in numerous ways (Hoffman & Bazerman 2007). For example, green marketing has been considered interchangeable with environmental marketing, ecological marketing, and responsible marketing (Polonsky 1994, 2011). Similarly, green services are also labeled as eco-efficient services or environmentally sustainable services (Heiskanen & Jalas 2003). Despite the variety of terms used to describe the concepts, most definitions of environmental sustainability, green marketing, and green services share a common theme of satisfying customer needs while simultaneously minimizing the harmful environmental effects associated with economic activities (Polonsky 1994, 2011), including service delivery and service support activities (Chan et al. 2016; Wong et al. 2013).

Green prescriptions for reducing environmental degradation tend to focus attention on reducing the consumption of natural resources and/or minimizing waste during the production/delivery processes by both manufacturing and service firms (e.g., Polonsky 1994; Wong et al. 2013). For instance, a firm's green initiatives may include: developing offerings that conserve energy and other natural resources in the production process (Harrington et al. 2008), reducing pollutants and conserving resources in the transportation of goods to market (Patton 2010; Rodrigue, Comtois, & Slack 2009; Science News 2010), advertising green products effectively (Chan, Leung, & Wang 2006; Chang 2011), and a host of other marketing-related practices. Although such environmentally friendly prescriptions are intended to slow the depletion of natural resources and decelerate the growth in environmental damage, they do not address the necessity of replenishing the earth's natural resources or repairing environmental damage. Consequently, environmental sustainability (or environmental responsibility) necessitates the creation of new and radical challenges to the management of service operations (Gummesson 1994).

For service organizations, the challenge of becoming environmentally sustainable is exacerbated by the complexity associated with linking together environmental responsibility and economic advantages (Parry 2012), and becomes even more complex when including social/ethical responsibility. Creating a balance among environmental responsibility, economic value, and social/ethical responsibility forms the triple bottom line framework for managing environmental sustainability (Elkington 2018; Junior, de Oliveira, & Helleno 2018). Yet, instead of dealing with the complexity associated with achieving environmental sustainability, service managers often fail to recognize the environmental impact of their service operations and tend to treat it as a secondary concern (Brown 1996; Gummesson 1994; Kirk 1995). In other cases, efforts to implement environmentally friendly policies tends to expose conflicts between service delivery methods and environmental activities (Kirk 1995).

For instance, service organizations are often unable to regulate the service-related behaviors of their customers, which result in environmental waste (Tzschentke, Kirk, & Lynch 2004). Similarly, many service customers are unwilling to accept a lower quality service experience that may accompany a reduction in environmental waste (Kirk 1995). Correspondingly, many services have financial constraints that reduce their abilities to implement environmental policies. As a result, financially constrained companies may be unwilling to implement environmental policy unless it is required by law (Gummesson 1994; Parry 2012) or provides an immediate and commensurate financial benefit or valued tangible benefit (Brown 1996). Such actions slow or deter service organizations from becoming environmentally sustainable.

When service organizations adopt environmentally responsible practices, the implementation of these green practices tends to be gradual and to occur when upgrading equipment, replacing equipment, or seeking ways to reduce operating costs (Tzschentke et al. 2004). Moreover, two types of environmental management practices are typically used to reduce/manage waste that occurs as a by-product of the service creation process. One approach controls waste after it is created, and is referred to as "end-of-pipe" efforts (Hart 1995; Polonsky 1994). Another approach prevents waste from occurring at the beginning (i.e., "beginning-of-pipe" efforts); if this continues throughout the service creation process (Hart 1995; Polonsky 1994) it is referred to as "source reduction efforts" (Porter & van der Linde 1995). Of the two approaches, the latter is considered to be less expensive than dealing with waste after its creation and is more commonly employed (Hart 1995; Kirk 1995). Since the late 1980s, manufacturing organizations worldwide have engaged in environmental management practices that have emphasized the minimization of emissions and pollution (Hart 1995; Sroufe 2003). The limited research that is available into the environmental practices of service organizations concludes that they are similar to manufacturing organizations in that they emphasize waste and pollution abatement (Foster, Sampson, & Dunn 2000; Salzman 2000). In addition, some types of services (e.g., small independently owned hotels consisting of less than 50 rooms) consider environmental responsibility as a peripheral business activity and gradually adopt environmental practices that enable the service to increase operational efficiency through cost reduction (Tzschentke et al. 2004). Consistent with these findings, Parry (2012) found that environmental practices within micro-businesses tend to evolve in an incremental manner.

Service organizations tend to gradually implement pollution reduction and prevention practices, during which time they encounter two types of costs, including the cost of incorporating environmentally sustainable practices and that of dealing with pollution after it is created. The increase in operating costs resulting from the incorporation of environmental practices jeopardizes cash flow and profitability (Hart 1995). Regrettably, there is little research on the best environmental management practices of service organizations (Makower 2006). This chapter provides an overview of the research that has been done, and creates a plan for future research that develops and describes environmental management needs, particularly for services.

The remainder of the chapter provides a framework to better understand the extent to which services and the service sector can effectively contribute to environmental sustainability. The next section summarizes the evolution of green marketing practices, from managing environmental waste to the current emphasis on achieving environmental sustainability. The evolution of green marketing practices to address environmental sustainability represents a fundamental transformation in an organization's frame of reference for defining and achieving environmental sustainability. Traditionally, green marketing practices were considered from a production-oriented perspective, which enabled micro-level analyses for managing environmental degradation; this focused attention on the production processes for creating goods and services. Although such a production-oriented approach helped to reduce a company's impact on the environment, it did not decrease the combined environmental degradation across companies and industries. The underperformance of firm-based green marketing efforts in terms of effectively reducing aggregate environmental degradation led to the consideration of environmental sustainability from a consumption-oriented perspective.

From the latter perspective, the examination of factors contributing to environmental degradation shifted from how goods and services are produced to how they are used and by whom. This shift from a production-oriented lens to a consumption-oriented lens broadened the analysis of environmental sustainability to a macro-level analysis that extends beyond the production process to include an investigation of consumer demand for goods and services. For instance, a macro-level analysis of environmental degradation reveals that production-based (i.e., company-based) efforts to become more environmentally sustainable may be suppressed (offset) by increases in overall consumption and consumer demand for products (goods and services) to maintain a particular lifestyle or state of well-being. Consequently, achieving environmental sustainability requires an understanding of both micro-level and macro-level factors.

In subsequent sections, this chapter explores how micro- and macro-level factors influence both service organizations and the service sector's effectiveness in achieving environmental sustainability. The chapter concludes by maintaining that the service sector's potential for contributing to environmental sustainability requires both reengineering of service organizations, individually and as a collective, and fundamental changes toward the reduction of environmental degradation within society as a whole. Without consideration of environmental sustainability from both micro- and macro-levels, continued efforts to improve environmental management practices in services from a micro-level (production-oriented) perspective will be ineffective, allowing environmental degradation to continue.

Evolution of green marketing practices

Peattie and Crane (2005) maintain that green marketing practices have evolved through three stages: ecological green marketing, environmental green marketing, and sustainable marketing. The first two stages focus on the production process and take a micro-level perspective. In contrast, the sustainable marketing stage takes a macro-level perspective by considering the influence of consumer lifestyles (i.e., consumption behaviors) on the earth's natural resources. More specifically, during the ecological green marketing stage, which began during the 1960s and 1970s, manufacturing was the primary economic driver of industrialized Western societies, and the pollution created by manufacturing processes became a serious public concern (Peattie & Crane 2005). In response, environmental legislation was passed to reduce pollution created by production processes and products. This approach emphasized end-of-pipe efforts to clean up environmental waste; however, such efforts could result in shifting waste to other parts of the production process rather than reducing environmental degradation (Polonsky 1994). Although the ecological green marketing stage was characterized primarily by increased environmental legislation, the environmental impact occurring during this stage and continuing into the sustainable marketing stage was influenced by transition of the U.S. from a manufacturing economy to a service economy (The Economics Daily 2014). This transition resulted in the use of cleaner energy and, consequently, a belief that the country was transitioning to employing sustainable marketing practices.

The sustainable marketing stage emerged during the late 1980s, when public concerns about the environment were raised after witnessing several major environmental disasters, including the discovery of a hole in the earth's ozone, the Chernobyl nuclear accident, and the Exxon Valdez oil spill accident (Peattie & Crane 2005). The World Commission on Environment and Development prepared its Brundtland Report, which brought attention to the environmental challenges facing the earth and called for a balance between economic growth and environmental protection (Collins, Roper, & Lawrence 2010). This report is considered to be the primary motivating factor for the emergence of the current sustainability movement (Collins et al. 2010) and the sustainable marketing stage (Peattie & Crane 2005).

The sustainable marketing stage witnessed a shift in green marketing activities from managing environmental waste after it occurred, to reducing environmental damage and appealing to increased consumer demand for green solutions (Peattie & Crane 2005). However, these sustainable marketing efforts have not reached their potential for simultaneously improving consumer well-being and the natural ecosystem (Polonsky 2011). For example, the emergence of green-oriented consumers resulted in the recognition that businesses could achieve competitive advantages by engaging in pro-environmental practices (Porter & van der Linde 1995). Correspondingly, business efforts to engage in sustainable marketing activities transitioned from end-of-pipe pollution cleanup to beginning-of-pipe activities (activities at the process design and product design stages) that emphasized the use of cleaner technology to reduce or eliminate waste (Peattie & Crane 2005). These efforts continue, as evidenced by an increasing number of consumers who profess a concern for the environment and are green-oriented. According to one survey, roughly 80% of American consumers claim to buy green products (Environmental Leader 2009). Many service organizations attempt to capitalize on public interest in green issues by positioning themselves as green organizations and making a commitment to be environmentally responsible (Glasser 2009). Despite consumer interest in green-oriented goods and services, many companies continue to find it difficult to gain competitive advantage by using pro-environmental practices to appeal effectively to the green-oriented consumer. Part of the difficulty in achieving a competitive advantage through green practices is attributed to consumer difficulty in recognizing and validating the effectiveness of green claims, practices, and performances (Cronin, Smith, Gleim, Ramírez, & Martinez 2011; Parry 2012; Peattie & Crane 2005).

Although the 1980s and 1990s witnessed substantial improvements in technologies and production systems that reduced pollution by individual companies and increased resource conservation, available evidence indicates no significant improvement in environmental sustainability (Peattie & Crane 2005). For instance, the U.S. transition to a service economy contributed to reducing the environmental impact of individual companies; however, the increase in aggregate economic activity from services was thought to have a net negative impact on the environment (Kassinis & Soteriou 2003; Salzman 2000). Consequently, the pressure to achieve environmental sustainability during the late 1990s and early 2000s triggered the beginning of a transition to the sustainable marketing stage (Peattie & Crane 2005). This stage is characterized by an emphasis on business practices that create profit, benefit current and future generations, and reduce the degradation of the earth and its limited natural resources (Connelly, Ketchen, & Slater 2011; Kotler 2011; Polonsky 2011; Shrivastava 1995). In contrast to the earlier two green marketing stages, understanding and managing environmental sustainability shifted from a production focus to a consumption focus (Schaeffer & Crane 2005). Examining sustainable marketing from a consumption perspective resulted in examining sustainable marketing from a macro-level perspective, rather than from a micro-level perspective (Polonsky 2011). This shift in perspective requires major transformations in both business and consumer viewpoints regarding relationships with the natural environment (Kotler 2011; Polonsky 2011). Such new viewpoints may result in radical changes in business practices benefitting future stakeholders (Peattie & Crane 2005). For example, a shift to environmental sustainability requires businesses to modify their marketing programs to promote quality of life and personal happiness through the encouragement of more responsible consumption, rather than through unlimited consumption (Fisk 1973; Kotler 2011). Additionally, business and consumer acceptance of environmental sustainability necessitates a change from beliefs that the earth has an abundance of natural resources and unlimited capacity to carry waste, to beliefs that the earth has limited resources and limited capacity to carry waste (Kotler 2011).

The transition of industrial societies to service economies coincided with the emergence of research into green services (Grove et al. 1996). However, green services research continues to be embryonic, appearing primarily outside of mainstream services literature. Furthermore, much of the existing green services research tends to address issues concerning consumer preference for green services or the use of environmental control systems within service organizations to reduce environmental harm. These research issues correspond to those examined within the manufacturing sector during the environmental green marketing stage. Because service research is currently inadequate, more work is needed to examine issues pertaining to the sustainable stage of green marketing efforts. Issues that must be considered include the interaction of micro- and macro-level factors that influence the abilities of service providers to achieve environmental sustainability.

Service-related challenges to becoming environmentally sustainable

From a service-dominant logic perspective (Vargo & Lusch 2004), there is little difference in the environmental impact of service organizations and manufacturing organizations, in that both consume nonrenewable natural resources and create waste and pollution (Wong et al. 2013). Nevertheless, compared to a manufacturing or smokestack context (Makower 2006), services are generally considered to be environmentally cleaner, as their impact on the natural environment is less noticeable (Brown 1996). Yet, for the same reason, services have been described as a silent destroyer of the environment (Aykol & Leonidou 2015). The 2011 Greenhouse Gas Inventory Report concluded that service industries, including transportation, had higher carbon emissions levels than manufacturing industries (Wong et al. 2013). Although the U.S. transition to a service economy reduced its greenhouse gas intensity (per unit of GDP), it increased the total amount of U.S. emissions because service creation and delivery both increased the total GDP and often utilized manufactured goods (Suh 2006). Household consumption of services was found to account for more than 37% of total U.S. greenhouse gas emissions, much of which was due to use of electricity and transportation; furthermore, total emissions linked to electricity production and consumption by services was greater than that caused by manufacturing (Suh 2006).

Customer participation in the production of a service outcome can both positively and negatively impact a service organization's environmental initiatives. For instance, customer co-production during a service encounter can contribute positively to the service provider's environmental initiatives by raising customer awareness of the initiatives; however, customer participation in service creation can also adversely impact the service organization's environmental initiatives, if customers demand improved service that is harmful to the environment (Foster et al. 2000).

At the micro-level, the environmental impact of individual service organizations is often negligible (Lawrence, Collins, Pavlovich, & Arunachalam 2006). Yet, there are instances where a single service organization can have a substantial impact on the environment. For example, McDonald's (a U.S.-based fast-food restaurant) recently announced several environmental initiatives. By 2025, McDonald's plans to have 100% of its customer packaging come from renewable, recycled, or certified sources, and to have recycling available in all of its restaurants (Carrig 2018). McDonald's also announced a 2030 goal of reducing the intensity of its greenhouse emissions levels by 31% across its supply chain (McDonalds.com 2018).

At the macro-level, the sheer size of the service sector means that ecological considerations pertaining to materials and resources can potentially have a major impact upon the environment (Kirk 1995). This impact can be obtained by reducing waste and environmental degradation through the traditional 3Rs of environmental management (i.e., reusing, recycling, and reducing), according to Grove et al. (1996). Although the 3Rs' approach to environmental management slows environmental degradation, these steps do not stop or replenish the world's nonrenewable resources. Continued consumption of nonrenewable natural resources jeopardizes both the environment and marketing practices over the long-term. Thus, there is a need to consider the possibility of adding a fourth R to the environmental management formula, which is 'renewing' environmental resources. When service organizations adopt environmentally conscious policies and practices, they can contribute to environmental preservation.

Micro-level factors influencing environmental sustainability of green services

How service organizations can become more environmentally sustainable

Environmentally responsible service organizations traditionally focus their efforts on one or more of three broad conservation-related activities: reusing, recycling, and reducing, also referred to as the '3Rs formula for environmental management.' These practices are designed to control the waste of natural resources that often accompanies organizational pursuits. By *reusing* packaging (e.g., offering products in refillable containers), *recycling* materials (e.g., reclaiming materials from used products), and *reducing* resource usage (e.g., conserving precious resources in the production process), organizations can minimize their impact on the environment. An overriding objective of these green practices is to accommodate environmental well-being while meeting the demands of the marketplace, such that the long-term impact on the earth is reduced (Lubin & Esty 2010).

Many environmental prescriptions are necessary to preserve the environment and slow environmental degradation; for instance, it is important for industry sectors and societies to replenish and/or renew natural resources and make environmental reparations (e.g., Connelly et al. 2011; Kotler 2011). Hence, as suggested above, it makes sense to introduce a fourth R – 'renewing' – to the environmental well-being formula described, to emphasize the importance of embedding the notion of sustainability into conscientious decision-making efforts concerning the other three R's (Fisk & Grove 2008). Renewing the earth's natural resources can contribute to environmental sustainability, but to date such efforts tend to be limited, and emphasis continues to be directed toward minimization and control of environmental waste (i.e., the original three Rs).

To become more environmentally responsible, service organizations typically require some type of reworking or 'reengineering' of service processes to limit their impact on the environment. Such practices can help to position a service organization as a champion of green initiatives in the public perception, and can attract an increasingly large, environmentally concerned customer segment. Implementing green practices can also enhance a service organization's brand equity (Namkung & Jang 2013).

Despite the advantages associated with green marketing initiatives, smaller firms, including services, tend to take a reactive and ad hoc approach when dealing with environmental issues (Brown 1996; Moore & Spence 2006; Parry 2012). Moreover, many service organizations implement a hodgepodge of environmentally friendly initiatives without having an overarching vision or plan, which should include an assessment of whether or not the changes are truly sustainable (Lubin & Esty 2010). For example, within the hotel industry, adoption of environmentally friendly practices, such as replacing or updating equipment to reduce operating costs (and gain more control over hotel guests' energy use), was found to be a gradual process prompted by efforts to improve financial performance (Tzschentke et al. 2004). Additionally, even if organizations incorporated environmental friendly programs into their business practices, managers oftentimes were unable to determine the extent to which the programs contributed to the organization's strategic or financial performances (Cronin et al. 2011).Thus, it appears that many organizations have not reengineered their service-oriented processes to include ecologically sound practices, and those that do tend to proceed piecemeal without a clear understanding of how the ecologically reengineered service impacts the customer experience. Such approaches are inefficient, can negatively impact the environment, and can impair the customer service experience. Greenprinting (Patrício et al. 2009) is proposed as an approach to help service providers design or reengineer their service offerings to include ecologically sound practices that contribute favorably to the customer experience.

Greenprinting: reengineering service operations to be environmentally sustainable

Improvements in ecological well-being driven by the services sector can only occur when service organizations incorporate environmentally sound practices into their service delivery processes without harming the customer experience. Environmental management systems (such as ISO 14001 and BS 7750) provide formal certification requirements aimed at improving the ecological soundness of service delivery (Chan 2009; ISO 2009; Kassinis & Soteriou 2003; Kirk 1995; Sroufe 2003). Thus, they make recommendations for creating environmental policy, by identifying measures to record the environmental effects of organizational practices, establishing environmental objectives, performing environmental audits, and implementing systems to monitor, regulate, review, and control business process to support environmental initiatives (Kirk 1995).

However, implementing a certified environmental management system is not sufficient for identifying specific changes to be made in the efficient and effective design or redesign of a service. For example, a criticism is that they fail to provide management with an understanding of how changes in environmental practices impact the quality of the customer service experience and service performance (e.g., Kassinis & Soteriou 2003; Wong et al. 2013) or contribute effectively to environmental sustainability (e.g., Chanchitpricha & Bond 2013; Jay et al. 2007; Morgan 2012). Moreover, unlike formal (certified) environmental management systems, informal guidelines (uncertified environmental management systems) do not impose a rigid framework to achieve certification and were found to provide greater flexibility to services for introducing green practices while reducing costs (e.g., Wong et al. 2013). Thus, the flexibility associated with uncertified environmental management systems contributed favorably to reducing service costs while enhancing the service organization's environmental performance (Wong et al. 2013). There is a need for such a flexible methodology that helps service designers identify where environmentally sound practices can be incorporated into the service delivery process without harming the customer experience.

Greenprinting is an environmental management approach that service organizations can use to design and structure their service creation and delivery processes to become more environmentally responsible (Patrício et al. 2009). More specifically, greenprinting extends service blueprinting (Bitner, Ostrom, & Morgan 2008) by including a procedure to facilitate the discovery of ecologically sound best practices contributing to the prevention and control of waste, which may not be easily recognizable within each step of the service creation and delivery processes. Through greenprinting, managers can gain a deeper understanding into how environmentally sustainable practices may be implemented into the service delivery process without harming the customer service experience. For instance, consider the impact that might ensue when a hotel chain (such as Holiday Inn or Hilton) adopts an energy conservation policy that involves setting thermostats in the back regions and public areas two or three degrees closer to the outdoor temperature. It is unlikely that such a change would be noticeable by most guests or employees, yet it could substantially reduce energy consumption.

Greenprinting: mapping the ecological impact of a service process

Greenprinting, similar to service blueprinting, is an effective visual mapping technique that illustrates a dynamic service process, and it is adaptable to handle macro- or micro-levels of analyses (Bitner et al. 2008). When mapping a service and its environmental implications, greenprinting requires that the service delivery system be decomposed into a set of inter-related events (Bitner et al. 2008; Shostack 1987). Like service blueprints, service greenprints encourage creativity, preemptive problem-solving, and efficiency during service design or redesign, when compared to random or more piecemeal service development processes (Shostack 1984). Moreover, greenprinting is a flexible customer-focused approach that helps managers to design or redesign a service to ensure a high quality and uniform customer experience that is environmentally friendly (Bitner et al. 2008; Sampson 2012).

To begin reengineering a service operation to become more environmentally responsible, greenprinting begins by decomposing the service activity into a specific set of events (unit acts) that facilitate the identification and assessment of ecological impact. Because most investigations into action are based on similar conceptualizations (Darden & Dorsch 1990), the Theory of Action (Parsons 1937) provides an appropriate framework for examining the structure of a service event. According to this theory, the structure of an action requires the establishment of an appropriate frame of reference that specifies the boundaries of the action. Furthermore, an action can often be decomposed into a set of interrelated unit acts, or events. The unit act or event is the smallest useful building block for structuring an action (Parsons 1937). Therefore, to incorporate green considerations into service design or redesign via greenprinting, it is important to decompose the service into a set of distinct and easily recognizable unit acts. This allows service designers to establish specific parameters to help determine the specific resources needed to perform the act, and clarifies the environmental impact of using these resources.

Structuring a service event

Each unit act or event within a service delivery process represents a change or transition from one state of affairs to another (Von Wright 1970) and may be specified with respect to its identifiable characteristics. At a minimum, each event can be described in terms of four identifiable characteristics (Parsons 1937). First, an event has an agency or actor who expends energy. For example, an actor may be the customer, a service employee, or a machine. Second, an event has an end that represents a desired future state/outcome. The outcome of each unit act or event influences the structure of subsequent events in the sequence/chain that forms the service delivery process. Third, the event occurs within a particular setting. Part of the setting is not controllable by the actor and represents the constraints under which the unit act must be performed. Other parts of the setting are controllable by the actor and correspond to the decisions about how to perform the unit act. Fourth, an event is normatively regulated; thus, there is a set of rules that the actor uses to determine both the means and ends of the event. For example, hotel waste management practices must conform to the firm's policies, industry codes, and prevailing legislation.

Identifying ecological issues

The interrelationships among the unit acts that comprise an action (a service delivery process) tend to influence and constrain the set of feasible alternatives used to structure each successive event in the sequence (Nowakowski 1973, 1981). For instance, each service event may be defined by a descriptor that identifies the outcome of the event, and the set of descriptors depicts the entire service process. Although verbal descriptors enable a general understanding of each step in a service delivery process, they are unable to determine the ecological impact of each event. Greenprinting broadens service blueprinting methodology to include such an assessment. More specifically, greenprinting utilizes the service blueprint to identify each unit act in the service delivery system. Next, the event frame of reference is determined by structuring the unit act in terms of its identifiable characteristics. Then, each event is examined, to identify the renewable and nonrenewable resources required to complete the unit act. For example, if waste is created during a particular step in the service delivery process (such as recording room service orders on paper), then the management and control of waste must be handled in a subsequent step/event (e.g., discarding paper trash into recycling bins or in bins to be taken to a landfill). Finally, alternative courses of action are identified and evaluated to determine the most ecologically sound practices that enable the firm to maintain or enhance the quality of the corresponding customer experience at each step throughout the entire service delivery process. For example, the management of waste created during the service delivery process should not result in a customer service experience that falls short of customer expectations.

Performance related decisions may or may not include explicit consideration of the renewable and nonrenewable resources required to complete the act. For example, hotels may be constrained in terms of how they can effectively manage the amount of waste water resulting from high-pressure hot water showers or the laundering required for maintaining an adequate supply of towels and linen. Additionally, when making lighting decisions, a hotel may consider installing motion-sensor lighting and/or low-energy light bulbs in hotel rooms and/or hallways to conserve energy.

Greenprinting: contributing to greening of the service mosaic

Lovelock (1994) proposed the idea of a "service mosaic" to capture the notion that customer perceptions of service excellence are formed – like a mosaic's creation, piece by piece – by organizations successfully attending to various customer touchpoints in the service process. With each additional touchpoint successfully addressed, a clearer image of service excellence is perceived by organizational customers. Expanding upon Lovelock's logic, this chapter suggests that, for each successfully implemented green initiative within an organization's service blueprint, an image of the organization's environmental dedication comes into focus. As with a service mosaic in general, a mosaic that reflects shades of green is accomplished over time and across various points in the service process. It bears noting that the creation of a green mosaic, like its general counterpart, can be expedited by first attending to those points or steps in the service process that offer a greater opportunity to have a significant environmental impact. Simply put, when enough of the steps in a service blueprint have been adapted to reflect the green imperatives of reducing, reusing, or recycling, a service mosaic of excellence in hues of green might be perceived by an organization's stakeholders – customers, workers, and others. Beyond the obvious contribution to the environment that occurs, the creation of a green service mosaic has the potential to serve as a powerful marketing communication and positioning tool (Ko, Kyung, & Kim 2013).

A good example of a service organization that is creating a service mosaic in shades of green is Caesars Entertainment (Posner & Kiron 2013). Based on feedback from its guests, it has made efforts to reduce energy consumption, recycle waste, and reuse materials; these efforts are made known to guests through advertising, and have led to a more positive customer experience and repeat business. To put its greening effort into operation, Caesars first relied on input from various constituencies, most notably its employees, for ideas and suggestions on how it could improve upon its environmental impact; the results were used to prioritize various efforts. Caesars recognized it could not realize an environmental imperative all at once, so – like creating a mosaic – it began implementing green initiatives one by one, starting first with those that were the easiest to realize given their potential benefits. Among the environmentally friendly actions taken by Caesars at its different properties was the introduction of low-flow showerheads, the creation of opt-out linen programs whereby guests could choose to forgo daily linen service, the installation of energy efficient lighting throughout the properties, reduction of water consumption in the laundry facilities, the development of second use systems and donation programs for food waste, and numerous other programs to reduce, reuse, and recycle.

Macro-level factors influencing environmental sustainability in services

Understanding the potential of services to effectively impact the natural environment requires a shift from micro- to macro-level considerations (Polonsky 1994, 2011). At the micro-level, service organizations develop their marketing strategies to encourage consumption that enhances consumer quality of life and well-being (Kilbourne, Dorsch, & Thyroff 2018; Martin & Schouten 2014). Implicit in these marketing strategies are assumptions that an abundance of natural resources exist to satisfy increased consumption, and that the earth has the capacity to store waste and pollution that result from consumption (Kotler 2011; Polonsky 1994, 2011). Unfortunately, this is not the case, as a negative by-product of consumption is that it damages the natural environment (Polonsky 2011). Consequently, there are calls to engage in responsible consumption and to reduce consumer consumption overall (e.g., Fisk 1973; Kilbourne et al. 2018; Wong et al. 2013). Nevertheless, in many Western industrialized societies, consumption is encouraged to achieve economic growth. Increased consumption and materialistic behaviors have been demonstrated to be influenced by a society's value system, referred to as its dominant social paradigm (DSP) (Kilbourne et al. 2009).

A society's DSP is the set of shared values, beliefs, and behaviors that correspond to the specific features/dimensions characterizing the society, including political, economic, technological, competitive, and anthropocentric dimensions (Kilbourne et al. 2009). Of these dimensions, the anthropocentric dimension concerns the relationship between a society member and the natural environment (Kilbourne et al. 2009; Polonsky 2011). For example, a shared belief among many members of Western industrialized societies is that the natural environment exists to serve humankind and that humans have mastery over the natural environment (Kilbourne et al. 2009). A guiding principle within an anthropocentric society is that control of natural resources through consumption enables the society to achieve economic growth, raises the standard of living, and enhances the well-being of its members. The increased consumption also results in environmental degradation through a reduction of natural resources and increased waste.

Given the current DSP of many industrialized societies, efforts by either companies or consumer groups to encourage environmentally sustainable practices tend to be met with resistance, especially if they mean reducing the standard of living. Therefore, the ability of a service sector to effectively encourage environmentally sustainable behaviors depends on a fundamental transformation in the DSP concerning interactions between societal members and the natural environment. Furthermore, this transformation will be slow; both consumers and businesses, including services, exhibit reluctance to adopt environmentally sustainable initiatives (Collins et al. 2010). Consequently, initiating societal transformation to encourage environmental sustainability can require government intervention (Kilbourne et al. 2018); this is further complicated by other DSP dimensions, such as the political and technological dimensions. Yet, even though government intervention through regulatory efforts can create pressure to become more environmentally sustainable, businesses often resist such actions in favor of voluntary efforts, which are slow to emerge (Collins et al. 2010). Furthermore, interactions between government and private enterprises are vulnerable to corrupt practices (e.g., bribery, collusion, and conflicts of interest), which can inhibit the effective implementation of environmentally sustainable practices (Williams & Dupuy 2017).

Government leaders, like managers, are prone to biases resulting from bounded rationality, which can result in decisions that benefit society in the short-term, but are harmful in the long-term (Bansal & Roth 2000). Nevertheless, as long as public pressure for sustainable businesses practices that improve consumer quality of life continues to increase, both service and non-service industries are expected to witness a transformation that encourages the adoption of green marketing practices and green corporate culture (Polonsky 2011), Moreover, sustainable marketing practices will require a more holistic and comprehensive approach to identify and effectively manage sustainability-related issues pertaining to economic, environmental, social, ethical, and technology considerations (Lim 2016).

Environmental sustainability requires collaboration among societies

Recognizing that societies differ in terms of their shared values and behaviors, it is expected that environmentally sustainable practices implemented by one society may be offset by non-environmentally sustainable practices of other societies. Owing to this situation, environmental degradation is likely to continue, albeit at a slower pace than if environmentally sustainable practices are adopted. Consequently, achieving environmental sustainability is a global issue that requires cooperation and collaboration among the world's societies. To achieve the necessary worldwide cooperation, societies would need to develop DSPs that have common sets of shared values regarding the nature of how humans interact with the natural environment, including the responsible consumption of natural resources. Implementing these shared values would require cooperation among the world's societies, and some redistribution of natural resources to increase well-being across all societies and improve the standard of living of impoverished societies. Thus, redistribution of the earth's natural resources would necessitate a reduction in resource consumption within those societies that currently enjoy higher standards of living, to enable increased consumption within societies with lower standards of living.

An important macro-level factor influencing the effectiveness of services in achieving environmental sustainability relates to the size and growth of the world's population, which increases the rate of consumption of the earth's natural resources. This, in turn, hastens their depletion and increases global environmental deterioration (Ehrlich & Holdren 1971). The total negative impact of a society on the environment (I) may be expressed in terms of a relationship among the society's population size (P), affluence level (A), and technological impact (T). This environmental impact model (IPAT), is expressed algebraically as I=PAT, or the product of population, affluence, and technology (Ehrlich & Holdren 1971; Newman 2006).

To estimate a society's environmental impact (I), the society's population size (P) is multiplied by a proxy of the society's affluence level (A), such as the GDP per capita (GDP/P), and a measure of the society's technological processes (T) used to obtain and transform natural resources into goods and waste. The estimation of T is tailored to the particular situation; for example, when applied to services, T could be estimated in terms of the service technologies used to create and distribute the service offerings. Alternatively, a (somewhat tautological) proxy for a society's technological impact (T) may be estimated as (I/GDP), where technology represents the overall environmental impact per unit of GDP. Expanding this identity, it appears as: I=P(GDP/P)(I/GDP).

The IPAT equation can be used to estimate the impact of services on a society's overall ecological footprint; the environmental impact represented by T, the technology component of the IPAT model, may be calculated by considering the percentage of GDP due to services as compared to production and consumption of goods. Although individual service organizations have a small ecological footprint and environmental impact, the IPAT calculations can be used to demonstrate that the ecological footprint and environmental impact of services in the aggregate is considerable and expanding. For example, all of the improvements in generating and distributing services are part of the technology domain. There are ways of minimizing their environmental impact by applying both physical and organizational improvements in service delivery. Furthermore, technological improvements within services are independent of both population size and affluence (consumption rate), except in rare situations such as health services related to human reproduction. Thus, based on use of the IPAT model, the net gains associated with technological improvements to enhance efficiency and effectiveness in achieving environmental sustainability are expected to eventually be offset by increases in the size of the population (P) and the rate of service consumption or affluence (A).

To estimate the degree to which service improvements enhance environmental sustainability, the current population size (P) and/or consumption/affluence level (A) might be increased while holding the amount of technology (T) at its current level. Because T represents the ecological footprint of services, it is possible to determine the amount of technological improvement that must be made to maintain the current ecological footprint for a specified number of years. This requires knowledge of the anticipated growth rates for P and GDP/P, and a decision as to the number of years to project. To illustrate, recent growth rates for P and A are approximately 1.1% and 1.6%, respectively (World Bank 2016). Thus, for a period of 50 years, the level of T (the ecological impact per unit of GDP) would need to decrease by 26% per unit to keep the ecological footprint at its current level. Whether the service sector can reduce its ecological footprint by 26% depends on the extent to which it is efficient in creating and delivering service offerings.

The illustration demonstrates that technological improvements for reducing the ecological footprint of services may be offset by population growth and consumption. Thus, obtaining an actual reduction in the ecological footprint requires a reduction in population size and/or consumption of goods/services. Such a recommendation conflicts with growth-based economic models employed by most societies, and represents a major hurdle in the quest for environmental sustainability. Thus, to achieve environmental sustainability, societies will need to adopt an economic model that encourages reduced production and more responsible consumption of goods and services.

Population growth has long been viewed as a potential problem, and attempts to deal with it have been made at both national and global levels. Although the population growth rate has declined to about half of what it was 50 years ago, this is not true of affluence (Goklany 2009). As a society's wealth increases, its population growth rate falls, because couples delay or avoid childbirth and engage in more personal consumption (Goklany 2009). Furthermore, there has been an unintended decline in the GDP growth rate over the past 50 years, which may be viewed as an economic failure. In an effort to stimulate economic growth, global policy was enacted through the World Bank, the International Monetary Fund, and the World Trade Organization to push affluence to its limits. Owing to this push, sustainable delivery of goods and services is viewed as a contrary goal. Some scholars therefore suggest that once a society's basic needs are met and the quality of life increases beyond the poverty level, it may be best to avoid emphasizing continuous increases in societal affluence, and instead begin to address environmental concerns.

According to Goklany (2009), once a society's basic needs are met, members begin to perceive that continued environmental degradation adversely impacts their quality of life; they may then begin to address environmental concerns, leading to slowed economic growth. This idea is based on the Kuznets curve hypothesis and its extension, the environmental transition hypothesis. The latter was supported by an observed inverted U-shaped relationship between economic growth and environmental impact among a cross section of countries (Goklany 2009). This inverted U-shaped relationship suggests that as a country's economy begins to grow, its environmental impact begins to get worse. Then, once the society achieves a certain level of economic development, environmental degradation reaches its highest point, and the society shifts its focus from continued economic growth to improving the environment by employing environmentally cleaner technologies (Goklany 2009). Correspondingly, wealthy countries tend to focus more attention on environmentally sustainable business practices, relative to underdeveloped or developing countries.

Although developing countries have yet to satisfy the basic needs of their members and therefore must focus attention on enhancing the well-being of their members, the diffusion of technologies worldwide (combined with some affluence) enables them to be better off than developed countries in earlier years when they were at the same level of economic affluence (Goklany 2009). Moreover, once developing societies achieve a desired level of societal well-being, they are able to redirect their efforts to improve technologies that address both economic development and environmental sustainability. Consequently, by accounting for both micro-level and macro-level factors, the development of environmentally sustainable business practices appears to be a real and achievable possibility.

Summary and conclusion

Kotler (2011) posited that companies need to make drastic changes in their marketing practices to reduce their environmental impacts. That, of course, is not an easy task or one that is undertaken without careful consideration (Olson 2012). A major goal of this chapter was to bring attention to the significant micro- and macro-level challenges facing service organizations in becoming environmentally sustainable. At the micro-level, this chapter describes greenprinting, an environmental management tool that enables service organizations to design and/or re-engineer their service creation and delivery processes to reduce their impact on environmental degradation. The purpose of greenprinting is to provoke thinking about how service organizations can adapt their service delivery processes to become more environmentally responsible, and to provide a broad framework to facilitate that endeavor.

At the macro-level, fundamental changes in DSPs must be combined with shared values that encourage and support environmental sustainability. Without global cooperation and collaboration, service efforts to become environmentally sustainable will be compromised. The general conclusion of this chapter is that based on the scope and sheer size of services in the global economy, if enough organizations were to institute a green imperative in the design of their service blueprints, a profound positive impact on the environment might be achieved. Thus, although greenprinting is useful for achieving sustainability, it, alone, is not sufficient to achieve it. Sustainability also requires fundamental changes to business models that few firms appear willing to accept. These fundamental changes are influenced by macro-level factors that call for more responsible consumption and improving standards of living among societal members.

References

Anderson, D. A. (2014). *Environmental economics and natural resource management*. New York: Routledge.

Aykol, B. & Leonidou, L. C. (2015). Researching the green practices of smaller service firms: A theoretical, methodological, and empirical assessment. *Journal of Small Business Management*, 53 (October), 1264–1288.

Bansal, P. & Roth, K. (2000). Why companies go green: A model of ecological responsiveness. *Academy of Management*, 43(August), 717–736.

Bitner, M. J., Ostrom, A. L. & Morgan, F. N. (2008). Service blueprinting: A practical technique for service innovation. *California Management Review*, 50(3), 66–94.

Brown, M. (1996). Environmental policy in the hotel sector: "Green" strategy or stratagem? *International Journal of Contemporary Hospitality Management*, 8(3), 18–23.

Carbon Footprint Ltd (2012). What is a carbon footprint? *Carbonfootprint.com*. Retrieved from www.carbonfootprint.com/carbonfootprint.html. (accessed 5 September 2014).

Carrig, D. (2018). McDonald's sets goal of recycling, 100% sustainable packaging by 2025. *USA TODAY*, January 17. Retrieved from www.usatoday.com/money/business/2018/01/16/mcdonalds-environmental-goals-sustainable-packaging-recycling/1037214001/. (accessed 21 April 2019).

Chan, R. K. Y., Leung, K. T. K. P. & Wang, Y. H. (2006). The effectiveness of environmental claims for services advertising. *Journal of Services Marketing*, 20(4), 233–250.

Chan, T., Wong, C. W. Y., Lai, K., Lun, V. Y. H., Ng, C. T. & Ngal, E. W. T. (2016). Green service: Construct development and measurement validation. *Production and Operations Management*, 25 (March), 432–457.

Chan, W. W. (2009). Environmental measures for hotels' environmental management systems ISO 14001. *International Journal of Contemporary Hospitality Management*, 21(5), 542–560.

Chanchitpricha, C. & Bond, A. (2013). Conceptualizing the effectiveness of impact processes. *Environmental Impact Assessment Review*, 43(November), 65–72.

Chang, C. (2011). Feeling ambivalent about going green: Implications for green advertising processing. *Journal of Advertising*, 40(4), 19–32.

CIA (2018). Field listing: GDP composition by sector. *The World Factbook*. Retrieved from www.cia. gov/library/publications/the-world-factbook/fields/2012.html. (accessed 13 April 2019).

Collins, E., Roper, J. & Lawrence, S. (2010). Sustainability practices: Trends in New Zealand. *Business Strategy and the Environment*, 19(December), 479–494.

Connelly, B. L., Ketchen, D. J., Jr. & Slater, S. F. (2011). Toward a "theoretical toolbox" for sustainability research in marketing. *Journal of the Academy of Marketing Science*, 39(1), 86–100.

Cronin, J. J., Jr., Smith, J. S., Gleim, M. R., Ramírez, E. & Martinez, J. D. (2011). Green marketing strategies: An extension of stakeholders and the opportunities they present. *Journal of the Academy of Marketing Science*, 39(February), 158–174.

Darden, W. R. & Dorsch, M. J. (1990). An action strategy approach to examining shopping behavior. *Journal of Business Research*, 21(3), 289–308.

Ehrlich, P. R. & Holdren, J. P. (1971). Impact of population growth. *Science*, 171(March 26), 1212–1217.

Elkington, J. (2018). 25 years ago I coined the phrase "triple bottom line." Here's why it's time to rethink it. *Harvard Business Review*, June 25. Retrieved from https://hbr.org/2018/06/25-years-ago-i-coined-the-phrase-triple-bottom-line-heres-why-im-giving-up-on-it? (accessed 9 July 2018).

Environmental Leader (2009). 82% of consumers buy green despite economy. *EnvironmentalLeader.com*. Retrieved from www.environmentalleader.com/2009/02/05/82-percent-of-consumers-buy-green-despite-economy/. (accessed 5 September 2014).

Fisk, G. (1973). Criteria for a theory of responsible consumption. *Journal of Marketing*, 37(April), 24–31.

Fisk, R. P. & Grove, S. J. (2008). Greening the service economy. Presentation at American Marketing Association Summer Educators' Conference, San Diego, CA.

Foster, S. T., Jr., Sampson, S. E. & Dunn, S. C. (2000). The impact of customer contact on environmental initiatives for service firms. *International Journal of Operations & Production Management*, 20(2), 187–203.

Glasser, L. (2009). Survey: 50 percent of companies going green. *Libn.com*. Retrieved from http://libn. com/2009/10/09/survey-50-percent-of-companies-going-green/. (accessed 5 September 2014).

Goklany, I. M. (2009). Have increases in population, affluence and technology worsened human and environmental well-being? *The Electronic Journal of Sustainable Development*, 1(3), 3–28.

Grove, S. J., Fisk, R. P., Pickett, G. M. & Kangun, N. (1996). Going green in the service sector: Social responsibility issues, implications and implementation. *European Journal of Marketing*, 30(5), 56–66.

Gummesson, E. (1994). Service management: An evaluation and the future. *International Journal of Service Industry Management*, 5(1), 77–96.

Harrington, D. R., Khanna, M. & Deltas, G. (2008). Striving to be green: The adoption of total quality environmental management. *Applied Economics*, 40(23), 2995–3007.

Harrison, E. B. (1993). *Going green: How to communicate your company's environmental commitment*. Homewood, IL: Business One Irwin.

Hart, S. L. (1995). A natural-resource-based view of the firm. *Academy of Management Review*, 20(4), 986–1014.

Hart, S. L. & Dowell, G. (2011). A natural-resource-based view of the firm: Fifteen years after. *Journal of Management*, 37(September), 1464–1479.

Heiskanen, E. & Jalas, M. (2003). Can services lead to radical eco-efficiency improvements? A review of the debate and evidence. *Corporate Social Responsibility and Environmental Management*, 10(December), 186–198.

Hoffman, A. J. & Bazerman, M. H. (2007). Changing practice on sustainability: Understanding and overcoming the organizational and psychological barriers to action. In S. S. M. Starik & B. Husted (Eds.), *Organizations and the sustainability mosaic: Crafting long-term ecological and societal solutions* (pp. 84–105). Northampton: Edward Elgar.

ISO (2009). *Environmental management: The ISO 14000 family of international standards.* Retrieved from www.iso.org/iso/theiso14000family_2009.pdf. (accessed 8 July 2018).

Jay, S., Jones, C., Slinn, P. & Wood, C. (2007). Environmental impact assessment: Retrospect and prospect. *Environmental Impact Review*, 27(May), 287–300.

Junior, A. N., de Oliveira, M. C. & Helleno, A. L. (2018). Sustainability evaluation model for manufacturing systems based on the correlation between triple bottom line dimensions and balanced scorecard perspectives. *Journal for Cleaner Production*, 190(July 20), 84–93.

Kassarjian, H. H. (1971). Incorporating ecology into marketing strategy: The case of air pollution. *Journal of Marketing*, 25(July), 61–65.

Kassinis, G. I. & Soteriou, A. C. (2003). Greening the service profit chain: The impact of environmental management practices. *Production and Operations Management*, 12(Fall), 386–403.

Kilbourne, W. E., Dorsch, M. J., McDonagh, P., Urien, B., Prothero, A., Grunhagen, M., Polonsky, M. J., Marshall, D., Foley, J. & Bradshaw, B. (2009). The institutional foundations of materialism in western societies: A conceptualization and empirical test. *Journal of Macromarketing*, 29 (September), 259–278.

Kilbourne, W. E., Dorsch, M. J. & Thyroff, A. (2018). Theorizing materialism through the institutional analysis and development framework. *Marketing Theory*, 18(March), 55–74.

Kinnear, T. C., Taylor, J. R. & Ahmed, S. A. (1974). Ecologically concerned consumers: Who are they? *Journal of Marketing*, 38(2), 20–24.

Kirk, D. (1995). Environmental management in hotels. *International Journal of Contemporary Hospitality Management*, 7(6), 3–8.

Ko, E., Kyung, Y. H. & Kim, E. Y. (2013). Green marketing's functions in building corporate image in the retail setting. *Journal of Business Research*, 66(10), 1709–1715.

Kotler, P. (2011). Reinventing marketing to manage the environmental imperative. *Journal of Marketing*, 75(4), 132–135.

Lawrence, S. R., Collins, E., Pavlovich, K. & Arunachalam, M. (2006). Sustainability practices of SMEs: The case of NZ. *Business Strategy and the Environment*, 15(July/August), 242–257.

Lee, M. A. & Mather, M. (2008). U.S. labor force trends. *Population Bulletin*, 63(2), 3–16.

Lim, W. M. (2016). A blueprint for sustainable marketing: Defining its conceptual boundaries for progress. *Marketing Theory*, 16(June), 232–249.

Lovelock, C. H. (1994). *Product plus.* New York: McGraw-Hill.

Lubin, D. A. & Esty, D. C. (2010). The sustainability imperative. *Harvard Business Review*, 88(5), 42–50.

Makower, J. (2006). Beyond smokestacks: The greening of the service sector. *GreenBiz.com*. Retrieved from http://makower.typepad.com/joel_makower/2006/03/beyondsmokesta.html. (accessed 8 July 2018).

Martin, D. M. & Schouten, J. W. (2014). Consumption-driven market emergence. *Journal of Consumer Research*, 40(February), 855–870.

McDonalds.com (2018). Retrieved from https://news.mcdonalds.com/news-releases/news-release-details/recap-mcdonalds-environmental-commitments-and-actions-2018. (accessed 21 April 2019).

Moore, G. & Spence, L. (2006). Editorial: Responsibility and small business. *Journal of Business Ethics*, 67 (September), 219–226.

Morgan, R. K. (2012). Environmental impact assessment: The state of the art. *Impact Assessment and Project Appraisal*, 30(March), 5–14.

Namkung, Y. & Jang, S. (2013). Effects of restaurant green practices on brand equity formation: Do green practices really matter? *International Journal of Hospitality Management*, 33, 85–95.

Newman, P. (2006). The environmental impact of cities. *Environment & Urbanization*, 18(October), 275–295.

Nowakowski, M. (1973). A formal theory of actions. *Behavioral Science*, 18(6), 393–416.

Nowakowski, M. (1981). Structure of situation and action: Some remarks on formal theory of actions. In D. Magnusson (Ed.), *Toward a psychology of situations: An integrated perspective* (pp. 211–227). Hillsdale, NJ: Erlbaum.

Olson, L. (2012). It's not easy being green: The effects of attribute tradeoffs on green product preference and choice. *Journal of the Academy of Marketing Science*, 41(2), 171–184.

Ottman, J. (2011). *The new rules of green marketing: Strategies, tools, and inspiration for sustainable branding.* San Francisco, CA: Berrett-Koehler Publishers.

Parry, S. (2012). Going green: The evolution of micro-business environmental practices. *Business Ethics: A European Review*, 21(2), 220–237.

Parsons, T. (1937). *The structure of action.* New York: McGraw-Hill.

Patrício, L., Fisk, R. P. & Grove, S. J. (2009). "Greenprinting": Designing service delivery systems for sustainability. 18th Annual Frontiers in Service Conference, Honolulu, Hawaii (October 29–November 1).

Patton, O. B. (2010). New bill would set national freight transportation policy. *Truckinginfo*, July 23. Retrieved from www.truckinginfo.com/news/newsdetail.asp. (accessed 5 September 2014).

Peattie, K. & Crane, A. (2005). Green marketing: Legend, myth, farce, or prophecy? *Qualitative Market Research: An International Journal*, 8(4), 357–370.

Polonsky, M. J. (1994). An introduction to green marketing. *Electronic Green Journal*, 1(2). Retrieved from http://escholarship.org/uc/item/49n325b7. (accessed 5 July 2018).

Polonsky, M. J. (2011). Transformative green marketing: Impediments and opportunities. *Journal of Business Research*, 64(December), 1311–1319.

Porter, M. E. & Reinhardt, F. L. (2007). A strategic approach to climate. *Harvard Business Review*, 85(10), 22–26.

Porter, M. E. & van der Linde, C. (1995). Competitive and green: Ending the stalemate. *Harvard Business Review*, 73(September/October), 120–134.

Posner, B. & Kiron, D. (2013). How Caesars Entertainment is betting on sustainability. *MIT Sloan Management Review*, 54(4), 63–71.

Rodrigue, J. P., Comtois, C. & Slack, B. (2009). *The geography of transport systems*. 2nd Edition. New York: Routledge.

Salzman, J. (2000). Environmental protection beyond the smokestack: Addressing the impact of the service economy. *Corporate Environmental Strategy*, 7(1), 20–37.

Sampson, S. E. (2012). Visualizing service operations. *Journal of Service Research*, 15(2), 182–198.

Schaeffer, A. & Crane, A. (2005). Addressing sustainability and consumption. *Journal of Macromarketing*, 25 (June), 76–92.

Science News (2010). Reducing emissions in shipping. *Science Daily*, December 20. Retrieved from www.sciencedaily.com/releases/2010/12/101220102735.htm. (accessed 5 September 2014).

Sheth, J. N. & Parvartiyar, A. (1995). Ecological imperatives and the role of marketing. In M. J. Polonsky & A. T. Mintu-Wimsatt (Eds.), *Environmental marketing: Strategies, practices, theory and research* (pp. 3–20). New York: Hawthorne Press.

Shostack, G. L. (1984). Designing services that deliver. *Harvard Business Review*, 62(1), 133–139.

Shostack, G. L. (1987). Service positioning through structural change. *Journal of Marketing*, 51(1), 34–43.

Shrivastava, P. (1995). The role of corporations in achieving ecological sustainability. *Academy of Management Review*, 20(October), 936–960.

Sroufe, R. (2003). Effects of environmental management systems on environmental management practices and operations. *Production and Operations Management*, 12(Fall), 416–431.

Suh, S. (2006). Are services better for climate change? *Environmental Science & Technology*, 40(21), 6555–6560.

The Economics Daily (2014). Largest industries by state, 1990–2013. *U.S. Bureau of Labor Statistics*, July 28. Retrieved from www.bls.gov/opub/ted/2014/ted_20140728.htm. (accessed 14 October 2018).

Thiele, L. P. (1999). *Environmentalism for a new millennium*. New York: Oxford University Press, Inc.

Tzschentke, N., Kirk, D. & Lynch, P. A. (2004). Reasons for going green in serviced accommodation establishments. *International Journal of Contemporary Hospitality Management*, 16(2), 116–124.

U. S. Census Bureau (2012). Average annual expenditure of all consumer units by selected major types of expenditure: 1990–2009. *The 2012 Statistical Abstract: The National Data Book*. Retrieved from www.census.gov/compendia/statab/2012/tables/12s0684.pdf. (accessed 5 September 2014).

Vargo, S. J. & Lusch, R. F. (2004). Evolving a new dominant logic for marketing. *Journal of Marketing*, 68 (1), 1–17.

Von Wright, G. H. (1970). The event approach: The logic of change and action. In M. Brand (Ed.), *The nature of human action* (pp. 302–342). Glenville, IL: Scott Foresman and Company.

Williams, A. & Dupuy, K. (2017). Deciding over nature: Corruption and environmental impact assessments. *Environmental Impact Assessment Review*, 65(July), 118–124.

Wong, C. W. Y., Wong, C. Y. & Boon-itt, S. (2013). Green service practices: Performance implications and the role of environmental management systems. *Service Science*, 5(March), 69–84.

World Bank. (2016). CO2 emissions (metric tons per capita) | Data. Retrieved July 21, 2016, from The World Bank website: http://data.worldbank.org/indicator/EN.ATM.CO2E.PC

23

The convergence of not-for-profit services and the social enterprise

Joshua Coleman and Marla Royne Stafford

Introduction

According to entrepreneur Mark Ecko, "The future of non-profit is for-profit" (Schiller, 2014). Not-for-profit services are facing unprecedented changes, as donor retention rates fall (Nilsen, 2017), Millennials engage in new methods of giving (Miller, 2017), and volunteer rates continue to decline (Nesbit & Christensen, 2018). In tandem, the social expectations placed on for-profit businesses are increasing to the point where businesses are expected to operate in ways that are sustainable, ethical, organic, environmentally friendly, and gluten-free, all while achieving profitable returns and eradicating worldwide poverty. As Barnett (2015, p. 8) states, "There is no question that the legal, ethical, and discretionary expectations placed on businesses are greater than ever before." The result of these marketplace trends is a convergence of not-for-profit and for-profit values and operations. The strategic combination of these traditionally conflicting missions – essentially, making money and giving it away – are perhaps best epitomized by the development and expansion of the social enterprise, a hybrid form of business that unites philanthropy with a for-profit business model.

When looking to the trends of not-for-profit services, one must consider the economic development that has led to the current state of the industry and the social enterprise. What began as loosely structured volunteer associations at the start of the American nation soon turned to more corporate and legal entities by the end of the 19th century. At that time, early emergence of social welfare among for-profit industry was seen in the tycoon philanthropy of the late 1800s and early 1900s, before giving way to welfare capitalism. Charitable services grew into company-wide corporate social responsibility (CSR) efforts, which drove consumer-focused marketing tactics known as cause-related marketing (CM) that emerged in the 1980s. During that time, not-for-profit services transitioned from fraternal organizations to a more individualistic approach that coincided with the suburban transition of Americans: as they discovered greater independence in their personal finances, homes, and lives, they sought the same motivations in their not-for-profit support. Thus, over the past century alone, one can observe a slow decline in the utility of and membership in fraternal organizations and labor unions, in tandem with a rise of more individualized approaches to not-for-profit support. The current state of not-for-profit organizations along with an increased demand for socially responsible efforts from

American companies, has led to the social enterprise, which seamlessly integrates not-for-profit and for-profit missions and operations into one hybrid organization.

This chapter begins by elaborating upon this historical development, as summarized in Table 23.1, to provide insights into the progression of not-for-profit services and the

Table 23.1 Historical overview of not-for-profit services

Time Period	Major Theme	Description
1776–1860	Colonial volunteers and free market economics	American hesitancy to embrace a centralized federal government led to loosely formed and transient local volunteer services to meet community needs.
1860–1900	Solidifying a nation economically and charitably	Big business boomed during the Industrial Revolution. While philanthropists like Andrew Carnegie advocated for the wealthy to distribute their wealth, labor unions and fraternal societies emerged in response to oppression in the workforce. These local chapters were part of a national organization, laying the foundation for a future system of not-for-profit services.
1900–1945	Democratized charity and welfare capitalism	Two World Wars and the Great Depression had a tremendous impact on the welfare of the nation. New charitable vehicles emerged – many of the emergency programs enacted in response to the Great Depression still exist today despite their intended short tenure – and ethical reform in the business world led to the rise of welfare capitalism.
1945–1980	The not-for-profit sector and corporate social responsibility	Governmental influence in not-for-profit services grew in the postwar years, while Americans moved to the suburbs and began pursuing their own ideals and goals. This extended to their involvement in charity, as support for not-for-profit services began shifting from collective fraternal organizations to personal gratification. Companies began investing in corporate social responsibility in a more intentional effort to show the societal impact of their operations.
1980–2000	The Conservative Revolution and cause-related marketing	The Conservative Revolution resulted in the breakdown of much of the governmental involvement in not-for-profit organizations, but this also led to a significant reduction in funding. Not-for-profits were forced to change tactics and begin operating in a more competitive arena, adopting for-profit strategies to survive. Cause-related marketing emerged as an even more intentional way for companies to drive charitable support with consumer activity.
2000–2018	The social enterprise	The social enterprise emerged as a hybrid form of business that aligns a social mission with profit-seeking operations. This congruence of not-for-profit and for-profit in one organization has made a significant impact in terms of consumer demand, marketplace potential, and not-for-profit operations.

convergence of traditional organizations with modern-day socially conscious businesses like social enterprises. The focus then turns to future trends that can be expected in not-for-profit services, based on the trajectory of historical progress. Among these future developments is the necessity of online fundraising, a careful reanalysis of not-for-profit supporters as donors and consumers, an increased demand for not-for-profit organizations to operate like for-profit businesses, an intentional focus on ensuring financial sustainability, and an increase in cross-sector collaborations. These insights and trends among not-for-profit services provide both academics and practitioners impetus for growth as the marketplace continues to evolve.

1776–1860: colonial volunteers and free market economics

As a new nation emerged from the oppression of an overseas empire, many new Americans were hesitant to trust any part of their citizenship to a federal government. Political and intellectual giants like Washington, Jefferson, and Hamilton established a representative democracy, but a centralized governing body still seemed to some too reminiscent of the British monarchy. As such, early voluntary associations – many of which were the forerunners of today's not-for-profit services – were organized and executed independently of any state or national accountability. In tandem with the overarching issues facing the newly minted nation, early political leaders debated whether to manage the often ragtag volunteer associations through state or federal government. Churches, schools, and universities flourished alongside private donations to public institutions separate from any governmental interference (Hall, 2010).

Around the same time, economist Adam Smith proposed the free market economic system, the original intentions of which may have been misinterpreted throughout the proceeding decades (Oslington, 2012). Smith's descriptions of a mysterious invisible hand guiding the marketplace and the necessity of the businessman to act in his own self-interest have led many to consider him the epitome of marketplace greed (Bevan & Werhane, 2015). In recent years, however, scholars have begun reassessing Smith's work in an attempt to determine the true meaning of his writings (e.g., Bragues, 2009; Brown & Forster, 2013; Gonin, 2015). Coase and Wang (2012, p. 36) stated, "The degree to which economics is isolated from the ordinary business of life is extraordinary and unfortunate." Concerning the free market economic system Smith proposed, under his original ideologies,

> Business activities are permeated by the values of the local community and remain under the constant scrutiny of the numerous neighbors, customers, and authorities. The virtuous entrepreneur does not only consider his/her own self-interest but also takes into consideration the norms, as well as the needs of the community when managing his enterprise.
>
> *(Gonin, 2015, p. 224)*

The basic cyclical premise of the baker making food for the carpenter who makes the house for the baker to make food for the carpenter paints a picture of a nation where the mere undisturbed interaction of organizations and individuals resulted in the meeting of societal needs (Barnett, 2015). Over the next half century, early suspicion of governmental and corporate interference with not-for-profit services would dissolve, but Smith's vision of a self-sustaining economical infrastructure would also dissolve, until new methods of attaining congruence between social services and for-profit businesses emerged over 200 years later.

1860–1900: solidifying a nation economically and charitably

By the mid-19th century, distrust among Americans toward a federal government had generally declined, and volunteer organizations played a significant role during the Civil War and postwar reconstruction era. Business leaders began replacing lawyers and clergymen on university governing boards as a profit-driven economic boom ushered in the Industrial Revolution. This proliferation of tycoon philanthropy was epitomized by Andrew Carnegie's 'Gospel of Wealth' that promulgated the idea of intelligent benevolence coming from the nation's wealthiest individuals. Big money was becoming attainable for an elite few, but it was being attained at the expense of the common man (Hall, 2010). Gone was the utopian vision of a self-regulating society in which social welfare was the natural by-product of conducting ethical and economically profitable business.

Though struggling under wretched labor conditions, the common man was not completely bereft of opportunities to contribute to the welfare of society. Substantial monetary donations might have been limited to tycoons, but laypeople began joining labor unions and fraternal organizations. Because many of these organizations were enacted through local chapters connected to larger, nationwide bodies, members were able to see the advantages of local benevolence organized through widespread, homogenized large-scale distribution (Hall, 2010). This was further evidence of how far the people had come from distrust of a federally organized body to embracing the gains of nationwide service. These organizations laid a foundation for local, social welfare efforts to thrive, but they also deepened the rift between not-for-profit services and big business, especially because many of them were enacted in response to the oppression of the nation's industrialized labor force and capitalism.

1900–1945: democratized charity and welfare capitalism

As many began viewing tycoons and corporations as too powerful, the public started expecting something more from the nation's corporate giants: increased attention to and investment in societal needs (Barnett, 2015). The 20th century ushered in the Progressive Era, with social change manifesting itself in suffrage for women, prohibition, and child labor laws (Muslic, 2018). Two World Wars and a Great Depression had significant impacts on the makeup of the nation's charitable services as well. Much like previous wars, World War II drew volunteers together into organized groups operating under a national umbrella for a more effective distribution of services than what was seen in the earlier formations of such services. As Hall (2010, p. 17) states, "In the 1930s, no one envisioned that the emergency powers assumed by the federal government to deal with the Great Depression would become permanent and central features of public life." In response to these landmark events, the federal government took an increasingly present role in the distribution of social welfare and the creation of not-for-profit organizations. New charitable vehicles emerged to assume this responsibility, such as grant-making foundations and corporate entities for the distribution of the fortunes of the nation's wealthiest (Hall, 2010).

Because expectations for social reform were growing in response to the oppression of the Industrial Revolution, for-profit businesses endorsed many of these charitable efforts. Welfare capitalism emerged and brought with it corporate donations to not-for-profit organizations, educational programs, social and athletic programs for employees and families, and pension plans (Hall, 2010), as well as the development of professional fundraising (Muslic, 2018). Charitable services were becoming democratized, welfare capitalism was improving the ethical standards of the nation's leading organizations, and the foundation was laid for a more intentional focus on embedding not-for-profit services into the very operations of a company.

1945–1980: the not-for-profit sector and CSR

The movements that took place during the years 1900–1945 led to the development of an official not-for-profit sector, referred to as the "third sector" by 1980 (Defourny, 2014; see also Muslic, 2018). The postwar period of the late 20th century saw Americans moving to the suburbs, as the middle class ushered in a wave of individual progress and self-sufficiency. Accompanying grassroots civil rights movements, American involvement with not-for-profit organizations rose along a more selective, personally gratifying path. Formal membership in traditional fraternal societies declined as involvement in religious institutions, social justice services, and parachurch not-for-profit organizations rose (Hall, 2010). A century previously, in the face of growing oppression by big business, Americans joined welfare organizations for the benevolence of the common man; during this period, Americans selectively chose which not-for-profit organizations would most satisfy their personal desires and goals.

The movement toward greater societal impact among businesses began emerging as CSR, defined as "the economic, legal, ethical, and discretionary (philanthropic) expectations that society has of organizations at a given point in time" (Carroll & Buchholtz, 2014, p. 32). The notion of giving back to society does not fit well with the idea of a profit-maximizing company, because it would likely be required to divert profit-making resources in order to do so (Brown & Forster, 2013). The prevailing thought toward CSR is that businesses should voluntarily seek solutions to some of society's greatest needs, regardless of how the social problems arose or whose responsibility it should be to provide aid (Barnett, 2015). Thus, as consumers moved toward independent lives in the suburbs and companies began providing opportunities to improve society through capitalism, a new form of social support emerged.

1980–2000: the Conservative Revolution and CM

The 1980s saw the Conservative Revolution breaking down the dominant presence of big government. For not-for-profit services, this resulted in unintended consequences. As Hall (2010, p. 23) states,

> What [President Reagan], like most Americans, failed to understand was the extent to which the not-for-profit sector had become dependent on government spending…The federal government had become the largest single source of revenue for secular not-for-profit organizations, and for this reason, massive cuts in government social spending would devastate the not-for-profit sector.

This decrease in governmental not-for-profit expenditures meant these organizations would need to attain funding from other sources. This necessitated the need for skilled business leaders, professionally trained managers, and entrepreneurs to manage not-for-profit organizations (Hall, 2010). Thus, not-for-profit services, many of which operated alongside or even in response to big business, began seeing an infiltration of entrepreneurialism that has persisted to this day.

While profitable business practices began influencing not-for-profits, the social missions of not-for-profits began moving into the corporate world by integrating the high-level ethics and welfare programs seen in CSR with consumerism. The 1980s witnessed the debut of CM. American Express enacted an innovative marketing campaign to donate to renovations of the Statue of Liberty, but these donations were contingent upon customers opening accounts with the company. The unparalleled success of the campaign paved the way for future, customer-dependent charitable efforts. Varadarajan and Menon (1988) published a seminal academic work on the subject, explicating the managerial implications and boundary conditions of CM. The authors also provided a much-needed definition of the term that is still used today: "the process of formulating and implementing marketing activities that are characterized by an offer from the firm to contribute a specified amount to a designated cause when customers engage in revenue-providing exchanges that satisfy organizational and individual objectives" (Varadarajan & Menon, 1988, p. 60).

In the same article, Varadarajan and Menon (1988) discussed the differences between tactical and strategic CM. (A summary is provided in Table 23.2). Tactical CM utilizes the cause affiliation to increase awareness and sales; at most, the marketing activity serves as a differentiated sales promotion. Strategic CM, on the other hand, is a long-term commitment that involves managerial input at all levels of the organization and a significantly greater investment of resources than is typical for tactical CM programs. Varadarajan and Menon (1988, p. 67) explained that the primary distinction between the two facets of CM involves "the notion of managerial behavior guided by a philosophy that explicitly recognizes the corporation's obligations to society versus managerial behavior primarily guided by profit or earnings goals."

Companies and scholars have spent the majority of their time on tactical CM (Andrews, Luo, Fang, & Aspara, 2014), with research linking the marketing effort to more positive brand evaluations (Lafferty & Goldsmith, 2005; Olson & Thjømøe, 2011), better brand positioning (Du, Bhattacharya, & Sen, 2007; Moosmayer & Fuljahn, 2013), and favorable behavioral responses (Bigné-Alcañiz, Currás-Pérez, Ruiz-Mafé, & Sanz-Blas, 2012). This distinction is particularly informative in the current American marketplace, as the full merits and utility of strategic CM were not explored in great depth until the past decade. (For a comprehensive review of empirical work see Andrews et al., 2014.) For not-for-profit organizations, CM has provided a valuable and innovative tool by which support can be received. However, not-for-profits cannot rely solely on the benevolence of such corporate partnerships to maintain long-term sustainability. Thus, CM should not be seen as a panacea for not-for-profit sustenance.

The truly significant impact of CM, then, is the inclusion of the consumer in connecting for-profit transactions to charitable donations. Prior to this point, if individuals desired to contribute funds to social welfare through not-for-profit organizations, their primary means of doing so was by donating to the not-for-profit itself. CM allowed them to purchase a self-satisfying product, whether utilitarian or hedonic in nature, and also contribute to a not-for-profit organization at the same time. This fundamental shift toward simultaneously gratifying personal needs and supporting societal needs paved the way for the social enterprise, a new type of organizational structure that intentionally unites the mission of not-for-profits with the capitalism of for-profits, with success on both fronts contingent upon the consumer.

Table 23.2 Tactical and strategic cause-related marketing

Tactical CM	*Strategic CM*
• top management's involvement in key decisions is very limited • commitment to the program is short-term • limited resources are necessary for the successful execution of the program	• top management is involved in key program decisions • commitment to the program is long-term • development and implementation necessitate substantial investments
Ex: CM is used as a differentiated positioning approach for a sales promotion	Ex: an entire line of products is marketed around the notion of CM

2000–2018: the social enterprise

In 2006, social entrepreneur Blake Mycoskie started a revolutionary company called TOMS in the pursuit of satisfying customers while meeting the needs of individuals in poverty. This type of company, called a social enterprise, simultaneously pursues the dual goals of profit and philanthropy (Thornley, 2013). TOMS coined the unique "One for One" phrase, describing how the company is committed to donating a pair of shoes to a needy child every time a consumer purchases a pair of shoes. This integration of CM with every level of the business, from the Chief Shoe Giver (TOMS' version of CEO) to the retail outlet salespeople, has enabled TOMS to become a pioneer for the use of strategic CM in the marketplace (Wydick, Katz, & Janet, 2014), embodying the convergence of for-profit economics with social responsibility.

Although it might have been one of the first social enterprises to garner international attention and unprecedented sales, TOMS was not the first social enterprise. The term had been around for many years (Defourny, 2001), and some social enterprises have been in operation for over three decades (Yunus, 2007). TOMS was, however, the first social enterprise to reach the attention of national and global markets, demonstrating to the world that businesses that operate with the dual purpose of making money and giving back can successfully compete on an international scale. As of 2013, the most recent time at which data were collected on a nationwide scale, social enterprises were estimated to employ over 10 million people with a collective revenue exceeding $500 billion, around 3.5% of total GDP (Thornley, 2013). In comparison, not-for-profit organizations were estimated to represent 5.4% of GDP (McKeever & Pettijohn, 2014).

The unprecedented growth and success of the social enterprise over the past decade is remarkable, but one problem has stymied the proliferation of academic research on the subject: there is very little agreement as to what a social enterprise is (Brown, 2014; Plerhoples, 2013). Czischke, Gruis, and Mullins (2012) highlight many different variations of the term throughout the U.S. and Europe, concluding that the term can imply completely different things from country to country. Table 23.3 presents a selection of definitions gleaned from current literature addressing social enterprises. Although some scholars have collected definitions of social entrepreneurs (the individuals creating and leading social enterprises) and social entrepreneurship (the act of creating and leading social enterprises) (Zahra, Gedajlovic, Neubaum, & Shulman, 2009), the table focuses solely on the entities themselves. Much of the confusion herein lies in the varied delineations among cultures and corporations, which have led some to declare social entrepreneurship an essentially contested concept, of which no single description can be identified (Choi & Majumdar, 2014).

Regardless of the absence of a universal definition for the term, as Von der Weppen and Cochrane (2012, p. 497) note: "Increasing academic scrutiny has resulted in a consensus that the primary goal of any social enterprise is the adoption of financially sustainable strategies to achieve social aims." Several common themes have emerged that differentiate the social enterprise from previously researched social efforts that have come before it. For one, social enterprises are marked by a need to invest surplus income into societal needs, not the maximization of profit (Chell, Nicolopoulou, & Karatas-Ozkan, 2010). This idea offers the opportunity for new insight into discussions of stakeholder theory due to the primary focus of the social enterprise as a beneficiary of company donations. Just as a social enterprise may draw a business away from an unwavering focus on profit, it may also draw in entrepreneurs unsatisfied with traditional business models (Zahra et al., 2009). Furthermore, whereas nearly all social enterprises seek community restoration, many also work toward social efforts in third world countries (Defourny, 2001).

What has not been discussed prolifically among social enterprise researchers is its connection to CM. The distinguishing feature of any CM campaign is its contingency upon consumer

Table 23.3 Definitions of Social Enterprise

Source	Definition
Brown (2014)	A practice which is motivated by the objective of solving social and/or environmental problems, but which uses the tools of capitalism, especially trade, to do so
Bugg-Levine, Kogut, & Kulatilaka (2012)	Entrepreneurial organizations that innovate to solve problems
Department for Trade and Industry (2002)	A business with primarily social objectives whose surpluses are principally reinvested for that purpose in the business or in the community, rather than being driven by the need to maximize profit for shareholder and owners
Dey & Teasdale (2013)	Market-based strategies aimed at achieving a social purpose
Domenico, Maria, Haugh, & Tracey (2010)	Seek to attain a particular social objective or set of objectives through the sale of products and/or services, and in doing so aim to achieve financial sustainability independent of government and other donors
Johanisova, Crabtree, & Fraňková (2013)	Participating to some extent in the market, having a degree of autonomy from public authorities, with a commitment toward job creation, an explicit aim to benefit the community or a specific group of people in its founding documents, decision-making power not based on capital ownership (democratic ownership structure), and exclusion of the profit-maximizing principle
Massetti (2012)	Organizations seeking to achieve social goals through sustainable profits
Miles, Verreynne, & Luke (2014)	Organizations with an overarching core social mission funded through market-based initiatives
Ohana and Meyer (2010)	Organizations which achieve social goals in an entrepreneurial way
Smith, Gonin, & Besharov (2013)	Seek to solve social problems through business ventures
Teasdale (2012)	Organizations trading in the marketplace to achieve a social purpose
Vickers and Lyon (2012)	A set of organizations with primarily social purposes, but which generate a significant amount of their income from trading in goods or services

interaction to succeed. That is, the donation to a social cause in a CM campaign would not be made unless a consumer completes a revenue-providing transaction. This is different from previously discussed social efforts such as CSR, in which corporate philanthropy is often proffered regardless of whether or not consumers buy a specific product. The social enterprise, on the other hand, seems to be the ultimate embodiment of strategic CM: instead of one product or product line being utilized as a marketing strategy to assist not-for-profits, the entire organization exists to support a social cause through business activities. Every transaction leads to not-for-profit support, and not-for-profit support does not occur without transactions. If a profit-seeking company decided today that its CM strategy would extend to every transaction and product, it would look strikingly similar to the social enterprise.

A truly interesting conclusion that can be drawn from social enterprises is the relationship to the history of not-for-profit services. At the founding of the nation, American involvement in voluntary and social organizations was local and personal, and Smith's free market economics promoted a vision of a self-sufficient, profit-seeking economic model that contributed to the general welfare of society. Presently, Americans are involved in not-for-profit organizations on local and personal levels, and social enterprises are conducting business to both make money and give it away. Whether the country is on the precipice of a new economic horizon or is realizing the utopian vision of a nation reeling from revolution, the challenges and opportunities facing not-for-profit services in the future are tremendous.

2020 and beyond: current and future trends

Over the course of American history, not-for-profit services have developed from loosely organized and largely transient volunteer associations to the third sector of societally beneficial organizations run like some of the nation's largest profit-seeking corporations. The for-profit sector has witnessed the inclusion of ethics, corporate philanthropy, and now consumer-driven CM efforts to drive both economic and social bottom lines. Not-for-profit organizations rely less on donor and governmental support, drawing sustainability instead from consumer transactions, while for-profit companies are integrating philanthropy into core business practices alongside traditional profit-seeking operations.

Thus, the demands placed on not-for-profit organizations moving forward are profound. The CM seen in the 1980s brought consumer transactions into the domain of not-for-profit services, and the social enterprise took this concept and made an entirely new organizational structure out of it. Not-for-profit managers must continually seek balance in the tension between remaining steadfast within the boundaries of the traditional not-for-profit sector while learning from and adapting to the philanthropy of today's socially conscious for-profit companies. This convergence of not-for-profit and social enterprise is manifesting itself in a myriad of ways; this chapter now turns from the development of today's not-for-profit services to a discussion of several current and future trends that can be expected in the rapidly changing world of not-for-profits and social enterprises. These trends are summarized in Table 23.4.

Digital fundraising

Much of the future success for not-for-profit services will depend on how well such organizations can adapt to the for-profit mind-sets embodied in the social enterprise. However, many not-for-profit services with deeply loyal customer bases must continue to rely in some part on external sources of funding and fundraising to remain competitive. Recent statistics indicate that the methods of attaining such funding are changing among generations, including Baby Boomers (born 1946–1965), Generation X (born 1966–1976), and Millennials (born 1977–1994) (WJSchroer, 2017). Among the Millennial generation, 62% of individuals donate to not-for-profit organizations through their mobile phones, and 47% donate through websites. For individuals in Generation X, 47% donate through mobile phones and 40%

Table 23.4 Future trends for not-for-profit services

Trend	Description
Digital fundraising	Statistics indicate that younger generations are donating online and through mobile phones more than any previous generation. Not-for-profit managers must adapt fundraising strategies to accommodate these platforms, and social media should be leveraged to utilize current donors' word-of-mouth marketing.
Redefining donors	As sources of funding shift from traditional sources of government and donor support, not-for-profit managers need to begin seeking opportunities to reach out to consumers in addition to donors. Filling marketplace needs will provide an extra source of income but must take strategic, intentional marketing efforts.
Operating like a business	Not-for-profit services must adopt for-profit operations to remain competitive in an increasingly crowded and complex marketplace. This includes strategies such as monitoring expenses, tracking return on investment, and investing in real-time data analytics.
Fostering sustainability	As traditional sources of funding like governments and donors continue to decline, not-for-profit services must find other ways to remain financially secure. This financial sustainability must also be aligned with sustainability for missional impact to ensure that the organization does not lose its purpose in an attempt to attain financial security.
Investing in partnerships	Not-for-profit managers must seek intentional, innovative partnerships moving forward. Working with for-profit companies will provide many benefits for not-for-profit organizations and can supply resources and needs that cannot currently be met through governmental and donor-based funding alone.

give through websites; 42% of Baby Boomers donate through websites (Morpus, 2017). These findings indicate that nearly half of all individuals within a vast portion of the population (Millennials, Generation X, and Baby Boomers) prefer to donate through digital channels. Traditional fundraising methods such as direct mail solicitations or honorariums are still used, but the fastest-growing age-groups are increasingly moving online. This is not a surprise, as these figures mirror overall trends in the marketplace, but their impact on not-for-profit services must be taken into consideration.

Not-for-profit managers should adapt their organizational fundraising strategies to the digital changes facing the industry, and they should ensure that any online donation method made available to customers is perceived as reliable. According to one study, individuals donate online "only when they perceive the organization as honest and trustworthy and consider the Internet a secure medium for financial transactions" (Pollach, Treiblmaier, & Floh, 2005, p. 178.2). Online donations must be easy, accessible, and preferably trackable to encourage participation, with one report suggesting that priority should be placed on increasing the navigability of an organization's website for donations before investing in email, search engine marketing, or social media (Haselwood, 2018).

Miller (2009) discusses "flipping the funnel." Traditionally, a mass audience of individuals was exposed to fundraising opportunities in the hopes that a few would respond, illustrated by the idea of many people entering the large end of a funnel but only a few coming out the other end.

Today, those few individuals who come out the small end of the funnel should be empowered to then communicate back through the funnel to the rest of the audience who were exposed but did not respond to fundraising opportunities. Not only will this allow a not-for-profit organization to leverage the power and influence of current and committed donors, reducing the labor and resources necessary to attain more funding, but these individuals will harness the word-of-mouth marketing that can be much more effective than traditional marketing efforts. Moreover, with the advent of social media, individuals are more connected to one another than ever before, so investing in influential donors can provide substantial fundraising results with reduced labor and resource expenditures. One study shows that donors already logged into Facebook comply with requests to ask their peers for donations 130% more often than individuals who are not already logged into Facebook, because of the reduction of nuisance costs associated with having to log in to a social network (Castillo, Petrie, & Wardell, 2014). Thus, investing in people who already support the organization and are already online can be a very effective way to leverage online fundraising.

As funding methods shift to digital platforms, not-for-profit managers must remember that donating to fundraisers is still an intimately personal decision. Although many factors play roles in determining the success of donation requests (e.g., the size of the organization, the individual's history with the organization, and whether or not a target or goal exists for the fundraising opportunity), keeping giving requests personal continues to result in greater fundraising success (Payne, Scharf, & Smith, 2014). Meer (2011) empirically demonstrates that personal requests for donations are more effective among university alumni than are non-personal requests. It can be easy to lose the personal connection when fundraising through the internet, but not-for-profit services must maintain this connection if they are to successfully adapt to new methods of raising money. Effective use of social media and empowerment of current donors can go a long way toward maintaining personal connections through potentially impersonal media outlets.

Redefining donors

Individual donors, compared to foundations or corporations, gave $286 billion to charitable organizations in 2017, accounting for 70% of all donations in that year (Charity Navigator, 2018). Analysts continue to navigate how to effectively leverage not-for-profit donors by identifying their needs and wants (e.g., clear message, desire to make a difference, and desire to feel a connection with the need; Arnold, 2018). However, while fundraising and donors are still the backbone of many not-for-profit services, managers should begin evaluating their organization's sources of funding. As not-for-profits increasingly operate more competitively with for-profits, attaining donors may need to be redefined as "seeking consumers."

St. Jude Children's Research Hospital provides an example of this redefined thinking. One of the most well-known charities in the nation (Charity Navigator, 2019), St. Jude benefits from tremendous donor support, and has increased fundraising by 350% over a 20-year span, raising more money than any other hospital in the nation (Advisory Board, 2012). St. Jude solicits donations from a variety of demographics, ranging from families to business people to college students (Advisory Board, 2012). However, St. Jude's hospital gift shop in Memphis, Tennessee and its accompanying website pose an interesting issue in terms of seeking donors. When an individual purchases themed products in the gift shop, proceeds from the sale support the organization. Therefore, a pertinent question is: should individuals buying the products in the gift shop be considered donors or consumers? The answer to this question impacts decisions regarding marketing and particularly advertising. Most advertisements for social causes (e.g., curing children's cancer) invoke guilt appeals (Cotte, Coulter, & Moore, 2005). These emotional appeals attempt to evoke negative feelings related to the social need in the viewer before providing an opportunity to remove those feelings by donating (Boudewyns, Turner, & Paquin, 2013). However, it has been shown that explicit negative appeals may not be as effective when marketing to consumers purchasing a good that is associated with donations or ethical attributes (Peloza, White, & Shang, 2013). Thus, if marketers for St. Jude's gift shop view patrons as donors, the advertising should use a negative emotional appeal such as guilt; however, if the patrons of the gift shop are viewed as consumers, advertisements should focus on positive appeals more consistent with competing for-profit businesses. This issue is not as pertinent for a company like TOMS, in which there is a clear demarcation between consumers and donors.

The St. Jude example illustrates the importance of understanding the audience of a not-for-profit service. Donors and consumers respond to marketing efforts very differently, as each has a different motivational need: donors seek positive feelings due to contributing to meet societal needs, whereas consumers often seek the fulfillment of their own material needs or desires. There can be effective overlap between these two groups, but managers must ensure they understand who their audience is, and from what sources their funding comes. In addition, as donor retention and volunteer rates decline (Nesbit & Christensen, 2018; Nilsen, 2017), not-for-profit managers may need to consider reaching both consumers and donors (if they are currently only seeking donors). Like St. Jude's physical and digital gift shops, there may be marketplace opportunities that can coexist with current fundraising and donor-supported activities. These opportunities can only be considered when managers take the focus off of the donor-only approach and begin seeking consumers as well.

Operating like a business

Changes in fundraising and reevaluation of donors and consumers are elements of some of the larger issues facing not-for-profit services. Not-for-profit organizations must increasingly operate like for-profit businesses to remain competitive (Worth, 2018). One author encourages not-for-profit managers to consider how they would fund their operations if their donors or governmental funds were to disappear (Kaplan, 2018). The example of St. Jude describes the necessity of understanding the differences between donors and consumers in a supplementary environment such as a gift shop. Not-for-profit managers must extend this type of thinking to every aspect of the organization to remain competitive in today's marketplace. Research has shown that not-for-profit organizations adopting proactive marketing orientations and seeking opportunities to generate revenue from commercial activities are best positioned to succeed in the face of decreased funding sources (Álvarez-González, García-Rodríguez, Rey-García, & Sanzo-Perez, 2017). Thus, to remain competitive in an increasingly crowded marketplace amidst decreasing traditional revenue streams, not-for-profits must begin to operate like for-profit businesses.

Members of the Forbes Nonprofit Council, an invitation-only group of senior-level executives from some of the most successful not-for-profit organizations, recently gave their expert advice on how not-for-profits can succeed in operating like businesses (Forbes Nonprofit Council, 2018). First, expenses should be treated as they are in for-profit companies. Funds raised through donor dollars are not properly managed if they are not monitored, evaluated, and, where necessary, eliminated. Revenue, whether it is earned through consumer transactions or gained through fundraising, should be matched to costs. This allows better decisions to be made in terms of how and where to reduce costs.

Next, the choice of a profitable mission reduces the dependency on philanthropy and outside donations. An example of such a mission is offered by an organization that employs individuals with barriers to employment, such as those with criminal backgrounds or disabled veterans. An organization that does this not only fulfills its mission, but also ensures that its staffing needs are covered. Using real-time data analytics may seem like the domain of large corporations, but it can be just as effective for a not-for-profit seeking to better understand donors and consumers. If used properly, this technique can offer an effective use of donor dollars.

Finally, focusing on the highest return on investment possible is not only recommended for businesses that want to make money. Strategies and tactics must be implemented with a focus on attaining the largest financial benefit at the lowest cost. Making money is not a bad thing for not-for-profits to do. For most not-for-profits, more financial resources can go a long way toward fulfilling the organization's mission. Not-for-profit managers must be aggressive and competitive, knowing that money raised or earned will ultimately be used for a greater purpose than financial profit. Not-for-profit managers must clearly look beyond the financial and visionary limitations inherent in a not-for-profit organization and should seek to avoid the mentality that they are simply managing social welfare organizations. Rather, those managers who embrace business practices while remaining consistent to their not-for-profit's mission should prove to be competitive in both not-for-profit and for-profit industries in the future.

Fostering sustainability

One key aspect of operating like a for-profit business is fostering a sustainable business model. Sustainability in the not-for-profit sector has been defined as "identifying reliable financial and other types of support by utilizing markets, forming partnerships across sectors, and responding to stakeholder needs to ensure that the solution will be enduring" (Weerawardena, McDonald, & Mort, 2010, p. 355). Not-for-profits that rely on donations as their only source of funding face tremendous difficulties as donor retention rates fall, because there are no other sources of income. Without donors, opportunities for funding the organization disappear. Further, studies show that overreliance on governmental funding can be detrimental for long-term financial sustainability (Besel, Williams, & Klak, 2011). Thus, not-for-profit managers must focus on fostering a sustainable financial model to ensure enduring success.

In their book on not-for-profit organizational sustainability, Besel, Williams, and Klak (2011) discuss the importance of attaining both financial sustainability and sustained missional impact. Bell et al. (2010, p. 3) explain,

> For nonprofits, financial sustainability and programmatic sustainability cannot be separated. It's not enough to have a high-impact program if there's no effective strategy for sustaining the organization financially. And neither is it enough to be financially stable; we build our organizations for impact, not for financial stability. Yet surprisingly, in the nonprofit sector financial information and information about missional impact are seldom discussed in an integrated way.

After a synthesis of the literature on sustainability, not-for-profit researchers concluded that the most effective way to achieve sustainability in both the short- and long-term is to create "a clear strategic plan that defines the social mission and builds programs, community support, and collaborative partnerships that closely align with the mission" (Sontag-Padilla, Staplefoote, & Morganti, 2012, p. 27). This dual focus on financial and social mission sustainability will be of tremendous importance to not-for-profit services in the coming years.

Investing in partnerships

An important point that must be considered is that most not-for-profit organizations simply cannot do all of the work alone. As external funding dries up for not-for-profit services, strategic cross-industry and sector-spanning partnerships must be formed to ensure long-term survival and growth. Sociologist Helmut Anheier outlines several scenarios facing not-for-profit organizations and states,

> At one level, nonprofits become parallel actors that may complement or even counteract state activities and compete with businesses … At another level, the state and nonprofits are part of ever more complex public-private partnerships; they work in complementary fashion with other agencies, public and private.
>
> *(Anheier, 2013)*.

This concept of collaboration is crucial for the future success of not-for-profit services.

What might these not-for-profit partnerships look like? Grameen Bank, a microfinancing platform providing crowdsourced solutions to social needs, partnered with Danone (creating Grameen Danone Foods) to build a yogurt factory in Bangladesh, providing jobs and boosting employment. Conducting research on the health needs of the citizens of Bogra, where the factory was built, nutritionists also created a specific type of yogurt that included the most-needed nutrients. Microfinanciers leveraged Danone's economies of scale and R&D to meet the needs of the people of Bogra, a task that would have taken substantially more time and expense otherwise (Werft, 2015). In another case, The Salvation Army, whose red donation buckets are a staple of the U.S. holiday shopping season, partnered with kiosk company DipJar to place specially branded kiosks at retail outlets where consumers could donate using credit cards. Thus, the Salvation Army not only responded to changing fundraising demographics by recognizing that not everyone carries cash anymore, but they also acted competitively by reaching new donors in ways that had not been used before by partnering with an established, for-profit company to provide innovative methods for donating (Double the Donation, 2018).

Collaborations like these are mutually beneficial. For not-for-profits, the benefits of partnerships include increased funding and donor bases, increased media coverage and brand recognition, professional development and training for employees, and opportunities to develop relations with business leaders in the community. For-profits benefit from such partnerships through increased sales, brand loyalty, and employee retention, increased shareholder return, recognition from communities and media outlets, and tax deductions for charitable contributions (DeVita, 2017). Furthermore, an increasingly globalized society means that these organizations must look outside domestic borders to navigate the intricacies of cross-cultural partnerships (Phillips & Blumberg, 2017). If the history of not-for-profit services in America shows nothing else, it is that the lines between not-for-profit and for-profit are becoming indistinct, as exemplified by the social enterprise. It only makes sense that these fuzzy lines would lead to strategic and innovative new partnerships for the future and enduring success of not-for-profit services.

Conclusion

Not-for-profit services fulfill social needs across a variety of channels and organizations. However, the ways by which this occurs today differ dramatically from years past. Not-for-profit managers may find comfort in tradition, but today's rapidly changing economic and societal landscapes require continual adaptation and innovation. This chapter has outlined the historical development of not-for-profit services in conjunction with the rise of social support among for-profit companies to discuss future implications across sectors. In short, not-for-profit organizations are no longer able to rely solely on governmental and donor support for long-term sustainability and impact, and for-profit organizations must increasingly focus on social impact in addition to profit maximization to satisfy consumer demands. This convergence of not-for-profit and for-profit will continue to strengthen and shape the nature of both sectors.

Not-for-profit managers must be on the forefront of organizational change if they are to remain competitive in the coming years. This change necessitates a restructuring of not-for-profit identity that must be grounded in history and tradition but also intentionally cognizant of future trends. For some not-for-profit services, implementing for-profit operations and strategies will be critical to long-term financial sustainability. For others, innovative cross-sector partnerships will promote future growth. For nearly all not-for-profit services, progressive movement toward online donations, fundraising, and operations is essential. The loosely banded, locally driven voluntary associations of the American Revolution were successful in meeting social needs at one time. Today, success among not-for-profit services is found through intentional, innovative, and integrated strategies that tie together not-for-profit organizations, for-profit businesses, governments, donors, and consumers. Although these challenges and opportunities are significant, if the history of not-for-profit services has shown anything, it is that the needs of a society will continually be met by those who work for its betterment, no matter what type of organizational structure is in place.

References

Advisory Board. (2012). How St. Jude built a "fundraising machine." *Advisory Board: The Daily Briefing*. Available at www.advisory.com/daily-briefing/2012/02/24/st-jude-fundraising-strategy.

Álvarez-González, L. I., García-Rodríguez, N., Rey-García, M., & Sanzo-Perez, M. J. (2017). Business-nonprofit partnerships as a driver of internal marketing in nonprofit organizations. Consequences for nonprofit performance and moderators. *BRQ Business Research Quarterly*, 20(2), 112–123.

Andrews, M., Luo, X., Fang, Z., & Aspara, J. (2014). Cause marketing effectiveness and the moderating role of price discounts. *Journal of Marketing*, 78(6), 120–142.

Anheier, H. (2013). The nonprofits of 2025. *Stanford Social Innovation Review*. Available at https://ssir.org/articles/entry/the_nonprofits_of_2025.

Arnold, R. (2018). 6 things nonprofit donors want. *Nonprofit Pro*. Available at www.nonprofitpro.com/post/6-things-nonprofit-donors-want/.

Barnett, T. (2015). Corporate social responsibility. *Encyclopedia of Business*, 2nd Edition. Available at www.referenceforbusiness.com/management/Comp-De/Corporate-Social-Responsibility.html.

Bell, J., Masaoka, J., & Zimmerman, S. (2010). *Nonprofit sustainability: Making strategic decisions for financial viability*. Hoboken, NJ: John Wiley & Sons.

Besel, K., Williams, C. L., & Klak, J. (2011). Nonprofit sustainability during times of uncertainty. *Nonprofit Management & Leadership*, 22(1), 53–65.

Bevan, D. & Werhane, P. (2015). The inexorable sociality of commerce: The individual and others in Adam Smith. *Journal of Business Ethics*, 127(2), 327–335.

Bigné-Alcañiz, E., Currás-Pérez, R., Ruiz-Mafé, C., & Sanz-Blas, S. (2012). Cause related marketing influence on consumer responses: The moderating effect of cause-brand fit. *Journal of Marketing Communications*, 18(4), 265–283.

Boudewyns, V., Turner, M. M., & Paquin, R. S. (2013). Shame-free guilt appeals: Testing the emotional and cognitive effects of shame and guilt appeals. *Psychology & Marketing*, 30(9), 811–825.

Bragues, G. (2009). Adam Smith's vision of the ethical manager. *Journal of Business Ethics*, 90(4), 447–460.

Brown, J. A. & Forster, W. R. (2013). CSR and stakeholder theory: A tale of Adam Smith. *Journal of Business Ethics*, 112(2), 301–312.

Brown, M. D. (2014). The praxis of social enterprise and human security: An applied research agenda. *Journal of Human Security*, 10(1), 4–11.

Bugg-Levine, A., Kogut, B., & Kulatilaka, N. (2012). A new approach to funding social enterprises. *Harvard Business Review*, 90(1/2), 118–123.

Carroll, A. B. & Buchholtz, A. (2014). *Business and society: Ethics, sustainability, and stakeholder management*. Boston, MA: Cengage Learning.

Castillo, M., Petrie, R., & Wardell, C. (2014). Fundraising through online social networks: A field experiment on peer-to-peer solicitation. *Journal of Public Economics*, 114, 29–35.

Charity Navigator. (2018). Giving statistics. *Charity Navigator*. Available at www.charitynavigator.org/index.cfm?bay=content.view&cpid=42.

Charity Navigator. (2019). 10 most followed charities. *Charity Navigator*. Available at www.charitynaviga tor.org/index.cfm?bay=topten.detail&listid=148.

Chell, E., Nicolopoulou, K., & Karatas-Ozkan, M. (2010). Social entrepreneurship and enterprise: International and innovation perspectives. *Entrepreneurship & Regional Development*, 22(6), 485–493.

Choi, N. & Majumdar, S. (2014). Social entrepreneurship as an essentially contested concept: Opening a new avenue for systematic future research. *Journal of Business Venturing*, 29, 363–376.

Coase, R. & Wang, N. (2012). Saving economics from the economists. *Harvard Business Review*, 90(12), 36.

Cotte, J., Coulter, R.A., & Moore, M. (2005), Enhancing or disrupting guilt: the role of ad credibility and perceived manipulative intent. Journal of Business Research, 58(3), 361–368.

Czischke, D., Gruis, V., & Mullins, D. (2012). Conceptualising social enterprise in housing organizations. *Housing Studies*, 27(4), 418–437.

Defourny, J. (2001). From third sector to social enterprise. In C. Borzago & J. Defourny (Eds.), *The emergence of social enterprise* (pp. 1–28). London and New York: Routledge.

Defourny, J. (2014). From third sector to social enterprise: A European research trajectory. In J. Defourny, L. Hulgård, & V. Pestoff (Eds.), *Social enterprise and the third sector: Changing European landscapes in a comparative perspective*(pp. 1–23). London: Routledge.

Department for Trade and Industry. (2002). *Social enterprise: A strategy for success*. Available at www.dti.gov.uk/socialenterprise.

DeVita, A. (2017). 10 Benefits that only nonprofits can bring to partnership. *TopNonprofits*. Available at https://topnonprofits.com/10-benefits-nonprofits-can-bring-partnership/.

Dey, P. & Teasdale, S. (2013). Social enterprise and dis/identification: The politics of identity work in the English third sector. *Administrative Theory & Praxis*, 35(2), 248–270.

Domenico, D., Maria, L., Haugh, H., & Tracey, P. (2010). Social bricolage: Theorizing social value creation in social enterprises. *Entrepreneurship Theory and Practice*, 34(4), 681–703.

Double the Donation. (2018). 10 surprising (and spectacular!) cause marketing campaign examples. *Double the Donation*. Available at https://doublethedonation.com/blog/2017/04/cause-marketing-examples/.

Du, S., Bhattacharya, C. B., & Sen, S. (2007). Reaping relational rewards from corporate social responsibility: The role of competitive positioning. *International Journal of Research in Marketing*, 24, 224–241.

Forbes Nonprofit Council. (2018). 12 effective ways to operate a nonprofit like a for-profit business. *Forbes*. Available at www.forbes.com/sites/forbesnonprofctcouncil/2018/03/07/12-effective-ways-to-operate-a-nonprofit-like-a-for-profit-business/#4a4ea4f234c6.

Gonin, M. (2015). Adam Smith's contribution to business ethics, then and now. *Journal of Business Ethics*, 129(1), 221–236.

Hall, P. D. (2010). Historical perspectives on nonprofit organizations in the United States. In D.O. Renz & R.D. Herman (Eds), *The Jossey-Bass handbook of nonprofit leadership and management* (pp. 3–41). Hoboken, NJ: Wiley.

Haselwood, J. (2018). Fundraising roadmap: How to prioritize your digital fundraising channels. *Forbes*. Available at www.forbes.com/sites/forbescommunicationscouncil/2018/05/02/fundraising-roadmap-how-to-prioritize-your-digital-fundraising-channels/#38de77401f3f.

Johanisova, N., Crabtree, T., & Fraňková, E. (2013). Social enterprises and non-market capitals: A path to degrowth? *Journal of Cleaner Production*, 38, 7–16.

Kaplan, S. (2018). The future of nonprofits: Run them like an innovative business. *Inc.* Available at www.inc.com/soren-kaplan/the-future-of-non-profits-run-it-like-an-innovative-business.html.

Lafferty, B. A. & Goldsmith, R. E. (2005). Cause-brand alliances: Does the cause help the brand or does the brand help the cause? *Journal of Business Research*, 58, 423–429.

Massetti, B. (2012). The duality of social enterprise: A framework for social action. *Review of Business*, 33(1), 50–64.

McKeever, B. S. & Pettijohn, S. L. (2014). *The nonprofit sector in brief*. Public Charities, Giving and Volunteering. Washington, DC: Urban Institute.

Meer, J. (2011). Brother, can you spare a dime: Peer pressure in charitable solicitation. *Journal of Public Economics*, 95, 926–941.

Miles, M. P., Verreynne, M., & Luke, B. (2014). Social enterprises and the performance advantages of a Vincentian marketing orientation. *Journal of Business Ethics*, 123, 549–556.

Miller, B. (2009). Community fundraising 2.0: The future of fundraising in a networked society? *International Journal of Nonprofit and Voluntary Sector Marketing*, 14(4), 365–370.

Miller, J. (2017). How millennials are changing the landscape of nonprofit giving. *Forbes*. Available at www.forbes.com/sites/forbesnonprofitcouncil/2017/10/11/how-millennials-are-changing-the-land scape-of-nonprofit-giving/#701c820f12b2.

Moosmayer, D. C. & Fuljahn, A. (2013). Corporate motive and fit in cause related marketing. *Journal of Product & Brand Management*, 22(3), 200–207.

Morpus, N. (2017). 5 nonprofit trends to keep in mind for 2018. *Capterra*. Available at https://blog.cap terra.com/5-nonprofit-trends-to-keep-in-mind-for-2018/.

Muslic, H. (2018). A brief history of nonprofit organizations (and what we can learn). *Nonprofit Hub*. Available at http://nonprofithub.org/starting-a-nonprofit/a-brief-history-of-nonprofit-organizations/.

Nesbit, R. & Christensen, R. (2018). How to get more Americans to volunteer. *The Conversation*. Available at http://theconversation.com/how-to-get-more-americans-to-volunteer-88835.

Nilsen, M. (2017). 2017 fundraising report reveals declining donor retention rate. *Philanthropy Today*. Available at www.philanthropydaily.com/2017-fundraising-effectiveness-report-reveals-declining-donor-retention-rate/.

Ohana, M. & Meyer, M. (2010). Should I stay or should I go now? Investigating the intention to quit of the permanent staff in social enterprises. *European Management Journal*, 28(6), 441–454.

Olson, E. L. & Thjømøe, H. M. (2011). Explaining and articulating the fit construct in sponsorship. *Journal of Advertising*, 40(1), 57–70.

Oslington, P. (2012). God and the market: Adam Smith's invisible hand. *Journal of Business Ethics*, 108(4), 429–438.

Payne, A., Scharf, K., & Smith, S. (2014). *Online fundraising: The perfect ask*. University of Warwick, Centre for Competitive Advantage in the Global Economy. Working Papers (194).

Peloza, J., White, K., & Shang, J. (2013). Good and guilt-free: The role of self-accountability in influencing preferences for products with ethical attributes. *Journal of Marketing*, 77(1), 104–119.

Phillips, S. D. & Blumberg, M. (2017). International trends in government-nonprofit relations. In E. Boris & C.E. Steuerle (Eds), *Nonprofits and government: Collaboration and conflict* (pp. 313–342). Rowman & Littlefield Publishing Group, Inc., Lanham, MD, copublished with Urban Institute Press.

Plerhoples, A. (2013). Representing social enterprise. *Clinical Law Review*, 20, 215–265.

Pollach, I., Treiblmaier, H., & Floh, A. (2005). Online fundraising for environmental nonprofit organizations. In *Proceedings of the 38th Annual Hawaii international conference on system sciences*. 178.2. Washington, DC: IEEE Computer Society.

Schiller, A. (2014). Is for-profit the future of non-profit? *The Atlantic*. Available at www.theatlantic.com/business/archive/2014/05/is-for-profit-the-future-of-non-profit/371336/.

Smith, W. K., Gonin, M., & Besharov, M. L. (2013). Managing social-business tensions: A review and research agenda for social enterprise. *Business Ethics Quarterly*, 23(3), 407–442.

Sontag-Padilla, L., Staplefoote, B. L., & Morganti, K. G. (2012). *Financial sustainability for nonprofit organizations*. Santa Monica, CA: Rand Corporation.

Teasdale, S. (2012). Negotiating tensions: How do social enterprises in the homelessness field balance social and commercial considerations? *Housing Studies*, 27(4), 514–532.

Thornley, B. (2013). The facts on U.S. social enterprise. *The Huffington Post*. Available at www.huffington post.com/ben-thornley/social-enterprise_b_2090144.html.

Varadarajan, R. & Menon, A. (1988). Cause-related marketing: A coalignment of marketing strategy and corporate philanthropy. *Journal of Marketing*, 52(3), 58–74.

Vickers, I. & Lyon, F. (2012). Beyond green niches? Growth strategies of environmentally-motivated social enterprises. *International Small Business Journal*, 3(4), 449–470.

Von der Weppen, J. & Cochrane, J. (2012). Social enterprises in tourism: An exploratory study of operational models and success factors. *Journal of Sustainable Tourism*, 20(3), 497–511.

Weerawardena, J., McDonald, R. E., & Mort, G. S. (2010). Sustainability of nonprofit organizations: An empirical investigation. *Journal of World Business*, 45(4), 346–356.

Werft, M. (2015). 7 surprising pairs of nonprofits and corporations. *Global Citizen*. Available at www.glo balcitizen.org/en/content/7-surprising-pairs-of-nonprofits-and-corporations/.

WJSchroer (2017). Generations X,Y, Z and the others. Available at http://socialmarketing.org/archives/generations-xy-z-and-the-others/.

Worth, M. J. (2018). *Nonprofit management: Principles and practice*. Newbury Park, CA: SAGE Publications.

Wydick, B., Katz, E., & Janet, B. (2014), Do in-kind transfers damage local markets? The case of TOMS shoe donations in El Salvador. Journal of Development Effectiveness, 6(3), 249–267.

Yunus, M. (2007). *Banker to the poor*. New Delhi, India: Penguin Books.

Zahra, S. A., Gedajlovic, E., Neubaum, D. O., & Shulman, J. M. (2009). A typology of social entrepreneurs: Motives, search processes and challenges. *Journal of Business Venturing*, 24, 519–532.

24

Providing service in multicultural environments

Elten Briggs and Detra Y. Montoya

Introduction

Multiculturalism and services

The cultural diversity of populations in more developed countries is increasing as the higher standard of living in these countries attracts immigrants from varying cultural backgrounds. Although many immigrants are motivated by economic or professional opportunities, others migrate due to safety concerns, as evidenced by the number of Syrian refugees that recently fled to neighboring countries, and nearby developed nations, especially Germany (Conner, 2018). Over the past 30 years, immigration has accounted for more population growth in developed regions than births. In fact, with fertility rates continuing to fall in developed nations, the United Nations (2017) projects that immigration will be the sole driver of population growth in these regions after 2020. As illustrated in Table 24.1, each of the G7 major developed economies (except Japan) had a net migration rate greater than zero in 2017, indicating that the number of people entering the country was greater than the number leaving the country (Central Intelligence Agency, 2018).

Services are typically the primary economic driver in developed nations. In fact, services made up over 69% of gross domestic product (GDP) and employment in all of the G7 countries (see Table 24.1). The issue of multicultural service delivery has received careful attention in the context of community services such as education and health care (Alexandre, 2009), where public policy plays a key role in bettering the well-being of individuals in a society. For instance, in the health care sector, research suggests that poor quality interactions between provider and patient can result in suboptimal outcomes for minorities (e.g., Ashton et al., 2003; Betancourt, Green, Emilio Carrillo, & Ananeh-Firempong, 2003). However, there has been an uptick in the literature involving the marketing of for-profit services, with a special issue of the *Journal of Services Marketing* published in 2018 titled, 'Challenges and opportunities for services marketers in a culturally diverse global marketplace.' In this issue, Sharma, Tam, and Wu (2018) provide an overview of research in the area and identify important research gaps for future investigation, such as business-to-business multicultural services, and interactions among service employees from different cultures. Hence, as the global environment continues down this path, services research involving multiculturalism should continue to expand.

Table 24.1 Migration rate and services economic contributions in G7 countries

Country	Net Migration Rate*	Services as a Percentage of GDP*	Services as a Percentage of Employment^
Canada	5.7	70.2	78
France	1.1	78.9	77
Germany	1.5	69.3	71
Italy	3.7	73.9	70
Japan	0.0	69.3	71
United Kingdom	2.5	80.4	81
United States	3.9	80.2	79

* From: CIA *World Factbook* (www.cia.gov/library/publications/resources/the-world-factbook/June2018)
^ From: The World Bank (https://data.worldbank.org/indicator/SL.SRV.EMPL.ZS, June 2018)

Ethnic minorities and multicultural service strategies

Alexandre (2009) offers definitions for the terms 'ethnic group' and 'cultural minority.' An ethnic group is described as "one that self-identifies or is recognized by others (the majority) as different because of its historical or biological particularities," whereas a cultural minority is "a group that self-identifies or is recognized by others as having different values, customs, and social practices from the main population" Alexandre (2009, p. 10). The focus of this chapter is on those segments of consumers that are both ethnic and cultural minorities in their societies. The terms multicultural consumers, ethnic minorities, or minority consumers are used to refer to these individuals.

There is a growing need for service providers in more developed countries to target minority consumers and cultivate multicultural marketing competencies in their organizations. Not only are these potential customer groups increasing in size, but their distinctive behavioral norms and societal statuses often result in consumption patterns that differ from those of mainstream consumers (Korzenny, 2008; Montoya & Briggs, 2013). In the United States, for example, the U.S. Census Bureau estimates that the Caucasian majority, which made up 64% of the U.S. population at the time of the 2010 census, will account for less than 44% of the U.S. population by the year 2060 (Colby & Ortman, 2015). Minority consumers disproportionately utilize many services, including media and technology-based offerings (Korzenny, 2008). Similar to other developed countries, the U.S. is comprised of one larger majority group and several smaller ethnic minority groups of varying sizes. As these minority groups have grown, it has become more common for them to hold on to aspects of their ethnic identities rather than to fully assimilate into the dominant culture (Alexandre, 2009; Burgos & Mobolade, 2011).

In practice, it can often be more difficult to develop effective multicultural service strategies than international service strategies. With regard to international marketing, strategies are devised to be effective in other nations. Often, companies adapt their marketing strategies across the nations in which they operate, such that an optimal marketing strategy is implemented in each country. On the other hand, Spratlen, Lum, Montoya, and Verchot (2016, p. 57) define multicultural marketing as "the process of using market exchange concepts, methods and techniques to recognize and respond to culturally-distinct group characteristics and preferences of individuals, organizations, and communities." When practicing multicultural marketing, the service

481

provider must serve different cultures as with international marketing, but must also take inter-actions between cultures into account. Because a minority ethnic group that is targeted by a multicultural service campaign is not separated from other targeted groups by natural or man-made barriers (as it would be in international efforts), multicultural service strategies must always consider the majority ethnic group being served. Thus, it is important for providers serving these groups to understand the key tenets of social identity theory (SIT) as described by Tajfel and Turner (1979), to better appreciate common dynamics affecting the interactions between targeted minority segments and other ethnic groups in a particular country.

Social identity and ethnic minorities

SIT (Tajfel, 1982; Tajfel & Turner, 1979) provides a foundation for understanding intergroup behavior; specifically, it predicts that individuals will favor in-group members over out-group members. Individuals incorporate their membership group's identity into their own social identity. The way that members of minority groups are typically accounted for is by having them self-identify as being of a particular race or ethnicity. Tajfel and Turner (1986) argue that simply cat-egorizing individuals into groups activates in-group favoritism. In-group favoritism refers to a group member's tendency to favor their own group (in-group) over a comparison group (out-group) (e.g., Hewstone, Rubin, & Willis, 2002). For example, members of a group may display a more favorable attitude toward their own group and allocate a disproportionate amount of group resources to in-group, rather than out-group, members. An individual's social identity benefits from his/her positive group association, encouraging in-group favoritism. Such preferential behav-ior toward in-group members also strengthens the cohesiveness of the group (Mullen, Brown, & Smith, 1992). Three key concepts of SIT which contribute to in-group favoritism are group mem-bership, social context, and relevant comparison groups (Tajfel & Turner, 1979).

The concepts of SIT are especially applicable to members of ethnic minority groups (Montoya & Briggs, 2013). First, *social group membership* enables individuals to distinguish themselves from other groups (Brewer & Kramer, 1985), which also spawns a desire to enhance one's self-esteem and membership group status (Branscombe, 1998). Because eth-nicity and race are strong indicators of similarity, it is likely that individuals who share the same ethnicity will "flock together" and form reference groups to direct individual behavior (Korzenny & Korzenny, 2005). Second, *social context* is a setting in which indi-viduals interact with others. Prior research suggests that the ethnic composition of a social context can influence the salience of one's ethnicity (Deshpande & Stayman, 1994; McGuire, McGuire, Child, & Fujioka, 1978) and behavior (Stayman & Deshpande, 1989). Minority group members are more likely to exhibit bias than those in the majority by evaluating in-group members more positively (Bettencourt, Miller, & Hume, 1999; Brewer, 1991). Finally, in-group members are more likely to engage in in-group favorit-ism when the *comparison group* (i.e., the out-group) is relevant and meaningful (Tajfel & Turner, 1979). Situations perceived as illegitimate or unstable by lower status groups are likely to instigate collective behavior to promote the disadvantaged group's status (Taylor, Moghaddam, Gamble, & Zellerer, 1987).

Chapter framework

Montoya and Briggs (2013) found that minorities tend to exhibit greater levels of ethnic identification, or perceptions of belongingness to their ethnic group, than do members of the majority culture. Coupled with the increased salience of ethnicity for minorities, it is critical that service providers account for minority consumers' identification and group attitudes when attempting to build relationships with these customers, who typically exhibit higher levels of loyalty to service providers (Pires & Stanton, 2000). This chapter adapts the services marketing triangle as an organizing framework to describe the challenges faced by service providers operating in multicultural environments (Bitner, 1995). Specifically, it applies insights from the extant literature to discuss how service firms can develop the appropriate marketing messages for their multicultural consumers (external marketing), improve front line employee service delivery to these multicultural consumers (interactive marketing), and develop a multicultural service orientation to properly equip front line employees (internal marketing). (See Figure 24.1.) These activities should facilitate positive service outcomes for customers, potential customers, and service firms in multicultural environments.

Developing marketing messages for multicultural consumers

The importance of inclusion

Communication challenges for services often relate to the intangibility of the service offering (Mittal, 1999). Because services lack physical properties, they cannot be shown in external marketing communications as they can for goods, making it harder for consumers to grasp the essence of the offering. Mittal (1999) refers to this property of services as *incorporeal existence*, and recommends showing some physical components of the service delivery system to overcome this issue in marketing communications. Another related issue is that of *mental impalpability*, which is the notion that some service processes are so complex that consumers would not be able to understand them without prior exposure to the service. To overcome this issue, Mittal (1999) recommends vividly documenting the service process step-by-step and/or presenting a case study indicating what the service firm actually did for a particular customer.

In many circumstances, it is necessary to include or depict humans (i.e., service employees and customers) to properly implement service advertising tactics. For people-based services,

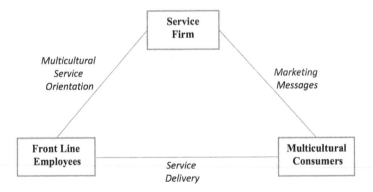

Figure 24.1 Multicultural service marketing triangle.

Note: Adapted from Bitner, M. J. (1995) 'Building service relationships: It's all about promises,' *Journal of the Academy of Marketing Science*, 23(4), p. 247 and from Zeithaml, V., Bitner, M. J., and Gremler, D. W. (2013), *Services Marketing: Integrating Customer Focus across the Firm*, 6th ed. New York, McGraw-Hill Irwin, p. 317.

service employees play a vital role in the service process and ultimate delivery. Due to the inseparable nature of services, customers commonly find themselves heavily involved in service processes. To depict specific cases of service delivery in advertising media, firms frequently need to include real customers or have actors play the role of customers. In multicultural environments, providers advertising their services need to make concentrated efforts to represent ethnic minority consumers in their marketing communications. Research suggests that ethnic consumers respond more favorably to advertisements that include members of their own minority groups (Torres & Briggs, 2005); therefore, it is recommended that advertisers of services incorporate ethnic minorities in marketing communications more frequently than do advertisers of goods (Briggs, Landry, & Torres, 2010).

When including ethnic minorities in advertisements, service providers should offer clear cues so that ethnic minority consumers can clearly identify the actor as a member of their in-group. Research suggests that minority consumers respond much more favorably to the inclusion of actors of their own ethnicity than to majority consumers (Lee, Fernandez, & Martin, 2002). *Physical appearance* is especially critical when using a visual communication medium, such as television, magazines, or online images. Members of an ethnic group can more accurately recognize fellow group members as opposed to dissimilar ethnic group members (Chance, Turner, & Goldstein, 1982; Zebrowitz, Bronstad, & Lee, 2007). Zebrowitz et al. (2007) posit that racial face familiarity contributes to in-group favoritism (e.g., likability, trustworthiness). These findings support the familiar face overgeneralization hypothesis, which suggests that responses to strangers vary based on their resemblance to more familiar individuals (Zebrowitz, 1996).

When a communication medium lacks visual cues, as with radio, some print, and some social media, then nonvisual cues take on increased importance. Spoken *language* is a strong group characteristic as well as an important differentiating factor for ethnic groups (Wallendorf & Reily, 1983). As ethnic groups integrate into the dominant culture, they often affect the speaking patterns of the majority culture. Thus, some phrases spoken in the minority consumers' language may be utilized in advertisements, because they are well understood by majority consumers. Finally, the use of *surnames* is an effective tool to identify ethnic group members (Mirowsky & Ross, 1980; Word & Perkins, 1996).

Beyond inclusion: incorporating cultural cues

The inclusion of minorities in service advertising is important, but not sufficient to develop a true competency in multicultural communications. Many cultural minorities are distinguished by traits (e.g., religion) that are not as easily addressed by casting the appropriate actors or actresses. Minority consumers find advertising more enjoyable when it includes cues relevant to their cultures, in addition to being portrayed by actors from these groups (Burgos & Mobolade, 2011). For example, in 2010, State Farm Insurance ran an advertising campaign in which its agents magically appear when called upon, and immediately fix their customers' problems. An advertisement targeted at Asian Indian consumers not only included actors of this ethnicity, but also referenced 'karma' – which would be well known to Asian Indian consumers, because it is an important tenet of Hinduism, the most common religion in India. There are many other aspects of culture that might be included in service communications to make them more culturally relevant (Burgos & Mobolade, 2011). Service marketers should attend closely to particularities in their ethnic targets' speaking patterns, senses of humor, nature of family interactions, and preferences for music, art, and food, any of which might distinguish them from the majority group.

When including cultural cues, the service marketer must weigh the potential responses from majority consumers, who will likely account for a dominant share of the service provider's base. Depending on the country, the receptivity of the majority group to diverse communications will differ. For example, North American countries have generally embraced diversity more readily than some European countries (Drake & Poushter, 2016). As discussed earlier, this leads to differences between the practice of multicultural marketing and the practice of international marketing. Service providers must take care when developing content targeting minority ethnic groups, especially when disseminating those communications in mainstream media. It is essential to pretest such communications with a sample of majority consumers to ensure there are no adverse reactions (Burgos & Mobolade, 2011).

When a communication targeting ethnic minority consumers appears in media that are primarily consumed by members of the minority group, further considerations arise. First, the marketer must ensure that the positioning of the service in the targeted media is not starkly juxtaposed to the mainstream positioning of the service. Though the service provider should seek to understand the distinctive value proposition for ethnic minority consumers and speak to the benefits desired by these consumers, it is important to note that these customers typically consume both mainstream and targeted media (Burgos & Mobolade, 2011). There must be some cohesion between the communications appearing in the mainstream and targeted media to avoid confusing the ethnic targets. Research by Bishop and Peterson (2010, 2011) further implies that the use of language to target ethic minority consumers should differ when communications appear in targeted as compared to mainstream media. These authors conducted an experiment in which a fictitious wireless service was advertised to Hispanic consumers in the U.S. The results indicated that print that included more English (majority language) than Spanish (ethnic minority language) actually fared better among Hispanic customers when placed in a mainstream media outlet (Bishop & Peterson, 2010, 2011). These findings illustrate the importance of considering the advertising medium when developing communications targeting ethnic minority consumers.

The role of multicultural brands

To serve a more diverse marketplace, brands must establish associations that resonate with multicultural consumers. Brands consist of associations and meanings in the minds of customers. Associations should be strong, favorable, and unique to help customers perceive meaningful differences between brands in a product category (Keller, 2013). Brand associations can be abstract or tangible, emotional and/or experiential. For example, the Bank of New Zealand developed meaningful associations between its service brand and Chinese customers in the country by making it easier for these customers to properly celebrate the Chinese New Year holiday (Direct Marketing Association, 2018). The company elaborately designed an ATM and placed it in the heart of one of the country's busiest central business districts to conveniently dispense the new currency and envelopes sought out by these consumers during this event. Many experiential brand associations include aspects of the servicescape, such as bilingual employees and/or signage, unique cultural products, and/or a more welcoming environment including ethnically diverse employees. Such experiential aspects are discussed in greater depth in the section on delivering service to multicultural consumers; the remainder of this section focuses on brand associations that can be cultivated through external service communications.

Brand associations that promote customer social identities can build brand loyalty and strong brand relationships (Keller, 1993). When targeting ethnic minority consumers, diversifying a brand's image may help ethnic customers connect with a brand. As previously discussed, ethnic spokespeople are more effective when targeting ethnic minorities (Torres & Briggs, 2005). An additional benefit of incorporating ethnic spokespeople or actors in advertisements is that a service firm can expand its brand image to be inclusive of minority segments. Another way to create such associations is by connecting the brand with other organizations and/or other brands (i.e., co-branding) that may be more familiar or appealing to multicultural customers. Co-branding provides a brand with an opportunity to access new market segments; this is especially relevant for a brand seeking to attract new and diverse customers. Service firms attempting to appeal to minority ethnic consumer groups should consider collaborating with local firms and organizations that have a strong presence in the targeted communities. For example, Verizon Wireless sponsored a contest that supported African-American churches and choirs in the United States in 2008 and 2009. The brand received endorsements from churches in many major cities across the country, from church pastors and other community leaders, which helped the brand to associate with this key segment.

Brands desiring to connect with multicultural customers must build a brand relationship, or brand resonance, which begins with a strong brand identity (e.g., Keller, 2013). Service brands serving multicultural customers need to ensure that they have brand recognition among these customers, including relevant brand associations. Brand can be strongly associated with a social group, which can strengthen the brand's cultural identity (John & Torelli, 2018). An effective brand communication strategy targeting multicultural customers can help to increase brand awareness in diverse communities. For example, AT&T launched its 'Mobile Movement' campaign targeting Hispanic millennials with ads using 'Spanglish' in 2014. The theme of the ads revolved around the difficulties of Hispanics balancing two different cultures in the U.S. AT&T was attempting to create associations to its wireless services that would resonate with a more diverse customer group (Wood, 2014). Although brands may have good intentions, their efforts can backfire, such as Dolce & Gabbana's ad in China that was criticized for mocking Chinese speech and emphasizing cultural stereotypes (Xu, 2018).

Service firms need to evaluate their brand elements, or brand identifiers, to increase their brands' abilities to attract a more diverse customer base. Brand elements may include a slogan, character, or jingle that can resonate with multicultural customers; as an example, the brand slogan should be assessed to determine whether it will translate to another language and be interpreted correctly. For example, Burger King introduced a new product in Europe called a 'Texican Whopper' in 2009; this product was described in an ad as "the Taste of Texas with a little spicy Mexican." This stereotypical portrayal of Mexicans was not received well, but even more offensive was the improper use of the Mexican national flag, which prompted a letter from Mexico's ambassador to Spain to the Burger King offices in the country.

Global brands can benefit from leveraging best practices across customer market segments. Many brands are expanding their service offerings, not only to new cultural segments, but also to global markets. One successful slogan for such a global brand was McDonald's "I'm lovin' it," according to Kohli, Thomas, and Suri (2013). Dropping the 'g' at the end of a word and replacing it with just the 'n' sound is commonly attributed to African-American vernacular (Rickford, 2019). Thus, this slogan was consistent with the company's decision to rely on ethnic minority consumers to set trends later pursued in the wider market (Helm, 2010). Service firms can leverage their brand elements and unique brand associations to expand into new markets, both domestically and globally, if they are very careful about market testing in the new culture.

Another way a service brand can address an increasingly diverse marketplace is to create a new sub-brand within its portfolio, or designate a brand within the portfolio to target a particular market segment. For example, in Arizona, a grocery firm has three retail store brands, each targeting a different segment of the market: AJ's, Bashas' and Food City. Specifically, AJ's targets a higher end market segment, Bashas' serves a mass market, and Food City targets Hispanic customers. Although Hispanic consumers may be able to find some of their desired brands in a Bashas' store, Food City has more diverse product offerings and is Arizona's largest retailer targeting the Hispanic community with 48 retail locations statewide (www.bashas.com). Food City has completely adapted its service delivery and servicescape to appeal to Hispanic customers. The store has bilingual signage, bilingual employees, aromas of typical Hispanic foods, Latin music playing throughout the store, and a large variety of brands/goods native to Latin America. The authors have personal experience with Food City stores, and note that most of the employees are Spanish-speaking, similar to their customers, and often members of the same local community. Thus, the employees, who are essentially front line representatives of the store brand, demonstrate a deep understanding of the customer and local community.

For those service firms that are unable or unwilling to create targeted sub-brands, care should be taken to ensure a welcoming environment to all customers, while preserving the rich cultural servicescape that targets a specific group. For example, Ranch Market, another local grocery store in Arizona that caters to Hispanic customers, includes a food court offering many prepared authentic Hispanic foods. Hispanic customers are able to enjoy their native food and, at the same time, the store environment offers a unique cultural experience for non-Hispanic customers. Non-Hispanics are able to enjoy foods with which they may not be familiar, engage with employees and customers from different ethnic backgrounds, and perhaps practice conversing in Spanish. Although some service firms may fear a backlash for catering to a particular cultural group, for these stores, non-Hispanic customers may welcome the unique cross-cultural shopping experience.

Another example of embracing a cross-cultural shopping experience happens in many U.S. cities boasting Asian marketplaces that include culturally relevant grocery stores and restaurants. Such Asian marketplaces offer their Asian customers a welcoming place where they can buy familiar brands and goods; at the same time, non-Asian customers can obtain a rich cross-cultural experience. For example, Uwajimaya is a popular family-owned Asian grocery store located in the Pacific Northwest. It offers unique Asian foods and gifts, which appeal to this minority group as well as to non-Asian customers.

Brands may also attempt to reach more culturally diverse customers through brand extensions, which extend a brand into a new product category. Aguirre-Rodriguez, Bóveda-Lambie, & Montoya (2014) examined the effects of crossover brand extensions on multicultural consumers. The authors define ethnic crossover brands as "brands associated with one ethnic group that crossover into a product category associated with another ethnic group" (Aguirre-Rodriguez et al., p. 457). Brands that extend into new categories can leverage the parent brand's equity, including brand associations, to appeal to a broader market. Although the intent is to build the brand's equity in a new product category, a lack of understanding of the brand's knowledge structures can result in a failed extension (e.g., John & Torelli, 2018). This is important to consider when a brand that caters to a predominantly Caucasian customer base (with appropriate brand associations) attempts to extend into a product category that would attract a more non-Caucasian customer base. Specifically, a brand that does not include ethnic minority spokespeople or common usage situations for ethnic minorities may not appeal to ethnic minority customers. Aguirre-Rodriguez, Bóveda-Lambie, & Montoya (2014) draw upon SIT (Tajfel, 1982) to understand how consumers evaluate crossover brand extensions. In particular, they argue that consumers are more likely to protect in-group cultural resources, such as brands that specifically target their own group. Customers construe brands concretely and product categories abstractly; these construal levels may influence their desire to protect in-group resources or, more specifically, to perceive a strong cultural fit of the crossover brand (e.g., Johnson, Lehmann, Fornell, & Horne, 1992). Moreover, customers are likely to use brands to strengthen their self-brand connections, which may in turn strengthen their group identification (Edson, 2004; John & Torelli, 2018). Product categories, because they are abstract, may contain many brand schemas. Thus, consumers are more likely to protect in-group brands than in-group product categories, as brands are perceived as a stronger in-group cultural resource than are categories.

Aguirre-Rodriguez, Bóveda-Lambie, & Montoya (2014) examined the effects of crossover brand extensions on perceived cultural fit, brand attitude, and self-brand connections. They found that an out-group brand (e.g., Campbell's) with an in-group extension (*caldo gallego*, a Spanish white bean soup) would produce greater cultural fit compared to an in-group brand (Goya) with an out-group product extension (New England clam chowder). The lower perceived cultural fit for the in-group brand with an out-group product extension (Goya New England Clam Chowder) results from a desire to protect a valuable cultural in-group resource (the Goya brand). Along the same line of reasoning, the researchers found that a cultural out-group brand with an in-group extension (Campbell's *caldo gallego*) results in more positive parent brand attitudes than does an in-group brand with an out-group extension (Keller, 1993; Loken & John, 1993). Hispanic customers clearly show a desire to protect the in-group brand and its brand image. The researchers also found that when customers perceived a crossover extension as intended for their cultural in-group, they were likely to rely upon perceived cultural fit to evaluate the new brand crossover extension. They were found to protect their cultural in-group resources when they perceived the crossover extension as intended for their cultural in-group, versus a cultural out-group. Finally, the researchers found that Hispanic customers use brands to strengthen their identification with their own ethnic group; brands have social and cultural meanings that customers build into their self-concepts (e.g., Aaker, Benet-Martinez, & Garolera, 2001; Edson, 2004). Customers can strengthen their cultural in-group brand identities by incorporating a brand's cultural associations.

These findings can be applied to service environments. Specifically, service marketers should consider how they position their service offerings to multicultural customers. A brand specifically designed to target a multicultural market, such as Food City or Uwajimaya, can effectively cater to its diverse clientele. However, when firms are considering crossover brand extensions, an out-group service brand (e.g., general market retailer) with an in-group product (e.g., ethnic products) may be perceived more favorably than an in-group service brand (e.g., ethnic retailer) offering out-group products (e.g., general market products). This is positive for retailers who want to attract more diverse customers. That is, it may be more beneficial for a firm to target multicultural consumers with a current brand and new ethnic products, rather than investing in an ethnic brand to target non-ethnic customers.

Improving service delivery to multicultural consumers

Interactions during service encounters

For service brands, consistency is essential; speaking in one voice is especially important for service firms who rely on direct, one-to-one interaction with clients. Front line service providers, who serve as a brand's ambassadors, should know the brand vision so they can effectively deliver the brand promise during every service encounter. However, unlike goods, delivery of a service is susceptible to variation across employees. This variance increases when delivery is directed towards multicultural customers with unique tastes and preferences. It is important for service providers to customize the service experience when interacting with ethnically diverse customers; therefore employee development and training are needed on standards for effectively providing service to the customer base.

Verbal and nonverbal communications are essential to providing a good customer experience, but can pose significant challenges for service delivery with a multicultural customer base. Verbal communications between service providers and customers who may not share a common native language can affect customer perceptions of service quality, as well as responses including loyalty, willingness to return, or positive word-of-mouth (Rosenbaum & Montoya, 2007). Bilingual employees can have a positive impact on a customer's experience, as research suggests that customers often prefer to speak in their first language during service encounters (e.g., Holmqvist, 2011). Accommodation theory suggests that individuals adjust their communication or speech to accommodate another individual (Giles, Taylor, & Bourhis, 1973). This is especially relevant in a multicultural environment, where customers may speak different languages or dialects. Trained front line service providers can identify situations when customers may require some additional assistance, and make efforts to adjust their speech or communication style to accommodate customer needs.

Communication between individuals is comprised of about 60% nonverbal behavior (Burgoon, 1994). There are nonverbal behaviors that are unique to a subculture, such as the appropriate level of eye contact or the amount of acceptable personal space between individuals (LaFrance & Mayo, 1978). For example, a female Japanese customer may feel uncomfortable if a service provider makes eye contact with her because of cultural communication norms. On the other hand, there are nonverbal behaviors that are relatively common across different subcultures, such as facial expressions that show interest and care for another (Elfenbein & Ambady, 2002, 2003; Winsted, 1997). Individuals interpret the nonverbal behaviors of persons from their own ethnic group more accurately than the nonverbal behaviors of members of a different ethnic group (Elfenbein & Ambady, 2002). This underscores the importance of hiring diverse employees, to improve intercultural communication during service encounters. A service firm should strive for a similar level of diversity in its front line employees as in the society in which it operates.

Adaptive selling is one technique that service providers can use to build better relationships with customers (e.g., Gwinner, Bitner, Brown, & Kumar, 2005; Park & Holloway, 2003). Front line service providers can assess the service exchange, and adjust their behaviors accordingly. Specifically, employees should strive to proactively identify customers who may require more attention due to a language barrier or lack of familiarity with a good or service. For example, a customer may be struggling to communicate, and the service provider can attempt to engage her in a shared language if possible. In situations where a customer is unable to communicate verbally with the employee, the customer may leave or fail to find a product that meets her needs; either of these outcomes is not positive for the customer or the firm. Service providers should adapt their verbal and nonverbal communications to effectively serve customers, and help them feel more welcome whenever possible (e.g., Rosenbaum & Montoya, 2007).

Emotional self-regulation refers to an individual's ability to respond to or cope with an emotional experience (e.g., Baumeister, Heatherton, & Tice, 1994). This ability can also influence interpersonal communication in a service environment. For example, how an employee responds to an emotional customer can substantially influence the service quality perceptions of both the focal customer and other customers in the service environment, and subsequently affect the firm's ability to establish or maintain a relationship with the customer. In addition, an employee's ability to respond to customer needs or handle a difficult situation can vary across cultures, because cultural norms may dictate appropriate responses to customer needs. In general, some cultural norms promote increased emotional self-regulation (e.g., France), whereas the norms of other cultures may not (e.g., US; Grandey, Fisk, & Steiner, 2005).

One consideration for service firms is how their efforts to customize interactions with minority ethnic customers might affect other customers in the servicescape. For example, how do customers from the majority group feel when an employee converses with a minority customer in their native language? Though the employee is trying to communicate effectively with the customer, consumers from other ethnic groups may feel excluded, or believe that they are not receiving the same level of service (e.g., Rosenbaum & Montoya, 2007). This dilemma illustrates an important principle. Although hiring bilingual employees for retail stores located in diverse communities is essential to delivering high-quality service, it is not sufficient to deliver basic service effectively to their diverse clientele. Training on cross-cultural communication is important to address the needs of diverse customers, especially as it pertains to addressing the needs of all customers without alienating any particular groups (e.g., Montoya & Briggs, 2013). Strong decoding ability for rapport-building with multicultural customers should be facilitated during employee training in highly diverse communities (e.g., Markos & Puccinelli, 2004). Front line service personnel need to develop an understanding of their potential markets, and adapt service delivery approaches appropriately to provide high-quality service experiences for ethnic minority customers, without simultaneously alienating customers from other groups.

The role of front line service employees

Research on multicultural service encounters supports the notion that service firms should strive to hire employees from ethnic groups representative of their potential markets. One stream of relevant research focuses on encounters involving different cultures (Sharma, Tam, & Kim, 2009; Sharma, Wu, & Su, 2016; Sharma & Wu, 2015). This research argues that increasing customer perceptions of cultural distance between themselves and service employees ultimately leads to decreased satisfaction with the service encounter. Perceived cultural distance makes customers uncomfortable in interactions with service employees, which can affect their perceptions of the service provided and, ultimately, their satisfaction with the encounters (Sharma et al., 2009). This research does find that the negative effects of cultural distance can be moderated by certain customer traits, such as competence interacting with other cultures, and personal independence (Sharma et al., 2016; Sharma & Wu, 2015), but because service firms have little control over customer traits, their best strategic option is to minimize perceived cultural distances.

There are other research streams that also suggest service firms should strive to hire employees representative of the ethnic groups they are targeting. For instance, Montoya and Briggs (2013) present a conceptual model depicting the effects of shared ethnicity awareness in face-to-face service encounters. Strong ethnic identification by Asian and Hispanic customers, especially when they are in minority groups, significantly affects their responses to retailers (i.e., satisfaction, loyalty, and word-of-mouth). Shared ethnicity awareness was activated by ethnic subculture membership cues including physical appearance (e.g., skin tone, hair color), surnames (e.g., common Hispanic surnames), and shared language (e.g., Spanish). For instance,

Hispanic customers in the study reported speaking with an accent when they believed the service provider also spoke Spanish, in an attempt to encourage Spanish language communications. Montoya and Briggs (2013) observe that ethnic minority consumers are motivated to disproportionately allocate resources to in-group members, owing to a desire to boost their group's status (Simon & Brown, 1987). Furthermore, they find that the exchange of particularistic resources (i.e., intangibles, such as love, status, or friendly service) (Foa & Foa, 1974) is especially prevalent when the customer and service provider are from the same ethnic minority group. Shared ethnicity among the minority consumers in this study was associated with higher satisfaction, greater loyalty to the service establishment, and increased likelihood to engage in positive word-of-mouth. These results underscore the value of hiring front line employees who are members of the same ethnic groups as the customers.

To assess the true value of hiring ethnically similar employees, service firms should also consider how strongly customers from the ethnic group identify with this ethnicity. The strength of ethnic identification influences shopping behavior (e.g., Deshpande et al., 1986) and expectation levels regarding customer service. Further, because shared ethnicity naturally alters the typical interactions between the service employee and customer (Montoya & Briggs, 2013), service firms may need to allow ethnic minority employees to adapt the established service script to more effectively serve ethnically similar customers when the effect on mainstream customers is not pronounced. For example, Comer and Nicholls (2000) found that Hispanic salespeople prefer to emphasize concern for the customer over concern for the sale during service encounters with Hispanic customers. Because Hispanic customers prefer an emphasis on relationships over discrete transactions and personal attention from service providers, they respond more positively to a more personal, relational approach to a service encounter (Kwak & Sojka, 2011; Seock, 2009). Language is another way to adapt the service encounter for a particular cultural group. Van Vaerenbergh and Holmqvist (2013) found a strong preference for service encounters to occur in a native language, especially with high-involvement services. These authors also observed that Hispanic customers are more likely to engage in positive word-of-mouth, and to provide a bigger tip to reward the enhanced service experience, compared to non-Hispanics.

Cultural norms affect how customers evaluate service encounters. For example, Asians and Hispanics are considered collectivists, because they tend to be more concerned about the group rather than the individual (Hofstede, 1980; Markus & Kitayama, 1991). In comparison, Westerners, including U.S. Caucasians, are generally considered more individualistic, having greater concern about the individual than the group. Asians and Hispanics are also generally more allocentric and interdependent, emphasizing the needs of the group rather than the individual (e.g., Comer & Nicholls, 2000). When minority ethnic consumers reside in country environments where the norms run counter to their own cultures, face-to-face service encounters can provide an opportunity for firms to meaningfully impact these customers through exchanges with service employees. Service employees are critical to helping ethnic minority customers feel comfortable and welcome in a service environment (Rosenbaum & Montoya, 2007). For example, Montoya and Briggs (2013) found that Asian and Hispanic customers responded positively to an employee's acknowledgment of their ethnic preferences/tastes, or to attempts to converse in a shared language. Thus, providing service employee training on cultural norms and the language of key ethnic minority segments is helpful when serving multicultural consumer segments, but it is not an adequate substitute for hiring ethnically similar employees on the front line.

The role of the servicescape

Bitner's (1992) servicescape framework considers customer response to physical elements such as ambient conditions, space/function, and artifacts, signs, and symbols. For example, an Asian grocery store exhibits fish in tanks, a Hispanic grocery store offers roasted chilies in the parking lot; bilingual signage or ethnic music are potential unique aspects of servicescapes. In addition to these physical elements, social elements in the service environment are important to customer behavior. The social servicescape includes interactions with other customers and employees (e.g., Rosenbaum & Montoya, 2007; Tombs & McColl-Kennedy, 2003). Customers take into account both physical cues (e.g., signage) and social cues to assess their place identity (Rosenbaum & Montoya, 2007). Place identity, or the manner in which an individual defines herself in relation to a physical environment (Proshansky, Fabian, & Kaminoff, 1983), is especially important in an increasingly diverse marketplace. As the percentages of ethnic minority consumers and their associated buying powers increase in a market, so do their options for having their needs and wants fulfilled. Such ethnic minority consumers can avoid the service environments that make them feel out of place. Rosenbaum and Montoya (2007) found that multicultural (e.g., Hispanic) customers assess their place identity in a service environment, and ethnicities of other employees and customers influence customer responses such as loyalty, word-of-mouth, and repeat purchases.

Customers evaluate their place identity through place likening, a process by which they assess the ethnicities of employees and other customers to establish their ethnic congruency. Rosenbaum and Montoya (2007) measured ethnic minority customers' approach/avoidance behaviors, finding that they are more likely to approach (avoid) retail establishments when they perceive congruency (incongruency) between their own ethnicity and that of other customers or employees. Customers rely upon verbal cues, such as language or personal greetings, and nonverbal cues, such as body language, to assess place identity and congruency. The study revealed that ethnic minority customer decisions regarding whether to patronize a service establishment are strongly related to how welcoming they perceive the service environment to be to members of their ethnic group. For example, unwelcoming behavior (e.g., walking customers to the 'discount rack') specifically due to their ethnicity was reported, which resulted in negative feelings toward the retail establishment. In a welcoming example, a friendly employee might greet a Hispanic customer in Spanish, or acknowledge extended family members, signage may be bilingual, and the variety of goods/service offerings might appeal to a multicultural customer base. Finally, the researchers found that customers were less likely to complain to others about any service failures at a preferred retail establishment; specifically, they kept any problems or issues 'in-house' to protect their favorite restaurant or retailer.

Developing a multicultural service orientation

Multicultural service orientation defined

A service orientation is an aspect of a firm's broader organizational climate (Lytle et al., 1998). The policies, practices, and procedures implemented by organizations affect employee perceptions of the behaviors that are expected, rewarded, and supported (Deshpande & Webster, 1989; Schein, 2010; Schneider, Wheeler, & Cox, 1992). Schneider, Macey, and

Young (2006, p. 117) describe the climate of an organization as a summary of employee impressions of "how we do things around here." Employee perceptions of service orientation affect their perceptions of the appropriate 'service-giving behaviors' to implement during encounters with customers.

A multicultural service orientation is critical so that firms can continually excel in communicating with and delivering services to a variety of cultures. Lacking this orientation, firms are left susceptible to systemic service failures directed at particular races, ethnicities, or cultures. For example, Harris, Henderson, and Williams (2005, p. 163) document several cases of accused consumer racial profiling, which they describe as "a type of differential treatment of the customer in the marketplace based on race/ethnicity that constitutes denial of or degradation in the products and/or services that are offered to the consumer." This differential treatment may be either subtle or overt. In several of the profiling cases noted in Harris et al. (2005), the employees' profiling behavior was encouraged by service managers and viewed as an acceptable practice.

Building on the definition of service orientation offered by Lytle and Timmerman (2006) and the insights on multicultural markets provided by Spratlen et al. (2016), this chapter defines multicultural service orientation as *a strategic organizational affinity or preference for excellence in how a company serves customers from a diversity of cultural groups.* Lytle, Hom, and Mokwa (1998) identifies four key dimensions of service orientation: service leadership practices (i.e., leadership and vision), service encounter practices (i.e., customer treatment and employee empowerment), human resources (HR) practices (i.e., training and rewards), and service system practices (i.e., failure prevention, failure recovery, technology, and standards communication). However, service delivery was considered in the previous section of this chapter, and two of the service orientation dimensions directly relate to service delivery – service encounter practices and service system practices (Briggs et al., 2020). Thus, the remainder of this chapter focuses on the two remaining dimensions of service orientation – service leadership practices and HR practices.

Service leadership practices

Service leaders occur at two levels in an organization: (1) managers and supervisors that directly supervise front line employees; (2) higher level or corporate leaders that are further removed from direct interactions with customers on a regular basis. The standards of managers at even the highest levels filter down to employees on the front line (Bridges, 2018). At any level, the behavior of service leaders plays a key role in conveying acceptable service standards to employees and influencing the organizational service climate (Hong, Liao, Jia, & Jiang, 2013). Supervising managers should demonstrate that they truly care about serving diverse groups, going beyond just giving 'lip service' and striving to be a practical example to employees of how to deliver service. Such managers are often required to step in and provide service to customers in retail or hospitality service organizations. As employees witness managers leading by example, serving customers and fulfilling promises to employees (Lytle et al., 1998; Jaramillo et al., 2009), they develop a clearer understanding of how to serve others. Thus, service managers can clearly demonstrate openness to customers and partners from differing cultural backgrounds, which facilitates multicultural service orientation.

One way that corporate level managers can demonstrate desired behaviors is by partnering with minority-owned businesses. Many firms, when targeting minority segments, employ marketing research providers or advertising agencies that are owned by individuals from these groups. This approach demonstrates openness to minority groups at the highest levels of the organization; it also improves relevant research insights and external communications by help-ing to avoid simple errors which can occur due to being out-group rather than in-group mem-bers. Burgos and Mobolade (2011) recommend matching a moderator with respondents of the same culture when conducting qualitative research, because there is a tendency for respondents to "self-censor" when dealing with a moderator of a different ethnicity.

It is important that the corporate leadership team also be diverse, to effectively convey this value to front line employees. Service firms must take a proactive approach to leader diversification, because leadership teams do not typically diversify naturally, due in part to the many barriers that tend to limit the advancement of ethnic minorities in organizations, including a lack of mentoring and exclusion from informal networks (Kilian, Hukai, & McCarty, 2005). Leadership diversity efforts will be greatly enhanced when senior service managers express their commitment to these goals as an aspect of their corporate visions, and enact diversity strategies to work toward top management diversification. As an example of what can occur when this is not done, in the mid-1990s Denny's restaurants had to pay out over $54 million to settle lawsuits by black customers who claimed that they were discrimin-ated against in Denny's restaurants. At the time of the lawsuits, the company's leaders were predominately Caucasian, but the firm became the first American company to hire a diversity officer who reported directly to its CEO (Speizer, 2004). In less than ten years, the company was able to diversify its board of directors and achieve 45% minority ownership of its franchises. Service organizations operating in multicultural environments can point to the diversity of their customer bases to justify the importance of leadership diversity.

HR practices

HR practices generally improve employee ability and motivation to perform, and many HR practices relate specifically to service (Hong et al., 2013). When constructing HR practices, service firms operating in multicultural environments should consider proactively hiring, socializing, and training employees based on the competencies critical for success in these set-tings. Customer orientation is widely acknowledged as a critical individual trait to be sought in service workers (Donavan, Brown, & Mowen, 2004), but it is also an aspect of the service climate that can be passed along to employees (Hartline, Maxham, III, & McKee, 2000). In addition, customer orientation relates to a set of individual behaviors that can be practiced by service employees, such as identifying customer needs and directly answering customer ques-tions (Kelley, 1992; Saxe & Weitz, 1982). In summary, service firms have become more aware of the need to hire customer-oriented employees, communicate customer-oriented culture, and train employees on customer-oriented behaviors.

Researchers have identified *intercultural competence* and *intercultural sensitivity* as important competencies of service employees for firms operating in multicultural environments (Sharma et al., 2009; Sizoo, 2006; Sizoo, Plank, Iskat, & Serrie, 2005; Tam, Sharma, & Kim, 2014). Intercultural competence is an "ability to think and act in appropriate ways with people from other cultures" (Sharma et al., 2009, p. 232), whereas intercultural sensitivity is an "attitude that enables an individual to interact effectively with people of different cul-tures" (Sizoo et al., 2005, p. 246). Employees inherently have differing levels of intercultural competence and sensitivity, and firms should approach the enhancement of these traits in current employees differently. Intercultural competence can be more effectively enhanced through employee training than socialization because it is a skill or ability that can be devel-oped. Conversely, as an attitude, intercultural sensitivity can be more effectively enhanced through employee socialization efforts than through training.

Intercultural competence may be assessed by considering the knowledge and associated comfort level of individuals who deal with people of different ethnicities, nationalities, languages, customs, and religious beliefs (Tam et al., 2014). Because an important aspect of intercultural competence relates to cultural intelligence, firms should train employees on common behavioral tendencies and communication styles of their targeted minority ethnic segments. Many service firms in the U.S. target Asian and Hispanic customers, so they should ensure that their employees are aware of the norms of these cultural groups, which may deviate from readily accepted norms in society. They should ensure their employees are aware that Asian customers may not make eye contact, and that this is not a sign of disrespect. They should ensure that employees are aware that Hispanic customers tend to shop with extended families, so employees will be better prepared for the occurrence of these encounters.

Service training along these lines should be proactive and occur at regular intervals. This is especially important in order to avoid (or at least reduce) service encounter failures that systemically relate to race, ethnicity, or culture. Starbucks Coffee is an example of a firm that took a reactive approach, rather than a proactive one, until forced to change. In 2018, the company received a great deal of negative publicity after videos surfaced of black consumers being arrested for trespassing after they were refused access to restrooms and then failed to place an order. The incidents seemed to highlight shortcomings inherent in the chain's service climate in regard to its treatment of minority customers. In response, on May 29th, 2018, Starbucks closed over 8,000 of its stores in North America so that its employees could complete racial bias training. The company belatedly realized its need for ongoing training to improve employees' intercultural competence.

Intercultural sensitivity is related to intercultural competence, but it is an attitude as opposed to a capability. It has been assessed in research studies by considering aspects of cross-cultural flexibility/openness, such as "liking for unfamiliar people and ideas," "tolerance toward others," and "flexibility with regard to experience" (Kelley & Meyers, 2001, p. 15). Perceptual acuity, which is related to how one communicates and interprets cues, is also measured (Sizoo et al., 2005). Research suggests that employees with higher intercultural sensitivities perform better in multicultural environments and also have better interpersonal interactions with coworkers (Sizoo, 2006; Sizoo et al., 2005). The interactions between more experienced employees and newer employees are especially critical to the dissemination of service communication tactics (Hartline et al., 2000). Importantly, intercultural sensitivity is not correlated with demographic traits, so service firms must go further than just diversifying their personnel. Rather, individual experiences such as living abroad and foreign language skills positively relate to intercultural sensitivity (Sizoo et al., 2005), so hiring employees with these traits can enhance firms' abilities to socialize new employees properly. Increasing the portion of employees with high levels of intercultural sensitivity favorably influences the climate for diversity and inclusion within the organization, which then makes it easier attract and retain a multicultural workforce (Madera, Dawson, & Neal, 2013). Service firms should also consider establishing formal relationships with mentors high in intercultural sensitivity at the managerial levels in the organization, as this is an especially efficient approach to socialization (Hartline et al., 2000).

Conclusion

This chapter discusses some of the challenges faced by service providers operating in multicultural environments, and some of the strategies that can be used to help such firms develop relationships with ethnic minority consumers. As the populations of highly developed nations have become increasingly diverse (see Table 24.1), and their economies increasingly service-driven, the need for service companies to enhance their multicultural marketing capabilities has increased markedly. Applying the services marketing triangle as an organizing framework, this chapter discusses and explains the rationale for approaches to enhance multicultural communications, deliver service to multicultural audiences, and develop firm service orientation. Through the use of company examples and research findings, the chapter highlights practical applications of many of these multicultural approaches in service organizations.

References

Aaker, J. L., Benet-Martinez, V., & Garolera, J. (2001). Consumption symbols as carriers of culture: A study of Japanese and Spanish brand personality constructs. *Journal of Personality and Social Psychology*, 81(3), 492–508.

Aguirre-Rodriguez, A., Bóveda-Lambie, A. M., & Montoya, D. Y. (2014). Ethnic consumer response to ethnic crossover brand extensions. *Journal of Business Research*, 67(4), 457–463.

Alexandre, M. (2009). *Delivering services in multicultural societies*. Washington, D.C.: World Bank.

Ashton, C. M., Haidet Paterniti, D. A. et al. (2003). Racial and ethnic disparities in the use of health services: Bias, preferences, or poor communication? *Journal of General Internal Medicine*, 18, 146–152.

Baumeister, R. F., Heatherton, T. F., & Tice, D. M. (1994). *Losing control: How and why people fail at self-regulation*. San Diego, CA: Academic Press.

Betancourt, J. R., Green, A. R., Emilio Carrillo, J., & Ananeh-Firempong, O. (2003). Defining cultural competence: A practical framework for addressing racial/ethnic disparities in health and health care. *Public Health Reports*, 118(4), 293–302.

Bettencourt, B. A., Miller, N., & Hume, D. L. (1999). Effects of numerical representations within cooperative settings: Examining the Role of Salience in In-Group Favoritism. *British Journal of Social Psychology*, 38, 265–287.

Bishop, M. M., & Peterson, M. (2010). The impact of medium context on bilingual consumers' responses to code-switched advertising. *Journal of Advertising*, 39(3), 55–67. doi:10.2753/JOA0091-3367390304.

Bishop, M. M., & Peterson, M. (2011). Comprende code switching? *Journal of Advertising Research*, 51(4), 648–659. doi:10.2501/JAR-51-4-648-659.

Bitner, M. J. (1992). Servicescapes: The impact of physical surroundings on customers and employees. *Journal of Marketing*, 56(April), 57–72.

Bitner, M. J. (1995). Building service relationships: It's all about promises. *Journal of the Academy of Marketing Science*, 23(4), 246–251.

Branscombe, N. R. (1998). Thinking about one's gender group's privileges or disadvantages: Consequences for well-being in women and men. *British Journal of Social Psychology*, 37, 167–184.

Brewer, M. B. (1991). The social self: On being the same and different at the same time. *Personality and Social Psychology Bulletin*, 17(October), 475–482.

Brewer, M. B., & Kramer, R. M. (1985). The psychology of intergroup attitudes and behavior. *Annual Review of Psychology*, 36, 219–243.

Bridges, E. (2018). Executive ethical decisions initiating organizational culture and values. *Journal of Service Theory and Practice*, 28(5), 576–608.

Briggs, E. F., Deretti, S., & Kato, H. T. (2020). Linking organizational service orientation to retailer profitability: Insights from the service-profit chain. *Journal of Business Research*, 107(February), 271–278.

Briggs, E., Landry, T. D., & Torres, I. M. (2010). Services' influence on minority portrayals in magazine advertising. *Journal of Services Marketing*, 24(3), 209–218.

Burgoon, J. K. (1994). Nonverbal signals. In M. L. Knapp & G. R. Miller (Eds.), *Handbook of interpersonal communication*, 2nd ed. (pp. 344–390). Beverly Hills, CA: SAGE.

Burgos, D., & Mobolade, O. (2011). *Marketing to the new majority*. New York: Millward Brown.

Central Intelligence Agency. (2018). *World Factbook*. Retrieved from www.cia.gov/library/publications/resources/the-world-factbook/.

Chance, J. E., Turner, A. L., & Goldstein, A. G. (1982). Development of differential recognition for own- and other-race faces. *Journal of Psychology*, 112, 29–37.

Colby, S., & Ortman, J. (2015). *Projections of the size and composition of the U.S. population: 2014 to 2060*. Washington, D.C.: U.S. Census Bureau.

Comer, L. B., & Nicholls, J. A. F. (2000). Communication between Hispanic salespeople and their customers: A first look. *Journal of Personal Selling & Sales Management*, 20(3), 121–127.

Conner, P. (2018). *Most displaced Syrians are in the Middle East, and about a million are in Europe*. Retrieved from http://pewrsr.ch/2Ekyze4.

Deshpande, R., Hoyer, W. D., & Donthu, N. (1986), The intensity of ethnic affiliation: A study of the sociology of Hispanic consumption. *Journal of Consumer Research*, 13(2), 214–220.

Deshpande, R., & Stayman, D. M. (1994). A tale of two cities: Distinctiveness theory and advertising effectiveness. *Journal of Marketing Research*, 31(February), 57–64.

Deshpande, R., & Webster, F. E., Jr. (1989), Organizational Culture and Marketing: Defining the Research Agenda. *Journal of Marketing*, 53(1), 3–15.

Direct Marketing Association. (2018). *Bank of New Zealand: The most prosperous ATM*. Retrieved March 20, 2019, from www.warc.com/SubscriberContent/article/dma/bank_of_new_zealand_the_most_prosperous_atm/123800.

Donavan, D. T., Brown, T. J., & Mowen, J. C. (2004). Internal benefits of service-worker customer orientation: Job satisfaction, commitment, and organizational citizenship behaviors. *Journal of Marketing*, 68(1), 128–146.

Drake, B., & Poushter, J. (2016). *In views of diversity, many Europeans are less positive than Americans*. Retrieved from http://pewrsr.ch/29BuWla.

Edson, J. E. (2004). Narrative processing: Building consumer connections to brands. *Journal of Consumer Psychology*, 14(1/2), 168–179.

Elfenbein, H. A., & Ambady, N. (2002). On the universality and cultural specificity of emotion recognition: A meta-analysis. *Psychological Bulletin*, 128(2), 203–235.

Elfenbein, H. A., & Ambady, N. (2003). Universals and cultural differences in recognizing emotions. *Current Directions in Psychological Science*, 12(5), 159–164.

Foa, U. G., & Foa, E. B. 1974. *Societal structures of the mind*. Springfield, IL, Charles C. Thomas.

Giles, H., Taylor, D. M., & Bourhis, R. (1973). Towards a theory of interpersonal accommodation through language: Some Canadian data. *Language and Society*, 2(2), 177–192.

Grandey, A. A., Fisk, G. M., & Steiner, D. D. (2005). Must "service with a smile" be stressful? The moderating role of personal control for American and French employees. *Journal of Applied Psychology*, 90, 893–904.

Gwinner, K. P., Bitner, M. J., Brown, S. W., & Kumar, A. (2005). Service customization through employee adaptiveness. *Journal of Service Research*, 8(2), 131–148.

Harris, A.-M. G., Henderson, G. R., & Williams, J. D. (2005). Courting customers: Assessing racial profiling and other marketplace discrimination. *Journal of Public Policy & Marketing*, 24(May), 163–171.

Hartline, M. D., Maxham, III J. G., & McKee, D. O. (2000). Corridors of influence in the dissemination of customer-oriented strategy to customer contact service employees. *Journal of Marketing*, 64(2), 35–50.

Helm, B. (2010). Ethnic marketing: McDonald's is lovin' it. *Bloomberg Businessweek*, July 8, 2010 22–24.

Hewstone, M., Rubin, M., & Willis, H. (2002). Intergroup bias. *Annual Review of Psychology*, 53, 575–604.

Hofstede, G. (1980). *Culture's consequences: International differences in work-related values*. Newbury Park, CA: SAGE Publications.

Holmqvist, J. (2011). Consumer language preferences in service encounters: A cross-cultural perspective. *Managing Service Quality*, 21(2), 178–191.

Hong, Y., Liao, H., Jia, H., & Jiang, K. (2013). Missing link in the service profit chain: A meta-analytic review of the antecedents, consequences, and moderators of service climate. *Journal of Applied Psychology*, 98(2), 237–267.

Jaramillo, F., Grisaffe, D. B., Chonko, L. B., & Roberts, J. A. (2009). Examining the impact of servant leadership on sales force performance. *Journal of Personal Selling & Sales Management*, 29(3), 257–275.

John, D. R., & Torelli, C. J. (2018). *Strategic brand management*. New York: Oxford University Press.

Johnson, M. D., Lehmann, D. R., Fornell, C., & Horne, D. R. (1992). Attribute abstraction, feature-dimensionality, and the scaling of product similarities. *International Journal of Research in Marketing*, 9(2), 131–147.

Keller, K. L. (1993). Conceptualizing, measuring, and managing customer-based brand equity. *Journal of Marketing*, 57(1), 1–22.

Keller, K. L. (2013). *Strategic brand management*. 4th ed. Upper Saddle River, NJ: Pearson.

Kelley, C., & Meyers, J. (2001). *CCAI: Cross-cultural adaptability inventory*. Minneapolis, MN: National Computer Systems.

Kelley, S. W. (1992). Developing customer orientation among service employees. *Journal of the Academy of Marketing Science*, 20(1), 27–36.

Kilian, C. M., Hukai, D., & McCarty, E. C. (2005). Building diversity in the pipeline to corporate leadership. *Journal of Management Development*, 24(2), 155–168. doi:10.1108/02621710510579618.

Kohli, C., Thomas, S., & Suri, R. (2013). Are you in good hands? Slogan recall: What really matters. *Journal of Advertising Research*, 53(1), 31–42.

Korzenny, F. (2008). Multicultural marketing and the reasons why. *Journal of Advertising Research*, 48(2), 173–176.

Korzenny, F., & Korzenny, B. A. (2005). *Hispanic marketing: A cultural perspective*. Burlington, MA: Elsevier Butterworth-Heinemann.

Kwak, L. E., & Sojka, J. Z. (2011). Salesperson preference among Hispanic and Asian immigrants. *American Journal of Business*, 26(2), 118–128.

LaFrance, M., & Mayo, C. (1978). Cultural aspects of nonverbal communication. *International Journal of Intercultural Relations*, 2(1), 71–89.

Lee, C. K., Fernandez, N., & Martin, A. S. (2002). Using self-referencing to explain the effectiveness of ethnic minority models in advertising. *International Journal of Advertising*, 21(3), 367–379.

Loken, B., & John, D. R. (1993). Diluting brand beliefs: When do brand extensions have a negative impact? *Journal of Marketing*, 57(3), 71–84.

Lytle, R. S., Hom, P. W., & Mokwa, M. P. (1998). SERV★OR: A Managerial Measure of Organizational Service-Orientation. *Journal of Retailing*, 74(4), 455–489.

Lytle, R. S., & Timmerman, J. E. (2006). Service orientation and performance: An organizational perspective. *Journal of Services Marketing*, 20(2), 136–147. doi:10.1108/08876040610657066.

Madera, J. M., Dawson, M., & Neal, J. A. (2013). Hotel managers' perceived diversity climate and job satisfaction: The mediating effects of role ambiguity and conflict. *International Journal of Hospitality Management*, 35(December), 28–34.

Markos, E., & Puccinelli, N. M. (2004). Nonverbal decoding and effective customer service. *Paper presented at the Society for Consumer Psychology*.

Markus, H., & Kitayama, S. (1991). Culture and the self: Implications for cognition, emotion, and motivation. *Psychological Review*, 98(2), 224–253.

McGuire, W. J., McGuire, C. V., Child, P., & Fujioka, T. (1978). Salience of ethnicity in the spontaneous self-concept as a function of one's ethnic distinctiveness in the social environment. *Journal of Personality and Social Psychology*, 36(5), 511–520.

Mirowsky, J., & Ross, C. E. (1980). Minority status, ethnic culture, and distress: A comparison of Blacks, Whites, Mexicans, and Mexican Americans. *American Journal of Sociology*, 86(November), 479–495.

Mittal, B. (1999). The advertising of services: Meeting the challenge of intangibility. *Journal of Service Research*, 2(1), 98–116.

Montoya, D. Y., & Briggs, E. (2013). Shared ethnicity effects on service encounters: A study across three U.S. subcultures. *Journal of Business Research*, 66(3), 314–320.

Mullen, B., Brown, R., & Smith, C. (1992). Ingroup bias as a function of salience, relevance, and status: An integration. *European Journal of Social Psychology*, 22(2), 103–122.

Park, J. E., & Holloway, B. B. (2003). Adaptive selling behavior revisited: An empirical examination of learning orientation, sales performance, and job satisfaction. *Journal of Personal Selling & Sales Management*, 23(3), 239–251.

Pires, G., & Stanton, J. (2000). Marketing services to ethnic consumers in culturally diverse markets: Issues and implications. *Journal of Services Marketing*, 14(67), 607–618.

Proshansky, H. M., Fabian, A. K., & Kaminoff, R. (1983). Place-identity: Physical world socialization of the self. *Journal of Environmental Psychology*, 3(1), 57–83.

Rickford, J. R. (2019). *What is Ebonics? (African American English)*. Accessed on February 27, 2019 from www.linguisticsociety.org/content/what-ebonics-african-american-english.

Rosenbaum, M. S., & Montoya, D. Y. (2007). Am I welcome here? Exploring how ethnic consumers assess their place identity. *Journal of Business Research*, 60(3), 206–214.

Saxe, R., & Weitz, B. A. (1982). The SOCO scale: A measure of the customer orientation of salespeople. *Journal of Marketing Research*, 19(3), 343–351.

Schein, E. H. (2010). The Role of Organization Development in the Human Resource Function. *OD Practitioner*, 42(4), 6–11.

Schneider, B., Macey, W. H., & Young, S. A. (2006). The climate for service: A review of the construct with implications for achieving CLV goals. *Journal of Relationship Marketing*, 5(2–3), 111–132.

Schneider, B., Wheeler, J. K., & Cox, J. F. (1992), Journal of Applied Psychology, 77(5), 705–716.

Seock, Y-K. (2009). Influence of retail store environment cues on consumer patronage behavior across different retail store formats: An empirical analysis of U.S. Hispanic consumers. *Journal of Retailing and Consumer Sciences*, 16(5), 329–339.

Sharma, P., Tam, J. L. M., & Kim, N. (2009). Demystifying intercultural service encounters: Toward a comprehensive conceptual framework. *Journal of Service Research*, 12(2), 227–242. doi:10.1177/1094670509338312.

Sharma, P., Tam, J., & Wu, Z. (2018). Challenges and opportunities for services marketers in a culturally diverse global marketplace. *Journal of Services Marketing*, 32(5), 521–529.

Sharma, P., & Wu, Z. (2015). Customer ethnocentrism vs. intercultural competence as moderators in intercultural service encounters. *Journal of Services Marketing*, 29(2), 93–102.

Sharma, P., Wu, Z., & Su, Y. (2016). Role of personal cultural orientations in intercultural service encounters. *Journal of Services Marketing*, 30(2), 223–237.

Simon, B., & Brown, R. (1987). Perceived intragroup homogeneity in minority-majority contexts. *Journal of Personality and Social Psychology*, 53(4), 703–711.

Sizoo, S. (2006). A comparison of the effect of intercultural sensitivity on employee performance in cross-cultural service encounters: London vs. Florida. *Journal of Euromarketing*, 15(4), 77–100. doi:10.1300/J037v13n04-05.

Sizoo, S., Plank, R., Iskat, W., & Serrie, H. (2005). The effect of intercultural sensitivity on employee performance in cross-cultural service encounters. *Journal of Services Marketing*, 19(4), 245–255. doi:10.1108/08876040510605271.

Speizer, I. (2004). *Diversity on the menu*. Accessed on March 20, 2019 from www.workforce.com/2004/11/01/diversity-on-the-menu/.

Spratlen, T., Lum, L., Montoya, D., & Verchot, M. (2016). *Business consulting in a multicultural America*. Spokane, WA: University of Washington Press.

Stayman, D. M., & Deshpande, R. (1989). Situational ethnicity and consumer behavior. *Journal of Consumer Research*, 16(December), 361–371.

Tajfel, H. (1982). Social psychology of intergroup relations. *Annual Review of Psychology*, 33, 1–39.

Tajfel, H., & Turner, J. C. (1986). The social identity theory of intergroup behavior. In S. Worchel & L. W. Austin (Eds.), *Psychology of intergroup relations*. (pp. 7–24). Chicago, IL: Nelson-Hall.

Tajfel, H., & Turner, J. C. (1979). An integrative theory of intergroup conflict. In W. G. Austin & S. Worchel (Eds.), *The social psychology of intergroup relations*.. (pp. 33–47). Monterey, CA: Brooks/Cole Publishing Company.

Tam, J., Sharma, P., & Kim, N. (2014). Examining the role of attribution and intercultural competence in intercultural service encounters. *Journal of Services Marketing*, 28(2), 159–170. doi:10.1108/JSM-12-2012-0266.

Taylor, D. M., Moghaddam, F. M., Gamble, I., & Zellerer, E. (1987). Disadvantaged group responses to perceived inequality: From passive acceptance to collective action. *Journal of Social Psychology*, 127(3), 259–272.

Tombs, A., & McColl-Kennedy, J. R. (2003). Social-servicescape conceptual model. *Marketing Theory*, 3(4), 447–475.

Torres, I. M., & Briggs, E. D. (2005). Does Hispanic-targeted advertising work for services. *Journal of Services Marketing*, 19(3), 150–156.

United Nations. (2017). Migration and Population Change: Drivers and Impacts, *Population Facts*, December, No. 2017/8.

Van Vaerenbergh, Y., & Holmqvist, J. (2013). Speak my language if you want my money! Service language's influence on consumer tipping behavior. *European Journal of Marketing*, 47(8), 1276–1292.

Wallendorf, M., & Reily, M. D. (1983). Ethnic migration, assimilation, and consumption. *Journal of Consumer Research*, 10(December), 292–302.

Winsted, K. F. (1997). The service experience in two cultures: A behavioral perspective. *Journal of Retailing*, 73(3), 337–360.

Wood, S. P. (2014). AT&T, Vice Speak Spanglish to Attract Young Latinos. Retrieved Oct 11, 2018, from www.adweek.com/agencyspy/att-vice-speak-spanglish-to-attract-young-latinos/70123.

Word, D. L., & Perkins, R. C. Jr. (1996). *Building a Spanish surname list for the 1990s: A new approach to an old problem*. In Technical Working Paper 13. Washington, D.C.: U.S. Census Bureau.

Xu, Y. (2018). *Dolce & Gabbana ad (with chopsticks) provokes public outrage in China*. Retrieved from www.npr.org/sections/goatsandsoda/2018/12/01/671891818/dolce-gabbana-ad-with-chopsticks-provokes-public-outrage-in-china.

Zebrowitz, L. A. (1996). Physical appearance as a basis of stereotyping. In N. MacRae, M. Hewstone, & C. Stangor (Eds.), *Foundations of stereotypes and stereotyping.*. (pp. 79–120). New York: Guilford Press.

Zebrowitz, L. A., Bronstad, P. M., & Lee, H. K. (2007). The contribution of face familiarity to ingroup favoritism and stereotyping. *Social Cognition*, 25(2), 306–338.

Zeithaml, V., Bitner, M. J., & Gremler, D. W. (2013). *Services marketing: Integrating customer focus across the firm*. 6th ed. New York: McGraw-Hill Irwin.

Index

A2A *see* actor-to-actor orientation
Aal, K. 348
Abbas, M. 208
Abela, A. V. 395–396
Abernathy, W. J. 118
accommodation 18
accommodation theory 489
Acker, O. 205
ACSI *see* American Customer Satisfaction Index
actor-to-actor (A2A) orientation 6–7, 34, 36, 38, 347, 349
actors 6–7; business models 34; determination of value 10–11, 14; greenprinting 453; innovation 24–25, 32–33, 40, 113, 121, 122, 123–124; institutional contexts 27; markets 35–36, 40; networks 168, 169, 245; resource integration 10, 32, 33, 35, 345–350, 366–367; service ecosystems 39; service marketing research 150; value co-creation 7–8, 9–11, 12–15, 26, 326, 330; *see also* customers; employees
ad hoc innovation 136
Ada, E. 243
adaptive selling 202, 489
adaptiveness 303, 307, 315–316
advertising 355–356, 445, 472–473, 483–484, 486
affluence 456–457
African-American customers 430, 486
agency 27, 77; front line employees 132, 137, 142, 143–144; value co-creation 330
agency services 175–177, 179, 181, 183, 186, 187–193
agility 246, 247, 249–250, 251
aging issues 428–429
Aguirre-Rodriguez, A. 487–488
Ahn, H. J. 149
Ahtola, O. T. 352
AI *see* artificial intelligence
Airbnb 24–25, 117, 228
AJ's 487
Akaka, M. A. 119, 149, 150, 157
Åkesson, M. 134, 289
Akkad, F. 205

Aksoy, L. 258
Alexander, E. 337
Alexandre, M. 481
Algesheimer, R. 379
Alibaba Group 117
Allen, A. M. 208
Allen, J. A. 218
Aloysius, J. A. 152
alpha testing 236
Altinay, L. 346
Alvarez, F. 185
Alvarez, G. 246
Alves, H. 344–372
Amazon 24, 37, 192–193, 261; dual culture strategy 264, 265–266; Mechanical Turk 218; operations management approaches 269; standardization 272
ambidexterity 261, 262, 263–267, 271, 273, 275
ambient conditions 150–151, 160, 162
American Customer Satisfaction Index (ACSI) 258
American Express 466
Americans with Disabilities Act (ADA) 426, 431
amusement parks 233
analytical decision-making 410–411, 412, 413, 414–417, 418–419, 421
analytics 231, 289; industrialization 273; not-for-profit services 471, 474; social media 382
Anderson, E. G. 242
Anderson, L. 338
Anderson, S. T. 227–240
Andersson-Cederholm, E. 149
Andreu, L. 345
Andrews, M. C. 218
Ang, A. 132
Angot, J. 347
Anheier, H. 475
apologies 208
Apple 24, 293
apps 374
Arnould, E. J. 149, 155, 346, 351, 361
ART *see* Attention Restoration Theory
Arthur, W. B. 32, 38, 125